A COMPREHENSIVE HISTORY OF INDIA

A COMPREHENSIVE HISTORY OF INDIA

Vol. I, Part 1

Prehistory of India

Edited by

M.K. DHAVALIKAR

COMPREHENSIVE HISTORY OF INDIA SOCIETY

MANOHAR
2026

First published 2013
First paperback edition 2023
Reprinted 2024, 2025, 2026

ISBN 978-81-7304-974-3 (Hb)
ISBN 978-81-960546-9-4 (Pb)

Published by
Ajay Kumar Jain *for*
Manohar Publishers & Distributors
4753/23 Ansari Road, Daryaganj
New Delhi 110 002

Printed at
Replika Press Pvt. Ltd.

Foreword

This volume of the Comprehensive History of India Project covers the period of Early Stone Age to the Later Stone Age and Bronze Age as they developed in different parts of the country. Such a comprehensive contribution would, undoubtedly, be of considerable value for the scholars and the lay public. It also shows the advance of studies on India's pre-history by scholars since H.D. Sankalia's *Pre-history of India (1977)*. Dr. M.K. Dhavalikar, former Dean of Deccan College, Pune, and Editor of this volume has made great efforts to bring together the papers for this volume. We are grateful to him, and to all those who have contributed to the volume.

The Harappan or Bronze Age continues to be a matter of controversy among scholars: chiefly whether it was Aryan, or pre-Aryan. Both points of view have been presented in the volume. However, the question about the original homeland of the Aryans, their identity, the age of the *Rigveda*, etc., will be dealt with the following volume, Vol. I (pt. 2), *The Vedic Age*.

It is a matter of regret that this volume could not be printed during the lifetime of Professor R.S. Sharma, who was the first Chairman of the Comprehensive History of India Society, under whom the publication programme of the Society made steady progress.

At the end I would like to thank Shri Ramesh Jain of Manohar Publishers & Distributors, for his personal interest and the arduous labour of his associates in bringing this volume to press, and all those associated with the publication of this volume. In particular, I am grateful to Prof. R.C. Thakran for assisting in proof-reading, and making the volume ready for press.

New Delhi
March 2012

SATISH CHANDRA
Chairman
Comprehensive History of India Society

From the Publications Committee: Comprehensive History of India Society

The first edition of this volume of *A Comprehensive History of India* Series was published in 2013. It is very gratifying that despite a market slowdown following the worldwide pandemic, this monograph received substantive support from researchers and scholars of history. The edition has been out of print for quite some time. On the request of the publisher, the Publications Committee of the Comprehensive History of India Society decided to get the volume reprinted. Further, keeping the interests of students in mind it also decided to bring it out in paperback format.

I am thankful to Shri Ramesh Jain of Manohar Publishers & Distributors for undertaking the present initiative. I also thank his numerous associates for publishing the monograph speedily without compromising the quality and aesthetics.

New Delhi
15 February 2023

KRISHNA MOHAN SHRIMALI
Secretary-cum-Treasurer
Comprehensive History of India Society

Preface

The present volume is the first in the Comprehensive History of India series planned by the Indian History Congress of which some have already been published. It covers the entire prehistoric period starting from the advent of man in India up to the end of the Bronze or the Chalcolithic age (*c.* 1000 BC).

The contributors, who are leading authorities in their respective fields of specialization, readily agreed and sent in their contributions. They have placed us under a deep debt of gratitude. It may, however, be stated that the views expressed by them are their own.

Archaeology in India has been making rapid strides in the post-Independence period and naturally, therefore, what formerly could be covered in one chapter, 'Prehistoric Period', has to now be compressed in a massive tome. Every care has been taken to include the latest discoveries and their significance but, considering their pace, I can only say, following Sir Mortimer Wheeler, that fifty years ago, this book could not have been written, and I am sure it will have to be rewritten before long.

It is my bounden duty to record my grateful thanks to the Editorial Board, more particularly Prof. R.S. Sharma and Prof. Satish Chandra, who entrusted the task of editing this volume to me, as also to the scholars who have contributed chapters to the book.

Some of the illustrations have been made by Sri Srikant Pradhan, artist. Sri Sharad Gosavi did the computer typing. To them both, my thanks are due.

M.K. DHAVALIKAR

Contents

PART TWO

EARLY, MATURE, AND LATER BRONZE AGE

Illustrations

FIGURES

PLATES

Contributors

B. ARUNACHALAM, formerly Professor of Geography, University of Mumbai, Mumbai.

G.L. BADAM, formerly Reader in Palaeontology, Deccan College Post-Graduate Research Institute, Pune.

M.K. DHAVALIKAR, formerly Professor of Archaeology and Director, Deccan College Post-Graduate Research Institute, Pune.

VIDULA JAYASWAL, Professor of Archaeology, Banaras Hindu University, Varanasi.

KENNETH A.R. KENNEDY, Professor, Section of Ecology and Systematics, Cornell University, Ithaca, N.Y. (U.S.A.).

B.B. LAL, formerly Director General, Archaeological Survey of India, New Delhi.

SHEILA MISRA, Reader in Prehistory, Deccan College Post-Graduate Research Institute, Pune.

V.N. MISRA, formerly Professor of Prehistory and Director, Deccan College Post-Graduate Research Institute, Pune.

J.N. PAL, Professor of Archaeology, University of Allahabad, Allahabad.

P.C. PANT, formerly Professor of Prehistory, Banaras Hindu Univesity, Varanasi.

SURAJ BHAN, formerly Professor of Ancient Indian History and Archaeology, Kurukshetra University, Kurukshetra.

R.S. PAPPU, formerly Reader in Geomorphology. Deccan College Post-Graduate Research Institute, Pune.

PURUSHOTTAM SINGH, formerly Professor of Archaeology, Banaras Hindu University, Varanasi.

T.C. SHARMA, formerly Professor of Anthropology, University of Gauhati, Gauhati.

A. SUNDARA, formerly Professor of Ancient Indian History, Culture and Archaeology, Karnatak University, Dharwar.

THAKRAN, R.C. Professor of Ancient Indian History, University of Delhi, Delhi.

Abbreviations

AJPA	*American Journal of Physical Anthropology*
BDCRI	*Bulletin of Deccan College Research Institute*
CA	*Current Anthropology*
EW	*East and West*
JAS	*Journal of Asiatic Society*
JASB	*Journal of Asiatic Society of Bengal*
JIAS	*Journal of Indian Anthropological Society*
JIH	*Journal of Indian History*
JGSI	*Journal of Geological Society of India*
JNES	*Journal of Near Eastern Studies*
JOI	*Journal of Oriental Institute*
JRAI	*Journal of Royal Anthropological Institute*
MASI	*Memoir of Archaeological Survey of India*
ME	*Man and Environment*
PASB	Proceedings of Asiatic Society of Bengal
PPS	Proceedings of Prehistoric Society
RAIP	*Recent Advances in Indo-Pacific Prehistory*, ed. V.N. Misra and Peter Bellwood, New Delhi: Oxford IBH, 1985
SAA	South Asian Archaeology
SAS	South Asian Studies

PART ONE

PALAEOLITHIC, MESOLITHIC AND NEOLITHIC PHASES

Chapter 1

Geography and Environment

B. Arunachalam

India is the homeland of one of the oldest civilizations of the world. It stands in satisfactory comparison with the civilizations of the Nile, the Euphrates-Tigris and the Hwangho—the River valleys in the attainment of a firm agrarian economic base, secure and sedentary living, social cohesion and cultural identity. Initially evolved on the desert margins in the Indus Valley, the nucleus of organized human settlement was centred in the Punjab plains during the Vedic ages. Progressively, the frontiers of the pioneering fringe were pushed down the Ganga plains eastwards, so that by the beginning of the Christian era, a fairly prosperous agricultural community had spread over the north Indian plains as far east as Bengal, and Kalinga on the east coast (Fig. 1.1). The southward advance into the peninsular interior was, however, restricted, mainly through narrow migration corridors along the Gujarat coast in the west, the Khandwa-Burhanpur gap of the Tapti Valley in the middle and along the Kalinga coast in the east. Since the days of the *Mahābhārata*, small, independent, organized societies flourished in cloistered, near-total isolation in almost every river basin of the peninsula. About the beginning of the Christian era, an estimated population of about a hundred million was sustained by farming communities as a culturally advanced, progressive world society.

The beginning of settled life in the Indian subcontinent now goes back to about ten thousand years, as is evident from the excavation at Mehrgarh. Its agricultural prosperity and wealth of natural endowment, at a time when most of Europe and Afro-Asia were being overrun by nomads and barbarians, attracted repeated external pressures and interactions; these form the spice of Indian history as it unfolds. The rich Indian historical heritage is not without geographical bearings. The basis of its agrarian economy, its cultural identity, the flows of social cross-currents and the ethos of Indian philosophy and thought are well-grounded in its subcontinental status within the framework of a larger Asia and its tropical monsoonal rhythm.

The India of the historic past was not confined within the limits of the present Republic of India nor even the undivided Indian empire of the British colonial days. Very often, historic India stretched beyond the Hindukush ranges and the Pamirs; many times, India has been ruled from beyond, from

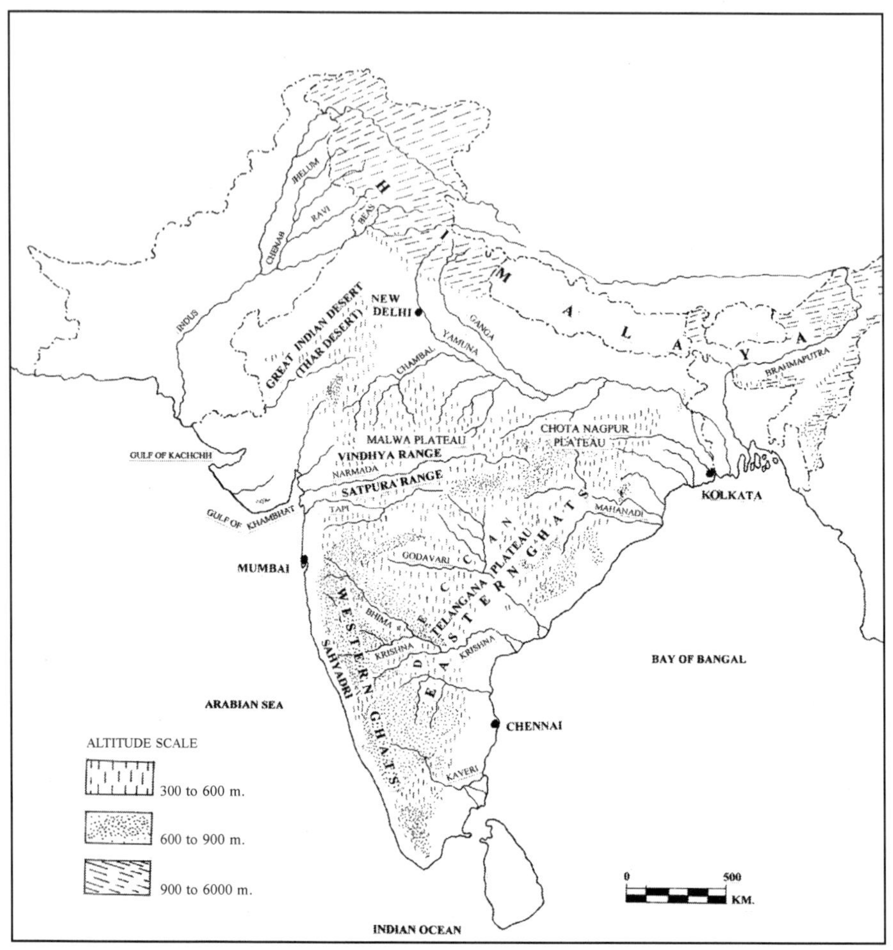

Fig. 1.1: India, physical features

places like Ghazni, and so on. The Delhi rule too extended into Afghan areas. The sway of Indian influence has persisted for long over South Asia. The historic traditions of India have been subject to the geographic controls of a larger Asia.

The mighty Himalayan ranges rising to snowy heights and running all along the northern limit for well over 2,200 km, and succeeded beyond by the similarly rising Karakorums and Kunluns, buttressed by a massive system of intermontane plateaus, form the essential nucleus of inner Asia. Sustaining a scanty population of pastoral nomads, eking out a meagre and hardy life in a chronically famine-infested, difficult environment, this plateau complex literally forms the human equator of the old world, separating the ethnic groups of Indo-Iranians to its south from the Chinese and nordic groups to its north. The very poverty of its resource base has, throughout the historic past, prompted, during stricken days, large waves of migrant nomadic groups descending on the agriculturally rich plains around, including those of India. Indian history is replete with such waves of migrants, entering the plains for loot but getting assimilated into the mainstream in course of time.

The Pamir knot on the apex of the convergence of mountain systems radiating all around is, literally, the roof of the world, sanctified in Indian traditions as Meru, the abode of the Gods, lying to the north of the land of Bharat. The Pamirs split the plateau complex into two: a smaller western one at lower heights and a broader eastern group at a much higher elevation, reinforcing the tremendous barrier effect of the snow-clad ranges, bereft of passes at accessible height. Each lobe of the plateaus lies in terraces at different levels, rimmed in by higher elevations, giving it a basin character. The highland backbone and the high plateaus within render communication across them between India and China almost impossible, except for the trickling trade of the Bhotias. The passageways to India are, thus, through the lesser plateaus to the west of the Pamirs, and the river valley passes at moderate heights in the Hindukush and Suleiman ranges that are to the north-west of the country. The Pamir knot has also functioned as the bridgeway on which converge transcontinental caravan trade routes, such as the Amber, Jade and Silk Routes that were important prior to the emergence of the sea-trade of the recent past. With the natural protection of its mountain-cum-desert fringes, the Pamirs provided tremendous scope for commercial and political expansion through history. Buddhism found its way from India into China through the Pamirs. Early Indo-China trade flowed through it; it was also the highway for all the Chinese pilgrims and Mongol invaders into India.

As all the early migrations and medieval political invasions reached India from the north-west, the Indus Valley and Punjab were the first recipients of frontier attacks. The coastal route along the less hospitable Iranian shores and Makran was much less frequented because of its difficult, barren terrain. Punjab has, thus, come to occupy the status of a transit zone in Indian history; no wonder Punjabis reveal excellent fighting qualities and the state contributes a lion's share to military recruitment. In contrast, the north-east, in spite of being in the lesser elevation of its hilly terrain, constitutes a formidable dual barrier of parallel hill ranges, narrow deep valleys and dense monsoon forests hosting many wild tribes. Throughout the early medieval and even modern historic periods, the guarding of the passes in the north-west and their control provided the key to the understanding of the events that engulfed the northern plains. Thus, the way into India, at least till the sixteenth century, was through the land gates of the north-west, and the door to the agricultural riches of the Ganga plains lay in Punjab on route corridor.

The signal importance of the Himalayas as a succession of parallel mountain chains with intervening narrow longitudinal valleys to the land and people of India cannot be underestimated (Fig. 1.2). No doubt its prime value lies in its imposition of physical isolation of India from the rest of Asia. Over

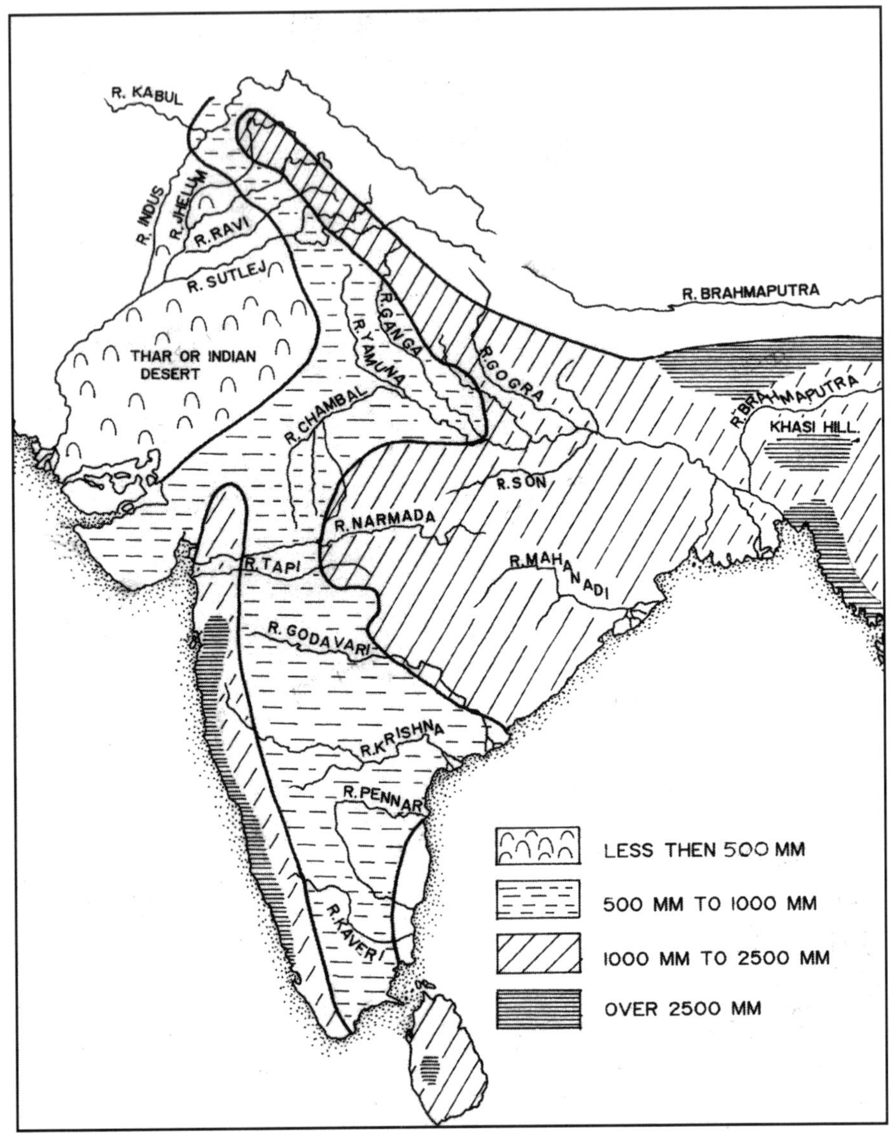

Fig. 1.2: India, rainfall pattern

centuries, it has acted as a natural frontier on the northern borders; though breached in the recent past, it has still not lost its value as a political frontier. Its secondary importance arises from the hydrological focus it provides for all the perennial snow-fed river systems that flow through the north Indian plains. The rich agricultural productivity of the well-watered river-transported alluvium is a direct gift of the Himalayas. While, on the one hand, the northern plains have been saved from bracing, snowy winters and harsh, cold, arctic winds, thanks to the Himalayan barrier, on the other, the generation of monsoon circulation and the accompanying copious orographic rains and warm tropical weather, notwithstanding the fact that the northern plains lie beyond the Tropic of Cancer, are endowments of the northern mountains. Protected by natural isolation, Indian society could afford to nurture a self-reliant resilient, agro-based community, living in relative peace and security. No wonder that in the Indian heritage, the Meru, Hima-Parvat and Ganga are held in high esteem and veneration.

The geographical tyranny of the external isolation imposed on India is made even more complete by the seas around that have few natural protected harbours to boast of, and are open to the fury of the monsoon and rough seas for a sizeable part of the year. No doubt, the commercial maritime trade relations of India with regions on the Indian Ocean borders, the Mediterranean countries of Europe, and China and Southeast Asia are centuries old, going back to the pre-Christian era. India enjoyed a favourable balance of trade, bringing in gold and silver in exchange for its trade commodities, such as spices, ivory, tropical timber, textiles, and tropical exotic birds and animals. The Gulf of Cambay, North Konkan, Malabar, the Tamil coast and Kalinga actively participated in this trade exchange across the sea. Yet the impact of maritime commercial relations was primarily confined to the coastal areas and communities, with only trickling effects being noticed inland through some routeways. In fact, maritime India lived apart from and relatively free of the happenings inland. The barrier effect of the surrounding oceans on India and its economy are no less profound than that of the land frontiers in the north. However, the occasional rise of a coastal power in Kalinga or the Tamil coast (the Cholas, with leanings towards the sea) produced cultural impacts in Ceylon and Southeast Asia. It is only with the coming in of European maritime trade colonies after the sixteenth century that the role of the seas changed; the gates to India became water gates and the external isolation, to an extent, was overcome.

This external isolation of the Indian land has led to the generation of an Indian society that is inward looking, tolerant and resilient to a degree. It absorbs and assimilates occasional incursions of religious and social ideas without much conflict or friction. Hinduism (and Buddhism and Jainism) lies at the root of the ethos and philosophy of Indian life and contributes to the cultural unity of India, notwithstanding the diversities within.

If external isolation is a dominant feature of the geography of India that has formed the strand-lines of its history, internal incoherence has dictated its historical heterogeneity and the dominance of regional hegemonies of power rather than a central power of authority, holding sway over the whole or most of the country. The very size of the country (almost half of Europe), with subcontinental dimensions, accounts for an immense variety of relief and climatic conditions, with a consequential diversity of farming and living patterns. India is a collection of lands and climates ranging between the desert and the rainforest, with multitudinous castes and tongues, not to mention its religious diversity. These necessarily lead to a persistent series of glaring contrasts and timeless antagonisms. The vastness of size and the lack of effective communication means never gave any reasonable hope of organizing itself much less the possibility of even organizing its surroundings. It was no wonder that political unity was late to emerge and had to overcome enormous hurdles.

Problems of internal communication and access between one part of the country and another was a major manifestation of its size and varied relief. Consolidation and the holding together effectively of large territorial areas for long periods of time was rendered difficult, if not impossible. The country's geography fostered the growth of a large number of languages and dialects with strong regional and local affinities, a host of religious faiths and beliefs under the common umbrella of Hinduism, and caste-bound societies that could live in mutual harmony and peace in a symbiotic fashion, fairly independent of each other, in pockets of cloistered, secure, regional environments surrounded by relatively less hospitable, if not hostile, surroundings. Regional friction leading to combat situations arose only when the wide frontiers, acting as zones of conflict, were breached by ambitious regional power centres. Thus, a number of nuclear zones naturally evolved in agriculturally rich enclaves, simultaneously or otherwise, but independent of each other. The zones of historical conflict, acting at times as potential conflict areas between adjoining nuclear areas, are set by major and minor geographical lineaments within the country; these have helped to structure the flow of the currents of Indian history.

Many nuclear zones of power have functioned as the determinants of Indian history. The marches or transit-zone of Punjab, the Awadh-Kosala region of UP, Malwa, coastal Kalinga, Magadha in Bihar, the lava shield of the middle Godavari Valley, the Tungabhadra lowlands, and coastal Tamil Nadu (Cholamandalam) are all examples of such enduring nuclear zones. Historically, Malwa reflects a duality of character. Its extensive agricultural base sustained by lava soils has given it an individuality; yet, as a land of passage on a vital routeway to the south, it constantly changed hands and remained 'the invincible appendage to the domains of every monarch' who became the master of the Ganga plains. The Middle Godavari plains in the lava shield of Maharashtra has a similar rich agro-base. Its distinctive historic personality arises from its status as a stronghold of Hinduism and the last bastion to fall to the foreign yoke. With a remarkable defence potential to retreat into the recesses of the Western Ghats, and a capacity to strike at will from hill fortresses with natural bastions in the Sahyadri, the Maratha power could hold at bay the much more powerful Mughals. The Tungabhadra country of north Karnataka, again with a rich agricultural base, was a transition area with cultural allegiance to the south and economic allegiance to the west coast. The Tamil coast in the deep south, together with Kerala, drew its strength of being nuclear power for its isolation from the rest of the country and its long-enduring maritime commercial contacts. It is 'the real old India, unravaged India, the India of unnumbered temples of indigenous art'. Kalinga on the east coast enjoyed a somewhat similar status, being at the terminal end of marches from the north. Awadh, Kosala and Magadha in the Ganga plains were agriculturally rich and had their safety in their interior locations, away from the routes of invasion.

The geographic lineaments that acted as segregators of regional power centres and compartmentalizing forces were mostly negative zones from the point of view of human settlement. They are the backbones of hill ranges, forest tracts, even marshes and deserts, that are all scantily peopled with tribal communities of a relatively low order of cultural development. At a national level, the Himalayan system is the most powerful historical barrier. Within the country, the most persistent geographical lineament of history is the central Indian watershed, a complex of hills and plateaus spreading east-west from Gujarat to Bengal and comprising the Vindhyas, the Satpuras, the Kaimur and Maikal ranges, and the plateaus of Bundelkhand, Rewa and Chotanagpur. Though not rising to high elevations, this multiple barrier of a formidable character has helped in defining Aryavarta as distinct from Dakshinapatha in the making of Indian history. While attempts to hold together the northern plains of Aryavarta occasionally bore fruit, as in the reigns of Asoka and the late Mughals, the rule of Delhi could never remain intact for long south of this lineament. In fact, the Deccan always remained politically fragmented by regional powers and owed little allegiance to the northern powers. The events that overtook the northern plains following the advance of Islam and the Muslim powers practically left the south undisturbed. The sole Muslim rule of the Bahamanis and, subsequently, the Nizam over Telangana was culturally and politically an Islamic enclave in the peninsula, with no areal contiguity with the Muslim rule in the north.

In view of the formidable nature of the obstruction offered by the central Indian lineament, the routeways through them and the pockets of internally organized communities within them assume historical significance. Thus, the Khandwa-Burhanpur gap assumed importance as the march route from the north into the Deccan, while Berar and the Tapti Valley became marshlands. The passage through Malwa leads to the Gujarat lowlands and onwards into Konkan; these areas, in spite of their maritime commercial interests, became politically unstable.

Within the Deccan, a minor lineament that has aided to keep the coastal communities away from the mainstream of inland history were the western and southern Ghats; they, thus, came to develop a maritime outlook.

The Terai in the foothills of the Himalayas was yet another pioneering fringe. Marwar to the west of the Aravalis was also a zone of conflict when regional powers emerged within it as did the Rajputs later. Towards the east, the Bengal lowlands with their riverine culture and water transport breathed its own historic air, while the Assam lowlands of the Brahmaputra Valley formed a natural *cul de sac*, difficult of approach and communication and, hence, formed a pocket of isolation. It is the last frontier of Indian settlement.

Lying between the marshlands of Punjab and the shock-absorbing Gangetic belt, between the Aravalis backed by the Thar and the Himalayan elevations, at the convergence of the Cambay, Malwa and Gwalior routeways, and at the head of the Jumna-Sutlej doab, Delhi epitomizes the history of Hindustan. It has come to represent all the great phases of development of the history of India – Hindu, Muslim and British. Its commanding position makes it the geographical pivot of Indian history. He who rules Delhi controls the northern plains.

The invincibility of the northern frontiers have been rudely shaken in the recent past. Internal incoherence is being overcome by means of modern transport and communication and a central authority of power. The persistent fundamentals of external isolation and internal incoherence have been breached to give way to a political unity, reinforcing the cultural unity. With the Indian ocean becoming the ocean of the future, the India of tomorrow has to gain a rising maritime status and convert the ocean into a bond of union.

Chapter 2

Early Hunter-Gatherers: The Lower Palaeolithic

R.S. Pappu

INTRODUCTION

The Lower Palaeolithic forms the earliest cultural stage in the history of mankind in India as elsewhere in the world and, in terms of geological time scale, covers the major portion of the Quaternary period. This cultural stage was earlier known by various terms such as the Early Stone Age,[1] Series I,[2] Madrasian[3] and Chopper-Biface element.[4] It has now been finally accepted that the European system of dividing the Stone Age into the Palaeolithic, Mesolithic and Neolithic, and subdividing the Palaeolithic into Lower, Middle and Upper is more appropriate to the Indian evidence.[5]

There is adequate evidence for the existence of two distinct Lower Palaeolithic cultural traditions in India, viz., the Soan tradition and the biface or handaxe-cleaver tradition. These were found to be concentrated in two different regions. The region lying to the north of the Indo-Gangetic plain (extra-peninsula) has mainly yielded lithic assemblages dominated by the first tool tradition, while the region lying to the south of this plain, viz., peninsular India, brought forth industries of the second tradition. The artefacts of the first cultural complex were first noticed by De Terra and Paterson (1939) in the Soan Valley in West Punjab (now in Pakistan) and, hence, this cultural complex was designated as the Soan culture after the river Soan.[6] Owing to the dominance of the chopper-chopping type of tools (pebble tools)

[1] Subbarao (1958), *The Personality of India*, M.S. University, Baroda.

[2] L.A. Cammiade, and M.C. Burkitt (1930), 'Fresh Light on the Stone Age of Southeast India', *Antiquity*, 4, pp. 327-39.

[3] H. De Terra, and T.T. Paterson (1939), *Studies on the Ice Age in India and Associated Human Cultures*, Carnegie Institution, Washington D.C.

[4] A.K. Ghosh (1974), 'Concept of Chopper/Chopping Tool Complex in India', in V.N. Misra and P. Bellwood (eds.), *Perspectives in Palaeoanthropology*, Firma K.L. Mukhopadhyay, Calcutta, pp. 221-34.

[5] V.N. Misra (1962), 'Problems of Terminology in Indian Prehistory', *Eastern Anthropologist*, 15(2), pp. 113-24.

[6] De Terra and Paterson (1939), op. cit.

in this complex, it is also referred to the chopper-chopping tool complex. This cultural phase seems to be related to chopper-chopping tool cultures in Southeast Asia, viz., the Anyathian culture of Myanmar (Burma), the Tampanian of Malaya, the Patjitanian of Indonesia and the Choukoutienian of China.[7]

Peninsular India happens to be the homeland of the second tradition, i.e. the handaxe-cleaver complex. Two substages, viz., the Abbevillian and the Acheulian have been recognized in the lithic industries of this tradition. These divisions are based on typo-technology, the former exhibiting inferior workmanship and the later displaying refined workmanship. The terms Abbevillian and Acheulian are derived from the sites Abbeville and Saint Acheul on the river Somme in France where lithic industries showing these typo-technological characters were first discovered. Lithic industries exhibiting a similar type of characters were subsequently noticed in other parts of the world, viz., Africa, the Near East and India, and the terms Abbevillian and Acheulian were used to describe these typo-technologically similar industries. Lower Palaeolithic assemblages in peninsular India are, by and large, dominated by tool-types showing Acheulian characters and the Abbevillian element is rather feeble. The term Acheulian for lithic industries in India has been considered mainly with reference to typo-technology and this tradition possesses its own distinct characteristic features. However, the broad similarity in typo-technology remains remarkable and that is why the term Acheulian continues to be used.

RESUME OF PALAEOLITHIC RESEARCH

The first discovery of a Palaeolithic artefact in India was made on 30 May 1863 at Pallavaram near Chennai in Tamil Nadu by Robert Bruce Foote of the Geological Survey of India.[8] The find was a handaxe which was recovered from the detrital laterite gravel deposit. Palaeolithic research in India is, thus, more than 135 years old and commenced more or less simultaneously with epoch-making discoveries regarding the origin and antiquity of man in Europe. Noteworthy developments, however, in Palaeolithic studies in India began only from 1950 onwards. These firmly established the existence of three cultural stages of the Palaeolithic, viz., the Lower, Middle and Upper in various parts of the Indian subcontinent.

Four broad phases could be identified in the development of Palaeolithic research in India: the first spanning 1863 to 1912, the second from 1930 to 1950, the third from 1950 to 1970, and the fourth from the 1970s to the present.

[7]H.L. Movius (Jr) (1948b), 'The Lower Palaeolithic Cultures of Southern and Eastern Asia', *Transactions of the American Philosophical Society,* New Series, Part IV, pp. 330-420.

[8]R.B. Foote (1916), *The Foote Collection of Indian Prehistoric and Prehistoric Antiquities*: *Notes on their Ages and Distributions,* Government Museum, Madras.

First Phase

After the first discovery of a Palaeolithic implement by Foote in 1863, a number of geologists of the Geological Survey of India and a few civil servants (King, Ball, Wynne, Hacket, Blandford, Oldham, Theobald, Cockburn, Rivetta-Carnac and many others) reported Palaeolithic artefacts from a number of river valleys in peninsular India.[9] Among these, the discoveries made by Foote occupy a prominent place. Foote took keen interest in the twin fields of prehistoric archaeology and Quaternary geology and carried out investigations in both these fields for more than thirty years in southern and western India. In the course of his routine geological field studies, he made an extensive collection of prehistoric antiquities of various types and ages, as also detailed notes of his finds which were published in two volumes in 1914 and 1916 by the Madras Government Museum.[10] The pioneering work undertaken during this phase (mainly by Foote and others) proved that the Indian subcontinent is extremely rich in prehistoric finds.

Second Phase

After Foote's pioneer work, there was a void in prehistoric studies during the first decades of the last century. Palaeolithic studies were revived in the mid-1930s when Cammiade and Burkitt (1930) carried out investigations in the Kurnool region of Andhra Pradesh.[11] The presence of four cultural stages, viz., Series I to IV based on differences in typo-technology, were recognized. These stages more or less coincided with the division of the Palaeolithic into the Lower, Middle and Upper Palaeolithic and the Mesolithic. This work was followed by the Yale-Cambridge expedition under the leadership of Helmut de Terra.[12] Explorations were undertaken by them in the glacial tracts of the Kashmir Valley, the adjacent periglacial region of the Chennai Potwar Plateau, the Narmada Valley in central India and the region around along the eastern coast. The expedition recognized a fourfold glacial succession in the Kashmir Valley, a record presumed to be parallel to that represented in the Alpine sequence in Europe. The sequence worked out in the Kashmir Valley was correlated with the terrace sequence observed on the river Soan in the Potwar Plateau. Pebble tools of the chopper-chopping tool tradition were recovered from these terraces in the Soan Valley. The pebble tool industry was designated as Soan and was divided into Lower, Middle and Upper. Tools of the handaxe-cleaver tradition were also noticed at a few localities. The expedition studied

[9]Dasgupta, R.C. (1931), 'Bibliography of Prehistoric Indian Antiquities', Journal and Proceedings of *ASB* (New Series), 27, 1, pp. 1-96.

[10]R.B. Foote (1914), *The Foote Collection of Indian Prehistoric and Prehistoric Antiquities: Catalogue Raisonne*, Government Museum, Madras. Also Foote (1916), op. cit.

[11]Cammiade and Burkitt (1930), op. cit.

[12]De Terra and Paterson (1939), op. cit.

the Narmada Valley between Hoshangabad and Narsinghpur in Madhya Pradesh. The alluvium having a total thickness of about 45 m was divided into three groups, viz., the Lower, Upper and Cotton soil group. This alluvium yielded a sequence of lithic industries of Abbevillian and Acheulian characters with a large number of mammalian fossils. The Kortalayar Valley in Tamil Nadu around Madras was thoroughly investigated by Krishnaswami.[13] He observed three distinct terraces and recovered from them lithic industries showing stratigraphical as well as typological evolution based on patination, staining and state of preservation.

Todd (1939) discovered a stratigraphic sequence near Bombay in the Kandivali-Borivali region along the western coast in Maharashtra which yielded lithic industries ranging from the Lower Palaeolithic to the Mesolithic.[14] N.K. Bose and D. Sen (1948) undertook investigations in the Mayurbhanj region of Orissa.[15] Lower Palaeolithic tool-bearing lateritic gravel was excavated at Kuliana and a lithic industry showing Abbevillio-Acheulian characters was recovered. This site has the distinction of being the first Palaeolithic site to be excavated in the Indian subcontinent. H.D. Sankalia (1946), on the basis of clues left by Foote in north Gujarat, carried out investigations in the Sabarmati, Mahi, Karjan and other river valleys which brought to light the evidence of lithic industries showing Abbevillio-Acheulian characters.[16]

Third Phase

In contrast with the limited work undertaken during the first two phases, there was a phenomenal expansion of Palaeolithic studies in the third phase stretching between 1950 to 1970. The late H.D. Sankalia of the Deccan College Postgraduate and Research Institute, Pune, was in the lead and organized planned explorations in diverse geographical regions of India. These were carried out by himself, his colleagues and his research scholars. Sankalia was fully aware of the contribution of geology in the development of Palaeolithic studies and, therefore, invited F.E. Zeuner, Professor of Environmental Archaeology at the Institute of Archaeology, London, in 1949-50. Expeditions were arranged under Zeuner's leadership to study the environmental aspects of Palaeolithic and Mesolithic sites in different river valleys of peninsular India. A monograph was published giving the preliminary

[13] V.D. Krishnaswami (1938), 'Environmental and Cultural Changes of the Prehistoric Man near Madras', *Journal of Madras Geographical Association*, 13, pp. 58-90.

[14] K.R.U. Tod (1939), 'Palaeolithic Industries of Bombay', *JRAI*, LXIV, pp. 257-72.

[15] N.K. Bose and D. Sen (1948), *Excavations in Mayurbhanj*, Calcutta University, Calcutta.

[16] H.D. Sankalia (1946), *Investigations into the Prehistoric Archaeology of Gujarat*, Baroda State Government, Baroda.

findings of the expedition in Gujarat and Maharashtra.[17] These studies laid the foundation of environmental archaeology in India.

The most significant contribution of Zeuner's work in India is the use of river deposits like gravels and silts for building up regional stratigraphic-cum-climatic sequences. The gravel-silt and humid-dry phases approach towards understanding the past environment and the correlation of Stone Age cultures with climatic phases emerged as a dominant research paradigm in Indian Palaeolithic studies during this phase.[18] Efforts were made to fix the relative stratigraphic-chronological contexts of lithic assemblages by ascertaining their sedimentary contexts in gravel and silt deposits forming alluvial cliff sections. Two, three or even more cycles of aggradation, each beginning with gravels and ending with silts, were noticed in a number of river valleys. Deposits at the base of the first aggradation cycle have generally yielded Lower Palaeolithic tools. Artefacts recovered from the gravel beds are often in rolled condition, thereby indicating their transportation over considerable distances from the original place of manufacture. These, therefore, are secondary occurrences of cultural materials in river gravels and only have a limited value in reconstructing past human lifestyle.

Fourth Phase

Realizing the limitations of the study of cultural materials from secondary sites, prehistorians in India from the 1970s onwards concentrated their investigations on the discovery and systematic excavation of sites in primary or semi-primary contexts. A number of Lower Palaeolithic Acheulian sites were discovered in such contexts and were excavated. Attempts were made to obtain precise information for both cultural and ecological reconstruction on the basis of the evidence from these sites. There has been a gradual shift in the methodology, techniques, and concepts used in Palaeolithic research. Since 1970, prehistorians in India have began to adopt the processual approach. Studies are now aimed at (a) recovery of homogeneous stone artefacts from excavated primary sites and their detailed typo-technological analysis, (b) reconstruction of the nature of hominid activities at primary sites, (c) study of strategies for the utilization of water, plant and animal food resources, and (d) study of sites in relation to various biophysical aspects of the surrounding environment with a view to understanding past human adaptations.

An important development since 1970 concerns the application of methods, techniques and concepts from the discipline of earth sciences to the field of

[17] F.E. Zeuner (1950), *Stone Age and Pleistocene Chronology in Gujarat*, Deccan College, Poona.

[18] K. Paddayya (1994), 'Investigation of Man-Environment Relationship in Indian Archaeology: Some Theoretical Considerations', *ME*, XIX, 1-2, pp. 1-28.

Palaeolithic archaeology.[19] Geoarchaeologists in India have made a significant contribution to Palaeolithic studies and attempts have been made by these scholars to resolve problems pertaining to stratigraphy, palaeoenvironment, sea level changes, river behaviour, neo-tectonics, settlement pattern, site catchment analysis, site formation processes and chronology.

DISTRIBUTION OF SETTLEMENTS

Investigations undertaken in different parts of India during the last three or four decades have brought to light a large number of sites of the Lower Palaeolithic culture and this has substantially increased our knowledge of their distribution pattern (Fig. 2.1). Twenty-two sites of this cultural phase in peninsular India (Fig. 2.2) and one in the extra-peninsula in a primary or semi-primary context have been excavated. The excavation of living sites has added a new dimension to Lower Palaeolithic studies in India and has helped to a great extent in the interpretation of the behavioural pattern of Lower Palaeolithic communities. This cultural phase may now be said to have extended practicallly all over the country, though their density is greater in some areas. The absence or sparseness of sites in some parts of the country is mainly due to ecological factors. The total absence of sites in the Indo-Gangetic plains is obviously due to the non-availability of rocks necessary for preparing stone artefacts. There is also the possibility that if any sites existed here in the past, they were buried subsequently under the thick alluvium. Sites are sparse in north-east India and along the Western and Eastern Ghats due to the rugged terrain, heavy rainfall and thick vegetation.

Lower Palaeolithic sites are thus found in varied geographical situations in India, viz., on river terraces in the sub-Himalayan region of north-west India[20]

[19]R.S. Pappu (1995), 'The Contribution of the Earth Sciences to the Development of Indian Archaeology', in S. Wadia et al. (eds.), *Quaternary Environment and Geoarchaeology of India*, Geological Society of India, Bangalore, pp. 414-24.

[20] D. Sen (1955), 'Nalagarh Palaeolithic Culture', *Man in India*, 35, pp. 177-84; B.B. Lal (1956), 'Palaeoliths from the Beas and Banganga Valleys, Punjab', *AI*, 12, pp. 58-92; R.V. Joshi et. al. (1975), 'Early and Middle Palaeolithic Tools, from River Terraces in the Saketi Area, Markand Valley, Himachal Pradesh', *Current Science*, 44, pp. 464-5; R.V. Joshi et al. (1978), 'Environments and Cultures of Early Man in the North-west India: A Reappraisal, *JGSI*, 19, 2, pp. 83-6; G.C. Mohapatra (1966), 'Preliminary Report of the Exploration and Excavation of Stone Age Sites in Punjab', *BDCRI*, 25, pp. 221-37; idem (1975), 'Acheulia Element in the Soan Culture Area', *Journal of the Archaeological Society of Nippon*, 80, 4, pp. 4-18; idem (1982), 'Acheulian Distribution in the Siwalik of Punjab', in R.K. Sharma (ed.), *Indian Archaeology: New Perspectives*, Agam Kala Prakashan, Delhi, pp. 28-37; idem (1997), 'Reidentification of Acheulian Element in the Western Sub-Himalayan Lithic Complex in the Light of New Discoveries', in V.D. Misra and J.N. Pal (eds.), *Indian Prehistory: 1980*, University of Allahabad, Allahabad, pp. 43-50.

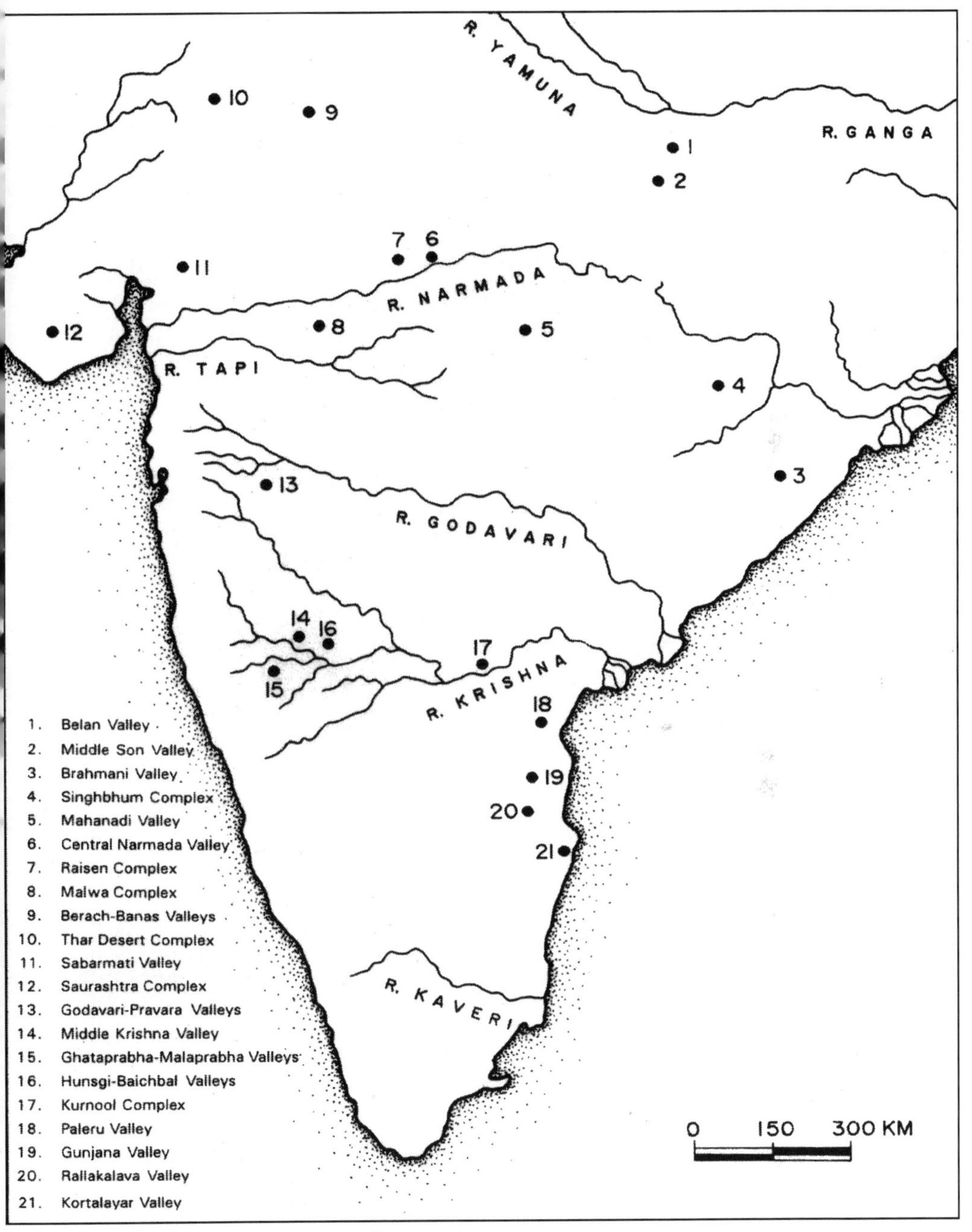

Fig. 2.1: Important Lower Palaeolithic sites and river valley complexes in Peninsular India

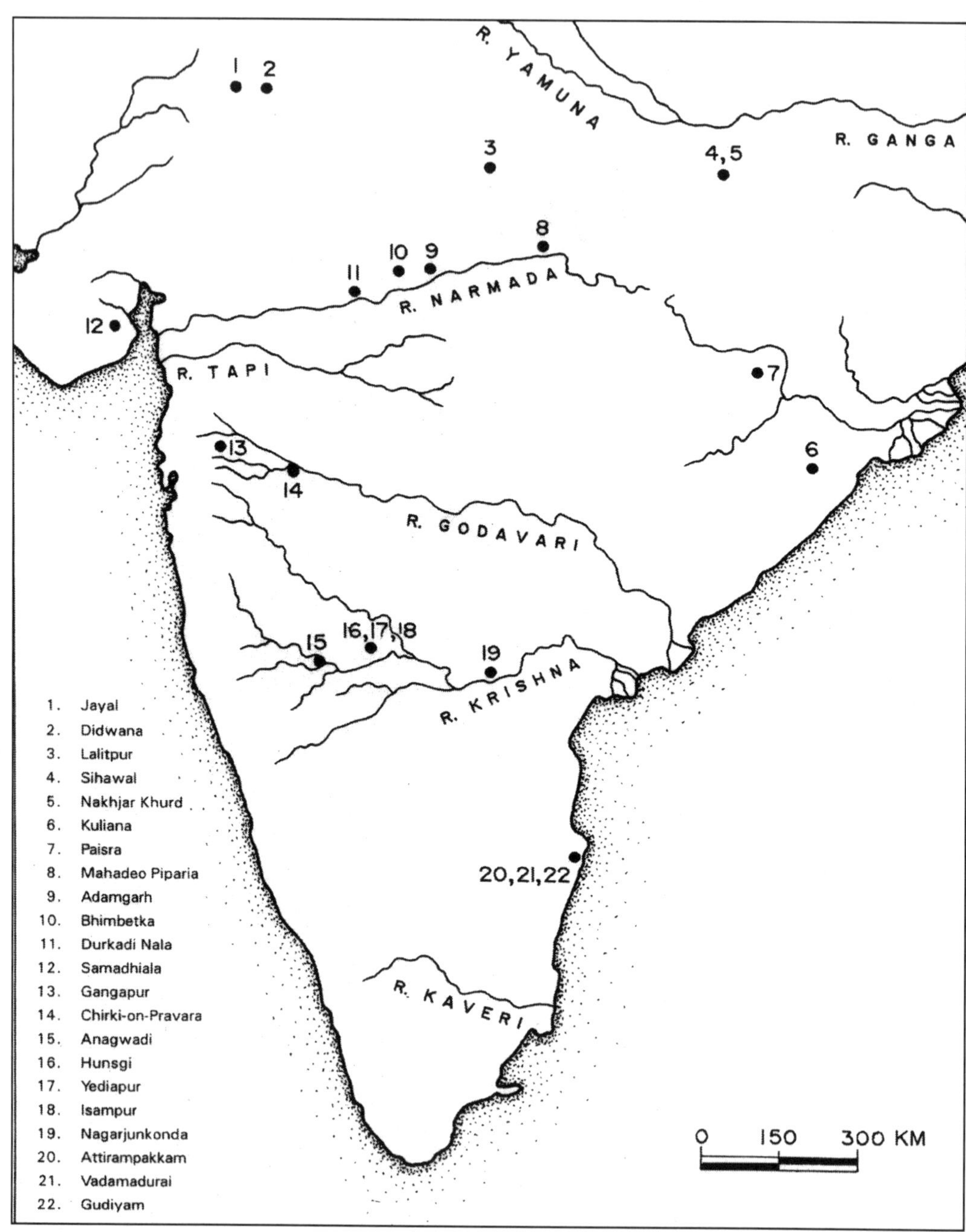

Fig. 2.2: Lower Palaeolithic excavated sites in Peninsular India

in arid to semi-arid regions in Western Rajasthan,[21] forested and hilly regions of Central India (Vindhyas)[22] and eastern India (Chota Nagpur plateau),[23] all along the east coast in the states of Orissa,[24] Andhra Pradesh and Tamil Nadu,[25] plateau regions of the Deccan upland,[26] near rock exposures in central India[27] in rocak shelters and caves in central India,[28] along the west

[21] V.N. Misra (1987), 'Middle Pleistocene Adaptations in India', in Olga Soffer (ed.), *The Pleistocene Old World: Regional Perspectives*, Plenum Press, New York, pp. 99-119; idem (1995), 'Geoarchaeology of the Thar Desert, Northwest India', in S. Wadia, R. Korisettar and V.S. Kale (eds.), *Quaternary Environments and Geoarchaeology of India*, Geological Society of India, Bangalore, pp. 210-24.

[22] G.R. Sharma (1973), 'Stone Age in the Vindhyas and the Ganga Valley', in D.P. Agarwal and A. Ghosh (eds.), *Radio Carbon and Indian Archaeology,* Tata Institute of Fundamental Research, Bombay, pp. 106-10; G.R. Sharma and J.D. Clark (1982), 'Palaeoenvironments and Prehistory in the Middle Son Valley, Northern Madhya Pradesh', *ME*, VI, pp. 56-62; idem (1983) (eds.), *Palaeoenvironments and Prehistory in the Middle Son Valley (Madhya Pradesh, North Central India)*, Abinash Prakashan, Allahabad.

[23] A.K. Ghosh (1970), 'The Palaeolithic Cultures of Singhbhum', *Transactions of the American Philosophical Society*, 60, 1, pp. 1-68; P.C. Pant and V. Jayaswal (1991), *Paisra: The Stone Age Settlement of Bihar*, Agam Kala Prakashan, Delhi.

[24] G.C. Mohapatra (1962), *The Stone Age Cultures of Orissa,* Deccan College, Poona. K.C. Tripathy (1980), *Lithic Industries in India: A Study of South-western Orissa*, Inter India Publications, New Delhi.

[25] K.T. Reddy (1994), 'Coastal Ecology and Archaeology: Evidence from the East Coast of India', *ME*, XIX, 1-2, pp. 43-56.

[26] R.V. Joshi (1955), *Pleistocene Studies in the Malaprabha Basin*, Deccan College, Poona; R.S. Pappu (1974), *Pleistocene Studies in the Upper Krishna Basin*, Deccan College, Poona; R.S. Pappu and S.G. Deo (1994), *Man-Land Relationships During Palaeolithic Times in the Kaladgi Basin, Karnataka,* Deccan College, Poona; R. Korisettar (1979), 'Prehistory and Geomorphology of the Middle Krishna Karnataka', Ph.D. dissertation (unpublished), University of Poona, Pune; idem (1985), 'The Acheulian Site of Almatti, Karnataka', in V.N. Misra and P. Bellwood (eds.), *Recent Advances in Indo-Pacific Prehistory*, Oxford-IBH, New Delhi, pp. 65-8; K. Paddaya (1982), *The Acheulian Culture of Hunsgi Valley (Peninsular India): A Settlement System Perspective*, Deccan College, Pune.

[27] J. Jacobson (1975), 'Early Stone Age Habitation Sites in Eastern Malwa', *Proceedings of the American Philosophical Society*, 119 pp. 280-97; idem (1985), 'Acheulian Surface Sites in Central India', in V.N. Misra and P. Bellwood (eds.), *Recent Advances in Indo-Pacific Prehistory*, op. cit., pp. 49-57.

[28] V.N. Misra (1978), 'The Acheulian Indusry of Rock Shelter III F-23 at Bhimbetka, Central India', *Australian Archaeology*, 8, pp. 63-106; idem (1985), 'The Acheulian Succession at Bhimbetka, Central India', in V.N. Misra and P. Bellwood (eds.), *Recent Advances in Indo-Pacific Prehistory*, op. cit., pp. 35-48; R.V. Joshi (1978), *Stone Age Cultures of Central India: Report on the Excavations of Rock-Shelters at Adamgarh, Madhya Pradesh*, Deccan College, Pune.

coast in Kerala,[29] Goa,[30] Konkan (Maharashtra coast),[31] Saurashtra[32] and Kutch.[33]

The Lower Palaeolithic communities thus seem to have adapted to all kinds of ecozones despite their regional differences. On the basis of the available evidence, it has now been firmly established that Indian subcontinent, in particular Peninsular India, is one of the richest areas for the Lower Palaeolithic cultural material in the Old World.

HABITATS

On the basis of the geomorphic settings of sites and the origin of associated deposits, Lower Palaeolithic Acheulian sites have been classified into five groups by Pappu (1985), viz., alluvial, coastal, slope, surface, and rockshelter and cave sites.[34] The first four groups fall into the category of open air sites. The rockshelter and cave category of sites are 'few in number if not altogether lacking'. The study of the locations of these sites suggests that early man lived mostly close to river banks, sea and lake shores, and in the foothill areas. The easy availability of perennial water supply, plant and animal foods and raw materials for fashioning stone artefacts were the main considerations while selecting the occupation sites.

Till 1970, a majority of the sites that were discovered were in riverine contexts. This pattern was due to the concentration of field studies in the river valleys. The artefacts from such deposits are disturbed, transported and

[29] P. Rajendran (1989), *The Prehistoric Cultures and Environments of Kerala*, Classical Publishing Company, New Delhi.

[30] L.D. Goudeller and Ravi Korisettar (1993), 'The First Discovery of Acheulian Bifaces in Goa: Implications for the Archaoelogy of West Coast of India', *ME*, XVIII, 1, pp. 35-42.

[31] Stativa Guzder (1980), *Quaternary Environment and Stone Age Cultures of the Konkan, Coastal Maharahtra, India*, Deccan College, Pune; R.V. Joshi and B.P. Bopardikar (1972), 'Stone Age Cultures of Konkan', in S.B. Deo (ed.), *Archaeological Congress and Seminar Papers*, Nagpur University, Nagpur, pp. 47-57.

[32] H.D. Sankalia (1965), 'Early Stone Age in Saurashtra Gujarat', *Miscelanes en Homenaje al Abate Henri Brenii (1877-1961)*, T.II, Institute de Prehistoria, Barcelona, pp. 327-46; V.S. Lele (1989), 'Quaternary Formations in the Bhadar Valley', *BDCRI*, 47-8, pp. 165-206; A.R. Marathe (1981), *Geoarchaeology of the Hiran Valley, Saurashtra, India*, Deccan College, Pune; S. Chakrabarti (1983), 'Acheulian Culture in Saurashtra in Relation to Pleistocene Stratigraphy: An Overview, *JIAS*, 18, 1, pp. 1-9; idem (1995), 'Late Quaternary Stratigraphy and an Upper Acheulian Occupation Site in the Kalubhar Valley, Saurashtra', in S. Wadia et al. (eds.), *Quaternary Environments and Geoarchaeology of India*, Geological Society of India, Bangalore, pp. 277-81.

[33] Z.D. Ansari and R.S. Pappu (1973), 'Stone Age in Kutch, Gujarat', *BDCRI* 31, pp. 150-67.

[34] R.S. Pappu (1985), 'Geomorphic Setting of Acheulian Sites in Peninsular India', in V.N. Misra and P. Bellwood (eds.), *Recent Advances in Indo-Pacific Prehistory*, op. cit., pp. 9-12.

redeposited, and have lost their primary context of utility. These sites only suggest that the makers and users of these tools were the inhabitants of the vicinity area. It is now realized that to obtain a comprehensive picture of the life of early hunting and food-gathering communities, it is essential to have data from excavated primary sites.[35] A number of such primary sites connected with occupation activities have been discovered and systematically investigated in recent years in different parts of peninsular India.

Open air primary occupation Acheulian sites are known from Chirki-Nevasa in Maharashtra,[36] Lalitpur in Uttar Pradesh,[37] Hunsgi-Baichbal valleys (Shorapur Doab) in Karnataka[38] the (Fig. 2.3), Paisra in Bihar[39] and the Raisen district in Madhya Pradesh.[40] Semi-primary Acheulian sites associated with alluvial

[35] K. Paddayya (1978), 'New Research Designs and Field Techniques in the Palaeolithic Archaeology of India', *World Archaeology*, 10, pp. 94-110.

[36] G. Corvinus (1981), *A Survey of Pravara River System in Western Maharashtra, India*, vol. 2; *The Excavations of the Acheulian Site of Chirki-on-Pravara, India*, Institute for Urgeschichte, Tubingen.

[37] R. Singh (1965), 'Palaeolithic Industries of Northern Bundelkhand', Ph.D. dissertation, (unpublished), University of Poona, Poona.

[38] K. Paddayya (1975), 'Investigations into the Acheulian Phase in the Shorapur Doab, Peninsular India', *Quarter*, 26, pp. 5-11; idem (1976), 'The Acheulian Culture of the Hunsgi Valley, South India', *CA*, 17, pp. 760-1; idem (1977), 'The Acheulian Culture of the Hunsgi Valley, Shorapur Doab, Peninsular India', *Proceedings of the American Philosophical Society*, 121, pp. 383-406; idem (1979a), 'Excavations of a New Acheulian Occupation Site at Hunsgi, Peninsular India', *Quarter*, 29-30, pp. 134-55; idem (1979b), 'Palaeoethnography *vis-a-vis* the Stone Age Cultures of India: Some Methodological Considerations', *BDCRI*, 38, pp. 63-90; idem (1982), *The Acheulian Culture of Hunsgi Valley (Peninsular India): A Settlement System Perspective*, Deccan College, Pune; idem (1985), 'Acheulian Occupation Sites and Associated Fossil Fauna from Hunsgi-Baichbal Valleys, Peninsular India', *Anthropas*, 80, pp. 653-8; idem (1987a), 'Excavation of an Acheulian Occupation Site at Yedipur, Peninsular India', *Anthropos*, 82, pp. 610-14; idem (1989), 'The Acheulian Culture Localities among the Fatehpur Nullah, Baichbal Valley, Karnataka, Peninsular India', in J.M. Kenoyer (ed.), *Old Problems and New Perspectives in the Archaeology of South Asia*, University of Wisconsin, Madison, pp. 21-8; idem (1991), 'The Acheulian Culture of the Hunsgi-Baichbal Valleys, Peninsular India, a Processual Study', *Quarter*, 41-2, pp. 111-38.

[39] Pant and Jayswal 1991, op. cit.

[40] J. Jacobson (1975), op. cit.; idem (1976), 'Evidence for Prehistoric Habitation Patterns in Eastern Malwa', in K.A.R. Kennedy and G. Possehl (eds.), *Ecological Backgrounds of South Asian Prehistory*, South Asia Occasional Papers and Theses, Cornell University of New York, pp. 1-63; idem (1985), 'Acheulian Surface Sites in Central India', in V.N. Misra and P. Bellwood (eds.), *Recent Advances in Indo-Pacific Prehistory*, op. cit., pp. 49-57.

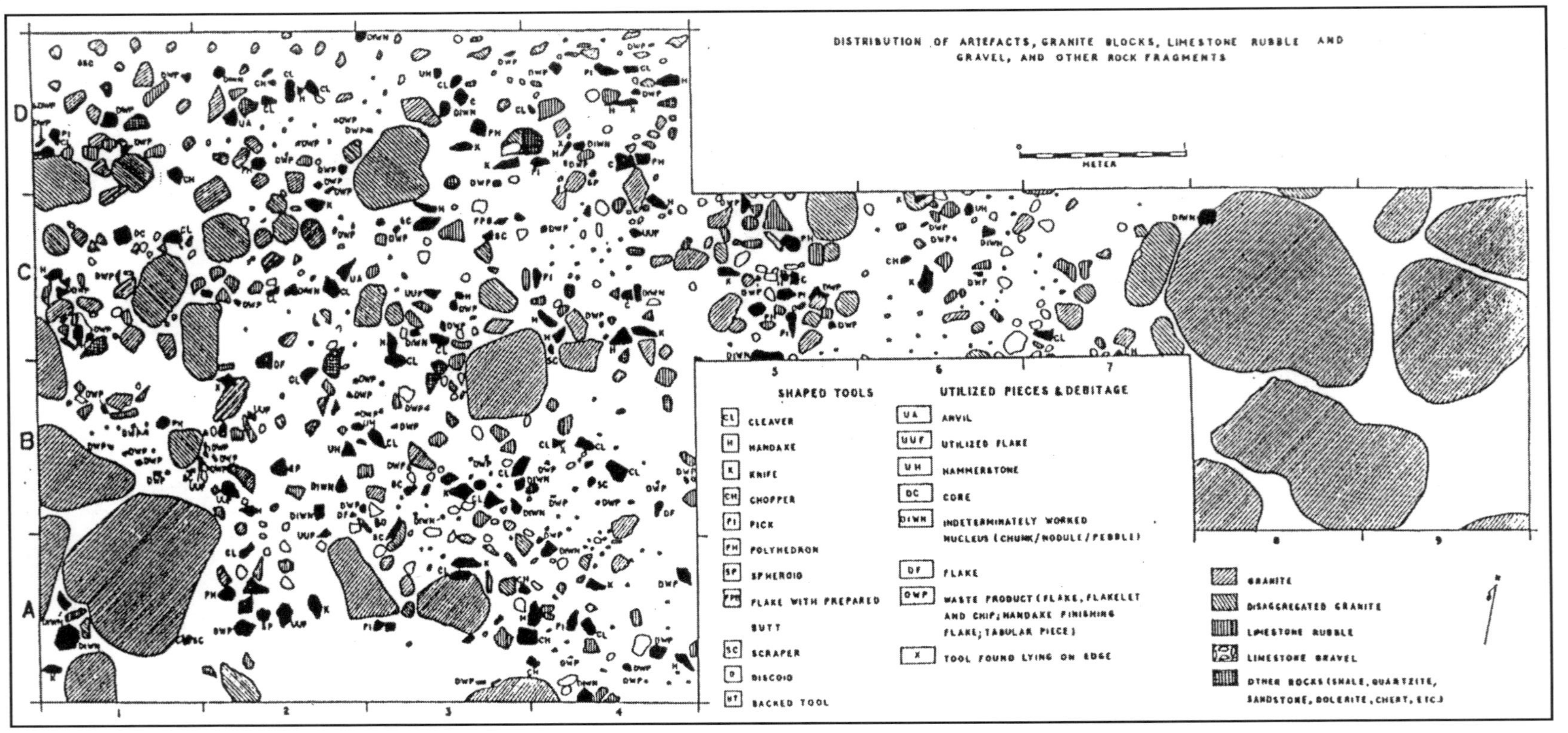

Fig. 2.3: Acheulian occupation floor, Trench 3, Locality V, Hunsgi (after Paddayya 1982)

deposits occur at Anagwadi,[41] Khyad,[42] in Karnataka, Gangapur[43] and Bori[44] in Maharashtra, Attirampakkam, Gudiyam and Vadamadurai in Tamil Nadu,[45] Samadhiala[46] in Gujarat, Belan Valley in Uttar Pradesh,[47] Son Valley in Madhya Pradesh[48] and Didwana in Rajasthan.[49] The rock shelters and caves at Adamgarh[50] and Bhimbetka[51] in Madhya Pradesh (Fig. 2.4) have also provided much better evidence of occupation sites. There is little evidence available on habitation structures or dwellings. However, a glimpse of the dwellings of these people can be had from excavations undertaken at a few primary occupation sites. At Bhimbetka, there is evidence of the erection of a wall of boulders for partitioning in one of the rock shelters during the Acheulian phase.[52] It appears that the rock shelters were occupied seasonally, particularly in the rainy

[41] R.S. Pappu (1974), op. cit.; idem (1990), 'Quaternary Environment and Palaeolithic Cultures of the Ghataprabha Basin, Karnataka', A. Sundara (ed.), *Archaeology in Karnataka*, Directorate of Archaeology and Museums, Mysore, pp. 17-22; Pappu and Deo (1994), op. cit.

[42] Joshi (1955), op. cit.; R.S. Pappu (1981), 'Recent Geoarchaeological Investigations around Badami District Bijapur, Karnataka', *BDCRI*, 39-40, pp. 170-9.

[43] R.V. Joshi et al. (1966), 'Animal Fossils and Early Stone Age Tools, from Gangapur on the Godavari River, Nasik District, Maharashtra State', *Current Science*, 35, p. 144; Arun Kumar (1985), 'Quaternary Studies of the Upper Godavari Valley: A Study in Environmental Archaeology', Ph.D. dissertation (unpublished) University of Poona, Pune; idem (1989), 'Almetrical Analysis of Handaxes and Cleavers from the Acheulian Site at Gangapur, Nasik District, Maharashtra', *ME* XIII, pp. 49-64.

[44] V.S. Kale et al. (1986), 'Discovery of an Acheulian Site at Bori, District Pune', *BDCRI*, 45, pp. 46-9; R. Korisettar et al. (1989a), 'Age of the Bori Volcanic Ash and Lower Palaeolithic Culture of the Kukdi Valley, Maharashtra', *BDCRI*, 47-8, pp. 135-7; R. Korisettar et al. (1989b), 'Discovery of a Tephra bed in the Quaternary Alluvial Sediments of Pune District (Maharashtra), Peninsular India', *Current Science*, 58, 10, pp. 564-7.

[45] De Terra and Paterson (1939), op. cit.; Krishnaswami (1938), op. cit.; *IAR* 1962-3, 1963-4, 1964-5, 1966-7; V. Jayaswal (1985), 'The Acheulian Industry of Vadamadurai', in V.N. Misra and P. Bellwood (eds.), *Recent Advances in Indo-Pocific Prehistory*, Oxford-IBH, New Delhi, pp. 73-6; Shanti Pappu (1996), 'Reinvestigation of the Prehistoric Archaeological Record in the Kortallayar Basin, Tamil Nadu', *ME*, XX, 1, pp. 1-23.

[46] Chakrabarti (1983), op. cit.; idem (1995), op. cit.

[47] Sharma (1973), op. cit.

[48] Sharma and Clark (1982), op. cit.; idem (1983), op. cit.

[49] Misra, (1995), op. cit.; V.N. Misra et al. (1982), 'Acheulian Occupation and Evolving Landscape around Didwana in the Thar Desert, India', *ME*, VI, pp. 72-86; idem (1988), 'Late Middle Pleistocene Environment of Acheulian Culture Around Didwana, Rajasthan'; C. Gaillard et al. (1983), 'Acheulian Occupation at Singi Talav in the Thar Desert: A Preliminary Report on 1982 Excavation', *ME*, VII, pp. 112-30; idem (1985), 'Acheulian Occupation in Singi Talav, Thar Desert: A Preliminary Report on 1981 Excavation', *BDCRI*, 44, pp. 141-52.

[50] Joshi (1978), op. cit.

[51] Misra (1978), op. cit.; idem (1985), op. cit.

[52] Ibid.

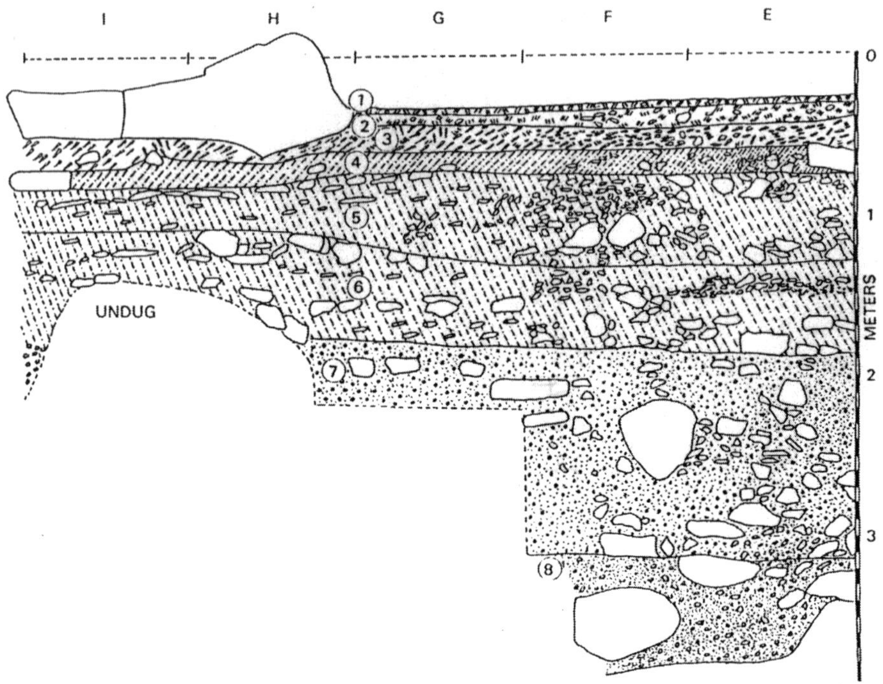

Fig. 2.4: Section through III F-23, Bhimbetka (after Misra 1985)

season, and the Acheulian groups mostly lived in the open. The open camp sites were probably provided with wind breaks. There is evidence available of wind breaks at Chirki-Nevasa and Hunsgi. At Chirki, a crude row of boulders is observed in one of the excavated occupation floor.[53] At Hunsgi, an oval-shaped living floor is surrounded by granite boulders on all sides, some of which must have been deliberately placed by the Acheulian men to facilitate the construction of a hutlike structure.[54] At Paisra, stone alignments were found associated with Acheulian habitation floors. These alignments are mostly in straight or somewhat curved lines. Postholes were also noticed at this site. These are of three types: single posthole, in pairs, or one or two postholes with some arranged stone alignments. Postholes and associated stone alignments show that small temporary structures were being constructed by the Acheulian settlers of Paisra.[55] These habitational structures represent temporary seasonal camps. It is a practice in modern hunter-gatherer groups to return to the same locality in the same season. It is inferred from this evidence that a similar mobility pattern was followed by Acheulian groups.

[53] Z.D. Ansari and R.S. Pappu (1975), 'Some Observations on the Excavation of Acheulian Site, Chirki-Nevasa, District Ahmednagar, Maharashtra', *BDCRI,* 35, pp. 1-8.

[54] Paddayya (1982), op. cit.

[55] Pant and Jayaswal (1991), op. cit.

TOOL TYPES

The tool kit of the Lower Palaeolithic culture consists of handaxes, cleavers, choppers, scrapers, discoids, points, borers, polyhedrons, spheroids and so on. Among these types, handaxes and cleavers of a variety of shapes and forms dominate. These two tool-types can be distinguished on the basis of their length, breadth, thickness and morphological outlines.

The most diagnostic tool type is the handaxe with its various subtypes. It is one of the standardized tool type. Handaxes are made both of cores and flakes and is invariably thick at one (butt) and pointed at the other (tip). They are bifacial tools characterized by flake scars on both surfaces. Handaxes are of various shapes: pear, almond, oval and triangular.

The next important tool type is the cleaver. This is characterized by an axe-like broad cutting edge which is at right angles to the long axis. A majority of the cleavers are fashioned on flakes. They are broadly classified into two types on the basis of the shape of their butt ends, viz., the rounded butt or U-shaped and the pointed butt or V-shaped. The cutting edge is straight, oblique or convex. The other main typological forms are choppers and scrapers. Choppers are generally made of pebbles and are divided into two types: unifacial choppers and bifacial choppers. The former have round or almost straight working edges along one side or the end of the pebble is made by flaking in one direction and at one face alone; the latter are characterized by flaking on both the faces. The working edge is formed by the intersection of alternate flake scars removed from both surfaces and in two directions along one end or the side of the pebble. H.L. Movius (1957) has distinguished a scraper from a chopper on the basis of a gross difference in size.[56] The term scraper is used for smaller tools made both of cores and flakes. Scholars like D. Sen (1957) give more stress on the functional aspects of the two tool types.[57]

On the whole, the appearance of choppers and handaxes is simultaneous. Cleavers mostly appear later. It is quite evident that during Lower Palaeolithic times, all the three major types, choppers, handaxes and cleavers, were present and toolmakers were acquainted with all these types in terms of morphology, technology and functions. These tool types are found to occur in different proportions in Lower Palaeolithic assemblages from different parts of the country. It is rather difficult to explain the reasons behind these differences. It is possible that tool types partially represent the specific needs of the people and, thus, reflect adaptive mechanisms specific to various ecological zones.[58]

[56] Hallam L. Movius (Jr) (1957), 'Pebble Tool Terminology in India and Pakistan', *Man in India*, 37, 2, pp. 149-56.

[57] D. Sen (1957), 'The Soanian and the Pebble Tool Terminology in India', *Man in India*, 37, 2, pp. 157-9.

[58] A.K. Ghosh (1985), 'An Attempt to Understand the Acheulian Succession in India

TECHNOLOGY

The techniques employed for preparing stone tools from blanks (pebbles, cores and flakes) into finished forms are basically similar to those known from other parts of the world, viz., Europe and Africa. During the Lower Palaeolithic stage, three main techniques were in use: the block-on-block, the stone hammer (heavy and light), and the soft hammer or cylinder hammer. The first technique was employed to obtain large, massive, wide-angled flakes. A rough outline of the tool was achieved by means of the heavy stone hammer technique. The desired shape of the tool was further obtained by means of the light stone hammer technique. The final finishing, dressing and trimming were made by the soft hammer technique. The majority of the flakes were detached from the blanks by Clactonian technique which consisted of the removal of the flake from the pebble or block by direct percussion. A few tools in the Acheulian assemblages from some sites suggest the use of the prepared core technique (Levelloisian) in which a flake is shaped prior to its detachment from the nucleus.

NATURE OF ASSEMBLAGES

As mentioned earlier, the Lower Palaeolithic culture in India comprises two distinct traditions, viz., the Soan represented by the pebble tools (also known as the chopper-chopping tool tradition) and the biface or handaxe cleaver tradition (also referred to as the Madrasian). The region lying to the north of the Indo-Gangetic plain (extra-peninsula) has mainly yielded lithic assemblages dominated by the former tool complex (Fig. 2.5) while the peninsular region has brought forth industries of the handaxe-cleaver tradition. A number of scholars like H. De Terra and T.T. Paterson (1939), and V.D. Krishnaswami (1953), propagated a hypothesis for the existence of two independent cultures within the Lower Palaeolithic period of the Indian subcontinent. These two cultures are supposed to have met in the central region of the subcontinent. The Singrauli basin in Uttar Pradesh and the Central Narmada basin in central India were recognized as the probable meeting places of these two cultures.[59] This hypothesis of the meeting ground of two cultures was prevalent in Indian prehistoric studies for a long time. After a study of the typo-technological features of Lower Palaeolithic collections from different regions, it is now agreed that there is no sufficient evidence for interpreting these typo-technological variations in terms of distinct cultural groups.[60] R.V. Joshi after the study of large collections of

from Spatial Distribution', in V.N. Misra and P. Bellwood (eds.), *Recent Advances in Indo-Pacific Prehistory*, op. cit., pp. 29-34.

[59] V.D. Krishnaswami and K.V. Soundar Rajan (1951), 'The Lithic Tool-Industries of the Singrauli Basin, District Mirzapur', *AI*, 7, pp. 40-65.

[60] V. Jayaswal (1978), *Palaeohistory of India (A Study of Prepared Core Techniques of the Palaeolithic Cultures of India)*, Agam Kala Prakashan, Delhi.

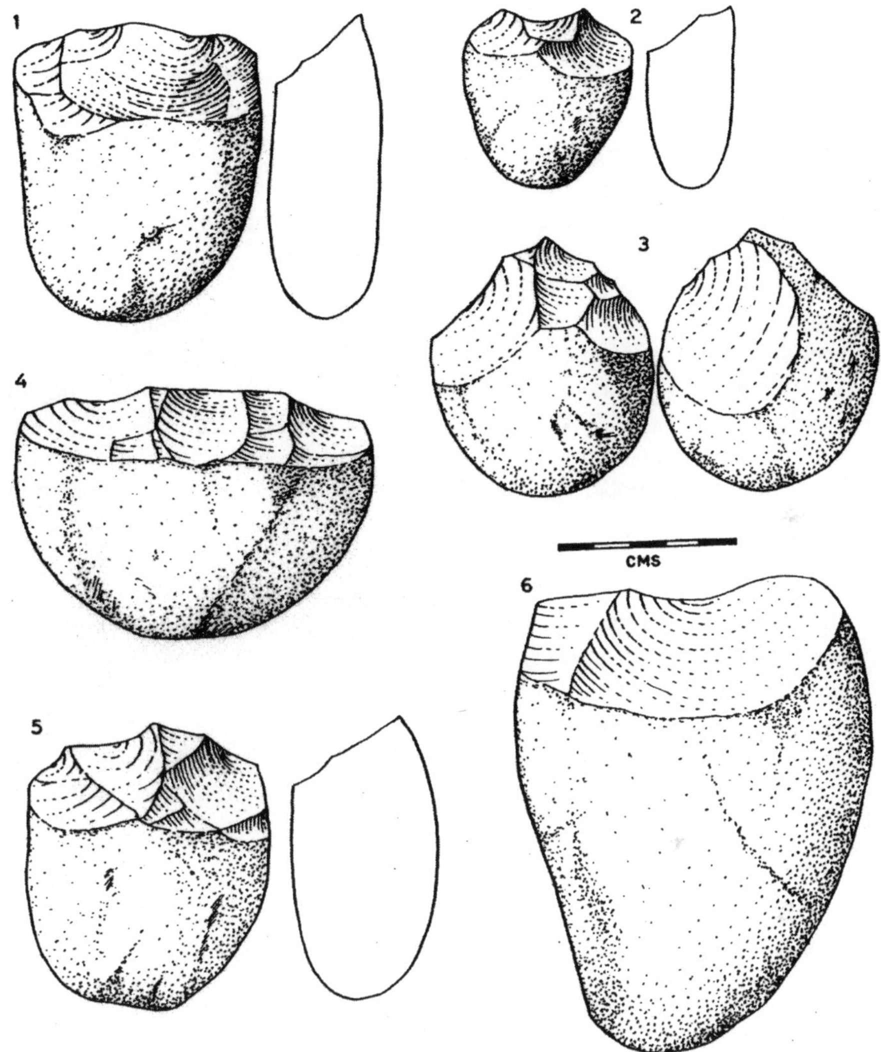

Fig. 2.5: Chopper-chopping tools, Bilaspur, Himachal Pradesh (after Jayaswal 1982) 1, 2, 4, 5, 6 unifacial choppers; 3 bifacial chopper

Lower Palaeolithic tools from various sites in India has indicated that the handaxe-cleaver culture is varied both in tool types and the proportion of each tool type.[61] In the areas where pebbles are abundant in river valleys, the chopper element group is dominant. Pebble tools present in appreciable numbers in any bandaxe-cleaver assemblage from the peninsula form an

[61] R.V. Joshi (1964), 'Acheulian Succession in Central India', *Asian Perspectives*, 8, 1, pp. 150-63; idem (1994), 'Southern Asia in the Period of Homo habilis and Homo erectus', in S.J. de Laed (ed.), *History of Humanity*, vol. 1: *Prehistory and Beginnings of Civilization*, UNESCO, Paris, pp. 77-85.

integral part of the handaxe-cleaver complex. The predominance of certain tool-types thus seems to be an ecological factor dependent on the environment.

Recent investigations have shown that the tool-types of the handaxe-cleaver tradition occur at a few localities in the extra-peninsula in the assemblages of the chopper-chopping tool tradition. G.C. Mohapatra has reported a large number of Acheulian sites in the sub-Himalayan region.[62] On the other hand, a few assemblages exclusively devoid of tool-types of the handaxe-cleaver complex were also noticed in the peninsular region. A few examples of this category are Nittur in Karnataka,[63] coastal Maharashtra (Konkan) in the Raigad and Sindhudurg districts[64] coastal Kerala[65] and coastal Andhra.[66]

A major focus of studies on the Lower Palaeolithic of the sub-Himalayan region has been to understand the Soan phenomenon in relation to the Acheulian. The Soan culture was once thought to belong to the chopper-chopping tool tradition of Southeast Asia.[67] In recent years, a few Soanian sites have been discovered in the sub-Himalayan tract in Punjab, Himachal Pradesh and Haryana, viz. the Beas-Banganga Valleys,[68] the Sirsa Valley,[69] the Markanda Valley[70] and the Siwalik frontal range.[71]

There are two opinions on the position of the Soan industry in the Indian subcontinent. According to one view, Soan constitutes a culture or tradition quite different from the Lower Palaeolithic Acheulian tradition of peninsular India. According to Mohapatra,[72] who discovered both Soanian and Acheulian sites in the Hoshiarpur-Chandigarh sector of the Siwalik hills, the Acheulian and Soanian populations inhabited two distinct types of environments, the former occupying the flat plain surfaces of the Siwalik frontal range and the

[62] Mohapatra (1966), op. cit.; idem (1975), op. cit.; idem (1981), 'Acheulian Discoveries in the Siwalik Frontal Range', *CA*, 22, 4 pp. 433-5; idem (1982), op. cit.; idem (1990), 'Soanian-Acheulian Relationship', *BDCRI*, 49, pp. 251-60; idem (1997), op. cit.

[63] Z.D. Ansari (1970), 'Pebble Tools from Nittur (Mysore State)', *IA* 4 (1-4), pp. 1-7.

[64] Joshi and Bopardikar (1972), op. cit.; Guzder (1980), op. cit.

[65] P. Rajendran (1989), *The Prehistoric Cultures and Environments of Kerala,* Classical Publishing Company, New Delhi.

[66] K.T. Reddy et al. (1995), 'A Pebble Tool Assemblage on the Vishakhapattanam Coast', *ME*, XX, 1, pp. 113-18.

[67] H.L. Movius (1948), op. cit.

[68] Lal (1956), op. cit.

[69] Sen (1955), op. cit.

[70] R.V. Joshi et al. (1975), op. cit.; idem (1978), 'Environments and Cultures of Early Man in the Northwest India: A Reappraisal', *JGSI*, 19, 2, pp. 83-6.

[71] Mohapatra (1966), op. cit.; idem (1975), op. cit.; idem (1981), op. cit.; idem (1982), op. cit.; idem (1990), op. cit.

[72] Mohapatra (1975), op. cit.; idem (1985), 'The Lower Palaeolithic in India', in K.N. Dikshit (ed.), *Archaeological Perspectives of India Since Independence*, Books and Books, New Delhi, pp. 1-8.

latter the *duns* or valleys of the Himalayan Hanks in the hilly region. Mohapatra considers that the Acheulian occurs in a geomorphic context which is later than the Soan and that it just touched the outer fringe of the western sub-Himalayas. He observed that Soanian tools are fashioned of waterworn cobbles and pebbles, while Acheulian communities utilized large flakes detached from boulders for preparing bifaces. According to the second view, pebble-based chopper-chopping tools are part and parcel of a single Lower Palaeolithic handaxe-cleaver complex, and there is no cultural dichotomy during the Lower Palaeolithic phase. Presently, however, differences in raw materials and ecological settings are considered more convincing factors in explaining variations in Lower Palaeolithic assemblages.[73]

There is no evidence so far for the presence of a pre-Acheulian cultural phase anywhere in India. A.P. Khatri (1962) earlier claimed to have discovered an industry exclusively made up of pebble tools in the lowermost red clay stratum of the Narmada River at Mahadeo Piparia.[74] He coined the term 'Mahadevian' for this pre-Acheulian industry and believed it to be the oldest in India, comparable to the Oldowan of East Africa. Excavations undertaken subsequently by S.G. Supekar (1985) at Mahadeo Piparia conclusively proved that there was no stratigraphical basis for postulating the existence of a pebble tool substratum underlying the Acheulian handaxe-cleaver industries.[75]

The Lower Palaeolithic industries of peninsular India, as mentioned earlier, essentially belong to the handaxe-cleaver tradition. The assemblages, by and large, are dominated by tool-types showing Acheulian characters. In India, we still lack precise and reliable stratigraphical evidence for distinguishing die sub-cultural phases of the Acheulian. No site anywhere in the Indian sub-continent has clearly revealed the Acheulian technological phases in a stratified context. At most Lower Palaeolithic sites, Acheulian artefacts occur in a mixed state. There is, as yet, no sound stratigraphical evidence to divide the Acheulian into various phase, as in Europe and Africa.

During the last three decades, there is an increasing trend of the application of statistical methods to the analysis of Lower Palaeolithic artefacts from different Acheulian sites in India. The main aim of the metrical analysis of tool-types like handaxes and cleavers is to objectively express their size, shape and refinement. These studies have been undertaken at the following

[73] V. Jayaswal (1982), *Chopper-Chopping Component of Palaeolithic in India*, Agam Kala Prakashan, Delhi.

[74] A.P. Khatri (1962), 'Mahadevian: An Oldowan Pebble Culture in India', *Asian Perspectives*, 6, pp. 186-96.

[75] S.G. Supekar (1985), 'Some Observations on the Quaternary Stratigrahy of the Central Narmada Valley', V.N. Misra and P. Bellwood (eds.), *Recent Advances in Indo-Pacific Prehistory*, op. cit., pp. 19-28.

Acheulian sites: Chirki-Nevasa,[76] Bhimbetka,[77] Peera Nullah,[78] the Banas-Berach basin,[79] Mayurbhanj,[80] Anagwadi,[81] Gunjana,[82] Paleru,[83] Rallakalava,[84] Didwana,[85] and Gangapur.[86]

On the basis of the metrical analysis of Acheulian artefacts from various sites, it is now possible to recognise two developmental phases within the Acheulian: Early and Late. The former is characterized by inferior workmanship as revealed by deep and irregular flake scars, thick bodies and asymmetrical forms. The Late Acheulian, on the other hand, includes finer types with smoother surfaces resulting from controlled flaking and symmetrical forms. To the first and earlier phase, we can assign the Acheulian industries from Lalitpur, Adamgarh, Kuliana (Mayurbhanj), Chirki-Nevasa (Fig. 2.6), Anagwadi, Singi Talav and Hunsgi (Fig. 2.7). These are characterized by a high percentage of chopper-chopping tools and bifaces, a low percentage of non-biface tools made of flakes, a high ratio of handaxes to cleavers, the low incidence of blades and Levalloisian flakes, and the predominance of the stone hammer flaking technique. To the second and later phase, one can assign the Acheulian assemblages from Bhimbetka (Fig. 2.8), Peera Nullah, the Berach Valley, the Rallakalava Valley, Attirampakkam, Vadamadurai, Raisen complex (Fig. 2.9), Paleru, Gunjana and Gangapur which are characterized by the use/presence of chopper-chopping tools, a low percentage

[76]R.V. Joshi and A.R. Marathe (1976), 'Material Analysis of Handaxes from Chirki-on-Pravara, W. Maharashtra, India', *Puratattva*, 8, pp. 3-12; idem (1985), 'A Comparative study of Matrical Data on Handaxes and their Cultural Interpretations', in V.N. Misra and P. Bellwood (eds.), *Recent Advances in Indo-Pacific Prehistory*, op. cit., pp. 77-80.

[77] D.M.S. Alam (1990), 'Morphometric Study of Palaeolithic Industries of Bhimbetka Central India', Ph.D. dissertation (unpublished), Pune University, Pune.

[78] C.A. Semans (1981), 'Analysis of an Acheulian Collection from Peerah Nullah, Narmada Valley, India', *ME*, V, pp. 13-31.

[79] V.N. Misra (1961a), 'Palaeolithic Culture of Western Rajputana', *BDCRI*, 21, pp. 85-186; idem (1961b) 'Palaeolithic Industry of the Banas, Eastern Rajputana', *JAS*, 34-5, pp. 138-60; idem (1967), *Pre- and Proto-History of the Berach Basin, South Rajasthan*, Deccan College, Poona.

[80]R. Ghosh and G. Ray (1964), 'A Technological Study of the Cleavers of Mayurbhanj', *Man in India,* 44, 1, pp. 50-74.

[81]Pappu (1974), op. cit.

[82]D.R. Raju (1985), 'Handaxe Assemblages from the Gunjana Valley, Andhra Pradesh: A Metrical Analysis', *Bulletin of the Indo-Pacific Prehistory Association,* 6, pp. 10-26; idem (1988), *Stone Age Hunter-Gatherers: An Ethnoarchaeology of Cuddapah Region, South-East India*, Ravish Publishers, Pune; idem (1989), 'The Lower Palaeolithic Culture in the Gunjana Valley on the Southeast Coast of India', *BDCRI*, 47/48, pp. 283-300.

[83]Joshi and Maratha (1985), op. cit.

[84]C. Gaillard and M.L.K. Murty (1988), 'Typo-Technological Comparison of Two Acheulian Assemblages at Renigunta, South India', *ME*, XII, pp. 125-33.

[85]C. Gaillard et al. (1986), 'Handaxe Assemblages from Didwana Region, Thar Desert, India: A Metrical Analysis', *PPS*, 52 pp. 189-214.

[86]Arunkumar (1989), op. cit.

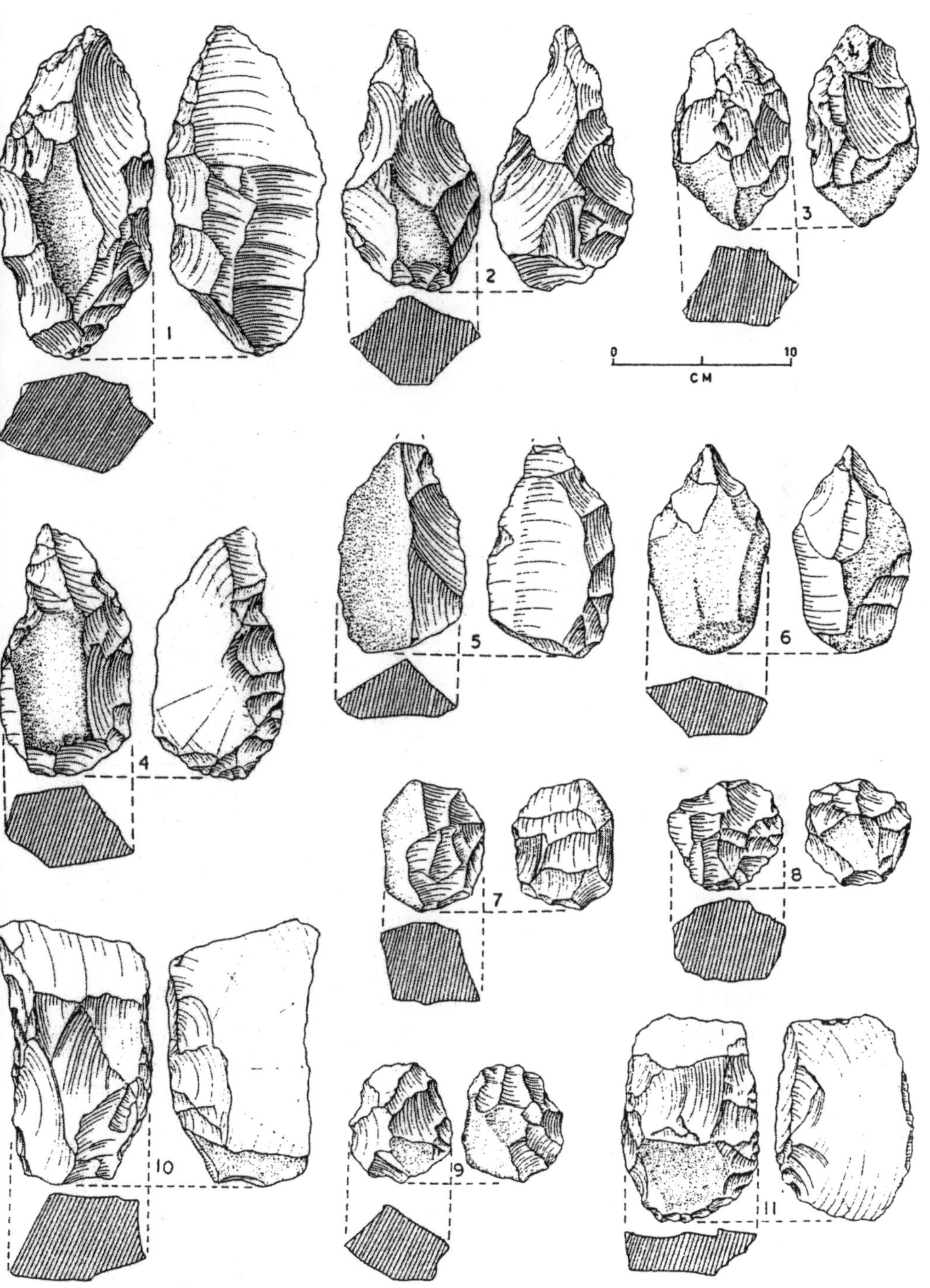

Fig. 2.6: Early Acheulian tools, Chirki (after Corvinus 1983) 1-3: Handaxes; 4: Knife, 5: Side scraper, 6: Pick; 7: Chopper; 8: Polyhedron; 9: Discoid; 10-11: Cleavers

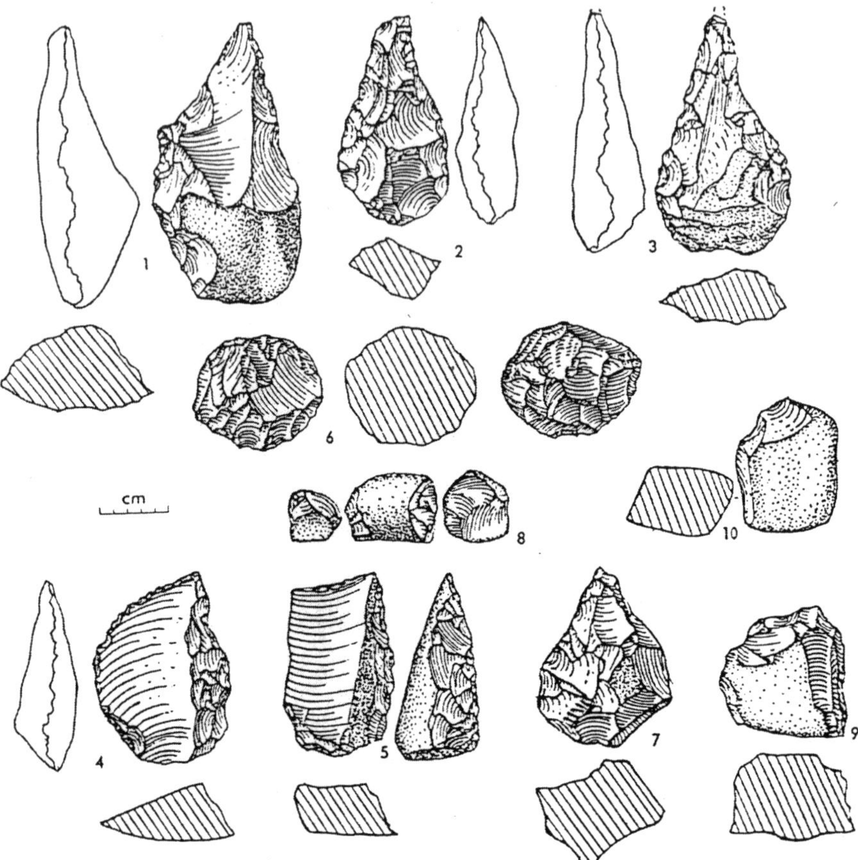

Fig. 2.7: Early Acheulian tools, Hunsgi (after Paddayya 1984). 1-3: Handaxes; 4: Knife, 5: Cleaver; 6: Polyhedron; 7: Pick; 8: Hammerstone; 9: Anvil stone; 10: Chopper

of bifaces, the high ratio of cleavers to handaxes, a very high percentage of and great diversity among non-biface tools, high indices of blades and Levalloisian flakes, and prominent use of the soft hammer flaking technique.[87]

Assemblages at different Acheulian sites show differences in the proportion of the main three tool-types, choppers, handaxes and cleavers. The proportion of handaxes and cleavers has also been taken into account as a indicator of technological evolution. Industries dominated by handaxes are treated as the Early to Middle Acheulian and those dominated by cleavers as the Late or Upper Acheulian. A statistical analysis of the relative proportion of handaxes and cleavers undertaken at a number of Acheulian sites show that the average

[87] Misra (1978), op. cit.

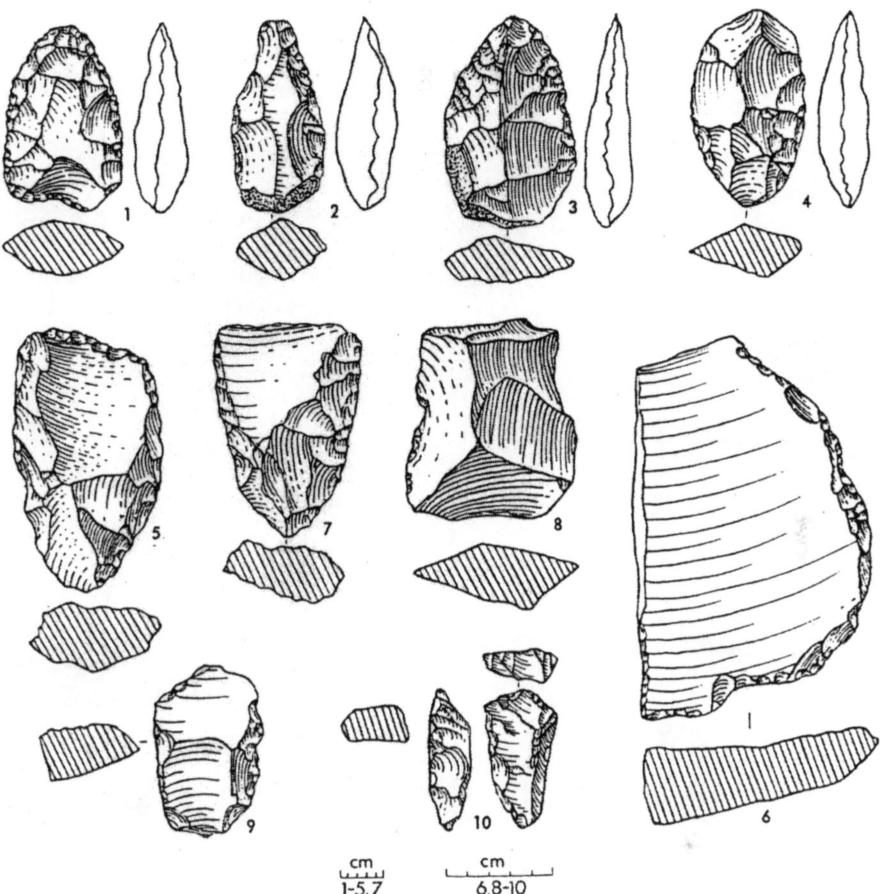

Fig. 2.8: Late Acheulian tools, Bhimbetka (after Misra 1985). 1-4: Handaxes; 5-7: Cleavers; 6, 9, 10: Scrapers; 8: Denticulate.

cleaver-handaxe ratio ranges from 1:1 to 1:2. At a few sites like Adamgarh, Bhimbetka and Gangapur, cleavers outnumber handaxes. Earlier it was suggested that the presence of cleavers in large numbers, in Acheulian assemblages reflect a well-wooded country and a moist climate[88] but detailed studies of various assemblages show that this was not the case. Typo-technologically, cleaver-dominated assemblages show an advanced Acheulian cultural stage. Flake blades and blades are found associated with Acheulian assemblages at Bhimbetka[89] in fairly large numbers, which is suggestive of the evolved character of the assemblage.

[88]F.E. Zeuner (1963), *Environment of Early Man with Special Reference to Tropical Regions*, M.S. University, Baroda.

[89]V.N. Misra (1982), 'Evolution of the Blade Element in the Stone Industries of the Rock Shelter III F-23, Bhimbetka', in R.K. Sharma (ed.), *Indian Archaeology: New Perspectives*, Agam Kala Prakashan, New Delhi, pp. 7-13.

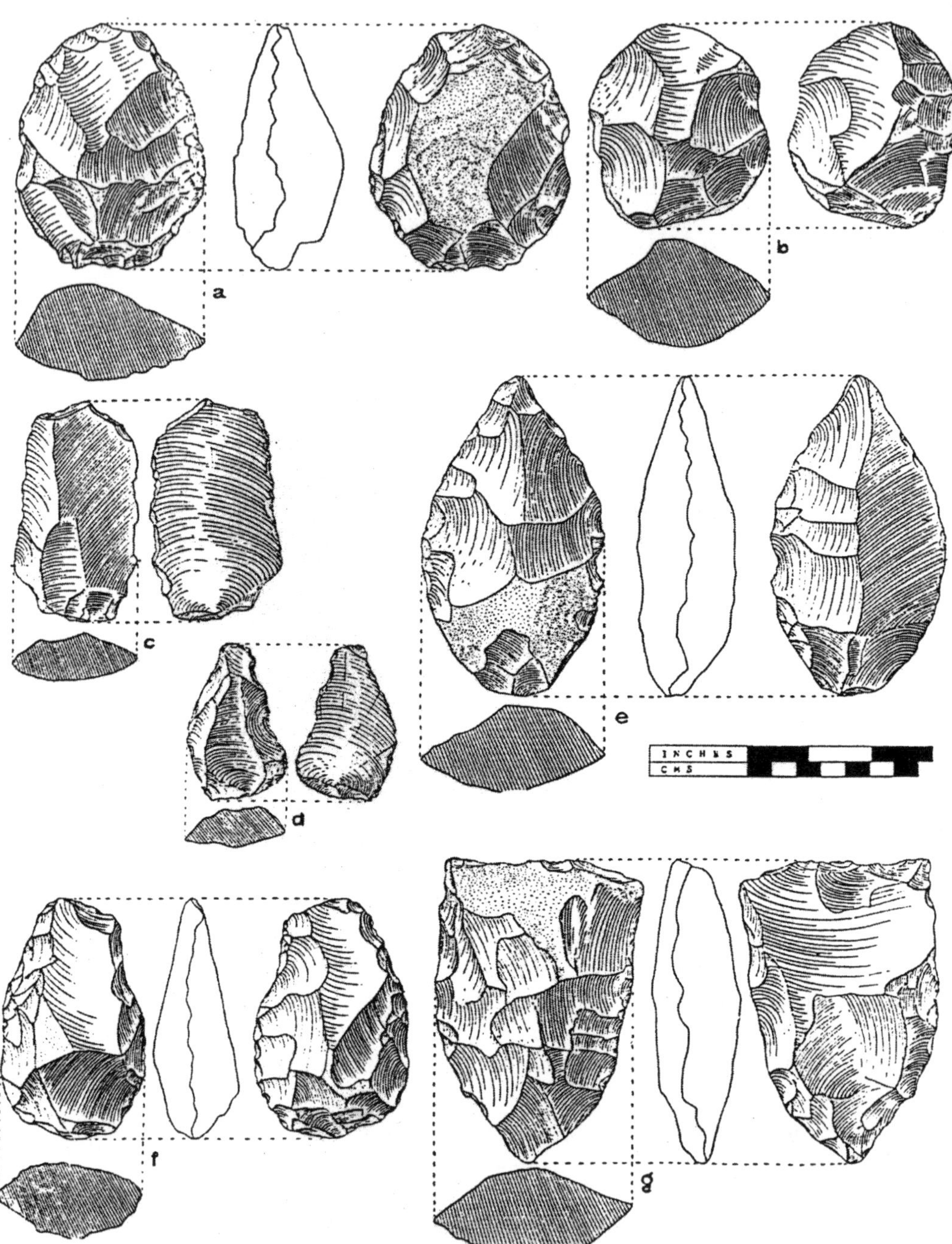

Fig. 2.9: Late Acheulian tools, Raisen Complex (after Jacobson 1975). a: Flake knife; b: Discoidal core; c, d: Scrapers; e: Handaxe; f, g: Cleavers

The Indian Acheulian industries have also been divided into two developmental stages by taking into consideration refinement indices, form and the number of trimming scars. The refinement index is expressed by T/B or T/L and the shape index is expressed by B/L (L—maximum length, T—maximum thickness, B—maximum breadth). A high value of T/B usually indicates an unrefined form while the low value of T/B shows a refined form. Similarly, a high number of trimming scars usually indicate a refined form while a low number of scars shows an unrefined form. Handaxes from Paleru (Late Acheulian site) have shown twenty trimming scars on an average in comparison to nine from Chirki-Nevasa (Early Acheulian) (Rao 1979).

FUNCTIONS OF TOOLS

The Lower Palaeolithic phase is so far removed from the present that even the most primitive tribes today are not known to manufacture the handaxe-cleaver type of tools. Comparatively, therefore, ethnography is not of much help in understanding the probable use of these tool types. Their functions can only be speculated by their shape and form, and also by making experiments with them. These tools were not directly useful for hunting purposes. They were perhaps employed in preparing larger weapons of wood and bone which have not survived. Some of the probable functions of the tool types may be listed as follows:

Choppers: Chopping and cutting meat and other organic materials.

Scrapers: Scraping of barks of trees and dressing of animal skins.

Handaxes: These might have served as all-purpose tools; the sharp lateral edges for skinning and cutting animal carcasses, the pointed tips for digging up roots and tubers and for opening up the bellies of animals, and the heavy butt for crushing purposes.

Cleavers: These were primarily used for cutting meat and bone and also possibly for cutting trees.

It is possible that some of the handaxes and cleavers were not used with naked hands but were hafted in wood or bamboo handles. This is evident from the fact that some handaxes and cleavers bear notches made deliberately on either side near the butt portions.

During the Lower Palaeolithic times, the shape of the Acheulian handaxe did not change for several hundred thousand years. D.P. Agarwal (1995) has suggested that even though the form of the Acheulian handaxe did not change its functions could have changed with the growing needs of the society.[90] A handaxe could have been used for a variety of functions: as an axe, adze, scraper and so on, without changing its form. A form is discarded and a new

[90]D.P. Agarwal (1995), 'Technology and Human Evolution', Datta et al. (eds.), *India at the Dawn of History*, Agam Kala Prakashan, Delhi, pp. 5-8.

one invented only when that form is rendered incapable of catering to further functional demands. If this hypothesis is correct, the acceleration of the pace of technological changes could not be exponential but only linear.

RAW MATERIALS

The distribution of Lower Palaeolithic sites is closely related to geological formations. Acheulian tool-makers, as elsewhere in the world, showed a preference for quartzite as the main raw material for making artefacts because of its hardness and good flaking qualities. Quartzites are of widespread occurrence in many parts of the Indian peninsula and form the major rock type in the Vindhyan, Aravalli, Delhi, Gondawana, Cuddapah and Kaladgi formations. Therefore, classical Acheulian localities occur in those parts of the country where quartzite outcrops are found in abundance. Quartzite, being hard and resistant to weathering, forms well-rounded pebbles due to transportation by running water. Pebbles of a suitable size, pebble flakes and blocks of quartzite obtained from natural outcrops were selected by Acheulian groups for preparing the desired tool types.

In non-quartzite regions, other rock types were preferred, e.g. the hard dense basalt and dolerite in the Deccan Trap region of Maharashtra,[91] granite in the Bundelkhand region of Uttar Pradesh[92] and cherty limestone in the Hunsgi Valley in the Shorapur *doab* of north Karnataka.[93]

The rarity of Acheulian sites in those parts of peninsula India where Deccan Trap basalt outcrops occur is due to the non-survival of basalt tools on the surface. A plausible explanation for this phenomenon, as suggested by Shiela Mishra (1986), is that basalt, which was the only rock available for tool-making in this region is highly susceptible to disintegration by weathering.[94] Thus, Acheulian sites that did not get buried under the alluvium cover soon after their use may have been totally destroyed by weathering processes. The pattern seen in the distribution of sites in the Deccan Trap region, therefore, reflects the working of geological processes such as weathering, transport and burial rather than hominid activities. Acheulian sites in this region are, therefore, preserved only in exceptional cases.

Although tools were fashioned of a variety of raw materials, they exhibit a remarkable similarity in form and technique, thereby indicating that Acheulian man handled varied raw materials with efficiency.

[91] Corvinus (1981), op. cit.; H.D. Sankalia (1952), *Godavari Palaeolithic Industry*, Deccan College, Pune; Joshi et al. (1966), op. cit.

[92] Singh (1965), op. cit.

[93] Paddayya (1982), op. cit.

[94] Sheila Mishra (1986), 'Archaeological Assemblages and Basalt Weathering: A Re-evaluation of the Nevasian', *ME X*, pp. 91-6.

ASSOCIATED QUATERNARY DEPOSITS

Quarternary formations associated with Lower Palaeolithic industries are represented by glacial fluvio-glacial, fluvial, littoral and colluvial deposits. These formations cover an immense area in the extra-peninsula whereas they have a restricted distribution in peninsular India. Among these deposits, those of fluvial origin have a widespread distribution all over the country and occur in present-day river valleys. They are associated at a number of places with Palaeolithic tool assemblages and occasionally with mammalian fossil remains. The stratigraphical sequence of these deposits has been worked out in different river valleys on the basis of the exposed alluvium in cliff sections and also buried alluvium. The salient characteristics of Quaternary deposits from six important regions in India have been described in the following pages.

SUB-HIMALAYAN REGION

A number of prehistorians have carried out investigations since Independence in the sub-Himalayan region on the Indian side of the river valleys of Sirsa, Beas, Banganga, Ravi, Markanda, Sutlej, etc., in the states of Punjab, Himachal Pradesh, Haryana, and Jammu & Kashmir.[95] These scholars have reported Palaeolithic sites yielding tool-assemblages mainly of the chopper-chopping tool complex and a few of the handaxe-cleaver complex which were found in association with river terraces (Fig. 2.10). However, there is no uniformity in the number of terraces, as two to seven are reported from different river valleys of the region. Joshi et al.[96] who worked in the Kangra Valley of Himachal Pradesh, did not find evidence of glaciation. They noted massive fluvio-glacial cones at various heights. According to them, the terraces on the rivers were not formed by glacial action but by the erosion of cones in the foothill region. Artefacts found scattered on the terraces would, thus, belong to a later date than the formation of the terraces. Cones developed on high level terraces indicate intensive fluvial action followed by a succession of upheavals, which, at intervals, raised the river basin in this region, thereby producing a series of terraces.

CENTRAL NARMADA VALLEY

The Narmada basin in Madhya Pradesh is one of the few regions in peninsular India where well-developed and well-preserved quaternary deposits occur in association with rich artefact assemblages and mammalian fossils. The trough-like nature of the Central Narmada Valley, formed as a result of tectonic

[95] Sen (1955), op. cit.; Lall (2956), op. cit.; Mohapatra (1966), op. cit.; idem (1982), op. cit.; idem (1990), op. cit.; idem (1997), op. cit.; Joshi et al. (1975), op. cit.; idem (1978), op. cit.

[96] Joshi et al. (1975), op. cit.

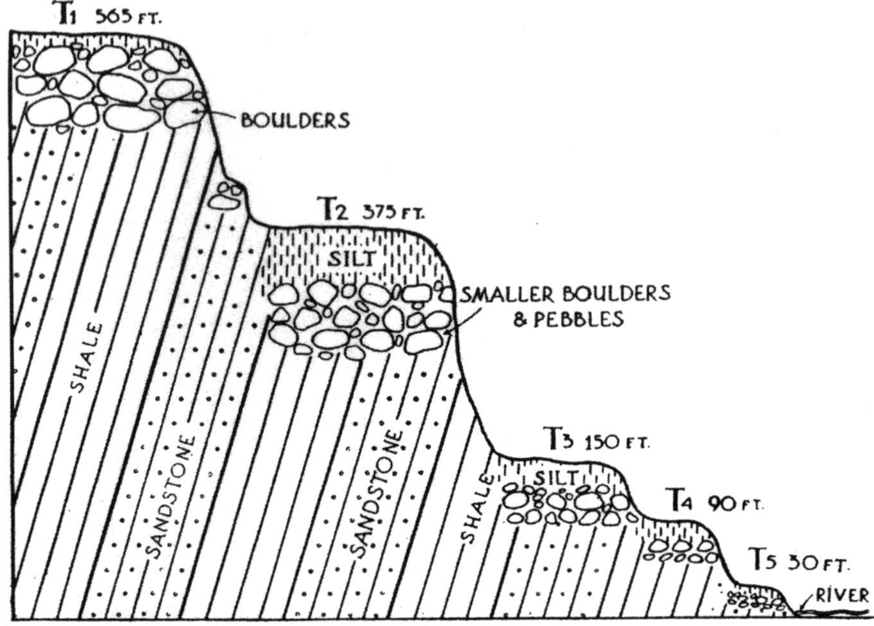

Fig. 2.10: Schematic section, Banganga terraces at Guler, Himachal Pradesh (after Lal 1956)

disturbances in the Late Tertiary and Early Pleistocene, has accumulated vast riverine deposits of the Middle and Upper Pleistocene age. The stratigraphical sequence in this region in relation to Palaeolithic industries was first worked out by H. De Terra and T.T. Paterson (1939) and this provided a standard yardstick for Pleistocene stratigraphy and the relative chronology in the peninsular region.

The Narmada River between Hoshangabad and Narsinghpur was explored by them. The stratigraphic sequence observed is as follows (from bottom to top (Fig. 2.11).

1. Laterite 2. Basal conglomerate 3. Red concretionary slip	Lower group
4. Gravel 5. Pink silt	Upper Group
6. Sandy gravel 7. Black soil	Newer Alluvium (Cotton Soil Goup)

From the Lower Group, thick flakes of the pre-Soan type, rolled handaxes of the Abbevillian and Acheulian characters (from basal conglomerate) and flakes and Acheulian bifaces (from the silty portion) were recovered in association with fossils of the Middle Pleistocene period. From the Newer Alluvium, a flake assemblage characterized by the absence of handaxes and

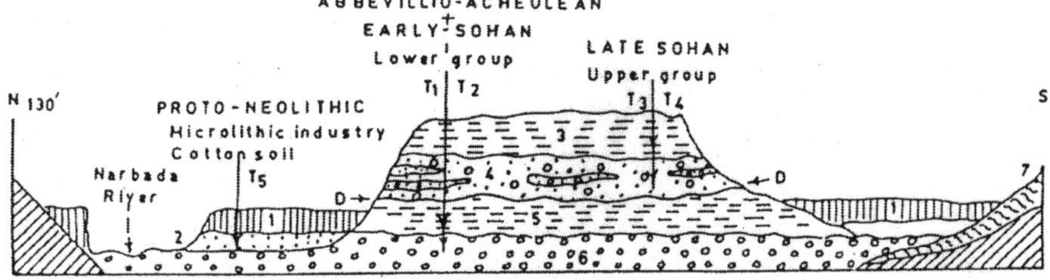

Fig. 2.11: Transverse section, Central Narmada Valley, Narsinghpur (after De Terra and Paterson 1939)

large cores and by the dominance of small blades and scrapers made of silica group minerals like jasper, chert and chalcedony was obtained. S.N. Rajguru et al. (1994) reinvestigated of the Central Narmada Valley of Narsinghpur district, Madhya Pradesh.[97] These studies were undertaken to revise the earlier concepts of litho- and bio-stratigraphy of the quaternary deposits. They indicate that the earlier classification of sediments on the basis of mega-vertebrate variation and the relative dating of sediments is no more tenable.

The Narmada has been flowing through the Narmada-Soan lineament since the geological past. This lineament extends up to the Lower Himalayas in the north. The litho-stratigraphy of the Narmada Valley is mainly in response to tectonic activity in the Himalayas. The average thickness of the exposed alluvium in the valley is about 30 m. However, on the basis of deep bore hole data, there is convincing evidence of a enormously thick mass of alluvium of over 300 m concealed below the surface. This thick, sub-surface alluvium is suggestive of Himalayan tectonic uplifts and also of fluvial activity on a larger scale in the geological past. The incorporation of sediments in the Narmada Valley alluvium is mainly from outcrops in the surrounding areas. The sediments, therefore, are of local origin. The feeding-in of sediments is more through lateral tributaries rather than through an integrated source of sedimentation.

Mammalian fossils and stone artefacts are also found in the secondary context. The reworking of sediments has resulted in the mixing of stone artefacts of different cultural periods. Hence, animal fossils and cultural materials are not useful in building up a litho- and-bio-stratigraphy. Investigators have suggested that factors as in morphology, the study of micro-vertebrate fossils, tectonic repercussions, ancient soil development, climate proxy-data and so on should be given priority in the building of a litho- and bio-stratigraphy of quaternary formations of the Central Narmada Valley (Rajaguru et al. 1994).

[97] S.N. Rajaguru et al. (1994), 'A Fresh Look at the Quaternary Lithostratigraphy of a Part of the Central Narmada Valley, Narsinghpur District, M.P.', in K.R. Dikshit et al. (eds.), *India-Geomorphological Diversity*, Rawat Publishers, New Delhi, pp. 435-52.

MIDDLE SON VALLEY

Four major alluvial and three widespread loess formations were identified in the Middle Son Valley of district Sidhi, Madhya Pradesh, viz., Sihawal, Patpara, Baghor and Khetaunhi[98] (Fig. 2.12).

The oldest formation (Middle Pleistocene) is the Sihawal formation (units 1 and 2) which consists of lower member-colluvial-alluvial clayey gravels and conglomerates with Lower Palaeolithic artefacts, and an upper member of mottled yellow-grey of aeolian provenance.

The Patpara formation (Late Middle to early Upper Pleistocene) lies over the Sihawal formation (units 3-5). The lower member is made up of gravel sands and sandy gravels, red brown in colour due to iron staining. These pass upwards into clay, rich in sands and gravels with massive red-brown clay in the upper levels. Transitional Late Acheulian to Middle Palaeolithic, artefacts, which are quite fresh, are found in these layers. A sample of the uppermost silty clay layer has given a TL date of 103, 800 + - 19800 years BP.

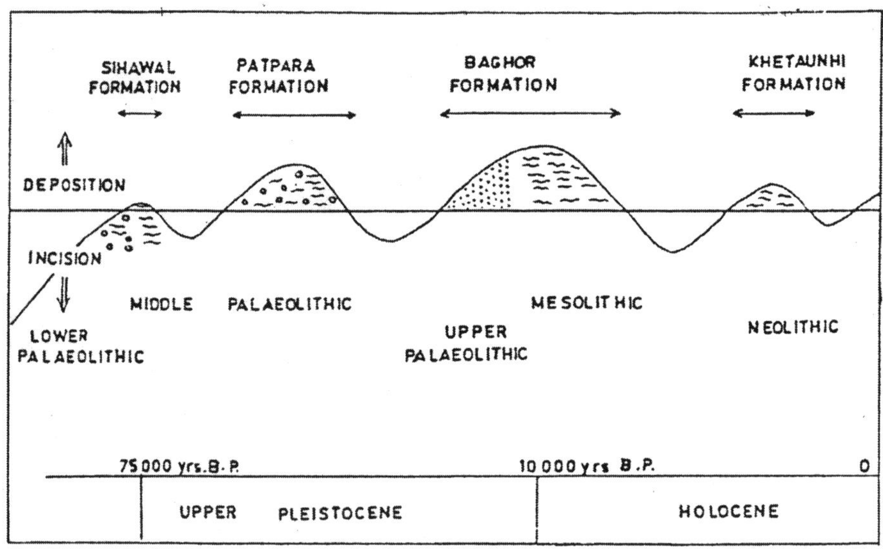

Fig. 2.12: Late quaternary erosion and deposition, Middle Son Valley (after Williams and Royca 1983)

[98] M.A.J. Willians and M.F. Clarke (1995), 'Quaternary Geology and Prehistoric Environments in the Soan and Belan Valleys, North Central India', in S. Wadia et al. (eds.), *Quaternary Environments and Geoarchaeology of India*, Geological Society of India, Bangalore, pp. 282-308; M.A.J. Williams and A. Royca (1983), 'Alluvial History of the Middle Son Valley, North Central India', in G.R. Sharma and J.D. Clark (eds.), *Palaeoenvironments and Prehistory in the Middle Son Valley*, Avinash Prakashan, Allahabad, pp. 9-21.

THAR DESERT

Three major geological formations, Jayal, Amarpura and Didwana, have been identified in the Thar region around Didwana and Jayal of Nagaur district, Rajasthan. The maximum depth of quaternary sediments recorded in the bore holes is over 100 m. The stratigraphical sequence is as follows (Fig. 2.13).

Formation	Lithology	Approximate Age
Jayal	Calcerated bouldery Gravel	Late Tertiary to Early Pleisctocene
Amarpura	Calc-pans, calcertised Alluvium and pedocalcic palaeosols.	Late Middle to Early Late Pleistocene.
Didwana	Stabilised aeolic sands, pedocalcic aplaeosols and playa sediments	Late Middle Pleistocene to Holocene

Jayal formation occurs in the form of a continuous, undulating gravel ridge with a width of 7-10 km and a height of up to 5 m above the surrounding plains. It is mainly composed of poorly sorted, clast-supported, bouldry-cobbly gravel deposits which were brought by high energy, bedload braided streams. Acheulian tools lie in hundreds on the surface of the ridge.

The Amarpura formation lies unconformably over the Jayal formation. It comprises calcareous loam, marl and Kankar clasts, and is extensively exposed in the low-lying areas. The total exposed thickness of this formation is approximately 15 to 20 m and comprises crude laminations, alternating layers of medium to coarse sand, with silty-clay, mottling weak calcratization with varying levels, an abundance of diffused carbonate almost throughout the formation, and a high content of calcereous clay. All these features suggest that these sediments were deposited in shallow water pans or in flood plain flats associated with playas. The occurrence of Lower Palaeolithic to Upper Palaeolithic artefacts in this formation suggest that it was deposited over a long period of time from the late Middle Pleistocene to the early Late Pleistocene. Didwana formations consist of two parts aeolian and lacustrine, both of which are extensively exposed in the Thar desert.

A number of Acheulian sites were discovered far away from existing streams. Several primary Palaeolithic sites were excavated around Didwana in Nagaur district. These sites have been buried in low energy fluvial, lacustral and aeolian sediments. In particular, the excavation of a 20 m deep profile in a fossil dune at 16 R locality, and its dating by a series of radiometric techniques like the Th/U series, thermoluminescence and C-14, have provided a history of sand deposition and stabilization of sand dunes, and of human occupation of aeolian surfaces over a period of more than 200,000 years. Acheulian hunter-gatherers camped along lakes and pools formed on the wide

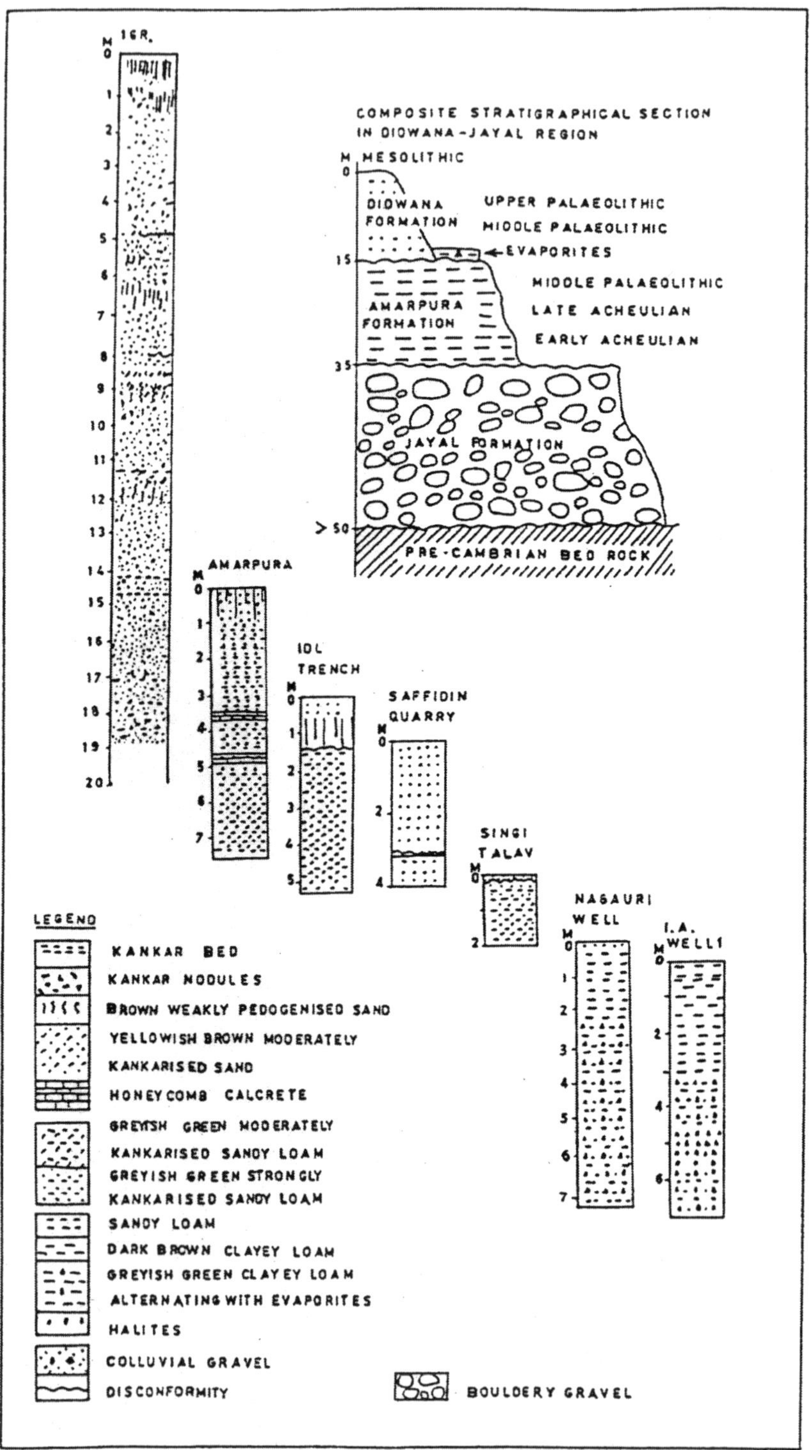

Fig. 2.13: Quaternary geological and archaeological sequence, Didwana (after Misra 1987)

flood plains of shallow, meandering streams. In addition, they also camped on stable sand dune surfaces and extensively exposed gravel beds.[99]

SAURASHTRA REGION

In the early 1960s, Sankalia (1965) discovered Acheulian and Middle Palaeolithic sites for the first time at Rajdi in the Bhadar Valley, Rajkot district, in the Saurashtra region of Gujarat.[100] On the basis of these clues, V.S. Lele (1989) explored the entire Bhadar Valley in the late 1960s and studied the problem of quaternary sea level changes in relation to Palaeolithic sites.[101] He observed that the chronology of the Palaeolithic cultures of Saurashtra was interlinked with miliolite formations in the area. A.R. Marathe carried out geoarchaeological investigations in the Hiran Valley, district Junagarh in the early 1970s.[102] At the Umrethi dam site on the river Hiran, he located Acheulian tools in a fluvial gravel, underlying a deposit of miliolite limestone (Fig. 2.14).

The quaternary geomorphic history of the Saurashtra peninsula has been reconstructed on the basis of erosional and depositional features preserved

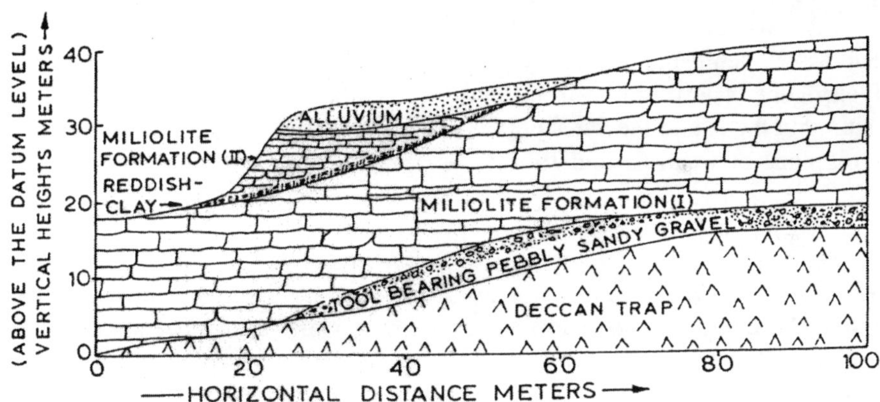

Fig. 2.14: Transverse section at Umrethi Dam site, river Hiran (after Marathe et al. 1977)

[99] Misra (1987), op. cit.; idem (1995), op. cit.; V.N. Misra et al. (1980), 'Prehistory and Palaeo-environments of Jayal, Western Rajasthan', *ME,* IV, pp. 9-31; idem (1982), op. cit.; C. Gaillard et al. (1983), 'Acheulian Occupation, at Singi Talav in the Thar Desert: A Preliminary Report on 1982 Excavation', *ME,* VII, pp. 112-30; idem (1985), 'Acheulian Occupation in the Singi Talav, Thar Desert: A Preliminary Report on 1981 Excavation', *BDCRI*, 44 pp. 141-52.

[100] Sankalia (1965), op. cit.

[101] Lele (1989), op. cit.

[102] Marathe (1981), op. cit.

in the river valleys. On the basis of well and bore-hole data, it appears that during the mid-quaternary, the rivers were flowing 10-15 m below their present bed levels and the presence of man is evidenced by the Acheulian artefacts discovered at Umrethi and Junagarh.

The basal bouldary/pebbly gravels laid down by the rivers contain Acheulian artefacts. There was a major transgressive phase of the sea which is represented by a miliolite formation (M-I), occurring at an elevation of 40-60 m AMSL at a number of places. This phase was followed by the rejuvenation of streams (3-5 m below the present bed levels) in response to the lowering of the sea level. The exact cause of the phenomenon may be eustatic, tectonic, or perhaps a combination of both. This phase, in turn, was followed by a major ubiquitous aggradational phase (base level higher by 5-10 m than at present) in all the river valleys, represented by fluvial gravels and silts. These gravel deposits have yielded Middle Palaeolithic tools. This terminal Pleistocene aggradational phase culminated in another transgressive phase represented by miliolite formation (M-II). The closing phase of the Pleistocene was one of a low sea-level during which coastal aeolianites were formed. The succeeding cycle of alluvial fills, beach rocks and oyster beds belong to the Early Holocene, a period of fluctuating sea-levels during when the Mesolithic and Harappan cultures flourished in Saurashtra. It is now fairly established that there were at least two phases of miliolite formations, and early man occupied the Saurashtra peninsula during the low sea-level phase of the Middle and Late Pleistocene. The miliolite from these regions have been dated by the Th/U dating methods and the dates obtained suggest that the Acheulian occupation took place between 69 and 190 kyr BP.[103]

Deccan Upland

The Deccan Upland area of Maharashtra is one of the regions in the peninsular India where intensive geoarchaeological investigations have been undertaken during the last three decades by S.N. Rajaguru and his students.[104] The quaternary

[103] M. Bhaskaran et al. (1986), 'Geochronology of Palaeolithic Cultures in the Hiran Valley, Saurashtra, India', *Journal of Archaeological Science,* 13, pp. 505-14; A.R. Marathe and S.N. Rajaguru (1977), 'The Chronology of the Early Man in Saurashtra', *Recent Researches in Geology*, 9, pp. 133-44; idem (1981), 'Middle Pleistocene Lithic Tools in Saurashtra, Western India', *BDCRI*, 40, pp. 110-22.

[104] S.N. Rajaguru and R. Korisetter (1987), 'Quaternary Geomorphic Environment and Cultural Succession in Western India', *Indian Journal of Earth Sciences*, 14, 3-4, pp. 349-61; S.N. Rajaguru et al. (1993), 'Changes in the Physical Environment of Western India During the Last 200 kyr B.P.: A Geoarchaeological Approach', *Proceedings of International Symposium and Global Change*, Waseda University, Tokyo, pp. 599-623; V.S. Kale and S.N. Rajaguru (1987) 'Late Quaternary Alluvial History of the North-western Deccan Upland Region', *Nature*, 325, pp. 612-14; R. Korisetter (1994), 'Quaternary Alluvial Stratigraphy and Sedimentation in the Upland Deccan Region, Western India', *ME*, XIX, 1-2, pp. 29-42.

sediments of this region are mainly of fluvial origin and occur in the present river valleys. They are occasionally associated with Palaeolithic tool assemblages and mammalian fossils. Five litho units have been recognized in this region in the Godavari, Bhima and Krishna river valleys, and have been designated as the Bori formation (BRF), Godavari formation (GDF), Upper Bhima formation (UBF), Chandanpuri formation (CPF) and the Post-Black soil formation (PBF) (Fig 2.15).[105]

The Bori formation (2-8 m) mainly represents the high sinuosity lithofacies sequence in the Kukdi River Valley near Bori village, Pune district, Maharashtra. The sediments are fine textured, dark brown, silty clays and gravels, and are associated with volcanic ash (tefra) of 1 to 1.5 m thickness. This tefra is found within the fissured clay deposit and has a non-conforming relationship with the overlying gravel bed containing the Lower Acheulian lithic assemblage. It has been dated by the chronometric K/Ar dating method at 1.4 myr BP, which suggests that the deposit is of the Early Pleistocene age.[106] However, recent investigations into the age of the ash by using the 39 Ar/40Ar dating method has revised the date to around 067 myr BP. On the basis of this evidence, the lithic assemblages from Bori can be considered to be the earliest Lower Palaeolithic industry in peninsular India.[107]

The Godavari formation (GDF) is represented by high level gravels which rest non-conformably on a rocky bench. These gravels occur at elevations ranging from 6 to 30 m above the present bed level of the rivers, and, in most cases, lie beyond the reach of the present flood levels at several locations on the Krishna, Bhima and Godavari river basins and their tributaries.[108] These deposits are the earliest quaternary alluvial formations to be preserved as terrace gravels. The characteristics of these deposits suggest a braided system of low sinuosity channels. In the absence of any datable material associated with the high level gravels, it is difficult to assign a precise age for this aggradational phase.

The Upper Bhima formation (UBF) rests against the Godavari formation and is the most ubiquitous of all quaternary deposits in the river valleys of the Deccan upland, thereby representing a major aggradational phase. It has a thickness of 5 to 30 m and has been divided into two major litho units: (a) a lower coarse grained unit and (b) an upper fine grained unit. The lower

[105] Rajaguru and Korisetter (1987), op. cit.

[106] R. Korisear et al. (1989 a and b), op. cit.

[107] Sheila Mishra (1995), 'Chronology of the Indian Stone Age: The Impact of the Recent Absolute and Relative Dating Attempts', *ME,* XX, 2, pp. 11-16.

[108] K. Paddayya (1971), 'High-Level Gravels of the Shorapur Doab, Peninsular India', *Quarter*, 22, pp. 95-110; R.V. Joshi et al. (1980), 'Excavations at Wadoli-Waghodi: A Middle Palaeolithic Site of the High Level Gravel of the Godavari River', *BDCRI*, 39, pp. 49-89; R.S. Pappu and J.V.P. Rao (1983), 'On the Problem of the Age and Origin of High Level Gravels around Moravakonda, District Kurnool, Andhra Pradesh', *BDCRI*, 42, pp. 119-30.

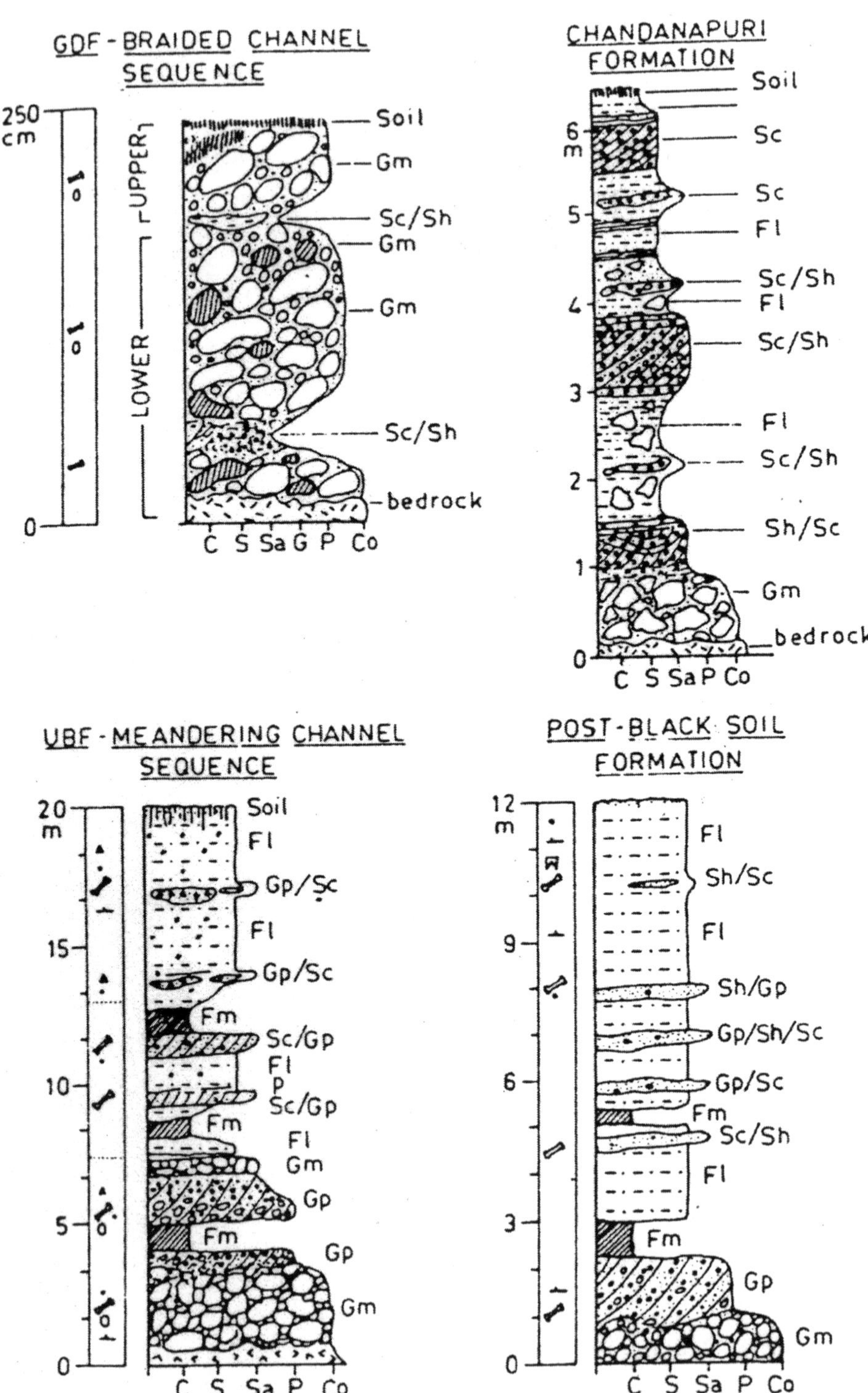

Fig. 2.15: Quaternary stratigraphy, Deccan upland region (after Rajaguru et al. 1993)

unit is a pebbly-cobbly gravel which is overlain by cross-bedded, pebbly-sandy gravels. Acheulian artefacts are frequently found in this deposit, at a few sites, fossils of *Equus*, *Elephas* and *Bos* have been found in this deposit. Th/U dates of indurated sandstones from Nevasa, Bori and Yedurwadi have given ages between 300 and > 350 kyr BP (Mishra 1992). The upper member is made up of predominantly sandy-pebbly gravel and yellow-brownish, bedded sandy silt. It has an average thickness of 8 m and rests non-conformably on the lower coarser unit. This member has yielded Middle Palaeolithic, Upper Palaeolithic and Epi-Palaeolithic artefacts, and fossilized animal bones, shells and drifted wood. About more than a dozen of C-14 dates on shells and bones indicate that this unit belongs to the Terminal Pleistocene.

The Chandanpuri formation (CPH) having a maximum thickness of about 6 m is mainly represented by colluvial deposits in the foothill zones of the valleys. The unit comprises pale yellow-brown, sandy silt and pebbly-sandy gravels. The basal part contains angular unweathered rubble of basalt. The th/u dates of the Kankar nodules (75-14 kyr BP) occurring in these deposits suggest that sediments were laid some time during the Late Pleistocene.

A geomorphic study of the above-mentioned fluvial sequence has facilitated the delineation of five major fluvial phases during the Late Quaternary in the Deccan Upland region as follows:

(1) Pre-Aggradational incision phase
(2) Ante-Holocene aggradational phase
(3) Early-Holocene rejuvenation phase
(4) Holocene alleviation phase
(5) Late Holocene incision phase

Changes in fluvial activity are attributed to changes in the base level, climatic changes and tectonic disturbances (Rajaguru and Kale 1985).

MAMMALIAN FOSSILS

Pleistocene fossiliferous localities have been observed in the Indian sub-continent for more than a century. Large and varied collections of mammalian fossils have been made from the Karewas of Kashmir, the Siwalik formations in the sub-Himalavan region in Punjab and Himachal Pradesh, the alluvia of Narmada and Mahanadi in Madhya Pradesh, the Belan Valley in Uttar Pradesh, Pravara, Godavari, Krishna, Ghod and Manjra in Maharashtra, and the Hunsgi Valley, Tungabhadra Valley and Ghataprabha Valley in Karnataka.[109] These faunal remains are associated with Lower Palaeolithic tools at a number of localities in the peninsular rivers.

[109]G.L. Badam (1979), *Pleistocene Fauna of India with Special Reference to the Siwaliks*, Deccan College, Pune; idem (1984), 'Pleistocene Faunal Succession of India', R.O. White (ed.), *The Evolution of the East Asian Environment*, vol. II, University of Hong Kong, Hong Kong, pp. 746-75.

The lower group of the Narmada stratigraphy which has yielded Acheulian tools contains fossils of *Elephas namadicus*, *Stegodon ganesa*, *Stegodon insignis*, *Bos namadicus*, *Equus namadicus*, *Bubalus palaeindicus*, *Cervus duvauceli*, *Rhinoceros unicornis*, *Hippopotamus palaeindicus*, *Leptobos fazeri*, *Ursus namadicus*, *Sus* sp., *Trionyx* sp. and *Emys* sp. In the Belan and Pravara valleys, similar types of fossil remains have been found. The presence of these animals during Acheulian times indicates the existence of both forest and open grass land environments, and the availability of plentiful water round the year.

A study of faunal remains has shown that fossils hitherto considered as an index for the Middle Pleistocene (*Equus namadicus* and *Bos namadicus*) range from the Middle to the Upper Pleistocene. Species like *Elephas maximus Cervus duvauceli* and *Rhinoceros unicornis* range from the Upper Pleistocene to the Holocene. Only *Hexaprotodon namadicus* and *Sus namadicus*, may be considered as index fossils for the Middle Pleistocene. The Upper Pleistocene is dated by a score of C-14 dates and contains a well-defined index of fossil assemblages.[110]

ASSOCIATED HUMAN REMAINS

A partial cranium of advanced *Homo erectus* or archaic *Homo sapiens* was discovered in 1982 in the basal gravels of the Narmada alluvium at Hathnora near Hoshangabad in Madhya Pradesh.[111] This is the first and, so far, the only hominid fossil discovery made in India. Tools of the Lower Palaeolithic Acheulian industry were also found from the same deposit. The cranium is heavily mineralized. Its position in the channel bar deposit of the Narmada combined with taphonomic features indicate that the cranium was redeposited in this sediment after having been transported over some distance. The hominid fossil and associated Acheulian tools come from a secondary context and, hence, a taphonomic study is necessary to arrive at a precise chronology, of the palaeoenvironmental aspects of the site.[112]

[110] Badam (1979), op. cit.; idem (1988), 'Quaternary Faunal Succession of India', *GSI, Special Publication II*, pp. 277-304.

[111] A. Sonakia (1984), 'The Shull-Cap of Early Man and Associated Mammalian Faun from the Narmada Valley Alluvium, Hoshangabad Area, Madhya Pradesh, India,' *Geological Survey of India Record*, 113, 6, pp. 159-72.

[112] Ibid., pp. 159-72; M.A. De Lumley, and A. Sonakia (1985a), 'Premieve Decouverted' un Homo erectus Sur le continent Indiana Hathnora, dans Moyenne Valle de la Narmada', *L'Anthropologic*, 89, pp. 13-61; idem (1985b), 'Contexte Stratigraphique at Archeologique de l' Homme de la Narmada, Hathnora, Madhya Pradesh, Inde', *L'Anthropologie*, 89, pp. 3-12; G.L. Badam (1989), 'Observations on the Fossil Hominid site at Hathnora, Madhya Pradesh, India', in A. Sahni and R. Gaur (eds.), *Perspectives in Human Evolution*, Renaissance Publishing Co., Delhi, pp. 153-71.

SUBSISTENCE PATTERN

The economy of the Acheulian culture was based on the hunting of the animals and gathering of wild plant foods. There is no direct convincing evidence in support of the subsistence practices of the Acheulian hunter-gatherers. This is because of the poor preservation of animal and plant remains at the excavated primary sites. The organic material which is essential to understand the subsistence practices of early man has been destroyed because of the tropical nature of the climate and acidic soil conditions.

The location of camp sites near perennial streams and in forests and grasslands provided good opportunities for hunting, fishing and gathering plant foods. There is evidence of fossils of contemporary animals in the river gravel deposits of the Narmada, Belan, Godavari, Bhima and other rivers which suggest that, in these areas, the wild elephant, wild ox, wild horse, wild buffalo, deer and other animals were present in large numbers. There were fishes, crocodiles and turtles in the rivers. In the marshy areas, lived the rhino and hippo.

No direct evidence is available to reconstruct the technique and equipment used for hunting. Large weapons made of organic materials like wood and bone have not survived. In some cases, stone artefacts like handaxes, cleavers and scrapers probably formed part of the hunting equipment. Pointed handaxes might have served as efficient spearheads, while the cleaver with its sharp cutting edges could have been used for cutting carcasses. There is little doubt that animal foods, acquired by hunting or scavenging, formed an important item of the diet of the Acheulian population.

Vegetable foods probably also formed an important part of the Acheulian diet. It has now been recognized that the meagre data available on the subsistence practices of Acheulian communities needs to be supplemented by ethno-archaeological, ethnobotanical and ethnozoological studies. Ethno-archeaological studies of some of the existing tribal communities like the bushmen of South Africa have convincingly shown that they derive their subsistence mainly from plant foods.[113] Ethnobotanical investigations undertaken in some parts like the Hunsgi Valley[114] and the Bhimbetka area[115] have revealed that the scrub jungle and deciduous vegetation tracts of peninsular India are extremely rich in wild plant foods of various kinds like fruits, berries, tubers, roots, nuts, seeds, greens, etc. These are still being exploited extensively by tribal groups like the Gonds, the Chenchus and the Yerkulas.[116]

[113]R.B. Lee (1969), 'Kung Bushman Subsistence: An Input-Output Analysis', in A.P. Vaidya (ed.), *Environment and Culture Behaviour*, Natural History Press, New York, pp. 47-79.

[114]Paddayya (1979b), op. cit.; idem (1982), op. cit.

[115]V.N. Misra et al. (1977), *Bhimbetka: Prehistoric Man and His Art in Central India*, Bhimbetka Souvenir Committee, Deccan College, Poona.

[116]M.L.K. Murty (1981), 'Hunter-Gatherer Ecosystems and Archaeological Patterns of Subsistence Behaviour on the Southeast Coast of India: An Ethnographic Model', *World*

PALAEOENVIRONMENT

Some idea of the past environment, particularly the palaeoclimate prevailing during Acheulian times, is provided by geoarchaeological studies carried out during the last three to four decades of fluvial, aeolian, colluvial, littoral and lacustrine deposits, with which Acheulian cultural remains are associated. These studies have established that there were climatic fluctuations, sea level changes and tectonic movements in the Indian subcontinent during the quaternary period.

In the Deccan upland region of Maharashtra, quaternary deposits are mostly of fluvial origin and are found in river valleys. Geoarchaeological studies conducted in several major river valleys of the Deccan have thrown considerable light on the behaviour of these streams in the vicinity of which Acheulian communities located their settlements. Fluvial phases of incision and aggradation have been recognized. The phases of fluvial activity were probably in response to regional climatic changes. The aggradational episodes were perhaps associated with semi-arid conditions, while incision phases were related to increase in rainfall. A comparison of the east-flowing rivers with the west-flowing ones revealed an inverse correlation between the two. During the period of low sea level, there was an increase in continentality and aridity, leading to aggradation on the leeward side of the Western Ghats. The high sea levels following the arid phases decreased continentality but led to increased runoff at which rivers began to cut down their beds.[117] These geomorphic events indicate that climatic fluctuations were not as drastic as in Rajasthan and the extra-peninsular region. The Deccan upland region, at present, enjoys a tropical, semi-arid, monsoonal climate, and more or less, the same pattern of climate, with minor fluctuations, prevailed during the Middle and Late Pleistocene. Pre-historic communities could very well have adapted themselves to such minor environmental changes.

The evidence for major climatic changes and the human response to these during the quaternary period comes from the semi-arid region of western Rajasthan. There is sufficient evidence to show that in present semi-arid western Rajasthan that is devoid of drainage, a mighty, well-organized stream existed during the Early Pleistocene. There is no evidence that man was

---

Archaeology, 13, 1, pp. 47-58; idem (1985), 'The Uses of Plant Foods by Some Hunter-Gatherers Communities in Andhra Pradesh', in V.N. Misra and P. Bellwood (eds.), *Recent Advances in Indo-Pacific Prehistory*, op. cit., pp. 329-36; Malati Nagar (1985), 'The Use of Wild Food and Plant Foods by Aboriginal Communities in Central India', in V.N. Misra and P. Bellwood (eds.), *Recent Advances in Indo-Pacific Prehistory*, Oxford-IBH, New Delhi, pp. 337-42.

[117] V.S. Kale and S.N. Rajaguru (1987), 'Late Quaternary Alluvial History of the Northwestern Deccan Upland Region', *Nature*, 325, pp. 612-14; idem et al. (1986), 'Relationship between Sea Levels and Continentality along Western Maharashtra During the Late Quaternary', *BDCRI*, 45, pp. 67-70; Rajaguru and Korisetter (1987), op. cit.

present in this area during this period. In the subsequent Mid- and Late Quaternary times, there were intensive climatic changes, and shallow streams flowing in wide flood plains deposited muds and calcareous clays in pans or shallow depressions. Acheulian artefacts in mint condition are found buried in these marly deposits at the site of Singi Talav in the Didwana region. The evidence shows that Acheulian man had adapted to the desert environment during mid-to-Late quaternary times. The Th/U date of > 390 kyr indicates an early date of the Acheulian culture. Acheulian man camped along pools and lakes in the flood plains.[118]

There were relative land and sea level changes during the quaternary, and there is ample evidence to show that the relationship between land and sea had fluctuated from 15 to 50 m. In recent years, investigations have been undertaken on the problem of quaternary sea level changes in relation to Palaeolithic sites in the Saurashtra region of Gujarat.[119] Two marine transgressive phases have been identified from the occurrence of marine deposits like miliolite formations, the first at the beginning of the late Middle Pleistocene about 1,70,000 yrs BP and the second around 30,000 yrs BP. Acheulian tools were located at Umrethi and Junagarh in gravel deposits underlying the first miliolite formation.

The major portion of the Indian peninsula has been regarded as tectonically stable since the post-Miocene or post-Tertiary times. Geomorphic studies undertaken in recent years in the peninsular region have shown that the Indian peninsula was not as stable as is generally believed.[120] There were tectonic disturbances of a epeirogenic type during the Late Tertiary and Pleistocene times. Rajaguru's studies in south-central Maharashtra indicated that the aggradational and erosional phase of the rivers have been controlled by large-scale, slow tectonic movements such as positive and negative epeiorgenic movements of the whole peninsular shields. The polycyclic nature of the landscape, the presence of peneplains at higher elevations, the superimposed and rejuvenated character of some of the rivers and entrenched meanders are attributed to the tectonic instability of the region. However, there is no direct evidence of tectonic activity in the form of structural displacements like folds and faults. Thus, these movements have not affected the landscape much or the archaeological settlements forming part of it. This is evident by the

[118]Misra (1987), op. cit.; idem (1995), op. cit.; Misra et al. (1982), op. cit.; Gaillard et al. (1983), op. cit.; idem (1985), op. cit.

[119]Lele (1989), op. cit.; Marathe (1981), op. cit.

[120]B.P. Radhakrishna (1952), 'The Mysoe Plateau: Its Structural and Physiographic Eovlution', *Bulletin of the Mysore Geologists Association*, 3, pp. 1-56; S.N. Rajaguru (1968), 'Some Aspects of Pleistocene Period in South Central Maharashtra', in F. Bordes and D. de Sonneville-Bordes (eds.), *La Prehistorie Problems et Tendances*, pp. 349-57; idem (1969), 'On the Late Pleistocene of the Deccan', *Quaternaria*, 11, pp. 241-53; R. Vaidyanathan (1977), 'Recent Advances in Geomorphic Studies of Peninsular India Review', *Indian Journal of Earth Sciences Ray Volume*, pp. 13-55.

preservation of fresh, unrolled artefacts in different geomorphic settings. The landscape has remained static, thereby indicating relative stability since the late Middle Pleistocene. Due to the inadequate knowledge of neo-tectonics in the region, it is rather difficult to ascertain the exact role played by tectonics in shaping varied geomorphic features.

SITE CATCHMENT ANALYSIS

The explicit realization that human groups procure resources from the regions immediately surrounding their settlements led to the introduction, in the late 1960s, of the analytical method of Site Catchment Analysis.[121] This concept is concerned with the exploitation of plant, animal and mineral resources by human groups in a particular territory. The catchment area of a site is the territory from which resources are taken to support human population and occur within a reasonable walking distance. On the basis of ethnographic data on the Kung bushmen in South Africa, two hours walking distance (10 km) has been suggested as the critical threshold for hunting-gathering economies.[122]

Over the last two decades, this hypothesis has been tested with great success at a number of Acheulian sites such as Chirki-Nevasa, Anagwadi, Khyad and Hunsgi. These studies have furnished evidence for the range of movement of Acheulian hunter-gatherers for resource exploitation and have confirmed that the resources occurred within a radius of 10 km.[123]

SETTLEMENT PATTERN

The concept of settlement pattern was first applied to archaeological studies by G.R. Willey (1953) in the Viru Valley, Peru, and offered a model framework for future investigations.[124] The analysis of past settlement patterns comprises the location of sites, their distribution and densities, and their relationship with ecology. In recent years, this concept has been successfully applied to the study of Palaeolithic sites in India.[125]

A large complex of open-air Acheulian sites was brought to light in the Hunsgi Valley of north Karnataka.[126] A detailed investigation of the location of the sites has given valuable clues about the probable annual activity cycle

[121] C. Vita-Finzi and E.S. Higgs (1970), 'Prehistoric Economy in the Mount Camel Area of Palestine: Site Catchment Analysis', *PPS*, 36, pp. 1-37.

[122] Lee (1969), op. cit.

[123] Pappu and Dev (1994), op. cit.; Paddayya (1982), op. cit.

[124] G.R. Willey (1953), 'Prehistoric Settlement Patterns in the Viru Valley, Peru', Bulletin Bureau of American Ethnology, 155, Washington D.C.

[125] Paddayya (1982), op. cit.; Pappu and Deo (1994), op. cit.; Raju (1988), op. cit.; R. Ray (1987), *Ancient Settlement Patterns of Eastern India*, Pearl Publishers, Calcutta.

[126] Paddayya (1982), op. cit.

of Acheulian groups and the nature of their seasonal settlement systems. They aggregated during the dry season at spring-fed water sources in the Hunsgi stream and dispersed during the wet season. It emerges that the wet season dispersal with an attendant reliance on plant foods and small fauna, and the dry season aggregation characterized by large game hunting were the governing principles of the Hunsgi Valley settlement system. Acheulian groups of the Hunsgi Valley practised a localized or restricted type of nomadism, mostly dependent on the seasonal availability of food and water resources.

The techniques and methods of geomorphology have been used to understand the settlement pattern and man-land relationship in the Kaladgi basin in north Karnataka.[127] The distribution of Acheulian sites in the Ghataprabha Valley of the northern part of the Kaladgi basin was found to have been influenced by morphometric parameters like relief, slope and drainage density, thereby indicating their role in the location of sites. Spatial point analysis results suggest that the sites were significantly concentrated in some parts of the basin, and the centrography of the basin revealed that the mean centre of Acheulian sites was located in the lower reaches. Based on these geomorphic investigations, three distinct archaeo-geomorphic zones, viz., the core zone, the marginal zone and the adverse zone, have been identified in the Ghataprabha basin.

Past natural processes and human activity contribute to the formation of an archaeological site. The study of the diverse processes of site formation is one of the most important aspects of modern archaeological research. This study provides a basis for interpreting the duration of human occupation, its continuity or intermittence, its intensity, the rate of deposit formation, post-depositional alterations and the effects of erosion on the preservation of cultural remains. In India a number of scholars have made attempts to study site formation processes.

K. Paddayya, M.D. Petraglia and R. Jhaldiyal made a study of site formation processes of Acheulian sites in the Hunsgi and Baichbal basins of north Karnataka.[128] The study aimed to identify and evaluate the natural and cultural processes responsible for the formation of Acheulian records in the basins. A majority of Acheulian sites in the basin are located away from the alluvial settings and occur as thin, unstratified artefact horizons which are on or very close to the surface. The cultural material at these sites lie completely exposed, partially exposed or buried under a shallow sediment cover. Acheulian artefacts occur in discrete clusters as isolated occurrences, and as horizontally diffused scatters in cultivated and uncultivated tracts of land.

The landscape on which Acheulian sites occur is a stable one where natural

[127] Pappu and Dev (1994), op. cit.

[128] Paddayya (1987 a and b), op. cit.; Petraglia (1995), op. cit.; R. Jhaldiyal (1997), 'Formation Processes of the Prehistoric sites in the Hunsgi-Baichbal Basins, Gulbarga District, Karnataka State', Ph.D. dissertation (unpublished), University of Pune, Pune.

processes operating on the landscape have been mainly low-energy, erosional processes. The varied preservational contexts in which Acheulian sites occur indicate that slow rates of sedimentation played a significant role in the preservation of the Acheulian record. The contemporary contexts of occurrence of the sites are the cumulative result of past and recent post-depositional processes. The weathering pattern analysis shows that the impact of processes on Acheulian sites before their burial was determined by the length of exposure, topographic location and nature of substrata. Sites located on soft sediments showed excellent preservation. An examination of the assemblage composition, the weathering analysis of artefacts and their spatial distribution in some of the excavated localities showed that the colluvial processes of sedimentation were clearly responsible for creating palimpset deposits containing artefacts discarded during different episodes of site occupation. The study of formation processes of surface and near-surface Acheulian sites shows that, in the absence of a vertical view, the documentation of the archaeological record at a regional level gives a better and more representative understanding of the character of natural processes operative on the landscape, and their impact on the archaeological record.[129]

GENESIS

To understand the genesis of the Lower Palaeolith Acheulian culture in the Indian subcontinent, it is necessary to know the evolutionary history of early man in other parts of the world. There are, at present, two contrasting views regarding this. According to the first, the ancestors of modern humans had their origins in Africa and from this continent they radiated to other parts of the world. Opposed to this view, some archaeologists have suggested the polycentric origin of early human cultures.

There is now convincing evidence to show that early man had his origin in sub-Saharan Africa. A tremendous amount of new evidence has come forward in support of this in the form of hominid fossil remains. The earliest hominid type is formed by the *Australopithecines* and is dated to four million years before the present. These were bipedal creatures who did not make any stone tools. The evidence of the first man-made stone tools in the archaeological record comes from Omo Valley in East Africa some 2.4-3.3 million years ago. These earliest simple tools were fashioned by the early forms of *Homo* known as *Homo habilis*. This hominid had a brain bigger than that of the *Australopithecines* and is significantly associated with the oldest evidence of tool-manufacture, known as the Oldawan stage. There appeared a new hominid type known as *Homo erectus* around 1.6-1.5 million years ago in Africa who had a higher stature and a brain larger than that of the *Homo habilis*. The

[129] Jhaldiyal (1997), op. cit.

arrival of die *Homo erectus* has always been regarded as marking an important stage in human evolution.

By about 1.5/1.4 million years ago, a large, bifacially worked tool-kit made its appearance in Africa. This is an industrial complex called the Acheulian. These stone artefacts showed a significant development over the Oldowan tool-kit and continued up to 1,25,000 years BP. They are the first standardized tools to appear in the archaeological record. Around one million years ago, *Homo erectus* moved out of Africa into the Asian tropics and then later into temperate Europe. Radiation and dispersal over wide areas are characteristics of evolutionary history. The earlier two hominid types, viz., *Australopithecines* and *Homo habilis*, never moved out of Africa and, therefore did not spread elsewhere. Sankalia[130] and Allchin[131] are impressed by African parallels and have postulated that the Acheulian culture was derived from this region to India via a new submerged continental shelf, or else through a land route connected by Arabia, Iran, Afghanistan and Baluchistan.

In recent years, new dates are available in different parts of the world for the Lower Palaeolithic culture which suggest that not one but several centres of human origin are likely. Such dates have come from Pakistan, Indonesia, Israel, Europe and Siberia.[132] These chronometric dates range from 2.5 million to 1.2 million years BP. This has necessitated a complete revision of earlier views.

CHRONOLOGY

Till recently, knowledge of the chronology of the Lower Palaeolithic Acheulian culture and its duration in India was far from satisfactory, as absolute dates for this cultural stage were not available. Its relative dating was based on palaeontological and geomorphological evidence. At times, the weathering of quaternary gravels and the flourine/phosphate ratios in fossil bones were used in estimating relative age.[133] In the last ten years, a significant number of absolute dates by the use of the Thorium-uranium (Th/U), Potassium-Argon (K/Ar) and Thermoluminesence (TL) methods have been made available.

[130] H.D. Sankalia (1974), *Prehistory and Protohistory of India and Pakistan*, Deccan College, Pune.

[131] B. Allchin, A. Goudie and K.T.M. Hegde (1979), *Prehistory and Palaeogeography of the Great Indian Desert*, London: Academic Press.

[132] P.G. Bahn (1996), 'The First Colonisation of Europe', in B.M. Fagan (ed.), *The Oxford Companion to Archaeology*, Oxford University Press, Oxford, pp. 224-5.

[133] S. Mishra et al. (1988), 'Relative Dating of the Quaternary Record from Upland Western Maharashtra', M.P. Patel and N. Desai (eds.), *National Seminar on Recent Quaternary Studies in India*, M.S. University, Baroda, pp. 267-8; R.V. Joshi and A.A. Kshirsagar (1986), *Flourine and Other Chemical Studies of Quaternary Animal of India*, Deccan College, Pune.

The Acheulian in the Indian subcontinent has been dated to the beginning of the Middle Pleistocene at the site of Bori in western Maharashtra,[134] and at Jalalpur and Dina in the Siwalik sediments in Pakistan.[135] At Bori, volcanic ash associated with an early Acheulian Industry has been dated between 670-530 kyr BP at Jalalpur and Dina. Achculian artefacts were found *in situ* in gravels just above the Bruhnes-Matuyam boundary and an age between 600-400 kyr BP has been estimated for the Acheulian culture at these sites. On the basis of palaeomagnetic stratigraphy, minimum dates of 190 kyr and 66 kyr were available on milliolite overlying gravels containing Acheulian artefacts in Saurashtra.[136] Th/U dates at the sites of Didwana, Yedurwadi and Nevasa show that the Acheulian is beyond the range of Th/U dating i.e. >350 kyr BP. In the Hunsgi-Baichbal valleys, one date is beyond the range of Th/U dating, and two further dates from the same context are close to the limit of Th/U dating.[137]

To conclude, dates from Umrethi and Adi Chad Vav in Saurashtra are suggestive of the minimum dates for the Acheulian culture in India. The dates obtained from Didwana, Tegginalli Nevasa and Yedurwadi are beyond the limits of the Th/U dating method. K/Ar of volcanic ash at Bori suggest that the Acheulian belongs to the early Middle Pleistocene. On the basis of this evidence, it is evident that the Acheulian in India falls within the time span of 600 kyr and 66 kyr BP. In terms of the geological time scale, it covers a period from the beginning of the early Middle Pleistocene to the mid Upper Pleistocene. The chronology of the Lower Palaeolithic Acheulian culture in India has thus been pushed backwards in time. This time framework compares fairly well with the chronology of the Acheulian in other parts of the world.

CONCLUSION

This review of the Lower Palaeolithic culture in India has brought to light varied aspects of this earliest phase of human occupation. The Indian sub-continent, particularly peninsular India, is one of the regions of the world with a long record of Acheulian hominid occupation. It is the most widespread and has the longest cultural tradition, as in Africa and Europe. Early man had adapted to a varying and changing environment. The diversity of habitats

[134] Mishra et al. (1995), 'Earliest Acheulian Industry from Peninsular India', *CA*, 36, pp. 847-51. P. Horn et al. (1993), 'K-Ar Fission Track and Thermoluminescene Ages of Quaternary Volcanic Tuffs and Their Bearing on Acheulian Artefacts from Bori, Kukdi Valley, Pune District, India', *Zectschrift der Deutschen Geologischen Gesellschaft*, 114, pp. 326-9.

[135] H. Rendell and R.W. Dennel (1985), 'Dated Lower Palaeolithic Artefacts from Northern Pakistan', *CA*, 26, 5, p. 393.

[136] Bhaskaran et al. (1986), op. cit.

[137] Mishra (1995), op. cit.

suggests that Lower Palaeolithic man was capable of a considerable degree of ecological adaptations. The Lower Palaeolithic phase in India, as elsewhere in the world, represents a very long and slowly evolving technology, thereby suggesting that behavioural changes were equally slow and gradual. The complete absence or only sparse presence of faunal and hominid remains at excavated primary or semi-primary sites precludes a full understanding of the Acheulian life. There are, thus, limitations in the ecological reconstruction of the Acheulian cultural system. Despite these limitations, Indian prehistorians in recent years have discovered a number of Lower Palaeolithic sites in a primary context and are undertaking systematic excavations by employing scientific techniques. It is hoped that in the coming years a significant and meaningful contribution will be achieved through their concentrated efforts.

APPENDIX

The Stone Age site of Attirampakkam (Tamil Nadu) was discovered in 1863 by Robert Bruce Foote which is incredibly rich in Lower Palaeolithic implements such as handaxes, cleavers, scrapers etc. Since then the site has been explored intensively but has been subjected to scientific excavation only recently by Dr Shanti Pappu who, with her colleagues, has discovered over 3500 Acheulian tools. Till now the Lower Palaeolithic implements in India were supposed to be about 0.5 million year old, but the Attirampakkam specimens, which were dated by the Cosmic Ray Exposure method, have been found to be about 1 to 1.5 million year old, that is, much older than those in Europe, indicating that the Stone Age man arrived in India from Africa much earlier than is generally thought. This is a very significant discovery which is consistent with the age of Acheulian implements in West and Southeast Asia, all belonging to Early Pleistocene.

Chapter 3

Early Hunter-Gatherers: The Middle Palaeolithic

P.C. Pant and Vidula Jayaswal

Though many scholars claimed to have found Palaeolithic implements of more than one series in the early part of the century,[1] the credit for recognizing distinct evidence of the Series 11 (Middle Palaeolithic) implements in stratified deposits at Nevasa on the Pravara in Maharashtra in 1954-5 goes to H.D. Sankalia (1956), the doyen of Indian prehistory, who called the industry' 'Nevasian'.[2] Since then, a very large number of industries of this phase have been recovered from different parts of the Indian subcontinent. Many of them are from definite stratigraphical horizons and an equal number of industries, if not more, have been acquired from factory sites. During the last four decades, enormous field data pertaining to the Middle Palaeolithic phase have been accumulated but scholars have hardly succeeded in projecting its distinct cultural identity.

As the name suggests, the Middle Palaeolithic occupies an intermediate stratigraphic position between the Lower and Upper Palaeolithic phases. In Europe, where Palaeolithic cultures have been best studied, it is a middle phase not only from the point of view of the stratigraphic and culture sequence, but it also appears to represent an intermediate stage of tool technology. However, this observation cannot be applied universally.

Nowadays the term Middle Palaeolithic has become more or less synonymous with 'Mousterian'. Earlier, Mousterian was regarded as one of the Middle Palaeolithic cultures of Europe, but sustained researches carried out by the Bordeaux group of prehistorians in France under the leadership of François Bordes (1969: 98 ff) and others have proved that it was a technological stage reached during the Middle Palaeolithic period, and was not limited to Europe. In fact, industries demonstrating the Mousterian stage of technology can be recognized even in various parts of Africa and Asia. The most important

[1]LA. Cammiade and M.C. Burkitt (1930), 'Fresh Light on the Stone Age of Southeast India', *Antiquity*, 4, pp. 327-30.

[2]H.D. Sankalia (1956), 'Animal Fossils and Paleolithic Industries from the Pravara Basin at Navasa, District Ahmednagar', *Ancient India*, 12, pp. 35-53.

feature of the Mousterian techno-typology is the occurrence of a variety of standardized flake implements. As far as Europe is concerned, this technological and typological level was perhaps reached in the last inter-glacial period, though most industries with clear evidence of the Mousterian level with all the techno-typological features occurred only in the earlier part of the Wurm glaciation (Wurm I & II of France and Wurm I of Central Europe) (ibid.), However, in many other parts of the world such as Africa and parts of Asia, including India, the Mousterian level appears to have been attained somewhat later.

In the present state of our knowledge, it may be stated that there are two sets of industries in the Middle Palaeolithic phase of India that show distinct evidence of the Mousterian level. They are

(1) Industries of the Soan tradition, mostly limited to the north and north-western part of the subcontinent, with sporadic occurrence in central India.

(2) Industries of the peninsular group distributed in almost the entire area earlier inhabited by the Lower Palaeolithic Acheulian man.

The two sets of industries are not only limited to two different regions having distinct ecological features but they are also distinguishable on account of their cultural material. The evidence for these two Middle Palaeolithic traditions are briefly discussed below.

MIDDLE PALAEOLITHIC CULTURE OF THE SOAN TRADITION (FIG. 3.1)

In view of their techno-typological level, some of the industries of the Potwar plateau of Pakistan, Himachal Pradesh, and the Vindhyan formations of the India can be safely grouped under the Middle Palaeolithic. Thus, many of the late Soan industries of H.D. Terra and T.T. Paterson,[3] particularly those included in the Late Soan B. and those of the Upper Soan of T.T. Paterson and J.N.T. Drummond may perhaps be termed as Middle Palaeolithic.[4] Besides, some flake industries of the Sirsa Valley in Himachal Pradesh and an industry from Lahchura in central India[5] also appear to exhibit the same general techno-typological features that are present among those of the Potwar region.

De Terra and Paterson claimed to have found the industries of the A and B phases of the Late Soan in two different strata but they assigned both of

[3] H. De Terra and T.T. Paterson (1939), *Studies in the Ice Age in India and Associated Human Cultures*, Pub. No. 393, Carnegie Inst of Washington, Washington.

[4] T.T. Paterson and J.N.J. Drummond (1962), *Soan: The Palaeolithic of Pakistan*, Karachi, Department of Archaeology, Government of Pakistan.

[5] P.C. Pant (1982), *Prehistoric Uttar Pradesh (A Study of the Old Stone Age)*, Agam Kala Prakashan, Delhi.

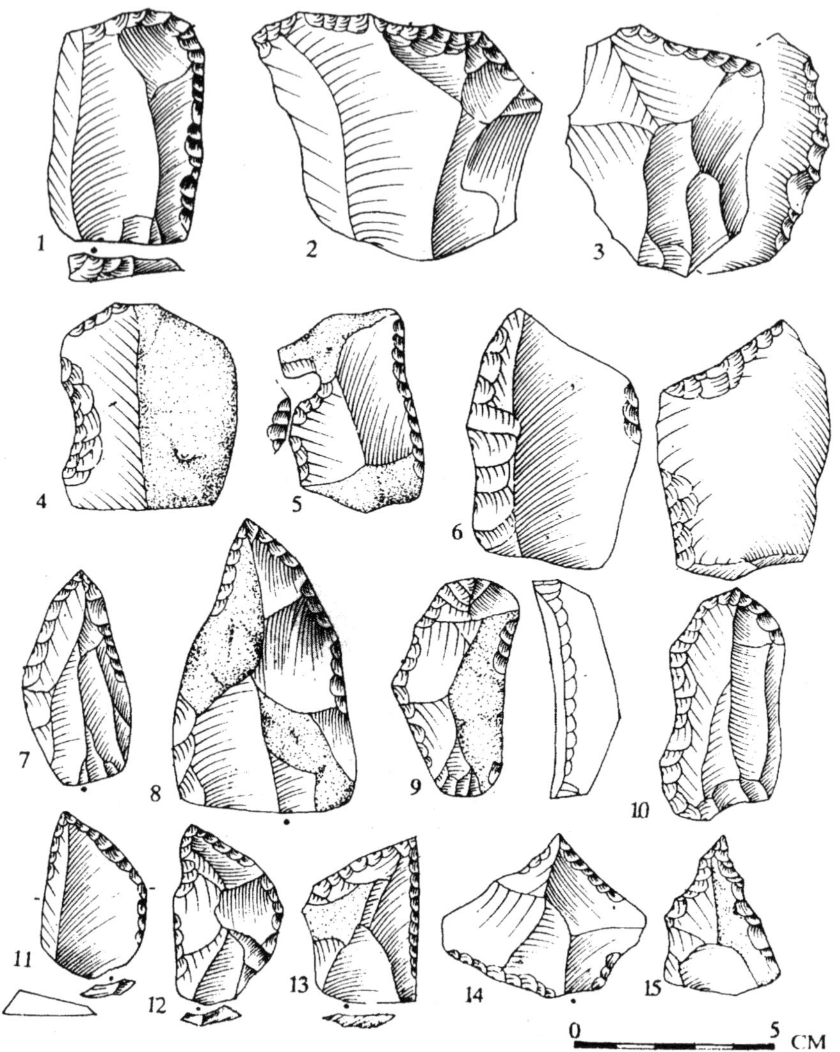

Fig. 3.1: Middle Palaeolithic tools

them to the third glaciation of the Himalayas. If this stratigraphical position and proposed chronology of the Late Soan are correct, it may be held that the Mousterian level was attained in this part of the world even earlier than in Europe. The British Mission, which recently re-examined the entire evidence of the Potwar region, however, questioned the stratigraphy, culture sequence as the well as the chronology proposed by the Yale-Cambridge Expedition.[6] In view of this, the proposed early geological context of the Late Soan needs reconsideration.

[6] R.W. Dennel et al. (1988), 'Early Tool-making in Asia: Two Million Year Old Artefacts in Pakistan', *Antiquity*, 62, pp. 98-106.

The techno-typological discussion of the lithic assemblages in the work of De Terra and Paterson is hardly adequate. However, even the brief notings and the accompanying line illustrations of implements are sufficient to indicate their Mousterian character. Both the phases of the Late Soan are said to be characterized by a good proportion of flake tools, besides a sizeable number of pebble tools. The accompanying line drawings in the work suggest the definite use of the Levallois technique and the occurrence of some notches and denticulates (Fig. 3.1). The Late Soan B phase also contains some blades.

Paterson and Drummond noted an Upper Soan phase and divided it into A and B, both assignable to the Upper Pleistocene.[7] However, while Upper Soan A belongs to the third glaciation of the Himalayas, according to the authors, phase B has been assigned to the subsequent inter-glacial. Among the various industries of the two phases, the one found at Ghila-khan of Upper Soan A, which contained 120 artefacts, appears to be the most significant. The two authors noted that 'about one-third are flakes, a third cores, and a third Soan type tools' in the industry.[8] The camp site of Adiala, belonging to Upper Soan B, yielded nearly 600 artefacts.[9] This industry, according to the authors, is characterized by an increase in the core-flake element, a definite advancement in the mode of core preparation and a decrease in the Soan-type pebble tools. In both the above representative industries, there are some flake tools with a regular marginal retouch, some of them resembling types occurring in some known Middle Palaeolithic industries. Unfortunately, the work does not specify either the precise types of implements or their exact number. However, it can be inferred from the accompanying line drawings of tools that many of the flakes and cores involved the use of the Levallois technique, and besides side-scrapers, some occasional denticulates and notched tools were also present in the industries.

As indicated above, Paterson and Drummond assigned Upper Soan A to the glacio-fluvial conglomerates of the third glacial period, which was characterized by a cool and wet climate. On the other hand, Upper Soan B belonged to fluvial gravels formed during warm and damp climatic conditions.[10] Thus, both the phases of the Upper Soan existed in an environment of sufficient precipitation, though the temperature must have differed widely. It is easy to presume that heavy rainfall must have given rise to forests, although the warm and humid climate of the latter phase would have been better suited to the growth of vegetation. It is indeed interesting to note that the warm inter-glacial climate of Upper Soan B did not bring about any fundamental changes in the tool-kit of the earlier phase, which existed in the cold peri-glacial climate. Of course, there are some distinctions in the tool-typology

[7]Paterson and Drummond (1962), op. cit.

[8]Ibid., p. 71.

[9]Ibid., p. 76.

[10]Ibid., pp. 42-3.

of these two groups of industries, but they appear to be more of a technological nature than functional. In view of these observations, it may perhaps be argued that the needs of the people of Upper Soan A and B were primarily related to the surrounding forests, and the fluctuations in temperature hardly brought about any significant change for them. Alternatively, the proposed evidence for the geology, palaeo-climate and chronology of industries is unreliable, as suggested by the British Mission (Dennell et al. 1987).

It is worthwhile to note, however, that the British mission, who reexamined the evidence of the Potwar plateau of Pakistan in the early 1980s, questioned the very existence of climatic terraces in the region as observed by the Yale-Cambridge expedition and other investigators. It noted that the region experienced various aggradational phases during the Pleistocene, as a result of which Upper Shivalik conglomerates. Lower Loess, Lei conglomerates and Upper Loess were deposited. In between these depositional phases, there were periods of erosion, and foldings and uplifting of rocks. According to H.M. Rendell and R.W. Dennell, some Middle Palaeolithic industries occurred between the Lei conglomerate and the Upper Loess, probably in an intervening erosional phase.[11] However, their precise techno-typological features have not been noted.

G.C. Mohapatra brought to light some industries in the Sirsa Valley of Himachal Pradesh,[12] which exhibit a general resemblance to the Late Soan of De Terra and Paterson and the Upper Soan of Paterson and Drummond. The tool-kit is said to be composed of some pebble choppers, prepared flakes, thick blades, small side-scrapers, incipient borers and fine bifacially flaked discoids. The term 'prepared flake' probably stands for the Levallois flake. The stratigraphical position is uncertain and, hence, no comment is possible on the palaeo-climate.

As many as three sites yielding pebble tools comparable with the Early Soan tool-kits of the Potwar region were located in the hilly tracts of Jhansi, the Hamirpur district of Uttar Pradesh and the adjoining Chhatarpur district of Madhya Pradesh in central India.[13] Among them the site of Lahchura is most significant for not only yielding the largest number of Lower Palaeolithic pebble tools, but also for an industry showing various Mousterian traits.[14]

This Middle Palaeolithic industry was found on the western slope at the foot of a long hill running almost parallel to the river Dhasan, nearly 500 m south of the village Lahchura Ghat, district Jhansi. Although the tool-kit consists of a variety of implements, the pebble element dominates throughout.

[11] H.M. Rendell and R.W. Dennel (1987), 'Thermoluminiscence Dating of an Upper Pleistocene Site, Northern Pakistan', *Geoarchaeology*, 2, pp. 63-7.

[12] G.C. Mohapatra (1974), 'Lithic Industries of Himachal Pradesh', in A.K. Ghosh (ed.), *Perspectives in Palaeo-anthropology*, Firma K.L. Mukhopadhyay, Calcutta, pp. 199-212.

[13] Pant (1982), op. cit., pp. 39-43.

[14] Ibid., pp. 72-6.

While pebble tools of the chopper-chopping group are mostly made of quartzite pebbles, crypto-crystalline silica and quartzite were used for other implements of the industry. Out of the total number of 102 artefacts, thirty-one are chopper-chopping tools, twenty-one scrapers, eight notches, six denticulates and six knives (Fig. 3.1). Among the side-scrapers, there are some perfect examples of convergent scrapers. A few specimens have a single or double shoulder near the base. Besides, there is a small proportion of roughly made burins. Levallois appears to be the dominant flake-detaching technique. However, the industry also contains some blades and blade cores. Thus, in view of its general typo-technological traits, the Lahchura industry compares favourably with those of the Potwar region in Pakistan, and the Sirsa Valley in Himachal Pradesh in India. Unfortunately, the implements were found on the surface and not in any geological formation. Obviously, nothing can be said about the palaeo-environment of the industry. Since central and peninsular India hardly experienced any noticeable influence of the glacial climate of the Himalayas during the pleistocene, it can be safely held that the Middle Palaeolithic man of Lahchura lived in an entirely different palaeo-environment. This also leads us to an obvious conclusion that environmental distinctions hardly brought about any noteworthy change in the techno-typology of tools of the Middle Palaeolithic cultures of the Soan tradition.

MIDDLE PALAEOLITHIC OF THE PENINSULAR INDIA

After the recognition of a distinct Middle Palaeolithic phase at Nevasa on the Pravara in Maharashtra, the distribution of this culture was traced to a very wide region, comprising almost the whole of the peninsula and the areas around the Aravalli, the Kaimur and the Chhotanagpur ranges. A recent analysis of the tool-kit from the Sanghao Cave excavated earlier by A.H. Dani reveals that the Middle palaeolithic industries of the peninsular group also occurred sporadically in Pakistan almost up to the Afghanistan border.[15] There is hardly any clear indication of distinct regional variations within this culture so far, although the possibility of such variations cannot be ruled out. One of the reasons may be that most of the investigators followed a set of techno-typological patterns established by Sankalia nearly three decades ago, and very often made efforts to recognize only 'scraper, point, and borer' in their assemblages.

Several localities in the India subcontinent have yielded Middle Palaeolithic industries which also contain a few handaxes, cleavers and/or choppers. Among such industries, particular mention may be made of those from Kurnool (Andhra Pradesh), Kutch and Saurashtra (Gujarat), Rankala

[15] A.H. Dani (1964), 'Sanghao Cave Excavation: The First Season 1963', *Ancient Pakistan*, Bulletin of Department of Archaeology, University of Peshawar, 14, pp. 1-50.

(Maharashtra), west Rajasthan,[16] and the Son Valley (Madhya Pradesh). It can be suggested that there are two distinct phases within the Middle Palaeolithic culture of the peninsular India, the earlier one being characterized by the occurrence of a few heavy duty implements of the Lower Palaeolithic tradition besides other Middle Palaeolithic tool types? It is worthwhile to mention here that G.R. Sharma and Desmond Clark[17] have indeed claimed to have found two distinct Middle Palaeolithic industries in the Son Valley, one excavated in the sediments of the Rehinala containing fresh flake tools along with small sub-triangular and cordiform handaxes, and the other from a site adjacent to Baghor I, consisting of the usual Middle Palaeolithic tool-kit. However, as long as we do not get confirmatory evidence from other sites that may determine the distinct stratigraphical horizons of the two suggested phases, it is difficult to arrive at any definite conclusion. It may be recalled that there are several advanced Acheulian industries from various parts of India, such as Bhimbetka[18] and Paisra,[19] which also contain tool-kits comparable with those of the Middle Palaeolithic. The Upper Acheulian of Western Europe is also characterized by a good number of well-made flake tools, similar to those from 'certain Mousterian industries of the Wurm glaciatioiv'.[20] Similarly, Bridget and Raymond Allchin opine that the Middle Palaeolithic culture of the Deccan and central India, extending through the Vindhyas up to the Ganga plains and sometimes referred to as Nevasian, is markedly different from the Middle Palaeolithic industries of the region lying west of the Aravalli Hills and north of the Saurashtra peninsula. The industries of the latter group, according to them, show great diversity and can be divided into 'lesser regional groups, and into what appear to be the outcome of a series of marked local, traditions'.[21]

Notwithstanding these occasional observations, there is little doubt that Nevasian-type Middle Palaeolithic industries are very widespread in the Indian subcontinent. They not only exhibit a marked homogeneity in their cultural contents but stratigraphically too they come from the deposits formed during the second aggradational phase of various rivers. Artefacts of this culture have been found almost everywhere in the thick gravel-sand deposits which overlie the boulder-cobble deposit and the clay or silt of an earlier

[16]H.D. Sankalia (1974), *Prehistory and Protohistory of India and Pakistan*, Deccan College, Poona, p. 199.

[17]G.R. Sharma and J.D. Clark (1983) (eds.), *Palaeoenvironment and Prehistory of the Middle Son Valley, M.P., North Central India*, Abinash Prakashan, Allahabad, pp. 9-21.

[18]V.N. Misra (1978), 'The Acheulian Industry of Rock Shelter III, F-23 at Bhimbetka, Central India', *Australian Archaeology*, 8, pp. 13-36.

[19]P.C. Pant and Vidula Jayaswal (1991), *Paisra: The Stone Age Settlement of Bihar*, Agam, Delhi.

[20]F. Bordes (1968), *The Old Stone Age*, McGraw Hill, New York, p. 59.

[21]B. Allchin and Raymond (1982), *The Rise of Civilization in India and Pakistan*, Cambridge University Press, Cambridge, p. 51.

aggradation. Good examples of stratigraphic successions have been noted in the Belan,[22] Son,[23] Narmada[24] and Pravara[25] valleys. Various investigators have observed that the gravels of the second aggradation are generally smaller than those of the earlier ones, and a good majority of them are fairly well-rounded, angular and sub-angular examples being rather rare. Further, the cross-bedding of sand and gravel-sheets appear to be a common feature of this deposit. It is also significant to note that this accumulation of gravels and sands has been found at many sites, particularly those located in the above-mentioned river valleys, and are fairly rich in the faunal remains of mammals. It is worthwhile to recall that mammalian fossil-fauna has also been found in large quantities from the earlier boulder-cobble deposit, which yielded evidence of the Acheulian culture. The sites of the Narmada Valley can be particularly mentioned in this respect. It is interesting to note, however, that the animal species represented by the fossil fauna of the two deposits, separated from each other perhaps by a very long interval, hardly differ from each other. Among the various animal species, the *Bos namadicus*. the *Equus namadicus*, the *Cerus* sp., and the *Elephas antiquus* appear to be the most frequent. Outside India, this group of fauna has been assigned to the Middle Pleistocene. However, in view of its occurrence in deposits associated with both the Lower and Middle Palaeolithic cultures, a similar time-bracket cannot be assigned to it in the Indian subcontinent. Moreover, there is sufficient evidence in India to suggest that some of the species of this group of fauna like *Bos namadicus* and *Palaeoloxodon* appear to have continued not only throughout the late Pleistocene but also occasionally in the early Holocene. Thus, the faunal evidence, considered hitherto very significant for dating purposes, cannot be relied upon for fixing the chronology of the Middle Palaeolithic culture of the peninsular region. Many scholars now believe that the culture cannot be dated prior to the late Pleistocene and probably belongs to its later half.[26] According to one estimate based on geological observations in the Belan Valley, the gravel-sand unit of the second aggradation and the culture associated with it perhaps mark the very end of the Pleistocene.[27] However, this view has not been found acceptable in the absence of adequate supporting evidence either from the Belan Valley or from any other sites.[28]

[22]Pant (1982), op. cit., p. 18.

[23]Sharma and Clark (1983) (eds.), op. cit., pp. 9-21.

[24]De Terra and Paterson (1939), op. cit., pp. 313-26.

[25]Sankalia (1956), op. cit.

[26]S.N. Rajguru and K.T.M. Hegde (1972), 'The Pleistocene Stratigraphy of India', in S.B. Deo (ed.), *Archaeological Congress and Seminar Papers*, Nagpur University, Nagpur, pp. 69-79.

[27]D.C. Dassarma and S. Biswas (1976), 'Quaternary Deposits of the Belan-Seoti Valleys, Allahabad District. U.P.', in M.S. Srinivasan (ed.), *Progs of the VI Indian Colloquium on Micro-Palaeontology and Stratigraphy*, Varanasi, pp. 33-6.

[28]Pant (1982), op. cit.

Fortunately, we now have some radiocarbon dates for the geological horizon associated with this cultural phase of a few sites in Maharashtra, Gujarat, Madhya Pradesh and Andhra Pradesh.[29] Although these radiocarbon dates differ widely from each other, a general time bracket of 40,000 to 5,000 BP may be assigned to this group of industries on this basis. The earliest date of more than 39,000 BP is from the Mula dam near Pune (Maharashtra), while the three dates from Bhimbetka (Madhya Pradesh) range between 17.670 and 15,370 BP (all dates are based on 5,568 BP half life). Although some dates like the one from Bardia Hill, Gujarat, are later, most of the other dates are higher than 15,000 BP. On the basis of a radiocarbon determination of carbonates in the clays of the Son Valley, which have an age of *c.* 25,000 BP, Clark and Williams think that the Middle Palaeolithic in this area may be about 40,000 or 50,000 years old, since the carbonates in the clays are actually post-depositional.[30] On the other hand, several TL and Uranium/Thorium decay series of fossil sand sheets of the 16 R locality at Didwana, north central Rajasthan, indicate that the Middle Palaeolithic industries have to be placed between 1,50,000 and 1,00,000 BP.[31] One does not know how reliable these dates are. Similarly, the reliability of the radiocarbon dates of shells, uncharred bones and carbonate samples from various deposits is also questionable. In view of the above discussion, it may be held that it is difficult to provide an absolute time-bracket for the Middle Palaeolithic culture of the peninsular India, at least for the present.

When compared with the European culture sequence, the Indian Middle Palaeolithic appears to be more or less contemporary with the pre-Magdalenian Upper Palaeolithic cultures, provided we discount the early TL and Uranium/Thorium decay series dates from Didwana. However, it may be borne in mind that the palaeolithic cultures of India seem to share more features with their counterparts in Africa than in Europe. Understandably, the culture under discussion has a comparatively late beginning, as is the case with the Sangoan-Charaman culture complex of South Africa.[32]

As noted above, the Middle Palaeolithic industries of the peninsular India have been found over almost the entire region from where the evidence for the earlier Acheulian culture was recovered. After the pioneering work of Sankalia at Nevasa, scholars of the Deccan College located a large number

[29] Gregory Possehl and Paul Rissman (1992), 'The Chronology of Prehistoric India: From Earliest Times to Iron Age', in R.W. Ehrich (ed.), *Chronologies in Old World Archaeology*, I and II, University of Chicago, Chicago, pp. 465-90 and 447-74.

[30] J.D. Clark and M.A. Williams (1986), 'Palaeoenvironments and Prehistory of North Central India: A Preliminary Report', in J. Jacobson (ed.), *Studies in the Archaeology of India and Pakistan*, Oxford-IBH, Delhi, pp. 19-41.

[31] V.N. Misra (1989), 'Stone Age India: A Ecological Perspective', *ME*, 14, pp. 21-2.

[32] C.G. Sampson (1974), *The Stone Age Archaeology of Southern Africa*, New York, pp. 140-2.

of Middle Palaeolithic sites in various parts of the country.[33] For obvious reasons, they all followed the techno-typological model of screening tool-kits, proposed earlier by Sankalia, and emphasized the tool types—scraper, point and borer—as the basic cultural components of this culture. The less frequent types are said to be the small chopper, small handaxe, small cleaver and burin. It was also claimed that the diagnostic tool types—scraper, point and borer are variously made of flakes, nodules and occasional cores. Among the different types of scrapers, the one named 'hollow scraper' appears to be more typical than others. The flake-detaching technique is basically non-Levallois, although the 'infrequent and sporadic' use of the Levallois technique has also been observed.[34] In a nutshell, in spite of the sporadic occurrence of a few choppers, handaxes and cleavers, the culture has been described as being characterized by 'light duty tools'.

The present authors have been working on the Middle Palaeolithic industries of Uttar Pradesh and Bihar for the last three decades, and the second author of this chapter had an opportunity to make a first-hand study of all the important Middle Palaeolithic assemblages housed in different centres in the country.[35] Our own observations, however, fail to support the above conclusions pertaining to the cultural composition of the Middle Palaeolithic complex of the peninsular India. It was noted that the conclusions regarding techno-typological features were drawn on the basis of artefact collections made from the river valleys. It was not realized that these collections are not well-suited for a standard techno-typological screening, since many of them may be thickly patinated so as to conceal finer marks of secondary working, or may bear various superfluous marks which might have been made on them in the course of their transportation. A closer examination of industries from primary sites will immediately impress upon any keen observer that most of the different tool-types are not classical in nature and sometimes appear to lack standardization. They can, at best, be described as degenerate or mediocre in quality. This applies more to the side-scrapers, which appear to predominate these industries. These implements very often do not bear evidence for a neat and regular marginal retouch, as is the case with their counterparts in industries of the Mousterian group of Europe, particularly those of Charentian (Bordes 1969: 101-2). Instead, several specimens of this tool-type contain marks of retouch on margins, partly from the dorsal and partly from the ventral surface on the same side. In no case have the authors encountered any typical Mousterian point, or what is sometimes termed as *Handspitze*. It may be recalled that Allchin also noticed the absence of a well-defined point in the Indian Middle Palaeolithic.[36] In rare industries, there are some convergent

[33] Sankalia (1974), op. cit., pp. 143-230.

[34] Ibid., p. 199.

[35] Vidula Jayaswal (1978), *Palaeohistory of India*, Agam Kala Prakashan, Delhi.

[36] B. Allchin (1966), *The Stone Tipped Arrow: Late Stone Age Hunters of the Tropical Old World*, Barnes and Noble, London, p. 78.

scrapers, which have sometimes been mistaken as points. Similarly, many artefacts have been identified as borers but there is hardly any specimen among them which contains notches, preferably retouched from alternate surfaces, one each on either side of the point, a feature usually associated with a typical borer. Thus, as per our observation, the Middle Palaeolithic industries of the peninsular India hardly contain any classical side-scrapers, or any typical Mousterian point, or borer.

On the contrary, if one minutely examines the tool-kits, one is bound to be impressed by the occurrence of numerous denticulates and notched tools, which appear to be the best-made implements. If the tools of both these categories are put together, they account for nearly 25-30 per cent of most of the industries.[37]

It is worthwhile to recall that they occur in the east up to West Bengal and in the west at the Sanghao cave in Pakistan.[38] Thus, they form a distinct and regular feature of the Middle Palaeolithic of the peninsular India and occupy a position which is only second to the group of side-scrapers. Among other tool types occurring in these industries besides side-scrapers, denticulate and notched tools, mention may be made of the knife, burin, end-scraper racelette, etc., but their proportion, though divergent, is usually very low and negligible. Industries like Jamalpur, Bhimbandh and Kandini in the Munger district of Bihar perhaps represent regional variations, as they also seem to be characterized by a few well-made knives, flake axes and some crude handaxes, besides the aforesaid components of the culture.[39]

From the point of view of technology too, the culture had attained a Mousterian level. In view of the flake-detaching technique, the Middle Palaeolithic culture of the peninsular India seems to have two clear divisions: (1) industries characterized by the overwhelming use of the Levallois technique, e.g. Ramgarwa, Cahinpura and Baithakwa industries of the Belan Valley and those of the Munger district, Bihar, and (2) those which are essentially non-Levallois, though in certain cases the Levallois makes its limited appearance. The industries of the second group have very often come from river deposits. The second author of this chapter has closely examined the question of the limited occurrence or otherwise of the Levallois technique among the Middle Palaeolithic industries of India and has come to the convincing conclusion that this technique appears to be predominant among industries which were made on quartzite like coarse-grained rocks, while it was very sparingly used in those which adopted crypto-crystalline silica as the raw material for manufacturing implements. Thus, the technological distinctions between the industries of the two groups appear to be related to

[37]A.K. Ghosh (1974), 'Denticulates in India: Examination of a Type Concept', *Journal of Hongkong Archaeological Society*, 5, pp. 47-56.

[38]Mohammad Salim (1986), *The Middle Stone Age Cultures of Northern Pakistan*, Islamabad.

[39]P.C. Pant and Vidula Jayaswal (1977-78), 'Jamalpur: A Typological Variant within the Middle Palaeolithic Culture Complex of India', *Puratattva*, 9, pp. 15-33.

the selection of rock as a raw material. It may be noted that most of the hills of peninsular India extending up to the Indo-Gangetic plains are formed by coarse-grained rocks like sandstone and quartzite, granite and gneiss, basalt, dolerite, etc. Obviously, this coarse-grained raw material was available to Palaeolithic man in abundance, mostly in the form of huge boulders, and he had to fashion his slender implements out of these blocks. The best course available to him to tackle the problem was perhaps preparation of the rocks (cores) in such a way that the desired flakes could be easily detached from them. On the contrary, in the case of industries using crypto-crystalline silica as raw material, man mostly exploited river cobbles and pebbles, but occasionally also veins of crypto-crystalline silica occurring in between the coarse-grained rocks. River pebbles and cobbles could not have been easily prepared in the Levallois fashion for obvious reasons.[40]

Another important feature pertaining to tool technology is the general lack of uniformity in retouch. It is either generally small and limited to the margins, or very bold, comparing somewhat with the type appearing on bifaces. In a good number of cases, particularly side-scrapers, it is partly from the dorsal and partly from the ventral surface on the same margin. The regular and neat retouch comparing with the scalariform retouch of the Quina-Ferrassie type[41] is either altogether absent or appears in a negligible proportion. This general lack of regularity and uniformity of retouch appears to be the main reason for the absence or sporadic occurrence of well-made classical implement types. However, the same does not apply to denticulates and notched tools, and many of the specimens of these categories compare favourably with their west European counterparts. They contain both 'clactonian notches' made by a fairly powerful single stroke as well as regular ones formed by a small neat retouch.[42]

In view of the short account of the techno-typological characteristics of the Indian Middle Palaeolithic of the peninsular India, it can be deduced that the culture is dominated by two groups of implements—different types of side-scrapers, generally showing workmanship of mediocre quality, and well-made denticulates and notched tools. The preponderance of side-scrapers makes the culture comparable with that of the Quina-ferrassic group of west Europe. Yet the mediocre quality of side-scrapers of the Indian Middle Palaeolithic and the near-absence of a neat scalariform retouch on them appears to negate any such possibility. However, in view of its techno-typological make-up and the occurrence of denticulates and notched tools in an appreciable proportion, it may be possible to compare the Indian Middle Palaeolithic culture with the Denticulate Mousterian of west Europe. The latter is said to be characterized by a 'Low to very low percentage of side-

[40]Vidula Jayaswal (1972-73), 'A Note on the Influence of Raw Material on the Block-debacking Technique', *Puratattva*, 6, pp. 64-70.

[41]Bordes (1968), op. cit., pp. 101-2.

[42]F. Bordes (1961) *Typology du Palaeolithic Ancien et Moyes*, 2 vols., Imprimeries Delmas, Bordeaux.

scrapers. often "degenerate", none being Quina type, high to very high percentage of denticulates and notches. Absence of true handaxes and absence or extreme rarity of backed knives, variable percentage of Levallois flakes.[43] Except for the scraper index, which is generally moderately high (30-5 per cent) in our industries, these features are also shared by the Indian Middle Palaeolithic of the peninsular India. Although the Denticulate Mousterian of France is said to include a high to very high proportion of denticulates and notches, some of the industries of west Europe also, e.g. the one coming from layer 38 of the cave Combe Grenal,[44] contain only a moderate proportion of these tool-types. In view of this and the near-absence of the typical neatly made Mousterian of the peninsular region it can be described as Denticulate Mousterian. However, points of distinctions between the Denticulate Mousterian of west Europe and Indian industries cannot be easily ignored. Perhaps the latter can, at best, be described as the Indian version of the Denticulate Mousterian.

Stratigraphically, the Middle Palaeolithic of the peninsular region belongs to the second aggradational phase of rivers. The gravel-sand deposit of 2-3 m thickness exhibits uniform features almost throughout the area of its distribution. Thus, the cross-bedding of sand and gravel sheets, better sorting and roundedness of pebbles, gravels, and sand particles appear to relate this deposit to certain distinct palaeo-environmental factors. These fluvial deposits appear to indicate that the rivers earned sufficient water, probably all through the year. The climate was perhaps wetter than that of modern times and, more importantly, the rainfall was better distributed during the year. Such a climate must have given rise to a thick vegetational cover on the land surface. However, fossil fauna recovered from second aggradational deposits suggest a savanna grassland environment. It may be noted that most of the factory and/or habitational sites of the Middle Palaeolithic culture of the peninsular region occur either on the river banks of rocky terrains, the gentle slopes of hill ranges or in the vicinity of small hillocks situated close to water sources. In western Rajasthan, the Middle Palaeolithic man settled on stable dune surfaces.[45] The evidence for his occupation of rock shelters is limited so far to those of Adamgarh[46] and Bhimbetka[47] in central India. However, the sites seldom occur in thick forests. This observation leads us to an obvious conclusion that he appeared to have avoided thickly forested regions, and

[43] F. Bordes and De Sounneville-Bordes (1970), 'Significance of Variability in Palaeolithic Assemblades', *World Archaeology*, 2, pp. 61-73.

[44] F. Bordes (1972), *A Tale of Two Caves*, Harper and Row, New York.

[45] V.N. Misra and S.N. Rajaguru (1986), 'Environment et Culture de l'Homme Prehistoric dans le desert du Thar, Rajasthan, Inde', *L'Anthropologie*, 90, pp. 407-37.

[46] R.V. Joshi (1978), *Stone Age Cultures of Central India: Report on the Excavations of Rock Shelters at Adamgarh, Madhya Pradesh*, Deccan College, Poona.

[47] V.N. Misra (1985), 'Acheulian Succession at Bhimbetka, Central India', in V.N. Misra and P. Bellwood (eds.), *Recent Advances in India Prehistory*, pp. 35-48.

preferred to inhabit only the fringes of the forests. Whether the specialized tools of denticulates and notches were primarily aimed at working on wood cannot be determined in the absence of any supporting evidence.

Thus, the two Middle Palaeolithic cultures of the Indian subcontinent apparently flourished in different ecological settings the only exception being the Lahchura industry belonging to the Soan tradition. This naturally leads us to think that the Soan tradition penetrated in central India at least up to Lahchura but in the absence of favourable ecological conditions, the tradition could not flourish in the region. It is also interesting to note that the Middle Palaeolithic of the Soan tradition placed more reliance upon heavy-duty chopper-chopping implements, though it did not possess any specimens which may be classified as hunting implements. On the contrary, the Middle Palaeolithic of the peninsular region appears to have generally lacked heavy-duty implements. Even the occasional handaxes, cleavers and choppers in some of the industries of this culture are considerably smaller than similar implements of the earlier Lower Palaeolithic phase. In fact, if we take into account the functional aspect of implements, we do not notice either any genuine cutting or hunting tool among the peninsular Middle Palaeolithic assemblages. There is hardly any true projectile point which could have been used as an effective arrow or lance head. Does it suggest that the human groups responsible for this culture-complex did not need them as they were basically vegetarian, fully exploiting the forest surroundings? Alternatively, perhaps they manufactured their hunting implements out of bone or wood, as was done by the Acheulian man of the twin-sites of Torralba and Ambrona in Spain,[48] or the Clactonian man of England, but these did not survive for posterity. This presumption is somewhat corroborated by the occurrence of a good number of notched tools, particularly those bearing a single notch on the margin of a flake or a flat nodule.

Most questions pertaining to the way of life of the Middle Palaeolithic people of India cannot be answered due to the paucity of reliable data from excavated habitational sites. No doubt two rock shelters, viz., Adamgarh[49] and Bhimbetka,[50] and one open air site of Samnapur,[51] all located in central India, have been excavated. However, the reportings of the evidence are so brief and insufficient that any meaningful discussion of the behavioural patterns of the people is very difficult to conduct. The evidence from the Sanghao cave in Pakistan, though significant, has not been properly studied either by A.H. Dani[52] or Mohmmad Salim[53] so as to make a reconstruction of their way of life possible.

[48]Bordes (1968), op. cit., p. 66, Fig. 18.
[49]Joshi (1978), op. cit.
[50]Misra (1985), op. cit.
[51]Misra (1989), op. cit., pp. 21-2.
[52]Dani (1964), op. cit.
[53]Salim (1986), op. cit.

Chapter 4

Early Hunter-Gatherers: The Upper Palaeolithic

Sheila Mishra

DEFINITION OF THE UPPER PALAEOLITHIC PHASE IN INDIAN PREHISTORY

The identification of a distinct Upper Palaeolithic phase in Indian prehistory was made in the late 1960s and early 1970s, with major contributions by M.L.K. Murty,[1] S.A. Sali[2] and G.R. Sharma.[3] The establishment of this phase required that the African terminology of the Early, Middle and Late Stone Age, adopted by Indian prehistorians in 1961 at the International Conference on Asian Archaeology in Delhi, be abandoned in favour of the European terminology of the Lower, Middle and Upper Palaeolithic. The major difference between the two terminologies is that the Late Stone Age of the African terminology includes both the Upper Palaeolithic and Mesolithic, as well as the Neolithic/Chalcolithic of the European terminology. This change to the European terminology was promoted primarily by H.D. Sankalia and G.R. Sharma (panel discussion in Agrawal and Ghosh 1973, pp. 504-8).

Murty, in identifying an Upper Palaeolithic phase in Andhra Pradesh, emphasized the distinctiveness of the blade and burin assemblages in the Renigunta and Kurnool regions of Andhra Pradesh as compared to the Mesolithic.[4] The assemblages that Murty described were mircrolithic, made of fine grained quartzite. He emphasized the presence of burins and bone tools, and the association of an extinct late Pleistocene fauna. Sali, however, based his definition of the Upper Palaeolithic phase primarily on the age of the assemblages rather than typo-technological differences. The archaeological

[1] M.L.K. Murty (1968), 'Blade and Burin Industries near Renigunta on the South East Coast of India', *PPS*, 35, pp. 83-101.

[2] S.A. Sali (1974), 'Upper Palaeolithic Research Since Independence', *BDCRI*, pp. 34-147.

[3] G.R. Sharma (1973), 'Stone Age in the Vindhyas and the Ganga Valley', in Agrawal and Ghosh (eds.), *Radiocarbon and Indian Archaeology*, TIFR, Bombay, pp. 106-10.

[4] M.L.K. Murty (1968), op. cit.; idem (1970), 'Blade and Burin and Late Stone Age Industries around Renigunta', *Indian Antiquary*, 1, pp. 106-27.

assemblages from Patne were microlithic, made of chalcedony nodules, but associated with a late Pleistocene colluvial sequence. An ostrich eggshell of the Late Upper Palaeolithic phase from the site was dated to 25 Ka by the radiocarbon method (see Table 4.1). Sharma also identified an Upper Palaeolithic phase in the quaternary stratigraphy of the Belan.[5] This was one of the earliest sites to be dated by radiocarbon and contributed to the acceptance of the Upper Palaeolithic phase as a distinct entity. Subsequent to the pioneering work of Sharma, Murty and Sali, an Upper Palaeolithic phase was identified from surface material from a number of areas.[6] Sali[7] and Murty[8] reviewed the available data for the Upper Palaeolithic.

Since Murty's review of the Upper Palaeolithic, a large number of dates have become available for this (Table 4.1). Important excavations of Upper Palaeolithic sites in the Son Valley,[9] Vodikalu[10] and the Narmada (Mishra, unpublished date), an extensive survey of the Chota Nagpur region of West Bengal,[11] geoarchaeological studies in Western Maharashtra,[12] and the identification of a Pleistocene microlithic industry from Nepal[13] have yielded important new information about the Upper Palaeolithic phase in India.

The typo-technological continuity of the Upper Palaeolithic and Mesolithic phases in Indian prehistory is well-established. Most of the Pleistocene blade tool industries are microlithic. Therefore, the equation of microliths with the

[5] Sharma (1973), op. cit.

[6] K. Paddayya (1970), 'The Blade Tool Industry of Shorapur Doab, Peninsular India', *Indian Antiquary*, 4, pp. 165-70; K.T. Reddy (1970), 'The Vemula Industry', *Indian Antiquary*, 41; R.P. Pandey (1987), 'An Upper Palaeolithic Phase in the Upper Mahanadi Valley, M.P.', *ME*, 1, pp. 149-60; K.T. Reddy and V. Sudarsen (1978), 'Prehistoric Investigations in Sagileru Basin', *ME*, 2, pp. 32-40; R.V. Joshi and R.S. Pappu (1979), 'Bhokar: An Upper Palaeolithic Factory Site from the Central Godavari Basin, Maharashtra', *ME*, 3, pp. 86-91.

[7] S.A. Sali (1974), op. cit.; idem (1990a), 'Quaternary Environments and Cultural Change in the Central Tapi Valley', *BDCRI*, 49, pp. 375-404; idem (1990b), *Stone Age India*, Shankar Publishers, Aurangabad.

[8] M.L.K. Murty (1979), 'Recent Research on the Upper Palaeolithic Phase in India', *Journal of Field Archaeology*, 6, pp. 321-30.

[9] J.M. Kenoyer et al. (1983), 'An Upper Palaeolithic Shrine in India', *Antiquity*, 57, pp. 88-94; idem, 'Preliminary Report on Excavations at the Late Palaeolithic Occupation Site at Bagor Locality', in Sharma and Clark (eds.), *Palaeoenvironments and Prehistory of the Middle Son Valley*, pp. 117-48.

[10] D.R. Raju (1986), 'The Upper Palaeolithic Industries of Cuddapah District', *RAIP*, Oxford and IBH; idem (1988), *Stone Age Hunter-Gatherers*, Ravish Publishers, Pune.

[11] D.K. Chakrabarti (1993), *The Archaeology of Eastern India*, Munshiram Manoharlal, Delhi.

[12] S.N. Rajaguru et al. (1980), 'The Terminal Pleistocene Microlithic Industry of Inamgaon, Maharashtra', *BDCRI*, 39, pp. 150-9.

[13] G. Corvinus (1994), 'Prehistoric Occupation Sites in the Dang-Deokhuri Valleys of Western Nepal', *ME*, 19, pp. 75-89.

Table 4.1: Absolute Data for the Upper Palaeolithic in India

Site Name	Lab. No.	Date	Material Dated	Reference
Bhedaghat	A6619	25,160,550+-	freshwater bivalve shell	Mishra and Rajguru (1993)
Belan Valley, Deoghat	TF 1245	19,175,240+-	freshwater shells	*IAR* 1972-73
Belan Valley, Deoghat	PFL 86	25,790,830,730+-	freshwater shells	Mandal (1983)
Chandrasal	GRN 10638	36,550,600+-	ostrich eggshell	Kumar (1988)
Chandrasal	GRN 10639	38,900,750+-	ostrich eggshell	Kumar (1988)
Dharampuri	BS 286	25,160,850+-	freshwater bivalve shells	Mishra (1985)
Gargaon	TF 1111	10,310,155+-	wood	Rajguru and Kale (1985)
Inamgaon	TF 1003	21,110,615,570+-	freshwater bivalve shells	*IAR* 1969-70
Inamgaon	TF 1177	19,290,360+-	freshwater bivalve shells.	Sankalia
Inamgaon	BS 146	11,700	freshwater bivalve shells	Rajguru et al. (1979)
Kurnool Caves	TL date	17,390 10%+-	burnt stones	Nambi and Murty (1983)
Mehgara	PRL 603	14,140,410, 390+-	freshwater shell	Mandal (1983)
Mehgara	PRL 602	11,200,130+-	freshwater shell	Mandal (1983)
Mehgara	SUA 1481	10,030,115+-	freshwater shell	Mandal (1983)
Mehtakheri	A6518	30,680, + 1040 - 920	freshwater bivalve shell	unpublished
Mehtakheri	AA8463	>41,900	ostrich eggshell	unpublished
Nagda	PRL 1196	>31,000	ostrich eggshell	Kumar (1988)
Nandipalle	PRL 293	25,360 + 660 - 710	freshwater gastropod shells	Reddy and Sudarsan (1979)
Nevasa	BS 517	12,850,190+-	freshwater bivalve shells	Rajguru and Kale (1985)
Nevasa	BS 575	16,420,200+-	freshwater bivalve shells	Rajguru and Kale (1985)
Patne	GRN 7200	85,000,200+-	ostrich eggshell	Sali (1989)
Ramnagar	PRL 1196	>31,000	ostrich eggshell	Kumar (1989)
Rampur	Beta 4752	11,870+-120	freshwater shells	Mandal (1983)
Rampur	Beta 4793	26,250,420+-		Mandal (1983)
Sangamner	PRL 470	12,890+-350	freshwater shells	*IAR* 1978/79:105
Sangamner	BS 78	24,670-710+-	freshwater	*IAR* 1978/79:105

'Mesolithic' creates serious misunderstandings about the age of the industries. Even geometric microliths are suspected to be of a possible Pleistocene age at some sites.[14] The separation of the Upper Palaeolithic and Mesolithic is not justified on the basis of typology alone. Blade technology, which begins around 40 kyr, is replaced only about 3 kyr ago when iron was introduced. Therefore, the period encompassed by the Upper Palaeolithic, Mesolithic and Neolithic/Chalcolithic, which together would be equivalent to the Late Stone Age, spans almost 40 kyr, during which the *Homo sapiens* underwent an evolution of culture from Pleistocene and Holocene hunter/gatherers to farmers and then with complex urban civilizations. In view of the tremendous scope of the changes, the European terminology is preferred for having more divisions.

Palaeoenvironmental data are now more abundant than it was twenty years ago. The transition from Pleistocene to Holocene climates was one of the most abrupt in the entire quaternary period. Not only did the global climate change from the maximum glacial stage to the maximum interglacial stage in 12,000 years (from 18 ka for the LGM to about 6 ka for the Holocene optimum) but, within this period, there were abrupt reversals of the climatic trend. Between 10-11 kyr, the process of deglaciation was reversed and a short period of glacial climate intervened. The onset and end of this period (Younger Dryas) was extremely abrupt, probably within decades.[15] Pleistocene environments were quite different from; Holocene environments, and so the use of the term Upper Palaeolithic to differentiate Late Pleistocene industries from those of the Holocene is useful. Therefore, Upper Palaeolithic in the discussion that follows encompasses blade-based industries, most of which are microlithic and belong to the Pleistocene. The term Mesolithic should be applied only to industries of the Holocene. Microlithic is a useful terminology when the age of the industry is not known.

UPPER PALAEOLITHIC PHASE AND HUMAN BIO-CULTURAL EVOLUTION

The beginning of the Upper Palaeolithic in Europe is placed around 40,000 years BC. It is associated with the probable replacement of the Neanderthal population with early modern humans. Compared to the Middle Palaeolithic, in the Upper Palaeolithic, the first large-scale use of bones and antlers for tools, and the first well-documented, fully developed art is found. The Upper Palaeolithic cave art of Europe is extremely sophisticated and proves to most prehistorians the definite existence of fully cultural behaviour. In West Asia,

[14]J.N. Pal (1984), 'Epi-Palaeolithic Sites in Pratapgarh District U.P.', *ME*, pp. 31-8; S.A. Sali (1989), *The Upper Palaeolithic and Mesolithic Cultures of Maharashtra*, Deccan College, Pune.

[15]E. Bard and Broecker (ed.) (1992), *The Last De-Glacialation: The Absolute and Radiocarbon Chronologies*, Springer Verlag Berlin,. Heidelberg.

early modern humans are associated with some of the Middle Palaeolithic industries at Kebar and Qafzah (Vandermeersch 1989). In the Sinai desert, A.E. Marks has documented what appears to be a technological transition from the Middle to the Upper Palaeolithic at around 40,000 BC years ago.[16] Most recently, a number of Upper Palaeolithic sites in Russia have been dated to about 43 kyr and >35 kyr and > 38 kyr.[17] Russian archaeologists, therefore, are beginning to suggest that the dating of the Middle/Upper Palaeolithic transition to 40 kyr, is an artefact of the dating limits of radiocarbon. The Upper Palaeolithic, therefore, represents a period when blades (long, narrow flakes), were used as easily replaceable working edges in composite tools. This phase dates from about 40 kyr to the end of the Pleistocene. During this period, the global climate was colder and drier than that of the present. A large part of the presently forested regions of the globe were replaced by grasslands, which supported herds of large herbivores. Many Upper Palaeolithic cultures emphasized big game hunting compared to Mesolithic cultures. The Upper Palaeolithic people were biologically similar to modern populations and their cultural behaviour was similar to that of the present. The study of the Upper Palaeolithic phase, therefore, is the study of a man similar to us but in a world where the environment was very different from the present.

DATING OF THE UPPER PALAEOLITHIC IN INDIA

A large number of C-14 dates are now available for the Upper Palaeolithic phase in India (Table 4.1). It is interesting that some of these dates are >20 kyr, >28 kyr and >41 kyr from different sites (Table 4.1). This implies that the beginning of the Upper Palaeolithic in India is probably around the same time as elsewhere. All of the older dates are on ostrich eggshells. The site of Mehtakheri has a date of 30 kyr on a mollusc shell and >41 kyr on an ostrich eggshell. While the mollusc shell could be subject to recrystallization of the calcite, the ostrich eggshell is quite stable, and so it is probable that the ostrich eggshell dates are more reliable than those of the former and are underestimating the age of the industries they are associated with. It is also possible that the ostrich eggshells are old shells collected by the upper Palaeolithic people. It is difficult to resolve this issue one way or the other. In any case, available evidence does suggest that the Upper Palaeolithic in India goes back to around 40 kyr as in other parts of the world. Quite a few dates centre around 25 kyr or slightly earlier. A few dates are between 16-20 kyr and many sites are dated to 11-12 kyr. Most of these dates are from shells

[16]A.E. Marks (1983), 'The Middle to Upper Palaeolithic Transition in the Levant', in F. Wendorf and A.E. Close (eds.), in *Advances in World Archaeology*, Academic Press, New York, pp. 51-97.

[17]T. Goebel and M. Aksenov (1995), 'Accelerator Radiocarbon Dating of the Initial Upper Palaeolithic of SE Siberia', *Antiquity*, 66, pp. 349-57; T. Goebel et al. (1993), 'Dating the Middle to Upper Palaleolithic Transition at Kara Bom', *CA*, 34, pp. 452-8.

collected from gravels which also contain Upper Palaeolithic tools. Recently we have argued that these episodes of gravel aggradation represent periods of maximum aridity during the Late Pleistocene.[18] Dates around 25 kyr represent one early arid phase, while the 16-20 kyr dates correlate well with the Last Glacial Maximum and the 11-12 kyr to the reversal of the warming/humid trend at the glacial holocene transition called the Younger Dryas.

UPPER PALAEOLITHIC SITES IN INDIA (FIG. 4.1)

Research on the Upper Palaeolithic phase in India can be divided into a number of regions where active groups of researchers have concentrated their

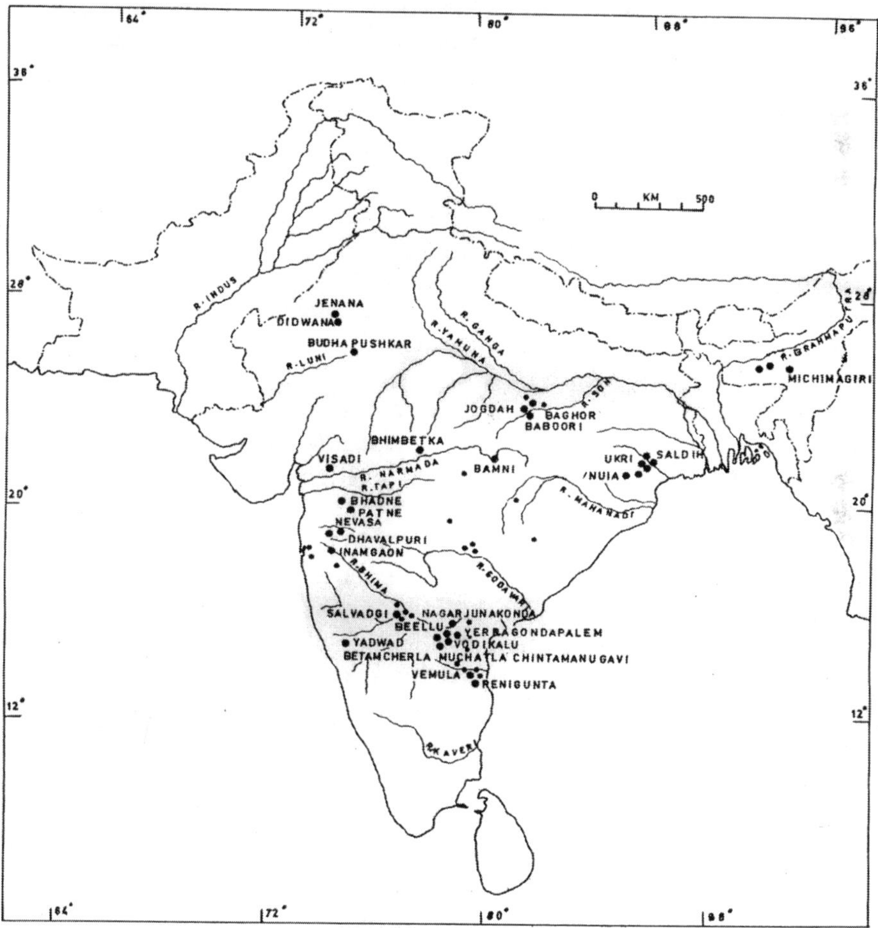

Fig. 4.1: Upper Palaeolithic sites

[18]N. Sadakata et al. (1995), 'Late Quaternary Environment, Change in the Pravara River Basin, Northwestern Deccan Upland, India', *Proceedings of the International Symposium on Palaeoenvironmental Change in Tropical Sub-Tropical Monsoon Asia*, Hiroshima Research Centre for Regional Geography, Hiroshima University, pp. 46-56.

efforts. These are Andhra Pradesh, especially the foothill region of the Eastern Ghats, the Chota Nagpur region of West Bengal, the Son and Belan valleys and other Vindhyan tributaries of the Ganga, and the western upland regions of Madhya Pradesh and Maharashtra. Each of these regions is discussed in turn followed by stray sites studied in other regions.

ANDHRA PRADESH

Andhra Pradesh is the first region where an Upper Palaeolithic phase was postulated as early as the last century by Foote, Cammiade and Burkitt (1930) also identified a phase, series IV which was equivalent to the Upper Palaeolithic. It was also here that a Pleistocene non-microlithic blade industry was identified by Murty.[19] Most of the work in the Andhra Pradesh region has centred around the Eastern Ghats and the streams draining the region. As many as six Ph.D. theses have been completed from the Deccan College alone which touch upon the Upper Palaeolithic phase in this region. Most of the work has been based on surface collections. In some cases, the sites are surface sites, but most of them are being exposed by the erosion of the sediments in which they were originally sealed. Small test pits taken by Murty at Nallagundlu.[20] K.T. Reddy and V. Sudarsen at Nandipalle in the Sagileru basin,[21] Reddy and Vijay Prakash at Madhyakadamam near Vishakhapatnam,[22] and D.R. Raju at Vodikallu[23] show that the same industry which occurs on the surface is also found in a stratified context sealed within a red silt deposit. Small-scale excavations were carried out by Murty at Muchchatla Chinamani Gavi cave in the Betamacherla region.[24] Here, however, the entire assemblage of stone tools was only 220. whereas bones, some of them with workings, were much more numerous. TL dating was attempted for a hearth belonging to the Upper Palaeolithic and a date of 17 kyr was obtained.[25] At Vodikallu, Raju's excavation was very interesting because it clearly showed that the Upper Palaeolithic artefact horizon was between 140-190 cm below the surface.[26] This 50-cm thick horizon yielded 1,425 artefacts within only a 2 × 2 m area, sealed by fine grained sediments. Raju was not only able to get artefacts but also associated quartzite rubble, grinding stones, rubbers and

[19]Murty (1970), op. cit.

[20]Ibid.

[21]Reddy and Sudarsen (1978), op. cit.

[22]K.T. Reddy and P. Vijay Prakash (1985), 'The Upper Palaeolithic and Mesolithic in the Gambheeram Valley, Northeastern Andhra Pradesh', *RAIP*, Oxford and IBH Publishing Co., New Delhi, pp. 157-8.

[23]Raju (1988), op. cit.

[24]M.L.K. Murty (1974), 'A Late Pleistocene Cave Site in Southern India', *Proceedings of the American Philosophical Society*, 118, pp. 196-230.

[25]K.V.S. Nambi and M.K.L. Murty (1983), 'An Upper Palacolithic Fireplace in the Kurnool Caves', *BDCRI*, 48, pp. 110-13.

[26]Raju (1988), op. cit.

a ringstone. Nine flakes were found at a depth of 260 to 270 cm below the surface which might belong to the Middle Palaeolithic, while a horizon above the Upper Palaeolithic yielded five flakes. The raw material used at Vodikallu is quartzite, lydanite and quartz. The model size of the blades is between 3-3.5 cm, so it is not a microlithic industry. At Madhyakadamam, Reddy and Prakash examined a 2 × 2 m trench. Microlithic blade tools made of milky and glassy quartz were found between 47-80 cm below the surface, while microlithic blade tools made of dark brown cherty quartz were found on the surface of a pellety lateritic gravel sealed by 110 cm of red soil.[27] Reddy and Prakash identify the microlithic horizon as 'mesolithic' and the macrolithic horizon as 'Upper Palaeolithic'. In the Sagileru basin too, both blade tool industries were found.[28] However, since there are a very large number of Pleistocene dates for similar microlithic industries and the horizon appears to be within a Pleistocene context, it is perhaps better to assign both to the Upper Palaeolithic. Once more, the density of artefacts in the excavated area is very high with 751 tools for the upper horizon and over 4,000 for the lower.

In the Renigunta region, Murty identified two blade tool industries, one macrolithic and the other microlithic, using different raw materials, which he referred to as the blade and burin, and the Late Stone Age, respectively.[29] It appears, however, that both, found now on the surface of a red silt/clay, are recently being eroded from a Pleistocene geological context. Reddy's Vemula industry is similar to the macrolithic blade industry of Renigunta.[30]

At Eleru, Murty and S.N. Rajaguru found Upper Palaeolithic tools from deposit in the upper part of the older fill.[31] The context of these tools is similar to that of the microliths found in gravels in other peninsular rivers. Microliths were also reported from the surface of a number of High Level Gravel occurrences by Rao (1992) and at the Early Historical site of Satanikota, district Kurnool,[32] where the habitational deposit covers the microliths. In the absence of dating, these occurrences have been assigned to the Mesolithic but it is quite likely that they belong to the Pleistocene period.

Chota Nagpur/West Bengal

Exploration in the rivers draining the eastern part of the peninsular regions in the Chota Nagpur area have yielded finds of 'microliths' from Late Pleistocene silty deposits. D.K. Chakrabarti has summarized much of this evidence collected by him and others.[33] Since most of the collections are

[27]Reddy and Prakash (1985), op. cit.
[28]Reddy and Sudarsen (1978), op. cit.
[29]Murty (1970), op. cit.
[30]Reddy (1970), op. cit.
[31]*IAR*, 1980-1, p. 1.
[32]*IAR*, 1977-8, p. 3.
[33] S. Chakrabarti, D.K. Bhattacharya and D.K. Chakrabarti (1982), 'The Context of

very small and no excavation has been attempted, it is difficult to evaluate this evidence. Recently B. Basak has explored the Tarefini basin, one of the areas for this complex.[34] Her collections reveal a microlithic industry primarily on black chert and fine grained quartzite. The material is exploited intensively and is scarce locally. In spite of the 'evolved' character of the assemblage, the context of the tools appears to be a red silt of the Pleistocene age, based on the fluorine/phosphate values of fossils from the same context. Chakrabarti and A.K. Datta have also avoided labelling these industries as 'Mesolithic', and have called only some of the sites 'Upper Palaeolithic', using the term microlithic instead. Basak's work establishing the Pleistocene is defined by the scope of this paper. Perhaps the best-studied blade tool site in West Bengal remains Birbanpur, excavated in 1953 by B.B. Lal.[35] Surface finds of microliths were found over an area of about 1 square mile of an upper terrace more than about 20 m above the highest flood area of the Damodar River today. Two large trenches were taken in this terrace. The microlithic horizon was found to be the top of a lateritic gravel which overlay weathered bedrock and was sealed by a sandy, light brown earth. Lal was aware that the geological context of the Birbanpur microliths implied some antiquity, and he also avoided calling them mesolithic. The microlithic industry from Birbanpur would appear, on the basis of Lal's work, to belong to the Pleistocene and so, should be included in the Upper Palaeolithic. The microliths from Birbanpur are made of quartz, chert, and chalcedony with some quartzite and basalt.

Microliths at Paruldanga', *ME*, 61, pp. 150-2; D.K. Chakrabarti, D.K. Bhattacharya and R.K. Chattopadhyay (1983), 'Lithic Industries of Purulia', *ME*, 7, pp. 131-41; D.K. Chakrabarti and R.K. Chattopadhyay (1984a), 'The Lithic Industries of the Tarafeni and Bhairavbanki Valleys, West Bengal', *The Calcutta Review*, 1 (2), pp. 41-63; idem (1984b), 'Prehistoric Stratigraphy in West Bengal: The Evidence from Burdwan and Midnapur', *ME*, 8, pp. 39-60; D.K. Chakrabarti, A.K. Nag and S. Chakrabarti (1978-9), 'An Archaeological Reconnaissance in Birbhum', *Puratattva*, 10, pp. 25-32; A.K. Datta (1991a), 'Upper Palaeolithic Culture in West Bengal: A District Regional Development', in A.K. Datta (ed.), *Studies in Archaeology*, Books and Books, New Delhi, pp. 67-76; idem (1991b), 'Blade and Blade Tool Association with Upper Palaeolithic and Mesolithic Periods: A Case Study from the "Mid-Kasai" Valley in the Jhargram Sub-division of Midnapur District, West Bengal', *ME*, 16, pp. 23-31; A.K. Datta and D.K. Ray (1988), 'Kattara, and Upper Palaeolithic Site in the Mid-Kasai Valley, District Midnapur, West Bengal', in D. Mitra et al. (eds.), *Studies in Art and Archaeology of Bihar/Bengal,* Delhi, pp. 309-19; A.K. Datta, D.K. Roy and B. Samanta (1984), 'Chamargora: The Microlithic Site of Tarafeni Basin, District Midnapur', in A. Ray et al. (eds.), *The Indian Studies: Essays Presented in Memory of Prof. Niharranjan Ray*, Caxton Publications, New Delhi, pp. 21-30.

[34]B. Basak et al., *Late Quaternary Environment, Palaeontology and Culture of Tarafeni Valley, Midnapur District, West Bengal: A Preliminary Study* (in press).

[35]B.B. Lal (1958), 'Birbhanpur: A Microlithic Site in the Damodar Valley, West Bengal', *Ancient India*, 14, pp. 4-48.

Vindhyan Tributaries of the Ganga

Important work has been done in this region, primarily by G.R. Sharma and his team from Allahabad University. Starting in the 1960s, Sharma carried out extensive explorations in the Son and Belan rivers and their tributaries. His best section was on the Belan near Deoghat where an 18 m section had a succession of Stone Age industries. Most of the artefacts were found in the gravel. Blade tools were found in gravels III and IV. Although some of the illustrated blades[36] are over 5 cm long and, therefore, not microlithic, Sharma did find microliths in gravel III itself. Shells from this section were dated to 26 and 19 kyr, establishing their Pleistocene age. Subsequently, a large number of additional sites were located in the region. In the early 1980s a multi-disciplinary project was organized to study the quaternary environments and Stone Age sites in the Middle Son Valley.[37] This collaborative project between Allahabad University and the University of California excavated a number of sites, obtained some additional radiocarbon dates and made a study of the quaternary context of Upper Palaeolithic sites.

Two localities were important for the Upper Palaeolithic phase in this collaborative work. At Baghor, three sites were studied, called Baghor I, II and III. Baghor I and III were considered Upper Palaeolithic and had geometric microlithic assemblages made mainly of chert. The Baghor II assemblage is made primarily of chalcedony.[38] The most extensively excavated site was Baghor I,[39] where a fairly large area was exposed. Along with stone tools, evidence for heat treatment of chert, quartzite rubble and grinding stones, and a broken ring stone were found. The arrangement of an elongated pebble on a rubble platform in the Baghor I excavation has been identified as a shrine.[40] Baghor III is stratigraphically older than Baghor I but its tools were slightly smaller.[41] Dates are available for both the sites, and are around 6 kyr for Baghor III and 8 kyr for Baghor I (see Table 4.1). These dates would place the industries in the Holocene and out of the scope of the Upper Palaeolithic as defined in this paper. However, a second locality in the Son Valley, Rampur, where a similar industry was found, gave dates of 11 kyr.[42] A date from the base of the Baghor formation exposed at Rampur dates to 26 kyr. Therefore, it is probable that the dates from Baghor are younger than

[36] Sharma (1973), op. cit.

[37] Sharma and Clark (1983), *Palaeoenvironments in the Middle Son Valley.*

[38] C. Susman et al. (1983), *Preliminary Report on the Excavation at the Mesolithic Occupation Site at Baghor II Locality*, pp. 161-96.

[39] Kenoyer et al. (1983b), op. cit.

[40] Kenoyer et al. (1983a), op. cit.

[41] J.D. Clark and R. Dreiman (1983), *An Occupation with Small Blade Technology in the Upper Member of the Baghor Formation in Baghor III Locality*, pp. 197-205.

[42] V.D. Misra et al. (1983), 'An Upper Palaeolithic Collection from Rampur', in Sharma and Clark (eds.), *Palaeoenvironments and Prehistory in the Middle Son Valley*, pp. 143-60.

the real age of the assemblage due to contamination of the sample with some modern carbon.

Gravels containing microliths in the Belan section have been dated to 19 and 25 kyr, and at Mahagara to 11-14 kyr.[43]

Western Peninsular Region

A great deal of work has been done in this region, starting with the excavation at Patne by Sali in 1972/3.[44] This site is crucial for understanding the Upper Palaeolithic. Five stratigraphically superimposed assemblages are found in addition to three Mesolithic and a Middle Palaeolithic phase. Patne is at the foot of the Ajanta range, about 20 km from Chalisgaon. The site consists of a series of colluvial deposits, which reflect the change in the late Pleistocene climate at the site. Some of the assemblages are associated with gravels, and other with soils and loess. The first phase of the Upper Palaeolithic (Patne IIA) is characterized by the presence of a backed knife, end-scrapers on blades, backed scrapers, and a greater proportion of blades as compared to the Middle Palaeolithic. Multicoloured cherts are the dominant material used to make tools, whose size is relatively large. In Phase IIB, the first fully-backed blades occur, and chalcedony occurs along with multicoloured chert. The chalcedony tools are microlithic in size. In Phase IIC, chalcedony becomes the dominant raw material and the industry becomes microlithic in size, although the chert tools are still relatively large. In phase IID, the richest horizon, being associated with a fossil soil, the industry shows the maximum reduction in size. Lunates occur for the first time. An ostrich eggshell was found in this layer and dated to 25 kyr. Saddle querns were found in association with this industry, along with grinding stones and hammerstones.[45] In phase IIE, geometric forms occur.

The site of Patne, therefore, provided the first indication that microliths were of the Pleistocene age. The evolution in the selection of raw material, the changes in the types of tools and the palaeoenvironmental information make Patne a key site for understanding the Upper Palaeolithic. In addition, a preceding Middle Palaeolithic horizon and three Mesolithic horizons succeeding the Upper Palaeolithic are also found.

Godavari and Bhima Basin of Western Maharashtra

In this region, a large number of microlithic sites of the Pleistocene age are known. Most of them are gravels, where microliths occur along with shells.

[43] D. Mandal (1983), 'A Note on the Radiocarbon Dates from the Middle Son Valley', in Sharma and Clark (eds.), *Palaeoenvironments and Prehistory of the Middle Son Valley*, pp. 284-9.

[44] S.A. Sali (1986), 'The Upper Palaeolithic Culture of Patne, District Jalgaon, Maharashtra', *RAIP*, pp. 137-46; idem (1989), op. cit.

[45] S.A. Sali (1990b), *Stone Age India*, Shankar Publishers, Aurangabad.

These shells have provided quite a few radiocarbon dates. The most important site is Inamgaon on the Ghod River. Here an excavation was carried out in the quaternary sediments. Microliths were recovered from two gravel horizons dated to 21 and 12 kyr. The microliths from the older horizon were compared to Patne IID by Sali,[46] while the microliths from the later horizon were labelled epi-paleolithic (Rajaguru et al. 1979). Gravels of different ages containing microliths have also been found at Sangamner and Nevasa.[47] Recently the site of Chandoli on the Ghod was reported.[48] Microliths were found from a gravel at the top of the Pleistocene terrace to Nandur Madmeshwar[49] on the Godavari River. At Harsul, in district Aurangabad, B.R. Mani of the Archaeological Survey of India reports the presence of geometric microliths in a gravel sealed by about half a metre of sediment.[50] In this region, all the blade tool assemblages reported so far are microlithic in nature. Most of them belong to the Pleistocene, attested by a large number of dates. In many cases, the artefacts are unabraded and in good concentration, so that it appears that the human activity was within the river channel itself.

Nimar region of Narmada Valley

The sites in the Narmada Valley were discovered during the period 1981-5 by V.N. Mishra (1985). They are interesting because dense, limited scatters of artefacts were found on recently eroded surfaces of Late Pleistocene silt. Systematic collections of this surface material was made at Pitnagar, Beda, Dharampuri, Nalway, Chot Barda and Nisarpur. These included ostrich eggshells from Pitnagar and Chota Barda. Burnt earth was found along with the artefacts, especially at Chota Barda. Mollusc shells from a layer associated with a collection of tools was dated to 25,160 at Dharampuri. The typological and technological features of the assemblages are similar to Patne IID. On the basis of stratigraphy and dating, these assemblages could be assigned to the Late Pleistocene. The collections are characterized by large amounts of waste flakes. Many raw material nodules were abandoned without striking any flakes. Only a few cores in any collection show any large number of blades removed. Many cores have only one or two blade removals. The blades arc microlithic with an average length of 2.5 cm baked blades are few. Points and lunates are the main types but they are not well standardized and it was noted that, in the half-dozen backed blades from different sites, none were exactly the same. The blades were made of chalcedony or chert, which occur

[46] Sali (1974), op. cit.

[47] G. Corvinus (1981), *A Survey of the Pravara River System in Western Maharashtra, India*, vol. I, Verlag Archaeologia Venatoria, Tubingen.

[48] Sadakata et al. (1995), op. cit.

[49] *IAR*, 1978-9, p. 17.

[50] *IAR*, 1986-7, p. 60.

as secondary minerals in the Deccan trap. In addition to the blade tools, quartzite was flaked. Quartzite flakes around 4-7 cm in size were occasionally retouched as scrappers. The sites of Dharampuri and Nisarpur show cores with more preparation, and a large number of blades removed from cores.

In 1991 and 1992, a small-scale excavation was earned out at Mehtakheri, one of the locations where artefacts had been noticed earlier. In this excavation, two Upper Palaeolithic horizons could be resolved compared to the surface collection. Mollusc shells associated with the artefacts appear to have been exploited as a food source. In addition to the artefacts and shells, a large amount of quartzite nibble was found. This is broken rather than flaked. It is definitely associated with the Upper Palaeolithic horizon but it is difficult to know which human activity produced it. It does not appear to be associated with any structures or even features. Perhaps it was produced by the stone boiling technique common at recent North American sites where containers, which could be directly placed on the fire, were absent. Alternatively, it was produced by some processing activity which required bashing with stones. Similar rubble in even greater amounts is reported from sites excavated in the Son Valley. It also appears to be present in sites in Andhra Pradesh and the grinding component is documented at Patne.

TECHNOLOGICAL EVOLUTION IN THE UPPER PALAEOLITHIC (FIG. 4.2)

Some general trends are noticed in the evolution of the Upper Palaeolithic blade technology. From both Patne and Andhra Pradesh, an Early Upper Palaeolithic Phase is present in which the blades are of a large size. The microlithic phase is associated with a change in the raw material selected to make tools and is later than the macrolithic phase, as seen in the stratigraphy of Patne and Madhyakadamam. The beginning of the microlithic phase pre-dates 25 kyr at Patne, while it is undated in the Andhra region. There appears to be an increasing standardization of the backed blade element. In earlier phases, each backed blade was slightly different but, in the later ones, points and lunates and geometric forms followed well-defined shapes and sizes. The preparation of the cores, and the efficiency and refinement of core exploitation, also appears to have increased in the later period. At Mehtakheri, dating to 30 kyr, even though the blades and backed blades are well-made, the quantity of debitage is considerable and very few blades are struck from any core.[51] In the same region, blade cores from mesolithic surface sites show the removal of dozens of blades from a single core and the debitage associated with the

[51] A. Ghosh (1993), 'Upper Palaeolithic Blade Technology: A Preliminary Analysis of Cores from Mehtakheri', *ME*, 18, 1, pp. 11-19.

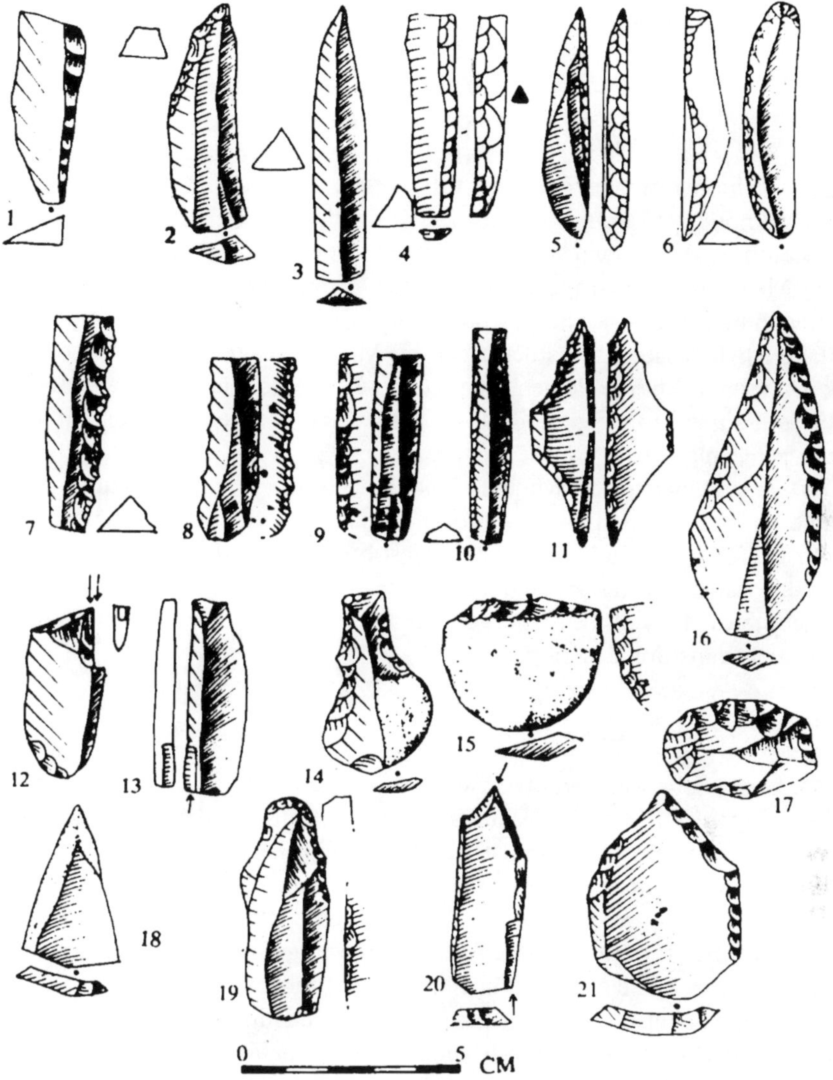

Fig. 4.2: Upper Palaeolithic tools

sites is much less.[52] Geometric microliths do appear to be later than non-geometric microliths, as seen at Patne, but some of them appear to be Pleistocene in age. Much more work has to be done to really trace the changes in blade technology through the Pleistocene.

Many of the Upper Palaeolithic sites are in context and little disturbed by natural processes. Excavations in the Son Valley showed the potential of

[52] Sheila Mishra (1985), 'Early Man and Environments in Western Madhya Pradesh', Ph.D. thesis (unpublished), Poona University.

some of the sites. Sites in Andhra Pradesh and West Bengal, as well as those in the Nimar region, are sealed within silty alluvium.

THE UPPER/MIDDLE PALAEOLITHIC TRANSITION

The transition from the Middle to the Upper Palaeolithic in India is so far poorly known. At Patne, the earliest horizon, labelled 'Advanced Middle Palaeolithic', shows some trends towards the Upper Palaeolithic. At Bhimbetka, V.N. Misra has shown the trend towards an increase in the blade element, although blade cores are not present.[53] Joshi's Wainganga B and some of the 'Flake Blade' assemblages described by Murty may be transitional between the Upper and Middle Palaeolithic.[54] At present, there are very few sites that can be assigned to the period 50-40 kyr, which is when this transition may have taken place.

While evidence for the Middle/Upper Palaeolithic transition is quite scanty, Patne and the Son Valley sites provide abundant evidence for the transition from the Upper Palaeolithic to the Mesolithic. There is abundant evidence that this transition was gradual and that the Mesolithic is rooted in the Upper Palaeolithic. Many of the gravels containing microliths date to the Pleistocene/ Holocene transitional period.

ART AND RELIGION

Ostrich eggshells were engraved with cross-hatch patterns between horizontal lines in phases IID and HE at Patne. At Nisarpur in the Nimar region, a broken disc of micaceous schist was found with Upper Palaeolithic tools. A piece of micaceous schist was also found at Patne and might show contact between the two groups. It might have served a decorative function in that the mica rubs off onto the skin. At Dharampuri and Mehtakheri, intertrapean fossil molluscs found at the site must have been collected by Upper Palaeolithic people. Wakankar collected green pigment pieces in the Upper Palaeolithic horizons at Bhimbetka, while fragments of red ochre are reported from the Baghor sites in the Son Valley. From Baghor there is evidence of a possible shrine. All this shows that some concern for art, decoration and religion was present in the Upper Palaeolithic period.

SUBSISTENCE

While very few sites have yielded bones from Upper Palaeolithic horizons, the presence of grinding stones and rubble from a number of sites shows that

[53]V.N. Misra (1982), 'Evolution of Blade Elements in the Stone Industries of Rockshelter III F23, Bhimbetka', in R.K. Sharma (ed.), *Indian Archaeology: New Perspectives*, Agam Kala Prakashan, New Delhi.

[54]Murty (1979), op. cit.

the processing of plant foods must have been practised. At Mehtakheri, freshwater clam shells associated with the site were possibly exploited for food. At many localities, there is increasing evidence of hearths, postholes and burnt sediments, indicating their more intensive use. It appears, therefore, that a fairly intensive hunting and gathering lifestyle was developed during the Upper Palaeolithic itself. Many of the sites show repeated occupation of the same location. The accumulation of thousand of artefacts is reported from Birbanpur and Vodikallu. This shows the repeated return to favoured localities. In some cases, the stone for making tools was acquired from distant locations for the absence of suitable raw material at the local level. This shows not only high mobility but also an intimate knowledge of available resources and how to exploit them.

CONCLUSION

Research in the Upper Palaeolithic phase in India has now achieved a certain maturity as a number of research groups have contributed to the understanding of its problems. The dating of a number of sites has given us an idea of the chronological range for this phase. A number of excavations have shown the potential of some of the sites to yield information about life in the Upper Palaeolithic period. In spite of these achievements, we are perhaps just beginning to learn about the many aspects of the Upper Palaeolithic in India.

Chapter 5

Palaeolithic Fauna of India

G.L. Badam

INTRODUCTION

Palaeontological researches of Palaeolithic cultures have taken great strides in India during the past two and a half decades. In fact, both Palaeolithic archaeology and vertebrate palaeontology have been useful in subdividing the Pleistocene period (which encompasses the Palaeolithic cultures) as a whole in India. Stone Age sites especially those associated with fauna, have received considerable attention for a better understanding of the man-animal relationship. Also, these sites are of great interest for the possibility of finding the physical remains of Early Man in India. Most Palaeolithic sites, generally located in central and peninsular India, represent a timespan ranging from the Middle to Terminal Pleistocene, as confirmed by the scores of C-14, TL, Fission Track and the Uranium series dates now available for them. However, some of the new dates suggest that a few sites may even go back to the Lower Pleistocene time bracket.

A large variety of animal fossils belonging to the ungulates, proboscideans, carnivores, reptiles, etc., have been discovered in profusion from the cultural sequences of the Son, Belan, Narmada, Godavari, Krishna and their various tributaries, and also from the cave deposits of Andhra Pradesh, being found in association with or in close proximity to the Acheulian and/or Middle and/or Upper Palaeolithic cultural material. However, in north-west India (Karewas of Kashmir and Siwaliks of India), the association of Palaeolithic cultural material with fossils is rather doubtful because the authenticity and *in situ* position of such artefacts is itself in doubt.

More importantly, the recent discovery of a partial cranium of *Homo erectus* from a Late Acheulian context in the central Narmada Valley has filled in the lacuna to some extent in our understanding of hominid evolution in South Asia as a whole. Needless to mention, though the handiwork of Early Man in the form of Stone Age tools has been found in abundance in various parts of India, the recent discovery of the cranium represents the only authentic evidence of his physical remains, besides a recently discovered claricle of a hominid from the same area.

The present section reviews the recent vertebrate faunal discoveries of the

Palaeolithic periods in India, and highlights their role in establishing biochronological and palaeoecological models during the Pleistocene. Remarks on the significance of the recently discovered *Homo erectus* cranium have also been added.

THE FAUNA

A large number of faunal elements of varied diversity have been discovered from various Palaeolithic cultures of India. However, no fossils have been found in association with the pebble tool industry of north-west India, though there is a report of fossils of *Bos namadicus* and *Bubalus* sp. having been found along with a pebble tool industry (of typical Soan type) at Nittur, on the right bank of the river Tungabhadra (a tributary of the Krishna) in Karnataka.[1]

This is just a solitary example of this type and, therefore, no inferences can be drawn on possible man-animal relationships during the period of the pebble tool industry in India.

Numerous fossils associated with Acheulian cultures have been found all over India except Rajasthan and Gujarat. In fact, as said earlier, scores of sites have yielded fossil in central India, and whole of peninsular India. However, it is not generally possible to separate Lower Palaeolithic cultures from the Middle at most of the sites because the tool types are found in a mixed context. Further, fauna is time-transgressive and does not, in most cases, help in putting the cultures into a proper chronological order. In view of this limitation, the faunal elements of the Lower and Middle Palaeolithic cultures are treated together in this work while those of the Upper Palaeolithic are dealt with separately.

FAUNA OF THE LOWER AND MIDDLE PALAEOLITHIC PERIOD

(A) *Son-Belan Complex*

This area represents one of the most important fossiliferous horizons in the country in association with Palaeolithic cultural materials. In the Son Valley, the fauna includes skulls, limb bones, dental and other osteological parts referable to *Bos namadicus*, *Bibos gaurus*, *Bubalus* sp., *Antilope cervicapra*, *Boselephas tragocamelus*, *Tetraceros quadncornis*, *Gazella gzella*, *Axis axis/ porcinus*, *Cervus unicolor*, *Cervus dyvauceli*, *Muntiacus muntjak*, *Sus* sp., *Hexaprotodon* sp., *Rhinoceros* sp., *Equus namadicus*, *Equus asinus/hemionus*, *Elephas* sp., *Gavialls* sp., *Trionyx* sp., *Emys* sp., carnivores (*Panthera*), rodents

[1] Z.D. Ansari (1970), 'Pebble Tools from Nittur, Mysore State', *Indian Antiquary*, 4, 1-4, pp. 1-7; G.L. Badam et al. (1988-9), 'Systematic Study of Fossil Bovids from Nittur, District Bellary, Karnataka', *Bulletin of the Deccan College Research Institute*, 47-8, pp. 1-9.

(Hysterix), etc.[2] Taphonomic observations suggest that about 50 per cent of the fauna are unabraded and have not suffered much fluvial activity. They are well-sorted and have preserved the evidence of sub-aerial weathering like cracking, flaking, splitting and different types of breakages. The cancellous tissues of the ends of long bones are affected by gnawing and, in some cases, by bacterial activity. The total complex is in favour of the Middle Pleistocene to Holocene time bracket and this agrees well with our studies in other parts of peninsular India. Some of the fossils like barking deer, hog deer, antelope, gazelle, nilgai, sambar deer, barasingha, etc., suggest that a few of these animals could have evolved indigenously.

Archaeological material ranging from the Lower Palaeolithic to the Neolithic are found in association with fauna. G.L. Badam et al.[3] suggest that a riverine environment, galleria forests along the flood plains of the rivers and tall grasses with sufficient pools were some of the factors responsible for the rich faunal survival. Hill slopes and areas away from the rivers must have supported thin grass, and the thorn and scrub cover. Flood plain zones, channel pools and the mixed grassland-woodland environment of the flood plains were favourable ecological niches.

In the Belan-Seoti valleys (Allahabad district), *Elephas* sp., *Bos* sp., *Bubalus* sp., *Antelope* sp., *Cervus* sp., *Equus* sp., *E. onager khur*, *Gazella* sp., *Gavialis* sp., *Trionyx* sp., have been reported along with Lower Palaeolithic to Mesolithic implements. Fossils are concentrated in the two lower units (boulder clays and gravel sands) without any apparent difference in the faunal assemblages from the two units. According to P.P. Satsangi and A.K. Dutta, this faunal assemblage is comparable to those of the Yamuna and Ganga[4] which have been assigned by H. Falconer[5] and G.E. Pilgrim,[6] respectively, to a horizon of the Pleistocene slightly younger than the Narmada alluvial deposits. D.K. Chakravarty assigned the Gangetic alluvium to the Upper Pleistocene.[7] However, the fauna and C-14 dates (19715 + - 340 BP) obtained from mollusc shells from the gravel sand unit support a Late Pleistocene-Early Holocene time bracket for the alluvium.

[2]G.L. Badam et al. (1989), 'A Preliminary Study of Pleistocene Fossils from the Middle Son Valley, Madhya Pradesh', *ME*, 13, pp. 41-7.

[3]Ibid.

[4]P.P. Satsangi and A.K. Dutta (1968), *Progress Report for the Field Season 1967-68* (unpublished), G.S.I. Report.

[5]H. Falconer (1865), 'Fluviatile Deposits of the Ganges', *Journal of the Geological Society of London*, 21, pp. 311-89.

[6]G.E. Pilgrim (1905), 'On the Occurrence of Elephas antiquus (namadicus) in the Godavari Alluvium with Remarks on the Species, its Distribution and the Age of the Associated Indian Deposits', *Records of the Geological Survey of India*, 32, 3, pp. 199-218.

[7]D.K. Chakravarty (1931), 'On a Stegodon Molar from the Older Gangetic Alluvium near Benaras', *Quarterly Journal of the Geological Mineralogical and Metalurgical Society of India*, 3, pp. 115-25.

A Late Pleistocene palaeontological site discovered in the Paimar Valley near Gaya in Bihar yielded fossils of *Cervus* sp., *Axis* sp., *Bos* sp., *Bubalus* sp., and *Emys* sp., along with Acheulian tools (ovates, handaxes, cleavers, scrapers, flakes).[8] Recently rich faunal material (crocodiles, turtles, bovids. cervids) has been discovered from the Diyara belt of the Ganga Valley near Bhagalpur in Bihar (personal communication: Arvind Mishra) and this has been studied in some detail.

(B) *Narmada Valley*

The Narmada Valley has yielded the richest deposits of mammalian fossils found in association with Stone Age tools, which makes it very significant as far as the origins of man are concerned. This region was one of the great hunting grounds of India during the Palaeolithic period. Even today, bears, blackbucks, deer, gaurs, large cats and other wild animals are found in the forests along the banks of the Narmada and its tributaries. Many of the ancestors of these animals lie buried in Pleistocene deposits, along with other animals like the elephant, hippopotamus, horse, rhinoceros, etc., fossils of which have been unearthed from the alluvial deposits in profusion from time to time.

G.E. Pilgrim (1905) gave the first authoritative list of vertebrate fossils from the Narmada Valley and equated the deposits of this valley with those of the Godavari Valley on the basis of the identity of fauna. The list includes *Bos namadicus*, *Bubalus palaeindicus*, *Cervus duvauceli*, *Equus namadicus*, *Hippopotamus namadicus*, *Hippopotamus palaindicus*, *Leptobos frazeri*, *Panqsura tectum*, *Rhinoceros unicornis*, *Stegodon genesa*, *Stegodon insignis*, *Sus* and *Ursus namadicus*. As we can see, some of the fauna listed above (e.g. buffalo, deer, turtles, etc.) still exist in the present day at the species level or as closely related to modern forms. A few forms like *Stegodon ganesa*, *Stegodon insignis*, *Equus namadicus* and *Hippopotamus namadicus* are survivals from the Siwaliks of north-west India.

De Terra and T.T. Paterson added a few more fossils of turtles (*Trionyx* and *Emys*) to the above list.[9] Subsequent workers added *Holarctos namadicus*, *Palaeoloxodon namadicus*,[10] and more advanced forms like *Elephas namadicus*, *Elephas hysudricus*, *Bubalus bubalis*, *Equus caballus* (this species which was wrongly identified is, in fact, *Equus namadicus*), *Crocodylus palaeindicus*, *Bibos gaurua* to the existing list of fauna.[11] In the most recent fieldwork

[8]G.L. Badam (1976), *Society of Vertebrate Paleontology, News Bulletin*, 108, pp. 39-41.

[9]H. De Terra and T.T. Paterson (1939), *Studies on the Ice-Age in India and Associated Human Cultures*, Carnegie Institute of Washington, 493, pp. 1-354.

[10]E.H. Colbert (1942), 'The Geological succession of the Proboscidea in India', in Osborn, H.F. Proboscidea, *American Museum of Natural History*, 2, pp. 1421-1521.

[11]S.G. Supekar (1968), 'Pleistocene Stratigraphy and Prehistoric Archaeology of the

(1993-4), fossilized remains of *Panthera leo* and *Ovis/Capra* were also discovered from the area around Devakachar.

On the basis of fossils and cultural material found in the Narmada deposits and of attempted correlations with other Pleistocene deposits in India (e.g. Manjra, Godavari, Ghod, etc.), various workers have assigned them from the Pilocene[12] to the Late Pleistocene.[13] Many of the fossil taxa that the older alluvium contains (*Cervus duvauceli, Antilope cervicapra, Bubalus bubalis, Bibos gaurus, Equus namadicus* and *Bos namadicus*) are closely related to modern forms and, hence, are not considered to be earlier than the Upper Pleistocene. However, *Equus namadicus* and *Bos namadicus* range from the Middle to Late Pleistocene and may, thus, no longer be considered the index fossils for the Middle Pleistocene.[14] A radiocarbon date of 31750 (+1770, - 1580) BP – TF 867 has been obtained on freshwater mollusc shells (with half-life periods of 5730 yr) from the sandy pebbly gravel horizon (upper group of the older alluvium) at Ratikarar, a few km downstream of Guarighat in the Devakachar area (Narsinghpur district), assigning it to the Upper Pleistocene.[15] Another C-14 date based on bivalve shells available from Bhadraghat is 25160 + – 50.[16]

A study of chemical assays to ascertain the relative dates of fossil bones gives the values of 5.322 and 5.18 for the fluorine/phosphate ratio (100 F/ P2 05) from the putative Upper Pleistocene at Devakachar which are consistent with values obtained elsewhere in India.[17]

Central Narmada Basin', Ph.D. thesis (unpublished), Poona University, Poona; G.L. Badam, (1979), *Pleistocene Fauna of India*, Deccan College, Postgraduate and Research Institute, Pune; R.V. Joshi et al. (1978), 'Fresh Data on the Quaternary Animal Fossils and Stone Age Cultures from the Central Narmada Valley, India', *Asian Perspectives*, 21, 2, pp. 164-81; G.L. Badam and C. Grigson (1990), 'A Cranium of Gaur, Bibos gaurus (Bovidae, Mammalia) from the Pleistocene of India', *Modern Geology*, 15, pp. 49-88.

[12] H. Falconer (1859), *Descriptive Catalogue of the Fossil Remains of Vertebrata from the Siwalik Hills, the Nerbudda, Perim Island, etc., in the Museum of the Asiatic Society of Bengal, Calcutta*; W. Theobald (1860), 'On the Tertiary and Alluvial Deposits of the Central Portion of the Narbudda Valley', *Memoirs of the Geological Survey of India,* 2, pp. 279-98.

[13] H.B. Medicott (1873), 'Note on a Celt found by Hackett in the Ossiferous Deposits of the Narbada Valley (Pliocene of Falconer): On the Age of the Deposits and on the Associated Shells', *Records of the Geological Survey of India*, 6, 3, pp. 49-54.

[14] G.L. Badam (1984), 'Pleistocene Faunal Succession of India', in R.O. Whyte (ed.), *The Evolution of East Asian Environment*, University of Hong Kong, Hong Kong, pp. 746-75.

[15] D.P. Agarwal and S. Kusumagar (1974), *Prehistoric Chronology and Radiocarbon Dating in India*, Munshiram Manoharlal, New Delhi, pp. 1-41.

[16] S. Mishra (2001), 'Quaternary Fluvial Geomorphology in Western India', *National Symposium on Role of Earth Sciences in Integrated Development and Related Societal Issues, Geological Survey of India Sp. Pub,* 65, 1, pp. ixxv-ixxxv.

[17] Anupama Kshirsagar and G.L. Badam (1990), 'Biochronology and Fluorine Analysis

Based on palaeomagnetic dating, the Narmada quaternary formations are stated to be younger than 0.7 my.[18] The hominid-bearing horizon at Hathnora in Hoshangabad district is estimated to be between 150,000 and 40,000 BP[19] (late Middle Pleistocene to early Upper Pleistocene) on the basis of archaeological associations.[20] However, some scholars consider the cranium to fall in the time bracket of 1,50,000 to 1,00,000 years BP[21] or 250,000 to 150,000 years BP.[22] If the later date is confirmed, some of the exposures may even go back to the Lower Pleistocene. Further, results of dates on volcanic ash discovered in several exposures of the Narmada alluvium have provided a better understanding of the chronological framework. The ash has been dated to 75 kyr ago and its cultural association is the Middle to Upper Palaeolithic.

The collection of fossils represents different types of preservation and weathering stages and shows interesting breakage patterns, various types of cracks, flakings and evidences of bacterial action, giving enough indications of biological/non-biological factors acting upon the bones at various times. The state of preservation and the distribution pattern of some fossils (especially those coming from the upper clayey, silty and sandy horizons) suggest that at least 30 per cent of the collection could be considered autochthonous with respect to local channels. In our excavations, we have discovered almost complete skeletons, without evidence of abrasion or transportation, of a fossil buffalo (at Barmanghat) and cattle (at Gurariaghat around Devakachar), and other medium-sized mammals, indicative of their complete burial/fossilization in an autochthonous situation.

The faunal evidence collected so far suggests that the vegetation during this period was of the savannah type with several backswamps and water pools suitable for the animals to thrive in the valley during the Middle-Late Pleistocene times. In this vast savannah land, punctuated by floodplain lakes and swamps, flourished a rich variety of hoofed mammals and reptiles. However, we would like to emphasize here that there were no significant

---

of Some Pleistocene Fossils from Central and Western India', *Bulletin of the Deccan College Research Institute,* 49, pp. 199-211.

[18]D.P. Agrawal et al. (1988), 'Chronology and Significance of the Narmada Formations', *Proceedings of the Indian National Science Academy,* 54 A, pp. 418-24.

[19]A. Sonakia (1984), 'The Skull Cap of Early Man and Associated Mammalian Fauna from Narmada Valley Alluvium, Hoshangabad Area, M.P. (India)', *Records of the Geological Survey of India*, 113, pp. 159-72.

[20]G.L. Badam (1989), Observations on the Fossil Hominid Site at Hathnora, Madhya Pradesh, India', in Ashok Sahni and Rajan Gaur (eds.), *Perspectives in Human Evolution,* Renaissance Publishing House, Delhi, pp. 153-71.

[21]E. Delson (1985), 'Late Pleistocene Human Fossils and Evolutionary Relationship', in E. Delson (ed.), *Ancestors: The Hard Evidence*, Alan R. Liss, Inc., New York, pp. 296-300.

[22]K.A.R. Kennedy et al. (1991), 'Principal-components Analysis of Prehistoric South Asian Crania', *American Journal of Physical Anthropology*, 64, pp. 105-18.

departures from the existing tropical climate in the area and, therefore, the valley provided a favourable ecosystem where some of the animals could survive till almost up to 30,000 years ago.

The recent discovery of a partial cranium of *Homo erectus narmadiensis* has evoked great interest amongst archaeologists and palaeontologists.[23] The cranium came from the cemented bouldery pebbly bed about 12 m from the top and 2 m from the base in the exposed section at Hathnora, 40 km north-east of Hoshangabad in Madhya Pradesh. From this unit, Late Acheulian Stone Age tools were collected by the author and his team during recent explorations. Outside India, numerous dates from various sites other Late Acheulian complexes spread between north Germany and East Africa range from 700,000 to 125,000 yrs BP.[24] Associated hominid fossils with late Acheulian complexes outside India have been morphologically assigned to archaic *Homo sapiens*.[25] The presence of archaic *Homo sapiens* in association with late Acheulian tools outside India, therefore, calls for a critical reinvestigation into the taxonomy of *Homo erectus narmadiensis*.[26]

(C) *Mahanadi Valley*

The Mahanadi, which is one of the major easterly flowing rivers of India has received scant attention from scholars so far. However, the lower reaches of the valley in Orissa have yielded lithic industries ranging from the Lower Palaeolithic to the Mesolithic.[27] Intensive explorations carried out two decades ago in the upper Mahanadi Valley have led to the discovery of several new Palaeolithic and Mesolithic sites in the Raipur, Bilaspur and Bastar districts of Chhatisgarh (formerly in MP).[28] A number of vertebrate fossils were also discovered from the valley for the first time. Middle Palaeolithic tools (borers, blades, scrapers, choppers, flakes, etc.) were, in fact, found associated with fossils at three of the four fossil localities, namely Somnath (21 34 N: 81 48 E), Sigma (21 37 N: 81 42E) and Nandghat (20 01 N: 81 48 E), located on the Seonath and Hasdeo rivers. At Rainandgaon (21 06 N: 81 02 E), no tools

[23] Sonakia (1984), op. cit.

[24] J.D. Clark (1976), 'The African Origins of Man, the Tool Maker', in G.L. Issac and E.R. McCown (eds.), *Human Origins: Louis Leakey and the East African Evidence*, W.A. Benjamin Inc, California, pp. 1-54.

[25] G.P. Rightmire (1983), 'The Fossil Evidence for Hominid Evolution in Southern Africa', in R.G. Klein (ed.), *South African Prehistory and Palaeoenvironment*, Rotterdam, Balkema.

[26] G.L. Badam et al. (1986), 'Evaluation of fossil Hominid the Maker of late Acheulian Tools at Hathnora, Madhya Pradesh, India', *Current Science*, 55, 3, pp. 143-5.

[27] G.C. Mohapatra (1962), *The Stone Age Cultures of Orissa*, Deccan College, Pune; K.C. Tripathy (1972), 'Lithic Industries of Southwestern Orissa', Ph.D. thesis (unpublished), Utkal University, Orissa.

[28] R.V. Joshi et al. (1980), 'Late Pleistocene Animal, Fossils and Stone Age Cultures in the Upper Mahanadi Valley, M.P.', *Eastern Anthropologist*, 33, 2, pp. 169-75.

were found. The fossils discovered include the dental and osteological remains of *Bos bubalus*, *Bos namadicus*, *Equus namadicus*, and *Ovis/Capra*. These were generally found scattered in the gravel beds of the rivers and exhibit some amount of rolling. We can envisage the presence of hard ground surrounding the water sheets in the valley, which must have been a vast savannah land with sufficient vegetation in which these ungulates flourished.

The Lower Palaeolithic sites discovered along the right bank of the Mahanadi on the foothill slopes near Bhilai (20 31 N: 81 23 E) and Haradula (20 28 N: 81 26 E) have not yielded any fossils so far nor did the only Upper Palaeolithic site located on the left bank of the Seonath near Amilidih (21 48 N: 81 55 E). However, a more exact correlation between the faunal and cultural stages in the Mahanadi Valley as a whole must await the discovery of sufficient faunal material from the implementiferous sites. However, the lack of thick alluvial deposits in the Mahanadi Valley as a whole poses some problems in this regard.

(D) *Gandheswary Valley*

Numerous vertebrate fossils have been collected from the quarternary deposits of the Bankura, Burdwan and Purulia districts of West Bengal. These deposits have been assigned a probable Middle Pleistocene to Late Pleistocene-Holocene age. Though W.T. Blanford (1869) had reported a few subfossils of *Bos* from these deposits along the banks of the rivers Damodar and Barakar, their palaeontological nature came to light only with the discovery of a wealth of faunal remains from the older alluvial beds of the river Gandheswary near the Susunia hills (23 23 30: 8b 58 06) in Bankura district.[29] A tentative Upper Pleistocene age was assigned to these fossiliferous deposits (Sastry, 1968) on the basis of the fact that the extinct forms show more progressive characters.[30]

The fossils include *Bos* cf. *B. namadicus*, *Bubalus bubalis*, *Boselephas namadicus*, *Palaeoloxodon* sp., *Hystrix crassidens* and *Crocuts* sp. Fossils of those animals extending up to the present day have retained some primitive characters and are of a late Pleistocene to early Holocene age.[31] These include *Antilope cervicapra*, *Cervus duvauceli*, *Cervus unicolor*, *Axis axis*, *Munticus muntjac*, *Sus cristatus*, *Equus onager*, *Panthera leo*, *Bataqur Baska* and

[29]D.C. Dassarma et al. (1982), 'Fossil Vertebratres from the Late Quaternary Deposits of Bankura, Burdwan and Purulia Districts, West Bengal', *Palaeontologia Indica*, 44, pp. 1-65; W.T. Blanford (1869), 'On the Geology of the Taptee and Lower Berbudda Valley and Some Adjoining Districts', *Memoirs of the Geological Survey of India*, 6, 3, pp. 163-282.

[30]M.V.A. Sastry (1968), 'Pleistocene Vertebrates from Susunia, Bankura District, West Bengal', *Indian Minerals*, 22, p. 20.

[31]Dassarma et al. (1982), op. cit.

Gavialis gangeticus. The fauna seems to be closer to that of the Kurnool caves and the Gangetic older alluvium. However, in recent years, some of the above-mentioned fossils have also been found in the Narmada Valley.

More significant among the collections are *Panthera* cf. *Leo* (Lion) and *Crocuta* cf. *C. sivalensis* (spotted hyena), the former being the first definite record of the fossil lion from India and the latter is from Pleistocene deposits of peninsular India. It may be mentioned in passing that the only record, so far, of *Panthera leo* was that of an upper premolar and limb bones of a doubtful '*P.* cf. *tigris* or (*leo*)?' from the Pleistocene deposits of the Kurnool caves in Andhra Pradesh.[32] As stated earlier, we now have evidence of *Panthera leo* (?) also from the Narmada Valley.

There is evidence to suggest that the *Crocuta* had probably migrated from the Siwaliks of north-west India to peninsular India during the Pleistocene. Further, it is of interest to note that the spotted hyena (*Hyaena hyaena*), now restricted to Africa, had its origin in India, while the stripped hvena (*Crocuta crocuta*), mainly restricted to India today, originated in Africa.[33] Again it is to be noted that a probable ancestral form of both the lion and tiger has been described from the Lower Pleistocene of Africa.[34] The above fauna, therefore, sheds important light on the migration patterns of some animals during the Late Pleistocene.

From the same area, several thousand artefacts ranging from the Acheulian to the Neolithic have been collected but no clear geological stratification is available. In this connection, it may be noted that the recent discovery of the fossils of *Bos namadicus*, *Antilope cervicapra* and *Axis axis* from north-west Midnapur from the caliche context at Dhuliapur assumes great importance in so far as the proximity of some of the fossils to the Upper Palaeolithic-Mesolithic transitional blade industry is concerned.[35] It may be mentioned that the Upper Palaeolithic-Mesolithic industry is derived from the colluvial context overlying the caliche horizon and there is an imperceptible time gap between the two horizons.

A fairly good estimate of palaeoecology can be formed on the basis of the theory of actualism even though the faunal material discovered is scanty. *Antilope cervicapra* frequent relatively settled regions and open the countryside, avoiding forest areas. However, they survive in semi-arid areas as long as there is sufficient scattered vegetation. *Axis axis* is generally confined to the

[32]R. Lydekker (1886), 'The Fauna of Kurnool Caves', *Palaeontologia Indica*, Ser. C, 4, 2, pp. 23-58.

[33] B. Kurten (1968), *Pleistocene Mammals of Europe*, Weidenfeld and Nicholson, London.

[34]R.F. Ewer (1964), 'Large Carnivora of Bed II', in L.S.B. Leakey (ed.), *Olduvai Gorge*, 1951-61, Cambridge University Press, pp. 21-2.

[35]Bishnupriva Basak et al. (1998), 'Late Quaternary Environment, Palaeontology and Culture of Tarafeni Valley, Midnapur District, West Bengal: A Preliminary Study', *Journal of the Geological Society of India*, 51, pp. 731-40.

riverine forest in the plains and in areas of dense grass. On the whole, these two animals are found in forests at the base of the hills and practically throughout the peninsular region wherever there are jungles for grazing and a plentiful supply of water. *Bos namadicus* does frequent several habitats but is generally characterized by only one dietary pattern. However, this animal possesses adaptive capabilities to varied microenvironments. Foraging is the major factor that affects the geographical movement of these animals. We envisage the presence of considerable floral heterogeneity, abundant grasses towards the foothill region and grasslands generally associated with the riverine situation. Such a habitat in the north-west Midnapur district must have governed the distribution of these animals during the Terminal Pleistocene-Early Holocene times.

The entire region during the Quaternary was sub-humid when these animals lived in savannah habitats. Water pool situations, abundant grasses in the foothill region and hard ground towards the water sheets was the general ecological situation. However, within the sub-humid environment, there were minor fluctuations even in the semi-arid conditions (confirmed by the presence of the caliche horizons). This, however, did not affect the survival of the megavertebrates which are generally quite adaptable to varied ecosystems. The fauna was indigenous and we agree with D.C. Dassarma et al. that there has been a general westward shift in fauna, some of which found suitable home ranges in Rajasthan and Gujarat.[36] Detailed excavations in the entire area and the discovery of more fauna will help us appreciate better the man-land relationship in this part of the country.

(E) *Godavari Valley*

One of the earliest discoveries of fossil vertebrates from the Godavari Valley was made by Pilgrim who reported the presence of *Elephas antiquus*, *Hippopotamus palaeindicus*, *Equus namadicus* and *Crocodylus* from various localities in the valley.[37] C. Tripathi collected *Bos namadicus*, *Bubalus palaeindicus*, *Equus namadicus*, *Hexaprotodon namadicus*, *Cervus* sp., *Palaeoloxodon namadicus*, *Stegodon insignis*, and *Crocodylus* from the main channels of the Godavari and its tributaries, the Pravara and the Mula. Subsequently,[38] H.D. Sankalia, Joshi et. al., Rajaguru and Badam discovered more fossils from several localities in association with Early and Middle Palaeolithic tools.[39] Some of these discoveries included fossils of more recent

[36]Dassarma et al. (1982), op. cit.

[37]Pilgrim (1905), op. cit.

[38]C. Tripathi (1967), 'The Pleistocene alluvial deposits around Nevasa, Ahmednagar District, Maharashtra', *Records of the Geological Survey of India*, 25, 2, pp. 355-66.

[39]G.L. Badam (1973), 'Pleistocene Fossil Studies', *Buttetin of the Deccan College Research Institute*, 33, 1-4, pp. 21-40; H.D. Sankalia (1964), 'Middle Stone Age Cultures in India and Pakistan', *Science*, 146, 3642, pp. 365-75; R.V. Joshi et al. (1966), 'Animal

animals like *Elephas hysudricus*, *Bubalus bubalis*, *Elephas maximus* and *Cervus duvauceli*.

The alluvial deposits of the Godavari Valley were formerly believed to be equivalent to the Narmada deposits on the basis of identical faunal elements in both the valleys and assigned a Middle Pleistocene age.[40] Recent bio-stratigraphical studies support the observation, made on the basis of the scores of C-14, Th/U and other relative dates and comparative studies of the fauna, that the deposits may range from the Middle to Upper Pleistocene. We now have definite evidence of Middle Pleistocene index fossils, *Hexaprotodon namadicus* and *Sus namadicus*, in the valley. As far as the Godavari is concerned, there is, so far, only one single C-14 date of 19,000 BP for the upper part of the calcareous alluvium exposed around Paithan.[41] A few semi-rolled Middle Palaeolithic tools along with limb bones of *Bos* sp. were collected from the sandy gravels occurring slightly below this well-dated formation.[42] Several Middle Palaeolithic sites have been discovered at Shankatirth and Rakshasbhuvan on the main channels of the Godavari, and these have also yielded faunal remains in loose gravelly beds. We also suggest that *Bos namadicus* (found along with Lower Palaeolithic tools of a late Acheulian character at Gangapur), *Elephas namadicus*, *Equus namadicus* and *Bos namadicus* (found in association with Lower and Middle Palaeolithic tools in the older alluvium around Nevasa in the Pravara Valley and in the upper Godavari), are, in fact, of Middle Pleistocene age. However, a well-dated jaw of *Bos namadicus* (32,000 BP) recovered from the buried channel about 30 m below the surface of the Mula, a southerly tributary of the upper Godavari,[43] indicates an Upper Pleistocene age for some of the sections, further supported by a few C-14 assays on freshwater shells and driftwood found in the older alluvial fills from the source region of the Godavari.[44]

One of the best-documented and thoroughly studied quaternary sections in India is at Nevasa on the Pravara, a major tributary of the Godavari. It exposed a complete Stone Age sequence in the context of Pleistocene alluvial deposits. In recent years, S. Mishra used relative dating methods on the various gravel occurrences at Nevasa and reinterpreted archaeological evidence

---

Fossil and Early Stone Age tools from Gangapur on the Godavari River (Nasik District, Maharashtra State)', *Current Science*, 35, 13, p. 344; idem (1978), op. cit.; S.N. Rajaguru (1968-69), 'Some New Fossils Discoveries from Western Maharashtra, India', *Puratattva*, 2, pp. 16-22.

[40] Pilgrim (1905), op. cit.

[41] G. Corvinus et al. (1972/73), 'Some Observations on the Quaternary of Western Maharashtra (India)', *Quarter*, 23-4, pp. 53-69.

[42] Rajaguru (1968-69), op. cit.

[43] S.N. Rajaguru (1970), 'Studies in the Late Pleistocene of the Mula-Mutha Valley', Ph.D. thesis (unpublished), Poona University.

[44] S.N. Rajaguru and G.L. Badam (1976), 'Litho and Bio-stratigraphy of the Quaternary formations in the Central Godavari Valley, Maharashtra', *Seminar on Deccan Traps and Bauxites*, Geological Survey of India, Poona, p. 45.

from the site.[45] Mishra (1986) suggested an age of Early Middle Pleistocene for the Nevasa Acheulian. Based on her studies of weathering of bedrock, thinks that the high level gravel at Hathi predated the Acheulian by a long time interval and is, therefore, of pre-quarternary age. Therefore, the Acheulian in this area and the associated faunal material may have a long antiquity, even going back to the Lower Pleistocene time bracket.

One of the richest palaeontological treasures in peninsular India was discovered in the Manjra—a major southerly tributary of the Godavari.[46] The importance of the fossils with regard to provenance is enhanced by the rich complementary geological and archaeological data that the valley has yielded in recent times. A large number of fossils of *Elephas maximus*, *Elephas hysudricus*, *Stegodon insignis ganesa*, *Sus* sp., *Bos namadicus*, *Bubalus bubalis*, *Equus namadicus*, *Axis axis*, *Antilope vervicapra*, *Hexaprotodon* sp., *Cervus unicolor*, *Cervus duvauceli*, *Crocodylus* sp., and *Chelonia* were discovered in the low energy overbank flood deposits of the Upper Manjra at Dhanegaon (18 36 N: 76 10 E), Wangdari (18 35 N: 76 25 E), Tadula (18 35 N: 76 25 E) and Ganjur (18 35 N: 76 24 E). It is of interest to note that the fossils of *Proboscides* were predominantly found in the abandoned oxbow lake formations near Dhanegaon. The old channel deposits at Wangdari (about 30 km east of Dhanegaon) yielded the maximum number of ungulates out of which fossils of *Bos* account for nearly 75 per cent of the total collection. This situation, substantiated by sedimentological studies, points to the distribution of these animals being controlled by local ecological factors. The Manjra Valley had a good vegetation cover, probably a savannah forest with several deep water pools. It is interesting to note that the river had its origin in the semi-arid region of the Deccan and flowed mostly on the semi-arid tract but still preserved one of the richest animal habitats. The Manjra Valley, on palaeontological grounds, is assigned a late Pleistocene age, which is now confirmed by the two C-14 dates (26830 + - 750 BP—Wangdari; and 34470 + - 2070 BP—Tadula), both obtained on mollusc shells.

Middle and Upper Palaeolithic cultures have been discovered at a number of sites but very few in association with fossils. The former are concentrated on the lower reaches (Allanadurg, Salura, Chitgunda, Metkonda, etc). At Mugaon (18 45N: 77 27 E), there is clear evidence of a buried channel below the present level. Middle Palaeolithic tools and a few animal fossils were collected here from the loose gravelly spread. The absence of Lower Palaeolithic industries in the valley is rather surprising, particularly when there was no dearth of availability of suitable raw material. The fauna was plentiful and there was a thick vegetation cover during Late Pleistocene times.

[45] S. Mishra (1995), 'Chronology of the Indian Stone Age: Impact of Recent Absolute and Relative Dating Attempts', 20, 2, pp. 11-16.

[46] R.V. Joshi et al. (1981), 'Archaeological Studies in the Manjra Valley, Central Godavari Basin', *Bulletin of the Deccan College Research Institute*, 40, pp. 67-98.

(F) *The Krishna Valley*

The earliest record of fossils from the valley is by Foote (1876) who discovered fossils of *Bos namadicus* (?) and a new species of rhinoceros. *Rhinoceros deccanensis*, from the ossiferous deposits near Gokak in Belgaum district on the Ghatprabha River.[47] Subsequently, K. Paddayya (1969) discovered a fossiliferous Middle Palaeolithic site (*Bos namadicus*, *Cervus* sp. *Elephas* sp.) near Hagargundi on the left bank of the river Bhima.[48] These fossils were found in a clear-cut stratigraphic context. Hagargundi is perhaps one of the few sites in the Krishna Valley where Stone Age tools occur in association with vertebrate fossils.

As mentioned earlier, Z.D. Ansari (1970) reported, along with a pebble tool industry (of typical Sohan type), fossils of *Bos namadicus* at Nittur on the right bank of the river Tungabhadra in Karnataka.[49] Further discoveries include fossils of *Bos* along with Middle Palaeolithic tools near Dhond on the Bhima River, *Elephas* tusk fragments at Borkhal Dam on the main channels of the Krishna, and at Dhom near Mahabaleshwar. The last site is dated to 37640 + 9200 - 4250 BP.[50]

Tuffaceous beds containing plant impressions as well as Middle Palaeolithic tools were reported for the first time in India by R. Korisettar and others (1976-77) from Wajjal (16 29 N: 76 33 E), situated about 23 km west of Shorapur, Gulbarga district, Karnataka.[51] The section yielding the plant fossils is located on the right bank of the Hunsgi River, a northerly tributary of the Krishna.

More recently, Paddawa (1982) discovered numerous fossils (*Bos namadicus*, *Bubalus* sp., *Equus namadicus*, *Equus asignus*, *Elephas* sp., cervids and turtles) from various Acheulian occupation sites in the Hunsgi Valley in Karnataka, especially from the gullies.[52] These gulleys in the limestone escarpment, formed due to excessive erosion by rain waters, were probably a regular phenomenon in the past and might have served as a suitable place for scavengers to hide their prey. Several breakages found in the collection (irregular spiral and spiral) are probably postmortem. Some bones do have gnawing and chewing marks and indications of charring but these are not sufficient enough to be attributed to human activity at this stage. However,

[47]R.B. Foote (1876), 'The Geological Features of the South Maratha Country and Adjacent Districts', *Memoirs of the Geological Survey of India*, 12, 1, pp. 1-265.

[48]K. Paddayya (1969), 'Hagargundi: A Fossiliferous Middle Stone Age Site on the Bhima River', *Journal of the Asiatic Society of Bengal*, 11, 1-4, pp. 12-14.

[49]Ansari (1970), op. cit.

[50]Corvinus (1972-3), op. cit.

[51]R. Korisetter et al. (1976-77), 'On the Occurrence of Plant Fossils along with Middle Palaeolithic Tools at Wajjal, District Gulbarga, Karnataka', *Bulletin of the Deccan College Research Institute,* 36, 1-4, pp. 62-5.

[52]K. Paddayya (1982), *The Acheulian Culture of the Hunsgi Valley (Peninsular India): A Settlement System Perspective*, Deccan College, Pune.

the presence of almost similar fauna throughout the period ranging from the Acheulian to the Neolithic may indicate stability in the climatic conditions of the Hunsgi Valley. A dry and wet sub-humid climate existed in some pockets where animals flourished.

Recently, B.J. Szabo and others (1990) obtained half a dozen radiometric dates using the U-series technique on a faunal assemblage from the Hunsgi Valley.[53] The dates range from 21,900 to 350,000 and confirm the Middle Pleistocene-early Late Pleistocene time bracket for the Acheulian cultures in the area.

A few fossiliferous sites are located on the river Ghod, a tributary of the Bhima (in Maharashtra). However, the most important site is Wangdari, upstream of Inamgaon. Excavations have revealed the presence of Middle Palaeolithic tools (chiefly scrapers) along with fossils in the gravel beds while, in the overlying brown silty sand, unrolled Upper Palaeolithic blades of chalcedony were found associated with faunal material. This is perhaps one of the few sites suggesting a clear-cut separation of Middle and Upper Palaeolithic tools even though the fauna found in both the units is long-ranging.

The fossils identified are those of *Elephas maximus*, *Elephas hysudricus, Bos Namadicus, Bubalus* sp., *Cervus unifolor, Canis* sp., *Equus namadicus, Hexaprotodon* sp., *Trionyx* sp., *Sus* sp. and *Lebtobos* sp. The discovery of the fossil of the hipposptamus is of special significance as it increase the geographical range of the animal of the south of the Godavari before becoming extinct. This was found in a gravel bed associated with mollusc shells which have been C14 dated to 20,000 BP *Leptobos sp.* and *Sus sp.* have been reported from the Ghod Valley for the first time and, thus, have an important bearing on the palaeogeographical distribution of these animals in the past.[54]

The Chalcolithic mound of Inamgaon (*c.* 3700-*c.* 2900 BP), just opposite to the fossil site at Wangdari, has revealed important faunal data belonging both to the domesticated and wild varieties. Further, a Mesolithic site dating to *c.* 12000 BP has also been discovered in the area[55] but a palaeontological record for this period is lacking at present. Faunal material, if discovered from the Mesolithic site, would have thrown important light on the process of the domestication of some animals in this area since some of the Pleistocene animals discovered here are directly or indirectly related to a few domesticated animals found at the archaeological site.

[53] B.J. Szabo et al. (1990), 'On the Age of the Acheulian Culture of the Hunsgi-Baichbal Valleys, Peninsular India', *Bulletin of the Deccan College Research Institute*, 50, pp. 317-21.

[54] G.L. Badam (1985), 'The Late Quaternary Fauna of Inamgaon', V.N. Misra and Peter Bellwood (eds.), *Recent Advances in Indo-Pacific Prehistory*, Oxford and IBH, New Delhi, pp. 411-15.

[55] S.N. Rajaguru et al. (1980), 'The Terminal Pleistocene Microlithic Industry at Inamgaon, Maharashtra', *Bulletin of the Deccan College Research Institute*, 39, pp. 150-9.

The sedimentary formations in the Ghod Valley were deposited by a series of water pools within a braid bar or point bar. Such pools, probably with a tall grass cover, might have provided suitable habitats for water-loving species of animals such as *Hexaprotodon*. This animal would have normally inhabited swampy plain areas where sluggish water predominated, although the contemporary presence of elephants, horses, buffaloes, cattle, deer, carnivores, etc., indicates a tropical semi-arid monsoonal climate with plateaus and lowlands probably covered by dense grass and stunted trees.[56] The presence of Middle and Upper Palaeolithic tools in the same geological layers as the animal bones suggests that biotic factors played an important part in attracting Palaeolithic settlers to this location. However, the exact role of prehistoric man in exploiting the contemporary fauna will remain enigmatic till primary/ semi-primary sites are discovered and excavated in the area.

In more recent years, some more fossil localities have come to light in the valley. Important among these is the 2 m long tusk of *Elephas* sp., found in association with Acheulian artefacts in a channel bar deposit at Bori (19 06 N: 74 05 E) in the Kukdi Valley, which has been well-preserved because of the short phase event of flood.

Fauna from the Upper Palaeolithic Cultures

(A) *The Kurnool Caves*

The caves in the limestone formations of the Kurnool district, in Andhra Pradesh present ideal examples of stratified animal fossils in association with Upper Palaeolithic cultural material. The evidence throws important light on migration patterns, the palaeogeographic distribution of animals and the palaeoecology of the area during the late Pleistocene period in this part of the country. The other Upper Palaeolithic sites in India (e.g. Patna) have not yielded as interesting and diverse fauna as that of the Kurnool caves.

A diverse variety of fossils ranging from primates to amphibians have been reported from these caves.[57] Important among these are *Presbytis entellus*, *Papio* sp., *Panthera* spp., *Felis* spp., *Crocuta crocuta*, *Herpestes* spp., *Viverra Karnuliensis*, *Melursus ursinus*, *Equus asinus*, *Rhinoceros Karnuliensis, Bos Bubalus*, *Boselephas tragocamelus*, *Gazella gazella*, *Antilope cervicapra. Cervus unicolor*, *Tetraceros quadricornis*, *Axis axis*, *Muntiacus muntjak*, *Sus scrofa cristatus*, *Sus karnuliensis*, *Crocodylus* sp., and *Bufo* sp. Microvertebrates are represented by several rodents (*Tater*, *Bandicoota*, *Mus*, *Millardia*, *Golunda*, *Hystrix*, *Lepus*, etc.). In general, the fauna indicates an Upper

[56]M.D. Kajale et al. (1976), 'Late Quaternary History of the Ghod Valley, Maharashtra', *Geophytology*, 6, 1, pp. 122-32.

[57]M.L.K. Murty (1975), 'Late Pleistocene Fauna of Kurnool Caves, South India', in A.T. Clason (ed.), *Archaeozoological Studies*, North Holland Publishing Company, Amsterdam and New York, pp. 132-8.

Pleistocene to terminal Pleistocene time bracket. The animals of the antelope and deer family are closely related to contemporary animals on the species level. Microvertebrates represent the same species that have been discovered in the central Narmada Valley recently.[58] There is no faunal element which is earlier than the Upper Pleistocene.

In recent years, ESR dating was attempted by V.D. Gogte and M.L.K. Murty (1986) on a bone sample from the Kurnool caves.[59] The samples belonged to five layers at MCG II, and the dates of 16,686 and 19,224 BP obtained for trench B4 (150-65 and 165-80 cm depths) confirm the Upper Palaeolithic age of these levels. These dates are almost in agreement with the TL date of 17,390 BP[60] obtained for a burnt clay sediment from the 165-80 cm level).

The Kurnool fauna is, on the whole, important in understanding the evolutionary processes and migration patterns of some of the animals. For example, the civet (*Viverra*) and porcupine (*Hystrix*) found in the caves probably provide an evolutionary stage between the Siwalik representatives and the existing forms of these genera. The pig (*Sus falconeri*) of the Siwaliks may have given rise to the extinct *Sus karnuliensis* and also to the existing *Sus cristtus*.[61] *Rhinoceros Karnuliensis* shows characters intermediate between those of *R. etruscus* (European), *R. deccanensis* and *R. bicornis* (African).

There has also been free migration of animals between India and Africa as examplified by a variety of porcupine (*Atherura*), which is now totally unrepresented in India but occurs in Africa. Lion is a comparatively rare animal in India but very abundant in Africa. *Felis chaus* (jungle cat) is an example of a species which originated in India and also extended its range into Africa.

The presence of animals of the antelope and deer family in the area during Late Pleistocene times indicates a scrub-to-tree jungle in the hilly and plateau country, and a tall grass cover in the plains. The presence of bovids attests to the fact that the plateaus and areas along streams might have provided a plentiful supply of grass, while the hilly slopes had a tree cover. The presence of primates points to a small forest-type vegetation. Rhinoceroses inhabited this area when there were a large number of swamps present. The rest of the animals suggest a scanty bush jungle in the area. On the whole, a thicker vegetation cover in the area during the late Pleistocene times is the most probable environmental setting that can be envisaged.

The Kurnool area presents the most authentic evidence of the Upper

[58] Rajeev Patnaik et al. (1995), 'Discovery of Microvertebrates from the Pleistocene Deposits of the Central Narmada Valley, India', *Current Science*, 68, 8, pp. 828-30.

[59] V.D. Gogte and M.L.K. Murty (1986), 'ESR Dating of Kurnool Caves, South India', *ME*, 10, pp. 135-40.

[60] M.L.K. Murty and K.S.V. Nambi (1983), 'An Upper Palaeolithic Fireplace in Kurnool Caves, South India', *Bulletin of the Deccan College Research Institute*, 42, pp. 110-16.

[61] Lydekker (1986), op. cit.

Palaeolithic bone tool industry in India in association with fauna. It may be mentioned here that Upper Palaeolithic industries are also known from open-air sites in Rajasthan and central India, Deccan and the south-east coast. Cave occupations are known in the Vindhya-Kaimur region, in addition to the Kurnool area. The Upper Palaeolithic site of Patne in the Jalgaon district of Maharashtra is a primary habitation site with the earliest evidence of art in India, as the discovery of engraved ostrich eggshells suggests.[62] Ostrich egg-shells ranging in data from 25 kyr to 40 kyr BP have now been discovered from more than fifty sites, in Rajasthan, Madhya Pradesh and Maharashtra from Upper Palaeolithic cultural levels (Badam and Sathe, 1994). It has also yielded some fragmentary remains of fossil mammals like *Bos*, *Equus*, etc.

Some Additional Palaeolithic Fossiliferrous Sites

(A) A third metacarpal (cannon bone) of *Equus*, of *E. asinus Linn.* (1762) obtained by H.D. Sankalia from near Tajpur (23 22 02 : 73 04 05) in Gujarat forms the first record of a Middle Palaeolithic fossil from the mid-western portion of the Survey of India topo sheet No. 46 E/3 & 7, scale, 1″ = 1 mile (old no. 147). The height of the bank at this place varies from 6 to 9.5 m. The gravel, varying in thickness from 1 to 3 m, rests on the hard trap rock about 1.5 m thick and is covered by 3 to 3.6 m thick calcareous silt, which is overlaid by modern sandy silt of 0.5 to 1.25 m thickness. The gravel which yielded the fossil also produced a few Middle Palaeolithic tools like points and scrapers.

The Meshvo River originates on the southern slopes of the Aravalli mountains and flows for a distance of about 15 km in a southwesterly direction to meet the Sabarmati River which empties into the Gulf of Cambay.

Badam gave a detailed morphological account of the fossil and discussed its significance in the evolutionary tendencies of equids.[63] His studies suggest that the proportional length of the third metacarpal is important for the identification of different species of equids. A number of important changes take place in the third metacarpal, for instance, in the shape of the bone, facets and the area of attachment for ligaments and tendons, which can best be explained by the change in the locomotion apparatus.[64] The limbs of asses are slender—a feature that does not correspond to a particularly great speed.

[62] S.A. Sali (1980), 'Stone Age Cultures at Patne, Dist. Jalgaon, Maharashtra', Ph.D. thesis (unpublished), University of Poona, Poona.

[63] G.L. Badam (1977), 'First Record of a Middle Palaeolithic fossil from Gujarat, India', *Journal of the Palaeontological Society of India*, Orlo Memorial Volume, 20, pp. 314-19.

[64] P.Y. Sondaar (1968), 'The Osteology of the Manus of Fossil and Recent Equidae with Special Reference to Phylogeny and Function', *Kon. Ned. Akad. Weten. Eerste Reeks-Deel,* 25, 1, pp. 22-31.

Their hoofs are narrow and seem to be adapted to rocky ground. Asses appear in India only in the Late Pleistocene period.

(B) One of the most important palaeo-rock art sites in India is Daraki-Chattan, located in the Indragarh Vindhya hill near Bhanpura in Madhya Pradesh. This author studied the palaeoecological history of the region, especially the section exposed by the excavation of the spill channel of the Indragarh dam and the agricultural fields near Lotkhedi, rich in fossils and observed that fossils are scattered all over a vast stretch of the field.[65] The fossils have been broken into fragments and are disturbed because of ploughing activity. Though the sediment in which they are found is generally red, their antiquity cannot be ascertained unless some trial trenches are dug to understand the history and chronology of the site. A few exposed sections of the gullies of the fields indicate a thickness of about 2.4 m.

Hundreds of carapace and plastron fragments of different varieties of turtles have been collected. Limb bones, vertebrae and crocodilian teeth are easily identifiable in the field. The fossils were encrusted with lateritic soil, hence these were chemically treated with a mixture of acetic acid and water in the ratio of 1:3, and this has helped in deciphering some of the features on the carapaces and plastrons.

The crocodilian teeth scattered in the area are sharp, strong and of various sizes, with a conical hollow at their base. Some are slightly curved, indicating their position in the dentition. The teeth may belong to *Crocodylus palaeindicus* since it is the only species of crocodile described from central India.[66]

The carapace fragments of turtles are generally big, thick and stouter in appearance. Various fragments preserve characteristics of neurals, pleurals and marginals. In some fragments, the pygal and nuchal plates can also be recognized. Plastron fragments generally preserve characteristics of meso-plastron and xiphiplastron. The fragments may belong to Tgestudinidae—the largest family of the order Chelonia, which includes both turtles and tortoises. The shape of some of the carapaces as ascertained from the fragments, indicates that they were moderately, convex and low-arched. Few carapace fragments belong to the genus *Trionyx* as revealed by the ornamentation pattern on their dorsal surface.

Also scattered in the fields are numerous Lower and Middle Palaeolithic stone artefacts like handaxes, scrapers, flakes, etc., some of them unrolled and in mint condition.

It appears reasonable to postulate that the area was occupied by lakes and swamps and might have been subjected to various episodes as revealed by the alteration of coarse and fine sediments, indicating a rhythmic deposition during a long period. The movement of water must have been slow as the

[65] G.L. Badam (2002b), 'A Preliminary Note on the Fossils of Bhanpura Region', *Purakala,* 13, 1-2, pp. 37-8.

[66] Badam (1979), op. cit.

pools and basins in the area were stagnant. Subsequently, man must have inhabited the area because of the availability of water and game. Gradually, climatic changes and the scarcity of water must have forced the water levels to recede and the pools must have dried up, thereby trapping the animals and resulting in their death *en masse*. We may call the site a 'Turtle graveyard'. The geological succession of the area, the causes for the concentration of turtle bones and other taphonomic aspects should be looked into, which calls for a detailed excavation of a multidisciplinary nature.

CONCLUSION

The discovery of more fossil-yielding and well-dated Palaeolithic sites in recent years has enabled us to revise the chronological ranges of various animal species, and to add new information on the palaeogeographic distribution and palaeoecological attributes of these species of the past. Also, our concepts of what should constitute the index fossil/fossils for the Lower, Middle and Upper Pleistocene periods in India are now becoming clearer and acceptable with the availability of more faunal data and the radiometric dates for these periods. The diverse fauna also throws a flood of light on the migration pattern of animals within India during Palaeolithic times and also intermigration with other countries. It has now been possible to study the palaeoecology of the sites and the taphonomy of biological remains with a fair amount of accuracy, using a multidisciplinary approach. As indicated in the preceding pages, some of the species have a direct or indirect bearing on a few domesticated animals found in India since Mesolithic times, as many animals like cattle, pig, buffalo and elephant have probably been indigenously domesticated.

It can thus be seen from the above account that the fauna during the Palaeolithic period has undergone tremendous refinement as far as their chronological sequence are concerned. The identifications are generally conservative, considering individual variations on account of sexual dimorphism, age, geographical and physical abnormalities, and other related factors like individual variations. Some of the earlier identifications have been updated. This author has generally tried to avoid splitting species because of the factors mentioned above.

During the last three decades many fossil complexes, individual sites and new species have been discovered which have contributed to a better understanding of the faunal wealth of our country during Palaeolithic times and its related aspects. The relationship of one faunal complex to another, taxonomic diversities, and the assessment of palaeoecology and living habitats can now be attempted more accurately. All this new data has put the information on Indian Palaeolithic fauna on as sound a footing as perhaps in Africa or Southeast Asia.

Remarks on correlations of Palaeolithic archaeology and faunal materials, as also the evolution and migration of individual animal species, have already been published elsewhere,[67] and need not be repeated here. However, the new dimensions of palaeontological research are shown in Fig. 5.1, and the Pleistocene fossiliferous localities encompassing some of the Palaeolithic sites in Fig. 5.2. The distribution of fauna in relation to Palaeolithic cultures is shown in Table 5.1, a summary of the quaternary bio-cultural and chrono-stratigraphy in India is given in Table 5.2, and the chronological sequence of Palaeolithic/Pleistocene fossils in India in Table. 5.3.

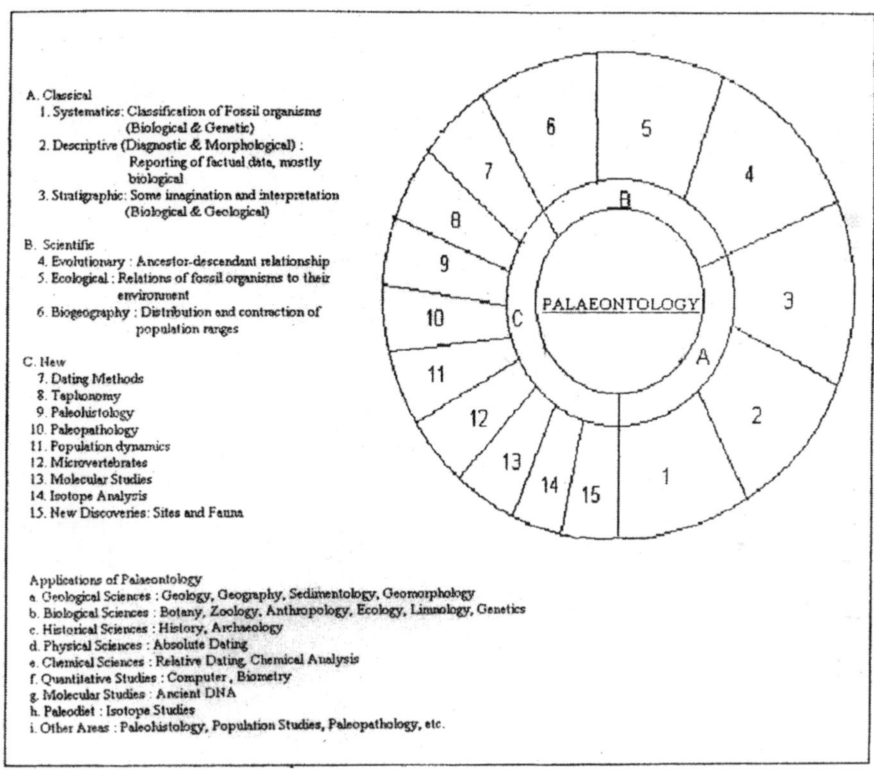

Fig. 5.1: New dimensions of palaeontological research

[67]Badam (1979), op. cit.; idem (1984), op. cit.; idem (2000), 'Pleistocene Vertebrate Palaeontology in India at the Threshold of the Millennium', *Journal of the Palaeontological Society of India*, 45, pp. 1-24; idem (2002a), 'Quaternary Vertebrate Palaeontology in India: Fifty Years of Research', in S. Setter and Ravi Korisettar (eds.), *Indian Archaeology in Retrospect*, vol. III, Indian Council of Historical Research and Manohar, New Delhi, pp. 209-46.

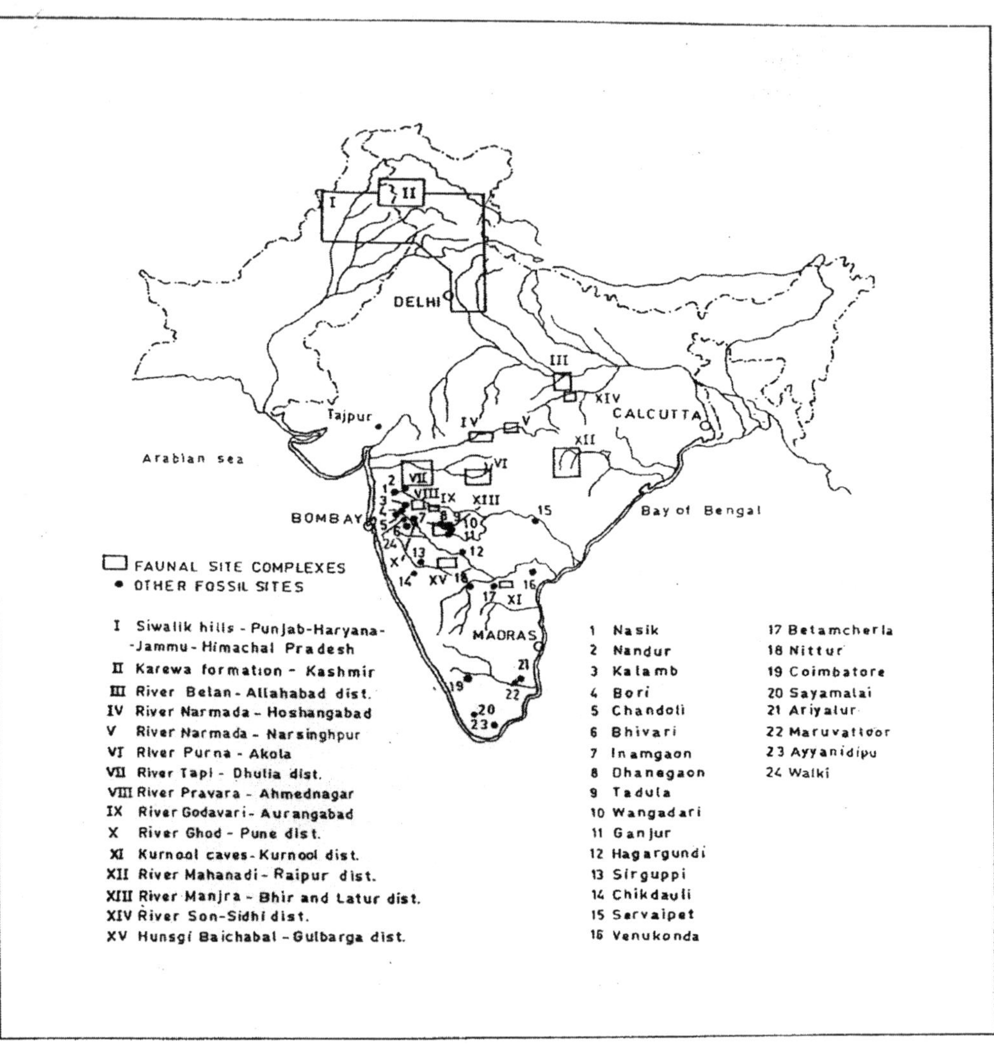

Fig. 5.2: Pleistocene fossiliferous localities encompassing some palaeolithic sites

Table 5.1: Distribution of Fauna in Relation to Palaeolithic Cultures in India

Locality	Important fauna	Stone Age Tools	Associated Cultures	Probable Age	Environment
Kurnool, Ghod, Manjra, Pravara, Godavari	*Canis* sp., *Bubalus* sp., *Cervus* sp., *Bos namadicus*	Bone tools, Burins, Blades, Points	Upper Palaeolithic	Late Upper Pleistocene (also dated by C-14; 40,000 to 15,000 BP.)	Savannah type with pockets of forests and swamps (humid in Kurnool)
	Elephas hysudricus, *Elephas maximus*, *Rhinoceros unicornis*, *Bos indicus*, *Hexaprotodon palaeindicus*	Scrapers, Flakes, Blades, Points, Borers	Late Middle Palaeolithic		
Central Narmada (Upper group); Paimar	*Equus namadicus*, *Bos namadicus*, *Hexaprotodon palaeindicus*, *Elephas hysudricus, Stegodon insignis ganesa*, *Cervus* sp.	Scrapers, Flakes, Flake-blades, Points, Borers, Handaxes, Cleavers, Polyhedrals, Discoids, Choppers	Middle Palaeolithic (Late Acheulian)	Early Upper Pleistocene	Savannah grassland interspersed with swamps
Central Narmada (Lower group)	*Equus namadicus*, *Bos namadicus*, *Hexaprotodon namadicus*, *Sus namadicus*, *Elephas hysudricus*, *Stegodon insignis ganesa*	Choppers, Handaxes, Cleavers, Flakes	Lower Palaeolithic (Acheulian)	Middle Pleistocene (not well established)	Savannah grassland interspersed with swamps
Lower Karewa, Pinjor of Upper Siwaliks	*Equus sivalensis*, *Rhinoceros sivalensis*, *Rhinoceros palaeindicus*, *Bos acutifrons*, *Archidiskodon planifrons*, *Sivatherium giganteum*	No authentic or *in situ* Stone Age Tools		Lower Pleistocene	Valley and open Savannah grassland with lakes and swamps

Table 5.2: Quaternary Bio-Cultural and Chrono-Stratigraphy in India

Geo Time Scale	Archaeo Time Scale	Approx Age	Significant Cultural Traits	Fauna	Dominant Climate
Late Holocene	Historical (Iron Age)	3000 BP onwards	Writing, iron technology and advanced agriculture known	Modern animals	Good monsoons prior to AD 1000, Bad monsoons, between 14th and 17th century AD
Mid Holocene	Chalcolithic/Neolithic	4500-3000 BP	Use of copper and stone, beginning of agriculture, advance town planning, knowledge of writing, polished tool technology	Domesticated and wild animals	Weak monsoons around 3000 BP
Early Holocene	Mesolithic	10-12,000 to 4,000 BP	Composite tool-technology, pastoralism and fishing dominant	Beginning of domestication of animals	Very good monsoons (8000-4000 BP), winter rains strong
Terminal Pleistocene	Upper Palaeolithic	40,000 to 10-12000 BP	Palaeolithic art and blade tool technology, hunting and food gathering	*Equus hemionus*, *Bos namadicus*, *Rhinoceros* sp., *Bubalus* sp., *Elephas maximus*, *Cervus* sp., etc.	Poor monsoons
Late Pleistocene	Middle Palaeolithic	130,000 to 40,000 BP	Hunting and food gathering, use of fine grained chalcedony, chert, etc., for making scrapers and flake tools, use of quartzite and basalt continues	Same as above + *Equus namadicus*, *Bos namadicus*, *Hexaprotodon* sp., *Elephas hysudricus*, *Sus* sp., etc.	Good monsoons around 120,000 BP, moderate to weak monsoons from 75,000 yrs onwards

Middle Pleistocene	Lower Palaeolithic (Early to Late Acheulian)	700,000-130,000 BP	Hunting and food gathering, use of quartzite, basalt for making handaxes, scrapers, cleavers, flakes, choppers, etc.	Same as above + *Hexaprotodon namadicus*, *Sus namadicus*, etc.	Fluctuating monsoons, strong to weak.
Lower Pleistocene	Suspected Lower Palaeolithic in Pakistan (Peshawar) and India (Maharashtra)	2.0 my-0.7 my (Peshawar: 2 my, Bori: 670,000 yrs)	Hunting and food gathering, use of basalt for making flakes and choppers	*Equus sivalensis*, *Bos acutifrons*, *Rhinoceros sivalensis*, *Hexaprotodon sivalensis*, *Stegodon Insignis ganesa*, *Archidiskodon planifrons*, etc.	Fluctuating monsoons, strong to weak.
Plio-Pleistocene		2.47 my – 1.87 my		First appearance of *Equus* and extinction of *Hipparion*	Transition from tropical humid climate to seasonal monsoonic climate
Pliocene		5 my – 2.5 my		*Hipparion* predominant	Tropical humid climate
Miocene		20 my – 5 my			

Notes: C-14 dates up to 40,000 BP
UR-Th dates up to 400,000 BP
K/AR dates for period 1 my and beyond

Source: Table compiled by G.L. Badam and S.N. Rajaguru and updated up to 2002.

Table 5.3: Chronological Sequence of Pleistocene/Palaeolithic Mammals in India

Lower Pleistocene	*Equus sivalensis*, Bos acutifrons*, Rhinoceros sivalensis, Hexaprotodon sivalensis, Archidiskodon planifrons*, Cervus punjabiensis**
Lower to Upper Pleistocene	*Elephas hysudricus, Stegodon insignis ganesa*
Middle to Upper Pleistocene	*Equus namadicus, Bos namadicus, Bubalus palaeindicus*
Middle Pleistocene*	*Elephas namadicus, Sus namadicus, Hexaprotodon namadicus*
Upper Pleistocene*	*Sus palaeindicus, Hexaprotodon palaeindicus*
Upper Pleistocene to Holocene	*Antilope cervicapra, Cervus unicolor, Cervus duvauceli, Axis axis, Ovis/Capra, Boselephas tragocamelus, Equus asinus, Elephas maximus*

Notes: * Index fossils

The above biochronological sequence, which revises our earlier concepts, is based on our work in various fossil localities in India especially Karewas, Siwaliks, Narmada Valley, Son and Belan Valleys, Tarafeni Valley, western Maharashtra, etc.

Chapter 6

Mesolithic Culture

V.N. Misra

INTRODUCTION

The existence of a Stone Age stage in the history of humankind was first recognized in the 1830s, following the discovery of chipped stone tools in association with fossilized bones of extinct animals in the geological deposits of the Somme River at Abbeville in France by the amateur archaeologist, J.C. Boucher de Perthes. Although ground stone tools belonging to a later age had been collected from the surface at many places in India and Europe from a much earlier date, no one believed that they were made by humans. They were thought to be thunderbolts with mysterious and magical properties. In India, they were often collected by village people from agricultural fields, and were placed at the foot of a tree or on a platform and worshipped as idols of Shiva, one of the three most important Hindu divinities. However, around 1854, following a severe drought, lake levels in Switzerland fell considerably and remains of ancient dwellings were exposed. These remains comprised ruins of wooden structures, baked clay polyground stone implements, bones of domesticated animals and charred seeds of cultivated plants.

With these discoveries, archaeologists realized that they represented a younger and different Stone Age. While the older Stone Age was characterized by chipped stone tools, extinct wild animals and a hunting-gathering economy, the new and younger one was marked by ground stone tools, living fauna and an agricultural economy. The French prehistorians gave descriptive names of the Chipped Stone Age and the Polished Stone Age to these two stages. Later, in 1865, the British banker, magistrate and amateur archaeologist, Sir John Lubbock, coined the terms Palaeolithic and Neolithic for these stages in his book, *The Prehistoric Times.*

However, at no place in Europe, where the study of prehistory first began, was a continuous succession of cultures from the Palaeolithic to the Neolithic found. On the contrary, in the caves in France where prehistoric materials were being excavated, there was always a sterile deposit between the Palaeolithic and Neolithic, denoting a cultural and stratigraphic gap or hiatus. At this stage, it was believed that agriculture originated in the near east and was introduced into Europe by farmers from Asia. This was the reason for the stratigraphic gap between the Palaeolithic and Neolithic.

However, discoveries by A.C.L. Carlleyle, an assistant to General Alexandar Cunningham, the first Director General of the Archaeological Survey of India, in rockshelters in the Vindhya hills of central India in the late 1860s revealed microlithic tools which were different from both Palaeolithic and Neolithic tools and belonged to an intermediate stage. Carlleyle realized that there was no break or hiatus between the Palaeolithic and Neolithic and coined the term Mesolithic for this transitional stage.[1]

Mesolithic is a brief period whose duration varies from a few centuries in the near east to some thirty-five millennia in Sri Lanka. The period has enormous culture-historical importance in old world prehistory. The technological hallmark of this period is tiny stone tools or 'microliths'. This much-abused term is strictly to be applied only to tools made of microblades or bladelets (having a maximum length of 50 mm and a width of 12 mm) or occasionally on small flakes, by blunting one or more margins by a steep retouch. The microliths comprise non-geometric forms like rectangular, blunted back blades and points, and geometric forms like crescents, lunates, triangles or trapezes. These microliths were too small to be used individually; instead, they were used as components of tools and weapons by being hafted on bone, wood or reed handles and shafts. A groove was cut in the wooden, reed or bone handle or shaft, and a number of microliths arranged serially into it and glued together by a natural adhesive like gum or resin. The microblade was blunted to prevent the cutting of the haft and thereby the loosening of the microliths during the use of the tool or weapon. Microliths were used as tips and barbs of arrowheads and spearheads, and as cutting edges of knives, sickles, daggers and harpoons. Discoveries of halted microliths from many excavated sites in Europe, the near east, Africa and India, as also their depiction in central Indian rock shelter paintings, testify to the use of microliths in this manner.[2]

According to L.R. Binford, 'Carlleyle was also one of the early questioners of the validity of the hiatus between the Palaeolithic and Neolithic. Carlleyle's excavations yielded typical crescents, trapezoids, and other geometric microliths; it was asserted that these implements were found both with late Palaeolithic tools and pottery. This led him to propose that there was no hiatus in India and that the microliths constituted an intermediate industry to which he applied the term 'mesolithic'. These materials were exhibited in England in 1888 at the Royal Albert Hall'.[3]

Utilizing the intimate knowledge of animal and plant behaviour accumulated by their Palaeolithic ancestors during the preceding several million years, the

[1]A.C.L. Carlleyle (1883), 'Notes on Lately Discovered Sepulchral Mounds, Cairns, Caves, Cave-paintings and Stone Implements', *PASB*, 49, February, Bengal.

[2]V.N. Misra (1974), 'Archaeological and Ethnographic Evidence for the Hafting and use of Microliths and Related Tools', *Puratattva*, 7, pp. 3-12.

[3]L.R. Binford (1968), 'Post-Pleistocene Adaptations', in S.R. Binford and L.R. Binford (eds.), *New Perspectives in Archaeology* Aldine, Chicago, pp. 313-41.

Mesolithic people started animal domestication and plant cultivation around nine thousand years ago in the vast stretch of land lying between the east coast of the Mediterranean Sea and the western edge of the Indus plain in Pakistan. The knowledge and practice of agriculture was diffused by the Neolithic people through the medium of their predecessors, the Mesolithic people, over much of the old world. It is the Mesolithic people who became the pioneering farmers, and their descendants established permanent settlements or villages which slowly grew into towns and eventually into cities, the Neolithic people cleared primeval vegetation with ground stone axes to establish farms and villages.

Once the Neolithic people learnt the extraction and smelting of copper, their culture came to be known as Chalcolithic. The Chalcolithic people learnt to produce the first man-made metal, bronze, by alloying copper with tin and arsenic, which was harder than copper. The Bronze-using people eventually invented civilization around five-and-a-half thousand years ago, and, therefore, Bronze Age and civilization have become synonymous. It was not possible to clear the dense and tangled forests of sub-humid regions with stone and bronze tools. For this reason, the earliest civilizations of the world were confined to the sparsely vegetated desert regions of the Nile Valley of Egypt, the Tigris-Euphrates Valley of ancient Mesopotamia or present-day Iraq, and the Indus-Saraswati Valleys of Pakistan and India.

However, despite the nine thousand-year-old history of agriculture, the five-and-a-half thousand years of urban life, and two hundred years of the industrial revolution and extensive urbanization, the atavistic hunting-gathering way of life did not disappear and still persists in many parts of the world, including India in the twenty-first century. Both farmers and hunter-gatherers have made a significant contribution to the evolution of the uniquely Indian social phenomenon of caste. I shall elaborate on this observation towards the end of this essay.

For a variety of reasons, evidence for the Mesolithic period in India, even though it has a duration of only a few thousand years, is far richer than that of the preceding Palaeolithic period which lasted more than a million years. First, all the dated Mesolithic sites belong to the Holocene and since there have been no significant geomorphic changes during this period, the sites are fairly well-preserved. Second, several thousand sites of this period have been discovered all over the country, barring the greater part of the Ganga plains, north-eastern India and much of the Western Ghats. The number of these sites is several times larger than that of the sites of the preceding Palaeolithic period. Third, thirty-five sites of this period have been excavated in varying sizes, and they have provided a variety of cultural materials which throw light on technology, material culture, subsistence and disposal of the dead. Fourth, biological material, comprising animal and human skeletal remains is preserved in good quality and quantity at a number of sites. Fifth, eight excavated sites have yielded human skeletal remains. Barring the solitary Pleistocene human fossil find from Hathnora in the Narmada Valley, these are the oldest human skeletal remains in the country. Analyses of these remains by biological anthropologists has thrown valuable light on the methods of disposing of the dead, the biological composition of contemporary human populations, the dietary habits, pathology and social organization of the Mesolithic communities. Sixth, there is an abundance of rock paintings associated with Mesolithic sites which, besides being a record of the aesthetic expression of the Mesolithic people, complements other archaeological data for reconstructing the technology, economy, social organization, and religious beliefs and practices of the Mesolithic population. And finally, nearly fifty radiometric dates from several sites help in determining the antiquity and in understanding the process of evolution of the Mesolithic societies.

RESUME OF RESEARCH

Explorations

As already mentioned above, the first discovery of microliths in India was made by A.C.L. Carlleyle in the caves and rock shelters of the Kaimur range of the Vindhya hills, south of the Ganga River in the Mirzapur district of the then United Provinces of Agra and Oudh (present Uttar Pradesh). Subsequently, in 1880-1, Carlleyle excavated some of these shelters, including Morhana Pahar, and came across microliths and other stone tools, living floors with hearths containing animal bones, ash and charcoal, and human burials. On the walls and ceilings of these shelters, he noticed paintings which appeared to him 'to illustrate in a very stiff and archaic manner scenes in the life of the ancient stone chippers; others represent animals or hunts of animals by men armed with bows and arrows, spears and hatchets.[4]

Carlleyle's findings served to stimulate John Allen Brown who published an article summarizing his work.[5] In this article, Brown asked if there had been similar microlithic forms found in the British Isles, pointing out that they were already reported from Tunis, Egypt, Italy, Palestine, France, Portugal and the Crimea. Brown's main concern was documenting the widespread occurrence of microliths and he offered no chronological interpretation. Wilson (1894) reported that in 1892, the U.S. National Museum acquired much of Carlleyle's material, and he proposed the acceptance of the Mesolithic as a transitional period between the Palaeolithic and Neolithic.[6]

The following year, Brown published an extensive paper in which he discussed the problem of the hiatus.[7] He went on to argue in favour of an

[4] V.A. Smith (1906), 'Pigmy Flints', *Indian Antiquary*, XXXV, pp. 185-95.

[5] J.A. Brown (1889), 'On Some Small, Highly Specialized Forms of Stone Implements Found in Asia, North Africa, and Europe', *RAI*, XVIII, pp. 134-9.

[6] T. Wilson (1894), 'Minute Stone Implements from India', *Annual Report of the Smithsonian Institution*, Washington D.C., June 1892, pp. 455-60.

[7] J.A. Brown (1892), 'On the Continuity of the Palaeolithic and Neolithic Periods', *JRAI*, XXII, pp. 66-98.

unbroken continuity between the Palaeolithic and Neolithic, setting forth four stages: the Eolithic, Palaeolithic, Mesolithic, and Neolithic.[8]

Unfortunately, for reasons unknown to us, other than a one-page note submitted to the Asiatic Society of Bengal at Calcutta (now Kolkata), Carlleyle never published the results of his investigations. He handed over his field notes to his friend, Rev. Reginald Gatty, who, in turn, passed them on to his friend, Vincent Smith, an officer of the British Indian Civil Service and a noted historian of India. Smith published these notes in *The Indian Antiquary* in 1906.[9] Carlleyle sold his collection of microliths to various museums in Europe and the United States where they were carefully curated. It is these widely dispersed collections and a few publications on them which help us in learning about his pioneering and precocious contribution to our knowledge of the Mesolithic period. Carlleyle's collections were examined by Brown, Black and Wilson who published notes on them.[10] His contemporary, J. Cockburn, studied the rock paintings and fossil fauna found in the region.[11] Due to his failure to publish his findings, Carlleyle became a shadowy and mysterious figure. There is even a controversy regarding the spelling of his name, as is seen from the references to his work cited above. Even the site of Morhana Pahar investigated by him was forgotten because of its location in remote forested hills, unconnected to any town or village byroad. It was due to the persistent efforts of Bridget and Raymond Allchin that this site was rediscovered in 1958.[12] This rediscovery led to a renewal of interest in the investigation of the site. It was excavated afresh in 1963-4 by the Archaeology Department of the Allahabad University but no new human skeletal remains were found.[13] Carlleyle's collections have been freshly studied and published by Sieveking and Cook and Martingell.[14]

[8]Binford (1968), op. cit., p. 314.

[9]Smith (1906), op. cit.

[10]Brown (1889), op. cit.; Brown (1892), op. cit.; G.F. Black (1892), 'Stone Implements from Asia and Africa', *Proceedings of the Society of Antiquaries of Scotland*, 2, pp. 407-12.

[11]J. Cockburn (1883a) 'On the Recent Existence of *Rhinoceros indicus* in the North-West Provinces, and Description of an Archaic Rock Painting from Mirzapur, Representing the Hunting of an Animal', *JRASB*, 52, pp. 56-64; idem (1883b), 'A Short Account of the Petrographs in the Caves and Rock Shelters of the Kaimur Range in Mirzapore District', *PASB*, pp. 125-6; idem (1899), 'Cave Drawings in the Kaimur Range, North-West Provinces', *JASB*, 18, pp. 89-97.

[12]B. Allchin (1958), 'Morhana Pahar: A Rediscovery', *Man*, 58, pp. 153-5.

[13]V.N. Misra (1965), 'Mesolithic Phase in the Prehistory of India', in V.N. Misra and M.S. Mate (eds.), *Indian Prehistory 1964*, Deccan College, Poona, pp. 57-85; K.K. Varma (1965), 'Comments on Mesolithic Phase in the Prehistory of India', in V.N. Misra and M.S. Mate (eds.), *Indian Prehistory 1964*, Deccan College, Poona, pp. 73-6; idem (1986), *The Mesolithic Age in Mirzapur*, Paramjyoti Prakashan, Allahabad.

[14]G.D.G. Sieveking (1960), 'Morhana Pahar: Or the Mystery of A.C. Carlleyle', *Man*, 140, 1, pp. 98-100; J. Cook and H.E. Martingell (1994), *The Carlleyle Collection of Stone Age Artefacts from Central India*, Occasional Papers of the Department of Prehistoric and Romano-British Antiquities, No. 95, British Museum, London.

Carlleyle's contemporary, the well-known geologist, Robert Bruce Foote, who is rightly regarded as the father of Indian prehistory because of his pioneering work, discovered many microlithic sites in different parts of south India and in Gujarat, including the now famous site of Langhnaj in Gujarat, in the last four decades of the nineteenth century. Unlike Carlleyle, Foote studied his collections of microliths as well as palaeoliths and other antiquities very meticulously and published detailed accounts of them, illustrating the finds with photographs and line drawings.[15] He also preserved his collections carefully. These were eventually purchased by the Madras Government Museum and displayed in a specially built hall.

In the 1920s, L.A. Cammiade, another amateur archaeologist, made collections of palaeoliths and microliths from stratified river deposits in the Eastern Ghats. These collections were examined by the Cambridge University archaeologist, M.C. Burkitt, who, together with Cammiade, published an account of them in 1930.[16] These authors proposed an evolutionary sequence of four phases of Stone Age industries in the Eastern Ghats and named them Series I to IV. Series IV comprised microliths which represented the Mesolithic phase. Small-scale diggings of microlith-bearing deposits were carried out by G.R. Hunter[17] and D.H Gordon[18] in the rock shelters at Pachmarhi in Madhya Pradesh in the 1930s.

However, a significant advance to our knowledge of this period was made only when H.D. Sankalia undertook excavations at Langhnaj and other sites in Gujarat in the early 1940s. Sankalia was motivated to pursue a career in archaeology by his teacher, Rev. Father Henry Heros, at St Xavier's College in Bombay (now Mumbai). He was trained in archaeology at the London University where he completed his Ph.D. thesis on the historic archaeology of Gujarat under the guidance of K.D.B. Codrington and F.J. Richards in 1935. While in London, Sankalia read the two volumes by Bruce Foote, learnt to identify stone tools of different periods and decided to follow up Foote's work on his return to India. In 1939, he was appointed Professor of Archaeology in the newly reopened Deccan College at Poona (now Pune). He got an opportunity to pursue his dream of 'carrying' forward Bruce Foote's

[15] R.B. Foote (1914), *The Foote Collection of Prehistoric and Protohistoric Antiquities: Catalogue Raisonne*, Madras Government Museum, Madras; idem (1916), *The Foote Collection of Prehistoric and Protohistoric Antiquities: Notes on Their Ages and Distribution,* Madras Government Museum, Madras.

[16] L.A. Cammiade and M.C. Burkitt (1930), 'Fresh Light on the Stone Age in South-east India', *Antiquity*, 4, pp. 327-39.

[17] G.R. Hunter (1935), 'Interim Report of the Excavation in the Dorothy Deep Shelter No. 1', *Nagpur University Journal*, 1, pp. 28-57; idem (1936), 'Final Report on the Excavation in the Mahadeo Hills', *Nagpur University Journal,* 2, pp. 127-44.

[18] D.H. Gordon (1938), 'The Microlithic Industries of India', *Man*, 38, pp. 91-100; idem (1950), 'Stone Industries of the Holocene in India and Pakistan', *Ancient India*, 6, pp. 64-90; idem (1958), *The Prehistoric Background of Indian Culture*, N.M. Tripathi Pvt. Ltd., Bombay.

work in Gujarat when, in 1940, Rai Bahadur K.N. Dikshit, then Director General of the Archaeological Survey of India, invited him to lead a prehistory expedition to Gujarat. He re-examined all the microlithic as well as Palaeolithic sites earlier discovered by Foote along the banks of the Sabarmati River, and carried out excavations at Langhnaj, Valasana, Akhaj and Hirpura. He excavated Langhnaj on several occasions from 1941 to 1949 and regularly published the results of his excavations.[19] He also enlisted the cooperation of biological anthropologists, Irawati Karve, his colleague at the Deccan College, and G.M. Kurulkar, an entomologist of the Govardhandas Medical College in Bombay for the study of human skeletal remains discovered from Langhnaj.[20]

In 1949, on the advice of Sir Mortimer Wheeler, a former Director General of the Archaeological Survey of India, Sankalia invited F.E. Zeuner, the well-known expert on quaternary climate and environment at the Institute of Archaeology, University of London, to examine the possibility of the presence of a buried soil horizon in the dune profile at Langhnaj. Zeuner succeeded in locating a faint soil horizon which was indicative of a moist interlude in the otherwise arid climate during the accumulation of the dune. He also examined the microlithic industry and faunal remains from the site. After examining the bruised surface of a rhinoceros shoulder blade, Zeuner drew the inference that the bone had probably been used as an anvil for producing microliths. He also examined the alluvial deposits of the Sabarmati, Mahi and Godavari rivers, and published several accounts of the prehistory and environment of western India.[21]

Zeuner took the faunal collection of Langhnaj with him to London where it was studied by his student, Juliet Clutton-Brock. This study was later published by the Deccan College as a monograph.[22] Zeuner returned to India

[19]H.D. Sankalia (1942), 'In Search of Early Man along the Sabarmati', *Journal of Gujarat Research Society*, 4, pp. 75-80; idem (1943), 'Pre and Protohistory of Gujarat', in K.M. Munshi (ed.), *The Glory That was Gurjar Desh*, Bharatiya Vidya Bhavan, Bombay, pp. 12-40; idem (1944), 'The Second Gujarat Prehistoric Expedition: A Preliminary Account of the Search of "Microlithic Man" in Gujarat', *New Indian Antiquary*, 7, 1, pp. 1-5; idem (1946a), 'The Age of Microlithic Culture in Gujarat', *Current Science*, 15, 1, pp. 11-13; idem (1946b), *Investigations into the Prehistoric Archaeology of Gujarat*, Baroda; idem (1955), 'Excavations at Langhraj, Gujarat', *Man*, 55, 33, p. 26; idem (1965), *Excavations at Langhraj: 1944-63*, Part I, *Archaeology*, Deccan College, Poona.

[20]I. Karve and G.M. Kurulkar (1945a), *A Preliminary Report on the Human Remains Found at Langhnaj in February and December 1944*, *Times of India*, Bombay; idem (1945b), *Human Remains Discovered So Far*, *Times of India*, Bombay; H.D. Sankalia and Irawati Karve (1949), 'Early Premitive Microlithic Culture and People of Gujarat', *American Anthropologist*, 51, pp. 28-34.

[21]F.E. Zeuner (1950), *The Stone Age and Pleistocene Chronology in Gujarat*, Deccan College, Poona; idem (1951), *Prehistory in India*, Deccan College, Poona; idem (1952), 'The Microlithic Industry of Langhnaj, Gujarat', *Man*, II, p. 182.

[22]J. Clutton-Brock (1965), *Excavations at Langhnaj 1944-63*, Part II: *The Fauna*, Deccan College, Poona.

in 1962 to deliver lectures at the M.S. University of Baroda on the prehistory and quaternary environment of India. These lectures were published as a monograph by the University.[23] On Sankalia's invitation, the human skeletal remains from Langhnaj were studied by the German and American anthropologists, Sophie Ehrhardt and Kenneth A.R. Kennedy. Their study was also published by the Deccan College.[24]

In 1949, Zeuner led an expedition on behalf of the Archaeological Survey of India to Balia Nalli in the Singrauli basin of the Mirzapur district of Uttar Pradesh and *teri* coastal dune sites in Tamil Nadu. A number of young prehistorians participated in this expedition. This resulted, among other things, in the publications of the palaeolithic and microlithic industries of the Singrauli basin by V.D. Krishnaswami and K.V. Soundara Rajan,[25] and the microlithic industry of the *teri* dunes by Zeuner and Bridget Allchin.[26]

In addition to his personal research, Sankalia inspired a large number of young researchers, both at the Deccan College and in other institutions in the country, to pursue research in prehistory. In 1949, one of Sankalia's brightest students, B. Subbarao, was appointed as the founding faculty of the newly established Department of Archaeology at the M.S. University of Baroda. As his first research project, Subbarao undertook an exploration of the Mahi River Valley in Gujarat. This exploration led to the discovery of a large number of Mesolithic sites. One of these, Amrapur, was excavated by Subbarao on a small scale.[27]

Sankalia was a pioneering leader of Indian prehistory with a unique devotion to the discipline of archaeology. When he began his research career, very few regions of the country had been systematically explored for prehistoric remains. He, therefore, encouraged his Ph.D. students to take up survey work as their research topics. As a result of this policy, several virgin regions were systematically explored and a large number of sites of different periods, including the Mesolithic, were discovered. Among these surveys, mention should be made of the following: V.N. Misra in Rajasthan;[28]

[23] F.E. Zeuner (1963), 'Environment of Early Man with Special Reference to the Tropical Regions', M.S. University, Baroda.

[24] S. Ehrhardt and K.A.R. Kennedy (1965), *Excavations at Langhnaj 1944-63*, Part III: *The Human Remains*, Deccan College, Poona.

[25] V.D. Krishnaswami and K.V. Soundara Rajan (1951), 'The Lithic Tool-industries of the Singrauli Basin', *Ancient India*, 7, pp. 40-5.

[26] F.E. Zeuner and B. Allchin (1956), 'The Microlithic Sites of Tinnevelly District, Madras State', *Ancient India*, 12, pp. 4-20.

[27] B. Subbarao (1952), 'Archaeological Explorations in the Mahi Valley', *Journal of the M.S. University of Baroda*, I, pp. 33-72.

[28] V.N. Misra (1961), 'The Stone Age Cultures of Rajputana', Ph.D. dissertation (unpublished), University of Poona, Poona.

A.P. Khatri,[29] Rameswar Singh,[30] Nisar Ahmed[31] and S.G. Supekar in Madhya Pradesh;[32] G.C. Mohapatra in Orissa;[33] S.A. Sali (1981) in Maharashtra; N. Isaac,[34] M.L.K. Murty,[35] S.N. Rao[36] and K.T. Reddy in Andhra Pradesh;[37] and K. Paddayya in Karnataka[38] (Fig. 6.1).

Among Sankalia's contemporaries who contributed to the study of the Mesolithic period, mention should be made of A. Aiyappan, K.R.U. Todd, S.M. Mathur, G.R. Sharma, and his students and colleagues. Aiyappan explored the *teri* site of Sawyerpuram and published an analysis of its microlithic industry.[39] Todd explored microlithic sites on the islands of Bombay.[40] S.M. Mathur located new microlithic sites in southern Mirzapur.[41] G.R. Sharma built one of the best departments of archaeology in the country at Allahabad University. Under his leadership, his former students and later colleagues, namely R.K. Varma, V.D. Misra, B.B. Misra, J.N. Pandey and J.N. Pal, discovered many Mesolithic sites in the Mirzapur district,[42] the Belan Valley in Allahabad district,[43] in the Ganga Valley in Allahabad and Pratapgarh

[29] A.P. Khatri (1958), 'Stone Age Cultures of Malwa', Ph.D. dissertation (unpublished) Poona University, Poona.

[30] Rameshwar Singh (1965), 'Palaeolithic Industries of Northern Bundelkhand', Ph.D. dissertation (unpublished), Poona University, Poona.

[31] N. Ahmed (1966), 'Stone Age Cultures of the Upper Son Valley', Ph.D. dissertation, Poona University, Poona.

[32] S.G. Supekar (1968), 'Pleistocene Stratigraphy and Prehistoric Archaeology of the Central Narmada Basin', Ph.D. dissertation (unpublished), Poona University, Poona.

[33] G.C. Mohapatra (1962), *The Stone Age Cultures of Orissa*, Deccan College, Poona.

[34] N. Isaac (1960), 'The Stone Age Cultures of Kurnool', Ph.D. dissertation (unpublished), University of Poona, Poona.

[35] Murty, M.L.K. (1966), 'Stone Age Cultures of Chittoor District', Ph.D. dissertation (unpublished), University of Poona, Poona.

[36] S.N. Rao (1966), 'Stone Age Cultures of Nalgonda', Ph.D. dissertation (unpublished), University of Poona, Poona.

[37] K.T. Reddy (1968), 'Prehistoric Cultures of the Cudappah Districts, Andhra Pradesh', Ph.D. dissertation (unpublished), University of Poona, Poona.

[38] K. Paddayya (1967), 'Hunsiholi: A Late Stone Age Site in the Krishna Valley', *Eastern Anthropologist*, 20, pp. 71-8.

[39] A. Aiyappan (1945), 'Mesolithic Artifacts from Sawyerpuram in Tinnevelly District, South India', *Spolia Zeylanica*, 24, 2, pp. 145-54.

[40] K.R.U. Todd (1950), 'Microlithic Industries of Bombay', *Ancient India*, 6, pp. 4-17.

[41] S.M. Mathur (1985), 'Notice of New Microlithic Sites from the Southern Mirzapur District, U.P.', *Science and Culture*, 20, pp. 446-7.

[42] Varma (1986), op. cit.

[43] G.R. Sharma et al. (1980), *Beginnings of Agriculture*, Abinash Prakashan, Allahabad.

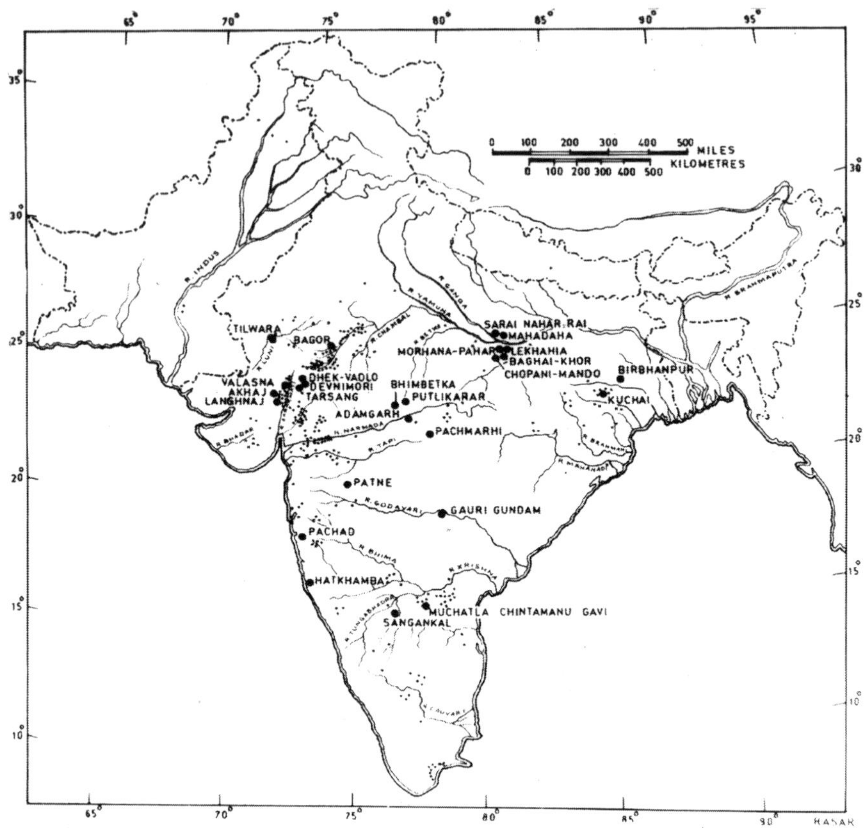

Fig. 6.1: Mesolithic sites in India

districts,[44] all in Uttar Pradesh, and in the Son Valley in the Rewa and Siddhi districts of Madhya Pradesh.[45]

After completing his Ph.D. work, V.N. Misra resumed his exploration of the Berach basin in south Rajasthan and discovered more than thirty Mesolithic sites.[46] In 1966, he and L.S. Leshnik carried out an archaeological exploration in Gujarat and Rajasthan and discovered a number of Mesolithic sites, including Tilwara and Bagor.[47]

[44]G.R. Sharma (1973), 'Mesolithic Lake Cultures in the Ganga Valley', *PPS* 39, pp. 129-46; idem (1975), 'Seasonal Migration and Mesolithic Lake Cultures of the Ganga Valley', in G.R. Sharma (ed.), *K.C. Chattopadhyaya Memorial Volume*, K.K. Dubey, Allahabad, pp. 1-20; Sharma et al. (1980), op. cit.

[45]G.R. Sharma and J.D. Clark (1983b), *Palaeoenvironments and Prehistory in the Middle Son Valley* (*Madhya Pradesh, North Central India*), Abinash Prakashan, Allahabad.

[46]V.N. Misra (1967), *Pre and Protohistory of the Berach Basin, South Rajasthan*, Deccan College, Poona.

[47]L.S. Leshnik (1968), 'Prehistoric Exploration in North Gujarat and Parts of Rajasthan', *EW* 18, 3-4, pp. 295-310; idem (1974), 'More Microliths from Gujarat and Some Thoughts on Langhnaj', in A. Ghosh (ed.), *Perspectives in Palaeoanthropology*, Firma K.L.

Explorations by Jerome Jacobson in Raisen district,[48] Zarine Cooper around the Chitrakoot Falls[49] on the Indravati River in Jagdalpur district, and Sheila Mishra in the Narmada Valley in Madhya Pradesh;[50] Sheila Mishra and her colleagues in the Godavari and Bhima valleys in western Maharashtra;[51] Ranjana Ray in some parts and Bishnupriya Basak in the Tarapheni Valley in the Midnapur district of West Bengal;[52] N. Isaac, M.L.K. Murty, S.N. Rao, K.T. Reddy, V.R. Reddy, V.V.M. Rao and P. Vijaya Prakash in Andhra Pradesh;[53] and P. Rajendran in Kerala[54] have led to the discovery of a large number of Mesolithic sites.

Mukhopadhyaya, Calcutta, pp. 249-58; V.N. Misra (1971a), 'Two Microlithic Sites in Rajasthan: A Preliminary Investigation', *Eastern Anthropologist*, XXIV, pp. 237-88; idem (1971b), 'Two Late Mesolithic Settlements in Rajasthan: A Brief Review of Investigations', *Poona University Journal* (Humanities), 35, pp. 59-79.

[48] J. Jacobson (1970), 'Microlithic Contexts in the Vindhyan Hills of Central India', Ph.D. dissertation (unpublished), Columbia University, New York; idem (1980), 'Investigations of Late Stone Age Adaptations in the Central Vindhyas', *ME*, IV, pp. 65-82.

[49] Zarine Cooper (1983a), 'CRT-19: A Mesolithic Site in Bastar District (M.P.), *ME*, VII, pp. 1-30; idem (1983b), 'Adaptation Patterns During the Late Stone Age in Bastar District, Madhya Pradesh', *Bulletin of the Indo-Pacific Prehistory Association*, 4, pp. 1-9; idem (1986), 'The Kuruk Fisherman of Bastar District, Central India', *Eastern Anthropologist*, 39, 1, pp. 1-20; idem (1997), *Prehistory of the Chitrakot Falls, Central India*, Ravish Publishers, Pune.

[50] S. Mishra (1999), 'Late Pleistocene Aridity in the Narmada Basin', in M.P. Tiwari and D.M. Mahabey (eds.), *Quaternary of India*, Gondwana Geological, Nagpur Society, p. 338..

[51] S. Mishra et al. (1998), 'Climatic Change during the Pleistocene/Holocene Transition in upland Western Maharashtra, Western India', in A.S. Issar and N. Brown (eds.), *Water, Environment and Society in Times of Climatic Change*, Kluwer Academic Publishers, Netherlands, pp. 323-33; idem (1999), 'Studies in the Geomorphology, Quaternary Palaeoenvironments and Archaeology of the Vel River, a Tributary of the Bhima in Western Maharashtra', *ME*, XXIV, 1, pp. 159-66; S. Mishra and S.N. Rajaguru (2001), 'Late Quaternary Palaeoclimates of Western India: A Geoarchaeological Approach', *Mansam*, 52, 1, pp. 286-96..

[52] Ranjana Ray (1975), 'Studies on the Blade-Bladelet Industries in India', Ph.D. dissertation (unpublished), Calcutta University, Calcutta; idem (1985), 'The "Blade-Bladelet" Industries of India', in V.N. Misra and P. Bellwood (eds.), *RAIP*, Oxford-IBH, New Delhi, pp. 123-7; Bishnupriya Basak (1997), 'Microlithic Sites in the Tarapheni Valley, Midnapur District, West Bengal: A Discussion', *ME*, XXII, 2, pp. 11-28.

[53] Issac (1960), op. cit.; Murty (1966), op. cit.; Rao (1966); op. cit.; K.T. Reddy (1968), op. cit.; V.R. Reddy (1968), op. cit.; V.V.M. Rao (1979), 'Stone Age Cultures of Prakasham District', Ph.D. dissertation (unpublished), Andhra University, Waltair; P.V. Prakash (1989), 'Mesolithic Adaptations: A Case Study from Visakhapatnam Region', *Andhra Pradesh History Congress*, 13, pp. 29-31; idem (1998), 'Vangasari: A Mesolithic Cave in the Eastern Ghats, Andhra Pradesh', *ME*, XXIII, 2, pp. 1-16.

[54] P. Rajendran (1983a), 'The Mesolithic Industries from South Kanara, Karnataka', *BDCRI*, 42, pp. 133-7; idem (1983b), 'The Coastal Mesolithic Industries of South India and their Chronology', *Bulletin of the Indo-Pacific Prehistory Association*, 3, pp. 18-31; idem (1984), 'A Preliminary Report on Tenmalai Rockshelter: A Late Mesolithic Site in

In western Maharashtra, Sheila Mishra and her associates have discovered microliths, often associated with burning activity and hearths, in alluvial deposits, dated by the radiocarbon method from the early to late Holocene, at Talegaon on the Vel River, a tributary of the Bhima, at Ranjegaon and Saksbalpimpri on the Sindhphana River, a tributary of the Godavari, at Akoni on the Nandi River, a tributary of the Bhima, and at Apegaon and Dharangaon on the Godavari.

One of the most intensively explored regions in the country is Orissa. Since the late 1950s, a number of archaeologists have been actively engaged in Stone Age research in this state. They include

G.C. Mohapatra,[55]
K.C. Tripathy,[56]
K.C. Tripathy and U.C. Mohanty,[57]
S.C. Nanda,[58]
S.B. Ota,[59]
S.K. Mishra,[60]
P.K. Behera,[61]

Kerala, South India', *Bulletin of the Indo-Pacific Prehistory Association*, 5, pp. 20-3; idem (1985), 'The Mesolithic Industries of North Kerala', *RAIP*, Oxford-IBH, New Delhi, pp. 165-70.

[55]Mohapatra (1962), op. cit.

[56]K.C. Tripathy (1970), 'Microlithic Industry of Bhubaneswar', *Prakruti, Utkal University Journal of Science*, 7, pp. 77-92; idem (1972), 'Lithic Industries of Southwestern Orissa', Ph.D. dissertation (unpublished), Utkal University, Bhubaneswar; idem (1973), 'South Orissan Prehistory: The First Record of Stone Age Tools', *Asian Perspectives*, 4, pp. 47-59; idem (1977), 'Prehistoric Studies in Orissa', in M.N. Das (ed.), *Sidelights on History and Culture of Orissa*, Vidyapuri, Cuttack, Orissa; idem (1980), *Lithic Industries in India: A Study of South-western Orissa*, Inter-India Publication, New Delhi.

[57]K.C. Tripathy and U.C. Mohanty (1972), 'Lithic Industries of South-western Orissa', *Prakruti, Utkal University Journal of Science*, 9, pp. 1-2.

[58]S.C. Nanda (1984), 'Stone Age Cultures of Indravati Basin, Koraput District, Orissa', Ph.D. dissertation (unpublished), University of Poona, Poona; idem (1985), The Microlithic Cultures of the Indravati Valley, District Koraput, Orissa', *RAIP*, Oxford-IBH, New Delhi, pp. 159-65.

[59]S.B. Ota (1982-83), 'New Research Designs in the Prehistoric Research in Orissa with Special Reference to Pebble Industry of North Boudh-Kondhmal District, Orissa', *Manav*, 1, pp. 160-80; idem (1986), 'Mesolithic Culture of the Phulbani District (Orissa): With Special Referance to the Heavy Duty Tol Implements', *BDCRI*, 45, pp. 47-56.

[60]S.K. Mishra (1987-8), 'Stone Age Antiquities of Joshipur, Orissa: A Survey', *Man in Society*, 3, pp. 81-8; idem (1990), 'Stone Age Remains and Palaeohuman Activities in the Burhabalang and Chipat River Valleys of Orissa', *Man in Society*, 4, pp. 21-33.

[61]P.K. Behera (1989), 'Archaeology of Sundargarh District with Special Reference to the Brahmani Valley, Orissa', Ph.D. dissertation (unpublished), Banaras Hindu University, Varanasi.

P.K. Mohanty,[62]
S. Chakrabarti,[63]
Balaram Tripathy[64] and
K.K. Basa.[65]

As a result of investigations by these archaeologists, several hundred Mesolithic sites have been discovered in Orissa. The sites are found in all the hilly and forested districts in the central and western parts of the state. These districts comprise Mayurbhanj, Sundargarh, Sambalpur, Bolangir, Kalahandi, Kondhmal, Dhenkanal, Koraput, Boudh, Phulbani, Ganjam, Bhubaneswar, Khurda, and Jajpur. The sites are mostly located along the banks of perennial rivers like the Mahanadi, Brahmani, and Baitarni, as well as along their tributaries like the Indravati, Jira, Chipat, Bagh, Tel, Salunki and Mehrni. Microlithic artefacts have been collected from the alluvial surfaces, river sections and rocky surfaces, away from the river banks.

G.C. Mohapatra explored the major rivers in the districts of Mayurbhanj, Keonjhar, Sundargarh, Sambalpur and Dhenkanal, and discovered some twenty-five Mesolithic sites.[66] S.C. Nanda discovered eighty-five Mesolithic sites in the Indravati Valley in the Koraput district, and attempted an ecological and ethnographic explanation for the location of the site, as also an insight into the adaptive strategies of the Mesolithic population.[67]

In the 1980s, P.K. Mohanty carried out investigations along the banks of small, seasonal streams in the Keonjhar district and discovered a number of sites. The artefact assemblage of this ecozone consists of microliths in association with heavy-duty implements like choppers and ring stones. He

[62]P. Mohanty (1988-89), 'The Mesolithic Cultures of Keonjhar District, Orissa with Special Reference to the Heavy-duty Tool Component: A Functional Interpretation', *BDCRI* 47-8, pp. 227-37; idem (1989), 'Mesolithic Settlement System of the Keonjhar District, Orissa', Ph.D. dissertation (unpublished), University of Poona, Poona; idem (1992), 'Stone Age Research in Orissa: An Overview', *Man in India*, 72, pp. 207-32; idem (1993), 'Mesolithic Hunter-gatherers of Keonjhar District, Orissa', *Asian Perspectives,* 32, pp. 85-104.

[63]S. Chakrabarti (1990), 'The Stone Age Prehistory of Khiching, Orissa', *ME*, XV, 1-2, pp. 13-21.

[64]B. Tripathy (1995), 'Prehistory of Boudh District, Orissa', *Boudh District Souvenir*, Satyanarayan Press, Cuttack, pp. 8-16; idem (1996-7), 'Archaeological Exploration Around Boudh District, Orissa: A Preliminary Report', *BDCRI*, 56-7, pp. 41-54; idem (2000), 'Archaeology of Boudh District: Central Orissa', in K.K. Basa and P. Mohanty (eds.), *Archaeology of Orissa*, Pratibha Prakashan, New Delhi, pp. 397-416; idem (2001), 'Archaeology of Boudh District, Orissa with Special Reference to Early Historic Settlement Pattern', Ph.D. dissertation (unpublished), Deccan College Postgraduate and Research Institute, Pune; P. Mohanty et al. (1997), 'Stone Age Cultures of Mayurbhanj District, Orissa, *Man in India*, 77, 2-3, pp. 159-77.

[65]Mohanty et al. (1997), op. cit.

[66]Mohapatra (1962), op. cit.

[67]Nanda (1984), op. cit.; idem (1985), op. cit.

also used ethnographic and ecological parameters as analytic tools for studying the lithic assemblages, and suggested the probable function of heavy-duty tools with the help of ethnographic parallels.[68]

Many Mesolithic sites were explored in the Moter and Behra River basins of the Brahmani valleys in the Kalahandi[69] and Dhenkanal districts by P.K. Singh[70] B.K. Khilar[71] and S. Biswal.[72]

In the districts of Boudh, a systematic exploration was carried out, in the Mahanadi and its tributaries, the Bagh and Tel, by S.B. Ota, who discovered thirty sites with microliths and heavy-duty tools in the alluvial deposits.[73] Later on, Balaram Tripathy explored the Mahanadi and Salunki River valleys and discovered fifteen Mesolithic sites.[74] All the sites have produced a typical microlithic industry, comprising both geometric and non-geometric tools. A large number of ring stones were associated with microliths/Ethnographic studies revealed the use of these stones for curing domestic animals of epilepsy. It is a belief in Orissa that if ring stones are kept in the cowshed, no evil spirit will harm the cattle.

In the last five decades or so, several thousand Mesolithic sites have been discovered in widely separated areas of India. Thirty-three of the explored Mesolithic sites have been excavated on varying scales.

These comprise:

Langhnaj,[75]

Valasana,[76]

Akhaj,[77]

[68]Mohanty (1988-9), op. cit.; idem (1989), op. cit.; idem (1992), op. cit.; idem (1993), op. cit.

[69]Behera (1989), op. cit.

[70]P.K. Singh (1988), 'Cultural Succession of Prehistoric Cultures in Central Orissa', in K.L. Bhowmick (ed.), *Culture of the Past*, Inter India Publications, New Delhi, pp. 87-99.

[71]B.K. Khilar (2001), 'Paleohistory of Parjang, District Dhenkanal', Ph.D. dissertation (unpublished), Utkal University, Bhubaneswar, Orissa.

[72]S. Biswal (2001), 'Palaeohistory of Kamakshanagar Region, District Dhenkanal', Ph.D. dissertation (unpublished) Utkal University, Bhubaneswar, Orissa.

[73]Ota (1982-3), op. cit.; idem (1986), op. cit.

[74]Tripathi (1995), op. cit.; idem (1996-97), op. cit.; idem (2000), op. cit.; idem (2001), op. cit.; P. Mohanty and B. Tripathy (1998), The Prehistoric, Protohistoric and the Early Historic Cultures of Oriss', *Pragdhara*, pp. 69-98.

[75]Sankalia (1942), op. cit.; idem (1943), op. cit.; idem (1944), op. cit.; idem (1946a), op. cit.; idem (1946b), op. cit.; idem (1955), op. cit.; idem (1965), op. cit.; Sankalia and Karve (1949), op. cit.; Karve and Kurulkar (1945a), op. cit.; idem (1945b), op. cit.; Zeuner (1952), op. cit.; G. Karve-Corvinus and K.A.R. Kennedy (1964), 'Preliminary Report on Langhnaj: The Preliminary Report of the 1963 Archaeological Expendition to Langhnaj, Northern Gujarat', *BDCRI*, 24, pp. 44-57; Ehrhardt and Kennedy (1965), op. cit.; Clutton-Brock (1965), op. cit.

[76]Sankalia (1946b), op. cit.

[77]Ibid.

Hirpura,[78]
Amarpura,[79]
Dhek Vadio,[80]
Devnimori,[81]
Tarsang,[82]
Dhansura in Gujarat,[83]
Tilwada,[84]
Bagor in Rajasthan,[85]
Patne (Sali 1989),
Pachad and Hathkamba in Maharashtra,[86]
Pachmarhi,[87]

[78] Ibid.

[79] Subbarao (1952), op. cit.

[80] S.C. Malik (1966), 'The Late Stone Age Industries from Excavated Sites in Gujarat, India', *Artibus Asiae*, XXVIII, pp. 167-74.

[81] Ibid.

[82] V.H. Sonawane (1983), 'The Microlithic Industry of Tarsang, Gujarat', *ME*, VII, pp. 31-8.

[83] V.N. Misra and Suman Pandya (1989), 'Mesolithic Occupations Around Dhansura, Sabarkantha District, Gujarat: A Preliminary Study', *ME*, XIV, 1, pp. 123-7.

[84] V.N. Misra (1968), 'Late Stone Age in Rajasthan', *Proceedings of the Rajasthan History Congress,* First Session, Jaipur, pp. 16-22; idem (1970a), 'Cultural Significance of Three Copper Arrowheads from Rajasthan, India', *JNES*, 29, 4, pp. 221-32; idem (1970b), 'Evidence for a New Chalcolithic Culture in Rajasthan', *Indian Antiquary* (Third Series) IV, 1-4, pp. 85-95; idem (1971a), op. cit.; idem (1971b), op. cit.

[85] V.N. Misra (1973a), 'Bagor: A Late Mesolithic Settlement in North-west India', *World Archaeology*, 5, 1, pp. 92-110; idem (1973c), 'New Light on the Mesolithic Period in India from Excavations at Bagor in Rajasthan', *The Researcher*, XII-XIII, pp. 1-14; idem (1973d), 'A New Prehistoric Ceramic from Rajasthan', *EW*, 23, 3-4, pp. 295-305; idem (1982), 'Bagor: The Archaeological Setting', in J.R. Lukacs et al. (eds.), *Bagor and Tilwana: Late Mesolithic Cultures of North-west India*, vol. 1: *The Human Skeletal Remains*, Deccan College, Poona, pp. 9-26; idem (1989c), 'Bagor', in A. Ghosh (ed.), *An Encyclopaedia of Indian Archaeology*, vol. 2, Munshiram Manoharlal, New Delhi, pp. 35-7; V.N. Misra and Malti Nagar (1981), 'The Microlithic Industry of Bagor, Rajasthan', in V.S. Srivastava (ed.), *Cultural Countries of India: Dr. Satya Prakash Felicitation Volume*, Abhinav, New Delhi, pp. 6-11; J.R. Lukacs (1982), 'Biological Anthropology of Human Skeletal from Bagor: Dentition', in J.R. Lukacs et al. (eds.), *Bagor and Tilwara: Late Mesolithic Cultures of North-west India*, vol. 1: *The Human Skeletal Remains*, Deccan College, Poona, pp. 61-94; K.A.R. Kennedy (1982), 'Biological Anthropology of Human Skeletal Remains from Bagor: Osteology', in J.R. Lukacs et al. (eds.), *Bagor and Tilwara: Late Mesolithic Cultures of Northwest India*, vol. I: *The Human Skeletal Remains*, Deccan College, Poona, pp. 27-60.

[86] R.V. Joshi and B.P. Bopardikar (1972), 'Stone Age Cultures of Konkan (Coastal Maharashtra)', in S.B. Deo (ed.), *Archaeological Congress and Seminar Papers*, Nagpur University Press, Nagpur, pp. 47-57.

[87] Hunter (1935), op. cit.; idem (1936), op. cit.; Gordon (1950), op. cit.

Adamgarh,[88]
Bhimbetka,[89]
Patli Karar[90]
Baghor II,[91]
Baghor III,[92]
Ghagharia I rockshelter in Madhya Pradesh;[93]

[88] R.V. Joshi (1978), *Stone Age Cultures of Central India*, Deccan College, Poona; R.V. Joshi and M.D. Khare (1966), 'Microlith-bearing Deposits of Adamgarh Rockshelters', in D. Sen and A.K. Ghosh (eds.), *Studies in Prehistory: Robert Bruce Foote Memorial Volume*, Firma K.L. Mukhopadhyaya, Calcutta, pp. 90-5.

[89] V.N. Misra (1985), 'Microlithic Industries in India', in V.N. Misra and P. Bellwood (eds.), *Recent Advances in Indo-Pacific Prehistory*, Oxford-IBH, New Delhi, pp. 111-22; idem (1989d), 'Bhimbetka', in A. Ghosh (eds.), *An Encylopaedia of Indian Archaeology*, Munshiram Manoharlal, New Delhi, pp. 69-73; idem (2002), 'Excavations of Human Burials', in K.A.R. Kennedy et al. (eds.), *The Biological Anthropology of Human Skeletal Remains from Bhimbetka, Central India*, Indian Society for Prehistoric and Quaternary Studies, Pune, pp. 7-25; V.N. Misra et al. (1977), *Bhimbetka: Prehistoric Man and His Art in Central India*, Exhibition Souvenir, Salak Press, Poona; K.A.R. Kennedy (2002), 'Skeletal Biology (Misra and Wakankar Series)', in K.A.R. Kennedy et al., *The Biological Anthropology of Human Skeletal Remains from Bhimbetka, Central India,* Indian Society for Prehistoric and Quaternary Studies, Pune, pp. 75-99; K.A.R. Kennedy et al. (1981), 'Dental Mutilations from Prehistoric India', *CA*, 22, 3, pp. 285-6; J.R. Lukacs (2002), 'Skeletal Biology (Haas Series)', in *The Biological Anthropology of Human Skeletal Remains from Bhimbetka, Central India*, Indian Society for Prehistoric and Quaternary Studies, Pune; J.R. Lukacs and K.A.R. Kennedy (2002), 'The Place of the Bhimbetka Skeletal Record in South Asian Palaeoanthropology', in K.A.R. Kennedy et al. (eds.), *The Biological Anthropology of Human Skeletal Remains from Bhimbetka, Central India,* Indian Society for Prehistoric and Quaternary Studies, Pune; K.A.R. Kennedy et al. (2002), *The Biological Anthropology of Human Skeletal Remains from Bhimbetka, Central India,* Indian Society for Prehistoric and Quaternary Studies, Pune; S.C. Tiwari (2002), 'Skeletal Biology (Misra Series)', in K.A.R. Kennedy et al. (eds.), *The Biological Anthropology of Human Skeletal Remains . . .*, pp. 27-40; V.S. Wakankar (1973), 'Bhimbetka Excavations', *JIH*, 51, pp. 23-32; idem (1975a), 'Bhimbetka: The Prehistoric Paradise', *Prachya Pratibha*, 3, 2, pp. 7-29; idem (1975b), 'Prehistoric Cave Paintings', *Marg*, 28, 4, pp. 17-34; idem (2002), 'Burial Systems in Bhimbetka', in K.A.R. Kennedy et al. (eds.), *The Biological Anthropology of Human Skeletal Remains*, pp. 1-5.

[90] Jacobson (1970), op. cit.; idem (1980), op. cit.

[91] C. Sussman (1893), 'Preliminary Report on Excavations at the Mesolithic Occupation Site at Baghor II Locality', in G.R. Sharma and J.D. Clark (eds.), *Palaeoenvironments and Prehistory in the Middle Son Valley* (*Madhya Pradesh, North Central India*), Abinash Prakashan, Allahabad, pp. 161-96.

[92] J.D. Clark and R. Dreiman (1983), 'An Occurrence with Small Blade Technology in the Upper Member of the Baghor Formation at the Baghor III Locality', in G.R. Sharma and J.D. Clark (eds.), *The Palaeoenvironments and Prehistory in the Middle Son Valley* (*Madhya Pradesh, North-Central India*), Abinash Prakashan, Allahabad, pp. 205-39.

[93] S.A. Brandt et al. (1983), 'Rockshelters with Paintings on the Top of the Kaimur Escarpment at Ghagharia and an Account of the Excavation and Analysis of the Mesolithic

Lekhania,[94]
Morhana Pahar,[95]
Baghai Khor,[96]
Sarai Nahar Rai,[97]
Mahadaha,[98]
Damdama,[99]
Chopani Mando in Uttar Pradesh,[100]
Sangankallu in Karnataka;[101]
Muchalta Chintaanu Gavi in Andhra Pradesh,[102]
Tenmalai in Kerala,[103]
Paisra in Bihar,[104]

Occupation at the Ghagharia I Shelter', in G.R. Sharma and J.D. Clark (eds.), *The Palaeoenvironments and Prehistory in the Middle Son Valley* (*Madhya Pradesh, North-Central India*), Abinash Prakashan, Allahabad, pp. 205-39.

[94]G.R. Sharma (1965), 'Comments on Mesolithic Phase in the Prehistory of India', in V.N. Misra and M.S. Mate (eds.), *Indian Prehistory 1964*, Deccan College, Poona, pp. 76-9; J.R. Lukacs and V.D. Misra (1997), 'The People of Lekhahia: A Bioarchaeological Analysis of Late Mesolithic Hunter-foragers of North India', in R. Allchin and B. Allchin (eds.), *SAA*, Oxford and IBH, New Delhi, pp. 873-89.

[95]Varma (1965), op. cit.

[96]Varma (1965), op. cit.; idem (1986), op. cit.; K.A.R. Kennedy (1990a), 'Porotic Hyperostosis on Human Remains from Mesolithic Baghai Khor', *BDCRI*, 49, pp. 183-98.

[97]Sharma (1973), op. cit.; idem (1975), op. cit.; Sharma et al. (1980), op. cit.; K.A.R. Kennedy et al. (1986), *Mesolithic Human Remains from the Gangetic Plain: Sarai Nahar Rai*, Cornell University, Ithaca.

[98]Sharma et al. (1980), op. cit.

[99]J.N. Pal (1986), 'Microlitic Industry of Damdama', *Puratattva*, 16, pp. 1-5; idem (1988), 'Mesolithic Double Burials from Recent Excavations at Damdama', *ME*, XII, pp. 115-22; idem (1992), 'Mesolithic Human Burials in the Gangetic Plain, North India', *ME*, XVII, 2, pp. 35-44; idem (1994), 'Mesolithic Settlements in the Ganga Plain', *ME*, XIX, 1-2, pp. 91-102; J.N. Pandey (1990), 'Mesolithic in the Middle Ganga Valley', *BDCRI*, 49, pp. 311-16; idem (1996), 'Burial Practices and Funerary Practices of Mesolithic India', in G.E. Afanas'ev et al. (eds.), *Bioarchaeology of Mesolithic India: An Integrated Approach*, Colloqurium XXXIII of the International Union of Prehistoric and Protohistoric Sciences, ABACO Edizioni, Forli, pp. 279-90; R.K. Varma et al. (1985), 'A Preliminary Report on the Excavations at Damdama (1982-4), *ME*, IX, pp. 45-65.

[100]Sharma et al. (1980), op. cit.

[101]H.D. Sankalia (1969), *Mesolithic and Pre-Mesolithic Industries from the Excavations at Sangankallu, Bellary*, Deccan College, Poona.

[102] M.L.K. Murty (1981), 'Hunter-gatherer Ecosystems and Archaeological Patterns of Subsistence Behaviour on the South-east Coast of India: An Ethnographic Model', *World Archaeology*, 13, 1, pp. 47-58.

[103]Rajendran (1984), op. cit.

[104]P.C. Pant and V. Jayaswal (1991), *Paisra: The Stone Age Settlement of Bihar*, Agam Kala Prakashan, Delhi.

Kuchai in Orissa,[105]
Birbhanpur in West Bengal.[106]

A list of the excavated sites with more details is given in Table 6.1. In addition to references to individual sites cited above, there are several other publications dealing with the Mesolithic sites of the Ganga plain.[107] From time to time, regional and national level reviews of Mesolithic studies have appeared which reflect the progress in Mesolithic research in the country.[108]

[105]B.K. Thapar (1989), 'Kuchai', in A. Ghosh (ed.), *An Encyclopaedia of Indian Archaeology* Munshiram Manoharlal, New Delhi, p. 240.

[106]B.B. Lal (1958), 'Birbhanpur, A Microlithic Site in the Damodar Valley, West Bengal', *Ancient India*, 14, pp. 4-48.

[107]V.D. Misra (1977), *Some Aspects of Indian Archaeology*, Prabhat Prakashan, Allahabad; idem (1996), 'History and Context of Mesolithic Research at Allahabad University, Allahabad, India', in G.E. Afanas'ev et al. (eds.), *Bioarchaeology of Mesolithic India: An Integrated Approach*, Colloquium XXXIII of the International Union of Prehistoric and Protohistoric Science, ABACO Edizioni, Forli, pp. 245-50; J.N. Pal (1992), op. cit.; idem (1994), op. cit.; idem (1996), 'Lithic Use Wear Analysis and Subsistence Activities among the Mesolithic People of North India', in G.E. Afanas'ev et al., *Bioarchaeology of Mesolithic India*, pp. 267-77; D.P. Sharma and M. Sharma (1987), 'A Reappraisal of the Chronology of the Mesolithic and Neolithic Cultures of the Vindhyas and Middle Ganga Valley', in B.M. Pande and B.D. Chattopadhyay (eds.), *Archaeology and History*, Agam Kala Prakashan, Delhi, pp. 57-66; I. Chattopadhyay and U. Chattopadhyay (1990), 'The Spatial Organization of Mortuary Practices in the Mesolithic Ganga Valley: Implications for Territoriality', in N.C. Ghosh and S. Chakrabarti (eds.), *Adaptations and Other Essays*, Visva-Bharati, Santiniketan, pp. 103-21.

[108]B. Allchin (1966), *The Stone-Tipped Arrow: Late Stone-Age Hunters of the Tropical Old World*, Barnes and Noble, New York; B. Allchin and R. Allchin (1982), *The Rise of Civilization in India and Pakistan*, Cambridge University Press, Cambridge; V.N. Misra (1965), op. cit.; idem (1966), 'Stone Age Research in Rajasthan: A Review', in D. Sen and A.K. Ghosh (eds.), *Studies in Prehistory: Robert Bruce Foote Memorial Volume*, Firma K.L. Mukhopadhyay, Calcutta; idem (1973b), 'Problems of Palaeoecology, Palaeoclimate and Chronology of the Microlithic Cultures of Western India', in D.P. Agrawal and A. Ghosh (eds.), *Radiocarbon and Indian Archaeology*, Tata Institute of Fundamental Research, Bombay, pp. 58-72; idem (1976a), 'Ecological Adaptations during the Terminal Stone Age in Western and Central India', in K.A.R. Kennedy and G.L. Possehl (eds.), *Ecological Backgrounds of South Asian Prehistory*, Cornell University, Ithaca, pp. 28-51; idem (1976c), 'Prehistory and Palaeoenvironment in Rajasthan', in D.P. Agrawal and B.M. Pande (eds.), *Archaeology and Palaeoenvironment in Western India*, Concept, New Delhi, pp. 31-54; idem (1985), op. cit.; idem (1989a), 'Stone Age India: An Ecologial Perspective', *ME*, XIV, 1, pp. 17-64; idem (1989b), 'Mesolithic Cultures', in A. Ghosh (ed.), *An Encyclopaedia of Indian Archaeology*, vol. 1, Munshiram Manoharlal, New Delhi, pp. 37-43; idem (1996), 'Mesolithic India: History and Current Status of Research', in G.E. Afanas'ev et al. (eds.), *Bioarchaeology of Misolithic India: An Integrated Approach*, Colloquium XXXIII of the International Union of Prehistoric and Protohistoric Sciences, ABACO, Edizioni, Forli, pp. 321-8; idem (2001), 'Prehistoric Human Colonization of India', *Journal of Bioscience*, 26, 4, Supplement Volume, pp. 491-531; V.N. Misra and

Table 6.1: List of Excavated Mesolithic Sites

Name of the site	Coordinates	District	State	References
Tilwara	72° 50′ : 25° 52′	Barmer	Rajasthan	Misra 1971a, 1971b
Bagor	74° 23′: 25° 21′	Bhilwara	Rajasthan	Misra 1971a, 1971b, 1973; Lukacs, Misra and Kennedy 1973
Langhnaj	72° 32′; 23° 27′	Mehsana	Gujarat	Sankalia 1946, 1956, 1965; Sankalia and Karve 1949; Corvinus and Kennedy 1964
Akhaj	72° 31′: 23° 28′	Mehsana	Gujarat	Sankalia 1946, 1965
Valasana	72° 15′: 23° 50′	Mehsana	Gujarat	Sankalia 1946, 1965
Hirpura	72°46′: 23° 35′	Mehsana	Gujarat	Sankalia 1946, 1965
Amrapur	73° 15′: 22° 38′	Baroda	Gujarat	Subbarao 1953
Devnimori	73° 23′: 23° 42′	Sabarkantha	Gujarat	Malik 1966
Dhek Vadio	73° 23′: 23° 42′	Sabarkantha	Gujarat	Malik 1966
Tarsang		Baroda	Gujarat	Sonawane 1983
Patne	74° 58′: 20° 19′	Jalgaon	Maharashtra	Sali 1974
Pachad	73° 24′: 18° 14′	Pune	Maharashtra	Joshi and Bopardikar 1972
Hathkamba	73°24′: 17° 00′	Ratnagiri	Maharashtra	Joshi and Bopardikar 1972
Morhana Pahar	82° 31′: 24° 30′	Mirzapur	Uttar Pradesh	Sharma 1965; Varma 1964, 1965
Lekhania		Mirzapur	Uttar Pradesh	Sharma 1965
Baghai Khor		Mirzapur	Uttar Pradesh	Varma 1963
Sarai Nahar Rai	81° 50′: 25° 48′	Pratapgarh	Uttar Pradesh	Sharma 1973, 1975

Malti Nagar (1976), 'Prehistoric Background of Rajasthan', in R. Subrahmanyam and N. Rameshan (eds.), *Somasekhara Sarma Commemoration Volume*, Government of Andhra Pradesh, Hyderabad, pp. 345-59; H.D. Sankalia (1963), *Prehistory and Protohistory in India and Pakistan*, University of Bombay, Bombay; idem (1974), *The Prehistory and Protohistory of India and Pakistan*, Deccan College, Poona; Kennedy (2000), op. cit.

Mahadaha	81° 11′: 25° 29′	Pratapgarh	Uttar Pradesh	Sharma et al. 1980
Damdama	82° 10: 26° 10′	Pratapgarh	Uttar Pradesh	Pal 1986, 1988, 1992, V.D. Misra 1992; Varma et al. 1985
Chopani Mando	82° 05′: 24° 56′	Allahabad	Uttar Pradesh	Sharma et al. 1980
Pachmarhi	78° 28′: 22° 26′	Hoshangabad	Madhya Pradesh	Hunter 1935, 1936; Gordon 1950
Adamgarh	77° 45′: 22° 45′	Hoshangabad	Madhya Pradesh	Joshi 1978
Putli Karar	79° 00′: 23° 15′	Raisen	Madhya Pradesh	Jacobson 1970
Bhimbetka	77° 37′: 22° 66′	Raisen	Madhya Pradesh	Misra et al. 1977; Wakankar 1976
Baghor II	82° 11′: 24° 35′	Sidhi	Madhya Pradesh	Sussman et al. 1983
Baghor III		Sidhi	Madhya Pradesh	Clark and Dreiman (eds.) 1983
Ghagharia I		Sidhi	Madhya Pradesh	Brandt et al. 1983
Paisra	86°26′: 25° 08′	Mungher	Bihar	Pant and Jayaswal 1991
Kuchai	86° 43′: 22° 21′	Mayurbhanj	Orissa	*IAR* 1961-62: 36
Birbhanpur	87° 17′: 23° 30′	Burdwan	West Bengal	Lal 1958
Sanganakkal	79° 55′: 15° 08′	Bellary	Karnataka	Subbarao 1948; Sankalia 1969
Tenmalai	08° 58′: 77° 04′	Quilon	Kerala	Rajendran 1984
Muchatla Chintamanu Gavi		Kumoo	Andhra Pradesh	Murty 1981

GEOGRAPHICAL DISTRIBUTION, SETTLEMENT PATTERN AND DEMOGRAPHIC IMPLICATIONS

Mesolithic sites are now known from almost all over India though their density is greater in some areas than in others (Fig. 6.1). The total absence of sites over much of the Ganga plain is obviously due to its remoteness from the sources of primary raw material, i.e. stone for making implements. Similarly, the absence of sites in north-east India and their sparseness in the Western Ghats and along the west coast is probably due to heavy rainfall

Fig. 6.2: Bhimbetka Hill showing rocks with shelters at their base on the densly wooded valley

and the consequent dense vegetation which is likely to have inhibited human habitation. Mesolithic people extended colonization into virgin areas like the Ganga plains and the peninsula south of the Kaveri River, as well as into previously inhabited areas. They settled in very different kinds of environments and exploited a great variety of food resources. In Gujarat, Marwar and, to some extent, Mewar as well, they settled on sand dunes. In Marwar, which is excessively arid today, microliths are found on top of almost every sand dune. The same is true of the Gujarat plain. Here the dunes are usually clustered in a circular form enclosing a lake which provided water to humans and animals, and was a source of aquatic food.

In the densely wooded and hilly country of central India and the Eastern Ghats, people inhabited caves and rock shelters (Fig. 6.2). The forests here are an abundant supply of plant and animal food.[109] On the islands around Bombay, they settled on the tops of low hills and rock outcrops near the sea shore.[110] Near the tip of the peninsula, they occupied coastal dunes. In both

[109]M.L.K. Murty (1985), 'The Uses of Plant Foods by Some Hunter-gatherer Communities in Andhra Pradesh', in V.N. Misra and P. Bellwood (eds.), *RAIP*, Oxford-IBH, New Delhi, pp. 329-36; M. Nagar (1985), 'The Use of Wild Plant Foods by Aboriginal Communities in Central India', in V.N. Misra and P. Bellwood (eds.), *RAIP*, Oxford-IBH, New Delhi, pp. 337-42.

[110]Todd (1950), op. cit.

these regions, marine food must have formed the main basis of subsistence. On the south-central margin of the Ganga plain, horse-shoe lakes formed by meandering rivers attracted Mesolithic populations. Biological remains from sites in this region show that the settlers exploited both terrestrial and aquatic fauna. Elsewhere, people lived in the open, on top of low hills, in the valleys and along the banks of perennial as well as seasonal streams. On the Deccan plateau, for example, microliths are found on the top of almost every hill and rocky eminence. The abundance of sites in such areas of limited and uncertain rainfall shows that settlements must have been of a seasonal nature.

The colonization of virgin areas like the Ganga plain, the peninsula south of the Kaveri River, and the intensification of habitation in previously colonized areas like Marwar, Mewar, central India and the Deccan plateau clearly suggest that the Mesolithic period witnessed a dramatic increase in human population. Several factors like the enhanced hunting yield made possible by the more efficient technology provided by microliths, greater yield from plant foods through processing by querns and grinders, and increased rainfall attested in several parts of the country would have led to an increase in animal and plant food resources, and could be responsible for this population growth.

PALAEOCLIMATE AND PALAEOENVIRONMENT

In several parts of the country, the climate and environment were vastly different during the Mesolithic period from that of today. The best evidence in this respect comes from the semi-arid and arid regions of western and north-western India, comprising Gujarat and north-west Rajasthan or Marwar. The alluvial plain of Gujarat and the whole of Marwar are totally covered by sand sheets and dunes, the latter reaching the form of hills in the hyper-arid western part of the Thar desert. In Gujarat and near the Aravalli hills in Marwar, which receive relatively higher rainfall, the dunes today are stable and covered with grass and tree vegetation. However, in the western part of the desert, which receives an annual rainfall of less than 250 mm, the dunes are still active, and being formed and reformed by blowing sand.

The existence of sand hills was noted by the geologist, W.T. Blanford, as early as the last quarter of the nineteenth century.[111] Blanford as well as subsequent investigators like T.D. La Touche and H.T. Verstappen postulated a highly arid climate during the period when the dunes were formed.[112]

[111] W.T. Blanford (1876), 'On the Physical Geography of the Great Indian Desert with Special Reference to the Former Existence of the Sea in the Indus Valley and on the Origin and Mode of Formation of the Sand Hills', *JASB*, 45, 2, pp. 86-103.

[112] T.H.D. La Touche (1902), 'The Geology of Western Rajputana', *MASI*, 35, 1, pp. 1-110; H.T. Verstappen (1970), 'Aeolian Geomorphology of the Thar Desert and Palaeoclimates', *Zeitschrift fur Geomorphologie*, 10 (Supplement Band), pp. 104-20.

However, multidisciplinary investigations carried out during the last four decades or so have considerably enlarged our knowledge of the process of dune formation and stabilization, and, consequently, of the climate during that period.

Palynological investigations carried out by Gurdip Singh and his associates in the salt lakes of Lunakavansar, Didwana and Sambhar in the 1960s revealed that lake sediments were resting on aeolian sands, and since these sediments were dated to the beginning of the Holocene the sands must have been deposited during the terminal Pleistocene or earlier.[113] Excavations in the 16R fossil dune at Didwana in the Nagaur district of Rajasthan and the dating of the dune profile by radiocarbon, TL and the Uranium-thorium decay series shows that the history of dune formation goes back to nearly 400,000 years ago. Weathering horizons within the profile show that there were multiple episodes of dune formation and stabilization. People camped on stable dune surfaces during humid phases as represented by the stone tool assemblages of the Lower, Middle and Upper Palaeolithic, and the Mesolithic periods.[114] The work of the Cambridge-Baroda expedition also shows that people camped on dune surfaces at Budha Pushkar near Ajmer in Rajasthan from the Middle Palaeolithic to Mesolithic times.[115]

On the basis of pollen data from the lakes, Gurdip Singh and his associates postulated two phases of increased rainfall. The first phase lasted from *c*. 8000 BC to *c*. 7500 BC. Rainfall during this period was at least 25 cm more than the present precipitation in western Rajasthan. After this phase, there was a slight decline in rainfall. The second phase lasted from *c*. 3000 BC to *c*. 1800 BC. This phase is characterized by a rather sudden and considerable increase in rainfall. The annual average rainfall during this phase was probably at least 50 cm more than the present rainfall in the arid belt. This increase in rainfall is also reflected in the deep brown weathering of the sand dunes. Microliths are found in this weathered horizon. A faint soil horizon was also detected in the Mesolithic dune at Langhnaj. The presence of the rhinoceros at Langhnaj during the Mesolithic period is also indicative of wetter conditions (Zetmer 1950, 1963). In central Indian rock shelters, Mesolithic remains are found in black soil which must have been brought into the shelters by the

[113]G. Singh et al. (1974), 'Late Quaternary History of Vegetation and Climate of the Rajasthan Desert, India', *Philosophical Transactions of the Royal Society*, 267B, pp. 467-501.

[114]V.N. Misra (1995), 'Evolution of Environment and Culture in the Rajasthan Desert during the Late Quaternary', in E. Johnson (ed.), *Ancient Peoples and Landscapes*, Texas Tech University Press, Lubbock, Texas, pp. 77-103.

[115]B. Allchin and A. Goudie (1978), 'Climatic Change in the Indian Desert and North-West India during the Late Pleistocene and Early Holocene', in W.C. Brice (ed.), *The Environmental History of the Near and the Middle East since the Last Ice Age*, Academic Press, London, pp. 307-18; B. Allchin et al. (1978), *The Prehistory and Palaeogeography of the Great Indian Desert*, Academic Press, London.

wind. The formation of black soil itself is indicative of a wetter climate than before and after. The increased rainfall must have stimulated the growth of vegetation and the animal population. This, in turn, would have accelerated the growth of the human population. Such a growth is clearly reflected in the sudden and dramatic increase in the number of Mesolithic sites all over the country, and also in the colonization of virgin areas by Mesolithic hunter-gatherers.

TECHNOLOGY AND MATERIAL CULTURE

The microlithic industries of India show considerable variations in the typology, technology and raw materials used in the manufacture of tools. Basically, these industries can be divided into two categories: non-geometric and geometric. The majority of sites belong to the second category. The greatest precision and symmetry in geometric microliths is seen at the sites of Bagor[116] (Fig. 6.3), Tilwara[117] (Fig. 6.4) and Bhimbetka.[118] Non-geometric industries are mainly represented at Sarai Nahar Rai[119] (Fig. 6.5), Birbhanpur[120] (Fig. 6.6) and the *teri* sites of Tamil Nadu[121] (Fig. 6.7). Associated with microliths are a variety of scrapers, borers, burins, flakes and blades. At the *teri* sites, pressure-flaked unifacial and bifacial points are common and, indeed, are unique to these sites.

At most of the sites, microliths were made on microblades removed from fluted or prismatic cores by the pressure technique. At Bagor, extreme miniaturization is seen. Here, many fluted cores are 10 mm or even lesser in size. At most sites, the preferred raw materials were fine-grained siliceous rocks like chert, chalcedony, agate and jasper but at sites like Bagor, Tilwara and Langhnaj, quartz was also used in large proportions. At the *teri* sites, quartz was the only material used. At Bhimbetka, microliths were also made of quartzite.

As attested to by the hafted tools from many Mesolithic and later sites in Europe, Africa, the near east, Iraq, Baluchistan and India, and by the depiction of arrows and spears that are barbed and tipped with microliths, microliths were clearly used as components of arrowheads, spearheads, sickles, daggers and harpoons.[122]

[116]Misra and Malti Nagar (1981), op. cit.

[117]Misra (1971a), op. cit.; idem (1971b), op. cit.

[118]Misra (1985), op. cit.; idem (1989d), op. cit.; Misra et al. (1977), op. cit.

[119]Sharma (1973), op. cit.

[120]Lal (1958), op. cit.

[121]Aiyappan (1945), op. cit.; Zeuner and Allchin (1956), op. cit.

[122]Misra (1974), op. cit.; Misra et al. (1977), op. cit.; Y. Mathpal (1984), 'Newly Discovered Rock Paintings in the Central India showing Honey Collection', *Deewar*, 65, 3, pp. 121-6; E. Neumayer (1983), *Prehistoric Indian Rock Paintings*, Oxford University Press, New Delhi; idem (1993), *Lines on Stone: The Prehistoric Rock Art of India*, Manohar, New Delhi.

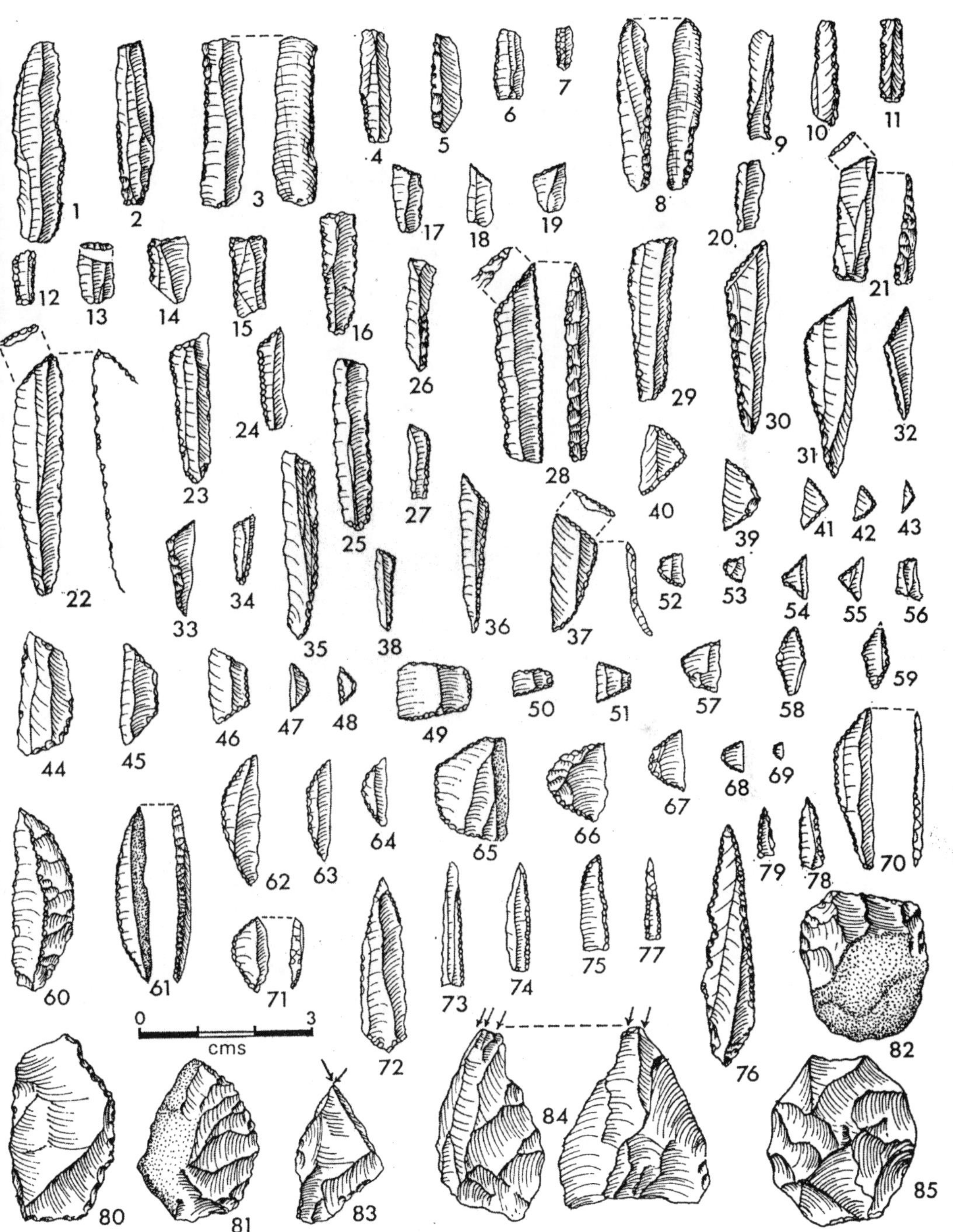

Fig. 6.3: Microlithic industry of Bagor

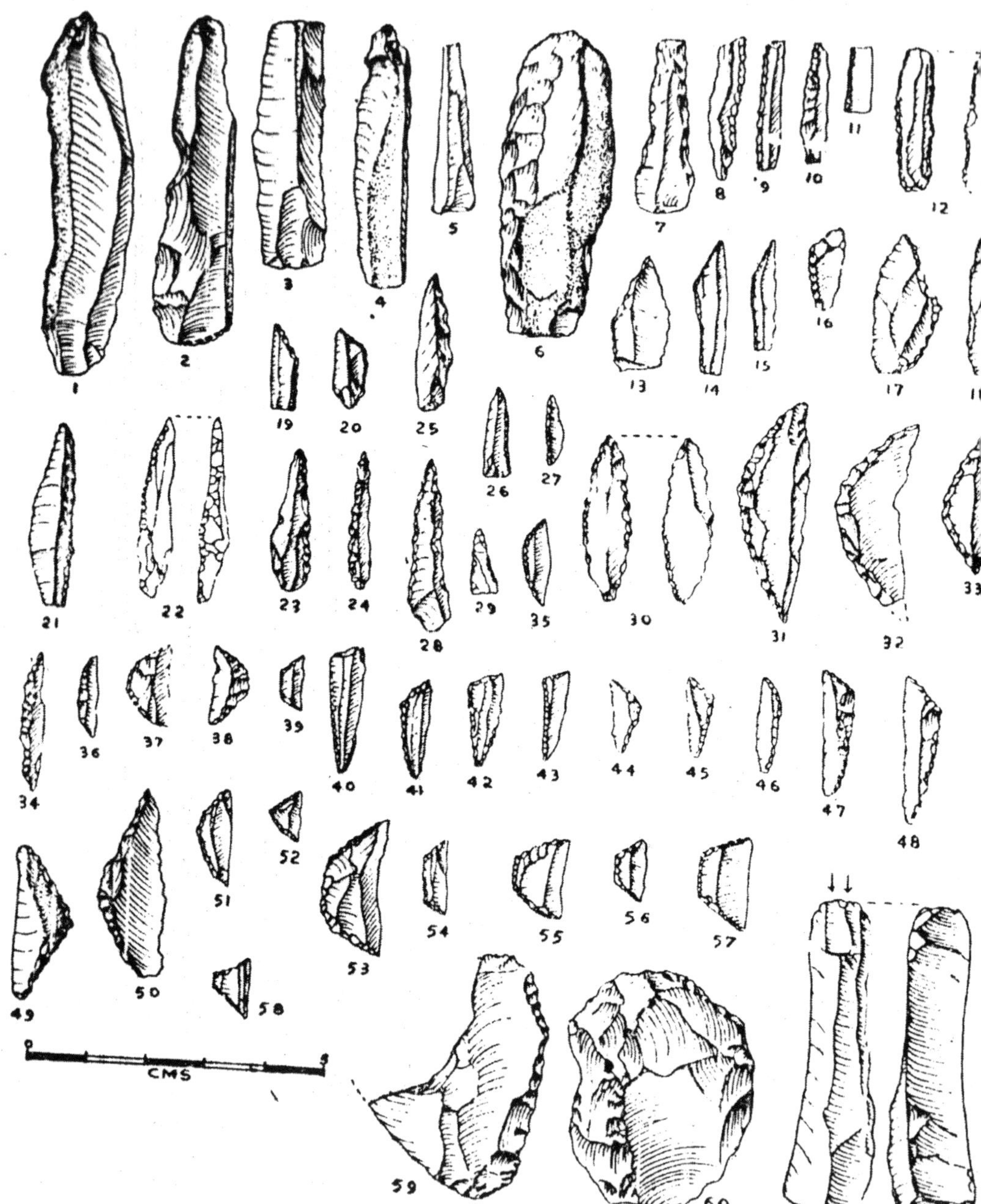

Fig. 6.4: Microlithic industry of Tilwara

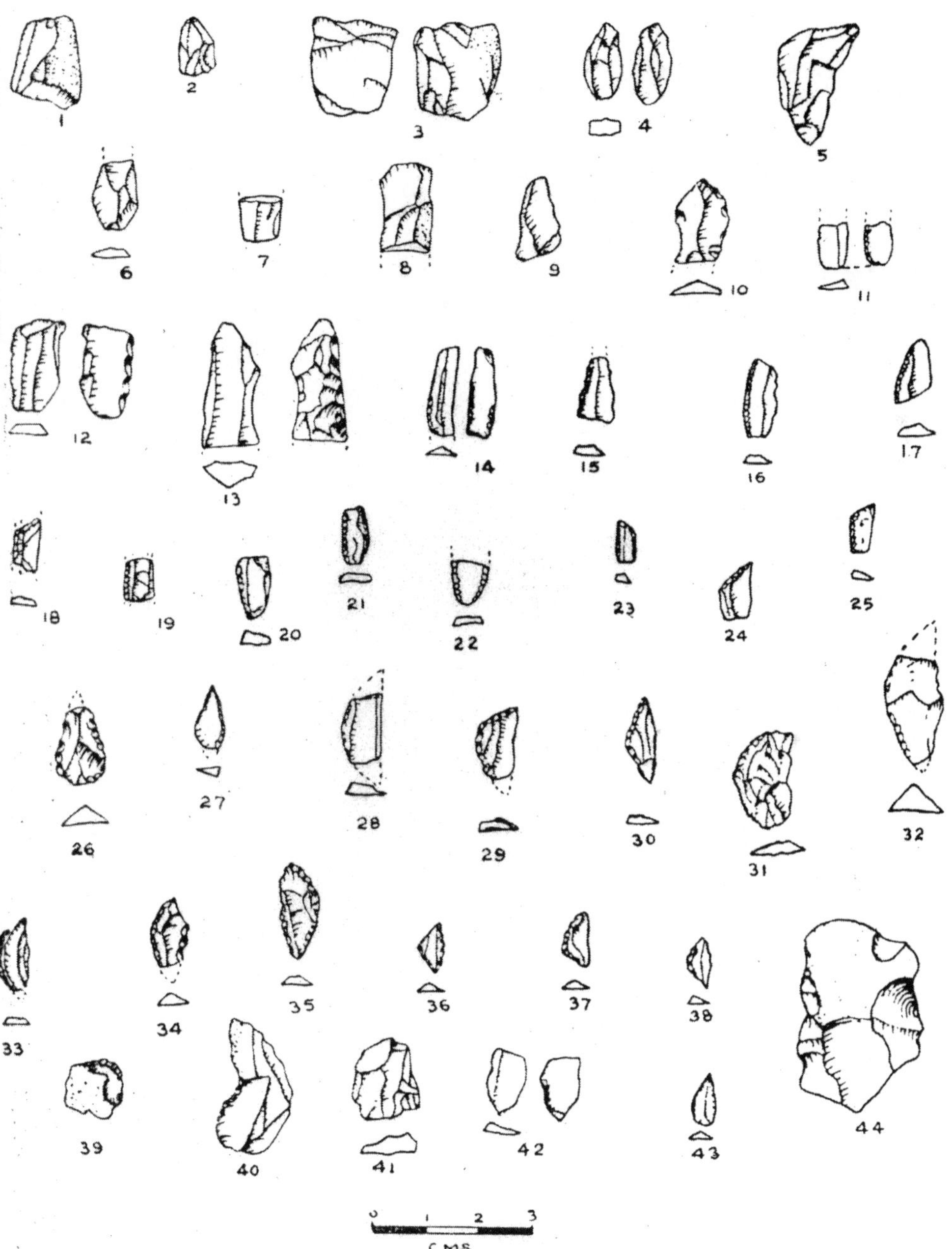

Fig. 6.5: Microlithic industry of Sarai Nahar Rai, U.P.

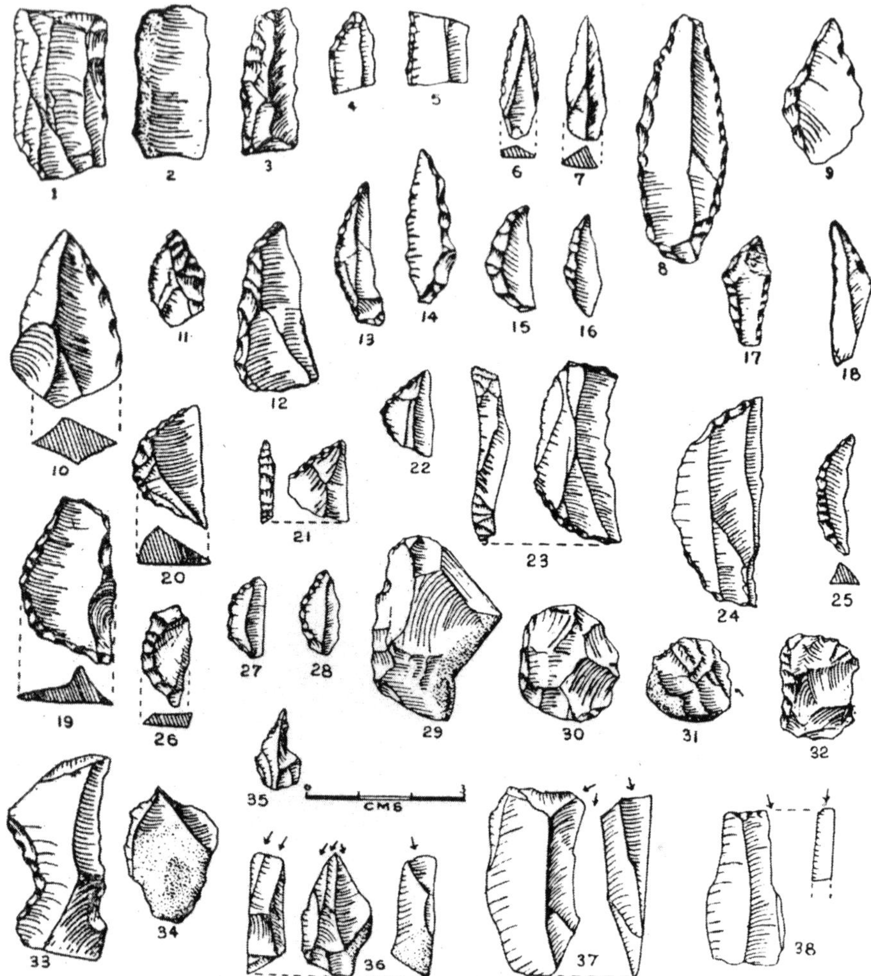

Fig. 6.6: Microlithic industry at Birbhanpur, West Bengal

At sites in Orissa[123] (Fig. 6.8), Bombay islands and the *teris*, heavy-duty tools like choppers, chopping tools and discoids are also found. Antlers with sharp cut marks and bone points occur at Bhimbetka, and antler, bone and horn tools have been found at Damdama. Ring stones, hammer stones and grinding stones have been found at many Mesolithic sites in different parts of the country.

Our knowledge of the material culture of the Mesolithic people is very limited, mainly because of the poor survival of items made of organic materials. In central India, these people often inhabited the naturally formed and readily

[123] Mohanty (1988-9), op. cit.; idem (1989), op. cit.; idem (1992), op. cit.; idem (1993), op. cit.

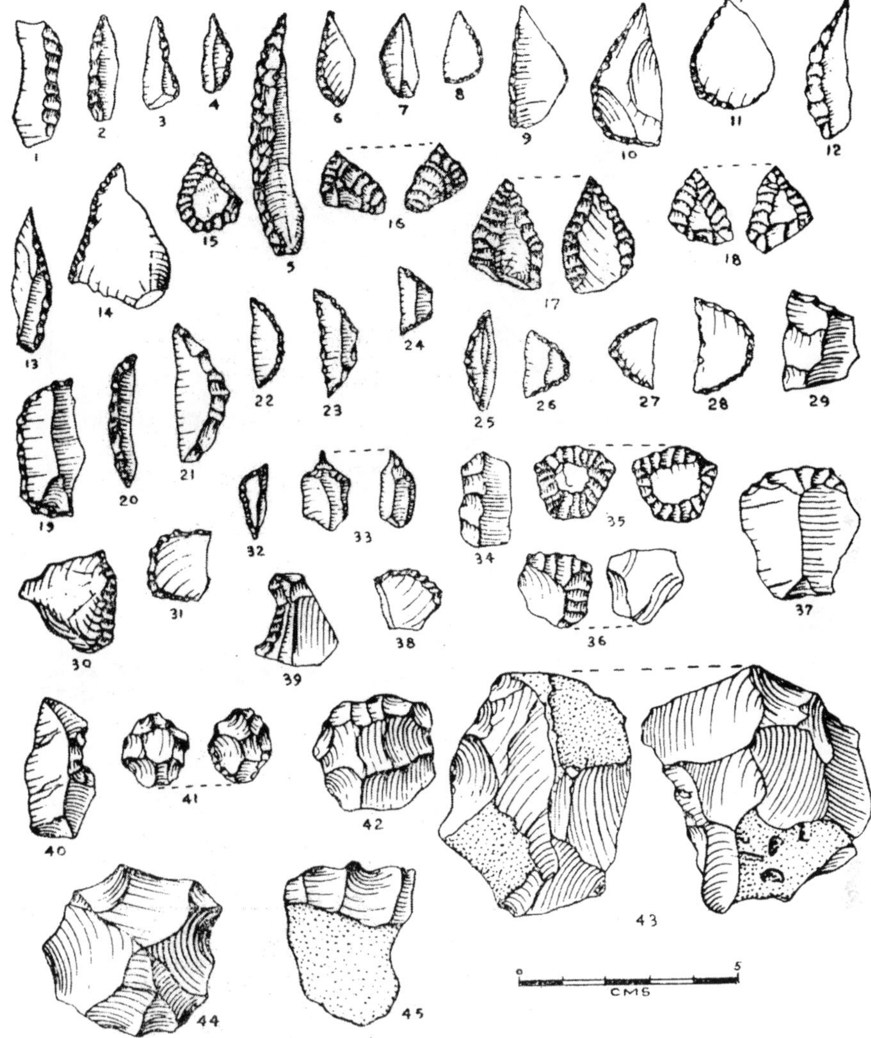

Fig. 6.7: Microlithic industry of Teri sites, Tamil Nadu

available rock shelters. But from one shelter at Bhimbetka, there is evidence that they raised a stone wall inside the shelter to partition off an area.[124] There is also evidence of circular stone-lined huts from Eagor and Tilwara. At Sarai Nahar Rai, a rectangular floor made by ramming burnt clay clods has been found.[125] Postholes found at the corners of the floor at this site, as also at Chopani Mando, Sharma suggest some kind of superstructure over the floor.[126]

[124]Misra (1989d), op. cit.
[125]Sharma (1973), op. cit.
[126]Sharma et al. (1980), op. cit.

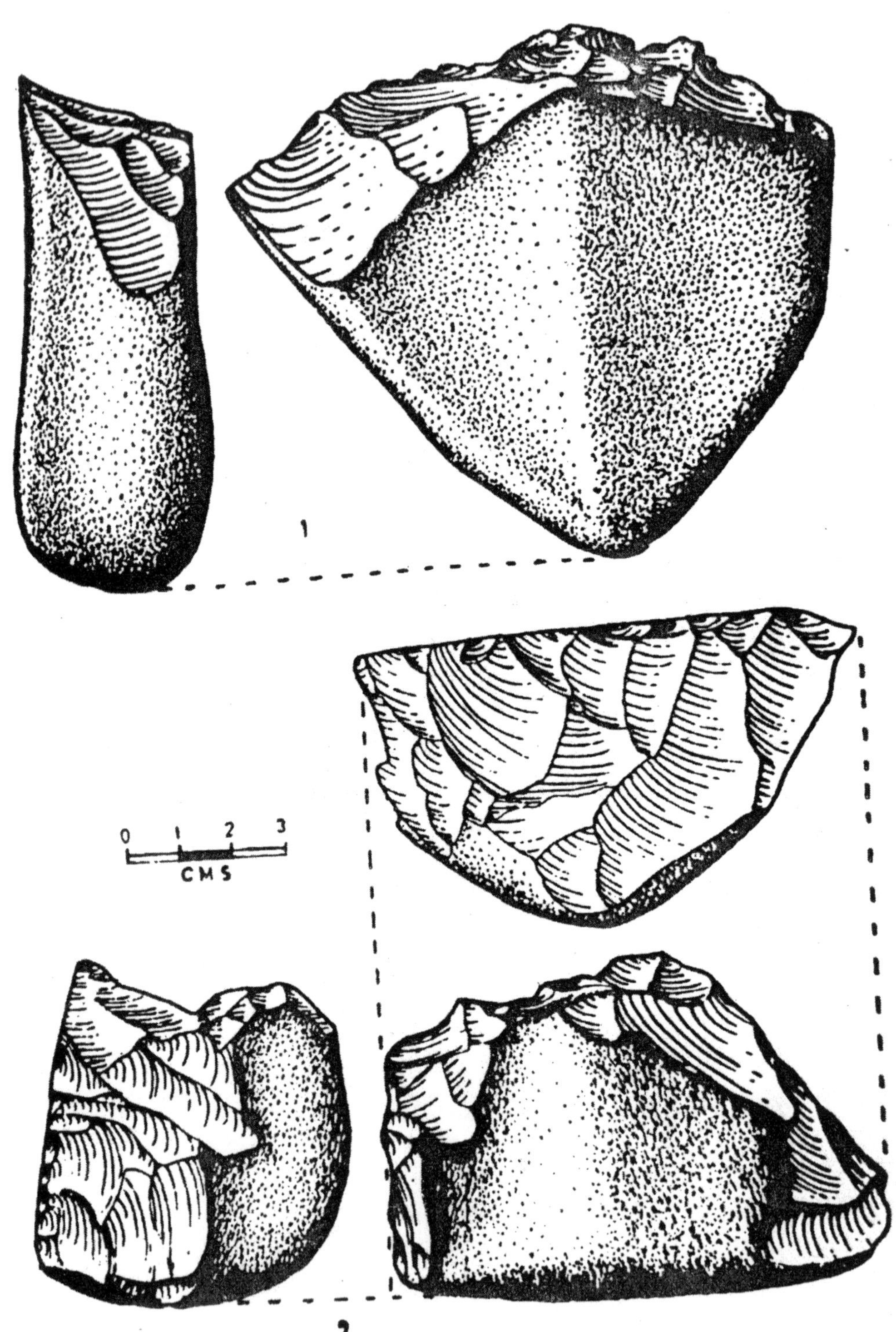

Fig. 6.8: Heavy duty tools from Phulbani, Orissa (after Ota 1986)

Rock paintings show circular huts made of tree branches and leaves.[127] The material possessions of the social units included bows and arrows, spears, traps and nets, grinding stones (Fig. 6.9) for processing food, stone hammers, sling balls, ring stones, and bone and antler tools and ornaments. Rock paintings also show that both men and women wore some kind of dress around the waist, probably made of leaves. Hunters are often shown wearing masks. Human skeletons in burials from Mahadaha in the Ganga Valley are shown wearing earrings and necklaces made of rings cut from antlers.

Fig. 6.9: Grinding stones, Bhimbetka

SUBSISTENCE

Our knowledge of the subsistence pattern of the Mesolithic people is mainly based the animal bones which have been found in large quantities and often in well-preserved condition at several sites. This is supplemented by the depiction of scenes of hunting, trapping, fishing and plant-food collecting in rock paintings. The animals most commonly represented in the bone record are the Indian humped cattle (*Bos indicus*), gaur (*Bos gaurns*), buffalo (*Bubalus bubalis*), sambar (*Cervus unicolor*), chital (*Axis axis*), gazelle (*Gazella gazella*), hog deer (*Axis porcinus*), nilgai (*Boselaphus tragncamelus*), fox (*Vulpes*

[127]Neumayer (1983), op. cit.; idem (1993), op. cit.

bengalensis) and the jackal (*Canis aureus*). The barasingha (*Cervus duvauceli*) and rhinoceros (*Rhinoceros unicornis*) were hunted at Langhnaj, Sarai Nahar Rai, Mahadaha and Damdama. Elephant (*Elephas maximus*) bones occur at all the Ganga Valley sites. In fact, the faunal record of this valley is extremely rich and its preservation excellent. At Damdama, faunal remains of thirty species of mammals, fish, birds, reptiles and molluscs have been identified. The principal species are chital, wild boar (*Sus serofa*), elephant, rhinoceros, gaur, wild cattle, and wild buffalo.[128] Porcupine (*Hystrix indica*) bones have been found at Adamgarh. At Eagor and Sarai Nahar Rai, there are bones of the turtle (*Chelonia* sp.) and fish.[129] Paintings at Bhimbetka and other sites show the hunting of a variety of animals by spear, bow and arrow, and by trapping and snaring. There are also scenes of the trapping of rats and of fishing. Besides, at Bagar and Adamgarh, there is evidence of the domestication of cattle, sheep (*Ovis aries*) and goat (*Capra hircus aegagrus*). At all the sites, bones occur in broken, split open and charred conditions, showing that meat was cooked on open fires and marrow was extracted from the bones. Efforts are also being made to reconstruct the palaeodiet from strontium isotopic ratios in human bones.[130]

Plant remains have been recovered from Damdama.[131] Paintings in rock shelters at Bhimbetka and other places show scenes of plant, food and honey collection. Besides, the deciduous forest region of central and eastern India, where a larger number of Mesolithic sites are concentrated, is very rich in a variety of plant foods which are extensively exploited by the local aboriginal and other rural populations even today, and there is no reason to believe that ancient hunter-gatherers did not do the same.

DISPOSAL OF THE DEAD

The only known method of disposing of the dead among the Mesolithic people was inhumation. Human burials have been excavated from eight sites.

[128] P.K. Thomas et al. (1995) 'A Preliminary Report of the Faunal Remains from Damdama', *ME*, XX, pp. 29-36.

[129] Clutton-Brock (1965), op. cit.; P.K. Thomas, and P.P. Joglekar (1994), 'Holocene Faunal Studies in India', *ME*, XX, 1-2, pp. 179-204.

[130] G.G. Goles and J.R. Lukacs (1996), 'Use of Strontium Isotopic Ratios in Studies of Human Palaeodiet: An Example from Alaska and a Proposed Application to the Mesolithic of North India', in G.E. Afanas'ev et al. (eds.), *Bioarchaeology of Mesolithic India: An Integrated Approach*, Colloquium XXXIII of the International Union of Prehistoric and Protohistoric Science, ABACO Edizioni, Forli, pp. 313-19.

[131] M.D. Kajale (1990), 'Some Initial Observations on Palaeobotanical Evidence for Mesolithic Plant Economy from Excavations at Damdama, Uttar Pradesh', in N.C. Ghosh and S. Chakrabarti (eds.), *Adaptation and Other Essays*, Visva-Bharati, Santiniketan, pp. 98-112; idem (1996), 'Plant Resources and Diet among the Mesolithic Hunters and Foragers', in S. Afanas'ev et al. (eds.), *Bioarchaeology of Mesolithic India: An Integrated Approach*, Colloquium XXXIII of the International Union of Prehistoric and Protohistoric Sciences, ABACO Edizioni, Forli, pp. 251-3.

These are: Langhnaj in Gujarat,[132] Bagor in Rajasthan,[133] Lekhahia,[134] Baghai,[135] Sarai Nahar Rai,[136] Mahadaha,[137] Damdama, all in Uttar Pradesh,[138] Bhimbetka in Madhya Pradesh.[139] In addition to publications on the human skeletal biology of individual sites referred to here, there are a number of others covering two or more sites.[140]

[132]Sankalia (1942), op. cit.; idem (1943), op. cit.; idem (1944), op. cit.; idem (1946), op. cit.; idem (1965), op. cit.; Sankalia and Karve (1949), op. cit.; Karve and Kurulkar (1945a), op. cit.; idem (1945b), op. cit.; Karve-Corvinus and Kennedy (1964), op. cit.; Ehrhardt and Kennedy (1965), op. cit.

[133]V.N. Misra (1972), 'Burials from Prehistoric Bagor, Rajasthan', in S.B. Deo (ed.), *Archaeological Congress and Seminar Papers*, Nagpur University, Nagpur, pp. 58-65; idem (1973a), op. cit.; idem (1982), op. cit.; Kennedy (1982), op. cit.; Lukacs (1982), op. cit.; J.R. Lukacs et al. (1982), *Bagor and Tilwara: Late Mesolithic Cultures of Northwest India*, vol. 1: *The Human Skeletal Remains*, Deccan College, Poona, pp. 61-94.

[134]Sharma (1965), op. cit.; Varma (1986), op. cit.; Lukacs and Misra (1997), op. cit.; Kennedy (2000), op. cit.

[135]Varma (1986), op. cit.; Kennedy (1990a), op. cit.; idem (2000), op. cit.

[136]Sharma (1973), op. cit.; idem (1975), op. cit.; K.A.R Kennedy (1996), 'Skeletal Adaptations of Mesolithic Hunter-foragers of North India: Mahadaha and Sarai Nahar Rai Compared', in G.E. Afanas'ev et al. (eds.), *Bioarchaeology of Mesolithic India: An Integrated Approach*, Colloquium XXXIII of the International Union of Prehistoric and Protohistoric Sciences, ABACO Edizioni, Forli, pp. 291-300; Kennedy et al. (1986), op. cit.

[137]Sharma et al. (1980), op. cit.; Pal (1985), op. cit.; K.A.R. Kennedy et al. (1992), *Human Skeletal Remains from Mahadaha: A Gangetic Mesolithic Site*, Cornell University, Ithaca.

[138]Pal (1988), op. cit.; Varma et al (1985), op. cit.; Kennedy et al. (2000), op. cit.

[139]Misra (1989d), op. cit.; idem (2002), op. cit.; Misra et al. (1977), op. cit.; Kennedy (2000), op. cit.; idem (2002), op. cit.; Kennedy et al. (1981), op. cit.; idem (2002), op. cit.; Lukacs (2002), op. cit.; Lukacs and Kennedy (2002), op. cit.; Tiwari (2002), op. cit.; Wakankar (1973), op. cit.; idem (1975), op. cit.; idem (2002), op. cit.

[140]K.A.R. Kennedy (1973), 'Biological Anthropology of Prehistoric South Asians', *Anthropologist*, 17, 1-2, pp. 1-13; idem (1976), 'Biological Anthropology of Prehistoric Populations in South Asia: A Summary of Current Research Efforts', in K.A.R. Kennedy and G.L. Possehl (eds.), *Ecological Backgrounds of South Asian Prehistory*, Cornell University, Ithaca, pp. 166-78; idem (1980), 'Prehistoric Skeletal Record of Man in South Asia', *Annual Review of Anthropology*, 9, pp. 392-432; idem (1984a), 'Biological Adaptations and Affinities of Mesolithic South Asia', in J.R. Lukacs (ed.), *The People of South Asia: The Biological Authropology of India, Pakistan and Nepal*, Plenum Press, New York, pp. 29-57; idem (1984b), 'Growth, Nutrition and Pathology in Changing Palaeodemographic Settings in South Asia', in M.N. Cohen and G.L. Armelagos (eds.), *Palaeopathology at the Origins of Agriculture*, Academic Press, Orlando, pp. 169-92; idem (1990b), op. cit.; idem (1996), op. cit.; idem (1999), 'Palaeoanthropology of South Asia', *Evolutionary Anthropology*, 8, 5, pp. 165-85; K.A.R. Kennedy and P.C. Caldwell (1984), 'South Asian Prehistoric Human Skeletal Remains and Burial Practices', in J.R. Lukacs (ed.), *The People of South Asia*, Plenum, New York, pp. 159-97; Misra (1977), op. cit.; idem (1996), op. cit.; J.R. Lukacs (1985), 'Tooth Size Variation in Prehistoric India', *American Anthropologist*, 87, 4, pp. 811-25; idem (1990), 'On Hunter-gatherers and Their Neighbours in Prehistoric India: Contact and Pathology', *CA*, 31, 2, pp. 183-6;

Both in the rock shelters of central India and at the open air sites of Rajasthan, Gujarat and the Ganga Valley, the dead were buried within the habitation area. In the Baghai Khor rock shelter, a single burial was laid in an extended position and the rock was dressed to provide raised platforms for the head and feet. At Lekhahia, as many as seventeen burials, with all the skeletons being incomplete, were found in a single shelter in a very thin deposit. Most of the burials from Bhimbetka were also placed in an extended position, with legs only slightly folded. At Bagor in Mewar, the only skeleton in Phase I of Period I, i.e. the Mesolithic, was laid in an extended position, while the three skeletons in Phase II, containing pottery and copper tools, were placed in a crouched position, with both arms and legs folded upwards. At Langhnaj in Gujarat, all the fifteen skeletons were buried in a crouched position. At Sarai Nahar Rai, Mahadaha and Damdama, the dead were placed in shallow graves in an extended position with the head to the west and the right forearm placed diagonally over the abdomen. At Sarai Nahar Rai and Mahadaha, there are examples of double and even multiple burials in single graves. At Sarai Nahar Rai, microliths were found embedded in the bones of some skeletons, suggesting violent death.

Grave offerings to the dead were few and rarely made. At Bhimbetka, pieces of red ochre, bone points, decorated bone pieces, sharply cut and polished antler pieces and, in one case, a number of grinding stones, were placed with the body. Mention has already been made of the bone and antler earrings and necklaces found on the skeletons at Mahadaha. Here, as also at Sarai Nahar Rai, a variety of local freshwater shells was placed with the dead, probably as a food offering.

BIOLOGICAL ANTHROPOLOGY OF HUMAN SKELETAL REMAINS

Human skeletal remains recovered from all the excavated Mesolithic sites have been examined by biological anthropologists like Sophie Ehrhardt, Kenneth A.R. Kennedy, John R. Lukacs, and several colleagues and students of the last two scholars. Their studies have made a very significant contribution to our knowledge of the physical composition, pathology and dietary habits

idem (1992), 'Mesolithic Hunters and Foragers of the Gangetic Plain: A Summary of Current Research in Dental Anthropology', *Dental Anthropology Newsletter*, 6, 3, pp. 3-8; J.R. Lukacs and J.N. Pal (1992), 'Dental Anthropology of the Mesolithic Hunter-gatherers: A Preliminary Report', *ME*, XVII, 2, pp. 45-56; idem (1993), 'Mesolithic Subsistence in North India: Inferences from Dental Attributes', *CA*, 34, 5, pp. 745-65; J.R. Lukacs et al. (1996), 'Chronology and Diet in Mesolithic North India: A Preliminary Report of New AMS C^{14} dates, $§^{13}C$ Isotope Values, and Their Significance', in G.E. Afanas'ev et al. (eds.), *Bioarchaeology of Mesolithic India: An Integrated Approach*, Colloquium XXXIII of the International Union of Prehistoric and Protohistoric Sciences, ABACO Edizioni, Forli, pp. 301-11; Pal (1992), op. cit.; Pandey (1990), op. cit.; idem (1996), op. cit.

of the Mesolithic population. In general, it can be said that the Mesolithic people of the Ganga Valley were taller and more sturdily built than those of the Mirzapur rock shelters, Bagor, Langhnaj and Bhimbetka. The people of Bhimbetka were, to some extent, closer in stature and build to the later agriculturalist populations.

Excellent evidence for pathology has been provided by the Baghai Khor female skeleton, studied by K.A.R. Kennedy. 'The Baghai Khor skeleton is most important because of the presence of pathological markers on the frontal and parietal bores identified as porotic hyperostosis (symmetrical osteoporosis or spongy hyperostosis).' It is the first recorded case of this condition from a Mesolithic context in India, and its occurrence is unusual given the higher incidence of this abnormality in later food-producing populations in South Asia and other parts of the world. . . . The spongy appearance is formed by pressure atrophy of the diploic tissue between the external and internal tables, and additional bone remodelling results in a 'hair-on-end' pattern observable radiographically when the diploic bone increases to form a thickening of the cranial vault. When porosity occurs along the superior walls of the orbits, the condition is called *cribra orbitalia.* Potential bones may become affected as well (Angel 1966).

What were the causes of this abnormality in the young woman from Baghai Khor? Some forms of porotic hyperostosis are related to senile changes in the bone formation of older individuals and are diagnostic of an anaemic condition of a genetic or acquired origin. The major causes are the inheritance of abnormal haemoglobins (sickle cell anemia), the thalassemia, nutritional iron deficiency, hookworm, and congenital heart disease. However, present research into the causes of porotic hyperostosis indicates a close relationship of the condition with infectious diseases, growth irregularities, and generalized nutritional stress.[141]

At the nearby site of Lekhahia, although originally only seventeen skeletons were reported, their re-examination by J.R. Lukacs, J.N. Pal and V.D. Misra[142] has shown that twenty-seven individuals are represented by osteological and dental remains. Among them are eleven males, ten females and eight skeletons of undetermined sex; age ranges are from a child of six to eight years to an adult of fifty to fifty-five years. Fragments of a prenatal infant are present. There is a healed lesion on the proximal end on the left femur of skeleton 8, a fracture of the proximal end of the humerus of skeleton 11, and a parry fracture of the left ulna of skeleton 4a. The perforation of the olecranon fossae of the humeri of four individuals may be a marker of occupational stress, although genetic factors should not be ruled out.[143]

A study of some thirteen skeletons from Langhnaj indicates that these

[141] Kennedy (2000), op. cit., p. 225.
[142] Lukacs et al. (1996), op. cit.
[143] Kennedy (2000), op. cit., pp. 225-6.

hook-fisher folk betray mixed racial features: dolichocephalic head with fairly large cranial capacity, medium and long stature with thin legs due evidently to continuous movement, pronounced supraorbital ridges, and a slight prognathism of the mouth and probably a snub nose. The highly ground surface of the crown of the teeth suggests a coarse diet. All these features betray mix of Mediterranian and Veddid features, but not of a particular race alone.[144]

At Bagor in Rajasthan, four burials were found, one (Specimen I) from Phase I of Period I, which only yielded a microlithic industry and animal remains, and three (Specimens II, III and V) from Phase II which yielded pottery, copper tools, and stone and bone beads along with microliths. Specimen I was buried in a fully extended position with its head to the west, while Specimens II, III, and V were buried in a crouched position, with their heads to the east. An osteological examination was done by Kennedy[145] while the dentition was studied by Lukacs.[146] Specimens I and II belong to adult females, Specimen III to a child, and Specimen V to an adult male.

With respect to dentition, Specimen I exhibits a remarkably low degree of dental attrition. This is in striking contrast to the Mesolithic skeletons from Langhnaj. According to Lukacs,[147] 'This apparent inconsistency is readily explained by demographic differences in age structure between the Langhnaj skeletal series whose mean age at the time of death is about 35-40 years, and Bagor I, a young adult between 17 and 19 years of age.'

Dental attrition patterns exhibited by the two Phase II skeletons are very different due to the great disparity in their age at the time of death. Specimen III, seven and a half to eight years old at the time of death, is conspicuous by the absence of any noticeable dental wear on the enamel surface of its newly-erupted, permanent molar teeth. In contrast, Specimen II has two highly abraded molar teeth. The deep attritional basins present in these teeth can only partially be attributed to dental wear. The excavation of such deep and narrow pits requires the presence of an additional agent of dental destruction such as caries formation.

From eight rock shelters at Bhimbetka, a large number of human skeletons were excavated by V.S. Wakankar, V.N. Misra and Susanne Haas during 1972-7. The skeletons are in varying degrees of preservation. A detailed morphometric analysis of these skeletal remains by S.C. Tiwari. K.A.R. Kennedy, and J.R. Lukacs has been published.[148] The following summary is based on the conclusions drawn by Lukacs and Kennedy.[149] Their two main conclusions are: (1) There is considerable biological diversity present in the

[144]Ehrhardt and Kennedy (1965), op. cit., XV.

[145]Kennedy (1982), op. cit.

[146]Lukacs (1982), op. cit.

[147]Ibid., p. 81.

[148]Kennedy et al. (2002), op. cit.

[149]Lukacs & Kennedy (2002), op. cit., pp. 101-7.

bones and teeth; and (2) Archaeological and stratigraphical data testify to an ancient and relatively continuous occupation of this region of rock shelters and open-air sites.

A clearer picture of the ancient Bhimbetkans emerges from a comparative study of phenotypic variables with those of other prehistoric South Asian populations. The total crown size area (TCA) for the Haas series is 1198 mm^2. The mesolithic foragers of Damdama have a larger TCA of 1396 mm^2 (males only) and their neighbours at Mahadaha have a TCA of 1322 mm^2 (males only). The size of the Bhimbetka dentition is, thus, smaller than that of the Mesolithic people of the Ganga Valley. The TCA of the Bronze Age people of Harappa is 1194 mm, which is not very different from that of the Haas series. Although many factors—environmental and genetic—impinge upon variations in tooth size, this research provides new insights into the dental attrition of the people of Bhimbetka. These results are largely consistent with the cultural and dietary model of tooth size variations.

The second example of contextualizing the Bhimbetka skeletons focuses on stature. The estimated stature of the skeleton of burial no. II-B-33, a female, is 151-7 cm, and specimen no. 170, a male, has an estimated stature of 165-70 cm. In comparison to the Mesolithic hunter-foragers of the Ganga Valley, the individuals from Bhimbetka are significantly shorter.

Stature estimates for male and female specimens from Bhimbetka also permit an assessment of sex dimorphism in stature for the site. The male (165-70 cm) and female (151-5 cm) values display an appropriate degree of variation in stature between the sexes. When the average of high and low stature estimates for each specimen is used in calculating the per cent dimorphism in stature (154 cm for burial no. 1; 167.5 cm for specimen no. 170), a value of 8.8 per cent is obtained. This degree of dimorphism in stature is slightly greater than the mean per cent dimorphism in stature calculated for the Chalcolithic human skeletons from Mehrgarh (8.0 per cent, n = 20). The per cent sex dimorphism in stature for the Mesolithic foragers from the Ganga plains exhibits a wide range of values, from a low of 4.9 per cent for Damdama to a high of 7.0 per cent for Mahadaha, while the people of the Lekhahia rock shelter in the Kaimur hills have the highest percentage dimorphism in stature, 9.7 per cent. In conclusion, while the Bhimbetka specimens are of shorter stature than their Mesolithic neighbours to the north, the degree of sex dimorphism at Bhimbetka fits into the mid-range of values reported for several south Asian skeletal series with foraging and semi-sedentary lifestyles.

Stresses of the hunting-foraging lifestyle are indicated in the dental record, as in the incidence of dental enamel hypoplasia, severe occlusal wear and antemortem tooth loss. More specific pathological conditions are represented by the case of probable osteomyelitis in the skeleton of specimen no. III-A-28 of late Pleistocene antiquity.[150]

[150] Ibid.

In striking contrast to the paucity and poor preservation of Mesolithic skeletal remains from Rajasthan, Gujarat and the Vindhya hills is the richness of the Ganga plain sites of Sarai Nahar Rai, Mahadaha and Damdama. Skeletal remains from these sites are impressive in appearance—large, heavily muscled, tall and hyper-robust people who appear to have attained their full ontogenetic potential in a demanding hunting-foraging lifestyle. When viewing photographs of these Gangetic hominids, the late K.P. Oakley was moved to remark, 'They look like European Cro-Magnon skeletons!'

There are fifteen well-preserved skeletons in the Sarai Nahar Rai series. Of the ten examined by Kennedy and his associates, seven are males and three are females. All seventeen are adults, with age ranges for males being sixteen to twenty-four years at the time of death and age ranges for females being fifteen to thirty-five years. These death age ranges are close to values obtained from other Mesolithic populations in South Asia and Eurasia. All but one of these individuals had attained full skeletal maturity, and both males and females were tall. In this respect, they share a physical resemblance with the Upper Palaeolithic populations of Europe and Western Asia, as well as with the skeletal series from Mahadaha.

Perhaps the most striking feature of the Sarai Nahar Rai males is their massive and robust skulls, which range from mesocrany to hyperdolichocrany with moderately elevated vaults surmounted by prominent supraorbital tori, moderately large to very large mastoid processes with well-defined supramastoid crests, and sharp temporal lines that extend posteriorly to the parietal bones. The development of the nuchal crests varies from slight to pronounced, some male skulls exhibiting very large external occipital protuberances. Parietal eminences are very large for skulls of both sexes. The facial architecture for males and females is broad (hypereuryprosopic and hypereuryene) with noses of narrow (leptorrhinic) to broad (chamacrrhinic) dimensions. The orbits have a rectangular shape and are low (charnaeconchic) rather than oval and high. When observed from the right or left side, the skulls of both sexes exhibit low foreheads, either slightly bulbous in females or vertical in males, with deep, nasal notches, slight projection of the face (mesognathism), but with projection of the tooth-bearing portions of the face (alveolar prognathism) in some individuals. Molar bones vary in size but are robust. The inter-orbital distance is great in all individuals. Palates are deep and broad (brachystaphaline), while the mandibles are massive with everted gonia and well-marked attachments of the Pterygoid muscles. In fact, one mandible of a male is so massive and robust that it resembles the *Homo erectus* lower jaws from Temifine (Tighenif) in north Africa and the Heidelberg mandible. But the Sarai Nahar Rai mandibles possess the prominent chins characterisitc of anatomically modern *sapiens.*

Our knowledge of the dental anthropology of the Gangetic Mesolithic populations is extensive, accurate, and of immense importance in learning more about their health status and lifestyles. The anterior and posterior permanent teeth of the Sarai Nahar Rai skeletons are large, an adaptive trait in a lifestyle demanding mastication of a tough diet and the use of the mouth as a tool for holding objects or for sharpening or breaking down fibrous materials. The enamel will endure for a longer period of time in a large tooth compared to a small one, hence its functional utility is extended. Teeth worn down to root stumps are still functional but are realigned and allow spaces to develop between adjacent teeth or else, in the case of pre-molars and molars, may be reoriented to form a continuous occlusal surface as the dental roots 'drift' in a mesial direction. Teeth specimens from Sarai Nahar Rai have mean values of 1,314 mm^2 for the TCA within a range of 1,083 to 1,530 mm^2 for comparative dental series of modern and prehistoric populations in Asia and Australia.

Dental pathology is low in the Sarai Nahar Rai series. Only one skeleton exhibits dental enamel hypoplasia of the canine and incisor teeth of upper and lower dentitions. The low caries rate is attributable to the relatively high protein and low carbohydrate nature of the hunting-foraging diet, as well as to the coarse texture of the foods and their methods of preparation. Antemortem tooth loss appears in the dentitions of Sarai Nahar Rai but not as a consequence of caries or abscess; rapid attrition and exposure of the pulp cavity is the major cause of tooth loss. This population, as with the ancient people of Mahadaha and Damdama, provides cases of dental enamel hypoplasia on the enamel surfaces of the teeth. These are markers of arrested growth affecting infants and children during those parts of the growth cycle when the dental enamel is fanning out prior to the eruption of the teeth. This condition may reflect a number of abnormal health conditions suffered by an individual in his early life that bear upon the frequencies and qualities of nutrients, interruptions of nutrient flow (as in periods of famine or illness when food is not taken), weaning to solid foods, and metabolic responses. Dental enamel hypoplasia is frequently encountered in food-producing sedentary populations, ancient and modern, so its relatively high incidence in individuals from these Mesolithic Gangetic sites is unusual. However, the tall stature of the Sarai Nahar Rai males and females testifies to their capability to attain full ontogenetic growth potential, and their post-cranial bones are remarkable for their robustness and large size.

With the exception of the dental enamel hypoplasia of one skeleton and an osteocartilaginous exostosis (osteochondromia) observed on the right radius and left first metatarsal of another skeleton, the pathological features of the Sarai Nahar Rai series are attributable to the degenerative patterns of arthritic bone modification. With respect to this, what is striking is the relatively early age of the onset of osteoarthritic changes of the bones of the post-cranial skeleton, particularly the lipping of vertebral bodies by the third decade of life.

Among other non-pathological anomalous features of the Sarai Nahar Rai series are three squatting facets on the distal ends of the male tibiae and the hyper-development of the Supinator and Anconeous crests of the male ulnae (although this is observed in two females as well). This stress marker is consistently more prominent in the right ulnae than in the left, and right-handedness is indicated for all of the individuals possessing this character. The Anconeous hyper extends the forearm while the Supinator allows the arm to turn with the palm facing upwards. When the muscular attachments for these muscles are hypertrophied, it is a good indication that vigorous brachial activity is involved, as in spear-throwing, hurling stones, or using a slingshot. This same feature has been observed in skeletons from Mahadaha and Bhimbetka, as well as in modern hunting populations such as the Eskimo.

Mahadaha, the second excavated Mesolithic site in the Ganga Valley, yielded thirty-two skeletons in twenty-eight graves. These include seventeen males, seven females, one adult of uncertain sex and three children. Age ranges are eighteen to forty years for males and thirty to sixty-five years for females, young adults from eighteen to thirty-four years predominating for both sexes. Like the Sarai Nahar Rai people, the Mahadahans were tall, and exhibit large and robust post-cranial bones. Their cranial morphology is characterized by dolichocranic to ultradolichocranic vaults with moderate cranial elevation (metriocranic to tapeinocranic), although one female has a relatively high vault (acrocranic). Males exhibit large supraorbital tori, sharp temporal lines, well-defined nuchal crests with a prominent external occipital protuberance; and massive mastoid processes with well-marked supramastoid crests. Mahadahan faces are very broad (hypereuryprosopic) with variable nasal forms ranging from narrow (leptorrhinic) to very broad (hyperchannel Thinic), high and rounded orbits (hypsiconchic), and narrow palates (leptostaphyline). Lower jaws, while massive, tend to be narrow or compressed (dolicho stenomandibular). Mid-facial and alveolar proguathism is moderately expressed. In short, the Mahadahans are very similar to the people of Sarai Nahar Rai in a number of craniofacial features, tall stature, and robust post-cranial bone architecture. Hyperdevelopment of the Anconeous and Supinator crests on the ulnae is present as well, and is a good marker of occupational stress, involving spear-throwing and related muscular-skeletal activities significant in a Mesolithic hunting-foraging lifestyle.

This is reflected, too, in dental anthropology, which indicates a very abrasive diet. The use of the teeth in non-dietary grasping and masticatory activities contributed to severe dental wear. The molar teeth are of equivalent size and are the largest in crown area reported thus far in India. Dental enamel hypoplasia occurs with relatively high frequency among Mahadahans but, whatever the causes for these episodic growth eruptions, there does not seem to have been any significant compromise of the attainment of full ontogenetic potential. This suggests that disruptions of nutrient resources were of brief duration during the early growth periods of infants and children. Other pathological indicators that are not of an osteoarthritic nature include an exostosis on the medial surface of a humeral diaphysis of a young adult male, unilateral auditory exostoses in two adult males, a unilateral bony irregularity of the same kind in another adult male, a possible osteosarcoma or chondrosarcoma on the right ilium of an adult male, and a low incidence of dental caries. Anomalies include squatting facets and the anterior-posterior bowing of lower limb bones (unless this curvature is due to rickets or osteomalacia, which seems unlikely).

The third excavated Mesolithic site in the Ganga Valley is Damdama. It yielded forty-seven human skeletons from forty-one graves. Lukacs and his associates,[151] who studied the skeletons determined that 50 per cent of them were male, 40 per cent female and nine of undetermined sex. Further laboratory analysis of the bones and teeth is in progress.

There is considerable evidence that these Ganga Valley hunter-foragers were closely interrelated both culturally and biologically. It is difficult to escape the fact that they may have been a relatively homogeneous group of Mesolithic communities that shared skeletal features of tall stature, robusticity of cranial and post-cranial muscular attachments and stress-bearing structures, teeth subject to heavy occcusal wear and low frequencies of dental pathology, and the realization of their full growth potential (despite the incidence of dental enamel-hypoplasia in some individuals). The results of a univariate and multivariate analysis and morphometric studies suggest that the Sarai Nahar Rai and Mahadaha skeletal specimens are representative of populations that shared a high frequency of discrete phenotypic characters of which some were under genetic control. Pending a complete analysis of the Damdama individuals, Lukacs has indicated their biological similarities with the other two series (Lukacs and Misra 1996).

It is likely that these similarities of phenotypic pattern represent genetic affinities and gene flow between the Gangetic lake culture people of the Mesolithic, although random effects of drift and evolutionary parallelism must not be overlooked. Perhaps these populations are regional enclaves of the same macro-population and the degree of contemporaneity between them is not greater than that of a separation by a few generations. This thesis finds support in the archaeological record of their socio-economic and technological practices, and burial customs. In short, the phenotypic pattern of the Gangetic Mesolithic people is unique, and when comparative studies with other prehistoric South Asian populations were conducted, it appeared that the degrees of relationship were distant, and that the people of Sarai Nahar Rai and Mahadaha contributed little biologically to later inhabitants of their regions and beyond. There is a superficial resemblance of the Gangetic Mesolithic people to European Upper Palaeolithic fossils but these phenotypic features are limited. More significant are questions about the evolutionary mechanisms that account for these biological parallels of larger body size

[151] Lukacs et al. (1996), op. cit.

and robusticity. How has natural selection operated, and why do populations like those of Sarai Nahar Rai, Mahadaha, and Damdama no longer exist in South Asia today?[152]

This last statement of one of the leading biological anthropologists needs to be examined in the light of the existing ethnic situation of the Ganga Valley where a number of communities are practising a hunting-foraging way of life right into the twenty-first century. These include the Kanjars, Haburas, Bediyas, Baheliyas, Sansis, Bhantus, Bawariyas and Bangalis. Males and females of these communities have a dark complexion, which is perhaps a result of their long adaptation to the hot and humid climate of the Ganga plains. Yet they are tall, sharp-nosed and extremely handsome. Due to the steady deforestation and consequent loss of wild animal and plant food resources in the Ganga plains, after the introduction of agriculture in the second millennium BC, the Mesolithic hunter-foragers were forced to assimilate themselves into the expanding agriculture-based multi-occupational society. Bereft of the resources for a hunting-foraging way of life and mentally unable to adopt agriculture and attendant occupations, these people took to crime, much like carnivores, who, deprived of their natural habitat due to agricultural expansion and the loss of forests, start preying on domestic animals and, in extreme situations, even on humans. The morphometric and genetic features, including DNA, of these surviving hunting-foraging communities need to be examined and compared with the same features of the Mesolithic hunter-foragers before a conclusion of this nature can be reached.

ART

Since the last quarter of the nineteenth century, a lot of research has been carried out on the prehistoric art of India.[153] As a result, a large body of information is available on the subject.

[152] Kennedy (2000), op. cit., pp. 224-31.

[153] Cockburn (1983a)(1983b), op. cit.; Smith (1906), op. cit.; M. Ghosh (1932), 'Rock Paintings and Other Antiquities of Prehistoric and Later Times', *MASI*, 24, Archaeological Survey of India, New Delhi; Gordon (1958), op. cit.; V.S. Wakankar (1962), 'Painted Rockshelters of India', *Rivista de Sciencz Perhistoriche*, 17, pp. 237-53; idem (1978), *The Dawn of Indian Art*, Vishnu Bhatnagar, Ujjain; R.R.R. Brooks and V.S. Wakankar (1976), *Stone Age Paintings in India*, D.B. Taraporevala and Sons, Bombay; J.P. Singh Deo (1976), 'Prehistoric Cave Paintings of Jogimath Dongar', *The Orissa Historical Research Journal*, XXII, 2, pp. 21-2; Mathpal (1984), op. cit.; V.N. Misra and Y. Mathpal (1979), 'Rock Art of Bhimbetka Region, Central India', *ME*, III, pp. 27-33; Misra et al. (1977), op. cit.; Giriraj Kumar (1981a), 'Aesthetic Sense in the Prehistoric Man', in M.D. Khare (ed.), *Malwa Through the Ages*, Directorate of Archaeology and Museums, Government of Madhya Pradesh, Bhopal; idem (1981b), 'Painted Rockshelters from Rajasthan', in V.S. Srivastava (ed.), *Cultural Contours of India: Dr. Satya Prakash Felicitation Volume*, Abhinav, New Delhi, pp. 277-85; idem (1983), 'Ostrich Eggshells and Early Rock Paintings in India', in K.K. Chakravarty (ed.), *Indian Rock Art*, New

While most of the art evidence belongs to the Mesolithic period, the earliest art goes back to the Upper Palaeolithic period and is dated to *c*. 35,000 years ago. It consists of cross-hatched engravings on ostrich eggshell pieces from Patne in the Dhule district of Maharashtra. Beads of eggshell pieces have been found from Patne and several other sites in Maharashtra, as well as from the Chambal Valley in Madhya Pradesh.[154]

Delhi, pp. 120-8; idem (1989), 'A Unique Ritualistic Dance Composition in Indian Rock Art', *Pictogram*, 2, 3, pp. 7-8; idem (1990), 'Ostrich Egg and the Prehistoric Man: Some More Evidence from Chambal Valley', in N.C. Ghosh and S. Chakravarti (eds.), *Adaptations and Other Essays*, Visva-Bharati, Santiniketan, pp. 69-74; idem (1992), 'Rock Art of Upper Chambal Valley: Some Observations', *Purakala*, 3, 1-2, pp. 56-67; idem (1995), 'Rock Art of Chambal Valley and Aravalli Hills: A Saga of the Achievements of Our Ancestors', *Researcher*, 16-17, pp. 5-10; idem (1996), 'Review of Rock Art Studies: The Post-Stylistic Era or Where Do We Go From Here?', *Purakala*, 7, 1-2, pp. 63-6; Giriraj Kumar and A.K. Sharma (1993), 'Sigiri-Agra Kshetra ki Shaila Chitrakala ki Kshetriya Visheshtayen evam inka Sanskritik Mahattva' (Hindi), *Purakala Souvenir*, pp. 27-8; Giriraj Kumar and Murarilal Sharma (1995), 'Petroglyph Sites in Kalapahar and Ganesh Hill: Documentation and Observations', *Purakala*, 6, 1-2, pp. 56-9; Kumar et al. (1992), 'Rock Art of Upper Chambal Valley: Rock Art and Rock Art Sites', *Purakala*, 3, 1-2, pp. 13-55; Neumayer (1983), op. cit.; idem (1993), op. cit.; V.H. Sonawane (1984), 'An Important Evidence to Date Rock Paintings of Mesolithic Period', in K.K. Chakravarty (ed.), *Rock Art in India*, New Delhi; idem (1996), 'Rock Paintings of Gujarat', in R.K. Sharma and K.K. Tripathi (eds.), *Recent Perspectives in Prehistoric Art in India and Allied Subjects*, Aryan Books International, New Delhi; K.K. Chakravarty (1984) (ed.), *Rock in India*, New Delhi; K.K. Chakravarty and O.P. Misra (1997) (ed.), *The Bounteous Tree-Treasures in Indian Art and Culture*, Sharada Publishing House, Delhi; K.K. Chakravarty and R.G. Bednarik (1997), *Indian Rock Art and Its Global Context*, Motilal Banarsidass and Indira Gandhi Rashtriya Manav Sangrahalaya, Delhi; R.G. Bednarik (1990), 'Rock Art Tour of India: A Report', *Purakala*, 1, 1, p. 16; idem (1993), 'Palaeolithic Art in India', *ME*, XVIII, 2, pp. 33-40; idem (1997), 'Rock Art, Taphonomy and Epistemology', *Purakala*, 8, 1-2, pp. 53-60; Bednarik et al. (1991), 'Petroglyphs from Central India', *Rock Art Research*, 8, 1, pp. 33-5; idem (1993), 'Petroglyphs from Central India', *Purakala*, 2, 1, pp. 24-6; N. Chandramouli (1991), 'Rock Paintings from Budagavi, Anantpur District, Andhra Pradesh, *ME*, XVI, 2, pp. 71-80; idem (1995), 'Petroglyphs from Naidupalli, Andhra Pradesh', *Purakala*, 6, 1-2, pp. 29-34; S.K. Pandey (1993), *Indian Rock Art*, Aryan Books International, New Delhi; S. Pradhan (1994), 'Painted Rockshelters of Orissa: A Case Study of Manikmoda', *Orissa Historical Research Journal*, XXXIX, 1-4, pp. 40-5; idem (1995), 'Rock Art of Orissa: A Study of Original Style', *Purakala*, 6, 1-2, pp. 5-13; idem (1995-6), 'Rock Engravings in the Rockshelters of Upland Orissa', *Puratattva*, 26, pp. 34-42; idem (1997), 'Prehistoric Art', in P.K. Mishra and J.K. Samal (eds.), *Comprehensive History and Culture of Orissa*, Kaveri Books, New Delhi, pp. 46-53; idem (1999), 'Painted Rockshelters of Orissa', in S. Pradhan (ed.), *Orissa History, Culture and Archaeology*, D.K. Printworld, New Delhi, pp. 39-46; idem (2000), 'Rock Art of Orissa', in A.N. Tiwari (ed.), *Reference Orissa*, Enterprising Publishers, Bhubaneswar, pp. 182-7; M.L. Sharma (1996), 'The Sahibee River Valley: A New Region of Rock Art in Rajasthan', in R.K. Sharma and K.K. Tripathi (eds.), *Recent Persepectives in Prehistoric Art in India and Allied Subjects*, Aryan Books International, New Delhi;

[154]Bednarik (l993), op. cit.; Kumar (1983), op. cit.; idem (1990), op. cit.; Giriraj Kumar

However, the real flowering of art took place during the Mesolithic period. The evidence mainly consists of paintings on walls and ceilings, and in the niches of naturally formed rock shelters though, occasionally, petroglyphs are also found.[155] Besides, there are two examples of engravings. One of them is on a prismatic core form Chandravati in Rajasthan. The engraved design consists of cross-hatched squares or a lattice.[156] The other example is an engraving over an area of 1.80 m in length and 25 cm in width on the exterior surface of the Tenmalai rock shelter in Kerala. The design consists of a row of interconnected and inverted Roman alphabet V (Fig. 3).[157]

The richest area of prehistoric paintings is the central part of the country extending from the Aravalli hills of Rajasthan and Sahyadri hills of Gujarat in the west to central Orissa in the east, although isolated examples are also known from Andhra Pradesh in the south. A considerable area of central India is covered with Vindhyan sandstone. This rock, because of its relatively soft nature, is easily susceptible to weathering and breakage which leads to the formation of shelters of various kinds. There are shallow as well as deep cave-like shelters and pseudo-shelters formed by two or more fallen rocks coming to rest against each other. Several thousand such shelters are known from the Mirzapur district of Uttar Pradesh, hilly tracts of Bihar, Jharkhand, Orissa, Madhya Pradesh, Chhattisgarh and eastern Rajasthan. While many of them were used for habitation by the Mesolithic people, and occasionally by Palaeolithic groups, almost all of them were used for executing paintings.

There is a broad uniformity in the whole area on the subject matter, technique, style and the pigments used in making the paintings. The majority of the paintings are in various shades of red and white but ones in green and yellow colours are also known. Very often, the later painters executed their work over already existing paintings and, therefore, several layers or superimpositions of paintings are known. These superimpositions are very useful in building the relative chronology of the paintings. Pieces of haematite with ground facets produced in the process of making pigments for paintings are common in Mesolithic habitation deposits in the shelters. Since the older paintings only depict a hunting-gathering way of life, they can be clearly associated with the Mesolithic phase.

On the basis of subject matter and style, the paintings can be divided into two broad chronological stages: (1) Prehistoric and (2) Historic. The most

---

et al. (1990), 'Archaeological Discoveries and a Study of Late Pleistocene Ostrich Eggshells and Eggshell Objects in India', *ME*, XV, 1, pp. 29-40.

[155]Kumar and Sharma (1995), op. cit.; Bednarik et al. (1991), op. cit.; idem (1993), op. cit.

[156]V.H. Sonawane (1987), 'An Engraved Mesolithic Core from Chandravati, Rajasthan', in B.M. Pande and B.D. Chattopadhyay (eds.), *Archaeology and History*, Agam Kala Prakashan, Delhi, pp. 53-6.

[157]Rajendran (1984), op. cit., p. 23, Fig. 3.

common subject of prehistoric paintings is wild animals. These include wild cattle (*Bos indicus*), the wild buffalo (*Bubalus bubalis*), gaur (*Bos gauros*), sambar (*Cervus unicolor*), chital (*Axis axis*), nilgai (*Boselaphus tragocarnelus*), blackbuck (*Antilope cervicapra*), elephant (*Elephas maximus*), rhinoceros (*Rhinoceros unicormis*), monkey, wild boar (*Sus Scrofa cristatis*), tiger (*Panthera tigris*), jackal (*Canis aureus*), dog (*Canis familiaris*), fox (*Vulpes bengalensis*), porcupine (*Hystrix indica*) and the rat (*Rattus rattus*). The animals are in standing, moving, running, grazing and frolicking postures, and are shown individually as well as in herds. They are very realistically drawn and are characterized by vitality and dynamism.

Next to the animals are scenes of hunting—both of single animals and of herds of animals—by individual hunters as well as by groups of hunters. A few paintings showing unusually large numbers of animals and hunters probably depict ceremonial group hunts, which are still common among the aboriginal populations of central India. The hunters are depicted using spears, bows and arrows, and traps and snares, the spearheads and arrowheads often being tipped and barbed with microliths. There are some paintings of animals of an unusually large size, and others of animals with composite characters. These are probably depictions of mythical animals which were worshipped and held in awe. A painting of a large animal with the body and face of a boar and the horns of a bull particularly belongs to this category. It has a fierce look and is chasing a small human figure which, in turn, is running behind a crab. This scene is depicted in three different shelters. Other subjects of painting include food-gathering scenes, with men and women climbing trees, sometimes with baskets on their backs, group dances, family groups, men running in a file, a nude female, and a man drinking from a vessel.

TECHNOLOGICAL AND CULTURAL EVOLUTION

There are very few sites where the evolution of Mesolithic culture is clearly seen. In the rockshelters and open-air sites at Morhana Pahar, excavators have reported a four-phase evolutionary sequence: (1) non-geometric microlithic industry, (2) geometric microlithic industry, (3) geometric microlithic industry with pottery, (4) diminutive microlithic industry with pottery.[158] In rockshelter IIB-33 at Bhimbetka, the stone industry of the lowest layer is characterized by a comparatively crude blade technique and a lower proportion of geometric forms than that of the upper layers. The microlithic industry of Birabhanpur lacking triangles and trapezes and with large crescents made on flakes or broad blades, is certainly more archaic than the industries of western and central India. The *ter*; industry with its pressure-flaked points, asymmetric geometric forms, and large tools like discoids and choppers, also tends to represent an older technological stage. At the other extreme end of the

[158] Sharma (1965), op. cit.; Varma (1965), op. cit.; idem (1986), op. cit.

technological spectrum are the industries of Bagor and Bhimbetka that are characterized by low proportion of flake tools and a very high degree of geometric precision. At Bagor, extreme miniaturization of microliths is seen.[159]

The evidence for cultural evolution among the Mesolithic people through contact with more advanced communities is clearer. The microlith-using hunter-gatherers came into contact with the metal and pottery-using settled agricultural communities, and borrowed, from the latter, traits like pottery, metal tools and stone, bone and terracotta beads. This contact eventually enabled them to give up the use of stone tools in favour of metal ones and reduce or eliminate their dependence on hunting-gathering by adopting an agricultural way of life. As the contact between the cave-dwelling hunter-gatherers and the farmers in the river valleys in the hilly country of central India grew, the former must have come down from the caves to settle in the plains at the foot of the hills. The aboriginal communities living today in villages at the foothills containing prehistoric shelters, and practising a mixed farming and hunting-gathering economy, are almost certainly in the direct line of descent of the cave-dwelling Stone Age hunter-gatherers.[160]

This process of the acculturation of Mesolithic societies is now documented at a number of archaeological sites.[161] At Langhnaj, a copper knife was found in the middle levels of the site.[162] This must certainly have come from one of the Harappan sites in the neighbourhood. At Bagor in phase II, three copper arrowheads, one spearhead, and awl, hand-made pottery, and numerous stone and bone beads were found in association with a microlithic industry.[163] All these indicate direct or indirect contact with the Harappan and Chalcolithic communities of Gujarat, north-west Rajasthan, and Mewar. At Bhimbetka, sherds of painted Chalcolithic pottery of the Malwa tradition and copper objects have been found in the middle levels of Mesolithic deposits.[164] At Langhnaj,[165] Bagor,[166] Bhimbetka,[167] and Lekhahia,[168] iron arrowheads and

[159] Misra and Nagar (1981), op. cit.

[160] M. Nagar (1983), 'Ethnoarchaeology of the Bhimbetka Region', *ME*, VII, pp. 61-9; M. Nagar and V.N. Misra (1994), 'Survival of the Hunting-gathering Tradition in the Ganga Plains and Central India', in B. Allchin (ed.), *Living Traditions: Studies in the Ethnoarchaeology of South Asia*, Oxford-IBH, New Delhi, pp. 169-91.

[161] V.N. Misra (1976b), 'Evidence of Culture Contact between Terminal Stone Age Hunter-gatherers and Contemporary Farmers', in U.V. Singh (ed.), *Archaeological Congress and Seminar: 1972*, Kurukshetra University, Kurukshetra, pp. 151-61; G. Possehl and K.A.R. Kennedy (1979), 'The Hunter-gatherer/Agricultural Exchange in Prehistory: An Example from India', *CA*, 20, 3, pp. 592-3; Lukacs (1990), op. cit.

[162] Sankalia (1965), op. cit.

[163] Misra (1973a), op. cit.

[164] Kennedy et al. (2002), op. cit.

[165] Sankalia (1965), op. cit.

[166] Misra (1973a), op. cit.

[167] Misra (1989d), op. cit.

[168] Sharma (1965), op. cit.

early historic wheel-made pottery have been found in the topmost levels of Mesolithic deposits, showing that the tradition of using microliths and associated stone tools persisted right up to the introduction of iron technology, and disappeared only after iron tools and weapons became freely available to the common people in the early historic period.

The process of assimilation of the Mesolithic hunter-foragers into the larger Indian society needs a little elaboration. Agriculture and its by-product, settled village life, first appeared in the Indian subcontinent at Mehrgarh at the junction of the Baluchistan plateau and the Indus alluvial plain around 6500 BC. It was based on the cultivation of wheat and barley, and the domestication of cattle, sheep and goat. All these crops and animals existed in a wild state in the vast stretch of land extending from the eastern edge of the Mediterranean Sea to the eastern edge of the Baluchistan plateau, bordering the Indus plain. One of the many consequences of the emergence of agriculture or food production was a dramatic rise in human population. Since Baluchistan is largely a hilly terrain and has only narrow alluvial valleys available for cultivation, it could not contain the dramatically expanding human population, which eventually spilled over into the vast and fertile alluvial plain of the Indus River. The immigrants from Baluchistan established villages which slowly grew into towns and eventually into the cities of the Indus/Harappan civilization around 3000 BC.

The second introduction of agriculture into India was from the east and it consisted of the introduction of rice, taro and yam cultivation, and the domestication of the pig. Rice as a wild grass grows today in the vast region extending from the east of Allahabad in Uttar Pradesh to southern China and Southeast Asia. The largest varieties of wild rice are found in Orissa. Taro and yams are important food crops in the central and eastern Ganga Valley, eastern and north-eastern India, and the south up to Maharashtra.

The third source of agricultural crops introduced into South Asia was Africa. From Ethiopia in Africa, three important crops, *jowar* (*Sorghum bicolor*), *bajra* (*Pennisetum typhoideum*) and *ragi* (*Eleusine coracana*) were introduced here.

The fourth source of the South Asian crops was indigenous. Crops like black gram or *urid* (*Vigna mungo*), green gram (*Phaseolus mungo*), Italian millet (*Setaria italica*), panicum millet (*Panicum miliaceum*), (*Eleusine indica*), *kodo* millet (*Paspalum scrobiculatum*), *kulith* (*Dolichos lahlab*), hyacinth bean (*Dolichos biflorus*), lentil (*Lens eaculenta*), *khesari* (*Lathruss sajivus*), common pea (*Pisum arvense*), pigeon pea (*Cajanus cajan*), groundnut (*Arachis hypogea*), linseed (*Linum usitatissimum*), *bori ber* or Indian jujube (*Zizyphus jujuba*), and the egg plant or brinjal (*Solanum melongena*) were indigenous to South Asia.

Once the knowledge and practice of agriculture was introduced into the country around six thousand years ago, it was quickly adopted by the Mesolithic hunter-foragers. Agriculture, comprising plant cultivation and the domestication of animals, had many advantages over the hunting-foraging way of life. It ensured a steady, regular and assured food supply, and made permanent settlement possible. It also caused a dramatic increase in the human population. Agriculture also necessitated subsidiary occupations like those of the coppersmith, goldsmith, silversmith, weaver, carpenter, potter, brick-maker, mason, architect, beadmaker, basketmaker, leatherworker, oilpresser, barber, washerman and many others. Surplus food production by enterprising farmers allowed a section of the population to utilize its talent and energies for these newly-emerging occupations. The society got diversified into different occupations. For the new crafts, raw materials like semi-precious stones, copper, gold, silver and cotton were required, which had to be procured from distant places. Similarly, manufactured goods had to be supplied to the people who needed them. Thus, a new class of businessmen and traders came into being.

Initially, villages came into existence. Slowly they grew into towns and eventually into cities. Around 5,000 years ago, urban life appeared in the Indus/Harappan civilization in the semi-arid and arid parts of north-west India. With the production of wealth, society became divided into the rich and poor, exploiters and exploited. As social and economic spheres became more complex, a formal administration was required to ensure the safety and security of citizens, particularly the wealthy and the trading class, from anti-social elements. Rules and laws had to be framed and enforced, citizens' grievances had to be redressed, and social harmony and peace had to be maintained. Thus, a system of bureaucracy, intelligence, police and judiciary came into existence. For the protection of society from external aggression, armed forces had to be created. For the political system to be able to provide all these facilities, it had to levy taxes on wealthy citizens. Around the same time, writing had to be invented to keep accounts of traders' transactions, the revenues collected by the administration from the citizens, and the expenditure incurred on the provision of civic amenities, including the salaries of administrative employees.

With the dramatic expansion of the population, the establishment of new villages, towns and the cities, and the creation of roads, ponds and other civic facilities, there was naturally a shrinkage of land under primeval forests and, consequently, a reduction in wild plant and animal food resources. As a consequence, the habitat of the Mesolithic hunter-foragers shrank. They had only two choices: (1) to assimilate themselves into the new emerging and steadily expanding agriculture-based rural and urban society, and enjoy the benefits of a secure food supply and abundant leisure after the closure of agricultural operations during the winter and summer, and (2) to enjoy the unrestricted freedom of a hunting-foraging way of life and suffer the insecurity of food unavailability. The majority of the hunter-foragers chose the former course and got assimilated into the newly-emerging rural and urban society by adopting agriculture or other occupations. However, a few of them prized their freedom more than food security, persisted with their hunting-foraging way of life, and are doing so right into the twenty-first century. As natural resources for their livelihood were considerably depleted, some of them took to other occupations to supplement their subsistence.

Hundreds of such hunting-foraging communities survive in India to this day. Among them are the Aheriyas of the Punjab (Ibbetson 1883), the Kanjars, Baheliyas, Haburas, Bawariyas, Bejdays, Sansis, Bhantus, and Bangalis of the Ganga plains;[169] the Van Vagris;[170] Bagris and Kalbeliyas of Rajasthan;[171] the Pardhis, Kuchbandhiyas and Kabutars of Madhya Pradesh;[172] the Pardhis of Gujarat;[173] the Pardhis and Vaids of Maharashtra;[174] the Baheliyas of Bihar;[175] the Birhors of Jharkhand;[176] the Makadias of Orissa;[177] the Yaruidis[178] and Chenchus of Andhra Pradesh; and the Kadars, Cholanaikams and Malapantarams of Kerala.[179]

Deprived of their natural food resources, these traditional hunting-foraging communities took to other occupations to supplement their resources for sheer survival. Using their traditional craft skills, they manufacture items useful to farmers and barter them for grain and other items. For example, the Kanjars of north India make nets from hemp string for storing and transporting wheat chaff, and for covering the mouths of bullocks during threshing. They dig the *khas* grass from riverbeds for making screens which were used before the introduction of coolers and air conditioners for cooling offices during summer. They also make grinding stones and roughen their surfaces. In addition, they collect honey from beehives located in the eaves of thatched roofs of village houses and share it with the houseowner. The

[169] J.C. Nesfield (1883), 'The Kanjars of Upper India', *Calcutta Review*, LXXVII, pp. 368-98; W. Crooke (1896), *The Tribes and Castes of Northwestern Provinces and Oudh*, vols. I-IV, Government of India, Calcutta; M. Nagar and V.N. Misra (1989), 'Hunter-gatherers in an Agrarian Setting: The Nineteenth Century Situations in the Ganga Plains', *ME*, XIII, pp. 65-78; idem (1990), 'The Kanjars: A Hunting-gathering Community of the Ganga Valley, Uttar Pradesh', *ME*, XV, 2, pp. 71-88.

[170] V.N. Misra (1990), 'The Van Vagris: "Lost" Hunters of the Thar Desert, Rajasthan', *ME*, pp. 89-108.

[171] U.B. Mathur (1969), *Ethnographic Atlas of Rajasthan (with Special Reference to Scheduled Castes and Scheduled Tribes*, Government of India, Delhi.

[172] R.V. Russell and R.B. Hira Lal (1961), *The Tribes and Castes of the Central Provinces of India*, Government of India Press, Delhi; M. Nagar and V.N. Misra (1993), 'The Pardhis: A Hunting-gathering Community of Central and Western India', *ME*, XVIII, 1, pp. 115-40.

[173] R.E. Enthoven (1922), *Tribes and Castes of Bombay*, Government Central Press, Bombay.

[174] Ibid.; K.C. Malhotra et al. (1983), 'Hunting Strategies among Three Non-pastoral Nomadic Groups of Maharashtra', *Man in India*, 63, 1, pp. 21-39.

[175] E.T. Dalton (1872), *Descriptive Ethnology of Bengal*, Government Press, Calcutta.

[176] S.C. Roy (1925), 'Birhors: A Little Known Tribe of Chota Nagpur, Ranchi', *Man in India*.

[177] Dalton (1872), op. cit.

[178] Murty (1981), op. cit.

[179] L.K. Iyer and Anantha Krishna (1935), *The Mysore Tribes and Castes*, The Mysore University Press, Mysore.

Van Vagris of the Thar desert work as contract watchmen for protecting the winter crops of farmers from wild and domestic animals and birds, and their women beg food from village homes.[180] The Pardhi women of Madhya Pradesh sell cosmetics and trinkets to village women, and the Kuchbandhiya women of the same state sell crockery. The Haburas of Uttar Pradesh go begging from house-to-house. They yell so loudly and frighteningly that housewives give them food or flour just to get rid of them.

Others utilize their singing and dancing skills for entertaining the rural folk. For example, the Bediya women entertain people of lower castes with song and dance at functions like the birth of a male child or a marriage, and their male family members accompany them as musicians. The Kalbeliyas of Rajasthan catch snakes and entertain people as snake charmers, and their women, like the Bediya women, entertain people with song and dance. The Bediya women also indulge in prostitution.

Barring a few hunter-foragers like the Van Vagris, Birhors, Chenchus, and Kadars, almost all others have taken to crimes like theft, burglary, highway robbery and dacoity. Many of them, if resisted, do not hesitate to resort to violence, including cruelly hitting their victims with iron rods and even committing cold-blooded murder in their pursuit of crime. The most notorious criminals are the Kanjars, Bawariyas, Sansis, Haburas and Pardhis. Among the Pardhis, young boys are mercilessly beaten by their elders so that, when caught and beaten by the police, they will not confess their crime. The yelling of the Haburas is so frightening that mothers put small children to sleep by telling them that a Habura has come.

The British government had designated these people as criminal tribes and put them into special settlements to keep a watch over them. After Independence, the government enacted a law by which this pejorative appellation was removed and they were designated as Denotified and Nomadic Tribes. They are being helped to give up crime and their nomadic habits, and settle down permanently.

The government provides them free land for housing and cultivation, and grants for buying livestock and agricultural inputs. They are also given special privileges for education and employment, and many of them have made effective use of these benefits. Today many members of these communities are well-educated and occupy important positions in government departments. Others have taken to trade and other occupations. Unfortunately, the members of a few communities, particularly the Sansis, Bawariyas and Pardhis, still continue to live by crime.

ASSIMILATION OF HUNTER-FORAGERS INTO THE HINDU CASTE SYSTEM

Towards the end of the second millennium BC, when the Harappan Civilization begun to decline, the Indo-Aryan or Sanskrit-speaking people appeared in

[180]Misra (1990), op. cit.

Table 6.2: Radiometric Dates from Mesolithic Sites

1. Radiocarbon Dates

Site Name	Lab No.	5730 BC			Calibration
# Apegaon 3	A 7637	6,280	+	210 - 205	
# Apegaon 6	A 7638	6,600	±	100	
Adamgarh	TF 120	5505	±	129	N.A.
Adamgarh	TF 116	900	±	108	1105 BC-805 BC
Akoni	BS 417	7,150	±	80	
Apegaon 2	A 7636	4,250	±	95	
Apegaon Chal	PRL 384	3,520	±	100	
Baghai Khor	TF 187	1670	±	124 AD	N.A.
Baghor	SUA 1422	3514	±	90	4110 BC-3795 BC
Baghor II	PRL 715	6385	±	227	N.A.
Bagor	TF 786	4480	±	206	5365 BC-4965 BC
Bagor	TF 1007	3840	±	129	4570 BC-4385 BC
Bagor	TF 1011/12	3295	±	88	3955 BC-3775 BC
Bagor	TF 1009	1775	±	108	3400 BC-3160 BC
Bagor	TF 1005/6	2115	±	93	2650 BC-2315 BC
Bhimbetka	PRL 17	5845	±	216	N.A.
Bhimbetka	PRL 50	4085	±	113	4950 BC-4560 BC
Bhimbetka	PRL 318	1715	±	103	2135 BC-1755 BC
Bhimbetka	PRL 306	955	±	113	1125 BC-825 BC
Bhimbetka	PRL 534	915	±	155	1125 BC-795 BC
Bhimbetka	PRL 18	780	±	129	890 BC-770 BC
Bhimbetka	PRL 317	615	±	103	795 BC-420 BC
Bhimbetka	PRL 310	440	±	103	445 BC-375 BC
Bhimbetka	PRL 51	106	±	113	185 BC-AD 35
Bhimbetka	PRL 316	40	±	103	35 BC-AD 95
Bhimbetka	PRL 315	135	±	185	AD 10-465
Bhimbetka	PRL 535	755	±	155	AD 790-1175
Bhimbetka	PRL 311	860	±	82	AD 870-1050
Damdama		8640	±	65	
		8865	±	65	
Dharangaon	BS 1422	7,000	±	190	
Inamgaon	BS 146	10100	±	155	N.A.
Langhnaj	TF 744	2040	±	108	2550 BC-2185 BC
Lekhahia	TF 419	2415	±	113	3035 BC-2780 BC
		3500-4200			

		8370 ± 75	
Nirgudsar	BS 43	38220 ± 3296	N.A.
Ranjegaon	BS 1256	7, 800 ± 130	
Sakshalpimpri	BS 1259	7,800 ± 100	
Sarai Nahar Rai	TF 1356/9	995 ± 124	1140 BC-865 BC
		4625-4465	
		4220-4075	
Sarai Nahar Rai	TF 1104	8400 ± 113	N.A.
Talegaon	BS 1421	10,390 ± 130	
Talegaon	BS 1427	6,930 ± 120	

2. THERMOLUMINESCENCE DATES FROM MESOLITHIC SITES

Site Name	Lab No.	Dates
Amarpura	PRL: TL: S 9	6140 BP
Amarpura	PRL: TL: S 8	14610 BP
Amarpura	PRL: TL: S 7	16190 BP
Langhnaj	PRL: TL: S 12	5180 BP
Langhnaj	PRL: TL: S 11	8630 BP
Langhnaj	PRL: TL: S 10	20280 BP
Bagor	PRL: TL: S 13	2100 BP
Bagor	PRL: TL: S 14	
Sarai Nahar Rai		2935 BP

north-west India. Their main focus, like that of the Harappan Civilization, was the Saraswati River, which even today survives as the dry bed of the Ghaggar-Hakra in Haryana, Rajasthan and Pakistan. On the banks of the Saraswati, the Aryan sages (*rishis*) composed the hymns of the *Rigveda*, which, though mainly intended as prayers to Aryan deities like Agni, Indra, Varuna, Mitra, Nasatyas and Usha, also reflect the social, political and economic life of the period. The Rigvedic society was divided into four *varnas*, Brahman, Kshatriya, Vaishya and Shudra, on the basis of occupation, biological composition and stature, the shape of the nose and complexion, the degrees by which they practised Vedic rituals, and their living habits.

After the introduction of iron technology, the spread of agriculture was accelerated in the middle and lower Ganga Valley because iron tools facilitated the cleaning of the dense and tangled forests of the sub-humid and humid Ganga plains. This naturally led to the rapid decrease of wild animal and plant food resources on which the Mesolithic hunter-foragers had depended for their livelihood. As a result, these communities were forced to assimilate themselves into the expanding agriculture-based and multi-occupational society. By this time, the fourfold *varna* system got divided into castes or *jatis*. Caste is a uniquely Hindu social phenomenon. It is based, first and foremost, on occupation. Its other features are a strict hierarchical order, endogamy, *anuloma* and *pratiloma* forms of marriage, rules relating to the sharing of food, ritual purity and pollution.[181] Hunter-foragers who had adopted agriculture or related occupations, or chosen to persist with their atavistic way of life, were placed into one or other of the *jatis*, depending on the prestige purity attached to their occupations, the level of ritual purity practised by them, and the cleanliness of their habits. Those who followed unclean occupations like the lifting of animal carcasses, working in leather, scavenging, keeping pigs, or practising omnivorous food habits, were placed at the very bottom of the hierarchical caste order and declared as untouchables. These, peoples are today designated as Scheduled Castes under the provisions of the Indian Constitution.[182]

The proportion of Scheduled Castes in the total population is highest in the Indo-Gangetic plains (Fig. 6.2), which, because of the fertile alluvial soil and plentiful availability of water, are under the most intensive cultivation and cleared of forests. This percentage is shown in Fig. 6.2 and Table 6.3.

This high percentage of Scheduled Castes in the Indo-Gangetic plains strongly affects the political life here, particularly of Uttar Pradesh. It also creates enormous social turmoil. As against the predominance of Scheduled Castes in the plains, in the hilly and forested belts of central India, the Eastern Ghats and north-eastern India, which were not suitable for intensive agriculture, hunting-foraging and a primitive agricultural way of life has persisted. In these areas, the Scheduled Tribes have a high proportion in the total population (Fig. 6.3, Table 6.3). This remarkably contrasting distribution of Scheduled Castes and Scheduled Tribes can be understood only against the background of the expansion of agriculture and the assimilation of hunter-foragers into the emerging farming-based *jati* society.

Table 6.3: The Percentage of Scheduled Castes and Scheduled Tribes in India

State	Scheduled Castes	Scheduled Tribes
Punjab	26.9	0.0
Himachal Pradesh	24.6	4.6
West Bengal	22.0	5.6
Uttar Pradesh	21.2	0.2

[181] J.H. Hutton (1946), *Caste in India: Its Nature, Function and Origins*, Cambridge University Press, Cambridge; Sir Denzil Ibbetson (1916), *Punjab Castes*, Punjab Government, Lahore; D.G. Mandelbaum (1972), *Society in India*, Popular Prakashan, Bombay.

[182] V.N. Misra and Malti Nagar (1997), 'From Tribe to Caste: An Ethnoarchaeological Perspective', in Dev Nathan (ed.), *From Tribe to Caste*, Indian Institute of Advanced Studies, Shimla, pp. 136-66.

Haryana	19.1	0.0
Tamil Nadu	18.4	1.1
Rajasthan	17.0	12.2
Karnataka	15.1	4.9
Tripura	15.1	28.4
	14.9	5.9
Orissa	14.7	22.4
Bihar	14.5	8.3
Madhya Pradesh	14.1	23.0
Kerala	10.0	1.0
Jammu & Kashmir	8.3	0.0
Gujarat	7.2	14.2
Maharashtra	7.1	9.2
Manipur	1.2	27.3
Arunachal Pradesh	0.5	69.8
Meghalaya	0.4	80.6
Nagaland	0.0	84.0
	0.0	93.6

CHRONOLOGY

Although not all the excavated sites have been dated by radiometric methods, the chronology of the Mesolithic period can be determined on the basis of around fifty uncaliberated radiocarbon dates from twenty sites and eleven TL dates from five sites. The oldest available date is 10100 +100 BP and it comes from the site of Inamgaon near Pune. A date of *c.* 10000 BP is known from Sarai Nahar Rai but as it is obtained from uncharred bone, its reliability is low. From Bhimbetka, the oldest date is 7790 BP, and from Adamgarh it is 6430 BP. The beginning of microlithic industries can, therefore, be assigned to *c.* 12000 BP. However, it needs to be pointed out that microlithic industries in Sri Lanka are dated by radiocarbon to as early as 35000 BP. Since the microlithic industry of the *teris* of Tamil Nadu is closely similar to that of the Sri Lankan caves, it is reasonable to assume that the *teri* microlithic industry should be of equal antiquity. Two dates from phase II of Bagor, which has an association of copper tools and pottery with microliths, are 4715 BP and 4060 BP. Several dates from the upper levels of the Bhimbetka shelters have readings between 3000 and 2000 BP. It is significant that the Mesolithic occupation in central Indian caves as well as on the sand dunes in western India came to an end soon after the beginning of the Christian era. Iron first appeared in the Ganga Valley at the beginning of the first millennium BP and slowly diffused to other parts of the country. As iron tools began to be available to the microlith-using hunter-gatherer communities, they started giving up the use of stone technology. Both archaeological data and radiocarbon dates suggest that the use of stone tools had completely disappeared by the beginning of the Christian era. The Stone Age finally ended after the introduction and diffusion of iron technology.

ACKNOWLEDGEMENTS

I am deeply grateful to Dr. Balaram Tripathi, Alok Kanungo and R.N. Singh for their help in typing the text. In the section on Biological Anthropology, while the portions on Langhnaj, Bagor and Bhimbetka are based on the summaries in Ehrhardt and Kennedy (1965), Lukacs et al. (1982), and Kennedy et al. (2002), respectively, those on Baghai Khor, Lekhahia, Sarai Nahar Rai, Mahadaha and Damdama are virtually reproduced unchanged, barring parts not relevant to the present text, from Kennedy (2000). It was not possible for me to summarize the concise and highly technical text of Kennedy. Putting the selected portions repeatedly into quotation marks would have interrupted the flow of reading. I have cited the authors by the year of publication and page numbers at appropriate places, and I sincerely hope that this candid confession adequately compensates for the omission of quotation marks.

Chapter 7

Beginning of Agriculture: Kashmir

M.K. Dhavalikar

INTRODUCTION

The transition from Mesolithic to Neolithic was a revolutionary change and was, therefore, referred to as the 'Neolithic revolution'. However, this change was gradual, spanning a few millennia. How and why did it happen? Mesolithic man lived a comfortable life because of a favourable environment which, however, started deteriorating and led to a culture change. Gordon V. Childe explained this as due to the increasing aridity in West Asia when desertification began and oases were formed.[1] This brought man and animals in close proximity to each other for water. Man watched the behaviour of animals and domesticated them. This ecological model has been challenged by the 'population stress' model developed by Mark Cohen which is based on ethnographic parallels.[2] In fact, demographic stress as an important factor in the domestication of plants and animals was first suggested by Leslie White (1959: 258). Lewis R. Binford, too, argued that population pressure during the Mesolithic was largely responsible for the beginning of agriculture.[3] It appears that the favourable environment during the Mesolithic (15000-10000 BP) led to an increase in population and at the end of this period the available food supply—plant and animal—was not sufficient to support the growing population. Hence, the domestication of plants and animals began in West Asia in the Kurdish hills of Iraq where wild species of wheat and barley grew abundantly, and wild sheep and goat roamed. The different stages of their domestication have now been well-documented in the archaeological record of West Asia.

The transition from food gathering to food production is clearly discernible in the Tahunian and Natufian cultures of Israel. The Tahunians led a seasonally settled life and subsisted on hunting-gathering and wild wheat and barley. They had stone querns for crushing and grinding purposes. Domesticated

[1]Gordon V. Childe (1928), *The Most Ancient East*, Routeledge and Kegan Paul, London.

[2]Mark Cohen (1977), *Food Crisis in Prehistory: Overpopulation and the Origins of Agriculture*, Yale University Press, New Haven.

[3]L.R. Binford (1963), 'Post-Pleistocene Adaptations', in S.R. and L.R. Binford (eds.), *New Perspectives in Archaeology*, pp. 313-41.

species of plants and animals began to occur towards the close of the Tahunian phase. The following Natufian culture represents the Neolithic phase. The knowledge of agriculture spread east and west in a short period of time.

In the subcontinent, the beginning of settled life now goes back to about 7500 BC as is clear from evidence from the excavations at Mehrgarh, located near Quetta on the Bolan River.[4] Here, the first two cultural periods are Neolithic and have been assigned, on the basis of radiocarbon determinations, to *c.* 7500-5000 BC. It may be noted that wild barley, and wild cattle, sheep and goat are present in the Indo-Iranian borderland and seem to have been independently domesticated, if the Mehrgarh evidence is any indication.[5]

The first cultural period (7000-6000 BC) at Mehrgarh marks the beginning of settled life in the Indian subcontinent, which is almost contemporaneous with that in West Asia. It represents the primary Neolithic stage which is aceramic, but baskets lined with bitumen and gourds were used as containers. People lived in multi-roomed mud brick houses of four or six small rooms with an entrance through the roof. The size of the mud bricks is regular: 33 × 14.5 × 7 cm and 28 × 14.5 × 7 cm which is especially noteworthy as it approximates the Early Harappan and Urban Harappan standards of 3 × 2 × 1 cm and 4 × 2 × 1 cm. There were hearths inside the houses, usually in corner rooms, one of which was lined with bricks and had a dome. There were compartmentalized storage structures. Grinding stones and querns have been found. Mention should be made of shell bangles, beads of calcite, lapis lazuli and turquoise, as also clay figurines. Rich evidence of a food economy has been recovered from Mehrgarh. The people domesticated barley, cattle and sheep/goat.

Hand-made pottery occurs in Period II (5000-4500 BC). Mud brick architecture continues and so does the subsistence pattern, the only noteworthy feature being the discovery of wheat and barley, which grow only in irrigated fields, suggesting some form of irrigation.

Human burials belonging to both the phases of the Neolithic have been unearthed. Of the 166 inhumations, eighty-five belong to Period I and the remaining to Period II. They have been described as 'wall graves' because the body was kept alongside a wall which was probably built after the burial. The body was decked with personal ornaments such as necklaces of beads of calcite, shell, turquoise and so on. In one case, a tool kit was placed in the burial which indicates that he was a craftsman. Bitumen baskets were found in a few burials. Children, too, were buried. A study of skeletal biology shows that the Neolithic people of Mehrgarh and also those of Southwest Asia were different from those of Europe.[6]

[4] J.F. Jarrige (1993), 'The Excavations at Mehrgarh: Their Significance for Understanding the Background of the Harappan Civilization', *HCRP*, pp. 79-84.

[5] Gregory L. Possehl (2002), *Indus Civilization: A Contemporary Perspective*, Alta Mira Press, New York.

[6] John R. Lukacs (1989), 'Biological Affinities from Dental Morphology from Neolithic Mehrgarh', in J.M. Kenoyer (ed), *OPNP*, Wisconsin Arch. Reports, Madison, pp. 75-88.

The third cultural period at the site marks the arrival of a new people who introduced many innovations in the cultural pattern.

In other parts of the country the Mesolithic phase lingered till about 3000 BC after which Neolithic food producing cultures emerged in these different regions:

(1) Kashmir Valley
(2) Mid-Ganga Valley, U.P. and Bihar
(3) South India
(4) Eastern India

Explorations and selective excavations have unearthed interesting evidence which throws light on the Neolithic farming communities, but that for the transition from hunting-gathering to food production is not available, except for Gufkral in the Kashmir Valley (Fig. 7.1). Gufkral literally means 'potter's

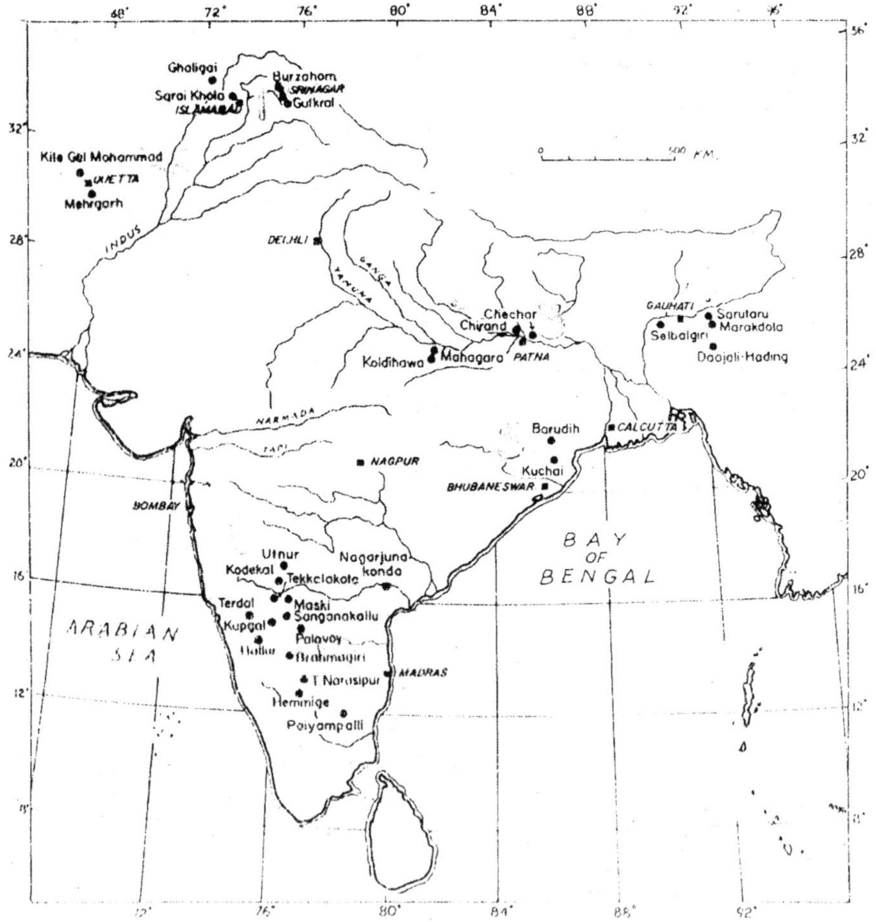

Fig. 7.1: Map showing important Neolithic sites in India

cave' (guf, potter; kral, cave). The ancient site (35 54′ N, 75 60′ E) is located 41 km south-east of Srinagar, on an extensive deposit of the upper Karewas in between two streams which join the Jhelum River. A few menhirs stand on the site.[7]

The excavation revealed a threefold culture: 1. Neolithic (2800-1500 BC), II. Megalithic (1000-500 BC), and III. Early Historic (300 BC-300 AD). The Neolithic habitation is divided into three sub-phases, viz., I-a pre-pottery Neolithic (2800-2500 BC), I-b early Neolithic (2500-2000 BC) and I-c late Neolithic (2000-1500 BC). The earliest inhabitants (I-a) lived in pit dwellings, either circular, oval or rectangular in plan (Fig. 7.2). Their dimensions varied

Fig. 7.2: Pit dwellings, Burzahom, Kashmir, Phase I-a

[7]A.K. Sharma (1980-1), 'Animal Bones from Gufkral: Evidence of Human and Non-human Activities', *Puratattva*, 12, pp. 31-6.

from 3.80 m to 1.50 m at the top, but they were considerably shallow, about 20 to 30 cm in depth; these can be better referred to as sunken floors.

One rectangular pit (3 × 1.50 m) was, however, 1 m deep. They contained hearths and storage pits. They had postholes around the periphery which supported the roof that was covered by birch (*bhurja* Sk) leaves, as is clear from the evidence at Burzahom near Srinagar. The dwelling pits had low mud walls, burnt portions of which have been recovered from excavations. The pits were cut into the loessic deposit and their floor decorated with red ochre.

Phase I-b at Gufkral is identical with the early Neolithic phase at Burzahom near Srinagar. It is characterized by pit dwellings cut deep (1.0 m) into the loessic deposit. These were bell-shaped, wide at the bottom and narrow at the top. At Burzahom, sunken floors (or shallow pit chambers) were noticed in the central area of the habitation (Fig. 7.3) whereas pit dwellings were

Fig. 7.3: Neolithic houses, Burzahom, Kashmir, Phase I-b

located along the periphery.[8] This is indicative of some sort of social hierarchy. The pit chambers had depressions on all four sides and, in the central part, were storage bins and hearths. The dwelling pits had stepped entrances and, in some cases, alcoves dug into the walls have been noticed. Sometimes two pit dwellings were joined by an arched passage. The pits of this phase (I-b) were dug deeper and the earlier ones enlarged. The floor was made of clay mixed with lime (*chunam*), and rammed hard and periodically plastered with mud. There was no hearth inside the pit but it was usually to be found in the courtyard which, too, was well-maintained. Oblong and circular ones have been noticed in this phase with their sides plastered with mud. One large round hearth (diameter 93 cm, 30 cm deep) had postholes around its margin; it may have been used for roasting hunted animals. Some dwellings had twin chambers. It is interesting to note that no dwelling pit contained a hearth, which was always located in the courtyard in the open. This shows that much of the life of the Neolithic folk in Kashmir, as elsewhere, was lived in the courtyard, as is the case at present, and hence, the area around the house was well-maintained by frequent plastering with mud. A wall built of pebble and a mud platform was probably a religious structure.

In Phase I-c, there is a marked change in the residential structures. Most of the earlier pits were filled up with debris and mud huts with walls 30-40 cm thick were built. The use of mud bricks is also attested. There were, however, a few dwelling pits which had no postholes, suggesting that their roofs were moveable.

POTTERY

Pottery appears in Phase I-b at Gufkral and at Burzahom in the earlier phase of the Neolithic occupation. It was all hand-made, predominantly grey ware with which a dull red ware is associated. The forms include jars, bowls basins and one stem of a dish-on-stand. The vessels had mat-impressed bases and punched decorations. Along with the thick, coarse grey and red pottery, a fine grey ware was also used. A pottery kiln of this phase, roughly circular in plan (diameter 1.70 cm and 20 cm deep) was encountered. Hand-made wares continue in the succeeding I-c phase when wheel-made pottery was also introduced. Besides, a burnished grey ware occurs which appears to be an improved variety of the fine grey ware of the preceding phase. It is represented by high-necked globular jars, bowls and basins. A fine red ware jar painted with a horned figure is probably an import from the Early Harappan period at Saraikhola, which is situated closeby in the Potwar plateau.

[8]R.N. Kaw (1979), 'The Neolithic Culture of Kashmir', in D.P. Agrawal and D.K. Chakrabarti (eds.), *Essays in Indian Protohistory*, D.K. Publishers, New Delhi, pp. 219-28.

SUBSISTENCE

The subsistence of the Neolithic settlers of the Kashmir Valley was based more on hunting than on agriculture. They cultivated six-row barley (*Hordeum vulgare Linn*), wheat (*Triticum* sp), lentils (*Lens esculenta Moonch*) and a weedy plant (*Lithospermum arvense*). They hunted wild sheep (*Ovis orientalis*), wild goat (*Capra aegagrus*), wild cattle (*Bos namadicus*), red deer (*Cervus elephus*), wolf (*Canis lupus*), Himalayan ibex (*Capra ibex*), Himalayan Tahr, relative of the wild goat (*Hemitragees jemlahicus*), serow (*Naemorhaedus bubalinus*) and bear (*Ursus*). Only sheep (*Ovis aries*) and goat (*Capra hircus*) were domesticated. In the succeeding I-b phase, the number of domesticated animals increased and included cattle. There is less reliance on hunting for subsistence and the increase of dog bones indicates that it assisted in hunting small game. Holes were bored in long bones for extracting the marrow within. Domestic fowl appears in I-b and so does common pea (*Pisum arvense Linn*).

The final phase (I-c) marks the complete domestication of cattle (*Bos indicus*), sheep and goat, which were reduced in size because of this. There was a greater reliance on small game as is evident from the bones of the hare (*Lepus*), hedgehog, rodents, beaver, pig (*Susscrofa*) and fish.

TOOL KIT (FIG. 7.4)

Ground and polished stone and bone tools occur from the beginning of habitation. In phase I-a, there were five stone celts along with picks, stones, drills, querns, pounders, pestles and points, besides two adzes of Himalayan schist of which one was painted with red ochre. Ring stones occur in phase I-b whereas sharpners come from phase I-c. A unique tool referred to as a harvester was also used in I-c; it has two holes. It does not seem to have been used for harvesting for microwear studies indicate that it was used as a pendant around the neck. These artefacts are called harvesters in China where the Yang Shao culture flourished in the Yellow River Valley.

The most interesting are the bone tools which have been recovered in large numbers, particularly from I-c levels. They mostly include points, but also harpoons, needles, awls and arrowheads. They are mostly made of the bones of the deer and a few from the antlers. Copper celts, arrowheads and spearheads need a special mention.

Personal ornaments include beads of agate and carnelian, bone beads, spiral-headed hairpins of copper, a tiger claw-shaped pendant of jade, besides copper bangles and rings.

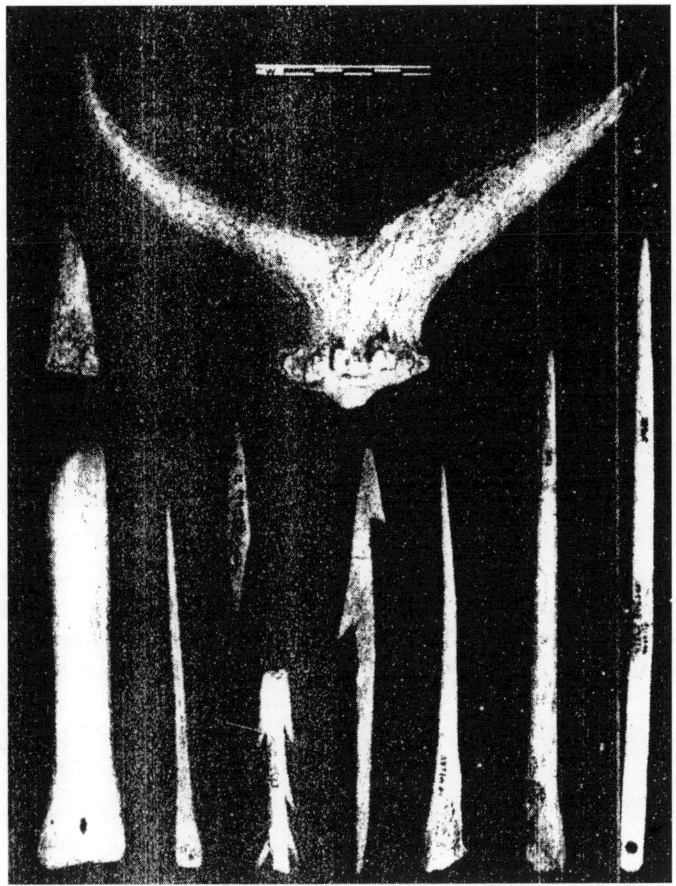

Fig. 7.4: Bone tools, Burzahom, Kashmir

BURIALS

Six human burials were exposed at Burzahom some of which were primary internments and some secondary.[9] The skeleton was placed in the pit in a crouching posture. There were animal burials, too, containing bones of wild dogs and antlers of the barasingha.[10]

[9]A.K. Sharma (1967), 'Neolithic Human Burials from Burzahom, Kashmir', *JOIB*, 16, pp. 239-42.

[10]A.K. Sharma (1968), 'Animal Burial from Burzahom: A Neolithic Settlement in Kashmir', *JOIB*, 18, pp. 40-4.

ART

The engraved stone slabs from Burzahom deserve special attention. One of them depicts a hunting scene and the other has been identified as a 'tectiform', which is a complex design of unclear meaning. The former was found to be a part of a rectangular structure made of stone slabs and rubble, which has been assigned to the late Neolithic phase of Burzahom.[11] It is clear that the slab was robbed from some other place and used in the structure. It is flat on both sides but the front face on which the scene is carved is smoothened. The hunting scene covers an area of 48 × 27 cm and depicts a stag hunt. The animal is in the middle with two hunters, one of whom is facing the animal and shooting it with a bow and arrow; one arrow has already pierced the chest of the animal. The other hunter is at the back at some distance, holding a long spear which he has thrust into the animal. Above are two sun symbols with rays and a dog. Of the two hunters, the one in front of the stag is a male as his organ is prominently shown, while the other to the right is a female as is clear from her protruding breasts. The stag is male and so is the dog.

The depiction of the two suns appears enigmatic. According to B.M. Pande, one of them represents the day and the other the day of successful return, which is in keeping with solar symbolisms among primitive people.[12] It is a realistic representation of sympathetic magic.

The same structure from which the slab with the hunting scene came also contained another slab on which a tectiform is carved. The 'tectiform' consists of a very complex pattern which is engraved on the slab and is unique because it is the only one of its kind in India. Although it appears as a sort of cobweb, Pande sees in it an abstract representation of a hut with a thatched domical roof and a broom-shaped spire,[13] as also the hind portion of an animal on the right. The hunting scene and the tectiform coming from the same structure are probably related, the former symbolizing ritual magic and the latter a trapped animal.

[11] B.M. Pande (1971), 'Neolithic Hunting Scene on a Stone Slab from Burzahom, Kashmir', *Asian Perspectives*, 14, pp. 134-7.

[12] Ibid.

[13] B.M. Pande (1972), 'A Neolithic Tectiform from Burzahom, District Srinagar, Kashmir', *JRAS*, 7, pp. 175-7.

Chapter 8

Beginning of Agriculture: Northern Vindhyas and the Middle Gangetic Plain

J.N. Pal

INTRODUCTION

The beginning of settled life in the Ganga Valley in north India has a high antiquity, as is clear from recent archaeological evidence. Much of this work was carried out by a team of archeologists from the University of Allahabad led by the late Professor G.R. Sharma.

The area under study lying between 24 N and 27 50′ N Latitude and 81 47′ 29 E and 87 50′ E Longitude is bound by the Himalayan *tarai* in the north and the Son in the south, the Allahabad-Faizabad railway line in the west, and Bihar and the West Bengal border in the east. The region comprises two contrasting ecological environments: (1) the rocky plateau of the northern Vindhyas in the south, and (2) the flat alluvial plains of the Ganga in the north (Fig. 7.1).

The northern Vindhyan plateau forms part of the Bundelkhand and Baghelkhand regions. It is a hilly tract marked by a rugged and diversed topography, which gradually merges with the alluvium of the Ganga plain. A number of small rivulets, tributaries and sub-tributaries of the Ganga and Son systems have fertile narrow basins. Many sites of the early Holocene period are located in these river basins. The main rivers and rivulets of the northern Vindhyas are the Tons, along with its tributaries, the Belan, Adwa, Lapari, Karmanasa and Chandraprabha of the Ganga system, and Kanhar, Pandu, Lauwa, Thema, Gopad and Narkuin of the Son system.

The middle Gangetic plain is drained by the Ganga and its tributaries, mainly the Ghaghra, Kuano, Chhoti Gandak, Burhi Gandak, Kosi, Varuna, Gomti, Son, etc. There are numerous oxbow lakes from which emerge the small rivers of the area.

The climate of the area is characterized by a long host summer, pleasant monsoon and cold winter. The annual average rainfall is about 976 mm. A variety of wild flora still survives in the Vindhyas while, in the Gangetic plain, due to extensive cultivation, the forests now are confined to isolated patches, especially of dhak (*Butea monosperma*), sihor (*Streblus asper*), etc. Among the wild floral species predominant in the Vindhyas, mention may be made of kardhai (*Anageissus*), dhawa (*Angeissus latifolia*), mahua (*wadhuca indca-Gmel*), salai (*Boswellia melanoxycon*), bahera (*Terminalia bellerica*), semal (*Salmaliama labrica*), babul (*Acacia arabica*), khair (*Acacia catechu*), etc., besides dhak and sihor.

Among the wild fauna still surviving in the Vindhyas despite reckless shooting and the destruction of forests are the leopard (*Panthera pardus*), wolf (*Canis lupus*), jackal (*Canis aureus*), fox (*Vulpes bengalensis*), bear (*Melursus ursinus*), hyena (*Hyaeuna striate*), boar (*Sus scrofa*), chital (*Axis axis*), black buck (*Antelope cervicapra*), nilgai (*Boselephas tragocamelas*), barking deer (*Muntiacus muntijak*), etc. Some of these, especially the deer, antelope and boar, used to roam in herds in the middle Gangetic plain some fifty years ago.

Due to the abundant flora-fauna and the easy availability of raw materials for tools, the Vindhyan plateau was inhabited by prehistoric man right from the middle Pleistocene period and we get a complete geological and cultural sequence of the Pleistocene and Holocene epochs in the Vindhyas. However, in the middle Gangetic plain, the evidence of human culture is dated to the terminal Pleistocene and early Holocene period when we get the cultural relics of the Epi-palaeolithic and Mesolithic cultures.

The antiquity of human cultures in the Vindhyas and the middle Gangetic plain goes back to this period when Vindhyan prehistoric human groups moved for the first time towards the north across the Yamuna and the Ganga to colonize the Gangetic plain. With ecologically and geomorphologically contrasting features, the hilly tract of the Vindhyas and the flat alluvial plain of the Ganga, as the archaeological evidence shows, continued till the early historic period, and the cultures of both regions influenced each other to a considerable extent.

HISTORY OF RESEARCH

Initial research on the Neolithic culture was restricted to the surface collections of celts, adzes and hammer stones. A large number of Neolithic celts were collected in the latter part of the nineteenth century.[1] Subsequently, during the 1950s to 1980s, archaeologists of the University of Allahabad and Banaras Hindu University collected a large number of Neolithic artefacts during surface explorations. A majority of them were found in a secondary context lying in the field or below the trees. Morphologically, Neolithic celts are divisible into two major groups: (1) triangular celts marked with curved

[1]Le Mesurier (1861), *Progs. of Asiatic Soc., Bengal*, 30, 1, pp. 81-5; W. Theobald (1862), 'Celts Found in Bundelkhand', *PASB*, p. 221; J. Cockburn (1879), 'Notes on the Stone Implements from the Khasi Hill and Banda and Vellor District', *JASB*, pp. 133-43; idem (1894), 'On the Flint Implements from the Kosi Ravines of South Mirzapur', *JASB*, 62, pp. 21-37; Rivet-Carnac (1883), 'On Stone Implements from North Provinces of India', *JASB*, 52, I-IV, pp. 221-30.

medial ground edges, corresponding to the principal type of south Indian Neolithic celt, and (2) rounded celts marked with a rectangular or ovaloid cross-section, fully ground and polished, corresponding to the eastern Indian Neolithic celts. It is interesting to note that the western part of the northern Vindhyas has, predominately, the first group of celts while, in the eastern part, the second group dominates. Archaeological investigations carried out in the eastern part have led to the discovery of some primary sites associated with a rounded variety of celts and excavations of these primary sites of the Neolithic culture have furnished valuable information regarding its different aspects.[2]

In the middle Gangetic plain, a large number of primary sites of the Mesolithic culture have been located in the western part. The sites, as indicated by continuous, thick, habitation deposits and heavily-utilized food-processing stone implements, represent semi-sedentary settlements. However, Neolithic sites are totally absent in this area.

From some of the sites of the early historic period of the middle Gangetic plain, stone celts were reported, but Neolithic artefacts in a primary context were found for the first time at Chirand,[3] which established the existence of the Neolithic culture in the Gangetic plain. Subsequent archaeological investigations carried out by the Gorakhpur University, Banaras Hindu University, Patna University, the Patna Circle of the Archaeological Survey of India and the Directorate of Archaeology and Museums, Bihar government, have brought to light several sites representing the beginnings of settled life in the central part of the middle Gangetic plain. The habitation sites, generally with thick overlying deposits of the chalcolithic and early historic period, pose practical difficulties in exposing the earlier horizon in a large area.

EXCAVATED SITE

The excavations of some of the habitation sites in the Vindhyas and the Gangetic plain have enriched our knowledge of the culture in these areas. Those in the northern Vindhyas include Koldihwa, Mahagara, Indari and Kunjhun, and those in the Gangetic plain, Chirand, Chechar-Kutubpur, Taradih, Senuwar and Soligaura.

Situated at a distance of 80 km south-east of Allahabad on the left bank of the Belan is Koldihwa in the Vindhyas, which yielded rounded celts and cord-impressed pottery, a diagnostic trait of the culture of the area (Fig. 8.1). The original mound, divided into several small mounds by rain *gullies* and *nalas*, has Neolithic deposits on its western and southern parts. The habitation deposit of 1.90 m is divisible into three cultural periods: (i) Neolithic,

[2] J.N. Pal (1983), 'Bases of the Neolithic Cultures of the Middle Ganga Valley', *Journal of G.N. Jha Kendriya Sanskrit Vidyapith.*

[3] *IAR*, 1962-3, p. 6.

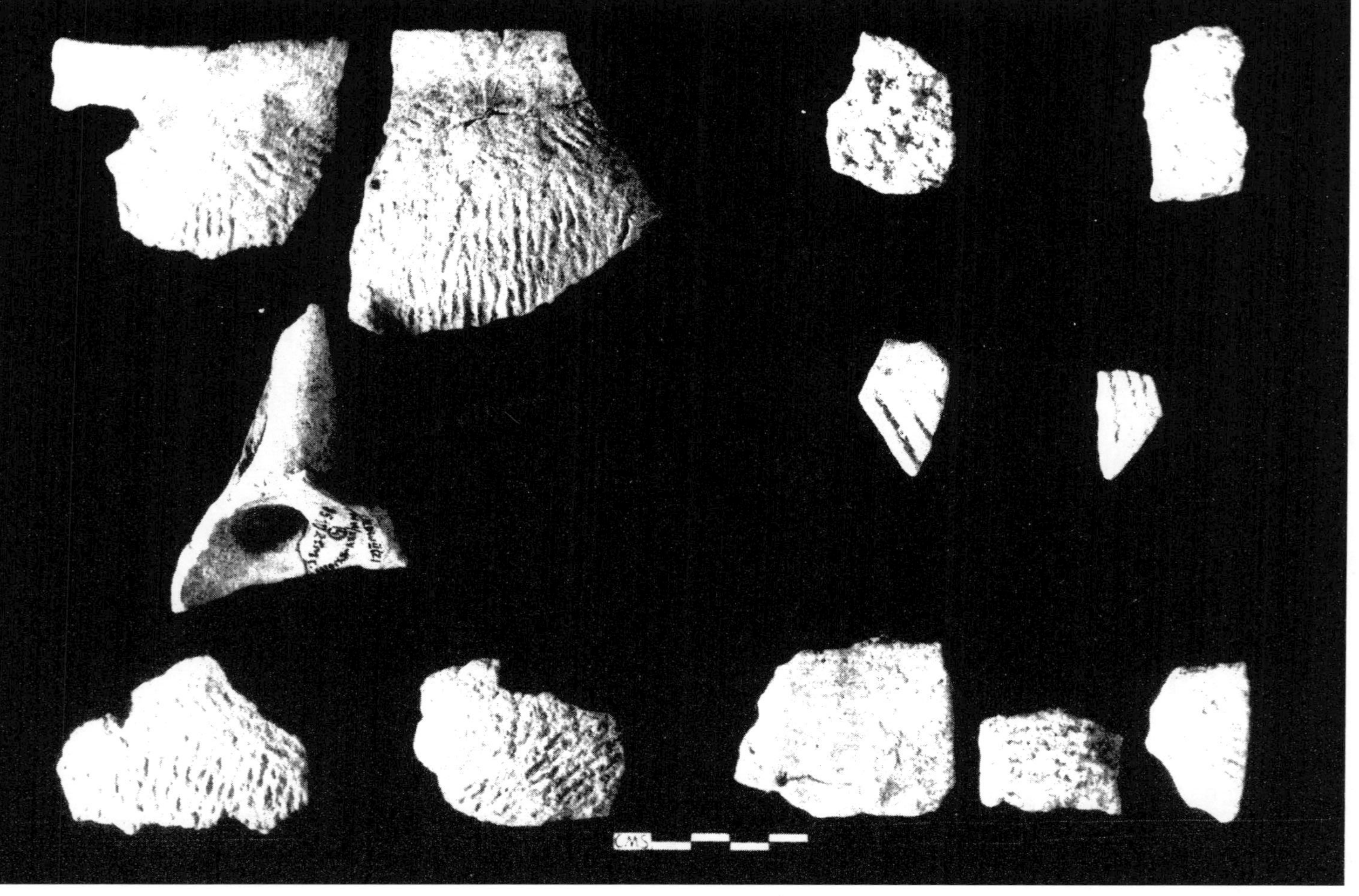

Fig. 8.1: Koldihwa, cord impressed pottery

(ii) Chalcolithic and (iii) Iron age. The Neolithic deposit of 45 cm divisible into two layers, yielded celts, bored stones, hand-made pottery, microliths, food-processing equipments in the form of querns, mullers and hammer stones, animal bone fragments, and burnt clay lumps with wattle and daub impressions.

Mahagara is situated just opposite Koldihwa on the right bank of the Belan near the confluence of the old and new Belans. The site, in a basin-shaped depression, is surrounded by a natural ridge of Pleistocene geological formations on the north, east and south. Trial excavations revealed a 2.60 m thick Neolithic deposit divisible into seventeen layers. The site, being a single culture site, was excavated horizontally in a 1622 sq m area (Fig. 8.2). It yielded evidence of a cattle pen, hut floors marked with pottery, celts, ring stones, sling balls, microliths, bone tools, burnt clay lumps, animal bone fragments, querns, mullers, hammers, anvils, perforated pottery discs, terracotta beads, etc. Yet another site, at Pachoh, located at a distance of 2.5 km north-west of Koldihwa near the right bank of the Belan, was also subjected to a small-scale excavation which yielded Neolithic artefacts in a 60 cm thick deposit. The site, being under cultivation, only has the basal deposit intact.

In the Adwa Valley, two Neolithic habitation sites, Indari and Baraunha, were located during surface explorations in the Mirzapur district, Indari, situated in a basin-shaped depression on the left bank of a *nala* of the Kahenjua, a tributary of the Adwa in the Mirzapur district, yielded Neolithic artefacts in a trial excavation.[4]

Kunjhun, located at a distance of 35 km north-east of Sidhi on the right bank of the Son in the Sidhi district of Madhya Pradesh, is the southernmost Neolithic settlement in the Vindhyas. The site is on the last terrace (Khetaunhi formation) of the Son.[5] A surface collection from the site included celts, bored stones, microliths, terracotta dabbers, pottery, animal bone fragments and terracotta bangle fragments in an area of about 3000 sq m. To the west of the habitation area, a few fresh potsherds, microliths and animal bone fragments were found deposited in the river section. The excavation in a step trench cut into the eroded cliff face revealed that these artefacts, coming from the neighbouring habitation site, were deposited in several levels in the Khetaunhi formation (the last terrace of the Son). The artefact-bearing horizons were characterized by a considerable amount of stone rubble, chert and chalcedony nodules, blades, debitage, pottery and animal bones (including *Bos gaurus*), a smaller bos species, cervids, tortoise, snake and dog.

Excavations in a 6 × 5 m area at Kunjhun II, another site some 0-.5 km upstream and 100 m south-southeast of the river terrace, revealed that it was a heat treatment area for the nodules. It demonstrates the method of heat

[4] *IAR*, 1980-1, p. 72.

[5] M.A.I. Williams and K. Royce (1983), 'Alluvial History of the Middle Son Valley', in G.R. Sharma and J.D. Clark (eds.), *Palaeoenvironment and Prehistory in the Middle Son Valley*, Abinash Prakashan, Allahabad, pp. 9-21.

Fig. 8.2: General view of excavation, Mahagara

treatment and the subsequent flaking technique of the microliths by the Neolithic people. The processing of the meat of hunted animals was also done here. Animal bones obtained from this area include the wild bison, large and medium-sized deer and the antelope.[6]

Chirand is situated on the left bank of the Ganga in the Saran district of Bihar. With a multicultural thick deposit ranging from the Neolithic to the Pala period, the site was excavated for a number of years.[7] The Neolithic level contained the structural remains of hut floors and a large number of artefacts, pottery, microliths, celts, bone tools, terracotta figurines and beads of semi-precious stones.[8]

A small-scale excavation at Chechar-Kutubpur, situated on the northern bank of the Ganga in the Vaishali district of Bihar, brought to light a three-fold cultural sequence. The earliest, Period I, is further divisible into three sub-periods—IA, IB and IC. Sub-period IA yielded artefacts similar to those in Period I at Chirand.[9]

Taradih, situated to the south-west of the Mahabodhi temple at Bodh Gaya (Gaya district, Bihar), also has a multicultural deposit ranging from the Neolithic to the historical period.[10] The site was excavated in 1981-2,[11] and 1984-5 but the Neolithic horizon was brought to light only during the excavations of 1984-5 when a 60 cm thick occupation deposit of Period I revealed hand-made pottery. Neolithic celts, microliths, bone objects, terracotta objects, burnt clay lumps with wattle and daub impressions, and hearths of different sizes.

The site of Senuwar was brought to light during an archaeological investigation in the Kaimur foothills in the Rohtas district of Bihar.[12] Many sites of the early farmers were brought to light in the alluvial plains near Kaimur foothills during an investigation in 1986-7. One of these, Senuwar, situated on the bank of the Kurda rivulet, was subjected to excavations. Like other sites of the plain, this too has a thick deposit of subsequent periods overlying the Neolithic debris. The cultural deposit, as revealed from the excavations, is divisible into four periods: (i) Neolithic, (ii) Chalcolithic, (iii) NBPW period, and (iv) Kushan period. The Neolithic phase is further divisible into two sub-phases, IA and IB. Phase IB has evidence of copper

[6]Desmond Clark and G.S. Khanna (1989), 'The Site of Kunjun II, middle Son Valley and its Relevance for the Neolithic of Central India', in J.M. Kenoyer (ed.), *Old Problems and New Perspectives in the Archaeology of South Asia*, Wisconsin Arch. Reports, vol. 2, University of Wisconsin, Wisconsin, pp. 29-45.

[7]L.A. Narain (1970), 'Neolithic Settlement at Chirand', *Journal of Bihar Research Society*, 56, pp. 16-35.

[8]B.P. Sinha (1979), *Archaeology and Art of India*, Sundeep Prakashan, Delhi.

[9]*IAR*, 1977-8, pp. 17-18.

[10]*IAR*, 1984-5, pp. 9f.

[11]*IAR*, 1981-2, pp. 10-12.

[12]B.P. Singh (1988), 'Early Farming Communities of Kaimur Foothills', (unpublished).

and may be termed as the transitional phase of the Neolithic and Chalcolithic cultures.[13] The site, located in a region between the Vindhyas and the Gangetic plain, is remarkable for its bone tools, ceramic industry and other Neolithic artefacts.

Sohgaura, situated on the confluence of the Ami and Rapti (Gorakhpur district, U.P.), also has a Neolithic base.[14] The excavations of the cultural deposit of 90 cm in the lowest level yielded hand-made pottery of the cord-impressed variety, as also rusticated and burnished red wares, along with burnt clay lumps, quern fragments, a hearth, and beads of bone and steatite.[15]

SETTLEMENT PATTERN

Neolithic sites are located on the banks of small rivers, generally above the flood plain. The easy availability of water and fertile land by annual inundation were the main factors responsible for establishing settlements on the river banks. Sites like Mahagara and Indari in the Vindhyas are located in a trough-shaped depression surrounded by a natural ridge, which provided security against cold/hot winds. The location of sites in close proximity to forests facilitated in exploiting wild plants and animals.

STRUCTURES

Evidence of structures have been uncovered in the form of circular or oval hut floors. At sites where excavations were done in a restricted area, the evidence of structures is found in the form of burnt clay lumps with wattle and daub impressions, suggesting thatched huts. Plans of circular hut floors have been unearthed at Mahagara and Indari in the Vindhyas, and Chirand in the Gangetic plain. Eighteen hut floors were exposed in the last phase of Neolithic occupation at Mahagara (Fig. 8.2). The average living area covered by the hut floors is 15.74 sq m. The diameter of the circular floors is 6.40 m. Whereas that of the longer ovaloid floors varies from 3.40 to 6.40 m and the shorter runs between 4.30 to 2.80 m.[16] The floors were surrounded by postholes, varying from six to nine in number on their periphery. The posts supported the upper roof as well as the side screen. Evidence of circular or semi-circular huts of about 2 m in diameter with a rammed floor have also been recovered at Chirand.

[13] Ibid.

[14] *IAR*, 1974-5, pp. 46 ff.

[15] S.N. Chaturvedi (1985), 'Advance of Vindhyan Neolithic and Chalcolithic Cultures in the Himalayan Terai: Excavations and Explorations in the Sarangpur Region of Uttar Pradesh', *ME*, 9, pp. 101-8.

[16] D. Mandal (1980), 'Neolithic Cultures of the Vindhyas: Excavations at Mahagara in Belan Valley' (unpublished).

The cattle pen exposed at Mahagara in the south-east sector of the site is irregular, rectangular in plan, measuring 12.5 × 7.5 m and demarcated by floors at its four corners. Clusters of hoof imprints of cattle of different age groups were also noticed in the cattle pen.[17]

SUBSISTENCE

The cultivation of plants and the domestication of animals are well-attested by the recovery of botanical and faunal remains from almost all the excavated sites. Rice was widely cultivated in the area. Almost all the sites, excavated as well as unexcavated, have produced evidence of rice in the form of rice husk used as a degraissant in pottery (Fig. 8.3). These include the cultivated *Oryza sativa*, the wild annual *Oryza nivara* and the perennial *Oryza rufigona*. The excavations at Chirand yielded a variety of cultivated grains such as wheat (*Triticum sphaerococcum*), barley (*Hordeum vulgare*), moong (*Vigna mungo*), masoor (*Lins esculent*), etc. Charred grains of barley (*Hordeum vulgare*) also have been found at Mahagara.[18] The evidence suggests that winter as well as summer crops were cultivated during the Neolithic period.

A large number of animal bones were unearthed during excavations. Though the final identification of animal species has not been done for most of the sites, the evidence of domesticated cattle, sheep and goat is noteworthy.[19] The terracotta figurine of a humped domestic bull, *Bos indicus*, and small *Bos faunal* remains at Kunjhun indicate that the Neolithic people possessed cattle. The early farming communities of the Vindhyas did not depend only on the cultivation of plants. Domestication is attested not only by hunting tools but also by faunal and floral remains of wild species. Wild rice (*Oryza nivara*) from Koldihwa, Mahagara, Indari, and Sanwa, *Echinochloa crusgalli* from Koldihwa, and bone fragments of the deer, antelope, boar and birds suggest that the hunting and collecting of wild food was as important as domestication and cultivation. Riverbank sites also provided food material in the form of the fish, snail, tortoise, etc., bones of which have been recovered from excavations. Other botanical remains include imprints of *Ischaemum rugosum* (a common weed grown in marshy paddy fields, and used as fodder) bamboo and jujube.

[17]G.R. Sharma and D. Mandal (1980), *Excavation at Mahagara*, University of Allahabad, Allahabad.

[18]Vishnu Mittre and Arun Sharma (1982), 'Neolithic-Chalcolithic Food Economy of Eastern Uttar Pradesh' (unpublished).

[19]K.R. Alur (1980), 'Faunal Remains from the Vindhyas and the Ganga Valley', in G.R. Sharma et al. (eds.), *Beginnings of Agriculture*, Allahabad.

Fig. 8.3: Mahagara: Rice husk imprints on pot-sherds

MATERIAL CULTURE

Pottery has been recovered in a large quantity from neolithic sites in the Vindhyas and the Gangetic plain. On the basis of surface treatment, the ceramic industry has been divided into four major groups: (i) Cord-impressed ware (ii) Rusticated ware (iii) Burnished red ware, and (iv) Burnished black ware.[20] The clay used for making pottery was not well-levigated, and contains calcium and iron particles. Profusely tempered with husk, leaves, straw and cowdung, the hand-made pottery has a coarse to medium fabric. Due to the organic temper and ill-firing, the colour of the core is blackish. The unslipped cord-impressed and rusticated wares have a dull red surface, and the burnished red and burnished black ware, due to the application of red slip, and black slip, respectively, generally have bright red and black surfaces. The utilitarian forms are simple but, to some extent, standardized, and include convex, straight or tapering-sided deep and shallow bowls, tubular spouted bowls, straight, concave or carinated necked jars, basins, *handis*, and platters (Figs. 8.4-8.5). The decoration of pottery is confined only to applique and incised designs. Some interesting pottery forms like a ladle, lids and a diminutive, crudely-made bowl were found at Kunjhur.

The ceramic industry of the Neolithic Gangetic plain is richer in ware, typology and decorative patterns. It is also technologically advanced in comparison to that of the Vindhyas. The pottery is hand-made and turntable-thrown. Besides cord-impressed and rusticated wares, red, grey, black and black-and-red wares have been reported from Chirand and Taradih. Burnishing has been done on the red and grey ware pots. Some of the grey burnished ware pots have post-firing ochre paintings on their rim and body. Decoration in the form of incised, thumbnail, rope and impressed designs have been found on pottery. Among the utilitarian shapes, mention may be made of globular jars, vases, *handis* with out-turned rims, perforated vessels, lipped or spouted bowls, deep bowls, cups with hollow ring bases, cups with solid stands, etc.

The ceramic industry of both the regions has many common features. Not only the manufacturing technique of the wares but even the shapes are similar to the ceramic assemblage of the Neolithic culture of both the regions. That the ceramic assemblage of the Gangetic plain is typo-technologically advanced as is evident from some peculiar forms restricted only to it.[21] These include the spouted vase with pointed base, footed bowls, perforated bowls on stand, channels, spouted vessels, lipped bowls, the spoon or ladle, and knobbed vessels. Applique decorations, consisting of rope and notch designs, are common to both regions. Post-firing ochre paintings, including linear, criss-cross, and concentric circles on some of the pottery from Chirand and Taradih, are new features not present in the Vindhyas. Some painted sherds analogous to those of the Malwa ware occur at Kunjhun, and may indicate some contact between the two regions.

[20] J.N. Pal (1986), *Archaeology of Southern Uttar Pradesh*, Swabha Prakashan, Allahabad.

[21] Pal (1983), op. cit.

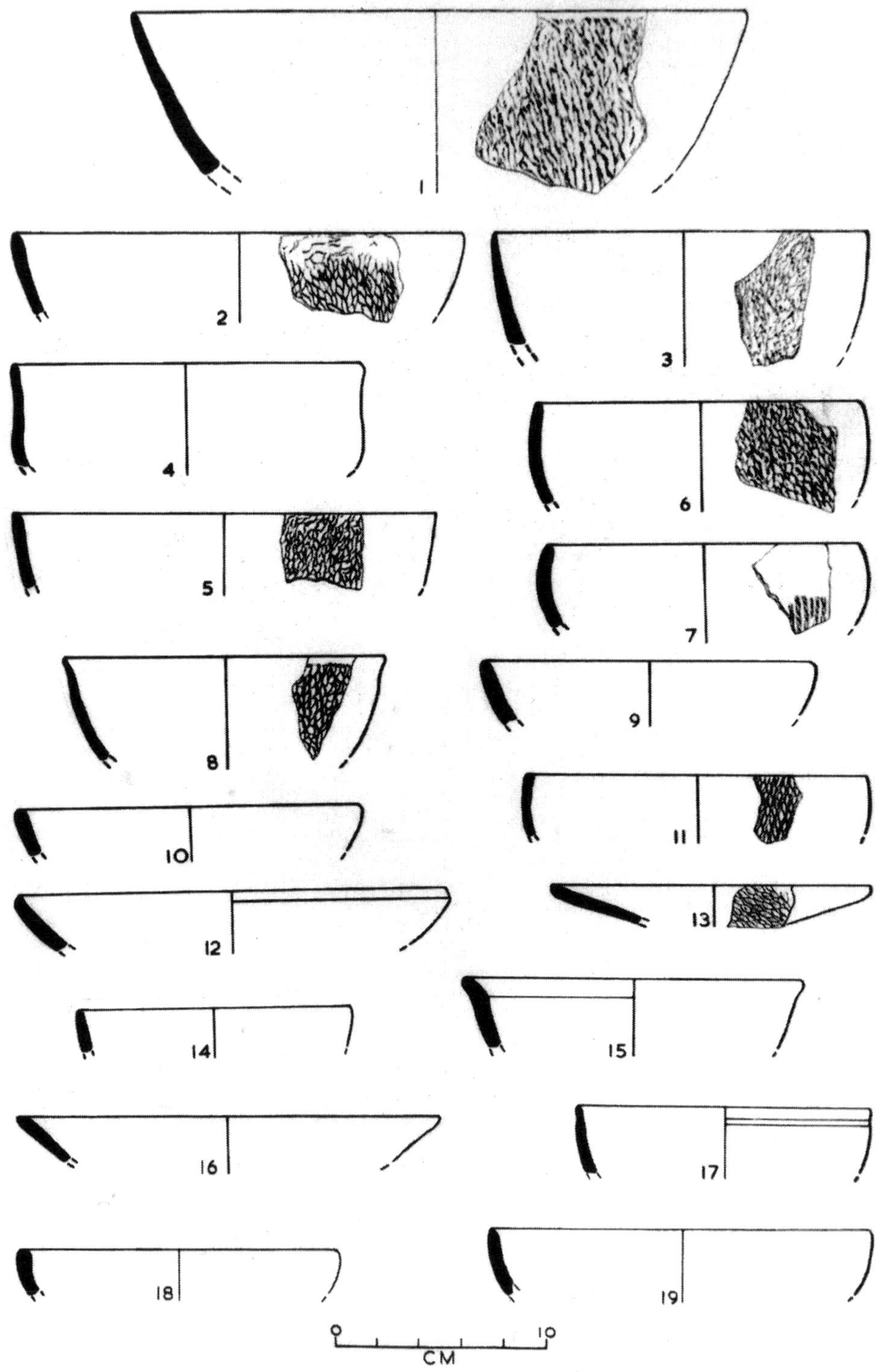

Fig. 8.4: Mahagara pottery

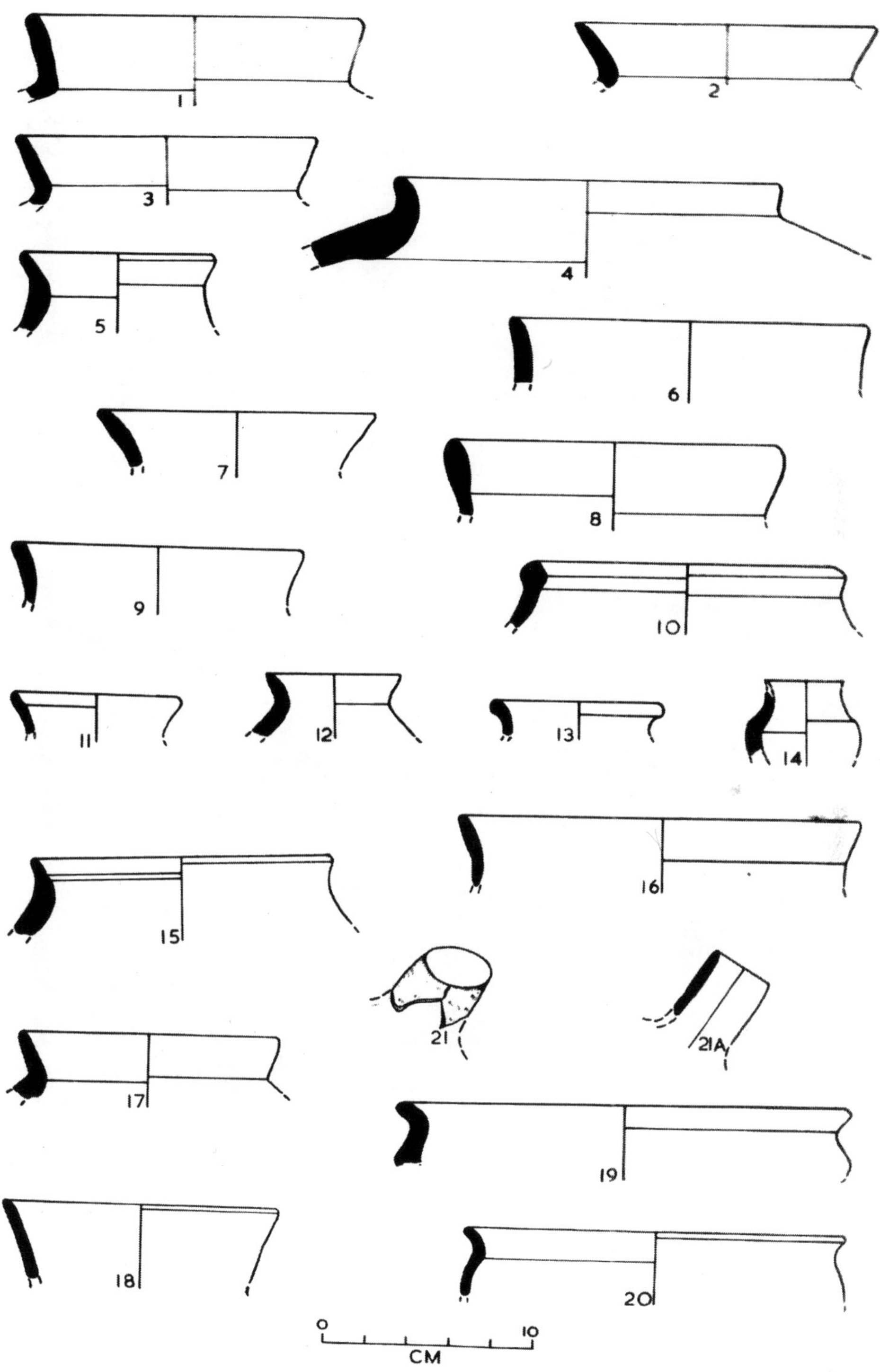

Fig. 8.5: Mahagara pottery

The ceramic industry, especially the cord-impressed ware forms the binding trait of the cultures of the hilly tracts and plains and distinctive ware of the eastern Asiatic Neolithic complex as a whole.[22]

Small, rounded celts and adzes are common in both regions. Fully-ground and polished neoliths are typologically divisible into celts, adzes and chisels. The celts are of a small, rounded variety with a rectangular or ovaloid cross-section (Fig. 8.6). The butt end is rounded but occasionally flattened. Many of the celts and adzes have use marks on their sharp working edges. They have been made of basalt, granite and quartzite. As there are no waste pieces, flakes or chips of the raw material of the neoliths, it may be assumed that these were manufactured at the source of the raw material and were brought to the settlement in a finished form. The possibility of primitive trade contact with the culture in the region of the source of the raw material cannot be ruled out.[23]

Artefacts fashioned on quartzite and sandstone by the pecking and grinding technique include querns, mutters, sharpeners, rubber stones, hammers, anvils, stone discs, sling balls and bored stones. Most of these were used as food-

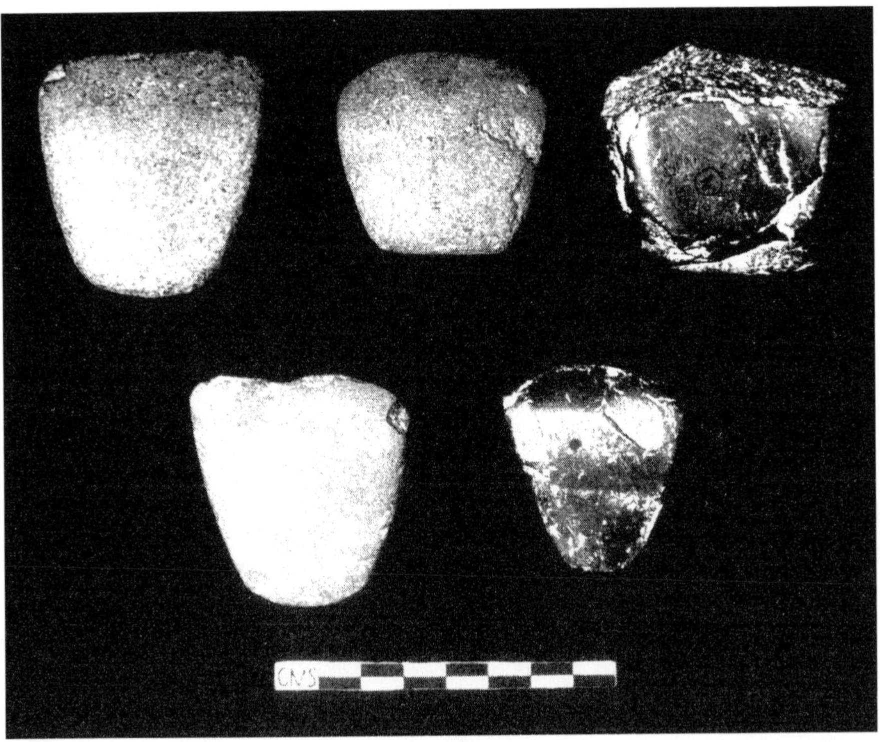

Fig. 8.6: Neolithic celts

[22]T.C. Sharma (1980), 'The Neolithic Pattern of Eastern India' (unpublished).

[23]L.A. Narain (1979), 'The Neolithic Cultures of Eastern India', in D.P. Agrawal and D.K. Chakrabarti (eds.), *Essays on Protohistory*, D.K. Publishers, Delhi, pp. 301-9.

processing equipment while some were tool fabricators and hunting tools. Querns fall into two groups: (i) basin-shaped concave querns with a smooth lustrous surface bearing concentric circular use marks, and (ii) flat querns with a pitted surface, whereas mullers are marked with smooth or pitted surface and have both unifacial as well as multifacial working surface.

Neolithic cultures of the Vindhyas and the Gangetic plain are also characterized by a microlithic industry, though it is not so prolific in the latter region. The microliths were made of chalcedony, chert, agate, carnelian and jasper (Fig. 8.7). The presence of chert and chalcedony nodules and waste material, i.e. cores, flakes, blades and chips, along with finished and utilized tools, suggests that they were made at the settlement itself. The tool types include retouched blades, backed blades, truncated blades, serrated blades, points, awls, scrapers, triangles, trapezes and lunates (Fig. 8.5). Some of the blades and flakes have use marks on their lateral edges. Edge polish on retouched and modified blades indicates that these were used on soft plant materials, wood and hide.

Bone artefacts are characteristic of the Gangetic Neolithic culture. In the Vindhyas, bone arrowheads with a single tang and pointed end have been found at Mahagara. A variety of bone tools and other utilitarian objects have been found at Chirand. Taradih,[24] Senuwar,[25] etc., in the middle Gangetic plain. Antlers, split shafts of long bones and tortoise shells were utilized for making these artefacts, which include the spearpoint, bodkin, borer, pin, arrowhead, divider, scraper, leather-cutting tool, wedge, chisel, weeding tool, drill, shaft straightener, hammer, barcelt, knife, socketed comb, pendant, disc, earring, bangle, etc.

Other artefacts peculiar to the Gangetic Neolithic culture include beads of semi-precious stones (from Chirand), steatite beads (from Sohgaura), terracotta bangles and figurines of the humped bull, bird and snake (from Chirand), a ball and an animal figurine (from Taradih), terracotta beads (from Mahagara), and bangles and a bull (from Kanjhun), and also occur at the Vindhya sites.

ORIGIN AND ANTIQUITY

We do not have stratigraphic evidence to show the evolution of the Neolithic farming culture from the earlier Mesolithic hunting-gathering culture. Many cultural traits such as the microlithic industry, bone tools, food-processing equipments, tool fabricators, hand-made pottery and hutments may be treated as surviving traits of the earlier culture in the Vindhyas. Some of the plants and animals which were domesticated in the Neolithic period are said to have been already present in a wild form. It seems that the Vindhyan Neolithic

[24]*IAR*, 1984-5, p. 10.

[25]Nina Thakur et al. (1988), 'Bone Tools from Senuwar' (unpublished).

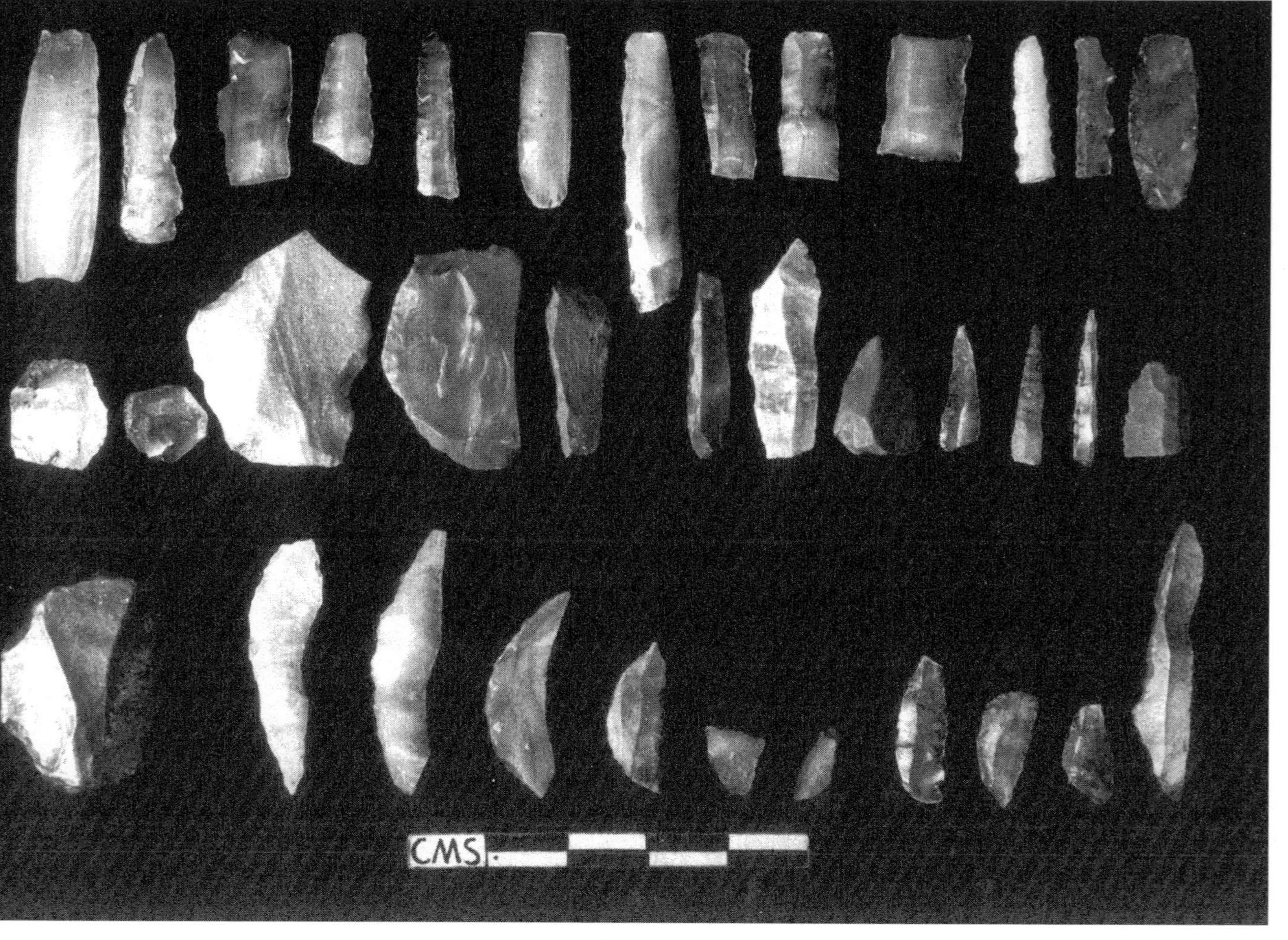

Fig. 8.7: Koldihwa microlithis

evolved from the Mesolithic of the area and, thus, its indigenous origin may be proposed. Available archaeological data from the Vindhyas and the Gangetic plain suggests that even though the early farming cultures of both regions have several common features, the latter appears to be technologically advanced. It is highly likely that the Gangetic Neolithic culture had its roots in the Vindhyan Neolithic culture and later developed certain distinctive features in bone artefacts, terracotta objects, beads of semi-precious stones and many new elements in the ceramic industry.

In the absence of dependable and consistent C-14 dates, the problem of the chronology of the culture is not resolved. C-14 dates from Koldihwa, assigning an early date to the Vindhyan Neolithic, are not dependable.[26] Those from Mahagara do not conform to the stratigraphy of the site, possibly due to the contamination of the samples. However, absolute dates obtained from Mahagara include two TL dates reading 2265 BC and 1616 BC, and four C-14 dates reading 1440+150 BC, 1330+120 BC, 1440+100 BC, and 1480+110 BC. A C-14 date for the transitional phase of the Neolithic to Chalcolithic at Koldihwa is 1440+120 BC. Kunjhun II activity site yielded C-14 dates of 2180+110 BC and 2380+126 BC.[27] For the Neolithic level of Chirand, nine C-14 dates are available of which three are consistent, viz., 1580+110 BC, 1675+140 BC, and 1775+155 BC. The Neolithic-Chalcolithic overlapping phase also has a C-14 date reading 1050+10 BC. These C-14 dates give a time bracket of 1800 to 1200 BC to the Neolithic at Chirand.[28] Period IB of the Neolithic-Chalcolithic level at Senuwar also has a C-14 date reading 1770+120 BC. Thus, the present evidence suggests a date of the third to the second millennium BC for the Neolithic culture of the northern Vindhyas and the middle Gangetic plain.

[26] Pal (1986), op. cit.

[27] Clark and Khanna (1989), op. cit.

[28] D.P. Agrawal and Sheela Kusumgar (1974), *Prehistoric Chronology and Radiocarbon Dating in India*, Tata Institute of Fundamental Research, New Delhi, p. 71.

Chapter 9

Beginning of Agriculture: South India

A. Sundara

INTRODUCTION

South India comprises the region south of the Godavari Valley, and includes southern Maharashtra, Andhra Pradesh, Karnataka, Kerala, and Tamil Nadu. The Neolithic culture which flourished in this region (Fig. 7.1) is found to be distinctive in many respects and, even within the region, it varies from one river valley to another as discussed below:

NEOLITHIC CULTURE IN SOUTH INDIA

(i) The material culture in the upper Godavari Valley is characterized by black-on-red painted pottery, besides a plain red ware, stone tools comprising parallel-sided blades produced by the 'Crested guiding ridge' technique, made of chalcedony and agate, and the use of copper objects, tools and ornaments on a restricted scale. Grey pottery is quantitatively less, and ground and polished stone axes are few and far between.

(ii) Along the middle Krishna Valley, up to the Krishna-Tungabhadra *doab* and as far down south as the Cuddapah region, the frequency of black-on-red painted pottery gradually decreases, except a site here or there, as, for instance, Singanapalle and Ramapuram. On the other hand, burnished and unburnished grey ware is dominant. There are also parallel-sided blades and microliths, mostly of chert and jasper. Polished stone tools occur in a large number but the use of copper is rare.

(iii) In the north-eastern part of Andhra Pradesh as at Jami, the Neolithic culture is characterized by a red pottery entirely different from that of the Krishna Valley. Apart from the triangular neolithic axe with a pointed butt end, typical of the south Indian Neolithic, there are rectangular axes like those in eastern India. This appears to be due to the overlap of two distinct cultural traditions: the eastern and the south Indian.

(iv) In the upper Tungabhadra and the middle-lower Kaveri valleys, black-on-red painted pottery is scarcely found. Blade tools usually made of black jasper occur in the last phase of the culture. On the other hand, quartz tools are present from the initial stage but Neolithic implements are far more numerous. Besides burnished grey pottery, there appears a hand-made, coarse, brown-and-black ware in profusion. Further, in the lower Kaveri Valley in the Shevroy (Dharmapuri district) area, there are sites with neoliths only on the surface, without any other items of cultural equipment such as pottery.

(v) In the Western Ghat belt from northern Goa, as, for instance, at Pila in the upper Mandovi area up to Quilon in southern Kerala, there occur stray Neolithic axes. Similarly, in the adjoining *ghat* from Anmod (district Uttara Kannada) to Koppa (Mysore district) only Neolithic axes were discovered. Neolithic pottery and stone tools have rarely survived in the later megalithic burials in Kerala. Northwards, in the Vidarbha area of Maharashtra, only a few neoliths have been picked up at a couple of sites, whereas at Kachgad (Bhandara district), grey ware pottery along with neoliths was discovered. In the lower Godavari-Mahanadi region, Neolithic remains occur at Chalcolithic sites. The north-eastern part, however, presents a different picture.

The Neolithic culture of the lower Godavari-Mahanadi has certain features which are very distinct from those of the other areas in the region.

It should be noted that these areawise variations are based on the limited evidence from excavations. Moreover, only a few excavations have been published in full. Hence, our knowledge of the material culture such as domestic architecture, economic activities, food habits, lapidary art, social structure, and religious beliefs and practices is extremely sketchy.

The Neolithic phase succeeds the Mesolithic and the various stages of this transition from a food-gathering to a food-producing culture have now been very clearly traced in West Asia but not in India. In the Indian subcontinent, the beginning of settled life now goes back to about 7500 BC, as is clear from the excavation at Mehrgarh in Baluchistan, but in, south India, it begins in the third millennium.

DISCOVERIES

The chance discovery of a stray neolith at Lingsugur (Karnataka) in 1842 by Mackenzie is perhaps the first in the south. In the valleys of the Tambraparni and Vaigai, Bruce Foote was the first to report Neolithic remains at Saidangallur, Sawyurupuram, Vellabakulam and Valimukkambay.[1] It may, however, be pointed out that except a mace head and a celt, from the first and the third localities, respectively, the rest are of doubtful Neolithic affiliation.

In the Tambraparni region, the Mesolithic was succeeded by the Iron Age Megalithic and there was no Neolithic stage in the entire region. However,

[1] R. Bruce Foote (1961), *Prehistoric and Protohistoric Antiquities of India*, Leeladevi Publications (rpt.), Delhi, pp. 43ff.

in recent times, an enigmatic picture of the Chalcolithic is emerging. The discovery of antennae-hilted copper swords with mid-ribs at Appukallu (Vellore district), Kuppa Chipadooru (Coimbatore district) and Shavanipatti (Ramanathapura district) is noteworthy in this context. They are almost identical with those from Kallur (Raichur district) discovered way back in 1937. They were found in a big rock cavity on the top of a hillock in the vicinity of a rock-engraving of two bisons and an ancient Neolithic-Chalcolithic site. In the upper Bhima at Chandoli (Maharashtra), a similar copper dagger with mid-rib was found in the Chalcolithic context. But the Appukallu excavation has revealed only two cultural stages: the Iron Age Megalithic and the Early Historical. What then is the cultural context of the copper swords from Tamil Nadu? This problem, the provenance of their manufacture and the agency responsible for their dispersal to places/areas such as Appukallu and as far south as Shavanipatti will have to be tackled by an intensive field survey, excavation of selected sites and technical studies.

Further northwards at Arikamedu, there is probably a Neolithic phase, as known from certain characteristic finds such as a polished stone axe (Wheeler 1946: figure 44) and grey ware, particularly the urn with a flaring rim type (ibid.: figure 24; 40-42b) from the pre-Arretine and pre-structural strata. Due attention could not be given to these finds at that time since hardly anything was known then about the Neolithic culture in the region. In the upper Ponnaiar Valley, particularly in the area of the Shevroy hills, Neolithic sites are of two kinds: those producing only polished stone tools and those with habitation debris, including polished stone tools. A few sites such as T. Narasipur in the Kaveri and Sanganakallu in the Krishna-Tungabhadra *doab* were the first of their kind with profuse habitational remains, including neoliths. It is from 1955 onwards that numerous Neolithic-Chalcolithic sites have been explored in the major river valleys from the Kaveri to the Godavari. Chalcolithic sites in the upper Godavari, the Bhima (Maharashtra), and the upper Krishna (Karnataka), and Neolithic sites in the lower Bhima, the middle-lower Krishna, the Tungabhadra Valley (north Karnataka) and the upper Kaveri are far too numerous and only a few of them have been excavated.*

Some scholars have critically reviewed the work done on the Neolithic phase in India.[2] However, it is only in recent years that archaeologists in India have begun giving due importance to the role of ecological factors in the study of pre and proto-historic cultures.[3] V.D. Krishnaswamy distinguished four major Neolithic zones, namely, the southern, the eastern, the central and

[2]B.B. Lal (1953), 'Protohistoric Investigations', *Ancient India*, 9, pp. 80-102; V.D. Krishnaswamy (1962), 'The Neolithic Pattern of India', *Ancient India*, 16, pp. 25-64; H.D. Sankalia (1974), *The Prehistory and Protohistory of India and Pakistan*, Deccan College, Poona, pp. 279-313.

[3]D.P. Agarwal (1982), *The Archaeology of India*, Curzon Press, London, pp. 99-100.

Kashmir.[4] The present writer has tried to demarcate different cultural zones in the Neolithic of Karnataka and ascertain their cultural affiliations with those of the neighbouring regions.[5] K. Paddayya has recognized five variants in the southern Neolithic culture.[6] The available evidence indicates that the Neolithic sites can be grouped as follows :

1. Early Neolithic with or without the preceding Mesolithic, as at Kappalavadi, Dayalmalai (Tamil Nadu); Dayyalankuntapalli, Hampapuram, etc. (Anantapuram district), and Peda Tadivada (Vishakhapatnam district).
2. Early and late Neolithic, i.e. the Neolithic-Chalcolithic stage, as at Nagarjunakonda, Gandluru, Garapadu (all in Guntur district), Channamarur and Pagidigutta (Mahabubnagar district), Kodekal and Budihal.
3. The Neolithic-Chalcolithic stage overlapping with the Iron Age Megalithic and Early Historical, as at Paiyampalli, T. Narasipur, Banahalli, Palvoy, Hulikallu, Ramapuram, Vemmiragutta, Utnur, Brahmagiri, Tekkalakota, Sanganakallu, Piklihal, Maski, Watgal, Hallur and Kachgad.
4. Sites with neoliths on the surface, the stratigraphic context of which is not known. There is a slight indication of the existence of an aceramic Neolithic stage sandwiched between the Mesolithic and early Neolithic as at Watgal.[7]

A large number of radiocarbon determinations are available and it is, therefore, possible to trace the development of the southern Neolithic as follows:

1. Aceramic Neolithic (*c.* 3000-2700 BC) in the western coastal belt and the adjacent *ghat*, as at Anmod, the Maski-Watgal of the Krishna-Tungabhadra Doab and Shevroy hill area.
2. Ceramic early Neolithic (*c.* 2700-2300 BC), as at Hallur IA, Sanganakallu IIA, Banahalli, early phase of Period I, the earliest phases at Gandluru and Garapadu, Nagarjunakonda, T. Narasipur, Hallur IB, Sanganakallu IIB, and Kachgad.
3. Neolithic-Chalcolithic (*c.* 2300-1700 BC), as at Maski, Brahmagiri IA, Tekkalakota, Piklihal and Utnur Early Neolithic and Late Phase (*c.* 1700-900 BC) and (*c.*1000-900/800 BC), respectively, overlapping with late Chalcolithic (Jorwe) and Iron Age Megalithic, as at Sanganakallu (III), Brahmagiri IIB, Hallur IB and Ramapuram IC.

[4] Krishnaswamy (1962), op. cit.

[5] A. Sundara (1970), 'Neolithic Cultural Patterns and Movements in North Mysore State', *Journal of Karnataka University (Social Science)*, 7, pp. 54-61, 109-10; idem (1971), 'Chalcolithic Phase in the Upper Krishna Valley', *Studies, History and Culture, P.B. Desai Felicitation Volume*, Dharwad, pp. 54-61.

[6] K. Paddayya (1973), *Investigations into the Neolithic Culture of the Shorapur Doab, South India*, E.J. Brill, Leiden, pp. 87-91.

[7] D.V. Devraj et al. (1995), 'The Watgal Excavations: An Interim Report', *ME*, 20, 2, pp. 57-74.

ENVIRONMENT

The environment in south India is congenial providing all the basic materials for human settlement. This seems to have been the condition even in the remote past. The whole region comprises wide bands of Dharwar rocks consisting of schist, iron-bearing haematite, quartzite and auriferous reefs, covering the western part in a northwest-southeast direction; the peninsular gneissic complex with dolerite dykes spread over a major part; and the sedimentary rock beddings of the Kaladgi, the Bhima and the Kurnool-Cuddapah series in the Bhima-Krishna. The Tungabhadra Valley is with inliers of fine-grained siliceous rock materials such as chert and jasper and veins of copper ore. The Deccan trap is with pockets of fine-grained siliceous chalcedony, agate, carnelian. Beside iron-bearing vein are located in the north-western parts of the landscape in addition to south-western and north-western parts of Maharashtra and Karnataka respectively. A thick mantle of soft laterite is confronted in the coastal areas all along, with enormous deposits of iron and manganese ores as well. It is also bestowed with a network of some major rivers and their tributaries; the Godavari with the Pravara and the Manjra-Karanja, the Krishna with the Bhima on the north, and the Gataprabha, the Malaprabha and the Tungabhadra on the south as major tributaries; the west-flowing Sharavati; the east-flowing Palar and Pennar; the Kaveri and the Tambraparni in the deep south.

All along the western coast, there are many more rivers such as the Mandovi-Zuari, the Kali, the Sita, the Netravati, the Pampa, etc., flowing into the Arabian Sea. While most of the upghat rivers rise at different spots of the Sahyadri (i.e. Western Ghats) and join the Bay of Bengal, the Sharavati and the coastal rivers flow into the Arabian Sea. The region is broadly divided into the plain with thin vegetation, covering mainly the wide middle area from the north to the deep south called the *maidan*; and the western part with hills and valleys covered with thick and wild evergreen forests comprising the upghat Malnad and the coastal areas. The eastern *ghats* are low and gently tilting towards the sea without any distinct demarcation between the two. The rainfall from east to west ranges from 600 to 8,300 mm. The upper Godavari and the Krishna generally has a thick cover of black cotton soil which is very fertile with the capacity of retaining moisture for a longer duration. The low-lying areas of these valleys have reddish-brown, sandy soil, and the remaining area is largely grey, sandy earth. All the river banks are usually overlain with alluvial soil due to the annual inundation.

A word about the climate of the past, particularly the proto-historic period as known from recent scientific studies: geo-archaeological studies in the upper Bhima area indicate that the rainfall was highly variable, like in the present, and there were frequent droughts, particularly during the Late Jorwe phase. This is indirectly evident from the notable increase in the bones of cattle, goat, sheep and pig, and from the presence of a higher level of strontium in human bones owing to the consumption of more fish and animal foods, implying decline in agriculture which is also evident from plant remains. There appears to be an increase in aridity from about 1000-800 BC. There was a cultural hiatus of nearly five to six centuries in the region, as evident at Nevasa and Bahal. However, the Neolithic zone in the south has not been scientifically investigated and the only study available is the pollen analysis of the Maski area indicating the prevalence of a temperate climate. There is no cultural hiatus between the end of the Neolithic and the beginning of the Iron Age Megalithic, and between the latter and the Early Historical (from the third century BC onwards); in fact, there was a distinct overlap between these phases.

ACERAMIC (*C.* 3000-2700 BC)

Open sites with an enormous quantity of Neolithic artefacts are found in the Shevroy hill area, particularly at Togarapalli, Dailmalai, Kappalavadi, Banahalli Period I (early phase), Nagarjunakonda, Gundlur, Garapadu (early phases), Sanganakallu IIA and IIB, Hallur Early Neolithic and Kachgad. They give some idea of the two earliest stages of Neolithic culture. At Watgal, the earliest cultural phase was Late Mesolithic, probably overlapping with an aceramic Neolithic with dolerite flakes, along with microliths comprising tiny chert and quartzite tools of geometrical types such as lunates, parallel-sided blades and cores.[8] The nature of the culture is still to be investigated. This phase is succeeded by the ceramic Neolithic phase. The painted flakes of dolerite at Sangankallu belong to a pre-Mesolithic stage but there was a cultural hiatus between the two stages. At Ramapuram, too there is some indication of the Neolithic being preceded by the Mesolithic or early Neolithic.[9] In the Vattalmali area, Mesolithic tools were found along with ground stone implements.[10]

There are also Neolithic factory sites at Bargur (58) Kappalavadi (Krishnagiri taluk, Dharmapuri district);[11] Dayyalakuntapalle, Krishnamareddypalle and Hampapuram all in Anantpur district,[12] Gangasagara, Kolar district[13] and Sanganakallu (Subba Rao, 1947) where rock material, waste flakes and tools in various stages of manufacture were found but no other cultural relics occurred. The most abundant occurrence of ground stone tools in all of south India is in the Shevroy hill range in the Dharmapuri and Salem districts, the Sanganakallu area and the Maski-Watgal area. In the Sahyadri Ghat, the adjacent coastal belt and in the Bhandara-Nagpur area, ground and partially

[8] Devraj et al. (1995), op. cit.

[9] *IAR*, 1983-4.

[10] Foote (1961), op. cit., pp. 70-1.

[11] Narasimhaiah (1980), *Neolithic and Megalithic Cultures in Western Tamil Nadu*, Sundeep Prakashan, Delhi, pp. 30-1.

[12] *IAR*, 1977-8, p. 1.

[13] *IAR*, 1974-5, p. 20.

polished stone axes occur sporadically on the surface without any other cultural materials. However, Neolithic habitation sites are absent in the adjacent Javadi and Tirumalai hills, which are otherwise rich in ground stone tools. The habitation sites are located at the foot of the Vattalmalai hills and in other such loci.

All these cultural ramifications seem to indicate that in some areas like the Shevroy lull range, Maski (surface finds) and Watgal I, there was an aceramic Neolithic cultural phase emerging towards the end of the Mesolithic which further developed into the early Neolithic at Gundlur IA, Sanganakallu IIA. Hallur Early Neolithic, Banahalli IA and T. Narasipur I marked by pit-dwellings and/or small circular huts; bone and stone tools with or without microliths, hand-made plain pottery and the disposal of the dead.

Early Neolithic

At Nagarjunakonda, Site 45 has been taken to represent the earliest Neolithic phase dated to *c*. 2500 BC or a little earlier (Sarkar 1975: 73, 82).** In view of the dwelling traces, the crude, hand-made, pale, reddish-brown pottery, blade tools of chert and a small quantity of ground stone tools, it appears that the people were also engaged in incipient agriculture. Their dwellings were of two kinds: pit-dwellings and structural huts. At Gundlur and Garapadu, about forty pit-dwellings of varying sizes cut into the ground were exposed. Around the mouth of the pits were postholes for wooden posts that supported the conical thatched roof. The pits were cylindrical, stepped, and bipartite, tripartite or even quadripartite. The floor was neatly chiselled. In one of the dwellings at Garapadu were found fragments of pottery vessels of hand-made coarse buff ware and burnished grey ware, and stone and bone tools suggesting the use of pits for dwelling. Similar huts also occurred at Gundlur and Banahalli. There may be hearths sometimes with pebbles inside which were used for retaining heat over a longer period. The floor was made of clay often with an apron of potsherds as at Banahalli or schist stone chips mixed with clay or river sand as at Hallur, all well-rammed. The post-holes around the floor contained wooden posts supporting the conical roof. In one of the houses was a pottery stand with a concave top indicating its use as a neck rest. One dish had an incised design suggestive of its being used for some special purpose. A Neolithic axe and charred grains of *ragi* (*Eleusine coracana*) occurred at Hallur. Other domestic articles include microliths, generally made of quartz and chert; bone points, ground stone axes as well as mullers, and rubber stone. The hand-made pottery, coarse red/grey or burnished black/grey, is usually plain. Occasionally, there may be post-firing red-ochre paintings on the edge of the mouth of the vessels. The most noteworthy discovery is that of two charred pieces of *Areca cache*, i.e. betelnut, found in a pit of the earliest phase of the period. This is the earliest evidence of the use of the plant in South Asia. There were burials of two kinds: primary inhumations for adults and sub-adults, and urn-burials for children. Generally the body was laid supine with hands crossed over the pelvis and oriented north, east or south. At Watgal, stones were placed over the body. There was no pottery as burial furniture accompanying the dead. In the case of child burials, the burial urn was placed in a vertical position and covered with a lid. The head is towards the east or south. On the basis of C-14 dates, the period IIA, i.e. Early Neolithic, is dated to *c*. 2700-2300 BC.

NEOLITHIC-CHALCOLITHIC STAGE (*c*. 1700-1400 BC)

Neolithic-Chalcolithic habitation sites are by far the most numerous and are spread all over a large tract from the lower Kaveri to north-eastern Andhra (excluding the Upper Bhima-Godavari-Tapi of western Maharashtra). Many of these sites were later occupied in the Iron Age Megalithic period and Early Historical period as at Mullikadu, Paiyampalli, T. Narasipur and Hemmige, in the Kaveri Valley; Banahalli in the Palar Valley; Brahmagiri (Figs. 9.1-9.2), Hallur, Piklihal, Maski, Watgal and Sanganakallu, in the Krishna-Tungabhadra Valley; and Pagidigutta,[14] Chinnamarur,[15] Utnur (Allchin, 1950); Vemmagirigutta (East Godavari),[16] Kini Ranjgol and Yenkura in the Manjra-Karanja Valley.[17] Generally there is an overlap between the Late Neolithic-Chalcolithic and the Iron Age Megalithic, or the Early Historical. The overlap between these cultures has been very useful in dating relatively the proto-historic cultures, the Neolithic-Chalcolithic and the Iron Age Megalithic. A few sites have been found to be exclusively with the remains of the Neolithic-Chalcolithic stage at Tekkalakota, Nagarjunakonda, Gundlur-Garapadu, Ramapuram. Thirty sites are found in the Palar-Kunderu Valley area. Infrequently, the culture is preceded by the early Neolithic in the upper Godavari. In particular, the sites in the Krishna-Tungabhadra *doab* indicate a feeble intrusion of the Upper Godavari culture, first identified at Jorwe, along the Bhima[18] into the *doab* area. Further, in the mid-lower Krishna, there is a considerable increase in the quantity of parallel-sided thin blades made of chert, jasper and chalcedony, produced by the crested guiding ridge technique; houses, some large and some of public utility, and black-on-red painted pottery of burnished grey and pinkish red ware fabrics, different in all respects from the painted Jorwe pottery of the subsequent late phase. Copper tools and ornaments such as long swords, celts, bangles and beads have been found at quite a few sites. Some have yielded terracotta figurines of humans and animals, as at Watgal.

[14] *IAR*, 1978-9.

[15] Ibid.

[16] *IAR*, 1989-90.

[17] R.M. Shadaksharaiah (1995), *Prehistoric and Early Historic Cultures in the Manjra and Karanja Valleys*, Kannada Research Institute, Karnataka University, Dharwad, pp. 107-28.

[18] Sundara (1970), op. cit.; idem (1971), op. cit.

Figs. 9.1-9.2: Brahmagiri, section showing culture sequence

The number of bone tools decreases. There were intimate cultural contacts between the Chalcolithic of the Krishna-Bhima-Godavari, covering the northern part of the Belgaum-Bijapur district and the southern part of western Maharashtra, and the Neolithic-Chalcolithic of the middle-lower Krishna Valley. Some traditions, e.g. the double or four pot burial, the burnished grey ware, Neolithic axes with a pointed butt end, the Jorwe black-on-red painted ware, and microliths are common to both.

Settlement Pattern

There is a heavy concentration of chalcolithic sites in the upper Godavari-Bhima-Krishna valleys, which are located in undulating plain fields of the black cotton soil zone. They range in extent from 1 to 8 hectares in area, and those on the banks of the rivers with water almost all the year round are extensive. They are situated close to one another, the average distance between the two being 5 to 8 km, which is more or less similar to the present pattern of village settlements. A large tract of the land of the middle and lower Krishna Valley is beset with chains of granitoid hill ranges with castellated terraces, rock-shelters and caves. The hill ranges with bands of dolerite dykes and auriferous quartz reefs overlooking expansive fields of red murrain or brown sandy soil, rich in flora and fauna which include fruit trees such as the Indian jujube (*Ziziphus mauritania* Lam), Cuddapah almond (*Buchnania lanzan* Sprenzel) jamoblana, Java plum (*Siziguium cumini* L), wild date, etc., as well as wild animals like tiger, deer and cattle, and birds like peacock. It has excellent natural shelters as also food supply and abundant rock materials for tools for people practising both pastoral and agricultural activities of a slightly advanced stage. Most of the hill terraces and valleys were used for habitation.

Dwellings

The dwellings are of two kinds: pit-dwellings and surface structures constructed of perishable materials. Paiyampalli, Sanganakallu, Hallur, Banahalli, Gundlur, Garapadu, etc., provide some information about the plan of dwellings, the materials used for construction and the village pattern. Dwelling pits have been exposed at Paiyampalli, Gundlur, Garapadu and Nagarjunakonda. However, their relative stratigraphical and other details are unknown.

The dwelling pits were cut into the natural soil and are circular or oblong in plan (Fig. 9.3). In one of the pits, a line of stones divides it into two parts. At the top and all round the edge of the pit are postholes supporting the thatched roof. They are of different types and sizes, and are bipartite, tripartite quadripartite in plan with a flight of steps for descending into them. In larger pits, a ramp is provided for this purpose. The floor is usually well chiselled. At Garapadu, there was a circular pit of about 1 m diameter and 1.94 m deep; it may have been a silo. In one of the pits a red ware jar was found on the

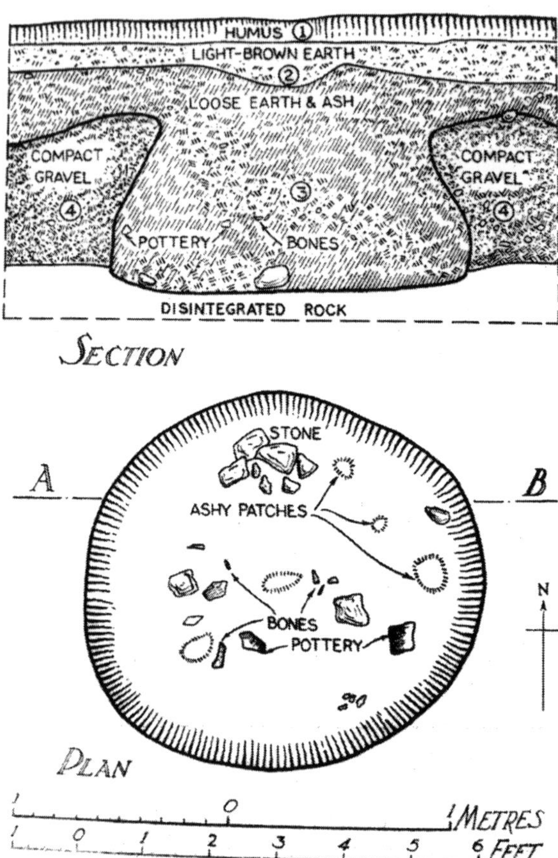

Fig. 9.3: Dwelling pit, Nagarjunakonda

floor. Pottery and animal bones occurred in these pits. Huts raised on the ground have been exposed at these sites, and also at Ramapuram (Figs. 9.4-9.5), Banahalli and Hallur (Fig. 9.6). There were traces of rammed floors with postholes along the exterior edge. Many houses, circular or oval in plan, were encountered at Ramapuram in all the three phases: IA, IB and IC. They had stone slabs along the margin and, in one case, there was a mud lining along the edge. In Phase IC, there was an apsidal floor. Occasionally, huts had open spaces of (23 × 15 m) in front of them. Many of them had pit silos, some with clay bins inside. Generally the diameter of the circular hut varies from 3 to 6 or even 8 m. Chunks of plastered clay-bearing impressions of wattle and daub pattern were noticed at some sites. Numerically, circular houses are by far the largest. There were also rectangular, semi-circular and apsidal floor plans, well-rammed with clay and stone chips of schist or granite.

Fig. 9.4: A circular house, Ramapuram, Neolithic-Chalcolithic phase

At Banahalli, there was an apron of clay mixed with potsherds along the raised edge for checking the flow of rainwater inwards whereas river sand was spread on the uneven floor at Hallur. Wooden posts supported the walls of wattle daub with clay and the conical roof was supported by the central post. At Sanganakallu, the uneven ground was paved with granite chips over which earth was rammed. What is interesting is the remains of a plastered wall mixed with kaolin and the impression of split bamboos. The hut probably had a conical roof covered with grass, as is evident from the remains of burnt grass. At Sanganakallu, there were three axes with polished edge, a sling ball, a hammer stone an oval-shaped stone rubber, a hearth consisting of three stones with marks of constant burning, and charcoal with ash. In the other part were two groups of four flat stones obviously meant for keeping a storage jar. In another hut was found a small oval-shaped hearth containing ash and a polished stone axe nearby. This evidence recurs at Tekkalakota as well.

Domestic Equipment

Among domestic articles, pottery constituted the major equipment for storing, cooking and serving food, as well as for interring bones of dead humans in the process of secondary burial. Owing to the long duration of the culture and varying geographical conditions and cultural practices, the pottery varies in form and fabric in different areas. Of course, certain simple and basic types are common all over the region. Broadly speaking, the two main pottery

Fig. 9.5: Plans of round huts, Ramapuram, Neolithic-Chalcolithic phase

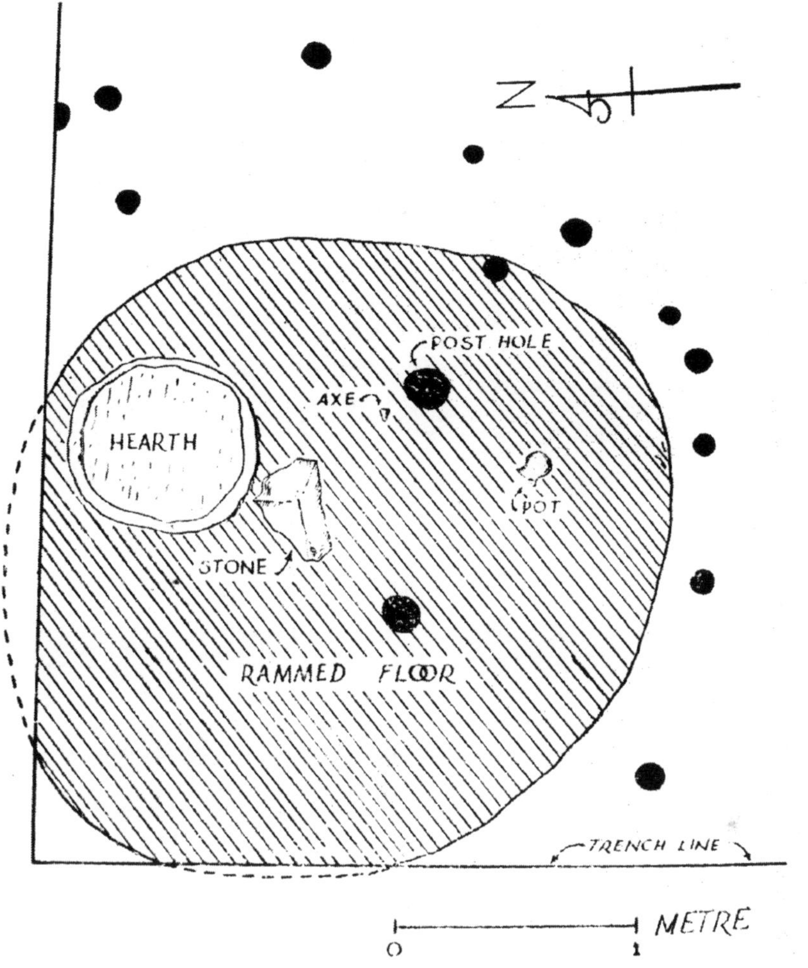

Fig. 9.6: A Round hut, Hallur

fabrics are the red ware and the grey ware, each having some varieties and both hand-made and turn-table made. The latter is usually burnished and micaceous. The forms include storage jars with globular body and out-curved rims, spouted vases, perforated jars, legged bowls, spouted bowls, platters, varieties of lids, goblets, head-rests, trough, basins, lamps, etc. (Figs. 9.7-9.9). Multi-lipped shallow bowls with perforations at the bottom reported from Ramapuram are rare. Head-rests, also known as neck-rests, seem to be peculiar to the Kaveri and upper Tungabhadra valleys, as they occur only in T. Narasipur and Hallur whereas in the upper Krishna and the Bhima-Godavari Valley, shallow bowls, platters, deep cups, varieties of lids, thick storage jars and dish-on-stand legged bowls are abundant. Basins and troughs are common in the upper Bhima and Godavari basins.

In the valley of the Manjra-Karanja, a tributary of the Godavari, the rimless

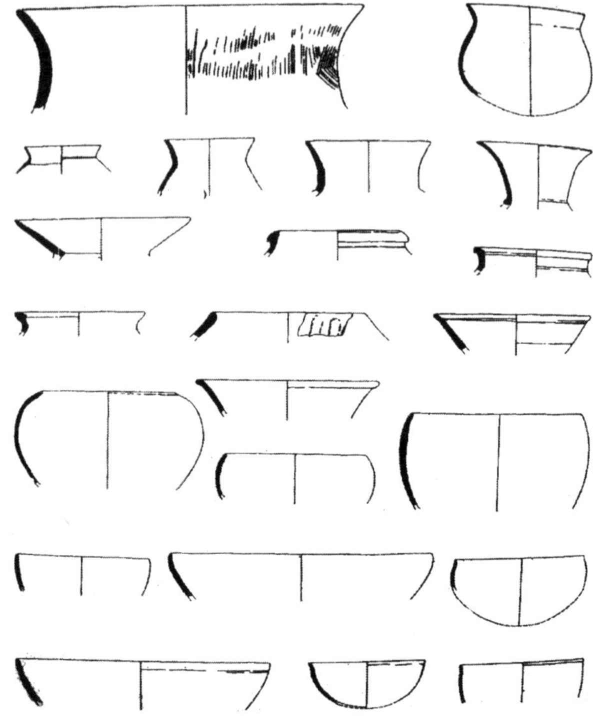

Fig. 9.7: Brahmagiri, Neolithic-Chalcolithic pottery types (greyware)

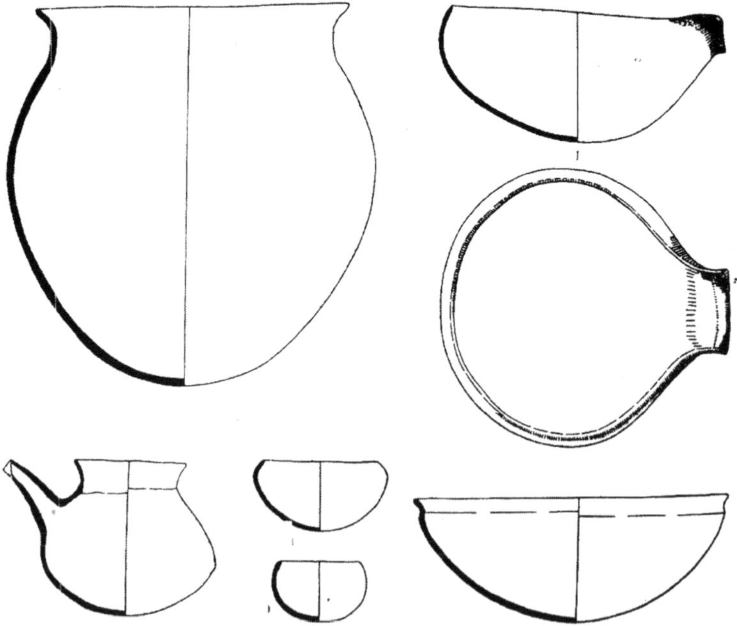

Fig. 9.8: Brahmagiri, Neolithic-Chalcolithic pottery types (greyware)

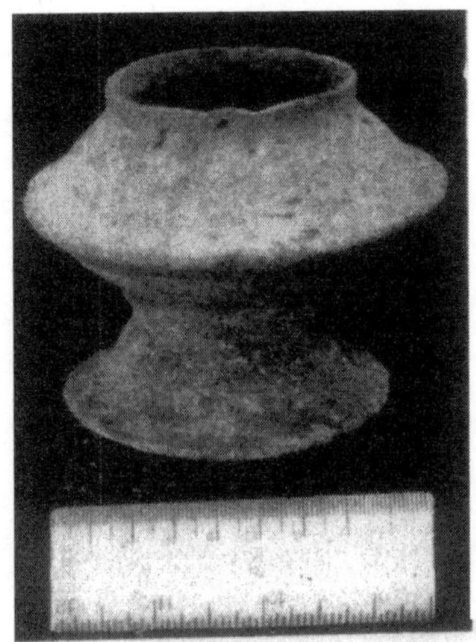

Fig. 9.9: Tekkalakota, Neolithic-Chalcolithic pottery, rare types

handi of grey ware and a bowl with straight sides are noteworthy. Occasionally the grey ware vases and bowls, burnished and unburnished, have post-firing red ochre painting along the edges. Big storage jars and vases have decorative fingered depressions on the rim or a chain pattern on the shoulder. A painted peacock on a pot from Satti and another with a painted bull from Ramapuram are fine specimens of realistic art. Besides, there are pre-firing incised decorative designs such as the herringbone pattern, on the shoulder of vases and the exterior of bowls. Burnished pottery in pinkish red as well as greyish black is decorated on the exterior with pre-firing dark purple geometrical patterns and rarely stylized plant and animal motifs. Some designs are complex and those from the upper Krishna sites deserve special mention. Bichrome paintings on a pinkish buff surface also occur and some pottery is decorated with simple lines in dull white.

Black-and-red pottery with white paintings is common at the Harappan sites of Gujarat and also at Chalcolithic sites in the Banas and Narmada valleys but is rare in the lower Deccan and Krishna-Tungabhadra Valley (Fig. 9.10). A few sherds of this pottery occur in the lower Krishna Valley, as at Kesarapalle. They are mostly varieties of bowls with simple linear patterns in dull white. Incidentally, excepting Kesarapalle, this pottery occurs in small numbers at all sites in burials alone but, in the upper Tungabhadra, it was common in the Early Iron Age culture and as burial furniture in megaliths. Strangely enough, it occasionally occurs at distant sites: in a megalith in Heggadehalli (Kodagu district) (Devaraj et al. 1998) and T. Kallupatti (Madurai district).[19]

The Jorwe red ware appears in the late or overlapping phase of the Neolithic-Chalcolithic stage. It was discovered first at Jorwe in 1950-1 and, hence, is

[19] *IAR*, 1976-7, pp. 46-7.

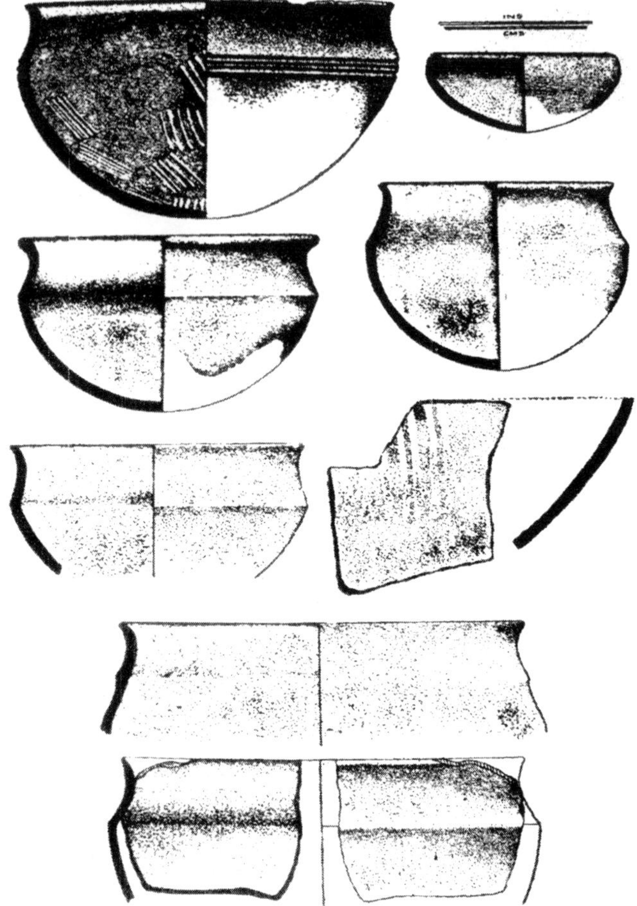

Fig. 9.10: Tekkalakota, white painted black-and-red ware bowls

named after the site. It occurs at several sites in the lower Bhima, the Krishna-Tungabhadra *doab* and the Upper Tungabhadra as far west as Hallur. It is wheel-made and the most common forms are: concave-sided carinated bowls, high-necked jars, spouted vessels with carinated or squat body and out-turned flaring rim, channel-spouted bowl, etc. Painted designs occur on the exterior and interior surface of the bowls as well. Black paintings largely comprising geometrical designs, animals such as tiger, deer or antelope, dog, birds and even human figures. Interestingly enough, this pottery occasionally bears graffiti marks caused by scratching on the exterior or interior. What these marks signify is still a problem. They are supposed to be potters, marks, religious symbols or the letters of the Harappan script.[20]

[20]K. Rajan et al. (1997), *Archaeology of Tamil Nadu* (*Kongu Country*), Book India Publishing Co., Delhi, pp. 116-22.

Tools and Weapons

Polished stone tools are characteristic of the Neolithic culture. They are generally made of dolerite, dyke, Deccan trap or hornblende and, rarely, of chlorite schist. The tool-types are chiefly the axe, adze, chisel, wedge and hoe and their varieties, the first being the most common (Fig. 9.11). The axes are generally triangular in form, and lenticular or ovaloid in section, with a pointed butt end and sharp working edge that is straight or crescentic. Rarely, the butt end may also be blunt like the axes from Kesarapalle. The tool is prepared on a selected rock nodule of suitable form by flaking, pecking, grinding and, finally, polishing. Usually the working edge but, rarely, the whole tool is polished. A stone axe from Kuduvelli is double-edged with a 'longish socket transversely cut'.[21] Another axe from Hasoodi (Shimoga district, Karnataka) with a thick rectangular butt end and a straight, sharp,

Fig. 9.11: Neolithic axes from Maski

[21] *IAR*, 1978-9, p. 92.

polished working edge has an engraving of a cattle in outline which is noteworthy. The chisel, wedge and, particularly, the hoe are specialized tools unlike the axe which is most commonly required for different purposes such as cutting, splitting, etc. Chisels and wedges are tools of carpentry and the hoe is an agricultural implement. A plough similar to the Harappan clay model from Banavali may have been used in the Neolithic period in south India. Many of the tools were probably hafted onto wooden handles. The other rather heavy tools are: sling balls for hunting and oval-shaped rubber stones for grinding and polishing, both of granite. Besides, there were microliths made of chert, jasper and chalcedony, comprising parallel-sided blades, backed blades, points, shouldered arrowheads, lunates, trapezes, and triangles. The blades were produced by employing the 'crested guiding ridge' technique (Fig. 9.12).

In the Tungabhadra-Krishna Valley, as also the Palar-Kaveri Valley, tools made of animal bones and horns were in use, as is clear from the evidence from Hallur, Sanganakallu, Tekkalakota, Kodekal, Garapadu, Banahalli,

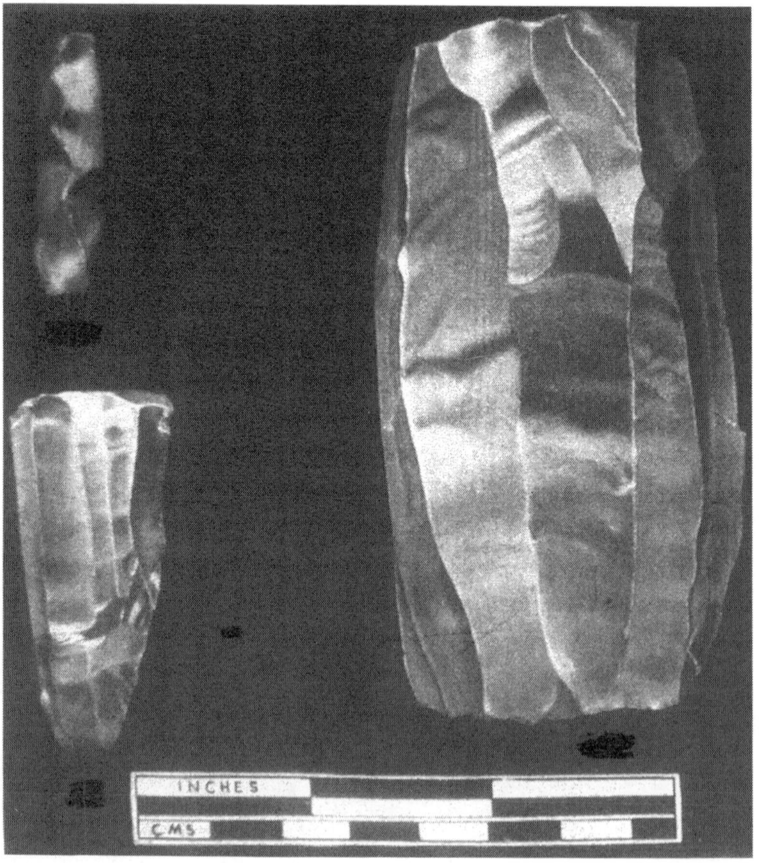

Fig. 9.12: Fluted cores and blade with crested guiding ridge, Maski

Palvoy, Paiyampalli, etc. They included points, axe-blades, chisels, etc., made of horns, long bones, splinters and scapula. Bone tools occur in a large number at Palvoy (Fig. 9.13).

Copper tools were also in use though they were rare. They included double-edged swords with a thin mid-rib and antennae hilt; daggers (as at Chandoli) of similar type; flat celts, chisels, fish hooks, axes, rods, etc. The accidental discovery at Kallur of three long swords with mid-rib and antennae hilt in a spot close to a Neolithic-Chalcolithic site is indeed noteworthy. Equally interesting are similar copper swords from Appukallu (Vellore district), Kupp Chipadooru (Coimbatore district) and Shavanipatti (Ramanathapuram district) in Tamil Nadu where the Chalcolithic cultural phase, particularly south of the Kaveri Valley, is poorly known. It may be stated that in the Tambraparni Valley, covering the Madurai and Ramanathapuram districts, there is a direct cultural succession from the Mesolithic to the Iron Age Megalithic. Copper was sparingly used for making tools and ornaments such as beads and bangles, as at Terdal, Chinnamarur, etc. A celt from Tekkalakota, chisel from Piklihal, axe from Brahmagiri, and a fish hook and a tiny axe from Hallur deserve special mention. Ramapuram was found to be rich in copper objects; it yielded triangular celt tongs, triangular parers with semi-circular expanded end and a double convex-edged tool, made on thin plate, thin spiral strips, convex

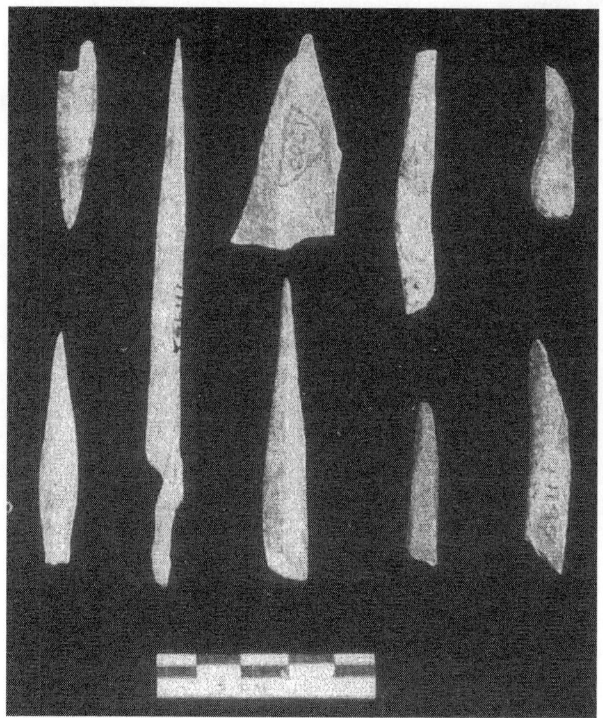

Fig. 9.13: Bone tools from Ramapuram

spiral beads, etc.[22] Copper tools of these varieties were in use in the upper Godavari-Krishna Valley (including western Maharashtra) and in northern Karnataka.

Agriculture

Agriculture, stock-raising, fishing and hunting were the main occupations of the Neolithic people. The meat of goat, sheep, deer and cattle constituted a substantial part of their diet. It was thus far believed that the horse was unknown to them and was introduced into the region from outside for the first time by the Iron Age megalith-builders but it is now reported from Hallur. Cattle was harnessed for cultivation of land and for hard labour. The wild animals included the elephant, horned rhinoceros, buffalo, black buck, nilgai, antelope, chital, sambar and barasinga. A variety of cultivated pulses, (black gram and green grams), beans and food grains (rice and ragi) came from the overlap phase of Hallur.

Foxtail and browntop millet from Hallur and Sangankallu appear to have been domesticated from the wild species in the Deccan but barley, emmer, free-threshing wheat, pearl millet, and ragi seem to have been introduced into the region from outside. *Setaria pumila*, Indian jujube, figs, little millet and kodo millet also occur.

Agricultural implements include a hoe for breaking the surface. It is not known if a plough was used. Wooden ploughs drawn by bullocks are presently used in the red soil zone of the eastern maidan and the sandy grey soil of the coastal area, and may have been in use in the past as well. Numerous corn-crushing stone troughs were found at some sites in the Krishna Valley; at Tekkalakota, their number is strikingly high.

Arts and Crafts

The village industries were tool-making, pot-making, making burnt clay figurines, etc. The discovery of copper swords with mid-rib and antennae hilt from Kallur is noteworthy. This was followed by the excavation of the site in which copper pyrites, suggesting copper smelting, were found. Later, in the area near the site, geologists of the Karnataka government discovered veins of minerals, containing prospective copper content, at a low depth from the surface in the plain field in the area. Mention may also be made of ancient copper, iron and gold workings in the Maski-Gadag area, the antiquity of which, however, is not known.

Mat impressions on the bottom of urns from Tekkalakota, Nagarjunakonda, Ramapuram and other sites give a clear idea about bamboo/reed mat weaving.

[22] *IAR*, 1981-2, Plate I; 1982-3, Plate II.

Varieties of finely polished beads of semi-precious stones, such as jasper, carnelian, agate, steatite, etc., attest to the prevalence of the lapidary craft.

Personal ornaments such as bangles and beads shed some light on the craft activity of the people. Plain copper bangles from Tekkalakota and Terdal, rings from Brahmagiri, various types of beads and bangles of semi-precious stones and shell and terracotta figurines from many Neolithic sites amply testify to the aesthetic sense of the people. Interestingly enough, Pusalapadu and Ramapuram have yielded hundreds of steatite beads (Fig. 9.14). In fact, Pusalapadu (*pusala* = bead; *padu* = heap), also known as Bandi Pusala Chenu, means a field of wheel-shaped beads. Varieties of beads of agate, carnelian, jasper and shell have been reported from many sites. Spiral ear ornaments of copper and gold from Brahmagiri and Tekkalakota, respectively, deserve special mention. A copper finger ring from Brahmagiri is a good instance of the use of this type of ornament by the people.

Terracotta figurines from Brahmagiri, Sanganakallu, Piklihal and Watgal are good specimens of Neolithic art. The figurine of a sheep from Brahmagiri is rather crude. Varieties of birds including the peacock, and human figures from Sanganakallu, Watgal and Piklihal, testify to the fine modelling. A bull figurine from Piklihal with a sturdy and robust body and prominent hump is superb in the delineation of the physical form and reminds us of the bulls on the Harappan seals. Occasionally, animal figurines are decorated with paintings on their body. A hollow pig with stripes painted in black on its body is worth mentioning. A male human figurine in the standing posture with a lamp (bowl) on his head from Watgal recalls the stone *yaksha* of *c.* first century BC from a Buddhist *chaityalaya* at Pitalkhora (Fig. 9.15).

Fig. 9.14: Steatite beads from Ramapuram

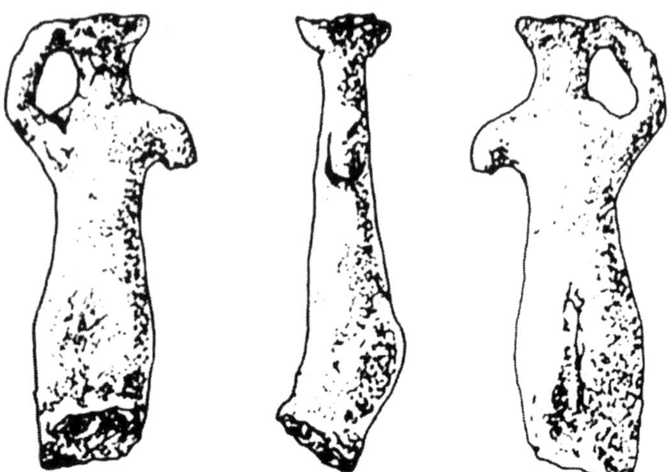

Fig. 9.15: Terracotta figurine from Watgal

The other technique of depicting the figures of animals was by puncturing on the pottery objects. A small lid from Tekkalakota is marked with punctured figures of the serpent, bull and deer, and a potsherd from Banahalli with the camel and bull (Fig. 9.16).

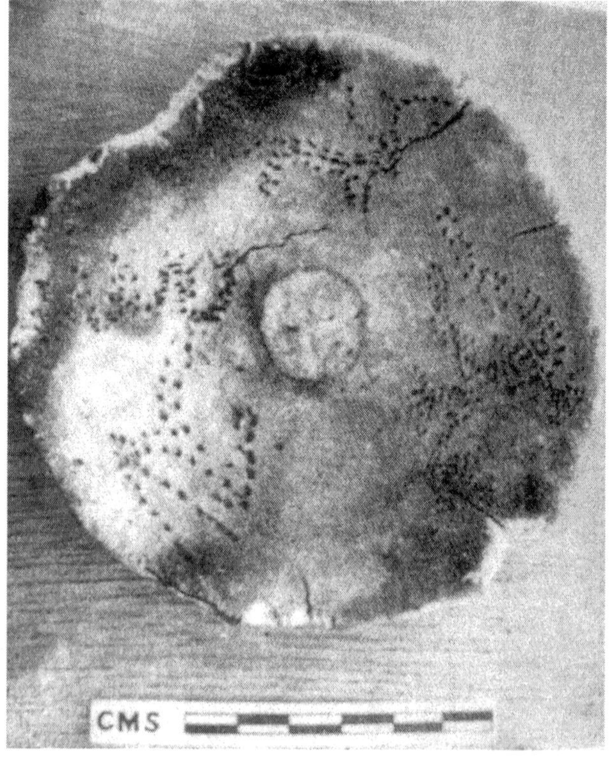

Fig. 9.16: Punctured designs on pottery from Tekkalakota

Religious Beliefs

The rock art of the Neolithic people throws light on their religious beliefs. It consists of paintings, bruisings and engravings which are scattered over south India (Fig. 9.17). The paintings are in red ochre and are depicted on the interior of rock shelters. There are two more categories of this kind of art: bruisintis executed with a hammer and stone, and engravings delineated with a sharp and pointed tool. They are found on the bare surface of isolated boulders usually overlooking or in the vicinity of Neolithic settlements. They may belong to different cultural periods from the prehistoric to the historical, but those which are stylistically akin to Neolithic examples on pottery can be taken as Neolithic. Generally the paintings and bruisings consist of human figures, and the dog, deer or lizard drawn either in outline and/or in silhouette

Fig. 9.17: Neolithic rock art

There are also curious geometrical designs. Although the art is simple in technique and symbolic it is executed with confidence and is forceful, thus making the figures, particularly the animals, lively. Some of the rock paintings and bruisings at Piklihal, Balachakra, Tekkalakota, Sanganakallu, Hampi, Vankatapura, etc., are typical examples of Neolithic rock art.

Disposal of the Dead

The dead were disposed of in two ways: by primary and secondary burial, the latter being more common. The secondary burial may be articulated or fractional. Invariably, the practice was to bury the dead within the habitation area and, in many cases, within the house. In the case of primary burial, the dead body was buried in an oblong or oval pit with the head towards the east or west and in an extended posture. The face may be turned towards the south. Besides, near the head, chest or waist were placed spouted or other vessels, probably containing food and drink at the time of the burial for the dead person to use in his life after death. The burials from T. Narasipur, Brahmagiri (Fig. 9.18) and Burial No. 5 in Tekkalakota illustrate this practice. In T. Narasipur, a head-rest was placed near the neck which revealed, for the first time, the function of this pottery object. The orientation of the body in an east-west direction or vice versa appears to be an early practice prevalent south of the Krishna. The body may also be placed in a north-south orientation, the head being towards the north. In Burial No. 2 of phase II at Tekkalakota, the well-preserved skeleton of a female was north-south oriented, with the face turned westwards. Seven pottery vessels comprising a spouted pot, two vases of grey ware and four black-and-red ware bowls with white paintings were placed near the feet. At Ramapuram (Fig. 9.19), which was excavated horizontally several burials were exposed, particularly from the IB and IC phases. They are of different types: the vertical or horizontal single urn burial, horizontal double pot burial, vertical single pot burial within an inverted vase, and shallow burial. The articulated burial, either primary or secondary, is almost invariably north-south oriented. The burial furniture includes some copper objects along with pottery. The curious feature of some of these burials is that the feet are cut-off. This part of the ritual implying an eschatological belief is noticed at some of the sites, but in the Kaveri and Palar Valley at T. Narasipur, Banahalli and Brahmagiri, this feature was absent.

The secondary burials are of two types: ceremoniously interring bones collected from the first burial or placing the skeletal remains of the dead in a natural anatomical order (to the extent possible) in a pit or in pots, two or three or four pots placed in a pit horizontally, in a mouth to mouth or with open bottom caused by breaking, which were accompanied with more pottery vessels as grave furniture. Such secondary pot burials were found at Nevasa, Piklihal, Watgal, Tekkalakota, Hallur, etc. Usually the pit-or-pot burial contains the skeletal remains of one individual. At Terdal, in a pit-burial, skeletal

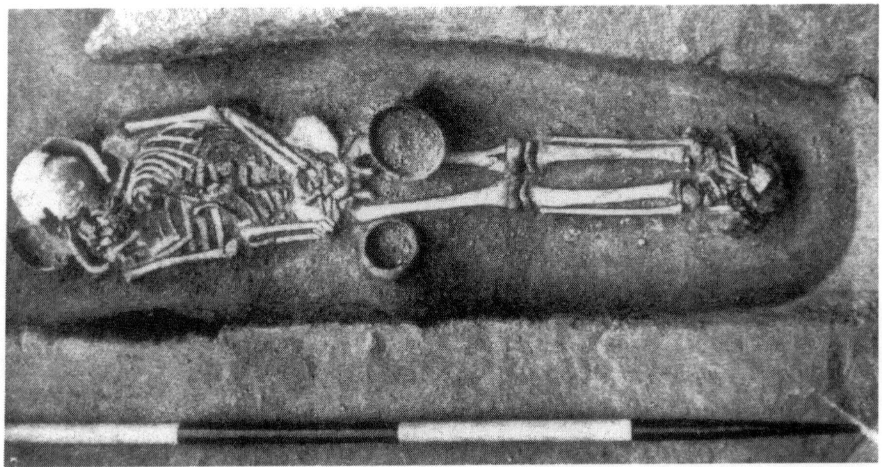

Fig. 9.18: A Neolithic burial, Brahmagiri (IB)

remains were found to be scanty; skull pieces, one or two ribs, and the thigh and long bones laid in an articulate order along the normal length, along with pottery and a copper bangle near the hands. Rarely, a pit burial may contain skeletal remains of more than one individual. The Tekkalakota Burial No. 1 (early phase) contained fragments of two skulls suggesting that it was a family burial. The double or treble pot-burial variety occurred at Hallur. Single pot-burials usually contained the skeletal remains of children. They are found in large numbers. A four-pot burial from Tekkalakota is of an adult. In some cases, the burial pot, bulging in the middle and narrow at the bottom, has two nipple-like projections and a chain-like design around the neck. The whole pot looks like a pregnant woman. Interring the bones of the dead in such pots seems to imply the symbolic return of the person into the mother's womb.

There is a pot-burial of a different kind at Banahalli, Brahmagiri, Watgal, etc.: a single urn containing the skeletal remains of a child with the mouth covered by a bowl or another pot, and without any other pottery vessels as part of the burial furniture. In the lower Krishna and Kaveri valleys, no pot burials have been found so far.

The People

Who are the people of this culture? There is no positive answer as yet. Their identity with any known community of the historical period is difficult to ascertain. The region is also too vast for the existence of a uniform type of one community. What is known about them at present is their different racial affinities from the study of skeletal remains from some of the sites. The skeleton from T. Narasipur seems to belong to the 'Mediterranean' type without any indications of admixture with Proto-Australoid as noticed at

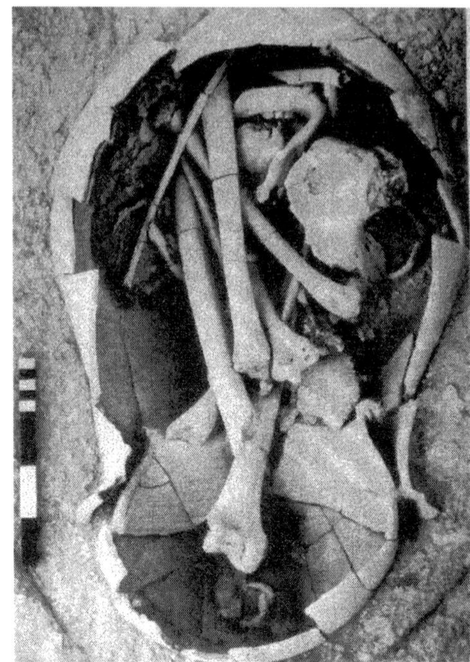

Fig. 9.19: Twin urn burial, Ramapuram

Piklihal, Tekkalakota (No. 5) and the female skull from Nagarjunakonda. Those from Brahmagiri belong to autochthonous Proto-Australoid; whereas at Tekkalakota, the Mediterranean predominates. On the whole, the people in the region are essentially of the Mediterranean-Proto-Australoid complex. But, of late, the scientific basis of such a racial identification is being questioned.

All these early opinions are now being viewed as incorrect and even baseless, and these proto-historic people are, to a large extent, being taken as indigenous. It should be noted that earlier theories were based on scanty evidence that was then available, and are not only provisional but vague. Further, nothing is known about the racial complex of the people of the pre-Neolithic stage in the south.

Cultural Contacts

Within the region under study, there was free movement of the people from one river valley to another at different periods, as attested by the occurrence of the characteristic cultural equipments of one area in the other. For instance, stone blades and microliths, Jorwe pottery and the double-pot or four-pot burial typical of the upper Godavari-Bhima Valley are also noticed in the Shorapur and Raichur *doabs*, the lower Bhima, and the middle Krishna and lower Tungabhadra valleys. Typical copper celts, swords and daggers occur in the Godavari-Bhima-Krishna valleys. Early black-on-red painted pottery of the Krishna of the type of Brahmagiri IA and long stone blade tools are found in the upper Tungabhadra, the lower Krishna and the Kaveri Valley. Likewise, neoliths of the south Indian type and burnished micaceous grey pottery occur in the upper Bhima-Godavari valleys and in the Vidarbha area.

Chronology

In the early stage of scientific excavations of some of the sites such as Brahmagiri and Maski, a sequence of three cultures, viz., the Neolithic, the Iron Age Megalithic and the early historical, was established. Accordingly, the chronology at Brahmagiri was based on the evidence of Roman coins, pottery such as rouletted ware and Satavahana coins. The three cultural periods were, therefore, dated from *c*. middle first century-third century AD (Period III), *c*. 200 BC of first century AD (Period II) and the early first millennium BC to 200 BC (Period I, Neolithic culture). It was accepted with marginal modification for Maski and Kesarapalle, and the latter site is dated to the middle of eighth to the middle of fifth century BC. But it should be made clear that this chronology was based on extremely limited data from a few individual sites. Since then, several sites have been excavated. Further, a series of C-14 dates are also now available. Of these, those from Watgal and Budihal are the earliest. On the basis of these absolute dates, the southern Neolithic-Chalcolithic culture is fairly well-dated. The sites in the Kaveri Valley (Paiyampalli, Palvoy) and in the upper Tungabhadra (the early and late Neolithic) are dated to *c*. 1800-800 BC; and in the upper and middle Krishna Valley from Terdal to Utnur to *c*. 2300-900/800 BC (Watgal Piklihal). There are two sub-phases, Early and Late, dated to *c*. 2300-1700 BC and *c*. 1700-800 BC (including the overlap phase), respectively. The earliest Neolithic as at Watgal and Nagarjunakonda may be dated to *c*. 3000-2700 BC.

The fag end of this cultural stage (*c*. 1200-900/800 BC) overlaps with some strikingly new traditions: the use of iron tools, implements and weapons for the first time, an increasingly large-scale production of pottery of new fabrics and types (black and red ware, black ware and red ware) and the use of stone slabs for lining the burial pit within the habitation area. All these are well-illustrated in Ramapuram IC where transepted oblong cist burials containing secondary articulated skeletal remains, copper and iron objects, and black-and-red ware pottery are found within the habitation area. Similar cultural situation recurs in Maski too. That iron objects were locally manufactured is evident from the discovery of iron smelting materials with iron slag and lumps of iron ore (Period III) at Banahalli. The wider of iron objects on a large scale resulted in ending the manufacture of stone tools and accelerated the process of urbanization.

Ash Mounds: Neolithic

Before closing the narration, a reference to the problem of the ash mounds of the Krishna-Tungabhadra valleys, located in or near many of the Neolithic sites, is necessary. There are more than eighty localities in the Krishna-Tungabhadra *doab* area with huge mounds of scoriaceous ash, which are referred to as ash mounds. All along the Krishna, from Kadoli where the river enters Karnataka, there are about twenty ash mounds. The biggest one is at Wandalli near Maski, measuring about 100 m long, 30 m wide and 3 m high. Of late, ash mounds have been noticed even in the upper Pennar Valley at Nagalapur (Tumkur district). The one at Appukallu near Vellore (Tamil Nadu) is isolated in the deep south but it is doubtful if it is an ash mound. There appears to be some relationship between Neolithic and Megalithic sites as at Palvoy, Utnur, Kodekal, Kupgal, Hulikallu, Budihal, Kudutini and others, of which the first six, as also the one at Appukallu, have been excavated to ascertain the causes for their formation, their purpose and their date. As far as Appukallu is concerned, excavations have largely revealed the cultural remains of the early Iron Age along with a few Neolithic cultural vestiges that had survived. The debris is ashy earth containing the cultural relics of human settlement and *not of scoriaceous ash*. Local people at a few of these sites narrate legends about the ash mounds: that they are due to the cremation of the great persons of the epics, the *Ramayana* and the *Mahabharata* such as Hidambasura, Vali, etc. In fact, the one in Venkatapura near Hampi is popularly called Vali *dibba* or *kastha*. Similarly, the ash mounds of Nagalapur, Yellappa Nayakana Halli and Yellappa Nayakana Hosakote (Tumkur district) are also locally known as Vali Dibba. Oral traditions prevalent in the Hampi area, and two Kannada inscriptions of 1069 from Devighat (about 10 km from Hampi) and 1234 from Shirsangi (Belgaum district) speak of the place as the Kishkindha of the *Ramayana*. The huge mound at Kudutini is believed to be the cremation spot of Hidimbasura of the *Mahabharata*.

Since the first notice of an ash mound in Kupgal by Mackenzie in 1834 to the present, various theories regarding their origin, purpose and significance have been advanced. Some scholars opined that they were composed of prehistoric volcanic or limestone slags, *kankar* or a petrified substance. It was Bruce Foote who tried to investigate them on scientific lines. He got some samples of ash chemically analysed and found them to be nothing but cow dung burnt at a very high temperature. After carefully considering the circumstantial evidence, he suggested that they belonged to the Neolithic period. In recent times, the excavations of ash mounds at Utnur, Kupgal, Palvoy and Budihal, and the laboratory tests of ash that followed, confirmed the first part of the theory postulated by Foote. Regarding the purpose of burning cow dung at such a high temperature (800 to 1200 centigrade) on a large scale, interpretations of the evidence differ. They are:

1. The sites are of cattle-pens of the Neolithic people; the periodical burning of accumulated cow dung was ritualistic; the formation of such mounds

came to an end in the beginning of the Iron Age and the practice survived in festivals such as Holi.

2. They were due to the iron smelting activity of the post-Neolithic Iron Age people.

This writer discovered scores of Chalcolithic sites, many of which contain the remnants of scoriaceous ash, in the Bhima-Krishna valleys, particularly in the upper Krishna valley.[23] Considering their distribution pattern and probable cultural affiliations, he observes that the activity resulting in the formation of ash mounds had diffused along the Krishna Valley towards the Bhima-Krishna-Tungabhadra *doab* and further south-eastwards, as far south as the upper Palar Valley. Second, the Neolithic people of the Kaveri Valley, middle-lower Krishna and Bhima Valley were not responsible for their formation. The ash mounds may chronologically be assigned from the last phase of the Chalcolithic culture overlapping with the Iron Age Megalithic.

On the basis of his findings in the excavation of twin ash mounds in Budihal, K. Paddayya has interpreted that the ash mounds are of the Neolithic stage datable to *c.* 1900-1400 BC.[24] It may be a little earlier, 2300 BC, a date that tallies with that of the Kodekal ash mound. They represent the burning of cow dung accumulated in cattle-pens near the habitation area. The people in this stage were chiefly pastoralists and, in order to keep away wild animals such as leopard and tigers from preying on their cattle, goat and sheep, the cow dung accumulated in the cattle-pen was burnt; the burning being a slow process. Incidentally, the unwanted dung was disposed off usefully in this manner.

At Hulikallu (Anantpur district), in the southern periphery of the ash mound were noticed some postholes and, in the south-eastern periphery, remains of a cattle-pen underlying the ash mound.[25] Near the pen were dumps of animal bones of the bovine species and black-and-red ware. The habitation at the site can be divided into two cultural periods: the Neolithic and the culture overlapping with the Iron Age Megalithic.

On the whole, the ash-mounds still remain an enigma; their authors and their purpose are not yet clear. Be that as it may, that the antiquity of many of them (as at Budihal and Kodekal) goes back to the beginning of the third millennium BC is firmly established.

* Besides the Neolithic habitation sites in the Ponnair Valley, there are some sites in the upper Kaveri (Krishnamurthy, 1971: A-12), Tungabhadra,[26]

[23]Sundara (1971), op. cit., pp. 13-30.

[24]K. Paddayya (1993a), 'Ash mound Investigations at Budihal, Gulbarga District, Karnataka', *Man and Environment*, 18, pp. 57-87; idem (1993b), 'Further Field Investigations at Budihal, Gulbarga District', *BDCRI*, 53, pp. 277-322.

[25]*IAR*, 1978-79, p. 6.

[26]M.S. Nagaraja Rao (1964), 'Recent Explorations in the Tungabhadra Basin: The Chalcolithic Phase', *BDCRI*, 23, pp. 55-7.

lower Krishna (I.K. Sarma 1967: 75-94) and the Godavari valleys.[27] Earlier, some were noticed by Bruce Foote.[28] A few of them such as Muttalavadi,[29] Hemmige Banahalli,[30] Tekkalakota,[31] Watgal (Jim Shaffer, 1995: 57-94), Budihal,[32] Utnur[33] and Kesarapalli (Sarkar 1966: 72-3), both lying in the lower Krishna Valley, have not yielded any ground stone tools, although they are found on the surface. Palvoy,[34] Hulikallu,[35] Kesarapalle (Sarkar 1966: 37-74), Nagarjunakonda (Sarkar 1975: 76-162), Virapuram (Sastri 1981: 1-8), Ramapuram,[36] Utnur,[37] Chinnamarur,[38] Kodekal,[39] Gandlur,[40] Garapadu,[41] Vemmarigutta (east Godavari district),[42] Polakonda,[43] Terdal, Maski,[44] Piklihal,[45] and Jami of the Gosthani Valley,[46] Peda Tadivada (Visakhapatnam, Andhra Pradesh),[47] etc., have been excavated.

**Section scraping at Mullikadu[48] and excavations at Paiyampalli[49] have exposed Neolithic cultural debris of considerable thickness, containing a few Neolithic, tools along with pottery and pit-dwellings (63).

In the upper Kaveri, at T. Narasipur, the early phase of the Neolithic was found to have no neoliths. Among the twenty-six illustrated specimens from the site, only one is from a late Neolithic level (Seshadri 1971: 60-4).

[27] Shadaksharaiah (1995), op. cit.

[28] Foote (1916), op. cit., pp. 68, 82-7.

[29] *IAR*, 1974-5, p. 20.

[30] *IAR*, 1985-6, pp. 42-6.

[31] M.S. Nagaraj Rao et al. (1965), *The Stone age Hill Dwellers of Tekkalakota*, Deccan College Poona.

[32] Paddayya (1993a), op. cit., pp. 57-87; idem (1993b), op. cit., pp. 277-322.

[33] F.R. Allchin (1961), *Utnur Excavations*, Government of Andhra Pradesh, Hyderabad, p. 50.

[34] V. Rami Reddy (1968), *Pre and Protohistory of South Western Andhra Pradesh, Hyderabad*, Government of Andhra Pradesh.

[35] *IAR*, 1978-9, p. 62.

[36] *IAR*, 1980-1, pp. 3-7; 1981-2, pp. 3-8; 1983-4, pp. 3-5.

[37] Allchin (1961), op. cit.

[38] *IAR*, 1978-9, p. 64.

[39] Paddayya (1973), op. cit.

[40] *IAR*, 1983-4, pp. 1-2.

[41] *IAR*, 1993-4, p. 2.

[42] *IAR*, 1989-90, p. 38.

[43] *IAR*, 1976-7, p. 5.

[44] Sundara (1971), op. cit.

[45] F.R. Allchin (1960), *Piklihal Excavations*, Government of Andhra Pradesh, Hyderabad.

[46] Ramachandraiya et al. (1976), 'Jami: A Summary of Excavation Results', *Journal of The Andhra Historical Research Society*, 25.

[47] *IAR*, 1989-90, p. 8.

[48] Narasimhaiah (1980), *Neolithic and Megalithic Cultures in Western Tamil Nadu*, Sundeep Prakashan, Delhi, p. 35.

[49] *IAR*, 1964-5, pp. 22-3; 1967-8, pp. 27-8.

The painted potsherds that are not of Jorwe fabric are probably intrusive.

In the Palar Valley, Banahalli (Kolar district), a rich habitation site, was continuously occupied from the early Neolithic (IA): Neolithic-Chalcolithic (IB); Chalcolithic overlapping with the Iron Age Megalithic (II), Iron Age Megalithic (III) and the Early Historical (IV). In the early and late Neolithic, circular and oval houses with rammed floors, plain red and tan pottery, burnished and unburnished pecked and ground stone tools, rubber stones, and other stone objects, bone tools including composite tools, and microliths mostly of quartz, were found.

Further northwards in the Tungabhadra Valley, in Phase I of Period I (early Neolithic) at Hallur, a few Neolithic tools made of locally available chlorite schist, along with coarse brown-and-black ware pottery, in Phase II, ground stone implements, floors of circular houses, grey ware pottery (burnished and unburnished), a few copper objects, double pot-burial, and, in the late levels of the phase, intrusive black-on-red ware pottery of Jorwe fabric, were found.[50]

In the Piklihal-Maski-Watgal area, between the Tungabhadra and the Krishna, Maski was found to have been strewn with numerous Neolithic tools on the surface but evidence of the Neolithic-Chalcolithic stage was discovered in 1954 during excavations (Thapar 1957: 101). The cultural stage of these surface neoliths, pre-creamic or aceramic, still remains unsolved. Period I corresponds to Brahmagiri IA, i.e. the Neolithic-Chalcolithic stage. Watgal seems to have been occupied in all the four stages from aceramic to Neolithic-Chalcolithic with the early Iron Age Megalithic.

Sanganakallu seems to indicate a consistent development from the early Neolithic (IIA) to the late Neolithic-Chalcolithic stage overlapping with the beginning of the Iron Age (III) through the advanced Neolithic (IIA). What is particularly noteworthy is the occurrence of a few Neolithic tools, as well as numerous waste flakes, implying the local manufacture of tools in the habitation area.

It is from the material remains of these sites that the everyday life of the early Neolithic communities can be perceived.

Further northwards in the Manjra-Karanja Valley of the middle Godavari, there are many Neolithic sites, generally without Neolithic tools and microliths. None of the sites have been excavated.

In the north-eastern area of Andhra Pradesh, as at Peda and Tadivada (Vishakhapatnam district), microliths of both Mesolithic and Neolithic phases, ground stone tools and other stone objects, grey ware pottery, etc., have been picked up.

[50]M.S. Nagaraja Rao (1971), *Protohistoric Cultures of the Tungabhadra Valley: A Report on Hallur Excavations*, Dharwad: The Author.

Chapter 10

Beginning of Agriculture: Eastern India

T.C. Sharma

The eastern Neolithic zone covers the landmass lying to the east of the Bengal delta, commonly known in geographical terms as north-east India. It comprises the states of Assam, Nagaland, Meghalaya, Arunachal Pradesh, Manipur, Mizoram and Tripura. Physiographically, the region is characterized by high mountains of the eastern Himalayas and Indo-Burma (Myanmar) ranges, which form a massive wall around the Brahmaputra Valley through which north-east India opens up to the great Indian plains. All the hills and the valley are covered with monsoon-soaked, dense rain forests. Nearly two-thirds of the area is covered by wide hill ranges which are inhabited by a large number of primitive tribes belonging to the Mongoloid racial stock. Through this region, India touches international borders with Tibet Plateau, China, Myanmar and Bangladesh. Racially, culturally and linguistically, this region of India actually forms a contact zone of two great races—the Caucasoid and the Mongoloid, as well as two great cultural traditions—the eastern and the western. All these factors contribute to creating the marked individuality of north-east India. The characteristic features of the north-east Indian individuality become clearly visible even during the Neolithic period when we analyse the typical cultural features of the region as discussed below.

A clear picture of the beginning of settled life in the eastern region has not yet emerged due to lack of sufficient excavated data from this region. Till 1960, surface finds of ground and polished stone tools constituted the only source material to write about the Neolithic culture of this region, and the study remained at the level of the typological classification of stone tools (Dani 1960). The first typological classification of a collection of stone tools from the Nage hills, attempted by J.H. Hutton while writing on the prehistory of undivided Assam, revealed two major types of stone tools: (1) the feebly shouldered or the quasi-shouldered celts, and (2) the triangular celt with pointed butt, the former showing affinities with the eastern Neolithic tradition and the latter with the pointed butt axe tradition of the south Indian Neolithic.[1]

E.C. Worman in his classification of the Neolithic tools of India identified

[1] J.H. Hutton (1928), 'Prehistory of Assam', *Man in India*, 8, pp. 228-32.

distinctive East Asiatic types among the stone tools found in the former undivided Assam, on the basis of which he proposed that the region served as a corridor through which celt-making techniques entered India.[2] The other typological classification attempted by A.H. Dani in his study of the collection of ground and smoothed stone tools from different parts of north-east India (now preserved in the Pitt Rivers Museum of Oxford University) made the Southeast Asian and Chinese connection with the Neolithic culture of the eastern region clearer after the identification, in the collection, of 'faceted tools' or the quadrangular type of axes, the curvilinear and rectilinear varieties of shouldered celts, and jadeite axes—the last one being a distinctly foreign intrusion from upper Burma or south-west China as jadeite is not locally available in India (Dani 1960: 44). T.C. Sharma in his comprehensive typo-technological classification of the large collection of stone tools from different parts of the region, including excavated materials from Daojali Hading, was able to identify the pre-neolithic Hoabinhian types, the early Neolithic types and the fully-developed late Neolithic types, in addition to showing very clear Southeast Asian and Chinese Neolithic influence on Neolithic culture of the region. Settled life or the evolution of Neolithic societies in the eastern region seems to be closely linked with the origin and evolution of Neolithic culture in China and Southeast Asia.

Several writers, while classifying ground and smoothed stone tools from different parts of the eastern region, could identify regional characteristics that appear to have been governed by geographical factors, mainly in the case of the availability of suitable rocks used as raw materials for the manufacture of stone tools, each region showing a preference for locally available, suitable rocks. The technique of manufacture also seems to vary from region to region depending upon the nature of the rocks used, thus giving rise to distinctive regional types. For example, the Neolithic industry of Assam was based upon the utilization of locally available, softer sedimentary rocks mainly shale and (rarely) sandstone, whereas the Neolithic industry of Garo hills was characterized by the utilization of locally available, igneous dyke rock-dolerite. In the case of Nagaland, it was an ultra-basic vein rock called diorite, commonly known as greenstone. Keeping this factor in view, Dani proposed that the Neolithic culture of this region could be studied by dividing the region into six Neolithic zones, viz.: (1) Cachar hill zone, (2) Naga hill zone, (3) Garo hill zone, (4) Khasi hill zone, (5) Sadiya frontier zone, and (6) Brahmaputra Valley zone. Subsequently, when Greater Assam was reorganized to constitute the hill states, it was found that newly-formed states followed, more or less, the pattern of regional Neolithic zones. In the present study, the newly-formed state-wise pattern of the Neolithic zones of the region would be followed.

Among all the states in the region, Assam is found to be rich in Neolithic

[2]E.C. Worman (Jr) (1949), 'The Neolithic Problem in the Prehistory of India', *Journal of Washington Academy of Sciences*, 39, pp. 181-200.

finds (Fig. 7.1). The present state of Assam includes the flat alluvial plains of the Brahmaputra Valley, which is flanked on the south by the north Cachar hills and, in the central part, by the hills of the Karbi Anglang district (Fig. 10.1). Both surface Finds and excavated materials are available from here. Surface finds of ground and polished stone tools have been reported from almost all parts of the state, among which those from the north Cachar hill district, now preserved in the Pitt Rivers Museum of Oxford University, are very significant. In addition to this, a stratified, chance find from Bishwanath

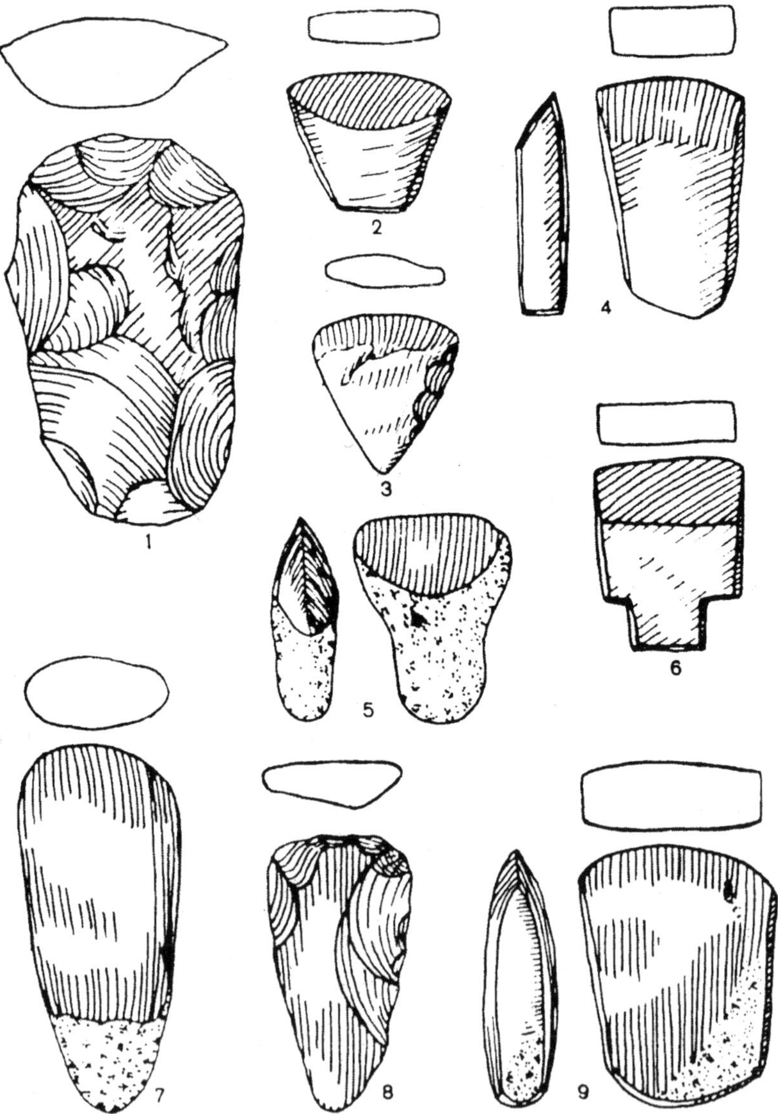

Fig. 10.1: Neolithic implements from eastern India: 1 NEFA; 2, 3 and 6 Cachar Hills; 4 and 8 Garo Hills; 5, 7 and 9 Nagaland

in the Sonitpur district of central Assam is noteworthy.[3] The collection includes, among other common types, some characteristic tools such as shouldered celts and grooved or belted hammer stones, which are found to be peculiar to the site. The excavated materials come from two sites: (1) Daojali Hading in the north Cachar Hills, and (2) Sarutaru in the Kamrup district.

Daojali Hading situated on a densely forested hilltop inside the Langting-Mupa reserve forest in the north Cachar hills, was excavated by M.C. Goswami and T.C. Sharma of Gauhati University during 1961-3 by exposing five trenches.[4] The stratigraphy in the trenches reveals that it is a single cultural site with a habitational deposit of 75 cm. The site yielded a large number of stone axes and adzes, grinding stones, querns, troughs, mullers and pestles, by-product flakes and pottery. Most of the axes and adzes are made of a kind of greyish indurated shale in addition to a few roughly made tools of sandstone and fossil wood, which are locally available. The stone tools made by fine chipping and grinding techniques are divisible into shouldered celts, small triangular celts, quadrangular axes and adzes, as well as edge-ground axes made of sandstone and fossil wood. The pottery (over 600 sherds), found only in small fragments, is coarse, ill-fired and hand-made. The dominant type at the site is of the cord-marked greyware class. Other rare types include sherds of stamped dull-red and plain brick-red wares. Most of the sherds are heavily weathered and yielded no shapes, being fragmentary in nature. The discovery of cord-impressed pottery in association with shouldered celts and quadrangular axes and adzes at the site, which are known to be characteristic eastern Asiatic Neolithic traditions, is very significant as it helps in tracing the origin and affinities of the Neolithic culture of the eastern region.

Sarutaru, situated on a low hillock close to the border of Meghalaya and Assam at a distance of about 25 km south-east of Guwahati, was excavated by S.N. Rao of Dibrugarh University during 1969-72. This is also a single-culture site with about a 60 cm thick habitational layer. The site yielded stone tools, pottery and charcoal. The dominant tool-type consists of shouldered celts and the common pottery type is coarse grey and cord-marked. The Neolithic assemblage of Sarutaru is found to be closely comparable with that of Daojali Hading.[5]

[3]Coggin-Brown (1914), 'Grooved Hammers from Assam and the Distribution of Similar forms in Eastern Asia', *JASB* (New Series) 10, pp. 107-9; idem (1917), *Catalogue Raisonne of Prehistoric Antiquities in the Indian Museum, Calcutta*, Simla, Government of India.

[4]M.C. Goswami and T.C. Sharma (1963), 'Further Report on the Investigation into the Prehistoric Archaeology of North Kachar Hills, Assam', *Journal of Gauhati University*, 14, pp. 45-7; T.C. Sharma (1966), 'Prehistoric Archaeology of Assam: A Study of Neolithic Culture of Assam', Ph.D. thesis (unpublished), University of London; H.D. Sankalia (1974), *Prehistory and Protohistory of India and Pakistan*, Deccan College, Poona, pp. 283ff.

[5]S.N. Rao (1974), 'The Neolithic Cultue of Sarutaru', *Bulletin of Department of Anthropology, Dibrugarh University*, 2, pp. 1-9; idem (1977), 'Excavation at Sarutaru: A Neolithic Site in Assam', *ME*, 1, pp. 39-40.

Meghalaya, constituted of the former districts of the Garo and Khasi-Jaintia hills, is found to be rich in Neolithic finds. Among these, the Garo hills district is particularly rich in Stone Age sites. From the Khasi-Jaintia hills, only four stray neoliths are known so far. Recently, a Neolithic site on a hillock near the dam-site of the Barapani (Umium) hydel project has been discovered. Some Neolithic axes and flakes from the surface of the site have been collected. The site has not yet been fully explored, excavated or reported.

Over a dozen Neolithic sites have been discovered and explored in the Rongram-Gand River Valley in the north-western part of the Garo hills, among which those at Rengchengiri Chitra-Abri, Ringigiri, Selbalgiri and Rangram Alagiri are found to be very rich. Among these, the last two sites were subjected to a small-scale excavation.

The site at Selbalgiri, located on a terrace of the Rangram River, was excavated by M.C. Goswami and T.C. Sharma during 1967-8. The cuttings revealed a sequence of three layers of reddish-brown earth mixed with a varying quantity of quartz gravels, of which layer one, 22 cm thick, yielded stone tools of the fully ground type, some chipped stone axes, flakes and pottery. Layer two, 2.20 m thick, yielded a fluted microlithic core, small flakes and some hammer stones, besides pottery. Layer three, 35 cm thick, yielded a large quantity of microliths with pottery. The discovery of microliths in a stratified Neolithic site in the Garo hills is very significant as they appear for the first time in the whole of the eastern region only at this site. All the tools found in the excavation, including the microliths, are made of dolerite. The tools are heavily patinated. The pottery found in association with neoliths as well as with microliths is hand-made, plain, coarse and gritty in texture, and grey, grayish-brown or dull red in colour. Cord-marked pottery is not present at the site.

The site at Rangram Alagiri, situated on a late Pleistocene terrace on the right bank of the Rangram River, yielded surface finds of chipped and ground stone tools, as well as very crudely flaked tools made of large pebbles of dolerite. A trial excavation conducted at the site by T.C. Sharma during 1978-9 revealed stratified cultural layers of reddish-brown silt of which the top layers, about 50 cm thick, yielded ground and polished stone tools. Below this, there occurs a thick habitational layer (about 120 mm thick) of paved floor with fattish river pebbles, which yielded a large quantity of very crudely flaked (some unifacially flaked) stone tools of a large size made up of river pebbles of dolerite, and chopper, scraper and axe types showing characteristic features of the Hoabinhian stone tool tradition of Southeast Asia.

Although Nagaland played an important part in bringing to light the evidence of the Stone Age culture of north-east India more than a century ago,[6]

[6]Lt. Brown (1872), 'A Note on the Stone implements from the Naga Hills', *JRAI*, 1, pp. 61-2.

archaeological explorations and excavations are yet to be utilized in this state as tools of uncovering the past. Due to this, the Neolithic culture of Nagaland is only known from surface finds of ground and polished stone tools. Pottery and other Neolithic traits are yet to be discovered in the state. The surface finds of neoliths made mainly by J.H. Mutton and J.P. Mills during 1920-30 were found mainly in the central part of the state, some of the find-places being Rokimi, Sirohi, Lazimi, Itumi and Lokhimi.

The Nagaland neoliths show distinctive regional characteristics with respect to raw material and the technique of manufacture. The main rock type used for the manufacture of tools in this state is a variety of ultra-basic vein rock called diorite, generally olive green in colour. It is locally available in the south-eastern part of the state bordering Manipur and Myanmar. It is a grained tough rock not easily amenable to flaking. The rock is, therefore, worked by the pecking technique as a primary stage of the manufacture of stone tools. The technique of grinding is normally applied for the preparation of the cutting edge. Other rarely used rocks for the manufacture of tools in the state are slate stone, shell and sandstone, which are worked by the flaking and grinding techniques. Some brightly coloured axes of jadeite have also been found in Nagaland suggesting the intrusion of foreign elements either from China or upper Burma, as jadeite is not locally available in Nagaland.

The Neolithic stone tool assemblage of Nagaland can be classified into two main types. The most common type is the quasi-shouldered Naga hill tanged axe—a variety of shouldered celt. The other common type is the triangular or pointed butt axe, very similar to the south Indian Neolithic axe.

Arunachal Pradesh, the north-easternmost hill-state of India occupying the eastern Himalayas parallel to Tibet and southern parts of China. The state is one of the least known regions of India with respect to prehistoric finds. Till recently, only a few stray finds of ground and polished stone tools were known from the Lohit, Siang and Kameng districts (Dani 1960: 46).[7] Arunachal neoliths are made of locally available rocks such as sandstone, schist and gneiss. Some tools made of jadeite, which is not a local resource have also been reported. Technologically, they are divisible into: (1) flaked and edge-ground tools, (2) pecked, edge-ground and fully ground tools. The common tools are shouldered celts, rounded butt axes, quadrangular axes and adzes.

A site at Parsi-Parlo situated on a terrace of the Kamla River in the lower Subansiri district was excavated by Abdulla Asraf Ali during 1981-2.[8] The cuttings reveal a stratigraphical sequence of three cultural periods within a depth varying between 50 to 100 cm above the gravel bed of the terrace. The bottom layers, layer 4 and layer 3, yielded cultural material of an aceramic

[7]M.C. Goswami et al. (1972), 'A Typological Study of Some Prehistoric Stone Tools from Kameng District, NEFA', *Journal of Assam Science Society*, 15, pp. 29-32.

[8]A.A. Ali (1991), *Prehistoric Arunachal*, Itanagar.

Neolithic phase, and layer 2 belongs to a ceramic Neolithic phase. The top layer yielded Neolithic tools with a few pieces of iron, which prompted the excavator to designate this cultural phase as Ferrolithic.[9] The association of iron with ground and polished stone tools suggests a continuation of the Neolithic way of life till a very late date in these isolated hilly terrains, and the introduction of iron into the Neolithic society without the intervention of copper and bronze.

The stone tools of the pre-pottery Neolithic phase consist of very crudely flaked palaeolith-like tools made of river pebbles, some of which are unifacially flaked like Hoabinhian tools, occurring in association with ground and polished tools. No pottery was encountered in this phase. This was succeeded by a ceramic Neolithic phase characterized by crudely flaked pebble tools, and ground and polished stone tools, occurring in association with a crude hand-made pottery showing square grid and honeycomb-type impressions. The shapes include bowls with a constricted neck and lipped pots with a globular body. This cultural phase was succeeded by the iron-using Neolithic, called the Ferrolithic phase by the excavator.

The stone tools found in the excavation are made of sandstone, quartzite, basalt, gneiss and jadeite. Except the last one, the others are locally available. Among the tool-types, crudely flaked pebble tools, which include choppers, large scrapers and a new type of tool familiar in Chinese archaeology as the 'waisted axe' showing a waist-like constriction in the middle of the tool (certainly a halting device not commonly found among the Palaeolithic and Neolithic assemblages of India) are very significant finds. Ground and polished Neolithic tool-types found in the excavation include triangular axes with pointed butt, rectangular types with broad butt, oval type of celts, crudely shouldered celts and elongated bar celts. Among these, the presence of unifacially flaked pebble choppers and scrapers clearly indicates the Southeast Asian pre-Neolithic Hoabinhian cultural influence on Arunachal Pradesh. Further, the find of waisted axes, jadeite tools and shouldered celts clearly points to the Eastern Asiatic origin of the Neolithic culture of Arunachal Pradesh.

Till recently, Tripura remained largely unknown with respect to its prehistoric cultures. Since 1980, some evidence of surface finds of ground and polished stone tools have begun to appear.[10] Excavated evidence is not yet available. Tools were picked up from the eroded surface of the terraces of the Khowai and Hoora rivers in the west Tripura district, within a radius of 50 km from Agartala, the state capital. Unlike other parts of north-east India, the Neolithic tools of Tripura are made of fossil wood, which is locally available as boulders and pebbles in the river bed. A detailed study of the

[9]Ibid.

[10]N.R. Romesh (1987), 'Evidence of Stone Age Culture in Pleistocene Sediments of Tripura', *Indian Journal of Earth Science*, 14, pp. 321-8.

Neolithic tool-types is not available. C-14 dates obtained from the tool and pottery-bearing layers of the terrace sediments give a sequence of the settled way of life in Tripura ranging from 1500 BC to AD 850.

From Manipur, surface finds of ground and smoothed stone tools, made of locally available rocks such as basalt, diorite, sandstone, shale, schist and quartzite, are known. The tools were made by applying the chipping, grinding and polishing techniques. The technique of sawing is known to have been applied in the manufacture of the quadrangular axes, showing square-cut shapes. Shouldered celts, quadrangular axes and adzes are the common types. A few triangular axes with pointed butt are also known.[11]

Mizoram is the least known state in north-east India with respect to Stone Age cultures. No archaeological activity has yet been reported from this state. So far, only one stray find of a stone axe is known. The axe, made of slate stone, is thin and broad with a fully ground smooth surface. Its unique feature consists of two bored holes at the butt end, evidently a hafting device of stone axes unknown in the Indian Neolithic context but common in China.

The characteristic ground and polished stone tools of the eastern Neolithic zone, consisting of a high frequency of shouldered celts occurring in all parts of the region, quadrangular axes and adzes found in association with cord-marked pottery, as well as the presence of a sufficient number of quadrangular axes of jadeite—a foreign rock type common in upper Burma and China, clearly suggest close affinities of the Neolithic culture of the eastern region with those of Southeast Asia and China. Further, the Neolithic culture of this region having contiguous land connection with China and Southeast Asia, which are known to have formed a common ecological zone with north-east India, where evolution of prehistoric cultures appears to have followed a pattern common to the whole region during the early Holocene period as once observed by E.C. Worman.[12] The discovery of Hoabinhian cultural remains in the Garo hills as well as in Arunachal Pradesh lends further support to Worman's hypothesis.

The problems of the origin, affinities and chronology of the eastern Neolithic cultures have, so far, remained at suggestive and speculative levels for want of confirmed radiometric dates. None of the excavated sites in Assam, Meghalaya and Arunachal Pradesh have been dated as a sufficient quantity of radiocarbon dating material was not available from them. The only C-14 date available from is Tripura (*c.* 1500 BC). The limited excavations conducted at Neolithic sites in Assam, Meghalaya and Arunachal Pradesh do not reveal a clear stratigraphical sequence of the Neolithic culture of this region. In the absence of scientific data, in order to provide firm dates of its origin and evolution through different phases of its development, as well as to reconstruct

[11] O.K. Singh and T.C. Sharma (1969), 'On the Discovery of Stone Age Relics from Manipura', *Journal of Assam Science Society*, 12, pp. 36-48.

[12] Worman (1949), op. cit., p. 198.

the economic pattern of the Neolithic societies of this region, the writers on the subject had to depend upon other available archaeological records, mainly the typological comparison of stone tools and the cross-cultural dating method.

The typological analysis of stone tools found in different parts of this region suggests (1) an early Neolithic phase characterized by wholly chipped and edge-ground implements, and (2) a late Neolithic phase characterized by pecked, ground and fully ground stone tools comprising shouldered celts, quadrangular axes and adzes occurring in association with cord-marked pottery. The early Neolithic phase appears to have occupied a cultural period between the pre-Neolithic Hoabinhian phase widespread in south-west China, Southeast Asia and Indonesia during which the settled way of life is known to have began in eastern Asia through early plant food exploitation.[13] The Daojali Hading assemblage of the late Neolithic phase shows a close affinity with that of south China and Southeast Asia. The presence of triangular axes with pointed butt, mainly in Nagaland, as well as of microliths with pottery at Selbalgiri in the Garo hills, occurring just below the Neolithic level suggests that the eastern Neolithic region served as a contact zone between the Neolithic traditions of north-east India and south-east regions.

[13] Chester Gorman (1971), 'The Hoabinhian and After: Subsistence Pattern in Southeast Asia during the Late Pleistocene and Early Holocene Periods', *World Archaeology*, 2, pp. 300-20.

PART TWO

EARLY, MATURE, AND LATER BRONZE AGE

Chapter 11

The First Urbanization: Bronze Age

B.B. Lal

INTRODUCTION

THRILL OF INITIAL DISCOVERY AND SAGA OF SUBSEQUENT ONES

If you pick up from the shelves of your nearest library the prestigious history book on ancient India, viz., *The Cambridge History of India*, vol. I, you will find in it a remark by Sir John Marshall, the then Director General of the Archaeological Survey of India, that India had nothing to offer by way of ancient remains prior to the cyclopean wall of Rajagriha, ascribable to *c.* sixth century BCE. The great irony of it all is that, while the book was being published (1922), one of Sir John's own officers in the Survey, Rai Bahadur Daya Ram Sahni, had in the previous year (1921), already unearthed at Harappa in the Montgomery (now called Sahiwal) district of Punjab archaeological remains which, in a single stroke, threw back the antiquity of civilization on the Indian subcontinent by nearly two thousand years. In the following year, 1922, Sahni's feat was repeated by another officer of the Survey, R.D. Banerji, at Mohenjo-daro in Sindh. These initial discoveries were followed by large-scale excavations at the latter site by many Indian officers of the Survey, under the overall direction of the Director General. Records, however, show a surprising fact that out of the nine seasons of sustained excavations at Mohenjo-daro, Sir John was at the site only during one season, and that too for a short period. There is hardly any record to indicate that he ever was at Harappa during the excavations. At the same time, credit must go to Sir John for organizing the work at Mohenjo-daro and publishing the monumental report, *Mohenjo-daro and the Indus Civilization* (1931). Subsequently, Mohenjo-daro was subjected to another spell of excavation by E.J.H. Mackay.[1] Harappa was excavated on a large-scale by M.S. Vats.[2]

With these excavations, it began to be universally recognized that India did have a civilization as old as those of Egypt and Mesopotamia. Nay, in

[1]E.J.H. Mackay (1938), *Further Excavations at Mohenjo-daro*, 2 vols., Government of India, Delhi.

[2]M.S. Vats (1940), *Excavations at Harappa*, 2 vols., Government of India, Delhi.

certain respects it even excelled them. For example, neither of the latter civilizations could boast of any kind of systematic town-planning, whereas the Indian civilization could. Here, the streets were oriented north-south and east-west, crossing each other at right angles. To cap it all, there were covered drains running underneath the streets with manholes at intervals for the discharge of sullage. The use of kiln-fired bricks was another innovation at the Indian sites—something unknown to their western counterparts. While the famous figure of the 'Priest King' from Mohenjo-daro and of the young naked male from Harappa, though small in size, are very good examples of art in stone, and the ravishing 'Dancing Girl' from the former site, of art in metal, nothing can beat the artistic grandeur and technical excellence of the carved steatite seals. Who would not be overwhelmed by the majesty of the zebu, with a vigourous body and face, pronounced hump, large incurved horns and swinging dewlap!

Once the remains of this great civilization were identified, it was but natural to look for more sites. In this context, N.G. Majumdar's explorations, including some excavations on a minor scale, in Sindh assumed great significance.[3] Amongst the more noteworthy sites investigated by him, particular mention may be made of Amri and Chanhu-daro, which were subsequently subjected to large-scale excavations, the former by J.M. Casal[4] and the latter by Mackay.[5] The brilliant career of Majumdar was cut short in 1938 when a gang of dacoits ran over his camp near Gaj Nai in Sindh, shooting him down and injuring some of his colleagues.

Another stalwart who needs to be mentioned in the context of these early discoveries is Aurel Stein. Not only did he do a great deal of valuable work in Chinese Turkestan and Iran, but his explorations in Swat, Waziristan, Gedrosia, Baluchistan and a part of the Ghaggar-Hakra Valley east of the Indus also yielded very fruitful results.[6]

In 1944 R.E. Mortimer Wheeler was appointed Director General of the Survey. One of the sites excavated by him was Harappa. Although an Indian officer posted at Harappa had already observed masses of mud bricks along the periphery of Mound AB at the site, it was left to Wheeler to dig this brickwork at a number of places and to identify it as a fortification-wall. The discovery was indeed epochal since, from 1921 to 1946, it was held that

[3]N.G. Majumdar (1934), *Explorations in Sind*, Mem. Arch. Surv. of India, no. 48. Government of India.

[4]J.M. Casal (1964), *Fouilles d'Amri,* 2 vols., Commission des Fouilles Archeologique, Paris.

[5]E.J.H. Mackay (1943), *Chanu-daro Excavations, 1935-36*, American Oriental Society, New Haven, Connecticut.

[6]A. Stein, (1929), *An Archaeological Tour in Waziristan and Northern Baluchistan,* Mem. Arch. Surv. of India, no. 37, Calcutta; idem (1931), *An Archaeological Tour in Gedrosia*, Mem. Arch. Surv. of India, no. 43, Calcutta.

Harappan settlements were unfortified. However, the great master erred on the historical conclusions that he drew from this great discovery. He stated that Indra, who is mentioned as *puramdara* (destroyer of forts) in the *Rigveda*, was responsible for the destruction of this fort. Extending his argument, he declared that it was the Aryans (whose cherished god India was) who invaded the Harappan settlements, as a result of which this civilization became 'extinct'. The fallacy of both these conclusions of Wheeler will be discussed later.

The midnight of 14-15 August 1947, was as dark for India as for Indian archaeology. A large chunk of the country was carved into Pakistan and with it went over the two famous sites of Mohenjo-daro and Harappa, along with a host of others. On the Indian side of the border, there hardly remained any site worth the name of this grand civilization. The leftovers included a tiny little site, Kotla Nihang, in Punjab and a slightly bigger one, Rangpur, in Gujarat, whose Harappan association, however, was doubtful.

Indian archaeologists bravely took up the challenge and, within a few decades, brought to light a large number of Harappan sites within the bounds of divided India. In fact, today, there are more sites associated with the various stages of the Harappan civilization in India than in Pakistan. Yet the number alone is not what matters, it is the new light that the Indian sites have thrown on the overall character of this civilization that is important. While we shall deal with this aspect in detail in subsequent pages, it may suffice to mention here that the Harappan site of Lothal in Gujarat has given to the world the earliest dockyard, dating back to *c*. 2300 BCE.[7] Dholavira, again in Gujarat, has thrown unique light on town-planning. It has three units, all individually fortified yet integrated into a single complex. Besides, it demonstrates how the Harappans dealt with the problem of water-supply. They harnessed the waters of seasonal streams and produced mighty reservoirs cut into the bed-rock.[8] The site of Kalibangan in Rajasthan has an Early Harappan occupation besides the Mature Harappan. Associated with the former, there was a ploughed agricultural field, which can easily claim the distinction of being the earliest (*c*. 2800 BCE) agricultural field ever discovered anywhere in the world through an archaeological excavation.[9] The Early Harappan occupation was destroyed

[7] S.R. Rao (1979), *Lothal: A Harappan Port Town (1955-62)*, vol. I, Archaeological Survey of India, Delhi; idem (1985), *Lothal: A Harappan Port Town (1955-62)*, vol. II, Archaeological Survey of India, Delhi.

[8] R.S. Bisht (1991), 'Dholavira: New Horizons of the Indus Civilization', *Puratattva*, 20, pp. 71-82; idem (1994), 'Dholavira', in J.P. Joshi and R.S. Bisht, *India and the Indus Civilization*, New Delhi, pp. 23-31.

[9] B.B. Lal (1970-71), 'Perhaps the Earliest Ploughed Field so far Excavated Anywhere in the World', *Puratattva*, 4, pp. 1-3; idem (1997), *The Earliest Civilization of South Asia*, Aryan Books International, New Delhi.

by an earthquake around 2700 BCE, which, incidentally, happens to be the earliest known earthquake in the archaeological records.[10]

While India evidently did the Herculean job of resurrecting the Harappan civilization on its side of the border, Pakistan did not lag behind. The work of its own archaeologists, supplemented, to a considerable extent, by that carried out by teams from England, France and USA, has revealed remarkable discoveries. While the details will come up at appropriate places later, one must point out here that the myth that the Harappan civilization owed its origin to civilizations in West Asia has completely been exploded by excavations at Mehrgarh and Nausharo in the piedmont area of Baluchistan, which have revealed a sequence of cultures beginning with an aceramic Neolithic in the seventh millennium BCE right up to the Harappan in the third.[11] Excavations at Amri and Kot Diji in Sindh[12] and at Gumla and Rehman Dheri in NWFP[13] have thrown valuable light on the Early Harappan stage. M. Rafique Mughal's explorations in Cholistan have given a picture of how this area, now a veritable desert, was variously occupied even from a stage prior to the Early Harappan.[14] The renewed and sustained excavations at Harappa have not only yielded a good deal of data about the transition from the Early Harappan to the Mature, on the one hand, and from the Mature to the Cemetery H on the other, but it has also brought to light what has been called the Ravi Phase, which antedated even the Early Harappan.[15]

From the above, it can be seen that sustained fieldwork on the Harappan civilization has added quite a lot to our knowledge since 1947, and one need not be surprised if this chapter would require a supplementary note within a decade or even earlier.[16]

[10]B.B. Lal (1984), 'The Earliest Datable Earthquake in India', *Science Age* (October 1984), Nehru Centre, Bombay, pp. 8-9; idem (1997), op. cit.

[11]Catherene and J.-F Jarrige (n.d.), *Mehrgarh: Field Reports 1974-1985, From Neolithic Times to the Indus Civilization*, Department of Culture and Tourism, Government of Sindh.

[12]Casal (1964), op. cit.; F.A. Khan (1965), 'Excavations at Kot Diji', *Pakistan Archaeology*, 2, pp. 11-85.

[13]A.H. Dani (1970-71), 'Excavations in the Gomal Valley', *Ancient Pakistan*, 5, pp. 1-177; F.A. Durrani et al. (1991), 'Further Excavations at Rehman Dheri', *Ancient Pakistan*, 7, pp. 61-146.

[14]M. Rafique Mughal (1992), 'The Consequences of River Changes for the Harappan Settlements in Cholistan', *The Eastern Anthropologist*, vol. 45, 1 & 2, pp. 105-16; idem (1997), *Ancient Cholistan*, Feroz Sons (Pvt.) Ltd., Rawalpindi.

[15]Richard H. Meadow, Jonathan Mark Kenoyer and Rita P. Wright (1991 ff.), Yearly Reports on Harappa Excavations, submitted to the Director General of Archaeology, Government of Pakistan and privately circulated.

[16]This paper was sent for publication more than a decade ago. Since then the site of Bhirrana in the Sarasvati Valley in Haryana has revealed a cultural stage which is earlier than even the Early Harappan. For it the C-14 dates are 4353 BCE, 4721 BCE and 6221 BCE.

Geographical Setting

At its maturity, the Harappan civilization covered an area approximately 1 million sq km, which is more than the area covered by the contemporary cultures of southern Mesopotamia, Sumer, Akkad, etc., put together. It is many times more than that of the Old Kingdom of Egypt, which was, at best, no more than 20,000 sq km. To give an idea of the spread of the Harappan civilization, it was a distance of 1,600 km from Sutkagendor on the western tip of Pakistani Baluchistan to Alamgirpur in the upper Ganga-Yamuna *doab* in the east, and 1,400 km from Manda in Jammu & Kashmir in the north to Daimabad in Maharashtra in the south (Fig. 11.1). The regions involved were not all plain, uniformly easy to travel across, but included the hilly terrains of Baluchistan and NWFP, the plains of the Indus and Sarasvati, the upper bits of the Ganga-Yamuna Valley and, southwards, the rocky terrain of Kachchha combined with the Gujarat plains. One wonders how exactly the Harappans of one region managed to communicate with their counterparts in a far-off one. Surely, bullock-carts were there and so were river boats, but it must have taken months to perform these arduous journeys. All this speaks volumes for the daring Harappans who not only maintained internal communication but also carried out trade with the distant lands of Central Asia in the north, and with Iran, Yemen, Bahrain and Iraq, over sea, in the west. Their capacity and determination to overcome all kinds of odds must be visualized and appreciated.

While discussing the geographical setting of the Harappan civilization, it must be kept in mind that the present-day political boundaries did not exist in the third millennium BCE. This fact is fully borne out by an independent source, literature. The *Rigveda*, which is the earliest known book of the Indian subcontinent and cannot be later than *c*. 2000 BCE, gives a very good insight into the geography of the times. Verses 5 and 6 of hymn 10.75, which is known as the *Nadi-stuti* (Prayer to the Rivers), refers to a continuous set of rivers from the Ganga in the east to the Indus along with its western tributaries on the west. It runs as follows:

Imam me Gange Yamune Sarasvati Sutudri stomam sachata Parusnya /
Asiknya Marudvridhe Vitastya Arjikiye srinudha Susomaya //5//

Tristamaya prathamam yatave sajuh Susartva Rasaya Svetya tya /
Tvam Sindho Kubhaya Gomatim Krumum Mehatnva saratham yabhiri yase //6//

O Ganga, Yamuna, Sarasvati, Sutudri (Sutlej) and Parusni (Ravi), O Marudvridha with Asikni (Chenab), O Arjikeya with Vitasta (Jhelum) and Susoma (Sohan), please listen to and accept this hymn of mine. //5//

O Sindhu (Indus), flowing you first meet the Tristama (and then) the Susartu, the Rasa, and the Sveta (Swat), and thereafter the Kubha (Kabul), the Gomati (Gomal), the Krumu (Kurram) with the Mehatnu; and (finally) you move on in the same chariot with them (i.e. carry their waters with you). //6//

There are two important points to be noted here. In the first place, these

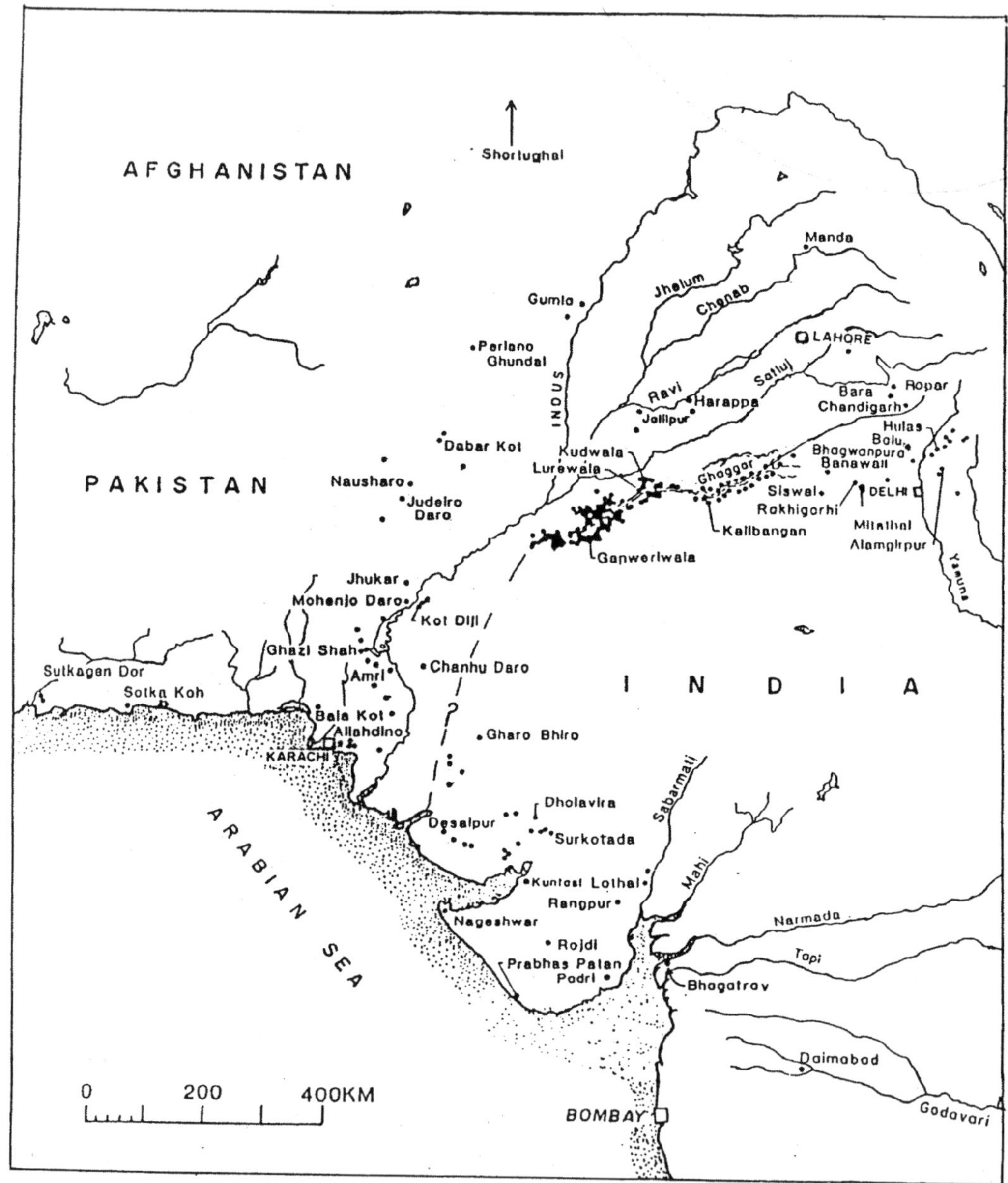

Fig. 11.1: Sites with mature and/or late Harappan remains

verses mention, besides the Indian rivers Ganga, Yamuna, Sarasvati, Sutlej, etc., the Indus, along with almost all its eastern tributaries which flow through present-day Pakistan, and its important western tributaries such as the Swat, Kabul, Gomal and Kurram, which originate in present-day Afghanistan. This would clearly imply that, according to the literary evidence, the territory with Afghanistan on the west and the Ganga-Yamuna *doab* on the east was regarded as one undifferentiated unit during the period prior to 2000 BCE.

The other point that surprisingly emerges from the above-mentioned Rigvedic geography is that the region traversed by the rivers mentioned in this text is almost identical with the extent of the Harappan civilization. The implications of this geographical overlap will be discussed in some detail at a later stage.

BIRTH AND ADOLESCENCE

For a very long time it had been held, evidently under the spell of the 'Diffusion Theory', that the Harappan civilization had its roots in the civilizations of ancient Iraq and Iran. Whenever these diffusionists were asked to cite concrete material evidence to substantiate their theory, they invariably fumbled, for there was nothing that they could produce. They then took shelter under the phrase 'ideas have wings' and suggested that even if the actual elements of the Harappan civilization had not been 'transplanted' from these western regions, at least the 'idea' of civilization must have come from there. However, intensive fieldwork for over half a century now in various regions of the Indo-Pak subcontinent have duly exploded the aforesaid theories and convincingly proved that the subcontinent itself was the motherland of the remarkable Harappan civilization (cf. Fig. 11.2).

Way back, Walter A. Fairservis had excavated Kile Ghul Mohammad and brought to light the evidence of a pre-pottery Neolithic culture in the lowest levels (Period I).[17] Though bereft of pottery, this period had elements of a settled village life. Houses were made of wattle-and-daub and their occupants had domesticated cattle, sheep and goat. Though no cereals were encountered (the finer technique of collecting cereals through 'floating' had not yet come into use), the presence of microliths, some of which may have been hafted as sickles for harvesting, would tend to suggest some kind of agricultural operation. As time passed, in Period II, a hand-made ware came to be used. It bore basket-impressions. A few specimens also bore simple painted designs. The pottery repertoire showed further changes in Period III. Now the wheel was used and the painted designs were more prolific: stars, triangles and loops in black pigment. There was also an important addition, viz., the use of metal. Rightly speaking, then, Kile Ghul Mohammad had entered the

[17]W.A. Fairservis (1956), *Excavations in the Quetta Valley, West Pakistan*, Anthropological Papers of American Museum on Natural History, vol. 45, pt. 2, pp. 169-402.

Fig. 11.2: Sites with pre-mature Harappan remains

'Chalcolithic Stage' of cultural evolution. The uppermost occupation (Period IV) was characterized by the use of a variety of colours in painting the pottery—red and white in addition to the usual black.

A more important point to note about the Kile Ghul Mohammad evidence is that as many as three radiocarbon dates, viz., 4352 BCE, 4346 BCE and 4210 BCE, were obtained for the uppermost levels of Period I.[18] With another 4 m of occupational strata that preceded these radiocarbon-dated levels, it is certain that the Neolithic settlement at Kile Ghul Mohammad must have begun in the sixth millennium BCE, if not even earlier. Yet, probably because of the long-held view, still persistent in the 1950s, that West Asia had the prerogative of starting the 'Neolithic revolution', the Kile Ghul Mohammad evidence was not taken due cognizance of.

[18] Gregory L. Possehl (1990), (ed.), *Radiocarbon Dates for South Asian Archaeology*, The University Museum, University of Pennsylvania, Philadelphia.

Some three decades later, the sustained work at Mehrgarh by J.F. Jarrige and his colleagues (final publication undated) duly confirmed that the beginnings of Neolithic settlements in the Indian subcontinent go back not just to the sixth but more likely to the seventh millennium BCE. At a distance of only 100 km from Kile Ghul Mohammad but in a different geophysical setting, Mehrgarh lies on the right bank of the Bolan River just where it enters the plains after leaving the hilly terrain where the former site is located. This change in topography, from the constricted hilly terrain to the plains, must have provided the Neolithic and subsequent Chalcolithic inhabitants of Mehrgarh a much-needed opportunity to expand.

The earliest settlement at Mehrgarh began along the Bolan River and, later, spread out well away from it. Thus, the ancient remains cover an overall area of about 1 km along the river and twice that at right angles to it. It must be made clear right away that not all this area was occupied simultaneously. There was a shift from area to area from time to time and, thus, the extent of the settlement at any given time was much smaller than the total area mentioned.

The excavators have divided the entire occupation at the site into six cultural periods, labelled I-VI from the bottom upwards. Period I, with a total deposit of about 10 m, is further divided into IA and IB. Both are ascribable to Neolithic times but there were two major differences. Thus, whereas IA was bereft of pottery, a hand-made coarse ware with basket-impressions made its appearance in IB. Again, while most of the faunal remains encountered in IA were those of wild animals such as wild cattle (*Bos namadicus*?), wild sheep (*Ovis orientalis*), gazelle (*Gazella dorcas*) and swamp deer (*Cervus duvauceli*), in IB, there was a profusion of domesticated ones amongst which cattle dominated over the sheep and goat. Here, it may be worth pointing out that, in contrast, in West Asia, the Neolithic people depended on the goat and sheep and not cattle. Another noteworthy feature of the fauna of the Mehrgarh Neolithic was the presence of the water buffalo (*Bos bubalis*); in south Asia, this would be the earliest evidence of its domestication.

In terms of agriculture, the Neolithic people of Mehrgarh produced two-row hulled barley (*Hordeum distichum*), six-row barley (*H. vulgare* and *H. vulgare* var. *nudum*) and at least three varieties of wheat, viz., bread wheat (*T. durum aestivum*), einkorn wheat (*T. monococcum*) and emmer wheat (*T. dicoccum*). Besides, there is evidence of fruits like dates and jujubes. It is likely that some of these cereals were stored for rainy days, as suggested by the presence of a few structure with small cells but without any doors. These and the living houses were made of mud bricks, some of which measured 28 × 14.5 × 7 cm—surprisingly yielding the typical Harappan ratio of 4:2:1.

Passing on to the other cultural constituents of the period, there were two kinds of lithic tools. The bigger ones comprised polished axes, adzes and chisels, which would appear to have been used for cutting down wood and shrubs to make the land cultivable. The smaller ones, consisting of retouched blades, scrapers, borers, lunates, triangles and trapezes, were variously used for harvesting, minor domestic jobs and hunting small game. There were bone tools, too, some of which, like awls, may have been used for stitching.

The burial practices of these Neolithic people offer some interesting insights into their belief in life after death, their technological excellence in certain crafts, their trade, as well as their social organization. The usual method was to place the body in a pit, either in an extended position or flexed, laid on the right side in the latter. Sometimes it was covered with red ochre and 'in one case the traces of a red-ochre-coloured textile were also visible on the bones'. Besides stone axes and microliths, grave-goods included stone vessels and baskets coated with bitumen. Ornaments recovered from the graves comprised necklaces of steatite micro-beads interspersed with those of turquoise and *lapis lazuli*, and some others made of seashells. What is at once striking is that none of these three materials, viz., turquoise, *lapis lazuli* and seashell, is locally available. The available sources in the case of turquoise were either some remote parts of Baluchistan or Iran/Central Asia. For *lapis lazuli*, these people must have looked to Afghanistan, while seashells must obviously have come from the Arabian coast south of Karachi. All this would imply long-distance trade, as well as an organizational set-up to execute the same. What is equally noteworthy is the occurrence of the bodies of the young ones of goats in two of the graves. This would suggest that the persons buried in these graves were richer and perhaps more important than the others—maybe the leaders of the community?

We may now have a look at the radiocarbon dates available for the Neolithic period of Mehrgarh. There are eight dates for Period IA and ten for IB. Unfortunately, these are not very consistent. Of the dates for IB, two are 31,680 + 3090, - 2265 and 11,790 +/ - 130, respectively—obviously too early to be accepted. Even in the case of the other dates, there is a great deal of overlap between those for Period IA and IB. Leaving aside these discrepancies, the earliest two dates for IA are 5980 BCE and 5749 BCE (Calib-2) and the latest are 4653/4648/4581 BCE and 4360 BCE. Likewise, the two earliest dates for IB are 4238 BCE and 5190/5058 BCE, and the latest, 4892/4887/4841 BCE and 4782 BCE. A time-range from *c*. 6000 BCE to *c*. 4500 BCE would be a good assessment for the Neolithic levels of Mehrgarh. One, however, does not know if there were any earlier deposits at the site which are not covered by these radiocarbon samples. If there were, it may well be that the settlement at Mehrgarh commenced some time in the seventh millennium BCE.

Without any break of occupation from the above is Period II with its subdivisions IIA, IIB and IIC. The hand-made, coarse and basket-impressed ware, met with for the first time in Period IB, increased in IIA and, by IIB, its clay was better levigated and the pots were well-fired. However, IIC was marked by the appearance of wheel-made, painted pottery. While the surface of the pots varied from buff to reddish, the designs were usually painted in black and included simple bands along the rim with curvilinear lines flowing downwards, and rows of dots and criss-cross squares on the body. Prominent shapes were globular vases with collared rims and bowls with tapering profiles. It may be added that this wheel-thrown, painted pottery is reminiscent of that from Kile Ghul Mohammad Period II and the earliest levels of Mundigak, a site in Afghanistan. This evidence is clearly indicative of the contacts which Mehrgarh had with the hilly areas further to the north-west. The discovery of a new variety of barley (*Hordeum sphaerococcum*), is of special interest since it requires irrigation and, thus, shows advanced farming. Equally noteworthy is the find of two 'sickles', made by setting three bladelets in wooden handles with bitumen. These specimens were recovered from within a compartmented structure which may well have been a granary, as indicated by the impressions of wheat and barley in it. While many other antiquities were recovered from Period II, particular mention may be made of a grooved elephant tusk, marking the earliest evidence of ivory-working. A ring and a bead of copper, while attesting to the use of metal, also indicated that it had yet to come in a big way. As in the case of Period I, the radiocarbon dates for Period II are also erratic. However, a time-range from *c.* 4500 BCE to 4000 BCE would be a reasonable assessment.

Besides the fact that the size of the settlement grew considerably in Period III, there was an overall development in various ways. In terms of agriculture, we come across a new variety of wheat (*Triticum sphaerococcum*). Also to be noted is the first occurrence of oats (*Avena* sp.). Amongst the structures, two call for special attention. Built more or less on a similar plan, each had a long north-south corridor on two sides of which were cells. In all probability, these may have been granaries. Due to their large size compared to earlier ones, it is most likely that these were controlled not by an individual houseowner but either the community as a whole or by the chief of the settlement. If that be so, these granaries may be regarded as the forerunners of the ones encountered at Harappa and Mohenjo-daro in the Mature Harappan levels.

There are some technological aspects of Period III which deserve to be mentioned. For example, the discovery of many fragments of crucibles with traces of melted copper clearly point to a spurt in metallurgy. Bun-shaped ingots of copper which anticipate those found in the Mature Harappan levels at Lothal and Mohenjo-daro were also found. Bead-making as a specialized craft is suggested by the occurrence of a large number of drill-bits, along with beads. The drills had a hollow at the end indicating that these were manipulated with a kind of bow. What is more interesting is that similar drill-bits have been found in pre-Harappan levels at Amri as well as in the Mature Harappan ones at Chanhu-daro, indicating the continuity of a technological tradition.

There was also a great spurt in painted designs on pottery. Besides the simple motifs noticed in Period II, there were faunal designs depicting cranes in a row and gazelles. Pottery painted with similar motifs has been found not only in nearby sites in Baluchistan (Togau A) but also in Afghanistan (Mundigak I, 3), and even as far away as Iran (Sialk III, Hissar IB and C) and Central Asia (Namazga II). All this shows much greater interaction between all these areas during the time represented by Period III of Mehrgarh, viz., the first half of the fourth millennium BCE.

Period IV is to be noted for the emergence of polychrome pottery. White and red colours were used in addition to the usual black. Amongst the antiquities, special mention may be made of terracotta female figurines with somewhat cylindrical heads, pinched noses and pendulous breasts, seated with outstretched legs. Stamp seals in bone as well as terracotta constitute another important category. In all likelihood, these may have been used for commercial transactions. While the radiocarbon dates for this period are somewhat erratic, in the general context of the other periods, Period IV may be placed between 3500 BCE and 3000 BCE.

Period V, of short duration, is to be noted for a decrease in polychrome pottery but the appearance of a grey (sometimes reddish) ware bearing floral and faunal motifs, such as the pipal leaf and fish. However, in Period VI, assignable to the first quarter of the third millennium BCE, there was, once again, an explosion in the variety of pottery, perhaps because of an increase in interaction with Afghanistan and Iran on the west and the Indus plains on the east. To be noted are the black-on-buff Quetta ware, sherds of the polychrome Nal ware, and painted designs like the humped bull with long horns and large dot-centred eyes in the typical Kulli style. Amongst the antiquities recovered from this period, attention may be drawn to compartmented seals in terracotta and stone, and a double-spiral-headed copper pin, all of which again attest to wide contacts. Period VII, with its subdivisions A, B and C, is to be noted particularly for a great proliferation in terracotta figurines, many of which with their pinched up nose and google-shaped eyes, are assignable to what is known as the Zhob style.

From this somewhat detailed treatment of Mehrgarh, it would appear that undue space has been given to this site in a chapter essentially meant to be devoted to the Harappan civilization. While this may be true, it needs to stated in defence that this is one site where a continual picture is available right from the aceramic Neolithic stage to the ceramic Neolithic and onwards to when metal begins to play an important role, small villages develop into towns and there is a cultural spread, more or less on a similar pattern of living (though not without regional variations in certain specific traits), in far-off areas from Afghanistan on west to well into the Indus Valley. This is, however, not to say that other sites do not deserve mention in this context. Thus, in the hilly tracts of Baluchistan, mention may be made of Rana Ghundai, which again shows a sequence from the Neolithic stage onwards. Then there are sites representing the Zhob and Kulli cultures. The latter, though contemporary with the Mature Harappan civilization, had its own distinctive features, especially the pottery style. There are also sites with a very distinctive pottery called the Nal ware: fine fabric, wheel-turned, well-fired, and with a variety of designs painted in black, blue, yellow and green.

Up in the north, two sites call for special attention: Gumla and Rehman Dheri, both within a radius of 25 km from Dera Ismail Khan in the North-West Frontier Province (NWFP). The former, excavated by A.H. Dani, has shown six periods of occupation, of which the first four are of immediate interest.[19] The earliest, Period I, was characterized by a Neolithic assemblage without pottery. Period II marked the arrival of newcomers who brought along with them the characteristic Chalcolithic tradition of painted pottery and metal (copper). A sterile layer between this and the succeeding Period III marks an interval, the duration of which can only be guessed. Interesting, however, was the presence in it of structures of mud bricks whose internal ratio was 4:2:1—so typical of the Mature Harappan times. Some of the pottery shapes and painted designs are similar to those from the Early Harappan levels of Kot Diji, a site which we shall deal with shortly. A layer of ash, charcoal and pottery overlay Period III, separating it from the succeeding deposits of Period IV. Besides retaining some material from the preceding period, Period IV yielded cubical weights, etched carnelian beads, perforated vessels and triangular terracotta cakes, clearly indicating the presence of the Mature Harappan civilization.

At Rehman Dheri, within a vertical deposit of about 6 m, the excavator, F.A. Durrani, has identified three occupational periods, numbered I-III from the bottom upwards.[20] Amongst the painted designs on the pottery of Period I, particular interest attaches to that of a 'horned deity', a motif occurring not only at the neighbouring site of Gumla but also having a much wider distribution—in the Early Harappan levels at Kot Diji in Sindh and in the Neolithic levels at Burzahom in Kashmir. Also noteworthy from these levels was an ivory 'seal' on one side of which are engraved two mountain goats, along with three symbols resembling, respectively, an arrow and two letters resembling Roman alphabet, I and T. The other side bears two scorpions, a frog and, again, a T-like symbol. The four radiocarbon dates available for this period place it around 3,000 BCE. Thus, if this object was really used as a seal, it throws valuable light on the organization of trade even during the pre-Mature Harappan times. In this context, one might recall the evidence of Mehrgarh Period IV and also that from Kunal, a site yet to be discussed.

Period II of Rehman Dheri yielded typical Kot Dijian pottery characterized by certain shapes and the use of two colours, usually black for the outline

[19]Dani (1970-71), op. cit.

[20]Durrani et al. (1991), op. cit.

and white for the filling in. The painted designs include motifs such as the peacock, pipal leaf and intersecting circles, which become characteristic of the Mature Harappan times. There was local manufacture of beads, as indicated by the presence of raw material and waste flakes. The former included *lapis lazuli* and turquoise both of which were brought from regions far away. Period III showed more elements of the Harappan times.

The foregoing discussion of the data from the mountain-grit and submontane sites of the Indo-Pakistan subcontinent brings out two important points. In the first place, there is little doubt that this area was occupied right from the Neolithic times dating back to the seventh millennium BCE, if not earlier, and that this Neolithic culture had its own entity inasmuch as in terms of agriculture barley dominated over wheat and amongst domesticated animals the cattle outnumbered sheep and goat. It may be recalled that in the Neolithic of West Asia, the position was the other way round. It is, therefore, clear that the Indian subcontinent was under no debt to West Asia as far as the beginning of settled village life is concerned. The old concept regarding this must be buried.

The second point relates to the identification of the region where the Harappan civilization actually grew. While we have noticed that Harappan elements did show up in the above-mentioned hilly and piedmont regions, there are no fully developed Mature Harappan settlements like Mohenjo-daro or Harappa. (A suspected site, Dabar Kot, has yet to be excavated to ascertain its actual status.) The Mature Harappan civilization, characterized by large metropolitan towns and a highly organized trade network, could have developed only in the vast plains on the east, namely those of the Indus and Sarasvati rivers, which provided the necessary geomorphological environment for unlimited agriculture to sustain the ever-increasing population and vast stretches of land for the laying out of large cities, along with satellite towns and villages.

We would have liked to begin this part of the story with the key site of Mohenjo-daro itself. Unfortunately, however, its lowest levels have so far defied excavation owing to subsoil water and, thus, we do not know what underlies the Mature Harappan remains. Hence, we go about 130 km south of it to Amri, excavated by J.M. Casal where we do have a continuous story, both before and after the Mature Harappan.[21] In all, five occupational periods have been identified, numbered, as follows, from the bottom upwards: IA-D, Amri Culture; IIA-B, Intermediate; IIIA, Mature Harappan; IIIB, transition; IIIC, Mohenjo-daro upper levels; IIID, Jhukar; IV, Jhangar; and VA and VB, medieval. The pottery of the Amri culture is greatly influenced by that from the Baluchi hills, in particular by the Togau ware, indicating the direction from which the earliest Amrians had come. That these people had entered the Chalcolithic stage is indicated by the presence of copper, though in a

[21] Casal (1964), op. cit.

somewhat limited amount. Radiocarbon dates indicate that this movement from the Baluchi hills to the Indus plains may have taken place some time in the first half of the fourth millennium BCE. Sub-period ID is significant because there occurred in it some pottery of the Kot Dijian type (to be described later) wherein some shapes and painted designs duly anticipate the Mature Harappan ones. These increase in Periods IIA-B while, by Period IIIA, the Mature Harappan is fully manifest. It also needs to be mentioned that right from Period IA, the pottery bore graffiti some of which are reminiscent of the Harappan signs.

Moving northwards, we have the site of Kot Diji opposite Mohenjo-daro on the eastern side of the Indus but, at present, a little away from it. It was excavated by F.A. Khan who found below a 4.5 m thick Mature Harappan occupation another 5 m deposit yielding a characteristic cultural complex, which has been named Kot Dijian after the site itself.[22] In between, there was a 45 cm thick layer which contained, besides mixed Kot Dijian and Harappan material, burnt earth, charcoal and ash. Made of mud/mud bricks, Kot Dijian houses were provided with a stone foundation and, although not much of the house plans were exposed, it is evident that these were oriented along the cardinal directions. However, no less important is the fact that the settlement was provided with a peripheral wall, although this was not exposed to any great length. As in the case of the house walls, the peripheral wall, too, had a stone foundation and superstructure of mud bricks. At places, it was extant to a height of 4.5 m. A further interesting fact is that the mud bricks had a length, breadth and thickness ratio of 4:2:1, so typical of the subsequent Mature Harappan times.

Kot Dijian pottery was essentially thin, reddish and usually painted in two colours, black and white. While simple bands along the rim were more common, the designs included a series of loops and an intersecting-circles-like pattern which may have given rise, respectively, to the Mature Harappan fish-scale and intersecting circles. While globular vases with short everted rims represent the distinctive Kot Dijian type, the pottery also included vessels with a flange below the neck and dishes-on-stand, which continued, with minor variations, in the subsequent Mature Harappan times. Other finds from the Kot Dijian levels included stone mullers and pestles, long notched/serrated blades of chert, leaf-shaped arrowheads and a bronze bangle. Last, but not the least, mention must be made of 'terracotta cakes', which constitute a characteristic feature of Mature Harappan times. Available radiocarbon dates would place the beginning of the Kot Dijian settlement around 3,000 BCE.

Proceeding further north, into the valley of the southernmost tributary of the Indus, we are at the key site of Harappa which has been yielding new surprises from time to time. Thus, when Vats[23] excavated it, the Mature

[22] Khan (1965), op. cit.
[23] Vats (1940), op. cit.

Harappan was the earliest level. Wheeler's[24] excavation in 1946 gave an indication that the site might have had an earlier beginning. Later on, when an American team under Dales,[25] Meadow[26] and Kenoyer[27] started further work, the earlier occupations began to unfold themselves (cf. Kenoyer 1998 and yearly reports by the team). Thus, not only has a Kot Diji-related Early Harappan settlement come to light but also an earlier occupation (Period I), termed by the excavators as the Ravi phase, dating back to *c*. 3300 BCE. The characteristic pottery of this period was a red ware, usually hand-made, painted in black pigment (sometimes with an additional white) with designs which included, besides linear and curvilinear motifs, faunal ones such as the crane. The vases had a slanting profile with a distinct carination at the junction of the upper part and the base. Some of the pots bore pre-firing or post-firing marks. While the former were most likely the potter's marks, one does have to think about the significance of the latter. Although no structures were seen, one has to leave the question open since the area excavated was very limited.

The above-mentioned Ravi phase, encountered in the northern part of Mound AB, was overlain by the remains of the Kot Diji period (Period II, 2800-2600 BCE). However, a more detailed picture of the latter was obtained in Mound E which lay south of AB. The structures of this period, oriented along the cardinal directions, were made of mud bricks with the length, breadth and thickness ratio of 4:2:1. It may be noted that the orientation of the walls as well as the proportion of the bricks are both typical of the subsequent Mature Harappan times. A little later, in what may be termed the 'Transitional Stage' between the Kot Diji and the Mature Harappan, a peripheral wall came up, identified in the north-western part of the mound. With a height of a little over 2 m and measuring about 2 m at the base, it has been traced up to a length of 15 m. It may be added that the general plan of this peripheral wall, as also of a street ascribable to the Transitional Stage, was followed during the Mature Harappan times (Period III). During this Transitional Stage, there also occurred 'terracotta cakes' as well as certain pottery forms with painted designs, both of which are, again, typical of the Mature Harappan period. Thus, there remains little doubt that the Mature Harappan civilization was a natural outcome of the earlier stages. We shall discuss this aspect at full length later.

We may now pass on to the valley of the ancient Sarasvati, which, in the Cholistan region of Pakistan, is now known as the Hakra. Here, M.R. Mughal

[24]R.E.M. Wheeler (1947), 'Harappa 1946: The Defences and Cemetery R-37', *Ancient India*, 3, pp. 58-130.

[25]G.F. Dales (1964), 'The Mythical Massacre at Mohenjo-darao', *Expedition*, 6, 3, pp. 36-43.

[26]Meadow et al. (1991 ff.), op. cit.

[27] Jonathan Mark Kenoyer (1998), *Ancient Cities of the Indus Civilization*, Oxford University Press and American Institute of Pakistan Studies, Karachi.

has explored as many as 377 ancient sites whose cultural association from the earliest is as follows: Hakra ware period, 99; Early Harappan, 40; Mature Harappan, 174; Late Harappan, 50; and Painted Grey Ware culture, 14.[28]

As no excavations have been carried out, there are no radiocarbon dates. However, it is estimated that Hakra ware may go back to the middle of the fourth millennium BCE. Under this generic name, there are a few distinctive varieties. Thus, there are pots whose exterior is coated with mud intermixed with tiny bits of pottery. Many bear sets of incised horizontal/oblique/ curvilinear lines. There is yet another category in which the pots have fine fabric, red/chocolate slip and are painted with broad black bands along the neck and/or shoulder. Other cultural components of the Hakra ware period include stone grinders, parallel-sided blades, scrapers, leaf-shaped arrowheads and, sometimes, bits of copper, too. Most of the Hakra sites seem to have been shifting camps though a few may have been regular ones.

Characterized by the Kot Dijian culture complex (described earlier), most of the Early Harappan sites in Cholistan were regular settlements as against the shifting Hakra ware camps. However, it is noteworthy that while nearly half of these sites were less than 5 ha in area, and one-fourth between 5 and 10 ha, some were large than those standards. For example, Jalawali and Gamanwala measured, respectively, 22.5 and 27.3 ha. This would indicate that by he Early Harappan times, there began to appear some large settlements amidst smaller ones—towns amidst villages. A kind of socio-political differentiation had begun to emerge.

Not only did the number of settlements increase by the Mature Harappan times but so did their size. Thus, for example, Ganweriwala covered as much as 81.5 ha—a size almost similar to that of Mohenjo-daro. During Late Harappan times, the curve took a downward turn, both in number and size, a fact that may be explained, amongst other factors, by the drying up of the Sarasvati.

Moving north-east along the Sarasvati Valley into the Indian side of the Indo-Pak border (which, of course, had no relevance in the fourth-third millennia BCE), we come to a large number of sites associated with the various stages of the Harappan civilization—Early, Mature and Late. Here, we shall take up only four, viz., Kunal, Rakhigarhi, Kalibangan and Banawali.

While the other sites mentioned above have a lot of subsequent occupation of the Mature Harappan times, making it somewhat difficult to make a thorough probe into the preceding Early Harappan levels, Kunal suffers from no such handicap. Located in district Hissar, Haryana, it has a 3-m thick deposit, which the excavators, J.S. Khatri and M. Acharya, have divided into three sub-periods, Ia, Ib and Ic.[29] Sub-period Ia is characterized by dwelling

[28] Mughal (1997), op. cit.

[29] J.S. Khatri and M. Acharya (1995), 'Kunal: A New Indus-Saraswati Site', *Puratattva*, 25, pp. 84-6.

pits which an average diameter of 2 m and a depth of 1 m. These were provided with thatched roofing, as indicated by a series of post-holes along their circumference. Pit-dwelling is an early feature (for example, of the Neolithic culture of Kashmir) and, thus, it is not unlikely that one day we may be able to locate the ancestors of these early Kunalians somewhere in the neighbourhood. The pits provided a welcome shelter from the northerly cold winds during winters and perhaps it was for this reason that such dwellings continued to be in vogue for some time even though these people had entered an advanced cultural stage, viz., Chalcolithic, wherein metal came to be used alongside stone and bone tools. Fish-hooks and arrowheads of metal (copper), have been found, signifying their use for fishing and hunting. The pottery, a red ware, was characterized by painted designs in black and white pigments—a feature, as already mentioned, that was shared by a large number of Early Harappan sites in Pakistan. Also to be noted were sherds of certain types in the Hakra ware, referred to earlier. The radiocarbon dates go back to 3016 BCE, although there is reported to be some deposit prior to the one which has yielded this date. Thus, the beginning of occupation at Kunal may well go back to about the middle of the fourth millennium BCE.

As time passed, in Ib, not only did the size of the pits increase but these were also lined with mud bricks. While the Hakra ware decreased, the bichrome one increased. It may be added that herein occurred painted designs such as the peacock and pipal leaf which became the hallmark of the Mature Harappan. Also to be noted was the presence of terracotta 'cakes'.

In sub-period Ic, pits were replaced by square or rectangular houses, the size of the bricks being in the typical Mature Harappan ratio of 4:2:1. Circular silos, used for storage point towards an increased grain production. That the Kunalians were growing more and more affluent is demonstrated by the discovery of a large number of beads of silver, gold and *lapis lazuli*, and of silver ornaments including two tiaras. The occurrence of a crucible with molten metal still sticking to it points to the local manufacture of copper objects, which included inverted V-shaped arrowheads, spearheads, coiled cones and coiled finger-rings, most of which call to mind their Mature Harappan counterparts. Likewise, discular beads of silver with a perforation along the diameter are exactly similar to gold ones from Lothal. Besides agricultural production, trade also seems to have boosted the economy of the Kunalians. Thus, while copper may have been obtained from the Khetri mines in Rajasthan, *lapis lazuli* could only have come from either Baluchistan or Afghanistan. That these people were engaged in trade is also suggested by the discovery of seven seals, six of steatite and one of shell. Like their Mature Harappan counterparts, these are square in shape and also have a perforated knob at the back. A major difference between the two, however, is that whereas the Mature Harappan examples bear animal and other motifs as well as inscriptions, the Kunal ones only have geometric designs. As far as the evidence of writing is concerned, while Kunal has yielded potsherds with post-firing graffiti marks, some of which are morphologically similar to the Mature Harappan signs, it remains uncertain whether the former had any phonetic value. However, the Kunal evidence does show that the way for the Mature Harappan was being paved slowly but certainly.

Located on the right bank of the Drishadvati, a tributary of the Sarasvati, Rakhigarhi has several mounds, named RGR-1 to RGR-7. Of these, RGR-6 was occupied only during Early Harappan times but the deposit is pretty thick, viz., 4.5 m. Within the top 2.5 m, the excavator, Amarendra Nath, encountered as many as four structural sub-periods.[30] The houses, made of mud bricks, were oriented along the cardinal directions with lanes in between. Although not completely exposed, one of the houses gives an idea of their planning. There was a courtyard around which the rooms were located—a pattern followed even by the Mature Harappans. The bricks, however, were made in the ratio of 3:2:1, as at Kalibangan, and not in the typical Mature Harappan ratio of 4:2:1. It appears that in the Early Harappan stage in the Sarasvati basin, bricks were manufactured in both these ratios (see Kunal, above) but the former was given up in Mature times.

Due to the structures in the upper levels, very little area was left for excavation in the lower ones. Hence, the nature of the earlier dwellings could not be made out but ash-cum-charcoal layers and made-up floors did testify to their existence. Unfortunately, we do not yet have any radiocarbon dates for the Early Harappan at Rakhigarhi, although some charcoal samples are stated to have been collected. One would like to know where exactly this site stands with reference to Kunal.

We may now turn our attention to Kalibangan in the Hanumangarh district of Rajasthan, excavated jointly by B.B. Lal, B.K. Thapar and J.P. Joshi.[31] As the radiocarbon dates reveal, the beginning of the Early Harappan settlement at Kalibangan, around 3000 BCE, was later than that at Kunal. This may perhaps explain some vital differences between the settlements at these two sites. Thus, for example, there were no pit-dwellings at Kalibangan. Right from the beginning, there were regular houses oriented along the cardinal directions. Of these, as many as five structural sub-periods were noted. The houses were laid out on the usual pattern with a central courtyard and living rooms around it. Although the houses were made of mud bricks (in the ratio of 3:2:1), the Kalibanganites had started the manufacture of kiln-fired bricks, as revealed by their use in drains. An interesting feature noted in the houses was the presence of *tandoors* (cooking ovens)—something we find even now in this part of Rajasthan, and also in neighbouring Punjab and Haryana.

[30]Amarendra Nath (1997-8), 'A Harappan Metropolis in the Sarasvati-Drishadvati Divide', *Puratattva*, 28, pp. 39-45; idem (1998-9), 'Further Excavations at Rakhigarhi', *Puratattva*, 29, pp. 46-9.

[31]B.B. Lal, B.K. Thapar and J.P. Joshi (in press), *Excavations at Kalibangan*, vol. I: *Early Harappan*, Archaeological Survey of India, New Delhi.

However, more noteworthy was the fact that the entire settlement was enclosed by a peripheral wall. Covering an area of about 240-50 m north-south and 170-80 m east-west, it had two structural phases. To begin with, it had a width of 1.9 m which was enlarged to 3-4 m. at least one gate, opening on the river-front, was duly identified, though there might have been more.

Associated with the Early Harappan period at Kalibangan was an agricultural field—the earliest one ever to have been discovered in an archaeological excavation. This had a very specific pattern of furrows.[32] There were two sets, running, respectively, north-south and east-west and, thus, cutting each other at right angles. The intermediary space in between the north-south furrows was 1.9 m, whereas that in between the east-west ones was only 30 cm. It is of great interest to note that this pattern of ploughing the fields obtains even today not only in Rajasthan but also in neighbouring Haryana, Punjab and even western Uttar Pradesh. In the widely-distanced furrows, farmers grow mustard, while, in the narrowly-spaced ones it is gram. The reason for this kind of planting is not far to seek. Both these plants are raised during the winter when the sun goes down to the southern hemisphere and casts longer northward shadows than it does in the summer. Thus, if the tall mustard plants were to be grown in the east-west furrows and the gram in the north-south ones, the shadows of the former would completely cover the latter, heavily affecting on their growth. As we have evidence of both mustard and gram during Harappan times, it is most likely that this very pattern of planting was followed even then. And, if that were so, should we not take our hats off to the Early Harappans for having devised this specific pattern of ploughing the fields?

Early Harappan pottery from Kalibangan also calls for attention. Six categories (A-C) have been identified on the basis of fabric but here we shall deal with only the three more noteworthy ones. In one category (A), which accounted for the bulk, pots were painted in two colours, usually with a black outline and white filling—a feature noted at most of the Early Harappan sites, right from Rehman Dheri in the north-west to Kunal in the east and south-west to at least Kot Diji. In another category (B) were jars whose exterior was coated with clay intermixed with sand-granules so as to obtain a rough surface—a treatment more or less in line with some of the pottery in the Hakra region, where, however, tiny bits of pottery were mixed with clay instead of sand. Under yet another category (C) were pots of finely levigated clay, well-fired and often provided with a plum to red slip. In this case, the painted designs were mostly, if not solely, in black. Many of these anticipated the Mature Harappan ones, as did some of the shapes.

The story of how the Early Harappan settlement at Kalibangan came to an end is no less exciting. Even within the limited area of these early levels that was exposed, there were shattered occupational strata and sheared walls.

[32]Lal (1970-1), op. cit.

Evidently, this could have happened only if there was a major shaking of the ground beneath—in other words, an earthquake. Perhaps the intensity was not very high and the incident took place at a time when the people were, by and large, out—for no buried skeletons were met with but the shock was enough to make them desert the settlement. The site was re-occupied only after a break of a century or so. It may, incidentally, be added that this is the earliest evidence of an earthquake recorded in an archaeological excavation.[33]

Banawali, in district Hissar, Haryana, is yet another site in the Sarasvati Valley which calls for attention. The excavator, R.S. Bisht, has identified three occupational periods, viz., I, Early Harappan; II, Mature Harappan and III, Post-Mature Harappan.[34] Period I has further been divided into three sub-periods: IA, IB and IC. The houses were oriented along the cardinal directions but a noteworthy point is that while at Kalibangan only mud bricks were used, at Banawali, kiln-fired bricks were also used. The internal ratio of the bricks in both cases was, however, the same, viz., 3:2:1. In sub-period IB, there was a peripheral wall and sub-period IC was marked by yet another important feature:

> drastic and diagnostic changes in architecture, planning and antiquities in an otherwise continuing cultural *milieu* of the preceding sub-period. The entire settlement was planned and constructed *de novo*. The dichotomous layout which the Harappans adopted was introduced during this sub-period. The fortification of the previous [sub-] period was externally chiselled or partially sliced away and doubled in width for housing the citadel, and the lower town was laid out contiguously towards the east as well as the north, while the position in the west remained unresolved.[35]

The pottery of Period I as a whole was similar to that from Early Harappan levels at various other sites in the Sarasvati Valley. But, in IC, there also occurred a ware with a deep red slip, some of the shapes and painted designs being typically Mature Harappan. Also to be noted were terracotta cakes and bricks in the ratio of 4:2:1. Amongst the other small finds of the period, particular mention may be made of a stone weight, 87.855 grams.

In the Indus and Sarasvati valleys, the cultural milieu that preceded the Mature Harappan civilization was, by and large, similar in nature. In Gujarat, it was rather different. Thus, for example, at Somnath/Prabhas Patan in district Junagarh (excavated by several archaeologists between 1955 and 1976)[36] has been identified a 'Pre-Prabhas Culture' which is characterized by pottery quite different from that found at sites like Kot Diji/Kalibangan/Kunal in the

[33]Lal (1984), op. cit.

[34]R.S. Bisht (1987), 'Further Excavation at Banawali: 1983-84', in B.M. Pande and B.D. Chattopadhyaya (eds.), *Archaeology and History: Essays in Memory of Shri A. Ghosh*, vol. I, Agam Kala Prakashan, Delhi, pp. 135-56.

[35]R.S. Bisht, in *Indian Archaeology: A Review*, p. 33.

[36]M.K. Dhavalikar (1997), *Indian Protohistory*, Books and Books, New Delhi, pp. 97 ff.

northern region. Yet, as radiocarbon dates indicate, it goes back to the first quarter of the third millennium BCE, i.e. well before the emergence of the Mature Harappan civilization. Again, at Padri in the Bhavnagar district,[37] the earliest strata may go back to well before 3000 BCE on the basis of radiocarbon data. Likewise, Nagwada in district Surendranagar had a pre-Mature Harappan beginning and so is the case with Rojdi, where work has been done jointly by G.L. Possehl and M.H. Rawal.[38] At Lothal, the well-known Mature Harappan site, S.R. Rao came across sherds of micaceous red and black-and-red ware in the earliest levels.[39] Likewise, Dholavira in Kachchh, excavated by R.S. Bisht, has yielded a good bit of non-Mature Harappan material in the basal levels.[40] Thus, the overall picture in the southerly domain seems to be that while there did exist a pre-Mature Harappan cultural substratum, it was different from that of the Indus-Sarasvati valleys.

We may now take an overall view of the foregoing data and try to answer two very vital questions about the Mature Harappan civilization: how and when did it emerge? In order to answer the first, we ought to spell out the characteristic features of the civilization and then look for its roots. These are:

(i) orientation of the houses and streets along the cardinal directions;
(ii) use of mud or kiln-fired bricks which had a length, breadth and thickness ratio of 4:2:1;
(iii) division of the urban settlements into at least two (if not more) major components, viz., a 'Citadel' and a 'Lower Towns;
(iv) the laying out of a peripheral/fortification wall around these separate units;
(v) a well laid-out drainage system at most of the urban centres;
(vi) monumental buildings like granary, bath, assembly hall, etc.;
(vii) a red ware which had certain specific shapes like dishes- and cups-on-stand, perforated cylindrical vases, ring-stands, S-shaped jars, Hanged jars, and flat-bottomed and flanged 'bread-containers';
(viii) most of these were painted in black with distinctive motifs such as the peacock, pipal and banana leaves, intersecting circles, fish-scales, and chessboard-like black-and-blank squares;
(ix) terracotta 'cakes';
(x) etched carnelian beads, faience bangles, bun-shaped ingots, specialized drill-bits;
(xi) monumental script;

[37] V.S. Shinde (1992), 'Padri and the Indus Civilization', *South Asian Studies*, 8, pp. 55-6.

[38] Gregory L. Possehl and M.H. Rawal (1989), *Harrappan Civilization and Rojdi*, Oxford and IBH, New Delhi.

[39] Rao (1979), op. cit.; idem (1985), op. cit.

[40] Bisht (1991), op. cit.; idem (1994), op. cit.

(xii) seals and sealings;
(xiii) cubical weights;
(xiv) measuring scales;
(xv) statuary in stone and metal; and
(xvi) long-distance overland and sea trade.

We may now re-examine the data from the various sites discussed so far and find out which of these features of the Mature Harappan civilization were already in existence and which emerged along with it. To begin with, town planning and the orientation of the houses and streets along the cardinal directions was already in evidence at a number of sites, for example, in Gumla Period III, Rehman Dheri Periods II/III, Kot Diji Period I, Kalibangan Period I and Rakhigarhi Period I, which variously fall in the first half of the third millennium BCE and, thus, antedate the Mature Harappan civilization. In fact, the concept of laying out buildings along the cardinal directions goes back to a much earlier period, as indicated by the granaries in Mehrgarh Period III, ascribable to the first half of the fourth millennium BCE. The use of bricks in the ratio of 4:2:1 was there not only in Kunal Ic or Kot Diji I or Banawali IC but even as early as Mehrgarh IB, datable to *c*. 4500 BCE. The firing of bricks is generally thought of as an innovation by the Mature Harappans, but this is not so since kiln-fired bricks had been used in a drain in Kalibangan Period I and in the houses of Period I at Banawali, both in the first half of the third millennium BCE. The only difference is that these were not used as liberally as in the Mature Harappan structures though it must also be noted that, except at Mohenjo-daro and Harappa, mud bricks were still used in most of the houses and platforms at Kalibangan, Lothal, etc. As for the building of a peripheral/fortification wall around the settlements during Early Harappan times, while Kot Diji, Rehman Dheri and Banawali have given reasonably good evidence, at Kalibangan, it has been exposed on all four sides to a considerable extent. This should leave no doubt in the matter. Further, though the concept of dividing the settlement into two parts, a citadel and a lower town, is characteristically Mature Harappan, it must not be overlooked that this feature made its first appearance towards the end of the Early Harappan times, as indicated by the evidence of Period IC at Banawali. As for the provision of a well laid-out underground drainage system, full credit must be given to the Mature Harappans; the Early Harappans had hardly any thing of that kind. The more or less the same regarding monumental public buildings, except for the fact that some kind of public granaries did emerge during Period III at Mehrgarh, ascribable to the first half of the fourth millennium BCE.

As mentioned earlier, Mature Harappan pottery is very distinctive: a sturdy red ware with specific shapes and painted designs in a single colour (black). On the other hand, Early Harappan pottery is not so sturdy, has shapes of its own and is painted in two colours, black as well as white. At the same time, collective evidence from various pre-Mature Harappan sites does show that many of the Mature Harappan shapes and painted designs had started appearing much earlier. Thus, for example, the flat-bottomed 'bread-container' with a flanged rim, the ring-stand and even the tall, cylindrical, perforated jar were there at Amri in Period IIB, which goes back to the first half of the third millennium BCE. Likewise, Kalibangan Period I has yielded storage jars with flanged rim, dishes and cups-on-stand, and even a tall, cylindrical jar, though without perforation. The same can be said of many of the painted designs. For example, the fish-scale pattern was there not only in Kalibangan I and Kot Diji I but as early as Amri IA and Mehrgarh III, i.e. in the first half of the fourth millennium BCE. Likewise, the chessboard-like black-and-blank-square design began as early as Amri IA and Mehrgarh III. Intersecting circles occurred in Amri IIB and Rehman Dheri II. The pipal leaf pattern has been noted in Rehman Dheri II, Amri IIA, Mehrgarh V and Kunal. At the last-named site, it has a black outline and white filling, so typical of the Early Harappan times. The same is the case with the portrayal of the peacock at Kunal. From all this, it is clear that the origin of many of the Mature Harappan pottery shapes and painted designs was much earlier. Likewise, the ubiquitous terracotta 'cakes' of the Mature Harappan times also had an earlier beginning.

Of the objects related to crafts, it may be stated that while carnelian beads go back to Early Harappan times, the characteristic etched ones were a speciality of the Mature times, as also perhaps the faience bangles. However, drill-bits of a specialized form found in the Mature Harappan levels do go back to earlier periods, for example, at Amri and Mehrgarh, dating back to the first half of the fourth millennium BCE in the latter case. Even bun-shaped ingots, found in the Mature Harappan levels at Lothal and other places, had an earlier beginning, for example, in Period III of Mehrgarh, assignable to the first half of the fourth millennium BCE.

We may now turn our attention to the other items, viz., writing, seals/sealings, weights, measuring scales, metal and stone statuary, and long-distance trade. It has to be admitted that inscriptions of the kind available during Mature Harappan times have not been met with in the Early Harappan strata. At the same time, it has also to be accepted that many of the Mature Harappan signs have a great antiquity. Thus, for example, at Harappa itself, well-known signs such as the 'V' with two downward strokes emerging from each of its two upper ends, the bow-with-oblique-arrow, the 'E'-like sign with multiple horizontal strokes and the *damaru*-like sign occurred as post-firing graffiti on pottery in Kot Dijian levels. Likewise, Kot Dijian horizons at a number of other sites (for example, Kunal, Kalibangan, etc.) have also yielded post-firing graffiti similar to some of those constituting the Mature Harappan signary. However, more noteworthy is the fact that a few graffiti marks resembling those in the Harappan script go back to Amri IB, ascribable to the second half of the fourth millennium BCE. Whether these pre-Mature Harappan graffiti marks were just symbols or had phonetic values is unclear since we do not yet have any regular inscription comprising at least a few juxtaposed signs from these levels. As an exception, however, one might note a debatable example from Rehman Dheri but, certainly, more evidence is needed to settle the issue.

The Mature Harappan seals and sealings are usually characterized by an inscription, below which there is an animal or some kind of scenic portrayal.

No such seal has yet been found from the Early Harappan levels. At the same time, it must be mentioned that the concept of having seals was already there. As stated earlier, Kunal, dating back to the first half of the third millennium BCE, has yielded seven seals, six of steatite and one of shell. These are square in shape and provided with a perforated knob on the reverse exactly in the manner of their Mature Harappan counterparts. However, the Kunal examples bear, on the obverse, only geometric designs and no inscription or animal figure. Still earlier, ascribable to the last quarter of the fourth millennium BCE, there is an ivory seal from Rehman Dheri. Seals in terracotta and bone have also been reported from Period IV of Mehrgarh, datable to *c*. 3500-3000 BCE.

With respect to weights, we only have two examples from the Early Harappan levels, one each from Banawali and Harappa. While the Banawali weight has already been described earlier, the one from Harappa, made of limestone, is cuboid in shape and weighs 1.7 grams, falling within the Mature Harappan category of 1.5-2.0 grams. As regards measuring scales, the writer is not aware of any specimen that may be assigned to the pre-Mature Harappan times. The same is the case with stone and metal sculpture.

Regarding trade, in the foregoing pages we had noted the occurrence of beads of turquoise and *lapis lazuli*, and objects of seashells and copper at many Early Harappan sites. In most cases, these materials were not available locally and had, therefore, to be imported either in the form of finished goods or raw material out of which the objects were prepared locally. In either case, an element of trade was involved, either direct or through an intermediary station. While seashells had to be procured from the coastal areas, copper may have come from the Khetri mines, which seem to have continued this supply even during the Mature Harappan times. However, *lapis lazuli* had to be obtained either from Baluchistan or Afghanistan and turquoise from as far as Turkmenia. However, certainly, the volume of Early Harappan trade was by no means as large as that of the Mature Harappan nor did it cover any maritime element for which the latter is well known.

The foregoing comparison between the Early and Mature Harappan stages brings out two important features. First, that the Mature Harappan civilization was not in the least an external 'import', as had been made out in the past, but grew on local soil, some of the roots penetrating as deep as the fourth millennium BCE. Second, even though it was growing gradually over centuries, there was a sudden blossoming, around the middle of the third millennium

BCE. There were both quantitative as well as qualitative changes, as though it was a case of 'revolution' within an ongoing 'evolution'. While it is not very easy to pinpoint the various causes that might have brought about these revolutionary changes, an attempt may, nevertheless, be made to probe the matter.

On the agricultural front, the Early Harappans had been doing quite well, as indicated by the innovative method of ploughing fields, noted at Kalibangan, which gave two kinds of crops in one stroke in the same field. That they and their predecessors had an agricultural surplus is borne out by the Mehrgarh III granaries, ascribable to the first half of the fourth millennium BCE. In those days, surplus agricultural wealth must have been the greatest of assets. On the 'industrial' side and internal trade, too, the Early Harappans were not badly off. They were producing copper, silver and gold objects, and beads of a variety of materials not only for their own local needs but also for their neighbouring settlements. That their trade network was spread over quite a wide territory is clearly established by the occurrence of objects of seashells hundreds of miles away from the coastal areas. The same can be said with respect to beads of turquoise and *lapis lazuli*, far away from their sources. By about the middle of the third millennium BCE, there seems to have been a much greater spurt in agricultural production and trade activities. The former is fully borne out by the great granaries at Harappa and Mohenjo-daro. On the 'industrial' side, there was not only immense growth in the production of already existing items such as bronze and copper objects, beads (a new etched variety was added), pottery, etc., but there also appeared on the scene new items such as measuring scales, or inscribed and sophisticated seals. Further, whereas the Early Harappan levels have, so far, yielded only two examples of weights, there are hundreds of them from the Mature levels. Again, even though the Early Harappans may stake their claim to writing, the Mature Harappan inscribed material stands out by itself. It is apparent that these items, namely weights, scales, seals and writing, are directly connected with trade. While weights and scales were used for weighing or measuring commodities that were sent out or brought in, seals were needed for sealing packages and the system of writing for keeping records. In this context, around the middle of the third millennium BCE, there was the opening of an altogether new vista in trade: over land with regions as far away as Central Asia, and by sea with the eastern horn of Saudi Arabia, Bahrain and Iraq (Mesopotamia).

This tremendous twofold boost in agricultural production as well as trade must have produced a surplus of wealth hitherto unknown. And it is this that would explain the coming into being of large urban settlements, elaborate planning, well laid-out drains, monumental buildings and, above all, a well-knit administrative system. With a surplus of wealth at their disposal, it was but natural for the people to think in terms of *objet d'art*. This is precisely what the Mature Harappan is all about when looked at through pre-Mature Harappan glasses.

IN FULL BLOOM: MATURE HARAPPAN CIVILIZATION

Towards the end of the previous section, we referred to the main characteristics of the Mature stage of the Harappan civilization. We shall take up the various items in detail as we proceed, and we begin with town planning.

LAYOUT OF SOME MAJOR SETTLEMENTS

It has often been said that, on achieving maturity, the Harappan civilization became monotonous. This is highly misleading. It is demonstrated, amongst other things, by the layout of the settlements. No two cities of the Mature Harappan civilization have an identical plan, be these Mohenjo-daro and Harappa in the Indus-Ravi valleys, or Kalibangan, Banawali and Rakhigarhi in the Sarasvati basin, or Lothal on the Gujarat plains, or Surkotada and Dholavira in Kachchh.

Mohenjo-daro

Mohenjo-daro is the anglicized rendering of the Sindhi word 'Muen-jo-daro', which means 'a mound of the dead'. At present, about 5 km away from the right bank of the Indus, the settlement seems to have been close to it in ancient times. It is divided into two major parts, a 'Citadel' in the west and a 'Lower Town' in the east, with a gap of about 200 m in between. The overall perimeter of these two parts is about 5 km, although there is evidence to suggest that there was some habitation even outside these mounds.

Rising to a height of about 12 m above the surrounding ground level and forming a rough rectangle, the citadel measures about 380 m north-south and 190 m east-west. Though the entire area has not been excavated, it appears that there was a basal mud-brick platform or several ones, as in the case of Kalibangan, over which various structures stood. The more noteworthy amongst these were a bath, a granary, a 'college of priests' and an 'assembly half'. In the bath complex, the tank measured 11.7 m north-south and 6.9 m east-west with a depth of 2.4 m. It was approached through two staircases, one each on the north and south. Around the tank were pillared corridors behind which there were rooms. In one of these, there was a well which supplied water to the tank. Every care was taken to make the tank watertight, particularly by using gypsum mortar. For the discharge of water, there was a corbelled drain in the south-west corner.

Immediately to the west of the bath was the granary of which only the basal part now remains. Measuring 45 m east-west and 22.5 m north-south, it consisted of twenty-seven blocks of kiln-fired bricks, arranged in three rows of nine each, over which there seems to have stood a superstructure of woodwork, now perished. The space in between these blocks provided passage for air so that the grain stored on the wooden floor of the granary could breathe and, thus, be saved from humidity.

On the eastern side of the bath across a street, there was a building measuring 69 × 23.4 m. It had a 10 m square courtyard, three verandas and many rooms. There were two staircases which evidently led to an upper storey. The immense size of the building and its proximity to the bath complex has led scholars to think that it may have been the residence of the high priest and his associates or a 'college' for them and visiting laymen.

Located in the southern part of the citadel, there was yet another building measuring 27-m square. With a large entrance on the north, it had twenty piers, laid in five east-west rows of four each. It has been surmised that this building may have functioned as an assembly hall, either for religious or secular purposes or both. Whether the citadel was fortified, as in the case of Harappa or Kalibangan, is not yet clear. However, the presence of a few towers along the periphery calls for further excavation to settle the issue.

Whether the lower town was surrounded by a wall remains uncertain, although on the western periphery, a massive mud-brick 'embankment' with a revetment of kiln-fired bricks on the exterior has been identified. Running across the town were at least two major north-south and an equal number of east-west streets, dividing it into nine major blocks. Each block was further subdivided into house complexes by minor streets and lanes. While the major streets were as much as 9 m in width, the lanes were only 1.5 m. An excellent underground drainage system was laid out through the streets, duly covered and provided with manholes at suitable places. As could be expected in a major metropolitan township like Mohenjo-daro, the size and layout of the houses varied considerably. Thus, for example, one of the big houses measured 75 m in length. It had two courtyards separated by a corridor and around each were living rooms. In the smaller of the courtyards, there was a bread-oven and one begins to wonder if the rooms around these smaller courtyard were used by the ladies, as has been the practice in the houses of big landlords in many parts of India even up to recent times. An average middle class house was relatively smaller but certainly much bigger than the houses which evidently belonged to the labour class. These last-named houses were in the form of barracks, each tenement having only two small rooms. Within the township, there were shops as well as workshops of potters, beadmakers, shellworkers, coppersmiths, etc.

Harappa

In the Sahiwal district of Punjab (Pakistan), Harappa lay on the left bank of the Ravi, which has since shifted its course to the north. A settlement almost as large as Mohenjo-daro, Harappa, however, has three clear-cut mounds, named from north to south as 'F', 'AB' and 'E' (Others of lesser importance are not discussed here.) Of these, Mound AB is the highest and is thought to represent the 'Citadel', encompassed by a thick mud-brick wall (Fig. 11.3). In a section cut across it along the southern part of the western periphery, the wall was found to stand on a mud-brick rampart that measured 13.5 m in width at the base but tapered upwards. On the exterior, there was a revetment of kiln-fired bricks, 1.2 m at the base. Along the north-western periphery, three successive rebuilds of the revetment were noted. In the section just referred to, a 6-m high mud-brick platform was juxtaposed to the back of the wall. On it six structural sub-phases were identified. Whether this platform ran through the entire citadel, providing a base for the superstructures could not be ascertained because of limited excavation in this trench but elsewhere, within the citadel, mud-brick masses were obviously met with in earlier excavations.

Mound F has yielded some very interesting structures. In its northern part, there stood a massive granary (cf. Fig. 11.3). It had two blocks, one each on the east and west, with a passage in between. Each block consisted of six units, each unit measuring externally 15 × 6 m. In a recent dig at the northern periphery of this mound, the remains of a thick mud-brick wall have been identified. If this wall is also traced along the other edges of the mound, it may well turnout that, like Mound AB, this one, too, was surrounded by a wall. Other noteworthy structures in this area are, 'pounding platforms' and workmen's quarters. So far, eighteen of these platforms, lying variously in five rows, have been unearthed but there may be many more. Circular in plan with an average diameter of about 3 m, the platforms were formed by laying a series of circular rings of bricks-on-edge. The central portion, has been found to be hollow, with stray remains of straw and husked barley. It has been surmised that a wooden mortar was fixed in this hollow in which cereals were thrashed, since a somewhat similar system was prevalent in many parts of the country until recently. To the south of these platforms were the workmen's quarters. These lay in a barrack-like fashion in two east-west rows, with a narrow gap in between. Each unit, measuring 17 × 7 m, comprised a room and a courtyard with an oblique entrance.

Mound E, with its adjunct called ET, is located to the south of Mound AB. It is this unit which can lay claim to being called the lower town. Here were streets, lanes, regular houses and drains. More importantly, it is now clear that this area was also enclosed by a peripheral wall, which has been exposed to a length of over 25 m on the southern side and for quite some distance in the north-east. At places, it is 6-7 m wide and of a height of about 2.5 m. On the southern side there was a gateway, flanked by two piers of kiln-fired bricks, each measuring 3 × 3 m, with an extant height of 2 m. In the eastern part of this mound, raw material and waste products have been found, indicating that units for the manufacture of steatite disc-beads, shell objects and weights were located here.

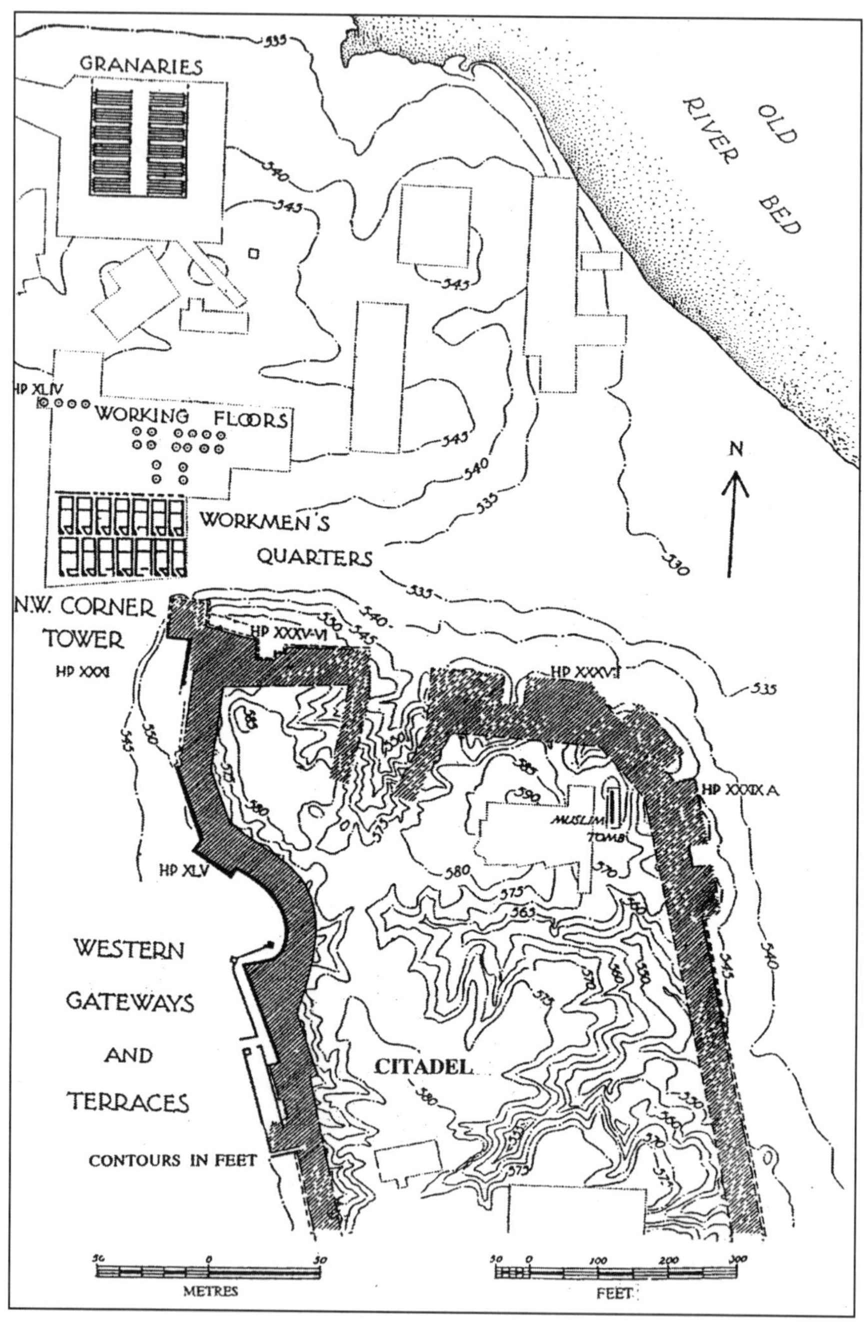

Fig. 11.3: Harappa: Citadel and structures under its shadow

Except for the Ravi Phase, which has so far been encountered only in the rain gully in the northern part of Mound AB, all the other cultural strata have been found in Mound E and these show a continuity from one to the other. The entire sequence at Harappa is as follows:

Period 1	Ravi Phase	> 3300 BCE–*c*.2800 BCE
Period 2	Kot Diji (Early Harappa) Phase	*c*. 2800 BCE–*c*.2600 BCE
Period 3A	Harappa Phase A	*c*. 2600 BCE–*c*.2450 BCE
Period 3B	Harappa Phase B	*c*. 2450 BCE–*c*.2200 BCE
Period 3C	Harappa Phase C	*c*. 2200 BCE–*c*.1900 BCE
Period 4	Harappa/Late Harappa Transitional	*c*. 1900 BCE–*c*.1800 BCE (?)
Period 5	Late Harappa Phase	*c*. 1800 BCE(?)–< 1300 BCE

As indicated above, Period 4 marks a transition from the Harappan phase towards that of Cemetery H, which is fully represented in Period 5. By the latter period, the pottery acquires a bright red slip and the paintings are executed in jet-black pigment. Some of the themes of the Cemetery H paintings are also different from those of the Mature Harappan.

To the south of Mound AB and west of Mound E, burials have been discovered, ascribable to the Harappa phase as well as the Cemetery H phase. In the Harappan burials, the body was laid supine in a grave-pit with the head towards the north. Some pottery and other goods were also placed in the grave. In Cemetery H, there were two kinds of burials. In the earlier stratum, the entire body was buried in a pit but in the later, only selected bones and the cranium were interred in large jars.

Kalibangan

Situated on the left bank of the ancient Sarasvati (now dry and going by the name of Ghaggar), Kalibangan falls in the Hanumangarh district of Rajasthan. There are three mounds (Fig. 11.4): from west to east KLB-1 (Citadel), KLB-2 (Lower Town) and KLB-3 (a small, essentially ritualistic complex). These have a total perimeter of 1.5-2 km. As stated earlier, occupation at Kalibangan began in Early Harappan times and had to be abandoned around 2700 BCE because of an earthquake. The site was re-occupied after an interval of about a century by which time the people had reached the Mature stage of development. These Mature Harappans built their 'Citadel' on the earlier remains so that it had a higher position. The peripheral wall that went around it was in the form of a parallelogram. The major axis running north-south measured 240 m, while the other one was half of it. The complex was further subdivided by a medial wall, running east-west, into two equal rhombs, each having its distinctive features. Thus, while the southern rhomb had a series of mud-brick platforms with specialized structures on them, the northern one had residential houses with a street in between. This street opened on the river-front in the north. There was one more entrance to the northern half from the east through which the residents of the lower town could get in.

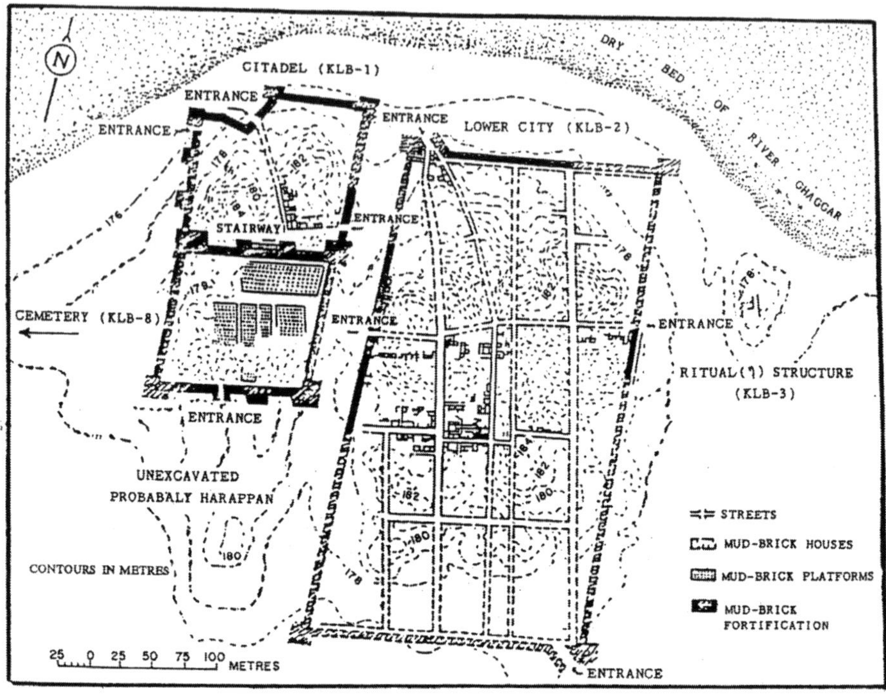

Fig. 11.4: Kalibangan: Harappan settlement, Period II

There was a stepped access from the northern half to the southern, connecting the two. Owing to the ravages of time and elements, many of the mud-brick platforms in the southern rhomb have been largely denuded but, on at least two, overlying complexes could be identified. On one, there was a brick-lined sacrificial pit containing bovine bones and antlers. In this context, it may be mentioned that engravings on a triangular terracotta cake discovered from the site shows how an animal, roped by the neck, was taken for sacrifice before a deity. On the other platform, there was a north-south row of seven contiguous 'fire-altars' (Pl. II). Though these have been disturbed over time, one can still see in them the remains of a central clay stele, circular-biconvex terracotta 'cakes' and pieces of charcoal. Close by lay the lower half of a jar containing ash and charcoal, which suggests that fire was kept ready for the ritual. Behind the row of altars was a north-south wall. It would, thus, appear that anyone who used these altars had to face the east. A little away to the north-west were a well and bathing pavement, which indicates that bathing formed a part of the worship. (Here, it may be necessary to mention that these 'fire-altars' have little in common with those used by the Parsis.)

These platforms were separated from one another, as also from the peripheral wall, by means of passages. As mentioned earlier, the southern rhomb was separated from the northern by a wall but there was a stepped access from one to the other. It has been surmised that in the residential buildings in the northern rhomb, there lived priests who supervised/conducted rituals performed on the platforms in the southern. Through the southern peripheral wall of the latter rhomb was an entrance which was stepped, indicating that no wheeled vehicles could enter this part. Thus, all worshippers were required to walk on the premises and not to ride about.

To the south of the citadel was an open, unfortified area. Though not much excavation was done in it, it was noted that the houses here were relatively smaller and, in one locale, a lot of pottery waste was also observed. It is likely that this area was occupied by a poorer segment of society.

About 40 m to the east of the citadel was the lower town. This, too, had a peripheral mud-brick wall. It formed a parallelogram in plan of which the longer axis had a north-south orientation, but the other deviated slightly from the east-west (Fig. 11.4). Since the eastern and western walls were traceable, it was easy to determine the width of the lower town, which was 240 m. While the northern wall was clearly identified, that in the south had largely disappeared. However, it is estimated that the north-south extent may have been in the neighbourhood of 360 m. Within this enclosed area, there were at least five north-south and four east-west streets, separating the blocks of houses. It is interesting to note that the lanes/streets followed a set ratio. Thus, while the narrowest lane was 1.8 m in width, the streets measured 3.6 m, 5.4 m and 7.2 m, respectively. Walking through the excavated remains, one observes, with a sense of satisfaction and amazement, that the residents of Kalibangan at no point of time during their seven hundred years of occupation of the site, ever encroached on the streets (Pl. III). This speaks volumes for their discipline, whether self-imposed or imposed by a vigilant civic authority. The only structures that could be seen projecting into the streets were small mud-brick platforms adjacent to the entrance, which were a planned part of the layout. An average house comprised a courtyard on three sides of which were rooms. Through the fourth was the entrance, wide enough to let even a bullock cart in. In the courtyard, there were long troughs where fodder and water were kept for the cattle. In some of the houses, the courtyard also had a well. Often, cooking was also done in a corner of the courtyard. The rooms were usually paved with mud-bricks but sometimes with kiln-fired tiles bearing the intersecting-circles design. In another case, the floor consisted of a soling of broken hard-fired nodules interspersed with charcoal, over which clay was laid. It is learnt that this particular kind of flooring is still in use in neighbouring villages to prevent sub-soil moisture from travelling up along the walls, as well as to act against termites. In some of the houses, a few large jars were found which were evidently used for storage of grains. Of further interest is the fact that one of the rooms seems to have been reserved for worship. In it, 'fire altars' have been noted in successive strata. An average altar consisted of a round-ended rectangular pit measuring about 1 × .5 m in plan and about 25 cm in depth. The sides were plastered with mud and the floor had turned red because of the fire that has left behind ash and charcoal. In the central part stood a cylindrical stele of clay about 10-15 cm in diameter and 30-40 cm in height. Around it had been placed circular-biconvex terracotta 'cakes', perhaps as offerings. (Earlier, we referred to a row of seven such fire altars in the citadel complex.)

The easternmost mound, the smallest of the three, revealed only fire altars. Perhaps it was exclusively used for ritualistic purposes. The area to the west of the citadel was used as a cemetery. Three different kinds of graves were discovered to which we shall refer later in detail while discussing the burial practices of the Mature Harappans.

Banawali

Proceeding about 120 km north-east along the now dry bed of the Ghaggar (ancient Sarasvati), one reaches Banawali in the Hissar district of Haryana. The main mound covers an area approximately 400 × 400 m and contains about 8 m of occupational deposits. Within it, three cultural periods, numbered I, II and III from the bottom upwards, have been identified. These represent the Early, Mature and post-Mature Harappan stages, respectively. While there was a continuity between Periods I and II, Period III came up after an interval of time.

The layout of the Mature Harappan settlement at Banawali was quite different from that at the three sites discussed earlier, viz., Mohenjo-daro, Harappa and Kalibangan. Thus, while in the latter cases, the citadel formed an exclusively separate unit, in Banawali it was not so. Here, the citadel lay within the overall area occupied by the lower town, the southern wall being common between the two. For the rest, the citadel had its own perimeter wall and formed a rough semi-ellipse in plan. Excavations revealed the existence of houses and north-south streets within the citadel. However, because of the limited dig, it could not be ascertained if the citadel contained platforms too, as it did at Kalibangan. There was a small opening in the peripheral wall on the east and a ramp paved with kiln-fired bricks, connecting the citadel with the lower town. The citadel wall had square bastions on the exterior.

The lower town had its own peripheral wall, also provided externally with square bastions. At one place on its east, a moat was identified. While the identification of a moat on the other sides remains a desideratum, it is interesting to note this new feature in the Harappan system of peripheral (fortification) walls. The lower town lay on three sides of the citadel. On the eastern and western sides, it formed rather narrow strips while on the northern, there was quite a bit of it. However, the layout of the township was not in the grid pattern, as elsewhere. On the other hand, fronting an entrance through the eastern wall was a piazza from where the streets forked out in various directions, not necessarily cardinal. Some of the houses in the lower town were pretty large and their contents suggested that they may have belonged to well-to-do people. In one case, many weights and seals were found and the toilet was provided with a wash basin placed on a high place in a corner near the drain which carried off the waste water into a sullage jar placed outside on the street. In another house, besides weights, there occurred a large number of beads of *lapis lazuli*, carnelian and gold. What is more noteworthy is the discovery of a touchstone bearing gold streaks of different hues, which clearly demonstrates that the method of testing the purity of gold, used even now in India, is at least 4,500 years old.

Rakhigarhi

While dealing with the Early Harappan cultures, we referred to the findings at Rakhigarhi. Covering an area of over 100 ha, it is easily amongst the largest Harappan sites. In district Hissar, Haryana, it lay on the right bank of the now dry Chautang, earlier known as the Drishadvati, a tributary of the Sarasvati.

Of the seven different areas marked out at the site and named RGR-1 to RGR-7, Mature Harappan remains have been obtained from RGR-1, RGR-2 and RGR-7 so far. In RGR-1, while there were the usual houses laid out along the cardinal directions, one structural feature deserves special attention. Located in a somewhat outlying area, it was circular in plan with two small semi-circular adjuncts, one each on the west and east. Altogether, it measured 5 m east-west and 2.92 m north-south, with a depth of 1.30 m. In the middle stood two independent shafts, arch-like in plan with a width of 46 cm. The side-walls of the entire complex, including those of the shafts, were burnt deep red, implying prolonged fire activity. At the bottom, there was a 30-cm thick deposit containing charcoal and ash. While no pots were actually found inside the complex, it is not unlikely that it may have been used for firing small-sized pots which had been taken out earlier.

RGR-2 has yielded some important information about the structural remains of the Mature Harappan times. In its southern part, two mud-brick platforms riveted with kiln-fired bricks have been identified. These are oriented along the cardinal directions. On their top lay sacrificial pits containing bones, horns, hoofs, etc., of cattle, and two 'fire altars' containing clay stele and circular terracotta cakes. The two fire altars were contiguous and behind them was a north-south wall, a situation similar to that at Kalibangan and implying that worshippers had to face the east.

On the western side of this mound, the remains of a peripheral wall have been identified. Oriented in a north-south direction and made of mud bricks, it measured 12 m in width at the base. It is extant to a height of 3 m and the exposed length so far is 30 m. The bricks, which are of the standard Mature Harappan ratio, 4:2:1, are placed in a stepped fashion in successive courses, both on the interior and exterior, with the result that the wall slopes back as it rises upwards. In an area a little to the south, the continuation of this wall has also been cleared. Over here, a construction of kiln-fired bricks seems to indicate a stepped entrance.

In RGR-7, which is located slightly to the north of RGR-1, a Mature Harappan cemetery has been discovered. The burials, as usual, were in pits, the body having been placed in an extended position with the head towards the north. In one case, the dead person wore shell bangles on the left wrist. Although the expert report is awaited, it is surmised that the body is that of a female. The significance of this will be discussed later.

Lothal

Situated in the Ahmedabad district of Gujarat, Lothal has given to the world its earliest dockyard, dating back to about the mid-third millennium BC (Pl IV). Passing by the site in ancient times was a river that joined the Bhogavo, a tributary of the Sabarmati, which, in turn, fell into the Gulf of Khambhat, an inlet of the Arabian Sea. Thus, there was a continuous riverine connection between Lothal and the sea. Located immediately to the east of the township, the dockyard formed a trapezoid in plan, with the longer axis north-south. Its retaining walls made of kiln-fired bricks measured, in length, in a clockwise direction from the west, 215 m, 37 m, 212 m and 35 m, respectively. In width, they were 1.5-1.8 m at the base but tapered upwards to only 1 m. At present, these are available to a maximum height of 3.3 m. The dockyard had two inlets, one in the northern arm measuring 12 m in width, and the other in the eastern with a width of only 7 m. It appears that the former was used first and the other in the second phase when the adjacent river shifted its course. In the southern wall, there was a stepped exit through which excess water drained out. The functioning of the dockyard seems to have been somewhat like this: taking advantage of the high tide in the sea, which had its impact way up on the connected watercourses, the cargo-loaded boats moved upwards and reached the dockyard. These were duly parked there, as indicated by the occurrence of stone anchors. The goods were unloaded onto the adjacent wharf. Meanwhile, the commodities to be exported were taken out of the nearby warehouse and brought to the wharf to be loaded into the boats, which were readied for the return journey to the sea. This trip was undertaken when another tide, reaching the dockyard, was on the wane, making it easier for the boats to follow it back to the sea.

The warehouse just referred to was constructed on a 40 × 40 m wide and 4 m high mud-brick podium. Over this podium lay a series of parallel mud-brick blocks, each measuring 3.6 × 3.6 × 0.9 m. Oriented along the cardinal directions, and these were separated from each other by a 1.2 m wide passage. The discovery of burnt wood and charcoal pieces in the passages suggests that the superstructure of the warehouse was of wood. No less interesting is the fact that, from within these passages, as many as sixty-five burnt clay sealings have been found. These have, on one side, the impressions of woven fibre and knotted cord and, on the other, of typical Harappan seals. This clearly indicates that, at the time the warehouse caught fire, packages duly sealed and evidently meant to be exported lay in it. In the context of sea trade, it must be mentioned that at Lothal itself has been found a seal of the typical 'Persian Gulf' style. It is circular in shape, with a flat obverse and convex reverse. The latter is perforated, and bears three incised lines and four circlets (features, all of which are different from those of the Harappan seals). On the obverse are engraved 'a reptile or dragon having two heads and flanked by two jumping goats or gazelle-like animals with protruding eyes and looking over the shoulders . . .' as described by S.R. Rao, the excavator. He adds, 'the goat-like animals on the seal . . . are more like Sumerian goats. Some of the late circular seals of Failaka . . . assigned by Dr. Bibby to the Sargonid period are identical in all details with the Lothal seal.' In this context, it may perhaps also be added that Lothal was a very important centre for the manufacture of beads, which were a hot favourite in Western Asia, particularly the etched ones.

We may now turn our attention to the general layout of the settlement which, it may be added, was different from the various sites discussed earlier. To pinpoint the issue, here the 'Citadel' was not separately located as at Mohenjo-daro, Harappa and Kalibangan. Again, whereas in the case of Banawali, the citadel, though integrated within the general complex of the lower town, had its own peripheral wall, this was not so in the case of the Lothal citadel. The only distinguishing feature between the citadel and the lower town at Lothal was that the former lay in an exclusive area on a 3.5-m high platform, with a core of mud and veneer of mud-bricks. In plan, it was trapezoidal, the various sides, beginning from the west in a clock-wise manner, measuring 118 m, 125 m, 118 m and 113 m, respectively. On it, there stood a series of large houses, a well, a row of twelve bathing floors and concomitant drains discharging into a bigger one. The row of bath pavements brings to mind the complexes at Mohenjo-daro and Kalibangan. Was the citadel at Lothal, too, used for some kind of religious purpose, housing priests in these buildings? To the south-east of these houses was the warehouse referred to earlier.

The entire settlement, inclusive of the citadel complex, was enclosed by a mud and mud-brick wall with an average thickness of 12-13 m and extant height of 1.8-2.4 m. It formed a rough rectangle oriented along the cardinal directions and measuring approximately 280 m north-south and 225 m east-west. Piercing the southern wall was an oblique entrance. The streets within were oriented along the cardinal directions, forming a gridiron pattern. The widest and narrowest measured, respectively, 12 m and 3.6 m. The houses had the usual plan: a courtyard surrounded by rooms on three sides and an entrance on the fourth. Fire altars, too, have been noted in some of the houses. The inmates were variously engaged in agricultural and industrial activities. The discovery of lots of beads in various stages of manufacture, of the raw material and even a kiln testifies to a thriving bead industry at Lothal. Likewise, copper artefacts were also manufactured locally, as evidenced by the discovery of ingots and crucibles, besides finished objects. Perhaps goldsmiths also constituted a part of the population. The site yielded a large number of tiny gold beads and seven of a special type, discular in shape with perforation along the diameter, similar to those found at Kunal in silver in an Early Harappan context. The other small finds included inscribed steatite seals, an ivory scale, an angle-measuring instrument and a terracotta figurine of a horse.

On the outskirts of the settlement towards the north-west, a cemetery has been identified. Besides the usual single-burial graves, there were three which contained two skeletons each. More will be said about these when we discuss the burial practices of the Harappans.

The occupational strata at Lothal, accounting for a total of 8.5 m, have been divided by the excavator into two periods, A and B. Period A has been further subdivided into four Phases, I-IV, while Period B has only one, V. Thus, while Phase I represents the beginning of the site, the township with its various nuances belongs to Phases II and III, the latter representing its peak. A general downward trend is visible in Phase IV while, by Phase V, the warehouse, dockyard and even the peripheral wall had fallen into disuse. The township was ill-maintained and the drainage system had become defunct. Clearly, the Harappan glory was on the decline.

Surkotada

The settlement at Surkotada located in Kachchh has yet another type of planning. Here, the citadel and the lower town were juxtaposed, with a common wall in between which had an opening for inter-communication. Both the units were square in plan, each measuring 60-5 m internally, the overall orientation being approximately along the cardinal directions. It is reported that whereas the structures in the citadel were placed on platforms, there were none beneath the houses in the lower town. Further, while each unit had an entrance on the southern side, that of the lower town was a simple one but the one to the citadel had a barbican, a ramp, steps and guard rooms The enclosure walls had a mud and mud-brick core with a veneer of stone-rubble, available locally in plenty.

The occupational deposits have been divided into three Sub-periods, IA, IB and IC. In Sub-period IA, specimens of the pointed-bottom goblet have been found, so it would appear that the settlement at Surkotada began well after the beginning of the Mature Phase. In the late levels of the site, there occurred the black-and-red ware which is characteristic of the contemporary Banas Valley culture of Rajasthan. This would indicate an influx of some people from that area to Kachchh. To the south-west of the citadel was the cemetery, which is characterized by lithic components. Further reference to it will be made later.

The site yielded the usual Harappan antiquities. However, most important was the discovery of the bones of the horse (*Equus caballus*) whose association with the Harappan civilization has been disputed by some scholars.

Dholavira

In Kachchh, there is yet another Harappan site, Dholavira, which is noteworthy in many respects: for a long-drawn culture sequence and innumerable antiquities, a unique town-plan, the use of stone pillars in construction, the earliest-known stadium, a remarkable system of water supply, unusual graves, and the largest Harappan inscription.

The settlement had three components, a citadel, a middle town and a lower town, all having their own enclosure walls yet interwoven into one complex. Oriented along the cardinal directions, the outermost enclosure walls formed a rectangle in plan, measuring approximately 770 m east-west and 615 m north-south (Fig. 11.5). These walls were made of mud-bricks, which were reinforced with stone veneer at strategic places. Besides, there were rectangular/square bastions at different points. Two seasonal streams flowed past this enclosure, one called Manosar on the northern side and another, Manhar, along the south-east and south. It is the water of these streams that was harnessed by the early engineers for the use of the inhabitants. We shall refer to this in some detail later.

The citadel complex, with its own enclosure wall and oriented along the cardinal directions, was divided into two more or less equal parts, eastern and western, called by the excavator, R.S. Bisht, as 'Castle' and 'Bailey'.

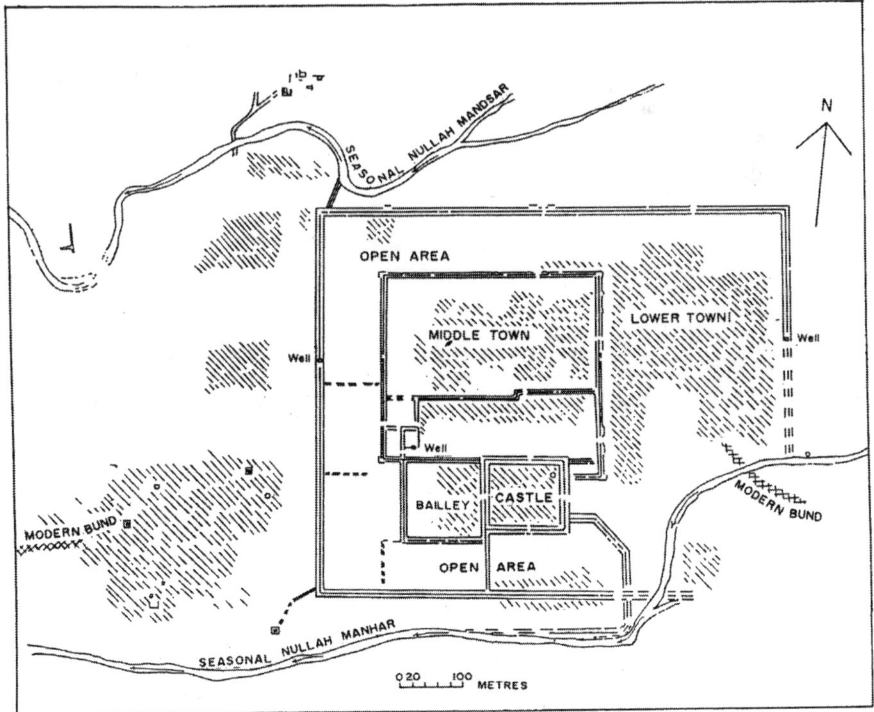

Fig. 11.5: Dholavira: Layout of Harappan settlement

Separated by a medial north-south wall, these parts were connected by a gate through it. The nature of the structures in these parts, however, differed, reminding one of a similar situation in the citadel at Kalibangan. The bailey seems to have had a residential character since many houses have been found within it. Also, there lay within the bailey a complex comprising four stone-lined, underground chambers, all juxtaposed and arranged in two rows of two each. Each chamber measured approximately 3 × 3 m in plan with a depth of 2.6 m. These chambers may have been used for storage, perhaps of grain, though no grains were actually found during the course of the excavation.

As far as the castle is concerned, it presented a different kind of planning. From its western gate, which has already been mentioned, there ran a 13-m wide west-east street leading to the eastern gateway. It divided the castle into two major parts, northern and southern. While the picture of the structures in the northern parts is still unclear (excavations are currently in progress), a major water-related complex has been identified in the southern. There was a stone-lined well with an internal diameter of 4 m. It has been excavated to a depth of 13 m without reaching the bottom. At one place, abutting the edge of the well, there was a trough with a stone slab at the base and three vertical slabs on each side, barring the edge of the well. There was an aperture at the bottom of the vertical slab in the south-west corner of the trough, through which water went into a covered drain which, after some distance, fell into a stone-lined tank, measuring 4.35 m north-south, 2.95 m east-west and 3.58 m in depth. It was provided with a flight of six steps, reaching the stone-paved floor. There is an indication of another tank nearby, the details of which have yet to be exposed. The entire complex reminds one of a more or less similar set-up in the citadel at Mohenjo-daro, and naturally one begins to think in terms of a ritualistic context. Also noteworthy in the castle was the presence of a large drain which, starting at the northern end and passing through the major street (already referred to), cascaded into the bailey finally to discharge into the open area outside.

The wall around the castle stands to a height of 9 m even now. It had a basal width of 18.5 m and was made of mud-bricks with a veneer of stones. Besides the western gate connecting the bailey and the castle, there were three more gates, one each on the north, east and south. These were laid out through the thickness of the enclosure wall and had a long flight of steps which descended to the floor of a passageway on the exterior. On either side of this passage were chambers and, in the front, an open terrace (Pl. V). On the floor of one of the chambers in the northern gateway complex, a large inscription comprising ten letters in the Harappan script has been found. These letters had a height of 35-7 cm and width of 25-7 cm, and were made from carefully sliced pieces of some 'crystalline material, maybe rock, mineral or paste'. In the side-chambers of the eastern gateway have been found parts of stone pillars, variously cubical, cylindrical and hourglass-like in shape.

Some of the parts still bear polish and, had these specimens not been found *in situ*, one would not have easily accepted their Harappan association.

Between the northern enclosure walls of the citadel and the bailey on the one hand and the southern enclosure wall of the middle town on the other, there is a wide open space which may have been used as a stadium. Though this will remain only a provisional assessment, one may note that, juxtaposed to the walls just referred to, facing the stadium and descending down to its floor level, there were terraces which may have been used by spectators to sit on in case the complex was really used as a stadium.

To the north of the stadium lay the middle town which, as already stated, had its own enclosure wall. Made of stone, it was oriented along the cardinal directions. Of its gateways, only the one on the eastern side has been excavated so far. It is about 3 m in width, with grooves in the vertical slabs to suggest the fixture of door frames. On both sides of the gate, vertical stones were placed as fender posts. The enclosure wall at this point was found to have a thickness of 5.2 m. The gate lay in front of an east-west street which measured 5 m in width. Within the middle town, there were many north-south and east-west streets/lanes, 5.75 m, 2.6 m, 1.8 m and 1.5 m in width. The houses were fairly large with provisions for a courtyard, peripheral living rooms, bathrooms, etc. There was a good drainage system.

To the east of the middle town was the lower town. The alignment of the major west-east street that ran up to the above-mentioned gate of the middle town was more or less followed by a street in the lower town, so that easy access was available from one to the other. Cutting this street at right angles were two major streets in the lower town, besides many other east-west and north-south streets. In one of the houses in the lower town, there were a stone-paved bathroom and stone-lined drain, besides a sullage-pit immediately outside. In another house, dressed stones were used in the walls and, interestingly, these stones measured 40 × 20 × 10 cm—exactly matching the standard size of mud-bricks. Some of the houses had storage jars and querns, too. The houses in the lower town did not in any way reflect a low economic level of the inhabitants. However, if we are looking for the less-privileged class at Dholavira, we have to turn our attention to areas outside the enclosed area where there is indication of habitation, though not yet excavated.

To the west of the main settlement there was the cemetery which yielded some new data, including the use of stone orthostats and capstones in the graves, and the erection of mud/mud-brick tumuli in a couple of cases. We shall refer to these later while dealing with the burial practices of the Harappans.

Finally, we turn to the culture sequence. Within the 12 m thick deposit in the citadel area, seven stages (numbered I-VII from the bottom upwards) have been identified. Briefly, their characteristic features are as follows: the first two stages may be regarded as pre-Mature Harappan, though such elements as the dish-on-stand, perforated jars, terracotta 'cakes' and bricks in the ratio of 4:2:l were met with in them. However, seals, weights and most of the other typical Mature Harappan pottery forms made their appearance only in Stage III. An interesting point has been observed by the excavator, R.S. Bisht, regarding the seals. These only had the animal figures but no inscriptions, the latter appearing only in Stage IV. With a thickness of about 5.5 m, this stage represented the Mature Harappan in its full bloom. The large inscription and the parts of the stone pillars (referred to earlier) seem to be ascribable to it. Then followed the decline, which is reflected in the loss of civic control and architectural degeneration in Stage V. At this point, the site was abandoned for a while. When it was re-occupied in Stage VI, there were some conspicuous differences. For example, seals were now without animal figures, although the weights continued. There were some changes in the pottery forms, too, besides the appearance of a new ceramic, a black-and-red ware (cf. a similar situation at Surkotada, above p. 292). There was, once again, a desertion. Stage VII, representing re-occupation after yet another gap, shows some major changes despite a continuity in some pottery forms and small finds. Thus, the houses were small and circular. There was no town plan and no drainage. A major decline had set in.

Some Other Noteworthy Sites

In the preceding pages, we discussed in some detail the layout of some major settlements of the Mature Harappan times. However, the picture will not be complete without reference to a few other sites which are important in one way or another. Thus, Sutkagen Dor, situated on the coastal area of Makran in Pakistan, is the westernmost site associated with this civilization. At a distance of some 1,600 km east-north-east in the upper Ganga Yamuna Valley in Uttar Pradesh lies Alamgirpur which, as of now, marks the easternmost extension of the Harappan civilization. In a similar manner, Manda in Jammu & Kashmir and Daimabad in the upper reaches of the Godavari in Maharashtra, spanning between them a distance of 1,400 km, mark, respectively, the northernmost and southernmost points. Of these, Daimabad has also yielded a cache of four animal figures in solid copper, having a total weight of about 65 kg. These include a rhinoceros, a buffalo, an elephant, and a chariot yoked to a pair of bullocks and driven by a man. It has been surmised that these figures may belong to the Harappan culture but, since these were found in a clandestine dig and not in a regular excavation, their stratigraphic horizon remains uncertain.

We may now refer to a few more sites, beginning from the coastal area of Pakistan. On the eastern side of the Sonmiani bay and about 90 km from Karachi lies the site of Balakot. It has yielded not only pre-Mature Harappan remains (called Balakotian), dating back to the first half of the fourth millennium BCE, but a substantial settlement of the Mature Harappan times, with a gap between the two. The latter had the usual gridiron street pattern but it is not clear if the settlement was enclosed by a wall. However, the site seems to have played an important role in the Harappan economy. It had a very prosperous shell industry, as indicated by the presence of thousands of specimens in various stages of manufacture, besides, of course, the finished ones. These were not only sent to inland home markets but were also exported. Balakot must have been a good halting port for ships commuting between the Gujarat coast and Iraq via the Persian Gulf.

Another port town participating in this trade may have been Allahdino, located about 40 km east of Karachi. Though small in size (about a 100 m each way), it had all the trappings of a prosperous township, as suggested by large-houses with wells and good drainage, and a rich yield of beads of semi-precious stones, copper objects, seals, and gold and silver ornaments.

Amri and Kot Diji in the upper region of Sindh played a very significant role during Early Harappan times. Both these continued into the Mature Harappan times as well. At Kot Diji, the thickness of the Harappan deposits was 4.5 m, which would imply a long duration of the settlement. Further, while Kot Diji came to an end during the Mature Harappan times, Amri continued to be occupied even later, showing a transition to the Jhukar stage.

On almost the same latitude as Amri but on the opposite side of the Indus is Chanhu-daro, a site to be noted for its many industries during the Mature Harappan times. There was a bead-making factory with a furnace, which covered an overall area of 9.9 × 3.75 m and was provided with 'a series of well-built flues, averaging $5\frac{1}{2}$ inches wide and 8 inches high'. In this area, there lay scattered on the floor a large number of beads, unfinished as well as finished. Elsewhere, chunks of raw material along with drills that were used in the process have also been found. Seal-making was another craft practised by the people of Chanhu-daro. This is indicated by the occurrence of eight unfinished seals in one place and of three in another. The finished ones had evidently been despatched to those who had ordered them, whether local merchants or outsiders. Likewise, weights were also manufactured at Chanhu-daro. Referring to these, the excavator, E.J.H. Mackay, observes: 'many of these weights are so highly finished that we suspect that they were used for testing purposes'. The succeeding occupation at the site has been designated as the 'Jhukar Culture', which, in fact, was a transformation of the Harappan itself. After a break, there appeared the Jhangar culture at the site, characterized by a burnished grey ware.

In northern Baluchistan lies Dabarkot. Over 150 × 135 m in plan, it has a very impressive height of 35 m. It is in urgent need of excavation since it has given full indication of both Early and Mature Harappan occupation. It also promises to be a good melting pot for the Harappan and local Baluchi cultures. Over here a male head in stone has also been found which seems to suggest Mesopotamian affinities.

Located further north are Gumla and Rehman Dheri, which have already been discussed in the context of the Early Harappan scenario. While the Harappan occupation at the latter site is rather limited, that at the former is much more. These, along with another nearby site, Hissam Dheri, however, clearly demonstrate that the Mature Harappan had extended to these far-off regions.

On the Indian side of the border, Siswal and Mitathal in the Hissar and Bhiwani districts of the Haryana, respectively, have yielded both Early and Mature Harappan remains. But the excavations carried out are so limited that not much can be said about the settlement pattern. The former is fairly large, 300 × 200 m, with a height of 12 m, while the latter has twin mounds. Thus, both these call for further work.

Balu in the district of Jind of the same state is yet another site deserving mention. It has all the three stages, viz., Early, Mature and Late Harappan. The Harappan occupation has given evidence of an enclosure wall laid around a 200 × 80 m settlement. The houses inside were laid along the cardinal directions. There was also a 10-m wide mud-brick platform which evidently was used for some specific purpose by the community.

Rupnagar (formerly called Ropar/Rupar) on the bank of the Sutlej in Punjab was the first Harappan site to have been excavated in India, after the Partition. It is extensive but a sizeable area is under current occupation. Excavation in the northern part, which is unencumbered and rises to a height of about 21 m, revealed six cultural periods, the earliest being Mature Harappan with an admixture of some Early Harappan pottery, signifying a continuity from one to the other. There was a break of occupation after the Harappan times, followed by the Painted Grey Ware, Northern Black Polished Ware, Sunga-Kushana, Gupta and medieval occupations. The Harappan levels yielded all the typical material and the burials, too. An interesting piece of evidence was the interment of a dog, perhaps a pet, beneath the master.

Located in the Saharanpur district of Uttar Pradesh, Hulas, like Rupnagar, has yielded several periods of occupation. However, the earliest was not the Mature but the Late Harappan in which, though there occurred a terracotta sealing with an inscription in the typical Harappan script, the pottery showed certain marked changes. Thus, for example, the dishes constituting the upper part of dishes-on-stand had a pronouncedly drooping rim and the jars had an unusually high neck with an everted rim. There was also a proliferation of miniature posts. Such features of pottery have also been noted at other Late Harappan sites in the Sarasvati and upper Ganga valleys, showing continuity and change in the Harappan assemblage.

Bhagwanpura, in the district of Kurukshetra in Haryana, takes the story of this devolution further. In a 2.7-m thick deposit, two sub-periods, IA and IB, have been identified by the excavator, J.P Joshi.[41] In IA, while some

[41] J.P. Joshi (1993), *Excavation at Bhagwanpura 1975-76*, Archaeological Survey of India, New Delhi.

Harappan shapes, like the dish-on-stand and flanged pots continued, there were certain changes in their features, as noted in the case of Hulas. Amongst the painted designs, too, only the *pipal* and banana leaves seem to have survived; no seals or sealings, let alone weights. On the whole, it was a poor shadow of the Harappan culture. Also noted was an amalgam of the late Baran and some Cemetery H influence. Though some mud platforms were noted, these did not carry any special buildings but were only put up to prevent the settlement from being flooded. Sub-period IB was a continuation of IA. Here, a new pottery called Painted Grey Ware made its appearance, with the earlier also continuing, to begin with, but finally petering out. Although no radiocarbon dates are available, for this overlap phase, the overall scenario from other sites suggests that it may have taken place towards the close of the second millennium BCE. No iron was found in this phase.

In the Gujarat region, besides Lothal, Surkotada and Dholavira, there are five other sites which deserve mention: Desalpur, Bet Dwarka, Kuntasi, Rojdi and Rangpur. Located on the north-western edge of the Little Rann of Kachchh, the settlement at Desalpur, approximately 130 × 100 m in plan, was enclosed by a wall. Made of mud-bricks with a veneer of stones, it had a basal width of 4 m and is extant to a height of 2.5 m. Two sub-periods of occupation, IA and IB, have been identified. While both these had the typical Mature Harappan material, the latter also yielded white/grey-painted black-and-red ware, indicating an influx of people from the Banas Valley in Rajasthan. Such a feature has also been noted at other sites in Gujarat (see, for example, Surkotada). Amongst the small finds, particular mention may be made of an inscribed copper seal since copper seals are rare in Gujarat but do occur in Sindh, at Mohenjo-daro. This would tend to justify the intermediary location of Desalpur between Sindh and Gujarat.

Situated on the north-western tip of the Kathiawar peninsula, Bet Dwarka has yielded the remains of a Harappan settlement, including a seal of chank-shell bearing an enigmatic three-headed animal. A part of the site is now under water, indicating that the sea level has risen since Harappan days. It is quite likely that, like other coastal Harappan sites, Dwarka, too, may have functioned as a port.

In the Rajkot district of Gujarat, Kuntasi lies on the right bank of the Phulki River which discharges into the Rann of Kachchh.[42] Being close to the ancient shoreline, it is likely that it may have functioned as an estuarine port during high tide. Though only 2 ha in area, the site has a sizeable occupational deposit: nearly 7 m. Two periods, numbered I and II from the bottom upwards, have been identified and assigned, respectively, to *c*. 2200-1900 BCE and *c*. 1900-1700 BCE, on the basis of radiocarbon dates.

Period I yielded most of the typical Mature Harappan assemblage. However, it is the layout that calls for attention. While the settlement was provided

[42] Dhavalikar (1997), op. cit., pp. 34-6.

with an enclosure wall, the houses and streets inside were not laid out in the customary gridiron pattern. Instead, the houses were placed along the periphery with the result that an open space was left in the centre, which may have been used for special community functions. One of the houses was very large, suggesting that it may have been the residence of the 'chief'. Period II was marked by an overall decline—shoddy houses, degeneration in pottery and lessening of small finds. Further, there also occurred the black-and-red ware of the Banas Valley type, indicating the arrival of some people from that area, as was the case at Surkotada, referred to earlier.

Though covered by the same general umbrella of the Harappan civilization, Rojdi in the heart of the Saurashtra plateau has its own story to tell, whether in terms of the layout of the settlement, the subsistence pattern or even the pottery forms and painted designs.[43] Following the course of the Bhadar River, the site is all length but much less width, viz., 500 × 150 m. Further, though a 2-m thick peripheral wall had been built around the settlement, there was no criss-cross pattern of streets and houses inside. As for the subsistence pattern, the main, crops were *jowar* (*Sorghum bicolor*), *bajara* (*Pennisetum typhoideum*) and *ragi* (*Eleusine coracana* and *E. Indica*), and not wheat and barley as in the Indus and Sarasvati valleys. As regard the pottery, it has been observed by the excavators that 'not more than 28 of the 98 Mohenjo-daro vessel types and sub-types are found at Rojdi. Several of the most important Rojdi forms, the very common convex-sided bowl and some dish-types, seem to be absent from Mohenjo-daro'. Considering all these differences, G.L. Possehl has named this complex 'Sorath Harappan'.

While dealing with Lothal, we referred to a general decline that had set in by Phase V. The story of this decline-cum-change is further available at Rangpur, a site hardly 50 km away from Lothal.[44] Here, three occupational periods have been identified, named I to III. Period I belonged to a pre-pottery Microlithic age with which we are not concerned right now. Period II has been subdivided into three, A, B and C, from the bottom upwards. Period IIA yielded a good deal of Harappan pottery, although there were also certain local 'Gujarati' shapes like the stud-handled bowl. From this period came weights and the bricks, too, conformed to Harappan measurements. Yet the glory of the Mature stage was not there. This was further on the wane in Periods IIB and IIC. Thus, for example, in IIB, in spite of a 3.6-m thick deposit, no brick structures were encountered. Instead, the presence of post-holes indicated that the houses were of wattle-and-daub. Period IIC showed some improvement since here were found a few metallic objects and pottery with a lustrous slip. Some new painted designs such as the running antelope or the bull with curly horns also made their appearance, while the Harappan

[43] Possehl and Rawal (1989), op. cit.

[44] S.R. Rao (1962-3), 'Excavation at Rangpur and Other Explorations in Gujarat', *Ancient India*, 18-19, pp. 5-207.

ones took a back-seat. The cult of 'fire-altars' continued and so did the Harappan graffiti tradition. In Period III, Lustrous Ware became more dominant and so also black-and-red ware with white-painted designs. The use of mud-bricks was noticed as also graffiti. Even the typical Harappan cubical dice marked with 1-6 dots were present. However, in spite of all these, there was no return to Harappan urbanism.

Sources of Wealth

Agriculture

Wheat and barley were the main crops raised by the Harappans. Of the former, at least three varieties have been identified, viz., the club wheat (*Triticum compactum*), the Indian dwarf wheat (*Triticum sphaerococcum*) and *Triticum aestivum.* As regards barley, besides the six-rowed variety (*Hordeum vulgare*) which preponderated, *Hordeum sphaerococcum* and *Hordeum vulgare nudum* have also been noted. While these cereals constituted the backbone of the food-economy in the riverine plains of the north, in the south-west domain of the Harappan civilization, particularly in the Saurashtra region of Gujarat, millets seem to have been popular. At Rojdi, as many as six varieties have been discovered, including *ragi* (*Eleusine* sp.), *kodon* (*Paspalum scrobiculatum*), *sawa* (*Enchinochloa colonum*) and *jowar* (Sorghum). Lothal, too, has yielded millets, for example, *kangni* (*Setaria italica* Beauv). Evidence is emerging for rice, too. At Lothal and Rangpur, its husk and spikelets were found mixed with clay lumps. Hulas has yielded actual grains though the context is Late Harappan. The Harappans also grew sesame and mustard. However, the most noteworthy aspect is the cultivation of cotton of which no evidence is yet available from other contemporary civilizations. In fact, Mehrgarh takes cotton back to the fifth millennium BCE.

That the agricultural production of the Harappans catered to more than their day-to-day needs is clearly indicated by large granaries in the metropolitan cities, as in Mohenjo-daro and Harappa. While these granaries may have functioned as special reserves under the control of some central authority to be used on special occasions or in an emergency, even individual householders had their own arrangements for storage. Clearly, agriculture formed the backbone of the Harappan economy.

One may, in passing, mention a few other items which the Harappans added to their diet, such as field peas, melons, dates and bananas. There is also a good deal of evidence about non-vegetarian food which we shall turn our attention to a little later. Meanwhile, it may interest the reader to know that the Harappans grew grapes and hyacinth beans, and even raised esoteric plants like *hena* (*Lawsonia inermis*), whose leaves are pounded and used even today for colouring palms and nails, and jasmine (*Jasminum* sp.) and *parijata* (*Nyctanthes arbortristris*) whose flowers provide excellent fragrance.

Animal Husbandry

The contribution of animal husbandry is often underrated while computing economic wealth though it cannot be denied that there are many countries, even in the present industrial age, where animals constitute the primary source of wealth. The Harappans domesticated the humped bull (*Bos indicus* Linn.) as well as the humpless one. These seem to have been used variously for ploughing the field, and for transporting men and material by harnessing them in carts or maybe even independently. The cow was a good source of milk and a variety of milk-products, such as curds, buttermilk, cheese and clarified butter (*ghee*). While cattle wealth may have been the principal one, other animals contributed to it. Thus, sheep (*Ovis orientalis vignei* Blyth) and goats (*Capra hircus asgrus* Erxleben), too, must have yielded milk. More importantly, these were used as food. The former provided wool (*urna*) as well. The pig (*Sus scrofa cristatus* Wagner) also contributed towards food. Wild animals such as the spotted deer (*Axis axis* Erxleben), blackbuck (*Antelope cervicapra* Linn) and *sambhar* (*Cervus unicolor Kerr*) were also hunted for food. This is indicated by their cut and charred bones. Of the aquatic creatures, the fish and turtle were also consumed as food. Of the former, many varieties have been found in the occupational debris: the *rohu* (*Labeo rohita*), *shingari* (*Mystus aor, M. seenghala*), *khagga* (*Rita rita*), etc. Though not found in abundance, there is evidence for the camel as well as the elephant. While the former was useful in transportation, particularly in the desert areas, the latter may have had multipurpose uses: not only in transportation and in uprooting trees but also by providing the much-sought-after ivory—indeed, a costly item.

We may now take up the case of the horse (*Equus cahallus* Linn.). While its association with the Harappan civilization has long been a matter of debate (and there are) even now sceptics, evidence is mounting about its presence at Harappan settlements. Way back, in his excavations at Mohenjo-daro, Mackay found a terracotta figure of the horse. Recently, Jarrige and his colleagues reported horse figurines from Nausharo. Then there is the terracotta horse from Lothal. Besides representations in terracotta, the actual bones and/or other remains of this animal have been found at a number of sites, such as Lothal, Kalibangan and Surkotada. Writing on the evidence from the last-named site, the internationally renowned archaeo-zoologist from Budapest, Sandor Bokonyi, states: 'The occurrence of true horse (*Equus caballus* Linn.) was evidenced by the enamel pattern of the upper and lower cheek and teeth and by the size and form of incisors and phalanges (toe bones).' This animal must have been of immense use in speedy travel as well as in the transportation of goods.

Marine, Mineral and Forest Resources

Though essentially laid across land, the Harappan civilization also had the advantage of a fairly long coastline along its southern fringe—from Gujarat via Sindh to Baluchistan. Thus, seafood must have supplemented that from the inland rivers. However, the exploitation of chank shell (*Xancus pyrum* Linn.), of which there is ample evidence, must have helped the economy considerably. Inlays, bangles and other ornaments were made from it not only for home consumption but also for export. Above all, the availability of a long coastal stretch with appropriate sheltered bays helped a great deal in the safe pursuit of seaborne trade with the contemporary Western world, to which we shall refer in a while.

Mountainous regions within the Harappan domain were duly exploited for 'the procurement of necessary stones and minerals. It seems that the Sukkur-Rohri hills were the prime source for the supply of chert of which a variety of small tools, such as borers, blades and arrowheads, were made. Likewise, some varieties of semi-precious stones for bead-making, e.g. agate, carnelian, etc., were obtained from Gujarat. However, certain other semi-precious stones had to come from long distances. It is not unlikely that the Harappan settlement of Shortughai in far-off Afghanistan might have been motivated, amongst other things, by a desire to exploit the local *lapis lazuli* mines. Some of it might have also come from the Chagai hills in Baluchistan. Turquoise, too, had to be brought from a long distance. The source of copper seems to have been the Khetri-Ganeshwar mines in Rajasthan and lead might have been obtained from Ajmer in the same region. For gold, the Harappans might have had to look southwards to Kolar and other mines in Karnataka.

Forest resources were equally important to the Harappans. For firing billions of bricks, as at Mohenjo-daro, Harappa, Lothal and other sites, they needed plenty of wood. Supply in the immediate neighbourhood being insufficient, far-off forests had to be exploited. For certain specialized woods, the Harappans did not hesitate to venture into the Himalayan regions. Thus, for example, for the coffin lid discovered in one of the graves at Harappa, the wood concerned, deodar (*Cedrus deodara* Loudon), must have come from this region. In fact, this discovery points to an important aspect of transportation. While in the case of the metals and minerals discussed above, land transport would have done the job, to bring the deodar down to Harappa all the way from the Himalayan region, the Harappans must have used the same method as now: to float logs of the wood down the river and collect them at relevant places downstream.

Some Industries

While agriculture and other resources provided the real base for the economic well-being of the Harappans, certain industries, too, must have augmented it. These related to bead-making, shell-working, ivory-carving, metal-smithies, working in clay and so on. Thus, for example, Lothal and Chanhu-daro were centres for bead-making. Regarding Lothal, S.R. Rao states:

> A bead factory with a working platform in the open courtyard surrounded by eleven rooms has been laid bare in Block E near the acropolis. Two earthen jars, one

containing 582 carnelian beads and another containing 212 beads of carnelian, shell and steatite, were found embedded in the platform. Several cores, flakes, ground and unbored beads were scattered all over the courtyard and in the rooms around. To the north-east of this factory is a kiln used for baking the raw material and finished product[45]. . . a drill-bit of bronze used in boring stone beads was found near the factory.

Mention must be made of the technique of etching carnelian beads, which were a hot favourite even of foreign buyers. The intended designs were drawn on the surface of the beads with alkali and then these were heated so that the alkaline material entered the softened surface and settled there to produce a red-on-white effect. There are some examples where a tricolour effect was obtained. The reddish surface of the bead was completely covered with alkaline material to make it white, after which the black design was produced, most probably with copper nitrate. It is interesting to note that bead-making is a flourishing industry in this part of Gujarat even today. As regards evidence from Chanhu-daro, we have already given some details of the bead factory and furnace at the site.

The shell industry was no less noteworthy. From Gujarat to Baluchistan was a vast seashore and sites located on or close to it were evidently places for the collection of sea shells, in particular the chank (*sankha*; *Xancus pyrum* Linn.). Many of these sites like Lothal in Gujarat and Balakot in Sindh have yielded unfinished and finished specimens, attesting to the local manufacture of shell objects which included bracelets, rings, pendants, beads, inlays, and even bowls, knives and gamesmen. The finished objects were traded inland and even abroad. But there were certain inland sites like Chanhu-daro which chose to import the raw material and manufacture the objects locally.

Yet another specialized industry was that of ivory-working. Sites like Mohenjo-daro and Lothal have yielded a great deal of evidence from raw material to finished goods to establish the manufacture of ivory objects. These included hairpins, combs, mirror handles, antimony rods, ear ornaments, gamesmen, and even seals and scales. Rao adds: ‘A small tapering rod of ivory on which stains of red ochre are seen at the tip must have been used for decorating lips or nail-tips. A chemical examination of the pigment reveals that a paint has been applied.’[46]

The metal-smithy seems to have been a ubiquitous industry. While copper and bronze were the metals more prolifically used, there is evidence of working in gold, silver and even lead. Copper, being soft, was often alloyed with tin, arsenic, nickel or lead in order to obtain the desired hardness. The techniques used included sinking, ‘raising’, cold working, annealing, lapping, closed casting and even *cire perdu* involving the ‘lost wax’ process. The last-named technique seems to have been employed in the making of the famous ‘dancing girl’ found at Mohenjo-daro.

[45]Rao (1985), op. cit., p. 580.

[46]Ibid., p. 630.

The copper/bronze objects produced by the Harappans catered to a variety of needs. Thus, to help in agricultural operations, which included the cutting down of unwanted forest accretions, they made axes (plain or with shaft-holes), adze axes and sickles. Chisels, straight or curved saws, plainer-bits, drills and awls were used in carpentry. For fishing and hunting, there were a variety of fishhooks and (hollow-based) arrowheads. The latter, along with tanged spearheads, could also have been used in warfare but no shield, body armour or helmet has been found so far to establish any warlike activity of the Harappans. For household use nails, chains, needles and knives (with curved ends) were used. No less noteworthy is the fact that pots and pans were also manufactured in copper/bronze. These included *thalis* (dishes), *handis* (carinated cooking pots), handled frying pans and goblets for drinking water from. Then there were ladies' ornaments such as bangles, rings, ear studs and hairpins, with single- or double-spiral heads. Objects of toiletry included circular mirrors with handle, antimony rods, and small narrow-mouthed vessels for keeping collyrium, and even (curved) razors for men. Interesting is a three-in-one gadget, similar to the one in use even now, whose components are used, respectively, for removing unwanted hair from the inner side of the eyelids, floss from the teeth and wax from the ears.

Silver and gold were used primarily for making ornaments though a few silver vessels have also been found. Ornaments included a variety of beads, pendants, amulets, brooches, etc. Particular attention may be drawn to a hollow conical ornament which is worn even now by women in Rajasthan and Haryana on their head but below the *dupatta* (head-scarf). A few objects of lead have been found including of some vases and plumb-bobs.

The ceramic industry may not have produced extra wealth like that of bead-making or shell-working but it did have an important part to play in the daily life of the people. Thus, for cooking food, there were *handi*s usually with a flanged rim to hold the lid. Large but shallow bowls were used for keeping the cooked food before being served. Three-legged *patas* were used to roll the bread on before it was toasted. There were cups and beakers to drink water from. Large jars were used for the storage of grains. Often, these had a narrow bottom so that they could be fixed into the ground and, thus, rendered safe. In case the jars were not fixed they were supported by ring-stands. The typical S-shaped jar, which was often painted, may have been used for the storage of some special items. Then there were dishes- and cups-on-stand which, too, seem to have had a distinctive role. However, the use of large, cylindrical, perforated jars remains unexplained though many guesses have been made in this regard. Usually these vessels were made from fine, levigated clay, and were wheel-turned and well-fired. Often, there was a reddish slip over which designs were executed in black pigment. These included characteristic motifs such as the banana-leaf, pipal-leaf, peacock, fish-scales, intersecting circles, chessboard and so on. Human and animal motifs were few and far between. However, some specialized scenes call for attention. Thus, from Lothal, there are two pots on one of which is depicted the story of 'The Thirsty Crow' and on the other that of 'The Cunning Fox'.

Terracotta figurines were made of fine clay and well-fired. These comprised humans as well as animals. Of the human figurines, the male ones are rather simple but the female somewhat elaborate. The latter have a thin waist and broad hips with a loin-cloth and girdle. The mouth is usually slit, the nose pinched up and the eyes indicated by small round pallets. Often, these are bedecked with necklaces and other ornaments. On the head is a fan-shaped gear and projecting from the lower part is a pannier on each side. Special attention may, however, be drawn to some female figurines which are painted in three colours, viz., yellow, black and red.

Animal figurines included the bull, elephant, rhinoceros, pig, monkey, dog, etc. Two examples of the bull, one from Kalibangan and the other from Mohenjo-daro, are to be noted for their forceful, dashing portrayal. Some dogs wore collars, while a few examples of the monkey were so designed that they could move up and down a string. There are also examples of birds placed in a cage.

Trade and Commerce

While the exploitation of natural resources and the production of goods lay at the base of economic growth, in actual terms, it was trade that converted commodities into wealth. The Harappans were well evolved with respect to trade—both internal as well as external. Earlier, we referred to some of the centres where beads or shell and copper objects were manufactured, though there were surely many more. It was from these centres that the commodities concerned were traded out. This may have been done either through a network in which middlemen were involved or even directly through a trader hailing from the consumer end. We have yet to work out this mechanism in detail, and, more particularly, the routes followed by the traders. As far as external trade is concerned, we have a reasonably good picture of the sea route and, to some extent, of the land route as well.

Sea trade was essentially along the coast since, in those days, high sea navigation was unknown. Ships starting, say, from the Gulf of Khambhat, near which a dockyard has been identified at Lothal, moved along the Gujarat coast, calling at ports like Bet Dwarka. Thereafter, these entered the coastal regions of Sindh and Baluchistan where ports like Allahdino and Sutkagen-dor were available. Proceeding further west, the ships passed through the Gulf of Oman and entered the Persian Gulf. On the way, they may have called at Ras-al-Junayz, Tell Abraq or Umm an-Nar (see Fig. 11.6). In the Persian Gulf, the island of Bahrain was a very important trading station and must have been greatly patronized by Harappan sailors. It is here that an Indian team has found a steatite seal which presents a good synthesis of the Harappan and Persian Gulf styles. Unlike the Harappan seals which are

Fig. 11.6: Some sites with Harappan artefacts (outside the homeland)

usually square, it is circular, typical of the Persian Gulf but the inscription on it is in the characteristic Harappan script. Further, the animal at the bottom is meant to be either a bull or a unicorn, which is, again, Harappan. Of great significance is the depiction in the central part of the seal of a bird, which, in all likelihood, represents the peacock. This seal seems to have been made locally under the orders of a Harappan merchant who had settled there. However, since the local seal-cutter was unfamiliar with the peacock, which is not a West Asian bird, he could not do full justice to its depiction. In this context, it also needs to be added that Mesopotamian texts mention a bird called *haja* in the list of imports from Meluhha, which is generally taken to be the zone of the Harappan civilization and this bird has been taken to be none other than the peacock. At the northern end of the Persian Gulf lay the vast land of Mesopotamia with its two massive rivers. In their valleys were situated many sites which have yielded a variety of objects of Harappan origin, such as beads (particularly the etched carnelian ones), dice, terracotta figurines, objects of conch-shell, and ivory. The sites from where these objects have been recovered are Tell Agrab, Tell Asmar, Ashur, Tepe Gawra, Kish, Lagash, Nippur, Umma and Ur. The archaeological strata of these objects range from pre-Sargonic times through the Akkadian, Ur III, Isin-i-arsa up to even the Kassite, i.e. broadly from about the middle of the third to the middle of the second millennium BCE with a greater concentration in the earlier part. This is precisely the period of the Harappan civilization as we shall discuss later. In the context of the Harappan-Mesopotamian trade, it needs to be added that Sargon of Akkad mentions in his records that in the harbour of his capital were berthed boats from Dilmun, Magan and Meluhha, which have been identified, respectively, with the Failaka-Bahrain region, the Oman and southeast Arabian region, and, as already stated, the Harappan civilization zone.

The overland trade was with Iran, on the one hand, and with Central Asia, on the other. Some of the sites from where Harappan material has been discovered in Iran are Tepe Yahya, Shahdad, Hissar and Shah Tepe. In Central Asia are the fertile valleys of the Amu Darya and its tributaries. Here, civilizational remains contemporary with the Harappan have been found. A more interesting point is that in the basin of the Amu Darya and its left-hand tributary, Kokcha, lies a full-fledged Mature Harappan site, Shortughai. It has a 2.5-3-m thick occupational deposit and covers an area of about 2.5 ha. This site might have functioned as an intermediary trading depot between the Harappan mainland and Central Asia, besides being a seat for the procurement of *lapis lazuli* from the nearby mines. Of the more important Central Asian sites which traded with the Harappans, particular mention may be made of Altyn-Depe, Namazga and Khapuz. The Harappan material found at these sites includes the usual beads, elongated ivory dice, copper spearheads and handled frying pans, and even some pottery such as the perforated jar, cylindrical vases and ring-stands. Special attention, however, needs to be drawn to a stone seal bearing two signs in the Harappan script and a silver pendant depicting a three-headed animal, which is conceptually similar to that found on Harappan seals.

Trade, which was not mere barter, required at least four supporting tools, namely weights and measures to weigh and measure the goods sent out or brought in, seals to mark the packages and a script to keep a record of the transactions. Although there is evidence of some of these items having originated in Early Harappan times, it was only during Mature Harappan days that we find them in abundance. This is expected since it was during the latter period that internal trade recorded an upward rise and external trade also dominated the scene, as shown above.

Made usually of chert, but sometimes of jasper and agate as well, weights were cubical in shape. While the smallest unit was of 0.871 gram, evidently used for weighing precious items like gold, the highest recorded was 10,865 gram which might have been used for weighing grains and other heavy material. These weights followed an upward ratio of 1, 2, $\frac{8}{3}$, 4, 8, 16, 32, 64, 160, 200, 320, 640, 1,600, 3,200, 6,400, 8,000 and 12,800. S.R. Rao records another set (from Lothal) where the smallest unit weighed 1.2184 and the largest 33.3052. As regards the units of linear measurement, it is difficult to arrive at any final conclusion since, unfortunately, all the four scales (one each discovered at Mohenjo-daro, Harappa, Kalibangan and Lothal), are incomplete (broken) and, hence, the markings on them cannot be categorically assessed. The material used for making these scales varied between ivory, bronze, shell and even clay.

Art in Metal and Stone

When a society comes of age and is economically well-off, it naturally begins to think big: big houses, monumental buildings, jewellery and other items of luxury. The Mature Harappans were no exception to this. In earlier sections, we dealt in detail with their town and house planning, monumental buildings and jewellery, and now we take up a brief account of their *objet d'art* both in metal and stone. While dealing with the various techniques employed by the Harappans for preparing their metal objects, we referred earlier to the famous bronze figure of the 'dancing girl' from Mohenjo-daro, prepared through the *cire perdu* (lost wax) technique (Pl. VII). In a fanciful description of this figure in a poem titled *Sindhu Satakam* (A Narrative of the Indus Civilization in English Verse), the present author wrote:

On cosy bed, one wint'ry night,
I lay in Cashmere blankets wrapped.
And lo! The room turned white with light
As someone at the door had tapped.

'Come in', I said. In came a lass
with neckless dangling 'tween her breasts.
Had she transparent or no dress?
In slimness she had passed all tests.

Muttering with protruding lips
Some charms, she posed her bangled hands,
The left on knee, the right on hips,
And whisked me off to unknown lands

Such is the charm of this mere 11-cm tall woman that she has rightly been regarded as one of the masterpieces of Harappan art. The ankles and feet are missing from this figure but there is another specimen from Mohenjo-daro with, unfortunately, only these parts, wearing an anklet as if to validate her 'dancing girl' aspect.

Art in copper/bronze was not limited to human figures. It embraced the animal world, too. These included, besides the elephant, dog, swan, etc., two most lively and forceful representations of a short-horned humpless bull from Kalibangan and a buffalo from Mohenjo-daro.

Stone was another medium which the Harappans used to express their artistic sensitivity. Altogether about a dozen sculptures have been recovered variously from Mohenjo-daro, Harappa, Dholavira, etc. However, here we shall refer to only four of these. From Mohenjo-daro comes a well-known figure, often called the 'priest king' or simply 'priest' (Pl. IX). About 18 cm in height and comprising only the upper part of the body, it is carved out of limestone. The reasons why it has been thought to represent a priest seem to lie in the following: it has introvert eyes, suggesting a meditative pose; on its forehead it has a band with a circular piece which may have some religious significance since a similar piece in gold was found at Lothal in association with a 'fire-altar'; and it wears a shawl in a manner which is typical of *pujari*s (priests) in India even now. The shawl has to be noted for its trefoil pattern, and the face for the well-groomed beard and shaven upper lip. From Harappa come two figures, both less than 10 cm in height. One of these, made of red sandstone (?), represents a naked youth with a well-built yet sensuous body. It is incomplete but what is to be noted is that it has three sockets, one on each shoulder and one in the neck. It is, thus, clear that the arms were fixed in the former and the head in the latter. The other figure from Harappa is to be noted for the uniqueness of its posture: its body is somewhat twisted and one of the legs is thrown sideways, as if in a dancing pose. Some scholars have gone to the extent of suggesting that it was a precursor of the later-day Shiva Nataraja (Lord Shiva in a dancing pose). From recent excavations at Dholavira comes a stone statue which is highly abraded but seems to be that of a seated male, most probably with *urdhva linga* (the organ in an erect position), as shown in the famous *Pashupati* seal from Mohenjo-daro.

Animals, too, were portrayed in stone and here we shall refer to two specimens. From Mohenjo-daro comes a composite figure—a seated bull with a ram's horns and an elephant's trunk. It may be added that the concept of composite animals is common on seals (to be discussed next). The recent dig at Dholavira has brought to light a lifesize and very artistic representation of a mongoose.

Glyptic Art

It is the glyptic art of the Harappans that remains unmatched by any other contemporary civilization, be it Egypt or Mesopotamia. Made of steatite and usually about 2-3 cm^2 in shape, the seals bear engravings of a very high order. Indeed, one cannot but be overawed by the majesty of the humped bull with a muscular yet graceful body, powerful facial expression, tall incurved horns and swinging dewlap. The seals have an average thickness of about 50-60 mm and, on the reverse, there is a convex knob, evidently perforated for the insertion of a thread for suspension. Besides the bull already referred to, the seals bear the figures of other animals like the elephant, rhinoceros, buffalo, unicorn, etc. There are combinations, too. For example, in one case, the hind part is of a tiger, the front of a ram/unicorn, the horns of a bull, the tusk and trunk of an elephant, and a humanlike face. On the top of these depictions, there is usually an inscription in the typical Harappan script. At many sites, clay lumps with impressions of such seals have been found, indicating that these were used primarily for sealing packages. The sealings bear impressions of the packing material as well as of the thread used. A classic example of this is the discovery of sixty-five sealings from the warehouse at Lothal. Not all the seals may have had mere commercial motivation. There are some which, in all likelihood, had some kind of religious association like the one with the figure of Pashupati or another showing a deity in a pipal-enclosure with an animal ushered in for sacrifice and a series of seven figures in the register below.

Other Aspects of the Civilization

Disposal of the Dead

Cemeteries have been encountered at Harappa, Kalibangan, Rakhigarhi, Lothal, Surkotada and Dholavira. The general mode of disposal of the dead seems to have been by burial. The dead body was usually laid supine in a rectangular pit in an extended position, the head being to the north. The dead sometimes continued to wear ornaments such as necklaces, rings and bangles. Also, placed alongside the dead were objects of toiletry such as mirrors, and antimony rods and pots whose number could be as large as seventy. A belief in life after death seems to be indicated not only by these grave goods but also by the presence of fowl-bones, indicative of food provision, and even of a lamp to provide light in the dark journey ahead. The grave-pit was sometimes lined with bricks (cf. Fig. 11.7) and, in one case at Harappa, a mud-brick tumulus was also erected over the grave. In a few cases, the body was placed in a coffin and, in one example (at Harappa), while the body of the coffin was made of rosewood, the lid was of deodar (*Cedrus deodara*), which evidently had to be procured from the Himalayan region.

While interring a single human body in one grave seems to have been the normal practice, Lothal has brought to light three examples in which two bodies were placed side by side. It has been surmised that these may represent the practice of *sati* (the wife joining the husband in death). However, the pity is that anthropological experts do not agree with one another about the identification of the sex of these skeletons to establish that, in each case, one is a male and the other a female.

There is yet another kind of enigmatic burial practice encountered at Kalibangan. In this case, there is no skeleton in the grave: of the sixteen graves excavated, only one yielded a piece of bone and, that too, was fragmentary. Further, in plan, these graves are circular or ovoid instead of rectangular, as is usually the case. Yet since these lie well within the general cemetery complex, their funerary association cannot be denied. They had articles usually met with in rectangular ones, such as pottery, beads and copper rings. Amidst the pots, there was always a large one occupying a prominent position. It was thought that this might contain ashes/charred bones in case these were post-cremation burials. However, if the internment was only of ash, that could have got so much mixed up with the earth inside that its identification was not easy. These burials call for further investigation.

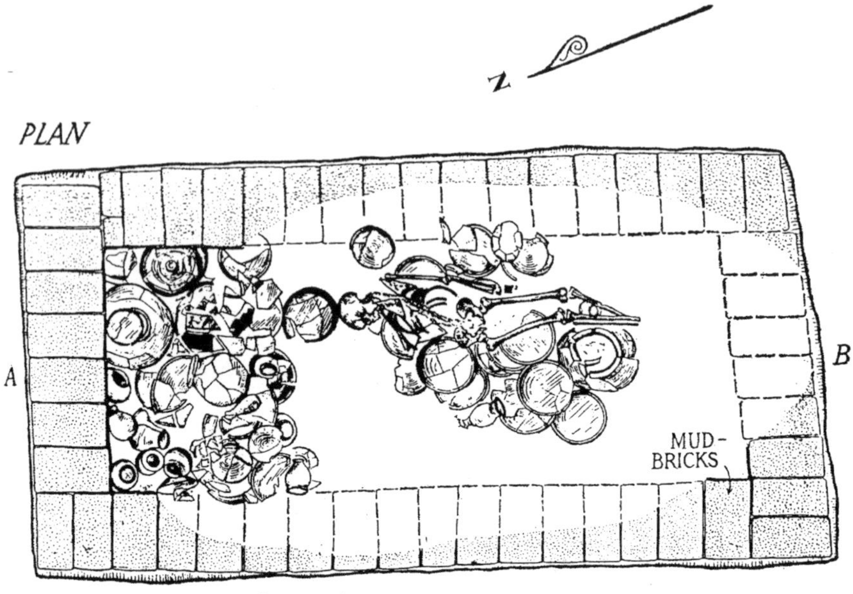

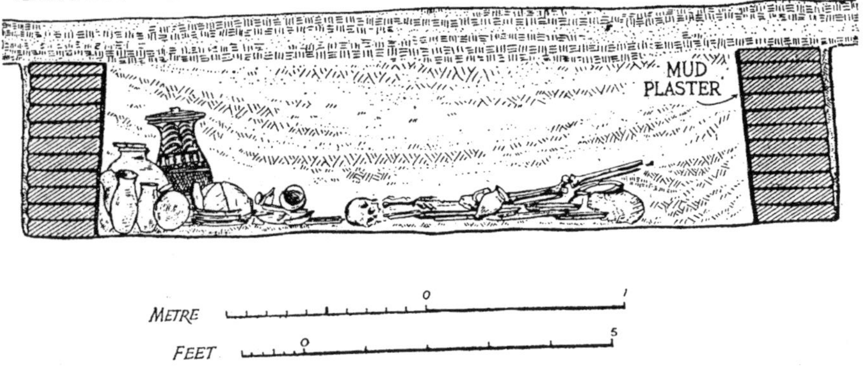

Fig. 11.7: Kalibangan, Grave 29

Alternatively, were these mere 'symbolic burials' for those who may have died elsewhere?

At Surkotada and, more particularly, at Dholavira, there is yet another feature which calls for attention. Though the graves contain the human body as usual, these are lined with stone slabs and often have a capstone and/or stone rubble at the top. If we look back at the Harappan or Kalibangan graves, we may recall that there, too, the pits were sometimes lined with mud-bricks and, at Harappa, there was also a mud-brick tumulus to mark the grave. As stone was available in plenty at both Surkotada and Dholavira, it may well be that the stone-slabs on the sides and the capstone-cum-rubble at the top merely represent a change from one material to another, readily available one and not any major conceptual departure.

Though meagre, the skeletal remains do throw some light on the composition of the Harappan population. It would appear that while the Caucasoids and Mediterraneans dominated the scene, there were also some Armenoids, Alpines, Australoids and Mongoloids. It is only to be expected that, in an area extending from Baluchistan to Uttar Pradesh and from Jammu & Kashmir to Maharashtra, the population would be a mixed one. As regards life expectancy, a study of ninety skeletons from Harappa revealed that while fifteen died before attaining the age of sixteen, thirty-five were in the age group of seventeen to thirty-four years, twenty-seven in thirty-five to fifty-five years, and thirteen lived beyond fifty-five.

Religion

Religion has two facets: one, metaphysical/philosophical and the other, practical/ritualistic. In the former, the seeker wants to know who he is, what is God and so on. In the latter, the person performs a variety of rituals through which he hopes to better for himself this world and the (already-taken-for-granted) next. Perhaps the Harappans, too, had a similar approach though not much can be said about this. Metaphysical/philosophical information can best be gleaned from books but, in the case of the Harappans, no such treatise is available and the little information that could have been gathered from the inscriptions on the seals remains blocked because of our inability to read them. Nevertheless, an indication about some kind of a practice, which we now call *yoga*, is given not only by the yogic *asanas* in which some of the terracotta figurines are depicted (Fig. 11.8) but also by the limestone statue of the 'priest' whose eyes are introverted and indicate a meditative pose (Pl.VIII). Some two thousand years later, the *asanas* as well as *dhyana* (meditation) were incorporated in the eightfold (*ashtanga*) path enunciated by Patanjali in his *Yogasutra.*

It appears that Shaivism in some form was prevalent during Harappan times. In this context, one may draw attention to the well-known seal from Mohenjo-daro which depicts a figure seated in a yogic posture on a dais (*chauki*), surrounded by animals. It has been held that the figure represents Shiva in his Pashupati (Lord of Animals) aspect. There are many other seals depicting this very form with minor variations. That Shaivism was really practised is now clearly established by the discovery at Kalibangan of a terracotta representation of a Shiva-*linga*-cum-*yoni* (Pl. IX). Some other deities are also likely to have been worshipped, as suggested by a seal which depicts, in the upper register, a female in a pipal enclosure and, in front of it, a kneeling devotee and a ram. There are seven other figures (worshippers?)

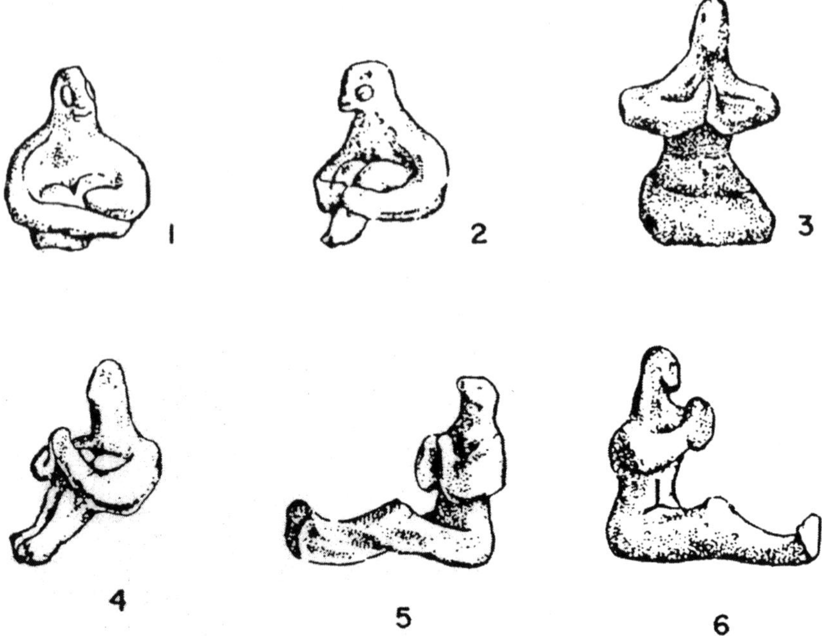

Fig. 11.8: Terracotta figurines in yogic *āsanas*: 1-4 from Harappa; 5 and 6 from Mohenjo-daro

in a row in the lower register. The cult of the Mother Goddess is attested to by a large number of terracotta figurines.

On the ritual side, at least two types are suggested by the available evidence. One relates to 'fire altars' and the other to animal sacrifice. In many of the houses in the lower town at Kalibangan, one of the rooms was reserved for rituals connected with what have been called 'fire altars' in the absence of a better name. These are, however, not to be confused with the fire altars of the Parsis. The Kalibangan altars were sunk to a depth of about 25 cm and not raised above the ground as those used by the Parsis. These were usually rectangular in plan and measure, on an average, about 1 × ½ m. The sides were plastered with mud. In the centre stood a cylindrical or faceted clay stele about 30-40 cm high and around it were placed circular-biconvex terracotta 'cakes', as if in offering. The presence of ash and charcoal testified to fire having been lit in these altars. In the citadel, the picture was somewhat different. As mentioned in earlier it was divided into two parts, a northern and a southern. While, in the former, there were residential houses, very likely those of the priests, in the latter stood individual platforms, each bearing a specific complex. Thus, on one of the platforms, there was a series of seven fire altars in a row, with the aforesaid features of stele, 'cake' and charcoal (Pl. II). In front, the lower half of a jar full of ashes and charcoal lay embedded in the ground. It is evident that fire was kept ready in it to be used in the altars. Behind the row of altars was a north-south wall, which suggests that anyone who used these altars had to face the east. Close to the altars on the north was a well along with a bath pavement. This indicates that anyone performing the ritual had to have a bath. Besides Kalibangan, Banawali, Rakhigarhi, Lothal and Rangpur have also yielded evidence of fire altars. Further, an apse-like enclosure wall going around the altar was noted at Banawali, which, might have constituted a part of some kind of an apsidal 'temple'.

Not far from the platform bearing fire altars at Kalibangan was yet another platform which carried a sacrificial pit. Lined with kiln-fired bricks, it measured 1.25 × 1 m. In it were found bovine bones and antlers, indicative of animal sacrifice. Evidence of animal sacrifice has also been obtained from Rakhigarhi and Lothal. The Lothal sacrificial pit measured 85 × 75 × 20 cm and in it were found 'charred fragments of the jaw-bones of an animal of the bovine group, a circular disk-shaped gold pendant, a carnelian bead, six sherds of a thick storage jar painted in chocolate over buff, and a large quantity of ash. . . .' There is also some very interesting though indirect evidence relating to animal sacrifice. On the two sides of a terracotta cake found at Kalibangan are engravings. On one, there is a man holding a rope which is tied to the neck of an animal. On the other is a deity which may be a proto-Shiva, as indicated by the headgear. Put together, the two sides show how an animal was brought in for sacrifice, in this context, reference must also be made to a plano-convex terracotta-tablet found recently in Harappa. It depicts, on the right, in a seated deity (in all likelihood, the proto-Shiva) and, on the left, a man and a buffalo. The man holds one of the horns of the animal with his left hand, pressing it with his right foot and piercing its back with a spear held in his right hand. Evidently the scene seeks to portray the sacrifice of the buffalo in front of the deity.

Social Stratification

Any question regarding the set-up of the Harappan society is not easy to answer. The short inscriptions that we have on seals and pottery might have borne surnames, caste names or the names of the profession of the persons concerned. Unfortunately, since the script remains undeciphered, we are helpless. Under the circumstances, all that we can do is look to other kinds of evidence which, however, can only be circumstantial in nature.

Going back to the layout of the settlement at Kalibangan, there were three major sectors, the lower town citadel (both of which were fortified) and an unfortified area to the south of the citadel. Further, in the lower town, there were fairly large houses with open courtyards for keeping cattle and facilities for the storage of grains. In many of the houses, seals and sealings were also found. All this would indicate that here lived a fairly well-to-do section of society, engaged in agriculture and trade activities. As opposed to this, the southern half of the citadel had ritualistic structures and in the northern half lived the priests who supervised/performed those rituals. In marked contrast to both the citadel and lower town was the area that lay to the south of the citadel. It was not fortified and the houses here were small. In one section lay a large amount of pottery and ashes, indicating that somewhere in the neighbourhood lived the potters. Though the excavation in this area was not extensive, it seems very likely that here lived the less-privileged working class. Indeed, a similar story is told by the workmen's quarters and working platforms located in the shadow of the citadel at Harappa. Recent excavations at Mound E at this site have brought to light another fortified area equivalent to the lower town at Kalibangan. This threefold division amongst the Harappan inhabitants is corroborated by evidence from Lothal and Dholavira as well. Further, the same class of people continued to live in their ancestral houses and usually followed the same profession. Such a situation is likely to have turned the profession-based class system into that of a caste system. If this be so, as seems to have been the case, the Harappan priestly class may have given rise to the Brahmans, the agricultural-cum-mercantile class to the Vaishyas and the underprivileged working class to what came to be known as the Shudras.

Political Set-up

Looking at the vast area covered by the Mature Harappan civilization, the efficient manner in which the metropolitan cities were maintained, the trade mechanism represented by a uniform system of weights and measures, the use of a single script all over the area and other factors, one is naturally curious to know what the administrative-cum-political set-up was in those days. The answer is not easy to get as, once again, we do not have any deciphered written documents to enlighten us on the subject. Thus, what follows is nothing more than an attempt at imaginative reconstruction. In the present state of our knowledge, any other exercise would be as good or bad as this one.

We may perhaps begin by posing a simple question: was there a Harappan empire, administering, from a single centre, the vast area from Sutkagen-dor on the west to Alamgirpur on the east and from Manda in the north to Daimabad in the south, or were there many 'States' located variously in this area? In searching for the answer, it may be worthwhile to have a look at the scenario that prevailed before the rise of the 'Mature' stage. During Early Harappan times, too, the area occupied was more or less the same, as indicated by far-flung sites such as Balakot, Amri and Kot Diji in Sindh, Gumla and Rehman Dheri in the north-west, Harappa in Punjab, Gamanwala in Cholistan, Kalibangan in Rajasthan, Banawali and Rakhigarhi in Haryana, and Padri, Lothal, etc., in Gujarat. The cultural level achieved by the Early Harappans was also of no mean order. As mentioned earlier, they, too, planned their houses and streets along the cardinal directions, laid a peripheral/fortification wall around some of their bigger settlements, standardized their bricks, inscribed their pots with signs (some of which may have given rise, at least morphologically, to the signs of the Harappan script), and engaged in long-distance trade as indicated by the presence of material such as turquoise, *lapis lazuli*, etc., at some of the sites. Amidst a cluster of smaller settlements, some of these. Early Harappan sites had also grown to a considerable size. For example, Gamanwala was as large as 27.3 ha. It would, thus, appear that even during Early Harappan times, some kind of hierarchy had begun to emerge. Thus, some of the sites may have 'dominated' others in the area around them. In other words, some kind of administrative set-up had already emerged during Early Harappan times. Perhaps these were chiefdoms or even 'Early States'. Thus, it is not unlikely that the same scenario with more sophistication and refinement may have persisted even during the Mature Harappan times.

It has often been argued that uniformity of material culture over such a vast area could not have been achieved unless it was enforced through the agency of an empire. Such a premise is basically faulty: 'empire' and 'cultural uniformity' are two different entities. For example, if we cast even a casual glance at a later-day situation, we find that around the middle of the first millennium BCE, there existed a more or less uniform material culture all over northern India—from Taxila in the north-west to Tamluk in the east and to the Narmada valley in the south. It was distinguished, amongst other items, by the well-known Northern Black Polished Ware, cylindrical weights of jasper/chert, and punched-marked and cast copper coins. At that point of time, there was no empire. Instead, there were several states, the *shodasa mahajanapadas*. Nothing prevents us from envisaging a similar situation during Harappan times.

One may also mention here why the theory of a Harappan 'empire' seems quite unsustainable. In the first place, an empire simultaneously envisages an emperor and, both in life and death, he must distinguish himself from the rest. In other words, there ought to be 'palaces' on the one hand and 'royal tombs' on the other. Unfortunately, we have neither. Attempts have been made to identify some of the structures at Mohenjo-daro as palaces but the case is far from satisfactory. And, certainly, there are no royal tombs. All the graves discovered so far, whether at Harappa, Kalibangan, Rakhigarhi or Lothal, are more or less of a modest order and none of them can lay claim to being that of an 'emperor'. Thus, the 'empire' theory will have to remain in a 'suspense account', at least for the time being.

Script and Language

Ever since the discovery of the Harappan civilization in 1921, many scholars have made attempts to decipher the script but, unfortunately, no one has succeeded so far. According to Asko Parpola,[47] Walter A. Fairservis[48] and I. Mahadevan,[49] the language was Dravidian. On the other hand, S.R. Rao,[50] M.V.N. Krishna Rao,[51] N. Jha[52] and others take it to be Sanskrit. In fact, a German scholar, Egbert Richter-Ushanas,[53] goes to the extent of reading actual Vedic verses in some of the inscriptions. Any successful decipherment should at least fulfil the following conditions: in the first place, there should be a sound reasoning for assigning a particular sound value to a given sign. Arbitrariness or 'intuition' is not the way. Second, once a particular sound has been assigned to a sign, it must be honoured all through the process of decipherment and not changed as per convenience. Finally, the resultant readings must follow the vocabulary and rules of the language arrived at, whether it is Dravidian, Sanskrit or some other language. It would not do to say that the Harappan language was 'some kind of proto-Dravidian or proto-Sanskrit, beyond the ken of any rules'. When put to these simple tests, all the attempts fail.[54] Hence, we are where we were in the 1920s, in this regard.

In the midst of such a dismal picture, some features of the script can, nevertheless, be stated. The direction of writing in this script (from the right to the left or the other way about) was long debated. A final end to the debate was offered by a couple of inscribed potsherds from Kalibangan where it was clear that successive signs on the right were overridden by those immediately on the left, thereby establishing that the one on the right was written before that on its left (Pl. X).[55] In other words, the direction of writing was from the right to the left. In case there was a second line in the inscription,

[47] A. Parpola (1969), *Decipherment of the Proto-Dravidian Inscriptions of the Indus Civilization*, Copenhagen.

[48] W.A. Fairservis (1992), *The Harappan Civilization and Its Writing*, Oxford and IBH, New Delhi.

[49] I. Mahadevan (1977), *The Indus Script: Text, Concordance and Tables*, Mem. Arch. Surv. of India, no. 77, Delhi.

[50] S.R. Rao (1982), *The Decipherment of the Indus Script*, Asia Publishing House, Bombay.

[51] M.V.N. Krishna Rao (1982), *Indus Script Deciphered*, Agam Kala Prakashan, Delhi.

[52] N. Jha (1996), *Vedic Glossary on Indus Seals*, Ganga Kaveri Publishing House, Varanasi.

[53] E. Richter-Ushanas (1992), *The Fifth Veda: The Indus Seals in Comparison with the Rigveda*, Germany.

[54] B.B. Lal (1970), 'Some Observations on the Harappan Script', in L. Chandra et al. (eds.), *India's Contribution to World Thought and Culture*, Madras, pp. 189-202; idem (1974), *Has the Indus Script been Deciphered?: An Assessment of Two Latest Claims*, Indian Institute of Advanced Study, Shimla; idem (1983), 'Reading the Indus Script', *Indian and Foreign Review*, 20, 13, pp. 33-6; Gregory L. Possehl (1996), *Indus Age: The Writing System*, Oxford and IBH, New Delhi.

[55] B.B. Lal (1996), 'The Direction of Writing in the Harappan Script', *Antiquity*, XL, 157, pp. 52-5.

the style was boustrophedon, i.e. the second line was from left to right. This was perhaps found expedient since the first sign in the second line had to be in immediate continuation of the last one in the first line.

As for the nature of the script, viz., whether it was logographic, syllabic or alphabetic, available evidence tends to suggest that it may most likely have been of the second category. In a logographic script like the Chinese, there is a sign for each word, thus letting the number of signs go up to tens of thousands. In a syllabic script, wherein a sign has a phonetic value and represents the combination of a couple of consonants along with a vowel, the number of signs drops down considerably. For example, the ancient Egyptian and Sumerian scripts, which were syllabic, had 100-50 signs. In an alphabetic language, each sign stands for a single sound, as in the case of the Devanagari or Roman script where the signs are, respectively, 48 and 26. In the case of the Harappan script, the total number of signs is still debated since some of them appear to be a combination of two or even more. Thus, estimates vary from 270 to 417. In all probability, therefore, the Harappan script may have been syllabic or syllabic-cum-logographic; in the latter case, some of the signs may have stood for words.

Inscriptions occur on a variety of objects: on seals, sealings, pottery, ivory objects, copper tablets and other metal objects like axes. While there are cases where only a single sign occurs, there are a few where the number goes as high as twenty-six. However, on an average, the number of signs in an inscription may be about four to six. As for the origin of the Harappan script, the view that it was derived from one of the West Asian scripts is hardly tenable. However, there is a greater possibility that it may have emerged on the Indian soil itself since many of the signs in the monumental Mature Harappan script have morphological parallels in the graffiti of Early Harappan pottery.[56] In cases where two or three signs occur in the Early context, it may well be that these had an inscriptional status. It is also clear that the script far outlived the Mature stage and there are examples of it even in a Megalithic context dating as late as the beginning of the first millennium BCE.[57] Once again, the script has kept all its secrets close to its chest.

Chronology

The first major account of the Harappan/Indus civilization is by John Marshall in his report on Mohenjo-daro. Here, went into its dating, which was done primarily on the basis of certain Harappan objects found at Mesopotamian sites. On this basis, he averred that the Indus civilization must go back to an

[56]B.B. Lal (1992), 'Antecedents of the Signs used in the Indus Script: A Discussion', in G.L Possehl (ed.), *South Asian Archaeology Studies,* Oxford and IBH, New Delhi, pp. 45-55.

[57]B.B. Lal (1960), 'From the Megalithic to the Harappan: Tracing Back the Graffiti on the Pottery', *Ancient India*, 16, pp. 4-24.

age before 2800 BCE. He, thus, proposed an overall bracket of 3250-2750 BCE for the Harappan civilization. However, there was a snag in Marshall's assessment. In the absence of any clear-cut evidence, he assumed that the Indus objects which found their way into Mesopotamia were from the 'Intermediary' levels. These could as well have been from the 'Early' levels. Reviewing the position, Mortimer Wheeler arrived at the following conclusion: 'It may now be postulated that the nuclear cities of the Indus civilization were founded some time before 2400 BC, and they endured in same shape to eighteenth century BC, always with the reservation that these brackets cannot be expected to fit closely and mechanically to Indus towns and villages of all sizes and in all location.'[58] Then came an era of 'shorter chronology' and its exponents suggested an overall data of 2300-2000 BCE. This phase was as short-lived as the proposition itself.

Finally came in the method of direct dating, namely that of radiocarbon. Though this method, too, has its pitfalls such as the contamination of samples with modern rootlets, successive changes in half-life value and revisions of 'calibrations' themselves, this method remains the best at present. An analysis of radiocarbon dates for Mature Harappan levels from as many as seventeen sites shows that the main span of the Harappan civilization ranged from *c*. 2600 BCE to *c*. 2000 BCE, with a possible though limited spillover on the latter side.[59]

MYTHS OF 'ARYAN INVASION' AND EXTINCTION' OF HARAPPAN CIVILIZATION

In the second half of the nineteenth century, a renowned German scholar, Max Müller, gave his estimate of the antiquity of the Vedas as 1200 BCE. He started with the Sutras, which he placed in the sixth-fifth century BCE, and assigned a duration of two hundred years to each of the literary periods, namely those of the Aranyakas, Brahmanas, and Vedas that preceded the Sutras. However, when some of his distinguished colleagues like Goldstucker, Whitney and Wilson questioned him and the criticism became unanswerable, he gave up his stand by admitting: 'If now we ask as to how we can fix the dates of these periods, it is quite clear that we cannot hope to fix a *terminum a qua* [*sic*]. Whether the Vedic hymns were composed [in] 1000 or 2000 or 3000 BC, no power on earth will ever determine.'[60] The unfortunate part, however, is that in spite of Müller's own confession of the inherent weakness of his thesis, many Western scholars and their devout followers on the

[58]R.E.M. Wheeler (1968), *The Indus Civilization*, Cambridge University Press, 3rd edn., p. 125.

[59]Lal (1997), op. cit., pp. 251-3.

[60]F. Max Müller (1890), *Physical Religion*, Asian Educational Service, New Delhi, rpt. 1979.

subcontinent still cling to the 1200-BCE datum line. It is against this background that we have to envision the formulation of the 'Aryan invasion' theory.

The 1920s saw the discovery of the Harappan civilization which, on the basis of its contacts with Mesopotamia, was dated by John Marshall to the third millennium BCE. However, since Müller's original writ about the Vedas being no earlier than 1200 BCE was still holding the field (despite his own withdrawal), Marshall had, perforce, to state that the Harappan civilization could not have been that of the Aryans. The only other ancient language spoken in the country was Dravidian and, hence, the conclusion that forced itself upon Marshall was that the Harappans were a Dravidian-speaking people. As a corollary, it was assumed that the Aryans invaded India around the middle of the second millennium BCE and destroyed the Harappan civilization.

Before proceeding further with the Aryan-invasion theory, let us examine whether the Harappan-Dravidian equation has any validity at all. It has been argued that when the Aryan nomads entered India and destroyed the Harappan civilization, the Harappan-Dravidians were pushed all the way down to south India and only a small fraction of the Dravidian population was left over in the north-west, which speaks the Brahui language. Not all scholars concur with the view that Brahui is a Dravidian language. Some even hold that it is akin to 'modern colloquial eastern Elamite'. There are still others according to whom the Brahui-speaking people moved to that area during the medieval times and, thus, have nothing to do with the Harappans.

In regard to the thesis that the Dravidian-speaking Harappans were driven all the way down to south India, one might ask whether there are any traces of the supposedly incoming Harappan civilization anywhere in south India, be it Tamil Nadu, Andhra Pradesh, Karnataka or Kerala. The only archaeological remains assignable to the third-second millennia BCE in this region are of the southern Neolithic culture which has nothing in common with the Harappan civilization. Are we then required to believe that the urban Harappans were completely transferred back to a Neolithic way of life by the invading Aryans and then sent down to south India?

There is yet another way of looking at the issue. If the Harappans were a Dravidian-speaking people, one expects that even after they left the area once occupied by them, there would still be some places, mountains and rivers which would continue to bear Dravidian names. This can be demonstrated by examples from many countries: in the United States of America, rivers like the Mississippi and Missouri or cities like Chicago and states like Massachusetts continue to bear the names given by the original inhabitants, the Red Indians, in spite of the fact that they have been ousted from the areas concerned by the invaders who speak European languages. Likewise, in Europe names of places, rivers, etc., in the older languages persist even though the new settlers speak a different language. From these analogies, it is expected that if the Harappans spoke the Dravidian language, at least some of the places, rivers and mountains would still bear their original names even if the Harappans themselves had been ousted. However, this is not the case. Within the entire area once occupied by the Harappans, there remains no such vestige!

There is yet another theory advanced by the protagonists of the Harappan-Dravidian equation. They hold that the invading Aryans borrowed from the Harappans the few Dravidian words that occur in the *Rigveda.* However, this is not the only way in which the borrowing can be explained. If, for argument's sake, it is assumed that the Harappans were a Sanskrit-speaking people, they could easily have borrowed Dravidian words from the south Indian Neolithic people with whom, as archaeological evidence suggests, they had some contacts. In all likelihood, it is the latter who spoke the Dravidian language which has continued ever since in that area. From this, it is abundantly clear that the Harappan-Dravidian equations stands on very slippery ground and is, therefore, untenable.

We may now turn our attention to the 'Aryan Invasion' theory. To Mortimer Wheeler must go the credit (?) of giving it the maximum boost. In 1946, he carried out excavations at Harappa and brought to light a massive fortification wall around one of the mounds called AB. While it was a welcome addition to our knowledge of the Harappan civilization, Wheeler's interpretation of it in historical terms was much more than warranted. Here is what he thought about it:

> The Aryan invasion of the Land of Seven Rivers, the Punjab and its environs, constantly assumes the form of an onslaught upon the walled cities of the aborigines. For these cities the term used in the *Rigveda* is *pur*, meaning a 'rampart', 'fort' or 'stronghold . . . Indra, the Aryan War-god, is *puramdara*, 'fort-destroyer'. He shatters 'ninety forts' for his Aryan protégé Divodasa. . . .
>
> Where are—or were—these citadels? It has in the past been supposed that they were mythical, or were 'merely places of refuge against attack, ramparts of hardened earth with palisades and a ditch'. The recent excavation at Harappa may be thought to have changed the picture. Here we have a slightly evolved civilization of essentially non-Aryan type, now known to have employed massive fortifications, and known also to have dominated the river-system of north-western India at a time not distant from the likely period of the earlier Aryan invasions of the region. What destroyed this firmly settled civilization? Climatic, economic, political deterioration may have weakened it, but its ultimate extinction is more likely to have been completed by deliberate and large-scale destruction. It may be no mere chance that at a late period of Mohenjo-daro men, women and children appear to have been massacred there. On circumstantial evidence, Indra stands accused.[61]

A scrutiny of Wheeler's thesis shows many flaws. To take up the first, the so-called 'massacre' at Mohenjo-daro: during nine years of excavation at this

[61] Wheeler (1947), *Ancient India*, no. 3, p. 82.

site, a total of thirty-seven skeletons were found, some compete and others fragmentary. All these came from the lower town (inhabited by the common folk) and not from the citadel where those who commanded the settlement dwelt. Does it not look strange that the (supposed) invaders deemed it necessary to attack and kill the commoners and carefully spare the 'rulers'? Second—and this is more important, should not the skeletons have come from the latest level of the site if it was an invasion and the site was destroyed on that account? Yet this was not the case. The skeletons belonged to different strata, some to the Intermediate and some to the Late. And, in fact, some are reported to have been found in deposits much later than the abandonment of the site. Third, it has been noted that a few skeletons bore cut-marks that had healed. Had death taken place as a result of a massacre, there would have been no time for the cuts to have healed. Finally, if it was an invasion, one expects the invaders to have left some vestiges at the site, by way of their arms or some other equipment. Nothing of the kind was found. In view of all these facts, George F. Dales rightly, though sarcastically, dubbed it as a 'mythical massacre'.[62]

If there is even the slightest truth in the Aryan invasion and destruction of the Harappan empire, one expects some of the other sites to corroborate the (misconstrued) Mohenjo-daro evidence. But the hard fact is that no other site has yielded any such evidence, be it Amri or Kot Diji, located not far from Mohenjo-daro, or Harappa itself in neighbouring Punjab, or Kalibangan in Rajasthan, or Banawali/Rakhigarhi in Haryana, or Lothal/Surkotada/Dholavira in Gujarat. Nor have any material remains of an alien culture been found at any of these sites. The so-called Jhukar Culture met with in the upper levels of Mohenjo-daro and Amri, has been demonstrated by Rafique Mughal to be nothing but a devolution of the Harappan civilization itself. Likewise, Richard Meadow and Mark Kenoyer have shown that the Cemetery H culture encountered in the upper levels at Harappa only represents a transition from the Harappa culture. The site of Kalibangan was abandoned due to the drying up of the nearby Sarasvati. Similar reasons were behind the desertion of Banawali and Rakhigarhi. Lothal, in Gujarat, shows a degeneration in the upper levels and the story is carried on to Rangpur where a transition to what is known as the Rangpur culture is clearly manifest. A similar kind of devolution took place in the upper levels of Dholavira. In the entire area covered by the Harappan civilization, nowhere are the vestiges of any wanton destruction or the presence of any alien culture. Thus, whether the protagonists of the 'Aryan Invasion' theory like it or not, 'Indra' no longer 'stands accused'. Indeed, he stands exonerated!

Commenting on Wheeler's theory, a distinguished archaeologist, Colin Renfrew, observed:

[62]Dales (1964), op. cit.

When Wheeler speaks of 'the Aryan invasion of the Land of Seven Rivers, the Punjab', he has no warranty at all, so far as I can see. If one checks the dozen references in the Rig Veda to the seven rivers, there is nothing in any of them that to me implies an invasion. . . . Despite Wheeler's comments, it is difficult to see what is particularly non-Aryan about the Indus valley.[63]

Jim G. Shaffer and Diane Lichtenstein (manuscript in press, copy sent to the present author in 1988) from across the Atlantic smell a rat in such allegations as the 'Aryan Invasion'.

A few scholars have proposed that there is nothing in the 'literature' firmly placing the Indo-Aryans outside of South Asia, and now archaeological record is confirming this. . . . As data accumulate to support cultural continuity in South Asian prehistoric and historic periods, a considerable restructuring of existing interpretive paradigms must take place. We reject most strongly the simplistic historical interpretations, which date back to the eighteenth century, that continue to be imposed on South Asian cultural history. These still prevailing interpretations are significantly diminished by European ethnocentrism, colonialism, racism and anti-semitism.

From this, it is clear that there is no basis for the 'Aryan Invasion' theory. Earlier, we also determined that there was little possibility for the Harappans having been a Dravidian-speaking people. All this leads us to another question: were the Vedic Aryans themselves the authors of this civilization? In answering this, we must first take into account the various objections raised against this equation. Broadly, these are: (i) the Vedic Aryans were nomads whereas the Harappans were highly advanced; (ii) the Vedas refer to the horse, whereas the Harappan civilization knows no horse; (iii) there is mention of the spoked wheel in the Vedas while the Harappan civilization is bereft of it; (iv) and finally, the Vedas, as per the computation of Muller, only go back to 1200 BCE, whereas the Harappan civilization belongs to the third millennium BCE.

The allegation that the Vedic Aryans were nomads is a sheer distortion of facts. The *Rigveda* refers to such terms as *samiti*, *sabha*, *samrat*, *rajan*, *rajaka*, etc. The first two terms clearly denote councils or assemblies which could not have been there amongst nomads shifting constantly from place to place. On the other hand, the next three terms show that in the Vedic set-up not only were there some rulers but there was a clear gradation amongst them. *RV* 6.27.8 refers to Abhyavarti Chayamana as a *samrat*, while *RV* 8.21.18 refers to Chitra as only *rajan*. In the latter verse, other kings are considered still inferior and the term used for them is *rajaka*. That these terms were not imaginary but really meant to denote the hierarchy amongst the rulers is evident from a clear-cut enunciation in the *Satapatha Brahmana* (V.1.1.12-13) which states: *avaram hi rajyam param samrajyam*, which not merely re-states that the two terms are separate but also emphasizes that the office

[63] C. Renfrew (1988), *Archaeology and Language*, Cambridge University Press, New York.

of the *rajan* is lower than that of the *samrat*. Could such fine distinctions have existed in nomadic society?

Not only were there many types of rulers but they were also militarily well-equipped. For example, the prayer in *RV* 10.101.8:

> *. . . varma si vyadhvam bahula prithuni.*
> *purah krinudhvamayasi rdhrista*

> . . . stitch ye [oh gods] the coats of armour, wide and many, make strong forts as of metal, safe from all assailants.

In fact, the devotee's prayer was that not only should there be a fort but it should also be very large so as to have a hundred arms, '*purbhava stabhujih*' (*RV* 7.15.14).

In matters of trade, too, the Rigvedic Aryans were evolved. Not only did they engage themselves in land trade but also that by sea. *RV* 9.33.6 says:

> *rayah samudranchaturo asmabhyam soma visvatah a pavasva sahasrinah*

> O Soma, from every side pour forth four seas filled with a thousandfold riches.

The boats used were very large, sometimes with as many as a hundred oars, as indicated by *RV* 1.116.5:

> *anarambhane tadvi rayethamanasthane agrabhane samudre*
> *yadasvina uhathurbhujyumastam sataritram navamatasthivansam*

> O Asvins, you have saved Bhujyu (from drowning) in deep sea where there was nothing to hold on, by lifting him up in a boat that had a hundred oars and by sending him to his place. This was indeed a brave act of yours.

From these examples relating to the system of governance, hierarchy of rulers, construction of forts and sea trade, it should be abundantly clear that the Rigvedic Aryans were no nomads but were enjoying a high degree of civilization.

Now to the absence of the horse from the Harappan civilization reporting on the terracotta figurines from Mohenjo-daro, Mackay categorically states: 'Perhaps the most interesting of the model animals is one that I personally take to represent a horse'.[64] This view was endorsed by Wheeler when he stated: 'One terracotta from a late level of Mohenjo-daro seems to represent a horse, reminding us that the jaw-bone of a horse is also recorded from the site, and that the horse was known at a considerably earlier period in northern Baluchistan.'[65] Unfortunately, despite such categorical statements by distinguished scholars associated with excavations at Harappan sites, the fate of the horse remained hung in balance.

However, fresh data recovered from many Harappan sites during the second half of the twentieth century has reaffirmed the presence of the horse in the

[64]Mackay (1938), op. cit., vol. I, p. 289; vol. II, Pl. LXXVIII, 11.
[65]Wheeler (1968), op. cit., p. 92.

Harappan context. For example, Lothal has yielded not only a terracotta figurine of the horse (P. VIB) but also a second upper molar of the animal. Commenting on the latter, Bhola Nath of the Zoological Survey of India and G.V. Sreenivas Rao of the Archaeological Survey stated: 'The tooth from Lothal resembles closely that of the modern horse and has pli-caballian (a minute fold near the base of the spur or protocone) which is a well distinguishable character of the cheek teeth of the horse.'[66] Kalibangan and Rupnagar (formerly known as Ropar) have also yielded remains of the horse. The material from the former site includes an upper molar, a fragment of the shaft of the distal end of the femur and the distal end of the left humerus.[67] Added to the foregoing is the considered view of Sandor Bokonyi, an internationally recognized authority on the horse, regarding the bones from Surkotada. After a thorough study of the material, he communicated this to the Director General of the Archaeological Survey: 'The occurrence of the true horse (*Equus caballus* L.) was evidenced by the enamel pattern of the upper and lower cheek and teeth and by the size and form of incisors and phalanges (toe bones). Since no wild horses lived in India in post-Pleistocene time, the domestic nature of the Surkotada horses is undoubtful. This is also supported by an intermaxilla fragment whose incisor tooth shows clear signs of crib biting, a bad habit only existing among domestic horses which 'are not extensively used for war'. Another very significant evidence comes from Nausharo in Pakistan where a few terracotta figurines of the horse have been found from the Harappan levels.[68] Thus, as I have stated elsewhere, 'the truant horse clears the hurdles',[69] though one would certainly welcome more evidence.

A for the wheel, based on the evidence of terracotta models of carts and, wheels, it has always been argued that the Harappans did not know the spoked wheel and only used the solid one.[70] This is far from the truth. Harappan levels at Kalibangan and Rakhigarhi have yielded terracotta wheels which clearly bear evidence of spokes. In these examples, radiating painted lines emerge from the hub which clearly represent the spokes (Pl. VIA). If these are not convincing one can look at the terracotta wheels from Banawali where the spokes are shown in low relief (Pl. VIA). This was the general technique adopted to show spokes even during the early historical times.

The Harappan-Aryan equation can be examined from another angle, that of time-space coordinates. The hydrological evidence produced by Raikes shows that Kalibangan was abandoned because of the drying up of the

[66] Cited in Rao (1985), op. cit., p. 641.

[67] A.K. Sharma (1993), 'The Harappan Horse was buried under the Dune of . . .', *Puratattva*, 23, pp. 30-4.

[68] Jarrige et al. (in press), op. cit.

[69] B.B. Lal (1998), *India 1947-1997: New Light on the Indus Civilization*, Aryan Books International, New Delhi.

[70] R.S. Sharma (1999), *Advent of the Aryans in India*, Manohar, New Delhi.

Sarasvati on whose bank it was located.[71] Radiocarbon dates indicate that this event took place around 2000 BCE. If we look at this data in the light of literary evidence, we get a very interesting insight. The *Rigveda* has several references to the Sarasvati, mentioning that it was a mighty flowing river (for example, *RV* 7.95.1 & 2; 6.612). On the other hand, it is learnt from the *Panchavimsa Brahmana* (XXV.10.16) that it had dried up by that time. It is, thus, clear that the *Rigveda* and *Panchavimsa Brahmana* are, respectively, anterior and posterior to the drying up of the Sarasvati. As seen earlier, the Sarasvati dried up around 2000 BCE, so it is abundantly clear that the *Rigveda* is earlier than that date but how many centuries is anybody's guess. To this evidence may be added the fact that the Rigvedic people occupied the entire area from the Indus on the west to the upper Ganga-Yamuna Doab on the east (*RV* 10.75.5 & 6). The most vital question now is: if the *Rigveda* is pre-2000 BCE and it covered the area just mentioned, with which archaeological remains can it be associated. It is clearly the Harappan civilization (Fig. 11.9).

Thus, not only are the various objections against an Harappan-Aryan equation giving way one by one but many new pieces of evidence are also emerging to support the equation.

Now to get back to Wheeler's other assertion, namely that the Harappan culture became 'extinct' because of the Aryan invasion. As noted earlier, there is no evidence whatsoever regarding any kind of invasion, much less by the Aryans. On the other hand, we noted that there was a transformation/devolution/degeneration of the urban Harappan civilization into various regional rural facets, such as the one called Jhukar in Sindh, Cemetery H in Punjab, Rangpur in Gujarat and so on. When the Sarasvati dried up in Rajasthan and Haryana, people shifted to the upper part of the Ganga-Yamuna Doab, to sites like Hulas and Alamgirpur.[72] The material obtained from these sites clearly shows that the Harappan civilization was no longer in its glorious form but had considerably 'degenerated'. The well-planned townships were relegated to the past, and so were the highly artistic sculptures and meticulously engraved seals. The pottery, too, underwent a change though there was enough in it to testify its continuity from the urban Harappan stage. Thus, for example, while the dish-on-stand confirmed, its dish-part developed a prominent drooping rim. The same was the case with the jars. Miniature pots began to appear in much larger numbers. Amongst the painted designs, many disappeared but some did continue like the peacock and the banana-leaf. Mention may also be made here of the occurrence of a terracotta sealing at

[71]Robert Raikes (1968), 'Kalibangan: Death from Natural Causes', *Antiquity*, XLII, pp. 286-91.

[72]K.N. Dikshit (1982), 'Hulas and the Late Harappan Complex in Western Uttar Pradesh', in G.L. Possehl (ed.), *Harappan Civilization: A Contemporary Perspective*, Oxford and IBH, New Delhi, pp. 339-51; Y.D. Sharma in *Indian Archaeology 1958-59: A Review*.

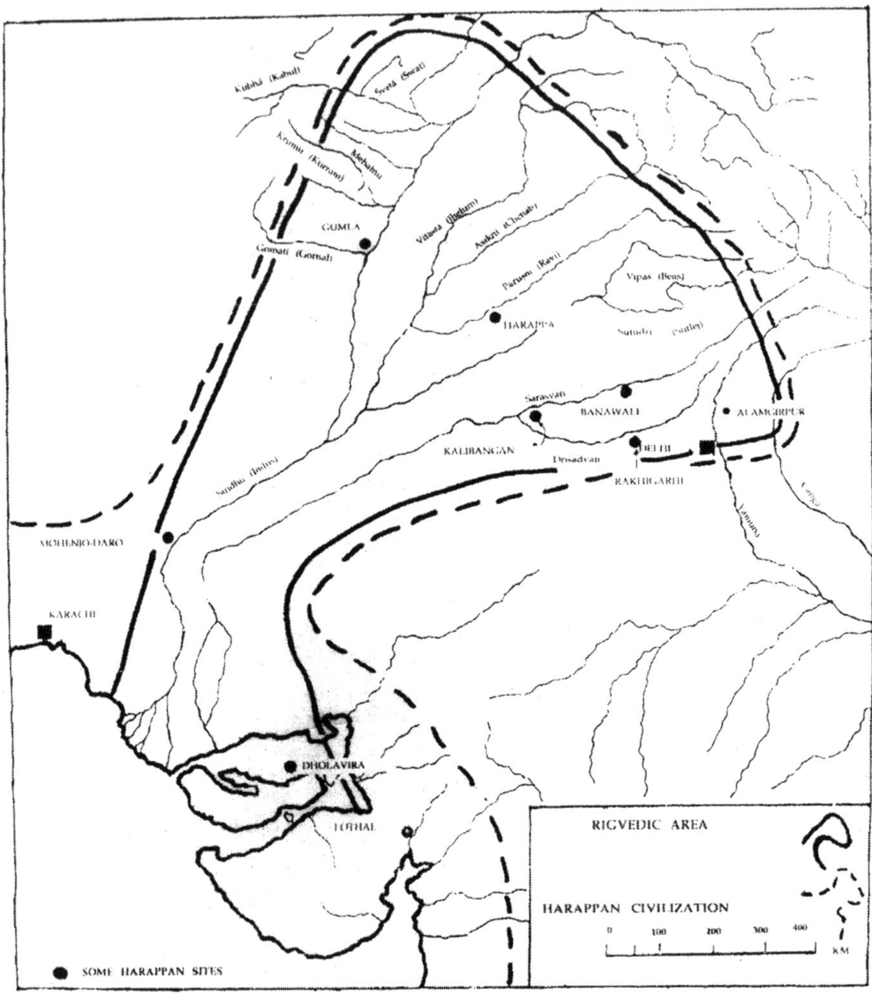

Fig. 11.9: Map showing a correlation between the Rigvedic area and the spread of the Harappan Civilization, before 2000 BCE

Hulas, and of an inscribed pot, some terracotta 'cakes' and even a cubical dice at Alamgirpur. Thus, the evidence from these two sites clearly points to a cultural continuity-cum-change. A still further devolved stage was noted at Bhagwanpura where the Harappan traits became very feeble. Finally, there was an overlap with the Painted Grey Ware culture some time in the second half of the second millennium BCE.[73]

The above-mentioned cultural continuity is also reflected in human continuity. After examining a series of human skeletons, Hemphill and his colleagues came to the following conclusion: 'As for the question of biological continuity within the Indus Valley, two discontinuities appear to exist. The

[73] Joshi (1993), op. cit.

first occurs between 6000 and 4500 BCE. . . . The second occurs after 800 BC and before 200 BC.'[74] It can, thus, be seen that, even population-wise, there was a continuity after the degeneration/transformation of the Mature phase of the Harappan civilization around 2000 BCE. Where, then, is a case for 'extinction'? All that happened was that because of various factors such as the drying up of the Sarasvati, a probable change in the climate, the wearing out of the landscape due to over-exploitation and a sharp fall in trade (internal as well as external), the flourishing urban civilization began to decline and moved back to a rural scenario. Thus, along with the highly organized town-planning, items like weights and measures, seals and sealings, the monumental script and fine artistic creations disappeared but, as will be demonstrated in the following pages, most of the other elements of the Harappan culture continued.

This continuity may be seen in almost every walk of life, be it house-construction, agriculture, cooking, transport, ornaments, toiletry, games, folk tales, social stratification or religion. This aspect has been dealt with in great detail in this author's *The Sarasvati Flows On* (in press). Hence, only the broad outlines are indicated here.

We may perhaps begin with house construction. To recall, an average Harappan house consisted of a courtyard on three sides of which there were the living rooms, while on the fourth was the entrance. Flanking the entrance on the exterior, there were small platforms used for sitting. In the courtyard, cattle were tied up and the bullock-cart was kept. Usually cooking was also done there. The material used for the construction of these houses was usually mud-bricks which were given a coating of mud. The roofs were flat and made by laying wooden beams, twigs and mud. It is interesting to note that the same kind of courtyard-centred plan and mud-brick houses were there throughout Rajasthan, Punjab, Haryana and western Uttar Pradesh up to the middle of the twentieth century when double-storeyed, courtyard-less, concrete houses began to proliferate. In fact, around that time, one could even see elderly people seated on small platforms (*chabutaras*) flanking the entrance, smoking the *hookah* (an Indian variety of pipe). Besides the general plan and the use of mud-bricks, there are a few other similarities which call for attention. It is difficult to believe the fact that the system of laying bricks in alternate courses of 'headers' and 'stretchers' (nowadays called the 'English Bond') goes back to Harappan times. The floors of the Harappan houses were paved with mud, mud-bricks, kiln-fired bricks or even decorated tiles. In certain cases, a unique technique was used: a soling of hard terracotta nodules intermixed with pieces of charcoal was provided over which the mud floor was laid. This was noticed for the first time at Kalibangan. The local public

[74]B.E. Hemphill et al. (1991), 'Biological Adaptations and Affinities of Bronze Age Harappans', in R.H. Meadow (ed.), *Harappa Excavations 1986-1990*, Prehistory Press, Madison, Wisconsin, p. 137.

works engineers informed the excavators that this is precisely what the local people do even now to ward off termites, and to prevent the sub-soil moisture from travelling up along the walls and damaging them. A continuity indeed!

While dealing with the Early Harappan settlement at Kalibangan we referred to an agricultural field (Pl. I). Its characteristic feature was the criss-cross pattern of the furrows. Precisely the same pattern is followed even now in north-western Rajasthan, Haryana and western Uttar Pradesh. Also, the plough used by the Harappans (as indicated by terracotta models) is similar to that used these days in northern India. At Harappa, circular brick-pavements with a central pit in which a wooden mortar was inserted for threshing grains were encountered. The same method of using mortar and pestles for pounding grains is used in rural areas even today, though the brick-pavement may not be there. Further, though many of the Harappan pot-forms have disappeared, there are many like the *handi*, *thali*, *lota* and handled frying pan which persist even now. Most surprising is the fact the *kamandalu* is as old as Harappan times. While cooking habits usually persist one is surprised to find that the *tandoor*, which is so popular in Punjab and Haryana these days, was encountered in the Early Harappan levels at Kalibangan. In modern times, a three-legged *pata* (also called *chakala*), made of wood or stone, is used all over northern India for rolling bread (*chapatti*). A similar *pata* in terracotta was discovered in Harappan levels at Alamgirpur.

Prior to the introduction of automobiles, bullock-carts were the major means of land transport in India. It is interesting to note that in shape, these are no different from their Harappan counterparts as reconstructed from terracotta models. However, the more exciting part is that even the gauge has not undergone any change. In 1946, ancient ruts were discovered during excavations at Harappa and it was noted that the distance between each pair was 1.08 m, which is precisely the gauge of carts even now in the region. The story is no different in the case of water transport. A seal from Mohenjo-daro depicts a boat with a central cabin, and a particular kind of disposition of prow and stern. Similar boats may still be seen ferrying on the Indus in that region.

It has been said that ladies are the bearers of tradition and culture. When we have a look at the ornaments and make-up of Indian women, we find that they owe a lot to Harappan times. In rural India, the ornaments worn by the womenfolk from head to foot are almost the same as the finds from Harappan sites. Rajasthani or Haryanavi women, more particularly the newly-married ones, may be seen wearing a conical ornament (called *chauk*) on their head (Pl. XIA) which is usually covered by a *dupatta* (scarf). Such ornaments have been found at Lothal, Harappa and other sites (Pl. XIB). In his report on Harappa, M.S. Vats writes: ‘By Hindus in northern India *chauks* are regarded among the essential ornaments which every man, rich or poor, has to give at the wedding of his daughter-in-law. This ornament is now worn chiefly on religious and important domestic ceremonies only.'[75] Who does not recall the beautiful bronze 'dancing girl' from Mohenjo-daro? She has to be noted not merely for her slim figure but also for the necklace dangling between her breasts and for her heavily bedecked arms (Pl. VIIA). The latter is a very specific style and it is interesting to note that womenfolk in Rajasthan and Haryana may be seen wearing a series of bangles on their arms even today (Pl. VII B). Likewise, the *karadhani* (girdle) and *payala* (anklet) worn during Harappan times are wore by women even now, though mostly in the rural areas and only rarely in cities. In the context of gold ornaments, it is interesting to note that the technique of testing the purity of gold these days, viz., by rubbing it against a touchstone, was also used by the Harappans. This is attested to by the discovery at Banawali of a touchstone bearing a series of golden streaks.

From ornaments, we pass on to make-up by women and objects of toiletry. In this context, attention ought to be drawn to certain terracotta female figurines from Nausharo (Pl. XII), dating back to *c.* 2800-2600 BCE, which are painted: the ornaments in yellow, indicating that these were made of gold; the hair on the head in black, to indicate that the lady is young and not grey-haired; and the partition-line in the middle of the hair in red. This last-named feature is very important. Readers must have observed that even now married Hindu women apply *sindura* to their *manga*. Indeed, how enduring a tradition can be!

The application of collyrium to the eyes also goes back to Harappan times, as indicated by terracotta figurines from Nausharo. However, the more interesting point is that even men did so. One need not be surprised at this since, as late as the middle of the twentieth century, menfolk applied collyrium to their eyes. Further, even the collyrium-stick used nowadays is similar to the Harappan. Of the various other toiletry gadgets used by the Harappans, there is one which calls for special attention. Made of copper, it comprised three objects put together by means of a small ring. A similar gadget is used even nowadays. Of these three, one is a small pointed rod and is used for cleaning spaces in between the teeth; the other rod, with a small cup at its end, is used for removing wax from the ears; and the third object is a tweezer, used for plucking small unwanted hair that sometimes grows on the inner side of the eyelids. The concept of three-in-one is indeed a remarkable continuity.

Continuity may be seen in games as well, whether played by children or adults. In villages, one sees children playing a game called *pittu* in which they strike a stack of pottery discs with a ball. This very game seems to have been played by the Harappans as indicated by the occurrence of pottery discs at almost all Harappan sites. At Rakhigarhi, a stack of about half-a-dozen discs was found *in situ*. Whether played by children or adults, the Harappans

[75] Vats (1940), op. cit., p. 442.

enjoyed a game in which cubes marked with 1, 2, 3, 4, 5 and 6 dots on respective sides were used. Exactly this kind of dice is used even now. No less interesting is the evidence regarding chess. Animal-headed gamesmen, similar to those used today in this game, have been found at various Harappan sites.[76] Of course, it would be too much to expect the wooden board to have survived the ravages of time and climate.

Many of the folk tales which grandmothers narrate to their grandchildren at bedtime seem to go back to Harappan times. Here, we present two of these, as reconstructed from the paintings on pottery from Lothal.[77] In one case, the scene depicts a deer who, having failed to drink water from a pitcher (because his head could not enter it on account of his long horns), walks away but then turns his head back only to find that a crow did the job by dropping a few pebbles into the pitcher, thereby raising the water level and quenching his thirst (Fig. 11.10). This is the story of 'The Thirsty Crow'. On

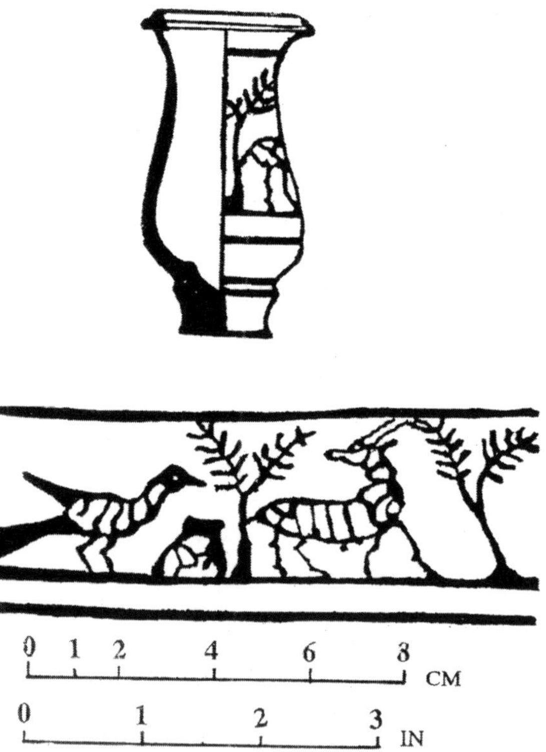

Fig. 11.10: Lothal: Painted vase, Period A

[76] Rao (1985), op. cit., Pl. CCXVIIB ff.
[77] Rao (1985), op. cit.

another pot is portrayed a scene in which two birds are seated on the branches of a tree, each holding a fish in the mouth. Down below, the painting is defaced, yet one may see a fox-like animal (as suggested by the tail) and a part of a fallen fish. If reconstructed, the story would appear to be that of 'The Cunning Fox' in which the fox, wanting to grab the food from the birds, praised them for being good singers. Puffed up by this, the birds started singing. The food fell from their mouth and the fox ran away with it.

We now pass on to an aspect of the Harappan civilization in regard to which no direct (i.e. written) evidence is available but which can safely be reconstructed from indirect evidence. As discussed in detail earlier, the Harappan society seems have had a threefold division, a priestly class, an agriculturist-cum-merchant class and an economically deprived 'lower class'. It has been surmised that these divisions, initially based on work and profession, may have fossilized, as centuries passed and professions became hereditary, into a caste-mould and may have given rise to the Brahmanas, Vaishyas and Shudras. When need arose, the Kshatriyas may also have come up to defend the community.

Regarding the Harappan religion we begin with the famous seal which depicts a deity in a seated yogic posture surrounded by animals. Marshall was of the view that the figure represents Lord Shiva in his Pashupati (Lord of Animals) aspect. This view is now generally accepted by scholars. In some of the seals, the association of snakes with this figure is shown. That Shaivism did exist during Harappan times is further confirmed by the discovery at Kalibangan of a *linga*-cum-*yoni* in terracotta (Pl. XI). From recent excavations at Harappa comes a sealing in which the Shiva-figure is seated and in front is a human being, perhaps a devotee, piercing a buffalo with a harpoon-like weapon, as if offering a sacrifice. That animal sacrifice was performed by the Harappans is amply clear from evidence from Kalibangan, Lothal and Rakhigarhi. At these places, sacrificial pits, sometimes even brick-lined, have been brought to light. These contained bovine bones and antlers.

That the Harappans performed certain rituals in which fire played an important role has already been discussed in detail. 'Fire altars' have been discovered at a host of sites—Kalibangan, Banawali, Rakhigarhi, Lothal and so on. The ritual was performed in individual houses as well as congregationally in public places. From time immemorial, Hindus have been known to perform *havanas* with which fire altars are associated. They also hold certain symbols as sacred and the *svastika* is one of these. Businessmen paint it on their safe-vaults while, in most houses, it is painted on Diwali alongside the worship altar on which the images of Lakshmi and Ganesha are placed. It is interesting that this symbol goes back to Harappan times.

One does not know if the Hindu way of greeting, the *namaste*, can be categorized as a part of religion or just seen as a social feature (Pl. XIIIA). The word itself, however, is loaded with meaning. It consists of two parts, *namah* plus *te*, meaning 'obeisance to you'. Harappan terracottas shown in this posture (Pl. XIII B) clearly establish that this kind of greeting goes back to the third millennium BCE.

Another religious feature, viz., the practice of yogic *asanas* and *dhyana*, goes back to the Harappan days. Many terracotta figurines depict yogic postures (Fig. 11.8) and there is the limestone 'priest' from Mohenjo-daro (Pl. VIII) which is in *dhyana-mudra* (meditative pose). Between the Harappan times and the present stands the *Yogasutra* of Patanjali which deals thoroughly with this matter.

From what has been stated in the preceding pages, it must have become amply clear that the theories of the 'Aryan invasion of India' and of the 'Extinction of the Harappa culture' are completely ill-founded. The sooner these are buried the better it would be for a proper understanding of the history of this country.

Plate I: Kalibangan: Criss-cross furrows of an early Harappan agricultural field

Plate II: Kalibangan, fire altars

Plate III: Kalibangan, a street in lower town

Plate IV: Lothal, dockyard

Plate V: Dholavira, terrace in front of northern gateway

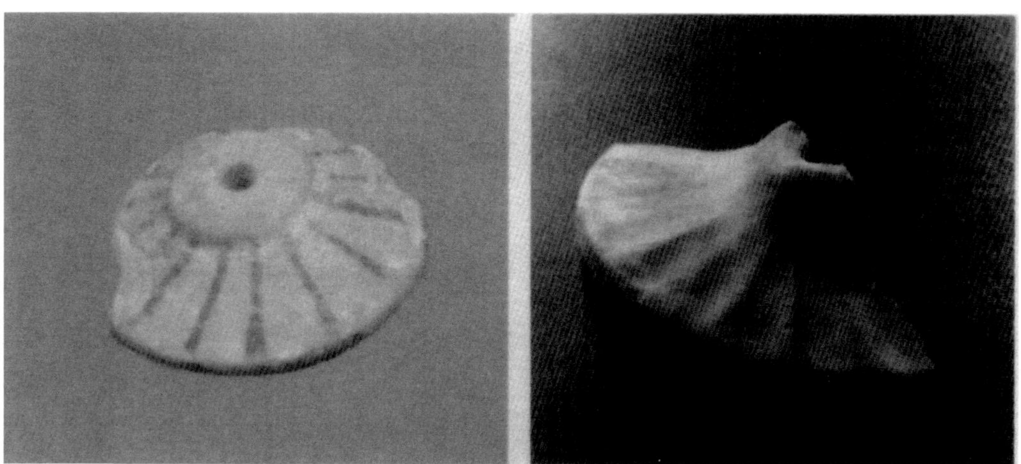

Plate VIA: Terracotta wheels from Kalibangan (left) and Banawali (right) showing spokes respectively in painting and low relief. Mature Harappan

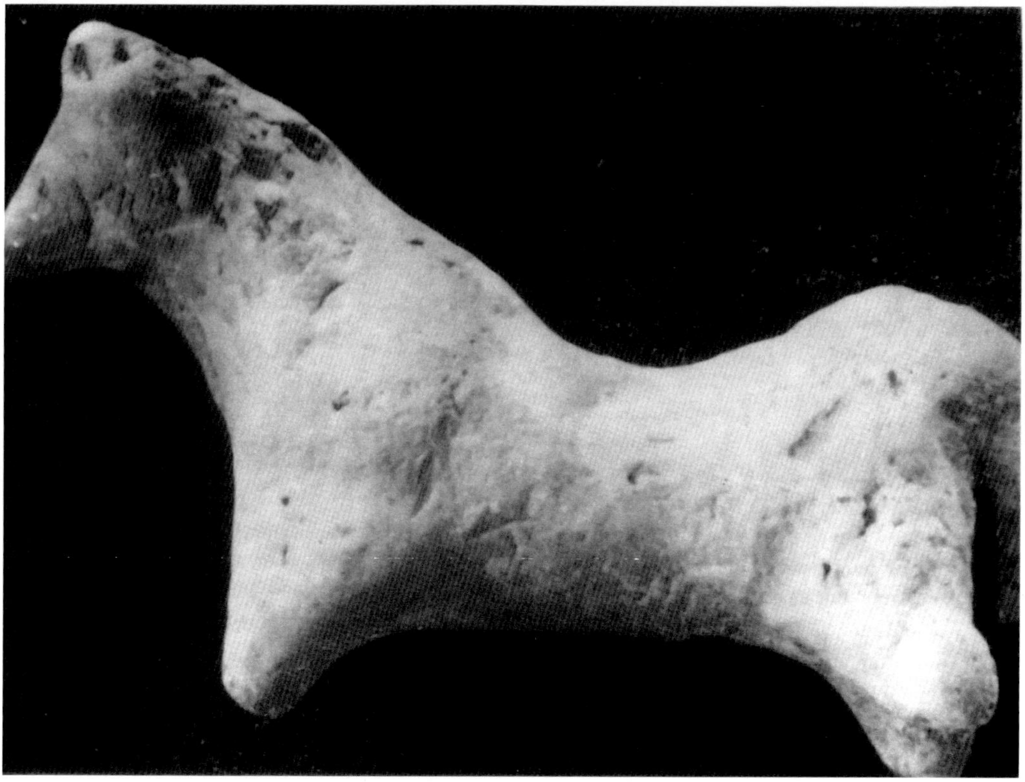

Plate VIB: Lothal: Terracotta horse. Mature Harappan

Plate VIIA: Mohenjo-daro: The famous bronze figure of 'dancing girl', wearing spiralled bangles on the upper left arm. Mature Harappan

Plate VIIB: A woman wearing spiralled bangles

Plate VIII: Mohenjo-daro, priest

Plate IXA: Modern Shivalinga

Plate IXB: Kalibangan, *linga*-cum-*yoni*

Plate X: Kalibangan, inscribed potsherd

Plate XIA. A newly-married lady, on the right, wearing a conical ornament on the head (covered by the *dupattā*). She also wears bangles all over her arms.

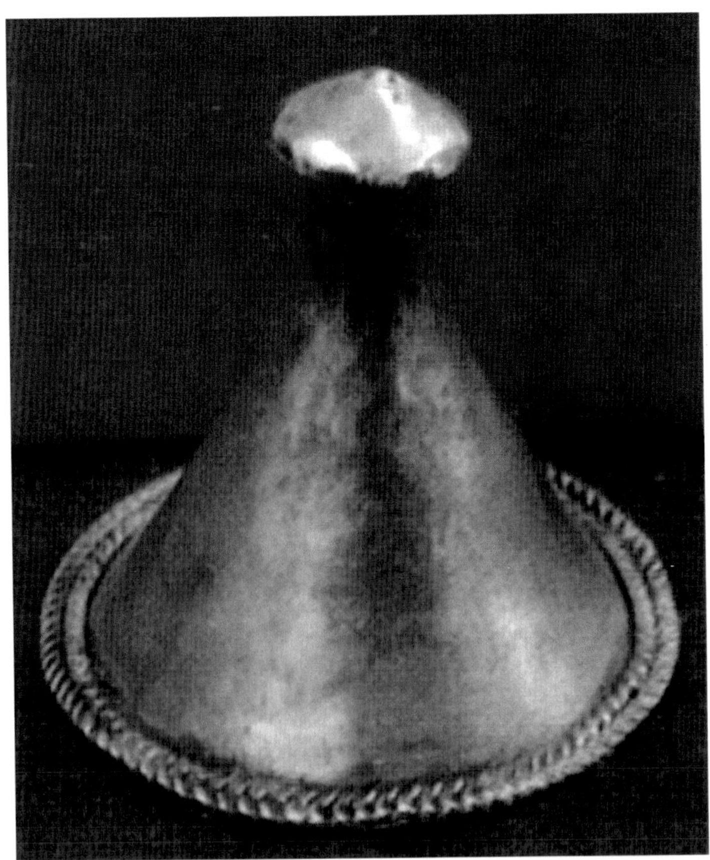

Plate XIB: Mohenjo-daro: Gold cone. Mature Harappan

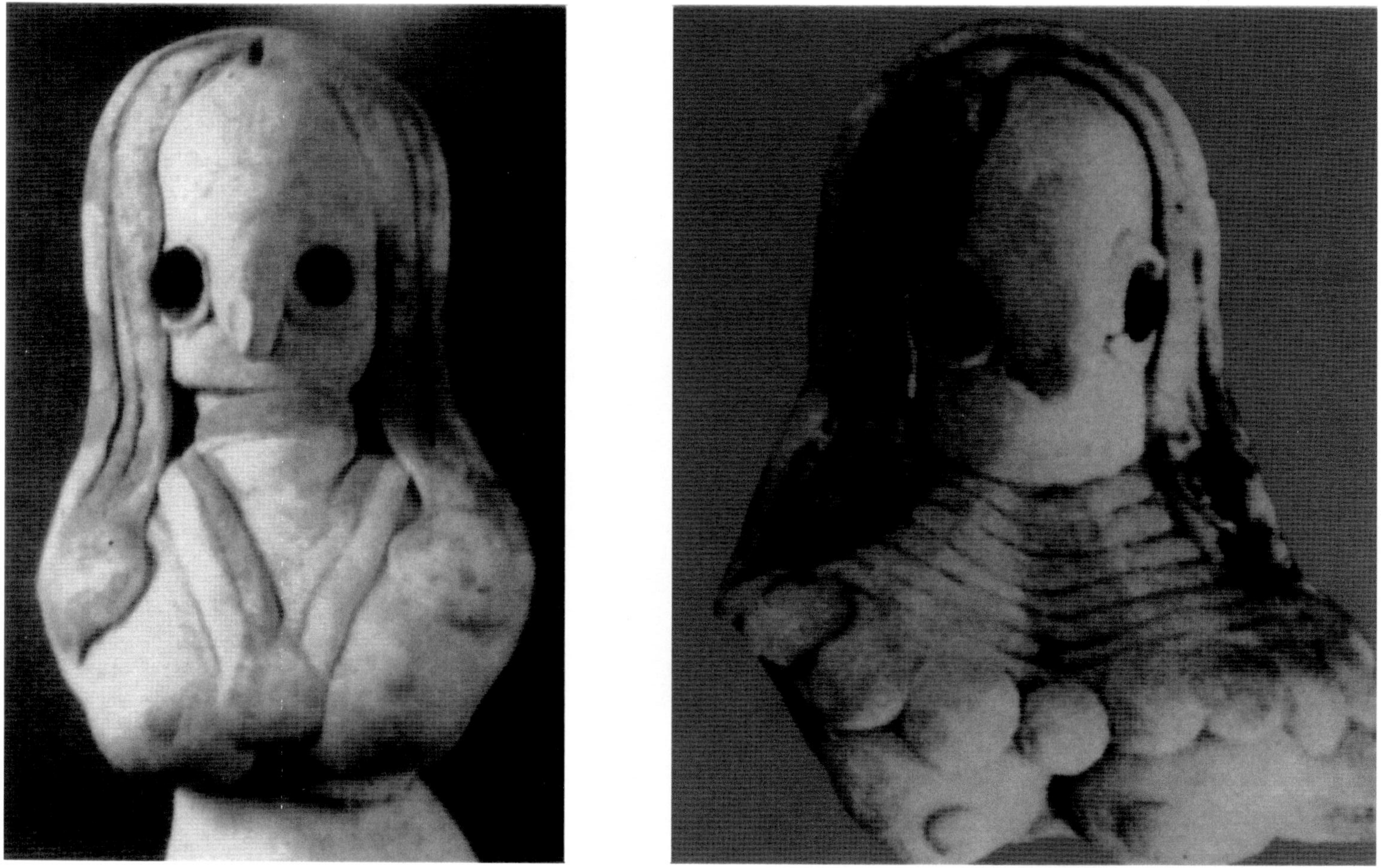

Plate XII A&B: Nausharo: Terracotta female figure, painted. The yellow colour on ornaments suggests that these were made of gold; the hair is black, while the red on the line of partition of the hair indicates the use of vermilion. Period IB, 2800-2600 BCE

Plate XIIIA: The President of India, Shri K.R. Narayanan (extreme left) being greeted with *namaste* by the Prime Minister, Shri Atal Behari Vajpayee (extreme right), and other dignitaries on the eve of the President's departure on a foreign tour.

Plate XIIIB: Harappan: A terracotta figurine greeting with *namaste*. Mature Harappan

Chapter 12

Bronze Age Civilization

Suraj Bhan and R.C. Thakran

INTRODUCTION

Nine decades after the first discovery of the remains of the Harappan civilization in the early 1920s,[1] we know its geographical limits, the trajectory of its expansion, the various stages of its evolution and devolution, the characteristics of the respective stages, the changes that occurred during them, the goods that were produced and exchanged internally as well as externally, along with their resource zones and production centres, the broad outline of the main subsistence activities and crops, the main features of the rural and urban settlements, the practices that were observed to dispose of dead persons, and so on and so forth. It pushed back the frontiers of our cultural antecedents by over a millennium and further intensified the debate on historical enquiry. Nevertheless, we are still grappling with the problematic aspects of the structure of state and society, the modes of production and distribution, the media of exchange and trade, and their alleged decline or fusion into regional entities, among others.

SUBDIVISIONS OF CIVILIZATION

The formative phase of the Harappa civilization covers a staggering time period in a phased manner, as one moves from west to east, it precedes the next stage (mature Harappa), and envelops a number of regional cultures such as Kulli[2] and Nal[3] in Baluchistan, Amri[4] and Kot Diji[5] in Sind,

[1] M.S. Vats (1940), *Excavations at Harappa*, vol. I, New Delhi.

[2] Stuart Piggot (1946), 'The Chronology of Prehistoric Northwest India', *AI*, I, ASI, New Delhi, rpt. 1983, p. 11; A. Stein, 'An Archaeological Tour in Waziristan and Northern Baluchistan', *MASI*, 43, Calcutta, 1931.

[3] H. Hargreaves (1954-5), 'Excavations in Baluchistan, 1925', in *MASI*, 35, Calcutta; D.H. Gordon, 'The Pottery Industries of the Indo-Iranian Border: A Re-Statement and Chronology', *AI*, 10-11, ASI, pp. 157-70.

[4] M.G. Majumdar (1934), 'Explorations in Sind', *MASI*, 48, ASI, New Delhi, pp. 24 ff; J.M. Casal (1964), *Excavations at Amri* (French edition); idem (1979), 'Amri: An Introduction to the History of the Indus', in D.P. Agrawal and D.K. Chakrabarti (eds.), *Essays in Indian Protohistory*, Delhi, pp. 99-112.

[5] F.A. Khan (1965), 'Excavations at Kot Diji', in *PA*, 2, pp. 13-85.

Ravi[6] and Hakra[7] in northern and southern Punjab (west), respectively, Kalibanga[8] and Sothi[9] in north-western Rajasthan, and Siswal-A[10] in Haryana. The material remains from these cultures do have strong regional variations but they are invariably the products of simple technological expertise and low economic development, primarily designed to sustain themselves. Their house-building activities are strictly limited to small wattle and daub, usually round, houses, though they knew the use of mud-bricks in the ratio of 1:2:3. Ceramics constitute the hub of artisanal activities and the use of the potter's slow wheel was a welcome addition to the tradition of hand-made pottery.

Better firing and surface treatment of the ceramic wares for these being applied with red wash or slip, and their decoration with thick black bands, wavy lines, strokes, slashes, mainly confined to the upper part, over red or white surface speak of the advancement attained during this phase. Besides, incised linear and wavy decorations on the inner as well as outer surface, and shapes such as vases, jars, bowls, cups, *handis*, dish-on-stand are all in tune with this process of general progression. The use of black, white and red colours turns this tradition into a polychrome ware, which becomes the hallmark of this industry along with the Kalibangan pottery types from A to F.[11] We lack any precise evidence of writing during this period, though graffiti marks of varied types do occur on ceramic ware, especially as post-firing engravings, which perhaps form a precursor to the Harappan script. The use of some exotic raw materials and the articles made of them is well-documented, which suggests the knowledge of and liking for such objects. Obviously, these objects were produced at certain places and transported to consumers at different settlements through some obscure mode of exchange. Significantly,

[6] Jonathan Mark Kenoyer (2008), 'Regional Cultures of the Greater Indus Valley: The Ravi and Kot Diji Phase', in *Cultural Relations Between the Indus and the Iranian Plateau During the Third Millennium* BCE, Indus Project, Research Institute for Humanity and Nature, Kyoto, Japan, 7-8 June 2008, pp. 46-51.

[7] M.R. Mughal (1980), 'New Archaeological Evidence from Bahawalpur', *ME*, IV, New Delhi, pp. 93-8; idem (1982), 'Recent Archaeological Researches in Cholistan', in G.L. Possehl (ed.), *Harappan Civilization*, New Delhi, pp. 85-96; idem (1990), 'Archaeological Field Research Since Independence', *Sindhological Studies*, Summer-Winter, pp. 31-8.

[8] *IAR*, 1960-69; B.B. Lal et al. (2003), 'Excavations at Kalibanga: The Early Harappa (1960-69)', *MASI*, ASI, New Delhi.

[9] A. Ghosh (1952), 'The Rajputana Desert: Its Archaeological Aspect', *Bulletin of the National Institute of Science of India*, I, pp. 37-42; K.N. Dikshit (1984), 'The Sothi Complex: Old Records and Fresh Observations', in B.B. Lal and S.P. Gupta (eds.), *Frontiers of Indus Civilizations*, Books and Books, New Delhi, pp. 531-7.

[10] Suraj Bhan (1971-72), 'Siswal: A Pre-Harappan Site in Drishadwati Valley', *Puratattva*, 5, pp. 44-6; idem (1975), *Excavations at Mitathal (1968) and other Explorations in the Sutlej-Yamuna Divide*, Kurukshetra University, Kurukshetra.

[11] Lal (2003), op. cit.

Gujarat[12] and the trans-Yamuna[13] zones remained outside the orbit of their movements during this phase. In both these regions, the process of the gradual shift of premature practices from the areas situated to their west and later, the graduation of these traditions to the mature stage are missing. Instead, what they demonstrate is only the arrival of the mature traditions in a phased manner and their diverse forms.

The next stage of development is the mature phase when features of town planning, defence, burnt brick (in the ratio of 1:2:4), houses, the art of writing, greater agricultural as well as artisanal production, standard weights and measures, internal and external trade, administrative and service personnel, advanced tool-technology and living conditions form an integral part. The area of influence, integrative power and the capacity to negotiate with natural as well as social agencies outstripped that of the preceding phase. The impact of this advancement is tangibly visible in its geographical expanse in one form or the other, which bring into focus the presence of some obscure agency/agencies to regulate/coordinate these activities. However, it becomes difficult for the power structure that be to sustain it in the course of time as has been suggested by the major deviations from the established norms in the uppermost levels of the mature phase.

The deviations are seen surfacing in the upper levels of the mature Harappan phase, which is christened the 'late mature Harappan phase' in archaeological discourse. They signal the creeping in of cracks in the system and, thereby, the increasing absence of diagnostic features of the mature phase in successive levels. The features of this phase include the weakening of law-enforcing agencies, work culture and respect for civic norms among people. This resulted in encroachments on public space[14] (streets, roads, etc.), on the one hand, and a non-performing attitude of personnel engaged in services like sanitation[15] (as suggested by the heaps of domestic waste in the streets and scattered human skeletons,[16] on the other. Further, demographic pressure[17] led to the apportioning of living space and the reuse of building material from previous houses for constructing hutments with single brick walls, a reduction in the production and consumption of luxury goods (especially of distant origin),

[12]V.H. Sonawane (1998-99), 'Harappan Civilization in Gujarat: A Recent Perspective', *Pragdhara*, 9, Uttar Pradesh State Archaeology Department, Lucknow, pp. 1-14; Kiran Dimri (1998-99), 'Assessing the Distribution of Harappan Culture in North-Eastern Saurastra: A Preliminary Report', *Praghdara*, 9, pp. 27-44; Abhijit Majumdar (1998-99), 'Early Harappan Settlements in Gujarat', *Pragdhara*, 9, Lucknow, pp. 15-25.

[13]*IAR*, 1958-9, pp. 50-1; K.N. Dikshit (1993), 'Hulas and the Late Harappan Complex in Western Uttar Pradesh', in Gregory L. Possehl (ed.), *Harappan Civilization*, 2nd rev. edn., Oxford and IBH Publishing Co., New Delhi, pp. 399-412.

[14]John Marshall (1931), *Mohenjodaro and the Indus Civilization*, London.

[15]Ibid.

[16]Ibid.

[17]Ibid.

standard weights, steatite seals and sealings, the weakening of long-distance trade, a decline in technical expertise,[18] so on and so forth. This is also discernible in the ceramic industry. These are bracketed between the mature and late Harappan phases.

The late Harappan phase succeeds the late mature Harappan levels in the undisturbed mature Harappan settlements and covers the major part of the second millennium BC. It embodies the continuation of some of the mature Harappan traditions, though in a substantially diluted form, as well as the introduction of new features. As a result of the changes, the practices of this phase are surely inferior to and disparate from those of the mature Harappan phase. During this phase, major shifts in the size, structure and hierarchy of settlements, the movement of people from the urban to the rural hinterland, the mode of artisanal and agricultural production, the swing from quality to mediocrity, the subsistence strategies and practices, the refined to utilitarian taste, the movement and exchange of goods, the level of interaction and social discourse, the rise of fissiparous tendencies and the resurgence of regional identities, the emergence of new cultural strands, etc., constitute the cultural order. These phases, especially the three main ones, have received a good deal of attention and yet deserve a relook.

TERMINOLOGICAL ISSUES

With regard to the multiple terminologies being used for each phase of the civilization, what we observe is a close connection between the various facets and the diverse nomenclatures being given to them by scholars. This would be abundantly clear if we note that cultural remains were named either after the place of their occurrence (Amri, Kot Diji, Sothi, Harappa, Siswal, Mitathal, Bara, etc.), the region (Sorath) or the river valleys (the Indus, the Ravi, the Hakra, the Saraswati, etc.), which call for a fresh look in sequential order.

When the civilizational remains came to light for the first time from the typesite of Harappa, nothing was known about their name, authors, geographical extent and so on. It was but natural to name them after the place where they had been discovered. Consequently, these became popular as the 'Harappa civilization'.

Later, as more remains were uncovered from Mohenjo-daro in 1922, 600 km further south in the Sind province. Both the sites of Harappa and Mohenjo-daro being urban settlements, produced a remarkable similarity in terms of their cultural remains and both situated along the Ravi and the Indus rivers respectively. The Ravi being a tributary of the Indus not only the geographical extent was thus extended by several hundred kilometres along the Indus but also the importance of the river valley was brought into sharp focus so far

[18] Shereen F. Ratnagar (1981), *Encounters: The Westerly Trade of the Harappa Civilization*, Delhi; idem (2000); *The End of The Great Harappan Tradition*, Manohar, Delhi.

as development of the civilization was concerned and consequently these remains were given a new name of 'the Indus civilization' after the river like the civilizations of the world (Egypt, Mesopotamia and China). This brings into sharp focus the relative importance of the natural properties of areas along perennial water courses and that of the areas situated away from them with respect to civilization. The constant supply of river water was considered a unique feature for its location and human existence, which, in a way, implied the inability of human beings to survive in its absence. This understanding was a product of the modern urban cultural background where water supply from rivers is very crucial in urban centres. Rivers, being powerful natural phenomena, were given supernatural status, generating a sense of awe and respect for them among the people and leading to their worship.

It is, however, a fact that water courses were not ubiquitous nor was their water accessible everywhere. Yet human presence is marked, though in varied frequency, over the entire Harappan geographical expanse. It is also a fact that these water courses were present there even before the emergence of the Harappan urban phase. The areas contiguous to the water courses, first did not find favour with the early settlers and, second, when these areas experienced human activities in a dispersed and restricted manner in the early stages, the pace of development was neither accelerated automatically nor instantly for their only being in the riverine environs, rather the pace of development took a winding route (in a phased manner) spanning over several hundred years and could attain the status of urbanization only through sustained human efforts. It was not that water courses did not offer the right opportunities to grow in the early stages of human presence but what was missing was the right working capacity to harness the opportunities offered by them and to accelerate the pace of development. This working capacity was not available in a ready form. Rather, it was to be acquired only through concerted efforts dispersed over time and space, and channellized in the proper direction with the right approach. Obviously, all this was bound to fructify over a period. Nothing was natural and spontaneous. Rather, it was the result of human labour.

The underlying premise of this terminological argument: that river water remained a pre-condition for urban centres in particular and the rural hinterland in general, was not supported by ethno-archaeological evidence. Harappan urban centres such as Rakhigarhi and Farmana in the Hisar and Rohtak districts of Haryana, respectively, and Dholavira in Kachchh (Gujarat) among others, are located in areas away from the rivers. Besides, the civilization did not only consist of urban settlements. It contained a very strong rural base as well, which was integral to it. Urbanization has not always been integral to the civilization.[19] Further, it is observed that the settlements were

[19]It is not always essential to have an urban centre as a precondition to attain the level of being civilized. The Egyptian civilization, one of the ancient civilizations, is an example to this effect where no substantial evidence of urbanization existed. Likewise, knowledge of writing is also not a precondition for being civilized; this is highlighted in the case of the Mayan civilization. Thus, there is a strong need to relook.

not located in a linear fashion along the rivers nor was water accessible to the vast majority of the dispersed settlements over the vast geographical expanse for drinking, let alone for agriculture. These settlements were located along or near local natural water bodies of varied denominations that appear to have formed the main lifeline. One wonders if the rivers were ever harnessed by the people on any substantial scale in the absence of effective technology and social organization.[20]

One may, however, still argue that urban centres such as Mohenjo-daro and Harappa, among others, harboured a sizeable population that needed an assured supply of water, which was not always obtained from the small natural water bodies. This assumption is a product of our modern cultural understanding and when societies of the remote past are viewed in terms of such standards, it leads to a serious mismatch between the degree of demand and supply of water in context of the past societies. In pre-modern urban centres, the life of the people was not comparable to that of modern cities in terms of water consumption levels. Primarily because of this factor, we fail to visualize a successful urban life without a regular supply of water from a perennial river. What was necessary for past centres was the availability of potable water for necessary daily chores. This might have been partly met by surface water available in local water bodies,[21] especially in areas away from riverine zones, and partly by harnessing the limited potable ground water generated by these bodies through percolation over a period by sinking wells, a technique that the Harappan were well-versed with.[22]

[20] Technology and social organization are two factors among others which define social working capacity to harness natural resources to social advantage. We lack evidence from excavated Harappan settlements for visualizing any substantial working capacity for regulating the rivers.

[21] All urban centres are not/were not located only along water courses, perennial or otherwise, as several are in areas where there is no evidence on the surface or sub-surface of any river. Nor is the quality of ground water potable. On the contrary, these are located along either local or regional depressions which received and contained rain water.

[22] Modern village ponds have generated a limited quantity of potable ground water through the process of the constant leaching of fresh water in the subsoil from them. In order to harness this transformed soil water, villagers make their wells along the margins of these ponds. There is a strong possibility that local as well as regional depressions might have transformed the ground water in some measure in the past as well. This water might have been tapped by the people by sinking wells (both *kachcha* and *pukka*). People were aware of the technique of making such wells during the Harappan period. R.C. Thakran (2003), 'The Myth of Saraswati Civilization: A Locational Analysis of Harappan Sites', in Kesavan Veluthat and P.P. Sudhakaran (eds.), *Advances in History*, Calicut, pp. 22-43; idem (2006-7), 'Recent Archaeological Explorations Along the Ghaggar in Rajasthan', *PIHC*, Delhi, pp. 992-1000; idem (2006), 'Was The River Water a Precondition for Human Existence?: Perspectives from Recent Explorations in Rajasthan', paper presented at The International Conference of the Association of South Asian Archaeology, held at Bombay University, Mumbai, 15-17 December.

With the progress of research, more and more settlements were discovered from different parts beyond the Indus system. In the light of new settlement data and expanding geographical frontiers, the nomenclature 'Indus civilization' became growingly untenable. Keeping in view the regional distribution of these settlements, a section of scholars claimed that the majority of the known settlements was located in the areas of a water course known as the Ghaggar in the Indian part and the Hakra in the contiguous Pakistani part, a seasonal river originating from the Siwaliks and traversing the southern parts of the Indian Punjab, the northern and western parts of Haryana, the north-western parts of Rajasthan and finally, the south-western parts of the Pakistani Punjab and the Bahawalpur area, in a north-east to south-west orientation. It is equated with the ancient Sarasvati. On the basis of this perception, another term 'Indus-Sarasvati' was assigned to these cultural remains.

The main argument in support of this term is that the majority of settlements are situated in areas along this water course and the river is referred to as the 'river *par-excellence*' in the *Rigveda*. The present-day Sarasvati river in Haryana is, however, a small stream, which travels for a short distance in the Kurukshetra district and then joins the Ghaggar. This certainly cannot match the grandeur of the Rigvedic river and, therefore, the present Ghaggar, the only other river of substance, is equated with the ancient Sarasvati of the *Rigveda*. Keeping in view the importance being attached to this river, it is deduced that the river was mighty as well as perennial during the Harappan period. The underlying premise is that the presence of such a river was very essential for the existence of such a high number of settlements in this region. To authenticate the high position of the river, it is further argued that it was fed by the Yamuna and the Sutlej to lead an independent course to the Arabian Sea through the western parts of Rajasthan.[23]

The argument of the greater concentration of the Harappan settlements in and around the riverine zones is, however, not borne out by actual location of the known Harappan settlements in this area. On the contrary, the majority of these sites are situated in areas away from the rivers where there is no tangible evidence of the river both on the surface as well in the sub-surface of the landscape.[24] In these areas, river water was not accessible in any form and nor was/is the ground water potable on a large scale by any standard.[25]

[23] S.P. Gupta (1999), 'The Indus-Saraswati Civilization Beginnings and Developments', in G.C. Pande (ed.), *The Dawn of Indian Civilization* (*up to c. 600 BC*), Centre for Studies in Civilizations, New Delhi, pp. 269-75; B.B. Lal (2002), *The Saraswati Flows On*, Aryan Books International, New Delhi; idem (1996), *The Indus-Saraswati Civilization*, Pratibha Prakashan, Delhi, 1996.

[24] R.C. Thakran (1998), 'Protohistoric Settlement Patterns in Haryana', in K.M. Shrimali, (ed.), *Reason and Archaeology*, Manohar, New Delhi, 1998, pp. 29-62; idem (2003), op. cit.

[25] In this belt, the nature of ground water in general is saline from top to bottom as most of its areas are devoid of any river and the sparse canal system is a recent phenomenon.

The rains were as erratic as in the recent times: they vary diurnally, weekly, fortnightly, monthly, seasonally and yearly from place to place during and after the monsoon season. The scarcity of water is not an isolated case concerning the ancient settlements along, as safe drinking water is not available even today to the inhabitants of most of the modern villages in these areas.[26] So much so the term does not represent the entire geographical expanse of the civilization.[27] Thus, in the light of the data, this river-centric terminology not only appears out of sync but also fails to appreciate the gigantic input of human labour in the development of this civilization. The interplay of the two integral variables (the natural and the social) in constant operation is controlled and guided by human agencies, and, in the process, human initiative and labour become the prime movers to chart out the course, pace and shape of prospective historical development.

A new nomenclature, 'Bronze Age Civilization', was proposed, which involves two very crucial ingredients: one, tools of copper and bronze (products of social labour) were being used for the first time; two, their application in productive activities and the resultant impact on production and consumption patterns is distinctly reflected during this period. The use of this term involves the role of human labour and tool-technology in determining the process of social production and, thereby, development.

We do not apprehend any major problem in the application of this term to the civilization except for one limiting factor regarding the civilizational process, which appears to have spanned, in terms of the time span, over the geographical landscape as one moves from the west to the east. We do not have anyone particular time span for one phase of the development over the entire region. The time period for a particular cultural phase appears to have been staggered over its expanse zone with the shift in activity loci from the west to the east despite cultural markers being constant in great measure. What we witness is that the early phase and its time period overlap with the mature phase and its time span as the former advanced from the areas west of the Indus to the east in an east-oriented movement, except for the region of Gujarat and the upper Ganga plains where there is no evidence of this evolutionary process. In the case of the former, what we notice is the arrival of the mature phase in an explosive manner[28] whereas, in the latter, only a

---

However, in areas of canal impact and along village ponds as well as natural depressions, a limited quantity of potable water in shallow aquifers is available.

[26]In the areas of the Harappan civilization, the quality of ground water is usually saline, except for riverine zones where the presence of Harappan settlements is limited and the availability of safe drinking water has always been a serious problem even in modern times, let alone the ancient past.

[27]Romila Thapar (1969), 'Presidential Address', *PIHC*, Varanasi, pp. 15-39. Besides, any term based on such narrow considerations cannot be inclusive in nature and, therefore, cannot encompass the entire zone of the Harappan civilization; it further exposes its inherent limitations.

[28]R.N. Mehta (1982), 'Some Rural Harappan Settlements in Gujarat', in Gregory L.

pale reflection of the mature phase is evidenced at a few locations[29] which, however, received greater attention in the succeeding late phase.[30] The difference in time of the spread of the early phase from the west to the east of the Indus speaks of the gradual dispersal of human activities in a phased manner. As the major features of this phase from the wide areas match among themselves and also broadly corresponds with those of the succeeding mature phase, the term 'Bronze Age Civilization' covers this early part as well.

The discussion on the terminological aspects also needs to take into account some other terms after the typesites. These include sites such as Harappa, Amri, Kulli, Nal, Kot Diji, Sothi, Kalibanga and Siswal among others. But instead of enumerating these terms, what is more important is to underline their connotation, especially for situating the very process of the evolution as well as the devolution of this civilization. Interestingly, these terms are neutral to the debate on the relative importance of the natural and social forces in this context. Simultaneously, these do represent the actual pocess in a stratified manner at the respective sites. Minute changes induced by local factors or otherwise are presented to demonstrate further their actual trajectory. These sites produce a cultural complex from the earliest to the mature levels in a stratified manner, which may not present one to one cultural parallels always for being situated in the vast and the diverse geographical regions that precluded any appreciable interaction leading to the consolidation of their independent regional identities, apparently looking so different from one another. Nevertheless, these early cultures do share among themselves certain broad similarities, especially in terms of their being agro-pastoral groups based on a primarily subsistence economy, the low level of overall techno-economic development, sheltering in wattle and daub houses (though some use of bricks was also in vogue), and a limited variety in their cultural equipment. This means that these groups shared common techno-economic growth patterns and outlooks. The use of the site-names for these cultural traditions leads us to a pool of such terms. However, if these are not rationalized by correlating the actual process of the development exposed there, it may further compound the confusion. What is crucial, in this regard, is to arrange the exposed cultural deposits at the respective sites in a sequential order on the basis of their dominant cultural markers.

In the mid-1970s, Rafiq Mughal used the term 'Pre-Harappa' for a cultural complex named 'Hakra' by him after the river. The so-called new cultural complex, supposedly anterior to the Kot Diji complex, was represented by

---

Possehl (ed.), *Harappan Civilization*, Oxford and IBH, New Delhi, pp. 167-74; Y.M. Chitalwala (1982), 'Harappan Settlements in Kuchchh-Saurastra Region: Patterns of Distribution and Routes of Communication', in G.L. Possehl (ed.), *Harappan Civilization*, pp. 197-204.

[29] Dikshit (1982), op. cit., pp. 399-412.

[30] J.P. Joshi et al. (1984), 'Indus Civilization: A Reconsideration on the Basis of Maps', in B.B. Lal and S.P. Gupta (eds.), *Frontiers of Indus Civilization*, Books and Books, Delhi, pp. 516, 522-3.

ninety-nine sites in Cholistan. The cultural complex comparable to the Kot Dijian complex is termed 'Early Harappa' by him on the basis of cultural and the chronological position between this group and that of the mature phase. Similar cultural material is said to have been discovered by him from the sites of Harappa, Saraikhola and Jalilpur among others in the upstream areas of west Punjab and the North West Frontier Provinces. The term 'Early Harappa' envisages a gradual development of early local cultures into the civilization,[31] though the evidence of systematic transition is missing. This term also does not embrace the diverse processes of development presented by the early sites.

With regard to the mature phase, there is no major difference of opinion in so far as it is equated with the urban phase, yet the process of urbanization has never been uniform in terms of its time frame and degree at each settlement. Besides, the features of this phase were not confined to the urban settlements alone but reached the contemporary settlements as well, though in a differential manner. This perhaps underlines the process of these settlements being integrated with the advanced system.

Later, in the uppermost levels of the mature phase, some signs of degeneration began to surface in one form or the other at some settlements. Here, what we notice is the continuation of some of the features of the mature phase and the appearance of degenerative tendencies simultaneously. This was neither a fully-advanced nor a degenerate phase but represents a transition from the mature to the late which signals the onset of the decline of the civilization. It is termed the 'Late Mature Phase'.[32]

The next phase of the civilization is generally designated as the 'Late Harappan Phase'. This succeeds the mature phase and spans over several hundred years during the second millennium BC before PGW and its contemporary cultures in other parts. Interestingly, during this phase in the currency of several cultural complexes in different simultaneously areas or an amalgam of diverse cultural traits with the predominance of some features of one cultural group during this period. These cultures have been characterized differently.

On these cultural complexes, we may enumerate the Jhukar,[33] Cemetery-H,[34] Mitathal IIB,[35] and the Late and Post-Harappa.[36] The first three are named

[31] Mughal (1980, 1982), op. cit..

[32] Mackay (1938), *Further Excavations at Mohenjodaro*, New Delhi.

[33] Casal (1964), op. cit.

[34] Mortimer Wheeler (1984), 'Harappa 1946: The Defences and Cemetery R-37', *AI*, 3, ASI, pp. 58-130; H.D. Sankalia (1972-3), 'The Cemetery-H Culture', *Puratattva*, 6, pp. 12-19.

[35] Suraj Bhan (1971-2), op. cit.

[36] R.C. Thakran (1981), 'The Sequel to the Indus Civilization in the Greater Indus Valley', unpublished M. Phil dissertation, Jawaharlal Nehru University, New Delhi, p. 3.

after the sites and also represents their respective regional associations whereas the last two (the Late Harappa and the Post-Harappa) speak of the chronological time period, as well as of the cultural affinity they represent across time and space. The 'Late Harappan phase' bears a close affinity to the preceding 'mature' phase through a stratigraphic continuum or with fresh habitation deposits. This phase embodies basic cultural shifts, i.e. the movement of population is reoriented to the rural hinterland, to agro-pastoralism and to more pristine areas.

The next term is 'The Post-Harappa', which is indiscriminately applied to the cultures subsequent to the mature phase. This, however, stands for particular cultural groups, which do not exhibit predominant cultural affinity with the Harappan tradition or have any stratigraphical continuity, though they occur in a chronological order. They represent a separate ancestry but are contemporary with the late Harappan as they broadly overlap in temporal but not geographical terms. These include the Jhukar and Cemetery-H cultures. Both the cultures are regional ones though the elements of the latter seem to have enjoyed greater acceptance in the northern Harappan zone.

GEOGRAPHICAL EXTENT AND DIVERSITIES

The civilization was spread over a vast geographical area of 1,600 km from Sutkagendor in the south-western part of Baluchistan in Pakistan to Alamgirpur near Meerut in western Uttar Pradesh, and 1,400 km from Manda in Jammu in the north to Daimabad in north-eastern Maharashtra in the south. This comes to a 1 million sq km area, which is bigger than the combined area of both the Mesopotamian and Egyptian civilizations. The vast geographical expanse envelops diverse natural settings as disparate as the mountainous areas of Baluchistan, western Sind, the North West Frontier Province, the Himalayan outliers and the Aravallis, the semi-arid plains of the Indus system, parts of the upper Ganga Doab, and the saline and rocky desert of the Kachchh, in addition to the plains and coastal regions, and the rocky and dry terrain of northern Maharashtra. These present a very interesting contrast in terms of their soil types, climate, rainfall, surface and sub-surface water sources, vegetation, mineral resources, cropping patterns, food habits, and lifestyles. These diversities offered a range of challenges and opportunities to those who lived there, and were harnessed by the people according to their working capacity.

PROBLEM OF AUTHORSHIP OF THE CIVILIZATION

The history of debate on the authorship of the civilization is as old as its discovery. Over time, several contrasting views came into play. Some scholars project similarities between the civilization and the Aryans on the following grounds: according to them, the geographical areas referred to in the *Rigveda* are synonymous with those of this civilization. But, on close scrutiny, one finds them different for the vast areas of southern Baluchistan, Sind and Gujarat among others do not find any mention in the *Rigveda*. In order to buttress their argument further, they suggest that the Ganga, Yamuna, Sarasvati and the Indus, along with its eastern (Sutlej, Ravi, Beas, Jhelum and Chenab) and western tributaries (Swat, Kabul, Gomal and Kurram), are mentioned in a sequential manner, which shows the accuracy of their geographical sense and the greater validity of these references in this context. We do not have any problem with their accurate sequential references nor their validity, at least in respect to these references, but with the absence of references to the numerous rivers (Zhob, Quetta, Pishin, Lora, Anambar and Bolan among others) covering vast areas of Baluchistan that contradict the basis of commonality of the area of activity between the two.

It is further argued by these scholars that the ancient Sarasvati River has been referred to as the river '*par-excellence*' for its mighty and perennial grandeur. This has also, according to them, been endorsed by the highest concentration of known Harappan settlements in its environs. On the basis of these factors, they conclude that the Rigvedic Aryans were the authors of this civilization.[37]

The argument of the Sarasvati being a mighty and perennial river has already been analysed above. To make our point clear, we will only state the essence of this discourse. The mightiness of the river is subject to the availability of a huge quantity of water the year round, which can only be ensured either by the origin of the river being from snow-capped mountains or by the even spread of good rains over the months of the year or by both. Interestingly, none of the features that make it a mighty and perennial river exist in case of this river from the remote ancient past. The river rises only from the lower Himalayas which do not experience snowfalls nor does the entire catchment of the river enjoy good rains through the year. However, the exponents of this view suggest that the river underwent a drastic change from ancient times and, as a result, dried up due to a variety of natural factors.[38] Without enumerating the absence of the factors that are supposed to have contributed towards its drying up, we note that we do not have any evidence with regard to the two incontrovertible signatures of such a 'Mighty' river: a thick sheet of river sand over its flood plain and huge fresh ground water reserves. These two will always be in tune with the size of a river and can also be identified, as is the case with the modern Sutlej and the Yamuna through a surface and sub-surface survey. The absence of these signatures from the areas of the Sarasvati and their presence in the areas of the present Sutlej and the Yamuna brings out clearly that these rivers never formed part

[37]Gupta (1999), op. cit.; Lal (2002), op. cit.

[38]Ibid.; R.S. Bisht (1999), 'Harappans and the Rigveda: Points of Convergence', in G.C. Pande (ed.), *The Dawn of Indian Civilization*, PHISPC, New Delhi, pp. 393-442.

of the Sarasvati and, therefore, there is no their question of shifting courses leading to their drying up.[39] These two rivers were inconsequential to the seasonal Sarasvati from ancient times. What we witness is about a 400-feet thick clayey silt deposit instead of any perennial river sand in the middle section, at least, of the Sarasvati which conforms to the kind of formations it originates from. The quantity of ground water is neither huge nor good in its major parts. Farmers rue the poor quantity and quality of ground water along its middle course.[40]

The argument of the very concentration of known Harappan settlements along it is also not true. The areas with its impact were very narrow and the emerging Harappan settlement pattern is not linear. Rather, it is of a dispersed order covering the vast geographical expanse between the Yamuna in the east and the Sutlej in the west. There is not reason to accept this argument. Besides, in these areas, no big impact of any river action is noticed in the Holocene period, let alone the seasonal Sarasvati. On close examination, one sees that almost all the ancient settlements are located in close proximity to multiple natural depressions; perhaps some of them were the product of human labour of varied denominations.[41] The ethnographic data of numerous modern villages which do possess a number of ponds close to their habitation areas and the majority of their wells are located along these very ponds. It shows how to manage water to survive in these rain deficient areas. Whatever limited quantity of ground water is generated through percolation along these ponds is harnessed through the wells for their daily use. These village ponds form the main lifeline for the survival of the people in modern times. Like these ponds, natural depressions in close proximity with past settlements seem to suggest to have constituted the main lifeline so far as the supply of water was concerned and also highlight their role in inducing a dispersed settlement pattern.[42]

As regards the highest importance being attached to the Sarasvati River in the *Rigveda*, we would like to make clear that it is earned by a water body, and for that matter by any thing, for being significant in the lives of the people than for only being a mighty and perennial. Mighty rivers had not always been important to the people, especially in the absence of technological know-how to harness them to their advantage. With a limited working capacity, such rivers posed insurmountable problems and appeared deadly to their very

[39] Aurel Stein (1942), 'A Survey of Ancient Sites Along the Lost Saraswati River', *GJ*, 99, pp. 73-182; R.D. Oldham (1887), 'On Probable Changes in the Geography of the Punjab and Its Rivers', *JASB*, 55, pp. 322-43.

[40] R.C. Thakran (2009), 'Was the Saraswati a Mighty Perennial River: An Archaeo-geohydrological Perspective', *Social Science Probings*, December, pp. 1-18.

[41] R.C. Thakran (2009), 'Rivers and Protohistoric Settlements: Negotiating Contrasting Perceptions in the Light of Recent Explorations in Rajasthan', in *Changing Perspectives in South Asian Archaeology*, forthcoming, K.P. Jayaswal Research Institute, Patna.

[42] Ibid.

existence instead of being the point of attraction. A seasonal river like the ancient Sarasvati only received rain water from its catchment areas primarily during the monsoon season. Such rivers do not support a good flow of water for long because they do not receive enough supply on a sustained basis due to erratic rains. Hence, they do not work as a lasting barrier, contrary to the mighty perennial rivers, for the movement of the Rigvedic pastoral people across the region. Moreover, the rain water coming to the river, can be retained in its lakes, as it is also known as the river of lakes in the *Rigveda*, through its length and breadth. This water can be used both by humans and their animals for most parts of the year. The absence of modern powerful devices to draw out the ground water on any considerable scale would have precluded the deepening of the water table and, thereby, reduced the loss of surface water through percolation. The occurrence of rains in the non-monsoon months in some measure would have replenished it from time to time in order to help retain it in these lakes for longer periods. The landscape, being rich in moisture content, would have supported a good vegetation cover during and after the rains for grazing animals. This could also have offered some suitable pockets with enough soil moisture reserve for raising certain crops on a small scale in a *Barani* (dry) fashion. Consequently, such water courses became very useful in the everyday life of the people and that made them dear to the people.[43]

The differences between the Harappan and Aryan lifestyles are well known. Yet the use of terms such as *samrat*, *rajan*, *rajak*, *sabha* and *samiti* in the *Rigveda* is enigmatic, to some scholars, in relation to the pastoral nature of the Rigvedic society. The use of these terms, according to them, announces the presence of a well-settled and hierarchically-developed society. This argument, however, is based on the Rigvedic literary compositions of varied times and also runs counter to ethnographic practices common among mobile groups who have both social institutions and a hierarchical arrangement of power-sharing. They assemble at mutually convenient points and perform the functions expected of them.[44]

The question of the knowledge of the horse to the Harappan has engaged the efforts of scholars over time. The proponents of Aryans as the creators of the Harappan civilization have tried hard to prove its presence during this period on varied grounds of biological, archaeological and stratigraphical-cum-chronological considerations. Among the archaeological evidences, they include terracotta animal figurines, one each from Nausharo, Mohenjo-daro and Lothal, which look like the horse, according to them.[45] Surprisingly, these are completely isolated instances among the numerous terracotta animal

[43] Thakran (2003), op. cit.

[44] Suraj Bhan (2000), 'Aryanization of the Indus', in Romila Thapar (ed.), *The Making of History*, Tulika, New Delhi, pp. 41-55.

[45] Bholanath and G.V. Sreenivas Rao (1985), 'Animal Remains from Lothal Excavations', in S.R. Rao, *Lothal: A Harappan Port Town (1995-62), MASI*, 78, vol. II, ASI, p. 641.

figurines coming from the Harappan settlements. Second, these only look like the horse and are not actual figurines of the animal. Third, the one from Nausharo belongs of the late Harappan levels and cannot be taken to represent the preceding mature phase. Moreover, the knowledge as well as the presence of the horse during late Harappan levels is not in dispute.[46]

As far as the biological evidence of the presence of the horse is concerned, some evidences of bones from Mohenjo-daro (a jaw bone), Lothal (a second upper molar), Kalibanga (an upper molar, fragments of the distal end of the femur and the distal end of the left humerus), Surkotada and Ropar are cited.[47] The remains from the last site are not clear in so far as their identification with a breed or stratum is concerned.[48] Evidence from Surkotada also comes from the late Harappan levels and has already been refuted convincingly.[49] Its authenticity was sought to be proved by presuming the absence of the wild horse from the Indian subcontinent in the post-Pleistocene period,[50] which, however, falls flat in the face of evidence from Mesolithic sites in Madhya Pradesh.[51] The remaining evidence quoted above stands isolated in comparison to the large body of faunal data from excavated Harappan sites, which make its presence even more doubtful.[52] On the contrary, its data, in all forms, are coming so spontaneously from late Harappan levels[53] that the need to manufacture them does not arise. This was because the horse was known to the people. Had the horse been integral to the Harappan people, it should have occurred spontaneously and profusely, as is the case with bull remains.

The other point of debate with regard to the Aryan authorship of the

[46] Giorgio Stacul (1989), 'Swat, Pirak and Connected Problems (Mid-2nd Millennium BC)', *SAA*, pp. 268-9; Marielle Santoni (1981), 'Sibri the South Cemetery of Mehrgarh: Third Millennium Connections, between Northern Kachhi Plain and Central Asia', *SAA*, p. 52.

[47] A.K. Sharma (1993), 'The Harappan Horse was Buried Under the Dune of . . .', *Puratattva*, 23, pp. 30-4.

[48] The details about these points are not forthcoming.

[49] Michael Witzel and Steve Farmer (2000), 'Piltdown Horse in Harappa', *Frontline*, 13 October, pp. 1-4; R.S. Sharma (2002), 'Rg Vedic and Harappan Cultures: Lexical and Archaeological Aspects', *Social Scientist*, vol. 30, nos. 7-8, July-August, pp. 1-11; Andrew Sherrat (1999), 'Sedentary Agriculture and Nomadic Pastoral Populations (3000-7000 BC)', in A.H. Dani (ed.), *History of Humanity*, UNESCO, vol. II, pp. 40-1; R.S. Sharma (2001), *Advent of the Aryans in India*, Manohar, New Delhi; idem (1995), *Looking for the Aryans*, Orient Longman, Madras, pp. 14-20.

[50] Sharma (1993), op. cit.

[51] D.K. Chakrabarti (1999), *India: An Archaeological History*, Oxford University Press, New Delhi, p. 101.

[52] Among the numerous faunal remains from the excavated Harappan sites, we get large amounts of evidence of both wild and domesticated animals. However, the evidence of horse is not forthcoming, so some colleagues strived hard and unsuccessfully to manufacture it.

[53] Stacul (1989), op. cit.

civilization is the presence or absence of the spoked wheel during this period. In support of its presence, the occurrence of terracotta wheels with painted spokes from Kalibanga and Rakhigarhi, and of wheels with spokes in relief from Banawali and Bhirdana, is mentioned.[54] There is, in fact, no denying that terracotta wheels, with or without the central hub, come naturally in a very good number from Harappan settlements, and, of them, with the central form the characteristic feature of mature Harappan advancement. Among them, we fail to mark the presence of the actual spoked wheel from any of the sites and there does not seem any valid reason for its presence since the people lacked the technical competence to produce it.[55]

In order to scientifically establish the authorship of the civilization, we need to take samples of human skeletons from the early and mature phases from as many settlements as possible. These should be analysed to understand the composition of populations in respective phases. Whatever evidence is with us as of now points to a mixed population composed of different stocks where the Aryans do not figure at all as a separate entity.[56] Even if we accept the face value of literary references, how do we explain the complete blackout of names of important Harappan settlements from literature when the names of rivers are stated so meticulously in a sequential order? There are many more gaps and perhaps future research might offer us convincing data to bridge them satisfactorily. Till such time, the question of Aryan authorship remains unsubstantiated.

THE PROCESS OF CIVILIZATIONAL DEVELOPMENT

In order to understand the process of the development of civilization, we need to take stock of the beginnings of human activities in a sequential manner in and around the Harappan zone, which can broadly be divided into three divisions: the area west of the Indus, the plains of the Indus and the areas east of the Indus. The first division covers the North West Frontier Province, Baluchistan and the western hilly parts of the Sind province. The second subdivision extends from the sub-Himalayas to the Arabian Sea along the Indus, while the third unit covers Punjab (east of the Indus), Haryana, western Uttar Pradesh, Rajasthan (north-western parts), Gujarat and the adjoining areas of northern Maharashtra.

Among these divisions, the earliest remains of sequential human activities come from the areas situated west of the Indus River and their antiquity goes

[54] L.S. Rao et al. (2003-4), 'Unearthing Harappan Settlement at Bhirrana (2003-04)', *Puratattva*, 34, p. 23.

[55] Shireen F. Ratnagar (1996), 'Revisionist at Work: A Chauvinistic Approach of the Aryan Theory', *Frontline*, 9 February, pp. 74-80.

[56] Whatever studies have been conducted so far on the skeletal remains from Harappan burials and what information we gather is of a mixed genome and also that continues even today (see reference no. 110).

back to the seventh-sixth millennium BC, as evidenced at Kile Ghul Mohmmad[57] and Mehrgarh[58] among others. Habitation begins at both the sites in aceramic Neolithic levels and the people subsisted on hunting and gathering. Later, hand-made pottery with basket impressions, decorated with linear designs, was introduced at both the sites. They also began domestication of animals for subsistence. Besides, at Mehrgarh (IB), people knew of barley and wheat (both west Asian native plants),[59] the construction of houses with mud-bricks in the ratio 1:2:4[60] (a standard followed later by the Harappans in the mature phase), the use of bone awls among other known stone tools, disposing of dead (in an extended as well as flexed manner which continued in mature Harappan times), its earliest known evidence comes from the Shanidar Cave site of middle Palaeolithic period in Mesopotamia,[61] with limited grave goods such as stone axes, microliths, baskets coated with bitumen, necklaces of steatite micro beads interspersed with those of turquoise, *lapis lazuli* and sea shells, and a stone vessel (an evidence of trans-regional contracts). The last four objects along with some others are of origin and imply long-distance inputs.

In period IIA at Mehrgarh, we notice the continuation of hand-made ware but this was prepared with well-levigated clay and enjoyed greater frequency, which turned out to be well-fired in Period IIB. Finally, this became wheel-made as well as painted with simple linear designs over globular vases with collared rims and bowls with tapering profiles in Period IIC. Besides, a new variety of barley (*Hordeum sphaerococuum*), two rudimentary sickles (prepared by fixing three bladelets in wooden handles), a grooved elephant tusk (perhaps being the earliest evidence of ivory working), a copper ring and a bead further point to the persistent development pattern. This is further strengthened with the introduction of a new variety of wheat (*Triticum sphaercocuum*), oat crop, crucibles for melting copper, drill bits with hollows at the end, bun-shaped copper ingots and faunal paintings (cranes in a row and the gazelle, which also occur in Namazga III in Central Asia, Sialk III, Hissar IB and IC in Iran and Mundigak I in southern Afghanistan) on ceramic ware in period III in the first half of the fourth millennium BC. These were turned into polychrome

[57] Fazal Dad Kakar (1992), 'The Antiquity of Human Settlements in the Quetta Valley', *PA*, 27, pp. 1-14.

[58] M.R. Mughal (1991), 'The Cultural Patterns of Ancient Pakistan and Neighboring Regions Circa 7000-1500 BC', *PA*, 26, p. 200.

[59] Hans Helbaek (1959), 'Domestication of Food Plants in the Old World', *Science*, 130, 14, August, p. 370; Lorenzo Constantini (1981), 'The Beginning of Agriculture in Kachi Plain: The Evidence from Mehrgarh', *SAA*, p. 31.

[60] J.F. Jarrige (1979), 'Economy and Society in the Early Chalcolithic/Bronze Age of Baluchistan: New Perspectives from Recent Excavations at Mehrgarh', *SAA*, pp. 93-114; idem (1981), 'Chronology of the earlier periods of the Greater Indus as seen from Mehrgarh, Pakistan', *SAA*, pp. 21-9.

[61] S.J. Francis Hours (1994), 'Western Asia in the Period of Homo habilis and Homo erectus', in E.J. De Laet (ed.), *History of Humanity*, vol. I, UNESCO, pp. 62-77.

ware with the application of black and white colour for painting designs over the plain red and red slipped surface in Period IV, dated between 3500-3000 BC.[62] The use of stamp seals in bone and terracotta (used first at the Tell Hassuna site dated between 5800-5500 BC in Mesopotamia) [63] and terracotta female figurines (with cylindrical heads, pinched noses, pendulous breasts, and in a sitting posture with outstretched legs), also continue in Mehrgarh VII, the mature phase, along with other human figurines.[64] One of them is said to have borne a red streak in the partition line of black hair, which is inadvertently interpreted as the application of *'Sindur in Mang'* as applied by married Hindu women in modern times.[65] However, this being an isolated ambiguous instance cannot be taken seriously to draw any major conclusion with utter disregard to the deductive instruments of scientific enquiry. Thus, all these are in tune with persisting progression. This has also been experienced during the short-lived Period V with decorations of the *pipal* (*Ficus religiosa*) leaf and fish-scale designs on grey ware in black and with the decreasing frequency of polychrome ware. This seems to have been further intensified by the integration of local as well as distant features through greater interaction, underlined by the circulation of diverse ware (Quetta, Nal, Kulli, etc.), stone as well as terracotta compartmented seals and double-spiral-copper pins in Period VI. Thus, this brings us to the mature phase in Period VII at Mehrgarh. Likewise, these are other sites of Rana Ghundai in the Loralai Valley,[66] and Gumla[67] and Rehman Dheri[68] in the Gomal Valley, which present a similar continuous cultural sequence from the Neolithic to the mature Harappan period that point to the common process of development.

The foregoing description brings out the following points: one, human interaction with natural forces began during the Neolithic levels in these areas; two, production of food and artisanal goods began in these levels in combination with sedentary life; three, among the staple crops, barley dominated over wheat like in the West Asian regions; four, these two crops

[62] J.F. Jarrige (1979), 'Excavations at Mehrgarh-Pakistan', *SAA*, pp. 76-87 and 93-114.

[63] J. Mellart (1975), *The Neolithic of the Near East,* London, pp. 70-90; George Roux (1992), *Ancient Iraq*, 3rd edn, pp. 48-52.

[64] Jarrige (1979), op. cit.

[65] B.B. Lal (2002), 'The Earliest Civilization of the Indian Subcontinent: Who could Have Its Authors? A Fresh Look', *ICHR* (xerox copy), Foundation Day Lecture delivered in New Delhi on 27 March, p. 3.

[66] Mughal (1991), op. cit., pp. 218-37.

[67] Ibid.; idem (1990), 'The Harappan Settlement Patterns in the Greater Indus Valley', *PA*, 25, pp. 1-73; A.H. Dani (1970-71), 'Excavations in the Gomal Valley', *AP*, 5, pp. 1-77. Among them, the site of Gumla presents a break between Period II and III but the duration is not elaborated.

[68] Farzand Ali Durrani (1988), *Excavations in the Gomal Valley-Rehman Dheri Excavations*, Department of Archaeology, University of Peshawar; F.A. Durrani et al. (1991), 'Further Excavations at Rehman Dheri', *AP*, 7, pp. 61-146.

seem to have travelled from parts of West Asia to these areas; five, among the domesticates, cattle enjoyed a commanding position unlike in the West Asian regions; six, integration of outside inputs with the local process of development is witnessed, which collectively helped shape the course of prospective developments.

The point as to where the civilization took shape, the second geographic region of the Indus where the two major exposed urban centres of Harappa and Mohenjo-daro exist, deserve discussion. Both are the earliest known sites, big in size and with a cultural sequence beginning with the antecedent phase, though the habitation being limited in the early stage, just like any other early village settlements, which grew into the urban centre in due course. It is believed that the civilization was shaped at these sites as there is no other site in the first zone to match their size and cultural richness.[69]

However, the site of Dabarkot in the Zhob Valley of Baluchistan which lies in the first zone is a strong contender at least in terms of size and antiquity of human activities.[70] The site has not yet been excavated. We are also reminded of the fact that the development of a civilization is not an incident; rather, it is part of a process. The legacy of this process goes back to early village settlements that emerged for the first time in the areas situated west of the Indus zone. These two cannot be separated for any rational analysis of the process of development. We also cannot elaborate each stage of this process of development for constraints of space, yet will take brief note of the early cultural composition at the site of Harappa. As expected by M.S. Vats, the excavator of the site, not only a Kot Dijian phase but also its anterior cultural deposits have been discovered here. These are termed the 'Ravi Phase' dated to 3300 BC.[71] Thus, it presents a fourfold cultural sequence from the 'Ravi Phase' to the Cemetery-H through the Kot Dijian and mature phases. The antiquity of the beginnings of human activities is surely posterior to and linked with the first zone.

Now we move on to the third geographical division, i.e. the areas situated east of the Indus, which include several important cultural zones and settlements. If we begin with the southern parts of this unit, the area of Cholistan (the northernmost extension of the Thar desert and the southernmost part of west Punjab) and the districts of Hanumangarh and Sri Ganganagar of Rajasthan in India are very crucial. Both these areas are traversed by a seasonal water course, which is known as the Hakra in the former and the Ghaggar in the latter. The former was intensively combed by Rafiq Mughal in the late 1960s and early 1970s[72] while the latter was intensively surveyed by A. Ghosh[73] in the early 1950s among others.[74]

[69]Mughal (1991), op. cit.; idem (1990), op. cit., pp. 1-77; 31-8.

[70]Ibid.

[71]Kenoyer (2008), op. cit..

[72]Mughal (1980), op. cit., pp. 93-8; idem (1982), op. cit., pp. 85-96.

[73]Ghosh (1952), op. cit.

[74]Thakran (2006-07), op. cit., pp. 992-1000; idem (2009), op. cit.; Katy Feroze Dalal

On the basis of his survey, Mughal proposed a fivefold cultural sequence from Hakra to PGW with intervening stages of the early, mature and late Harappa. The first three (Hakra/Pre-Harappa, early Harappa and mature Harappa) cultural stages are significant in order to understand the sequential beginnings of human activities and the development of civilization in this part, in particular, and all the regions, in general.

The Hakra culture with ninety-nine settlements is placed between 3500-3000 BC. The distinctive feature of this culture is said to have been a kind of ceramic ware with an uneven outer surface resulting from the application of mud mixed with tiny bits of pounded pottery. It is also decorated with incised (horizontal, curvilinear, oblique and panels of lines) and painted designs in black (block band on the rim and neck) over a red or chocolate slip. Its other cultural constituents include stone grinders, parallel-sided chert blades, scrapers, leaf-shaped arrow-heads and bits of copper. There are serious problems with this formulation because neither the ceramic ware nor other cultural equipments are different from the known cultural composition from the early levels of excavated sites in the third geographical subdivision. Neither have any sites from Cholistan been excavated to get us stratified cultural deposits in a sequential form nor have the deposits of the so-called Hakra culture been exposed from any other settlement of the civilization in a stratified form. In the given situation, we fail to understand how one can identify a new cultural group proceding the known sequence. In the absence of stratified Hakra remains, it is very difficult to segregate the cultural material of the so-called Hakra and the succeeding Kot Diji purely on the basis of the explored material. We also cannot suggest that the transient-looking small settlements represent the Hakra phase because these settlements belong to the pastoral people and form part of the sedentary groups. What appears to us is that the so-called Hakra and the succeeding Kot Diji cultural groups constitute only one cultural phase, i.e. the Kot Diji, and, consequent upon that, the antiquity of human activities is not anterior to the Kot Diji phase in this part. We further propose that among the numerous small and shifting settlements (99+40) of both the groups, there were the fairly large sedentary settlements of Jalwali (22.5 ha) and Gamanwala (27.3 ha). This aggradational trend later resulted in an increase in the number of settlements to 174 in the mature phase and the emergence of the bigger site of Ganweriwala (81.5 ha), a match to Mohenjo-daro in size at least but it has not been excavated.[75]

To the east of the Indo-Pakistan border is the site of Kalibanga in the Hanumangarh district of Rajasthan on the eastern bank of the Ghaggar. The earliest phase is dated to 2800 BC with the help of C-14 dates and Lal places it between 3000 and 2700 BC. Among the main features of this period are mud-brick houses (ratio 1:2:3), though burnt bricks were also known, a

---

(1980), 'A Short History of Explorations in Bikaner and Bahawalpur Along the Lost Saraswati River', *Indica*, vol. 17, 1, March, pp. 3-46.

[75]Mughal (1980), op. cit.

defence wall (with initial width of 1.90 m which later increased to 3-4 m with an opening towards the river), a ploughed field, the use of *tandoors*, six (A to F) pottery types with the impact of ceramic traditions from Rehman Dheri II in Baluchistan (where painted designs are outlined by black over the red surface) and Kot Diji I, as in the case of Fabric-A. This marks the direction of movement of this tradition from the west to the east. Another interesting point here is a gap between Kalibanga I and II but since the thickness of the sterile layer is not mentioned, it is impossible to make any conjecture about the time gap between the two periods.[76] Nonetheless, it underlines the absence of a continuous systematic evolutionary process.

The site of Banawali produced a cultural sequence from Period I to III, while Period I is further divided into IA to IC. Kalibanga I ceramic wares were used during Banawali IA to IC. A defence system in the form of a wall is marked in IB; it is made of mud-bricks (in a 1:2:3: ratio) that persisted in IC as well, though the brick ratio changes to 1:2:4. Some other mature Harappan ceramic features also arrive as precursors.[77] This suggests that the habitation is comparable to that of Kalibanga I but is also part of a gradual forward movement unlike it.

There is a 3-m thick cultural deposit at Kunal (district Hisar, Haryana) which is divisible into sub-periods IA to IC. During Period IA, the ceramic ware is comparable to Kalibanga I, Banawali IA to IC and Rakhigarhi, whose space was captured by bichrome ware with the application of black colour over a red surface for painting the peacock, the pipal leaf and mature Harappan designs.[78]

Besides, circular pits, of 2 m diameter and 1 m deep, perhaps being thatched in Period IA, which later were lined with mud-bricks in IB, and finally being replaced by square as well as rectangular mud-brick (1:2:4 ratio) houses in Period IC. This was coupled with the use of mud silos, a large number of beads (of silver, gold and *lapis lazuli*), two silver tiaras, copper objects (arrowheads, spearheads, coiled cones, finger rings) and their local manufacturing, as suggested by the occurrence of crucibles with copper content sticking to them. Discular silver beads from these levels with perforations along their diameter remind us of similar beads from Lothal and also of the adoption of this technique from steatite beads of this kind. Likewise, seven square seals (six of steatite and one of shell) with perforations in the back of their knobs contain animal motifs and inscriptions, unlike the geometric designs of mature Harappan seals.[79]

[76] *IAR*, 1960 to 1969; Lal (2003), op. cit.

[77] R.S. Bisht (1987), 'Further Excavations at Banawali: 1983-84', in B.M. Pande and B.D. Chattopadhyaya (eds.), *Archaeology and History: Essays in Memory of A. Ghosh*, vol. I, Agam Kala Prakashan, Delhi.

[78] J.S. Khatri and M. Acharya (1995), 'Kunal: A New Indus-Saraswati Site', *Puratattva*, 25, pp. 84-6.

[79] Ibid.

Excavations were conducted at Siswal (district Hisar, Haryana) where a 1.25-m cultural deposit was discovered, which was divided into two sub-periods: Siswal A and Siswal B. The former is comparable to that to Kalibanga I, Banawali I, Kunal IA and Rakhigarhi I with respect to ceramic tradition and other cultural equipments, while, in Siswal B, an admixture of the evolved ceramic ware of Siswal A (pottery shapes become sturdier and better potted than Kalibanga I with paintings in black colour, perhaps under the influence of the mature Harappan contact) and that of mature Harappan pottery, which include storage jars with ledged neck and flanged rim, S-shaped jars with flanged rim, vase with pointed base, perforated jars, dish on-stand with short out-curved rim, and broad squat stands.[80] The pottery is fast-wheel thrown, applied with bright red slip and decorated with linear designs in black. This points to the arrival of mature features from contiguous areas in the west rather than being evolved locally, on the one hand, and the same orientation of the movement, on the other. This is further corroborated by the cultural sequence exposed at Mitathal (district Bhiwani, Haryana) located east of the previous one. Here, habitation began in Mitathal I, which is comparable to evolved Siswal B where circulation of ceramic ware is limited to fabric A and C, and to a few shapes of the mature Harappan period. Mud bricks based on the ratio of 1:2:3 were still in vogue for house-building activities among other limited cultural objects. Habitation continued without any break in Mitathal IIA period with substantial circulation of mature Harappan ceramic types and cultural equipment.[81]

In the region of Gujarat, we encounter the beginnings of habitation during the phase preceding the mature Harappa at Somnath (Prabhash Patan) in the district of Junagarh,[82] Nagawada in Surendernagar,[83] Rojadi,[84] Lothal[85] and Dholavira[86] in Kachchh, and Padri in Bhavanagar.[87] None of these are comparable in temporal terms with the beginnings in the region west of the Indus (Padri is an exception for being dated to 3000 BC). They do not display any parallel with the succeeding mature Harappan cultural assemblage. On the contrary, they exhibit the arrival to the mature Harappan phase in a big way as an extension from areas in the west of Gujarat.

[80] Suraj Bhan (1971-2), op. cit.

[81] Suraj Bhan (1982), op. cit.

[82] Mehta (1982), op. cit.

[83] K.T.M. Hegde et al. (1988), 'Excavations at Negwada-1986-87: Preliminary Report', *ME*, 12, pp. 55-65.

[84] Mehta, op. cit.

[85] Rao, op. cit.; idem (1973), *Lothal and the Indus Civilization*, Asia Publishing House, New Delhi.

[86] R.S. Bisht (1989-90), 'Dholavira: A New Horizon of the Indus Civilization', *Puratattva*, 20, pp. 71-82.

[87] V.S. Shinde, 'Excavation at Padri (1990-91): Preliminary Report', *ME*, 17, I, pp. 79-86.

Generally, it is believed that the genesis of the civilization lies in the river valleys (Indus or Sarasvati) but what we have observed in the foregoing discourse is not in tune with this as the integral constituents of the civilization seem to have travelled to diverse provenances west of the Indus. And when the archaeological evidence from the Indus zone is juxtaposed with that of the other two zones, the ancient-most cultural background is associated only with the region west of the Indus (seventh millennium BC) followed by the Indus (mid-fourth millennium BC) and the east of the Indus (early third millennium BC) zones in a chronological order. We find the Indus zone as a transitional one with respect to its geographical position, natural properties, sequential spread of human activities, and in the transmission of the Harappan tradition to the eastern zone, but certainly not with regard to the beginnings and development of civilization.

TOWN PLANNING

The layout exposed at Mohenjo-daro and the AB mound of Harappan in the mature Harappan phase distinguishes it from the preceding as well as the succeeding phases. One of its features is the twin-mound system, which consists of a high mound (citadel) and a lower mound (residential area); the former is situated in the west and the latter in the east, both separated by an open space. The citadel measures 380 m north-south and 200 m east-west while it rises to a height of 12 m from the surrounding surface level at Mohenjo-daro. A mud-brick platform supported the superstructure of a granary, a college of priests and an assembly hall, in addition to a bathing tank.[88] While its counterpart at Harappa is marked by the presence of a high mound (measuring 240 × 120 m) in the west of the other two (E and F) mounds with signs of a peripheral wall (as part of defence system) atop a 13.5 m upward receding brick rampart with evidence of outer revetments. This is further divided into two (northern and southern) halves by a wall.[89]

However, a deviation is marked from this pattern at Banawali[90] (Haryana), Lothal[91] and Surkotada[92] (Gujarat), where both the mounds form part of only one complex. These (at Banawali and Surkotada) are encircled by a defence wall composed of mud, mud bricks or both with an outer covering of mud, burnt bricks or stone rubble, in contrast to Lothal where there is no defence wall. The complex is divided into two parts by a dividing line at Banawali and Surkotada, while, at Lothal, a 3.5-m high mud platform starting from the west clockwise measures 118, 125, 118 and 113 m) separates the two, which is provided with an opening for communication. In contrast to these

[88] Marshall (1931), op. cit.; Mackay (1938), op. cit.
[89] Vats (1940), op. cit.
[90] Bisht (1987), op. cit.
[91] Rao (1973), op. cit.
[92] J.P. Joshi (1990), 'Excavations at Surkotada and Exploration in Kutch', *MASI*, 87.

patterns, we encounter a three-tier system at Dholavira where the citadel is in the south instead of being in the north. The middle and lower towns are in the west and east directions, respectively. These have their separate defence wall around them. The longer axis of this combined unit (770 × 615 m) runs in an east-west direction, perhaps dictated by the presence of the two seasonal streams—the Manhar in the north and the Mansar in the south.[93]

The lower town, being the residential area, is bigger than the citadel at Mohenjo-daro and Harappa. It is divided into nine major blocks by two 9-m wide north-south main roads and two east-west streets cutting each other at right angles at Mohenjo-daro. Each block is further divided into a number of house complexes by minor streets and lanes of 1.5 m width. The drainage lines are in conformity with the roads, streets and lanes. These were provided with manholes at the intersections of major and minor drains at regular intervals for periodical clearing.

The diverse size houses based on a uniform plan with a courtyard and rooms around it are integral to this plan where the cooking space is reserved in the courtyard, adjacent to a street as a norm. Besides, independent spaces are earmarked for artisans, shopkeepers and service class personnel. The presence of a massive mud-brick embankment with an outer covering of burnt bricks in the western section points to defence measures.

Two parallel east-west barrack-like rows, each measuring 7 × 7 m with a narrow gap in between, are exposed at Mound F at Harappa. Two other blocks, facing each other in an east-west direction, each consisting of six units with a size of 15 × 6 m, were also discovered. Besides, eighteen circular platforms with a 3 m diameter, made of burnt bricks arranged in circular forms on their edge, are organized in five rows in unequal numbers. This combination of structures points to their specific use for husking and storing of grains.[94] The lower town measures 360 × 240 m north-south and east-west, respectively, with an orientation along the water course in a north-south direction at Kalibanga. Five north-south and four east-west intersecting streets divide it into blocks. Rooms are arranged around a central courtyard like at Harappa and Mohenjo-daro. Floors are paved primarily with mud-bricks after their soling at least in one of the rooms, with overfired bricks nodules interspersed with charcoal and clay.[95] Fire pits have been exposed in successive levels; the last two factors (five pits and mud floors) form part of houses in these areas even now. Such fire places also occur in some of the houses at Lothal in the lower town area. A courtyard is central to the house plan at Banawali, Lothal, Surkotada and Dholavira. But the same plan is not strictly observed at all these sites except the last one, where, in addition, some of

[93] Bisht (1987), op. cit.

[94] Vats (1940), op. cit.; Jonathan Mark Kenoyer (1998), *Ancient Cities of the Indus Civilization,* Oxford University Press, Delhi, p. 66 (see Fig. 3.29).

[95] Lal (2003), op. cit.

the houses possess stone-paved bathrooms and lined drains, sullage pits, storage jars and querns.[96]

ECONOMIC ACTIVITIES

Agriculture was the mainstay of Harappan society and economy. Available information on crops from this period (wheat, barely, gram, peas, mustard, sesame, cotton and so on) helps us discern two crop harvests (*rabi* and *kharif*) in one year. Among them, the *rabi* cereal crops (wheat, barley, gram, mustard and peas) seem to have formed the main food supply line. We, however, need to keep in mind that the raising of these crops was not confined to the so-called conducive pockets with irrigation facilities, as is generally perceived and projected; instead, it was extended over varied landscapes as per human manipulations of a host of variables. Millets (small and big) were perhaps added later to the list of *kharif* crops as sesame and cotton were already known.

Animal husbandry was another important economic activity as evidenced by a number of domesticates (cattle, sheep, goat, water buffalo, camel, pig) in the form of faunal remains, paintings on ceramic wares and seals, and clay and terracotta figurines from Harappan settlements. Animal husbandry assumes greater significance in the context of almost all past societies due to their low capacity for harnessing natural conditions to their advantage. The raising of a large number of herds does not demand any great investment in terms of money as well as expertise. It certainly calls for a great input in terms of human labour to manage the herds on a daily basis while it helps spread and minimize the risks posed by the uncertainties of food production under the rain-fed agriculture of this period.[97] However, they also resorted to hunting and gathering to supplement their food supply. This is supported by historic as well as ethnographic practices. Even now in vast areas of the civilization where the benefits of modern advancements have not reached the people and they only subsist on rain-fed agriculture, large herds are raised for their survival to compensate shortfalls in food supply.

Artisanal production activities were a significant constituent of the economy and, among them, the potters' profession enjoyed a predominant position for they supplied the bulk of household utensils among other things. They specialized in producing a range of ceramic ware and pottery types (dish-on-stand, beakers, goblets, s-shaped jars, storage jars, bowls, cups) decorated with painted designs (*pipal* leaf, peacock design, fish scale, intersecting

[96]Bisht (1991), op. cit.; idem (1997), 'Dholavira Excavations: 1990-94', in J.P. Joshi (ed.), *Facets of Indian Civilization: Recent Perspectives*, New Delhi, pp. 107-20.

[97] Shereen F. Ratnagar, 'Ancient River Basin Agriculture (The Bronze Age)', xeroxed copy, p. 7; idem (1991), 'Pastoralism as an Issue in Historical Research', *Studies in History*, 7, 2 (NS), pp. 181-94.

circles, chessboard pattern, triangles, diamonds, etc.) in fast jet black colour over a red slipped surface.

Besides, animate figurines enjoyed a lot of space; female figurines not only predominate numerically but also outsmart in sophistication (thin waist, loin-cloth and girdle on their hips, pinched-up nose, mouth and round pallet like eyes) and ornamentation (bedecked with necklaces, bracelets, some of them in yellow colour to look perhaps like gold). There are numerous instances of animal figurines both in clay and terracotta (bulls, pigs, dogs, elephants, monkeys among others). Some dog figurines are collared and monkeys are stringed to move back and forth as desired. The potters also produced toy cart frames (with or without a series of holes to receive pole supports), a range of dice (plain as well as numbered), balls, sling balls, a variety of cakes (oval, *idli* and triangular-shaped), diverse types of earthen lamps, flesh rubbers, gamesmen, beads, bangles and seals to cater to the diverse everyday needs of the people.

Varied stones continued being a powerful media of their artistic expressions. A large number of objects (finished and unfinished), raw materials and tools come from a number of Harappan settlements. Among them, Chanhu-daro stands out where beads (finished and unfinished), chunks of raw materials, drills and furnaces were discovered.[98] Likewise, two earthen jars (one containing 582 beads of carnelian and the other 212 assorted beads of carnelian, steatite and shell) were found embedded in a platform in Block E at Lothal.[99] Further, this also produced cores as raw material, flakes as debitage, beads in semi-finished form (grounded but unbored), a bronze drill-bit and a kiln point to there being a centre of production, distribution and consumption as well. There are beads of a number of other stones such as agate, turquoise and *lapis lazuli* among others, and these come from a wide range of settlements (rural and urban).[100] Besides the famous (so-called 'Priest king' in limestone from Mohenjo-daro (18-cm high, upper part of a bearded man, introverted eyes, a band on forehead), two other figurines less than 10-cm high in red sandstone (a naked youth with sensuous body, three sockets—two on shoulders and one on the neck—to receive the arms and head, and the other with outstretched legs) from Harappa, a highly braided statue from Dholavira, a composite figurine of a seated bull with horns of a ram and trunk of an

[98] Mackay, op. cit.; Lamerg Karlovsky, 'Archaeological and Metallurgical Technology in Prehistoric Afghanistan, India and Pakistan', *AA*, 69, pp. 145-62.

[99] Rao, op. cit.

[100] Ibid.; Some of these beads were discovered by us at the Harappan site of Dabadi in the Hanumangarh district of Rajasthan in 2007, and at Badali, district Jhajjar, 2008 [R.C. Thakran et al. (2009), 'Excavations at Harappan Site of Badali, District Jhajjar, Haryana', *Puratattva*, 39, New Delhi, 2009, pp. 165-71] and Manheru, district Bhiwani, Haryana in 2009 during excavations [R.C. Thakran et al. (2010), 'Manheru Excavations and Explorations in its Environs', *Aitihya: Journal of Ancient History Culture and Archaeology*, vol. I, M.J.P. Rohilkhand University, Bareilly, Uttar Pradesh, pp. 128-61].

elephant from Mohenjo-daro, and a lifesize realistic representation of a mongoose from Dholavira speak of the lapidary they had developed.

Shell working was an important constituent of the artisanal activities. These were procured from the coastal areas of Gujarat, Sind, Baluchistan and the Persian Gulf. The shoreline is also dotted with some important Harappan settlements. Negeshwar[101] (close to the Poshitra and Pinder bays) being a shell-cutting centre and Bagasra[102] (Harappan site close to the Gulf of Kachchh and production centre where many objects were found in different stages of production along with the shells in a large number), and Balakot in Sind (with finished as well as unfinished specimens of bracelets, rings, pendants and beads) are important in this context among others.[103] These activities also travelled to hinterland sites like Harappa where evidence of shell working comes from Mound E.

The use of steatite was known to the Harappan and it was utilized to make a range of beads (primarily micro, wheel-shaped and spacer beads) as well as seals; the latter become the hallmark of the mature Harappan period. This was, of course, locally available and in good quantity but it also demanded a kind of sophisticated expertise to process and turn into finished goods, especially the inscribed seals with animals engraved on them. Some of the micro-beads are as small as the tip of a needle point and many others, especially the wheel-shaped beads, are as thin as paper. The merit of these objects is compounded manifold due to the material being very fragile.

A good quantity of ivory goods such as combs, antimony rods, hairpins, mirror handles, ear ornaments, scales, seals and gamesmen come from Mohenjo-daro and Lothal among others. Although ivory is considered a difficult substance to work on its compact structure and composition would have enabled artisans of the past to carve a range of objects successfully given the limited expertise at their disposal.

In addition, some metals were also worked on by the people during this period. Among them, copper was the first to be identified and made use of. The reason for this was that its deposits were close to the soil surface and the metal was more malleable than any other raw material. Consequently, it was amenable to both cold and hot working techniques, perhaps transmitted from stone and ceramic workings, respectively. We have evidence of copper smelting and processing from a number of small and big settlements. Later, people acquired the expertise to produce an alloy by mixing tin or nickel or

[101] Louis Flam (1982), 'Towards an Ecological Analysis of Prehistoric Settlement Patterns in Sind, Pakistan', *Sindhological Studies*, Summer, pp. 5-6; Kuldeep Bhan and V.H. Sonawane (2004), 'MSU Experts Dig Up Rare Find at Harappan Site', *Indian Express News Service*, vol. I, March.

[102] Personal Communication with colleagues at the Department of Ancient Indian History and Archaeology, M.S. University, Vadodara, Gujarat.

[103] G.F. Dales (1974), 'Excavations at Balakot, Pakistan, 1973', *Journal of Field Archaeology*, 7, 1-2, pp. 1-22.

arsenic, if needed, in the right proportions. This enabled them to devise and employ the sinking, raising, annealing, lapping and closed-casting techniques to further appreciate the properties of known metals and techniques. The famous 'dancing girl' figurine was perhaps prepared with the help of 'lost wax' method. We also have copper axes, sickles, straight-sided or curved saws, drills, drill-bits, awls, chisels, fishhooks, arrowheads and a few spear-heads with a medial rib, knives (with or without curved ends), needles, nails, chains, dishes, pans, handled frying pans, pots, bangles, rings, earrings, hairpins, mirrors with tangs, antimony rods, and curved razors from different settlements; all these inform us about the presence of specialists involved in the procurement, manufacturing, transportation and trading of these goods. These also speak of their diverse tastes and the dimensions that their economy had acquired.

Besides, precious metals such as silver and gold were also employed, primarily to make ornaments such as beads, bangles, rings, pendants, brooches and amulets among others. Attention may also be drawn to conical-shaped hollow ornaments; this type of silver ornament was in vogue among ladies from Delhi, Haryana and Rajasthan till recently. In addition, silver was also used for making vases though on a highly restricted scale. These objects enlighten us on how the people aspired for such objects and the artistans catered to their needs, especially with the improvement in the economic condition of a few.

Neither natural nor human resources are dispersed over the landscape evenly nor are the latter given equal opportunities to grow alike. This leads to a situation of differential resources (natural and human); production and accessibility, on the one hand, and conditions of scarcity and abundance, on the other. Consequently, a vast space for economic discourses over land and water is offered. The location of Harappan sites like Ropar, Manda, Harappa, Chanhu-daro, and Mohenjo-daro along the hinterland water courses, on the one hand, and of Negeshwar, Bet Dwarka (Gujarat), Allahadino (Sind) and Sutkagendor along the coast, on the other, is a reminder of this.[104] The occurrence of Harappan etched carnelian beads and dice (shell and ivory) from contemporary Mesopotamian sites, and references to boats from Dilmum, Magan and Meluha (identified with Failaka in Bahrain, Oman and the south-east Arabian region, respectively) in the records of the Sargon of Akkad supports it further. Whereas pan-regional overland movements are suggested by the location of the Harappan site of Shortughai in north-east Afghanistan, near the source of fine quality *lapis lazuli* in the Kokach Valley[105] and the common occurrence of copper pans with handles formed by bending metal from Mohenjo-daro, Chanhu-daro and Mundigak (a contemporary site in southern Afghanistan), and among the specialized Harappan objects such as

[104] Ratnagar (2001), op. cit.
[105] Ibid.

the etched carnelian beads, ivory dice, perforated jars, cylindrical vases, ring stands from the Central Asian sites of Altyn Depe, Namzga and Khapuz and from the sites of Shahdad, Hissar, Shah Tepe among others in Iran.[106] Further, Tepe Yahya and Shahr-i-Sokhta in north-east Iran point towards for being the centre of production of *lapis lazuli* and black chlorite objects, respectively, and also for being the distribution centre of their articles. The discovery of chlorite beads from Mehrgarh, Chanhu-daro and Lothal is very significant evidence as it highlights the inward movement of goods in this context.[107] A steatite circular seal from Bahrain, unlike Harappan seals in this material, bears an inscription in the Harappan script. This also contains two obscure figures of a bird in the centre and of an animal at the bottom. Likewise, stone seals with two Harappan letters from these Central Asian sites are important examples. Both suggest not only trans-regional interactions but also a certain degree of fusion of traditions.

The foregoing commercial activities necessitate the application of weights and measures based on mutually agreed standards. We do have evidence to this effect from Harappan settlements, which suggest a whole range of chert weight denominations based on a fixed ratio. However, the occurrence of weights outnumber the measures and all denominations of these weights do not come from the major urban centres leave alone the majority (including rural) of the settlements. Nor do they come from the other settlements of contemporary civilizations. This may point to the absence of any mutually recognized medium among the civilizations. Perhaps the frequency of such interactions was not high or brisk.[108] Currency of unauthorized mediums of nearly comparable standards, especially in the form of local stones weight, seems to have occupied the available internal space because barter appears to have been the normal order at both levels.

[106] Shashi Asthana (1976), *History of Archaeology of India's Contacts with Other Countries from Earliest times to 3rd Century BC*, New Delhi; S.P. Gupta (1979), *Archaeology of Soviet Central Asia and the Indian Borderlands*, 2 vols., New Delhi; E.E. Kuzmina (1995), 'The Cultural Connections Between the Shepherds of the Steppes and South Central Asia, Afghanistan and India in the Bronze Age', *SAA*, Oxford, pp. 279-90; Shereen F. Ratnagar (2004), *Trading Encounters*, Oxford University Press, New Delhi.

[107] Macello Piperno (1973), 'Micro-drilling at Shahr-i-Sokhta: The Making and Use of Lithic Drill-heads', *SAA*, Duckworth, pp. 119-30; H.P. Francfort (1992), 'New Data Illustrating the Early Contacts Between Central Asia and North-West of the Subcontinent', *SAA*, Madison Wisconsin, pp. 97-102; idem (1979), 'The World Economic of West Asia in the Third Millennium BC', *SAA*, Naples, pp. 55-85.

[108] Bertille Lyonnat (1993), 'Relations Between Central Asia and the Indian World: New Interpretations in the Light of Comprehensive Study of Ceramics, *ME*, XVIII, 2, pp. 75-86; Philip Kohl (1978), 'Western Asian Trade in the Third Millennium BC', *Current Anthropology*, 19, pp. 463-92; Fleming Hojlund (1985), 'Some New Evidence of Harappan Influence in the Arabian Gulf', *SAA*, pp. 49-54; Shereen Ratnagar (2003), 'Theorising Bronze Age Inter Cultural Trade: The Evidence of Weight', *Palaeorient*, vol. 29, 1, pp. 79-92.

RELIGIOUS BELIEF SYSTEM

We do not have any solid evidence to suggest how the Harappans perceived ritualistic and philosophical aspects, yet there are some evidences which are interpreted to suggest a range of religious pursuits that the Harappan people observed in the light of historical and modern practices.

With the progress of mankind, people devised ways to dispose of the dead. This practice evolved in line with other developments as attested to by data obtained from the excavated sites of Harappa, Lothal, Surkotada, Dholavira, Kalibanga, Rakhigarhi, Sanauli and Farmana among others. The dead body was laid supine in an extended position in a north-south direction in a rectangular pit. Individual possessions (ceramic ware, antimony rods, bracelets, necklaces, rings, bangles and mirrors among others) formed part of the grave furniture. The number and quality of these articles were broadly subject to the social and economic status that the deceased enjoyed during his/her lifetime. There are also instances of pot-burials which are believed to have contained the partial remains of the decreased in the form of ashes and charred bones. These could also either represent the practice of child burials or symbolic burials for those whose remains were not available to dispose of properly.

The graves were occasionally lined with bricks (Harappa and Kalibanga) or stones (Surkotada and Dholavira) or with a mix of the above materials. The same was also used to make some kind of tumulus (Harappa) but we are not sure if this had any relation to the social and economic standing departed souls or if it was a mere device to protect the remains from stray and wild animals.

Scientific studies of some skeletons suggest that the Harappan population was composed of the Caucasoid, Mediterranean, Armenoids, Alpines, Australoids and Mongoloids, where the first two (Caucasoid and Mediterranean) predominated. Life expectancy was low as suggested by ninety skeletons from Harappa.[109]

A terracotta tablet from Harappa depicts a seated human figure on the right with a man and buffalo on the left side. The man holds one horn of the animal with his left hand and presses its head with his right foot, intending to pierce its back with the spear held in his right hand. This is mistakenly interpreted as displaying the sacrifice of the buffalo in front of the seated human figure. A terracotta cake from Kalibanga contains one human figure engraved on each side. The person on one side is shown holding a rope tied to an animal

[109] Kenneth A.R. Kennedy (1973), 'Biological Anthropology of Prehistoric Populations in South Asia: A Survey of Current Research Efforts', in Kenneth A.R. Kennedy and G.L. Possehl (ed.), *Ecological Background of South Asian Prehistory*, Cornell University, pp. 116-78; Brian E. Hemphill et al. (1991), 'Biological Adaptations and Affinities of Bronze Age Harappan', in Richard H. Meadow (ed.), *Harappan Excavations 1986-1990*, Madison Wisconsin, pp. 137-82; R.S. Sharma (1995 and 2001), op. cit., pp. 6-7.

whereas the person on the other side is shown with a headgear. The former is interpreted as taking the animal to the sacrificial altar, though this only demonstrates the act of taking the animal to some place held by a rope, as is usually done on a daily basis by people keeping animals. There is nothing unusual about it nor is there any evidence of an altar to interpret it this manner. A seal from Mohenjo-daro, depicts a human figure seated on a dais surrounded by animals and is erroneously equated with the cult of Shiva. Likewise, the cult of the mother goddess is seen by some in the depiction of a kneeling human figure and a ram in front of the female figure, in combination with seven figures in another register below in a *pipal* enclosure.

Besides, a combine of seven fireplaces in a row in association with a well on one side and a wall behind on the other are interesting. This encircling wall is taken as an apse-like enclosure and is equated with an apsidal temple. Another burnt brick-linked fire pit (1.25 × 1 m) with bovine bones and antlers an adjoining platform, as well as fire pits (plastered with mud, 25 cm deep) and a 30-40 cm high cylindrical stele fixed vertically among biconvex circular terracotta cakes with ash and charcoal from Kalibanga are presented as corroborative evidences of sacrificial practices. Further, a pit (85 × 75 × 20 cm) with charred fragments of jaw bones of an animal of the bovine group, a circular disc-shaped pendant, a carnelian bead, six sherds of a thick storage jar painted in chocolate over a buff surface and a lot of ash is also used to buttress this argument. Interestingly, these elements are not the sole preserve of religious activity; rather, they appear to have been associated with the more pressing daily needs of the people.[110]

The presence of fire pits in the Harappan levels is not misplaced in this context because these form an integral part of every household even today and these are meant for cooking purposes.[111] The cooking fire pits of the ancient past are likely to contain some of the elements of the dietary practices of the Harappan people as well as of their individual possessions, especially of those who worked on them, in the form of ornaments, etc. The occurrence of a stray bead and pendant is not out of sync in this context. Similarly, the presence of animal bones in any form in these pits is also part of their food habits, especially in association with sherds of a big storage jar or the jar itself. Such jars also form part of a cooking space along with fire pits and animal bones. This type of evidence is not wanting in the context of Harappan settlements. We have discovered a similar cooking context from the Harappan site of Badali in the Jhajjar district of Haryana during the 2007-9 excavations, where we exposed twin-hearths with terracotta cakes and a storage jar, the

[110] Lal (2003), op. cit. However, we would like to put the record straight in this context. We have discovered twin hearths and a fire pit along with a lot of ash and animal bones from the village Harappan site of Badali, district Jhajjar, Haryana, in 2008, which in no way suggests anything of the sort being inferred by Lal from such remains at Kalibanga.

[111] Thakran (2003), op. cit.

upper part being broken and the lower embedded in the mud floor, as also a fire pit with animal bones in ash.[112] The area of location of the seven fire pits, encircled by a wall on one side and a well on the other, in the southern part of the citadel is interesting for presenting a new context. These fireplaces, in fact, are neither part of the cooking activities of a family nor do they imply occasional cooking. Instead, what they seem to represent is the large-scale everyday cooking activity for a large group of personnel inhabiting the citadel. The so-called apse-like wall is only part of a device to safeguard the cooking space from the wind coming from that direction among other things. The well was to supply water for cooking and other necessary activities of the daily routine; there is nothing religious about it. In fact, the problem is that while we deal with the archaeological data from past societies, we try to perceive them through our own modern cultural lenses instead of the actual life parameters of the people of the past.

STATE AND STRUCTURE

We do not have any direct evidence regarding the structure of the Harappan administration. Whatever little information could have been contained from the numerous short inscriptions also remains elusive as they are not deciphered satisfactorily yet. Nevertheless, there are some indirect and circumstantial evidences in the form of the broadly uniform standards of town planning, bricks, weights and measures, defence, organized production, distribution and regulation of commercial transactions, and the congregation of a diverse population in the urban centre, which point to the need for and presence of some form of administration.[113]

The Harappan zone is generally presumed to be a static unit. This is erroneous because its frontiers continuously shifted during its lifetime. Nevertheless, there are some tangible constants in each phase. What we notice in the context of its early phase is a simple kind of house plan, building material, the 1:2:3 ratio of usually mud bricks, the low-hierarchy development of settlements, less diversity in simple productive forces, a largely subsistence economy, and regional ceramic identities which were later fused into pan-regional identities. This was perhaps the cumulative effect of multiple operative variables in the process of development guided by some moving force. Hence, what we notice is the interplay of a more advanced house plan, bricks in the ratio of 1:2:4 (both sun-dried as well as fired), a greater settlement hierarchy, surplus food economy, diverse and complex productive forces, predominant

[112] During the excavations at the Harappan site of Badali in 2008, these things were discovered. In no way can these be interpreted as suggesting any religious activity; rather, these are closely linked to the daily needs of the people. Each and every household contains these type of fire pits even today in the villages of this area.

[113] Shereen F. Ratnagar (1991), *Enquiries into the Political Organization of Harappan Society*, Ravish Publishers, Pune.

uniform ceramics, weights and measures, seals and sealings, substantial internal and external exchange of goods, and a defence apparatus. The element of greater uniformity may point to, the presence of some central authority, according to some scholars, though this is not always true. The ubiquitous defence mechanism, at least in case of urban settlements, is very significant, irrespective of its diverse forms. The residents of these urban settlements are not largely natives; they are not in any considerable percentage interrelated socially, geographically and in other persuasions, though they may represent commonality in their economic interests and safety concerns. They may not, individually or collectively, have addressed these safety concerns successively in any measure on their own for long. This necessitated the presence of some administrative machinery, including defence, on a regular basis. The question of its actual shape and structure, however, is still a point of debate and in the realm of conjecture.[114]

The above discussion clearly brings out at least three points: one, the need for a protective system was common to all urban centres irrespective of their size and functions; two, the protective measures effected were uniform in intent; three, these protective measures varied in their content in tune with threat perceptions based on the unique demands of respective settlements. The last point is elaborated by the presence of independent twin mounds at the big centres of Harappa and Mohenjo-daro, whereas the integration of the two in one mound at the small centres of Banawali, Surkotada and Lothal is noticed. This may also point to the existence of some kind of hierarchy in the administrative structure.

Substantial reversals are seen in the late phase where the resurgence of regional identities overshadows the pan-regional world-view of the preceding phase. We also experience its reflection on the defence system as well because evidence on the erstwhile system is not forthcoming from any of the settlements of this phase. It appears that whenever regional aspirations are not adequately addressed by the overarching system in place, such regional tendencies resurge to occupy centrestage. As a result, pan-regional formations are overtaken by regional outfits, though in a fragmented form.

SOCIAL STRUCTURE

Keeping in mind the advancements attained by the civilization, one gets the impression of a well-organized society. But the lack of literary information makes it difficult to comprehend its actual composition. The non-decipherment of the diverse inscriptions from the excavations (if some information is contained therein at all) compounds it further. There are, however, some circumstantial evidences, which perhaps can be made use of only in visualizing broad social contours but that will also remain in the realm of inference until proved either way with the discovery of hard data.

[114] Ibid.

The circumstantial data come in the form of well-finished goods, the products of established specialists. The diversity of data, the broad uniformity in their make and shape, and their persistent circulation, though in a differential frequency for a considerable time period further point to the division of labour as well as the presence of (at least in the mature phase) specialized groups and organized production. Among them, those who worked on land (for production and domestication of animals), clay (for producing a range of sun-dried as well as fired objects), stones (local as well as exotic), metals (both semi-precious and precious), marine shells, and ivory occupy greater space. Besides, those who specialized in service sectors such as planning, construction, trade, administration, defence and so on also seem to have formed part of the economic spectrum. They primarily represent economic units and professionals and cannot be equated with social entities such as the varnas and the castes of later times. The kind of space reservation for priests and the religious activities that is perceived in the northern and southern parts of the citadel at Kalibanga, respectively, is more an offshoot of personal persuasions than an outcome of scientific analysis of archaeological data.

The presence of spacious houses with open courtyards, grain-storing facilities, and seals and sealings from the lower town,[115] on the one hand, and the small houses with lots of pottery and ash in one section from the unfortified sector south of the citadel at Kalibanga, on the other, point to professional and economic diversity rather than an inherent privileged and non-privileged character of any profession as envisaged on the basis of this data. Likewise, the small hutments and (working) platforms from areas outside the citadel at Harappa also suggest this. Neither do this data underline any hierarchical arrangement of professions nor do they attach any ancestry to them despite professionals staying in their ancestral houses for generations. People live in their ancestral houses over generations but they do not necessarily engage in their respective ancestral occupations alone. We do not have any evidence to rule out inter-occupation mobility and, thereby, the reduction of these groups to a social institution such as caste. We cannot visualize the presence of these institutions in this period against the well-documented records from the early historical period onwards about their introduction and consolidation. What we need to do is to attempt a contextual analysis of the data to relieve the past lives rather than adding our own contexts to their data and drawing jaundiced conclusions.

THE ISSUE OF 'DECLINE'

The decline of this civilization was neither an event nor an incidence. Rather, it was a long-drawn out process like its evolution. Neither can it be attributed to any single factor nor to any one particular point in time. It appears to have

[115] Lal (2003), op. cit.

been a cumulative impact of the interplay of a host of factors added to it over time and space. In order to understand and dynamics of the decline, one has to take recourse to the interplay of natural and the social forces and find which of them played the role of the driving force in the collapse of this system.

We do not want to indulge in the details of the 'Aryan invasion' for neither is there any conclusive evidence nor can the breakdown of a system like this be satisfactorily explained by such an isolated encounter, if any. Moreover, literary references alone cannot be relied upon for the resolution of an archaeological problem of this nature despite some disjointed archaeological evidence from a few, isolated settlements. The evidence of seven (fragmentary or complete) skeletons from Mohenjo-daro fails to qualify this point of view. These come from different strata (intermediate, upper and post-desertion levels). These evidences cannot be treated as one body from a single stratum and this thereby reduces their relevance in proving any massive onslaught on the settlement. Moreover, their occurrence from only one settlement does not allow us to presume disturbances on any appreciable scale at all at the other important representative centres that led to the demise of the civilization. Thus, however, surely points to a possibility of some internal disturbance arising out of social and economic dissatisfaction.

Likewise, the settlement of Kalibanga is said to have been deserted by the drying up of the Sarasvati/Ghaggar River. The river dried up, according to the votaries of this viewpoint, because of the shifting of its two erstwhile tributaries in the form of the Sutlej in the west and the Yamuna in the east. Consequently, water became scarce which was further compounded by adverse changes in the realm of rains in this area. Interestingly, neither was the river ever fed by these two so-called east and west tributaries nor was it ever perennial, if new available data are any pointer. We do not have any supportive evidence to this effect in any form. The kind of signatures that the Sutlej and Yamuna are known for neither of them come from their vast intervening space nor from the Ghaggar as well. Besides, the site of Kalibanga was and is on the left bank of the Ghaggar; there is hardly any change in its relationship with the water course, nor do we have any hydrological or sedimentary evidences from the surface or sub-surface to this effect. This view is crystallized from the wide range of data that have been gathered from recent field researches in this area and, thus, the river has never been a perennial mighty water course as earlier envisaged.[116] As far as the availability of potable water for the survival of the settlement was concerned, it was neither tied up with the perennial or seasonal nature of the river nor with its continuous presence alone. We know that a certain quantity of potable ground water has always been available in shallow aquifers along the water course. What was needed was the knowledge of a device to harness this ground water reserve.

[116] Thakran (2009), op. cit.

Obviously, the Harappan people in general and the Kalibanga in particular knew how to sink brick-lined wells for drawing water from the sub-surface. Further, this water reserve was not depleted with this kind of exploitation for centuries together. Keeping this scenario in view, even if we accept the drying up of this water course (though there is no valid ground), the availability of ground water reserve would not have posed any threat to the existence of this settlement.

As regards the negative change in rainfall, we neither have any irrefutable evidence to prove it nor do we perceive an all-pervasive decrease in rainfall given the location of this region and the epochal nature of the rainfall system.[117] On the basis of available data, what we visualize is only oscillations within its broad outlines of highs and lows, and no major long-term departures before the independence period. These have also not been of a continental nature but rotated between local and regional contours. The situation was not substantially different from that on the eve of the introduction of canal irrigation by the British in the late nineteenth century in this area for the common people. Yet they, in more numbers than the Harappans, lived their lives successfully. Above all, rain water does not appear to have been the sole determining factor for the existence of a settlement in the landscape that the site of Kalibanga is located in. The so-called desertion of the settlement some time during the mature phase did not herald the simultaneous dislocation of all other contemporary settlements in the region in particular and the Harappan zone in general. Numerous settlements lived continuously through the mature and late phases without any stratigraphical interruption in contrast to Kalibanga. The point, however, is what led to the ultimate collapse of the civilization. The answer seems to rest with the stagnant social working capacity, especially tool-technology, which is closely linked with the quality of human resources. Whenever human resources do not evolve in tune with changing circumstantial needs to overcome ever-surfacing challenges in order to sustain growth, if not it increase, the society can only delay the impending decline instead of precluding it forever (the addition of millets to their crops serves as a reminder in this case). With the help of adaptive strategies, the society can only linger on a demise rather than rejuvenating itself to regain past growth levels. This is what we confront in this context. Social forces failed in evolving a new tool-technology to cope up with growing social demands and finally, the Harappan system succumbed under the constant pressures of growing demands.

[117] There is hardly any change in the physical location of this area in terms of its geo-coordinates since ancient times and, therefore, we do not visualize any abrupt, drastic shift in the realm of rainfall in this area during the ancient past, especially in the Holocene period. Its unpredictable character is a perennial feature which has been oscillating within low and high limits since the remote past, as it is governed by a host of natural factors.

Chapter 13

Post-urban Farming Cultures

M.K. Dhavalikar

The discovery of the Indus or Harappan civilization in the early 1920s created a hiatus between the end of that glorious civilization around 1600 BC and the beginning of the historical period in the sixth century BC. The discovery of the Neolithic phase at Brahmagiri by Mortimer Wheeler in 1947, and of the Chalcolithic culture at Jorwe and Nasik by H.D. Sankalia in 1950 showed that, during the hiatus in the post-Harappan period, rural farming communities lived in India. Subsequent excavations have shown that such farming communities occupied different parts of the country, particularly central and western India, and the Deccan, as also the middle and lower Ganga Valley (Fig. 13.1). They share many features in common, as, for instance, black-on-red painted pottery, a specialized blade/flake industry, and copper, which, being scarce, was used on a restricted scale for making tools and personal ornaments. Their mixed economy was based on subsistence agriculture, stock-raising and hunting-fishing. Many of these communities lived in the black cotton soil zone which is semi-arid with average precipitation ranging between 400-1000 mm. Although a few of them were contemporaries of the Harappans, most of them lived during the second millennium BC. They all, however, remained poor village folk and could not attain urban status; they vanished from the scene in the first half of the second millennium. Those living in the Ganga basin continued to survive well into the first quarter of the first millennium BC.

AHAR CULTURE

The Ahar culture also called the Banas culture after the river—is the earliest Chalcolithic culture contemporary with the Indus civilization if recent radiocarbon dates are any indication. It was first brought to light in excavations at Ahar (district Udaipur, Rajasthan) and, hence, is named after the type-site. Balathal (district Udaipur) and Ojyana[1] are smaller sites but Gilund (district Udaipur) is much larger and is being presently being excavated (Possehl and

[1] B.R. Meena and Alok Tripathi (2000-1), 'Further Excavation at Ojiyana', *Puratattva*, 31, pp. 73-8.

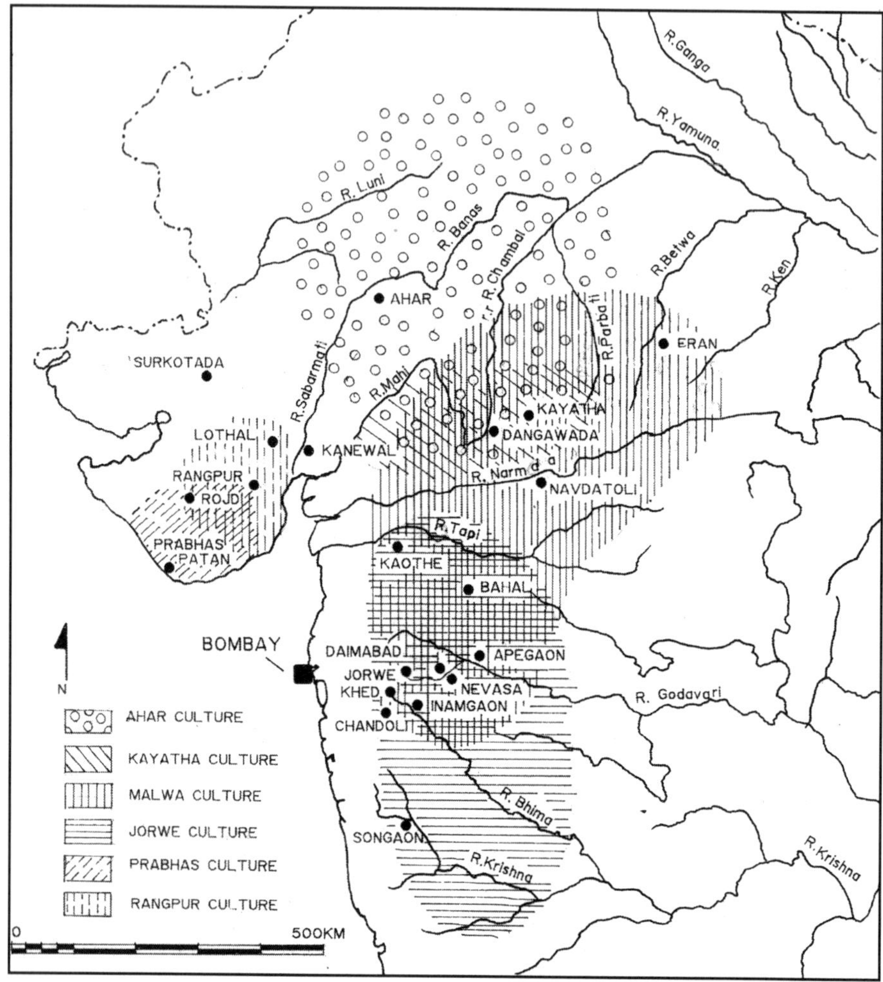

Fig. 13.1: Map showing distribution of Chalcolithic cultures

Shinde 2001). These sites have pushed back the antiquity of the Ahar culture to the beginning of the third millennium.

Ahar (ancient Aghatapur) is almost a suburb of the city of Udaipur. The ancient mound (500 × 275 m) is situated on the right bank of the Ahar River, a tributary of the Banas. It is interesting to note that Ahar was also known in ancient times as Tambavati Nagari, probably because of the availability of copper in the region. Mewar is a hilly region with a scrub forest but has alluvial patches in the Banas Valley in sharp contrast to Marwar, which is to the west of it. Even Mewar is poor with respect to its climate, rainfall and soils. The region around Ahar was earlier known as Medapataka from which the present name Mewar is derived. It is also likely that it is derived from Marwar. Which, in turn, owes it to the Mers or Meos, a pastoral nomadic tribe said to be of foreign origin.

Excavations revealed a threefold sequence of cultures of which the first is characterized by the Banas culture, after which the site remained unoccupied for over a thousand years only to be inhabited in the centuries around the Christian era (*c.* 100 BC-AD 100) and again in late medieval times.[2] The Banas culture does not seem to have developed at the site but the people appear to have arrived here from elsewhere. It is characterized by a distinctive black-and-red pottery decorated with white paintings. The first cultural period is divided into three different phases I-a (*c.* 2600-2150 BC), I-b (*c.* 2150-1950 BC) and I-c (*c.* 1950-1500 BC), on the basis of the ceramic evidence. The black-and-red ware (BRW) occurs in all three phases and, associated with it, are a red ware and a grey ware which also occur in all three phases, whereas a cream slipped ware is only confined to phase I-a.

Black-and-Red Ware

The BRW is the most enigmatic ceramic of ancient India. Earlier, it was thought to be characteristic of the Megalithic culture of south India, but it has now become clear that it has a hoary antiquity and the widest distribution of any ceramic ware in ancient India. The earliest evidence comes from western India where it is found in pre-Harappan levels at Prabhas Patan or Somnath (district Junagadh, Gujarat) and later, in Harappan levels at several sites in Kachchh and Saurashtra. It is also present at Chalcolithic sites in central and western India and the Deccan in the second millennium BC, and even in historical levels almost all over the country but vanishes from the scene after the second-third century AD, so much so that even the technique of its manufacture was totally forgotten. According to some, the pottery was made by inverted firing which produced the bi-colour effect[3] while others argue that it could be made only by double-firing.[4]

The BRW pottery is not found anywhere in the world except in Egypt and Greece where it occurs in Neolithic levels which are datable to the fourth-fifth millennium BC. Far more interesting is the BRW pottery from Nubia. Excavations at Tumas carried out by an Indian team led by B.B. Lal of the Archaeological Survey of India in the Nubian desert have also yielded BRW pottery which bears a striking resemblance to the Megalithic pottery from south India.[5] What is important is that the evidence shows that the BRW

[2]H.D. Sankalia, S.B. Deo and Z.D. Ansari (1969), *Excavations at Ahar (Tambavati)*, Deccan College, Poona.

[3]G.V. Childe (1937), 'On the Courses of Gray and Black Colouration in Prehistoric Pottery', *Man*, 37, p. Art. 55.

[4]G.G. Mujumdar (1969), 'Problem of Megalithic Black and Red Ware: A Technological Approach', in A.K. Narayan (ed.), *Seminar Papers on the Problem of Megaliths in India*, Banaras Hindu University, Varanasi, pp. 90-3.

[5]B.B. Lal (1963), 'The only Indian Expedition in Threatened Nubia: Work by Indian Mission in Afyeh and Tumas', *Illustrated London News*, 20, 4, p. 580.

pottery may have come to India as a result of cultural contact between India and Egypt in prehistoric times, as the technique is very specialized.

The BRW pottery constitutes the distinguishing feature of the Ahar or the Banas culture. The ceramic is represented mostly by bowls, rather sub-spherical and concave-sided, and sometimes burnished as well. The fabric is medium to coarse and, in some cases, the red portion appears brownish. Along with bowls, globular jars also occur in phase I-a whereas, in I-b, carinated bowls are introduced along with a step-sided dish, a bowl-on-stand, some time with a corrugated stem. In I-c, some new forms are introduced. Associated with the BRW, are a red ware, a chocolate or tan ware and a grey ware, all utilitarian ceramics represented by globular jars which, in red or tan ware, have ribbings on the shoulder. Pans, basins, dishes and bowls-on-stand also occur in this ware. The grey ware is very coarse in fabric and many of its vessels have their lower portions rusticated, which, along with black soot at the bottom, points to their being used for cooking.

The coarse grey and red ware vessels are sometimes decorated with incised and applique designs. The red ware was also (rarely) adorned with paintings in black. The BRW, however, is very exquisitely ornamented with painted patterns in white. They are mostly linear and geometric, and are usually formed by dotted patterns resembling *Bandhani* designs (tie-and-die) of the cotton fabrics which are used by women in Rajasthan and Gujarat. It is noteworthy that these garments are also usually black and red in colour, and bear white dotted patterns.

Structures (Fig. 13.2)

People of the Ahar culture lived in spacious houses built of schist slabs which are plentifully available locally. These stonewalled houses were quite large and rectangular in plan, sometimes enclosed by a stone wall. They had well-made floors in which sand mixed with silt was rammed hard. No postholes have been found and it is, therefore, clear that the roof was not supported by poles. Their absence can be explained by the fact that the region is more or less arid with very little rainfall, hence no sloping roof to drain rain-water was required. The flat roof was supported by low walls as is the case today. Large *chulhas* (three-walled hearths) have been found inside the houses; they had knob-like projections on the interior for supporting cooking vessels. Some of the large-mouthed *chulhas* were probably used for copper smelting.

The structure complex unearthed at Balathal is almost labyrinthine.[6] It is a small site, about 2.50 ha in extent, but half of it is presently under cultivation. The Chalcolithic habitation is divisible into two phases: I-a (*c*. 2800-2400 BC) and I-b (*c*. 2400-1800 BC). Period I-a is characterized by coarse, hand-

[6]V.N. Misra (1997), 'Balathal: A Chalcolithic Settlement in Mewar, Rajasthan, India-Result of First Three Seasons' Excavations', *SAS*, 13, pp. 251-73.

Fig. 13.2: Bronze Age houses, Ahar (Reconstruction), Rajasthan *c.* 2000 BC

made, plain and pained pottery. The people lived in round huts of mud and thatch. Tools were made of copper and stone blades are absent. Towards the end of this phase, wheel-made pottery appears: it is white-painted BRW associated with a thin red ware, a tan ware and a buff ware. Coarse, hand-made pottery, decorated with incised patterns also occurs.

The most important structure of phase I-b is a fortified enclosure (500 sq m) in the centre of the site. It is rectangular in plan with a rectangular bastion in the western corner; possibly there were such bastions at other corners too The structure, thus, looks like a citadel. It was built of stone-rubble set in mud mortar. Some residential complexes, too, were exposed, some with two-armed hearths and storages. A potter's kiln was also encountered.

Some interesting structures were unearthed at Gilund (25° 1′ N, 74° 15′ E), a site of crucial importance for the Ahar culture. The ancient site (district Rajsamand, Rajasthan) is quite extensive (500 × 250 m) and is located on the right bank of the Banas River in the Udaipur district, about 75 km north-east of Udaipur town. It was excavated by B.B. Lal.[7] The entire occupation is Chalcolithic and divisible into four sub-phases. A microlithic blade industry, which was conspicuously absent at Ahar, is present here. There are no stone-walled houses but mud-brick structures and even the use of burnt brick is attested. The twin mounds at the site, eastern and western, rising in height to 45′ and 25′, respectively, were occupied in Chalcolithic times but some later habitation took place on the former and, hence, its height is more. All the characteristic pottery as at Ahar occurs here besides, a painted black-on-red or buff ceramic.

A very unusual structure was encountered at Gilund. It covered a considerably large area of which 100 × 50 ft was exposed. It consisted of four parallel walls of mud-brick, the average size of which was 32.5 × 12.5 × 10 cm, laid in the headers and stretchers fashion, a characteristic feature of Harappan architecture. The four parallel walls running north-south joined an east-west wall at the southern end and, from the latter again, emerged three walls running north-south. The walls were about 75 × 90 cm in width and their extant height is about 1.80 m whereas the space in between them was filled with sand. This structure belongs to the earliest phase of the Chalcolithic (Period I).

A mud-brick house of the second sub-phase was exposed. A very interesting feature of this phase are the clay-lined pits, usually circular or oblong in plan, varying from 90 to 130 cm in diameter and about 30 cm deep. The thickness of the clay lining varying from 15 to 45 cm indicated that these were, in all probability, used as pit silos for storage. In fact, they may even be clay bins which were embedded in the ground, as at Inamgaon.[8] The houses of the

[7] *IAR*, 1959-60, pp. 23-46.

[8] M.K. Dhavalikar, H.D. Sankalia and Z.D. Ansari (1988), *Excavations at Inamgaon*, Deccan College, Poona, vol. I, pts. 1 and 2, fig. 11.60.

third sub-phase mark some degeneration; they were built of stone rubble and mud or mud-bricks with a thatched roof, and contained whitewashed earthen ovens.[9] A long wall built of burnt bricks was traced to a length of 8 m and another cutting across it were found. They had a plaster of mixed clay and sand an inch thick. The entrance with wooden posts shows that it was a large structure complex.[10]

In the last structural phase, a large circular pit (4.20 cm diameter) and 75 cm deep was encountered. It was plastered with mud mixed with sand and vegetable fibre. The very size and nature of the pit shows that it was a pit-dwelling, which indicates deterioration of economic conditions as a result of which people were gradually reverting to a seasonally settled life.

Recent excavations at Gilund have pushed back the beginnings of the Ahar culture to *c.* 3000 BC and has brought to light some of its new features. Gilund was subjected to excavation earlier by B.B. Lal[11] who found some concentric walls. It is the largest site of the Ahar culture, spread over 25 ha, and is represented by two mounds which are locally known as Modiya Magari (bald habitation mounds). It lies at the southern end of the Khetri copper belt. Recent excavations have revealed a threefold culture sequence which is as follows:[12]

Period I (*c.* 3000-2500 BC) is characterized by coarse, hand-made pottery used by the people who occupied a very small area at the site and who lived in circular mud huts of wattle-and-daub construction.

Period II (*c.* 2500-2000 BC) Gilund (GLD) became prosperous in the latter half of the third millennium when people started using fine wheel-made pottery, and lived in large rectangular houses of mud and mud-bricks. Two important structure complexes belong to this period. One consisted of parallel walls built of mud-bricks, externally plastered with mud. They formed long narrow (1 m wide) chambers used as a warehouse, as the evidence of pit silos dug into the floor and numerous seal impressions found deposited in a bin show. They are similar to those from Chanhu-daro, Pirak, Kot Diji and Nindowri and, are characteristic of the Bactria-Margiana-Archaeological Complex (BMAC) or the Oxus civilization, as it is now labelled. Another large structure complex was encountered to the south-west of the warehouse. Its floor was made of pebbles and gravel that was rammed hard.

It appears that GLD-I was probably the citadel area whereas GLD-II was similar to the lower town of the Harappans. In the industrial area in GLD-II, two large structures were exposed. One of them yielded chunks of highly vitrified material. Besides, there are a kiln and a hearth. Another structure

[9] *IAR*, 1959-60, p. 43, Pl. XLV, B.

[10] Ibid., pp. 43-4.

[11] Ibid., pp. 41-6.

[12] V.S. Shinde and G.L. Possehl (2001), 'A Report on the Excavations at Gilund 1999-2001', *SAA*, Paris.

built of mud and mud-bricks was partly uncovered. There was also a residential complex in GLD-II.

Remains of a fortification wall have also been traced. Another important discovery is that of a *tandoor* in the GLD-I area, which recalls to the mind that from Kalibangan. It may also be noted that an earlier habitation belonging to the Mesolithic phase has been found at the site. It has been divided into two phases: aceramic and ceramic, and is assigned to 5000-4000 BC.

Period III (2000-1500 BC) marks a decline, as mud-bricks were replaced by wattle and daub huts of which five were exposed. The settlement was finally abandoned in the middle of the second millennium BC.

The predominant pottery in all the periods is the white painted BRW associated with red and grey wares.[13]

The tools of the Ahar people were mostly made of copper. It is surprising that the microlithic blade industry which is present at other Ahar culture sites is totally absent at Ahar itself. Perhaps the abundance of copper in its neighbourhood was responsible for this. Copper deposits occur in the area around Ahar in the Aravalli region at Derbari, Delwara and Kotrj, which are situated within a radius of 20 km from Ahar. Besides, the Ambamata belt which extends from north Gujarat up to Khetri in Rajasthan is also rich in copper.[14] Large hearths uncovered in the course of excavations may probably have been used for smelting copper. Copper axes from Ahar were subjected to scientific examination which show that they were very probably fashioned from a crude earthen mould.[15]

SUBSISTENCE

The people at Balathal cultivated wheat (*Triticum* sp.), barley (*Hordeum vulgare*), lentil (*Lens esculenta*), common pea (*Pisum arvense*), finger millet (*Eleucine coracana*), Italian millet (*Setaria italica* Beauv) and panicum. The occurrence of jowar and bajra is not surprising since both are now reported from some of the Chalcolithic sites in the Deccan[16] and even from Harappan sites in Gujarat.[17] Their occurrence in West Asia is much earlier and it is,

[13]V.S. Shinde, G.L. Possehl and Shweta Sinha Deshpande (2001-2), 'The Ceramic Assemblage in Protohistoric Mewar Rajasthan with Special Reference to Gilund and Balathal', *Puratattva*, 32, pp. 5-24.

[14]N.L. Sharma (1968), 'A Note on the Old Copper Workings of Amba Mata near Abu Road Station, Gujarat', in *Copper: Progress on Symposium on Copper*, Geological Survey of India, Manager of Publication, Calcutta.

[15]Sankalia, et al. (1969), op. cit.

[16]M.D. Kajale (1991), 'Current Status of Indian Palaeo-ethnobotany', J. Renfrew (ed.), *New Light on Early Farming: Recent Development in Palaeoethnobotany*, Edinburgh University Press, Edinburgh, pp. 155-89.

[17]Weber, S.A. (1991), *Plants and Harappan Subsistence*, Oxford and IBH, New Delhi.

therefore, likely that thev may have been introduced in India by way of trade. The Aharians kept cattle, sheep/goat, buffaloes and even pigs.

Religious Beliefs

There is not much direct evidence for the religious beliefs of the people but the discovery of numerous terracotta bull figurines from the Ahar levels at Kayatha indicates that bull worship or a sort of bull cult was in vogue.[18] It is strange that such bull figurines should be absent at the most important site of the culture (Fig. 13.3). Yet, on going through the evidence, it becomes clear that a couple of bull figurines of the stylized variety have been found at Ahar[19] and also at Gilund. Again, in Rajasthan itself, the ancient site at Marmi has yielded some. The figurines are both realistic and stylized, and it is the latter variety which is very interesting as one can trace the evolution of the stylized form from the naturalistic. In this process, the hind part of the body is first reduced to a stem, then the head also vanishes and only a pair of horns on the pedestal remain. It is highly likely that these figurines were worn round the neck by means of a string, just as the Lingayats of Karnataka wear a *linga* today.

We do not know who the people of the Ahar culture were in the absence of skeletal remains. Excavators suggest that they may be the ancestors of the present-day Bhils who are living in that region.[20] Over fifty sites of the Ahar culture have been discovered in south-east Rajasthan and it was also spread over the adjoining area of Malwa in Madhya Pradesh. The site remained unoccupied for nearly a millennium and a half, after it was deserted by the Chalcolithic people around 1500 BC, and was re-occupied in the early centuries of the Christian era. It was then destroyed by fire and, hence, abandoned but again occupied in medieval times.

GUJARAT

Two farming cultures flourished in Saurashtra after the downfall of the Indus civilization. Of these, the Prabhas culture emerged in southern Saurashtra and the Rangpur culture in its upper part. Actually, both of them can justifiably be called sub-Indus cultures as they are clearly derived from the Harappan. Both are named after the type-sites where they were first noticed, respectively, at Prabhas Patan (district Junagarh) and Rangpur (district Limbdi).

[18] Z.D. Ansari and M.K. Dhavalikar (1971), 'New Light on the Prehistoric Cultures of Central India', *World Archaeology*, 2, pp. 337-46.

[19] Sankalia et al. (1969), op. cit., Fig. 117.4.

[20] Ibid., p. 224.

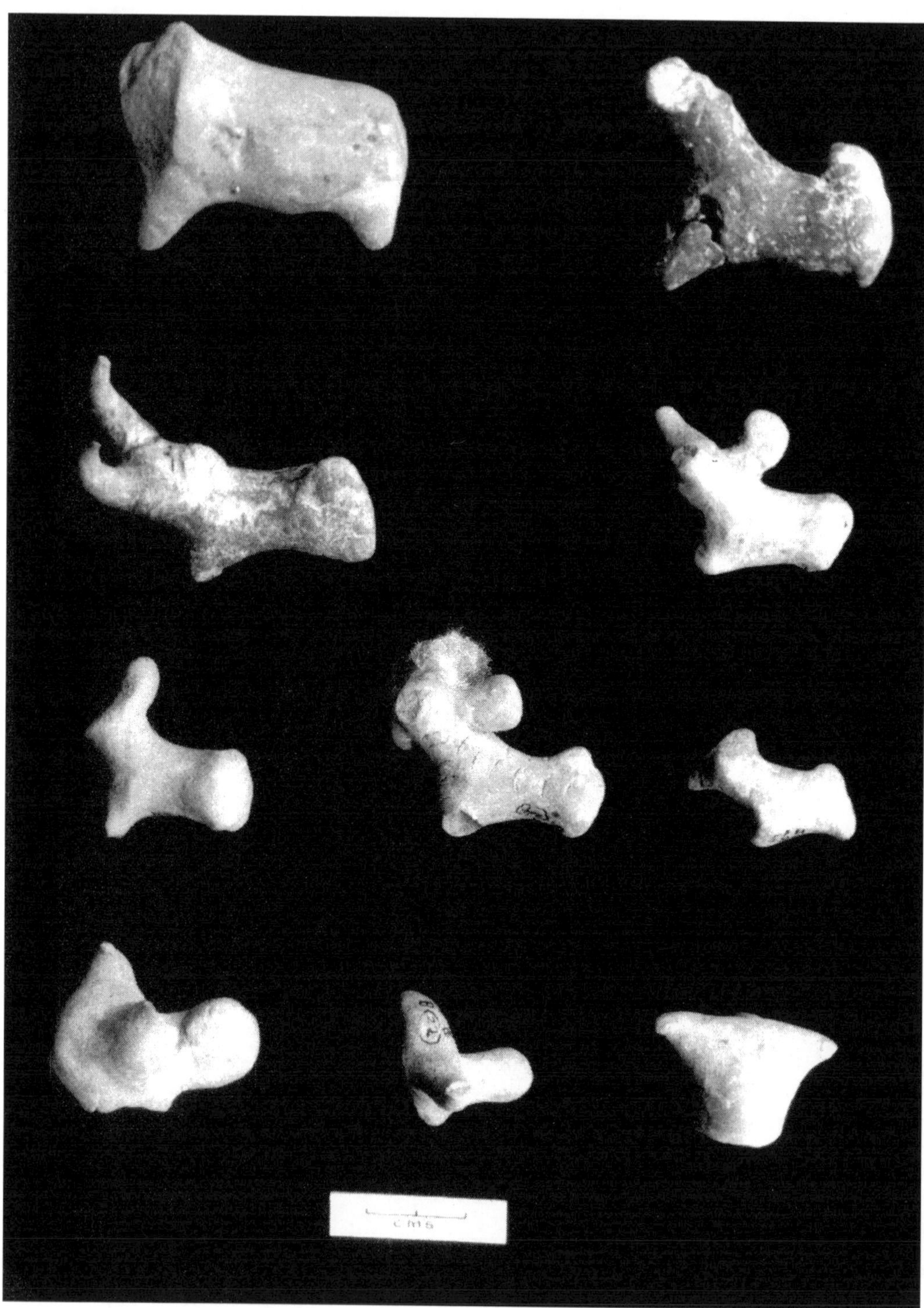

Fig. 13.3: Terracotta bull figurines, Kayatha, Ahar period

PRABHAS CULTURE (*c*. 1800-1500 BC)

The Prabhas culture was noticed in excavations at Prabhas Patan—also known as Somnath Patan—an important centre of pilgrimage because of the Somnath temple enshrining a *Jyotirlinga*. The ancient site, located on the Hiran River, was earlier excavated by the State Department of Archaeology and the MS University of Vadodara,[21] and later by the Deccan College, Pune.[22] The Prabhas culture has been divided into two phases: A. Early Prabhas; B. Late Prabhas. Excavation revealed that the site was occupied much earlier in the pre-Prabhas period (*c*. 3000-2800 BC), which is characterized by coarse pottery, red or grey, red slipped and BRW. An obsidian flake, and steatite faience beads, some of which were of the segmented variety, also occurred. The cultural debris of this period were washed away by marine transgressions. On the basis of radiocarbon dates, the pre-Prabhas phase can be assigned to *c*. 3000-2800 BC.

The site remained unoccupied for nearly a thousand years and was later inhabited by the Prabhas people who lived there for about six centuries from *c*. 1800-1200 BC (calib. dates 2000-1400 BC). The Prabhas culture has been divided into two phases on the basis of the presence of Rangpur lustrous red ware, which occurs from *c*. 1500-1200 BC (*c*. 1700-1400 BC calib.). The Prabhas ware which characterizes the Prabhas culture is clearly derived from typical Harappan pottery. It is of fine fabric, made of well-levigated clay, and is treated with a pinkish or orange wash which, in several cases, has turned greyish because of the peculiar firing conditions in the kiln. The painted designs are drawn in purple or dark brown. The repertoire of painted patterns is somewhat limited, and most of them are linear and geometric motifs which include vertical and oblique strokes, wavy lines, hatched triangles, loops, etc. The painted ornament is generally set in panels or registers and is confined to the upper part of the vessel. The predominant form is a sub-spherical bowl with a featureless rim, sometimes slightly incurved and internally sharpened (Fig. 13.4). Bowls occur in all sizes, small and big. Another form is a globular jar with an outcurved rim which was obviously used for storage. The Harappan forms are the dish-on-stand, the perforated jar and the stud-handled bowl. The dish-on-stand, however, has a flat dish and not a cup which occurs at Harappan sites. Its stem is solid. The perforated jar is a copy of the Harappan.

It is enigmatic that no stone tools were found save a solitary obsidian flake, which, however, may have been an import as it is not available locally. Obsidian is said to be available in the Osham hills in central Saurashtra but is much coarser than the specimen obtained from the excavations. Copper

[21] J.M. Nanavati et al. (1971), *Somnath (1965): Ahmedabad and Baroda*, Gujarat Government and M.S. University, Baroda.

[22] M.K. Dhavalikar (1978), 'An Early Warehouse on West Coast', *Puratattva*, 9, pp. 100-3.

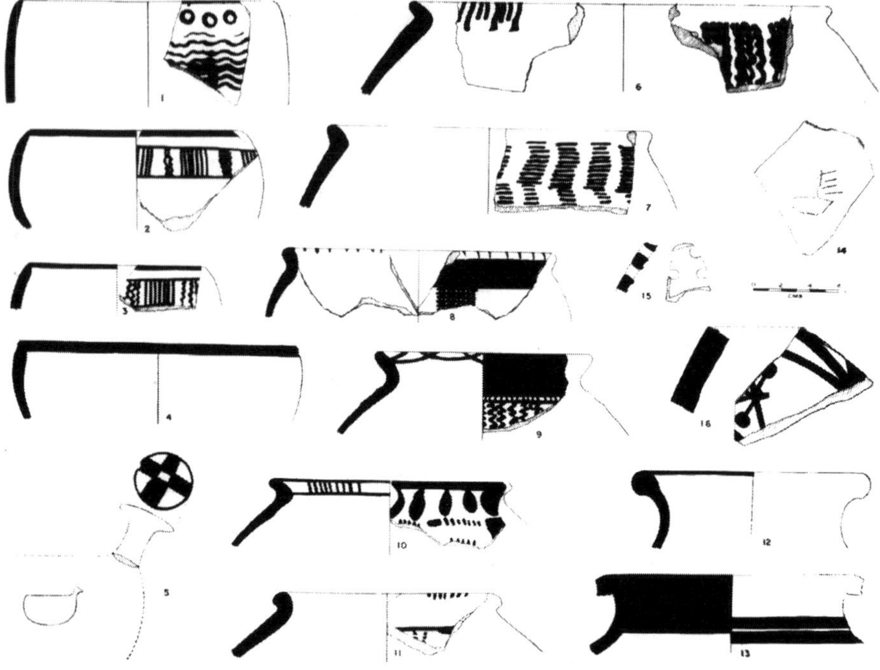

Fig. 13.4: Prabhas pottery

tools were in use for which the metal may have come from the Amreli district where the ore occurs (Lamberg-Karlovsky 1967:169). However, there exists a large copper belt from Ambamata in north Gujarat to Khetri in Rajasthan which was also exploited by the Harappans.[23] Agate and carnelian beads, along with segmented faience beads and dentalium shells, were quite common. Gold was rare as only one floral-shaped ear ornament was found. Cubical chert weights are exact copies of Harappan weights. Far more interesting is a steatite seal from the late Prabhas phase which is squarish with transverse perforation; it is engraved on both sides with seven stylized deer on one side and five on the other. The seal amulet is the only one of its kind of the post-Harappan times.

Structures (Fig. 13.5)

A huge structure complex was found built of stone-rubble in mud masonry, which belongs to about 1500 BC and is a good example of public architecture. Its criss-cross walls form small oblong chambers, some of 1.50 m^2, 2 × 1.50 m

[23] Sharma (1968), op. cit.

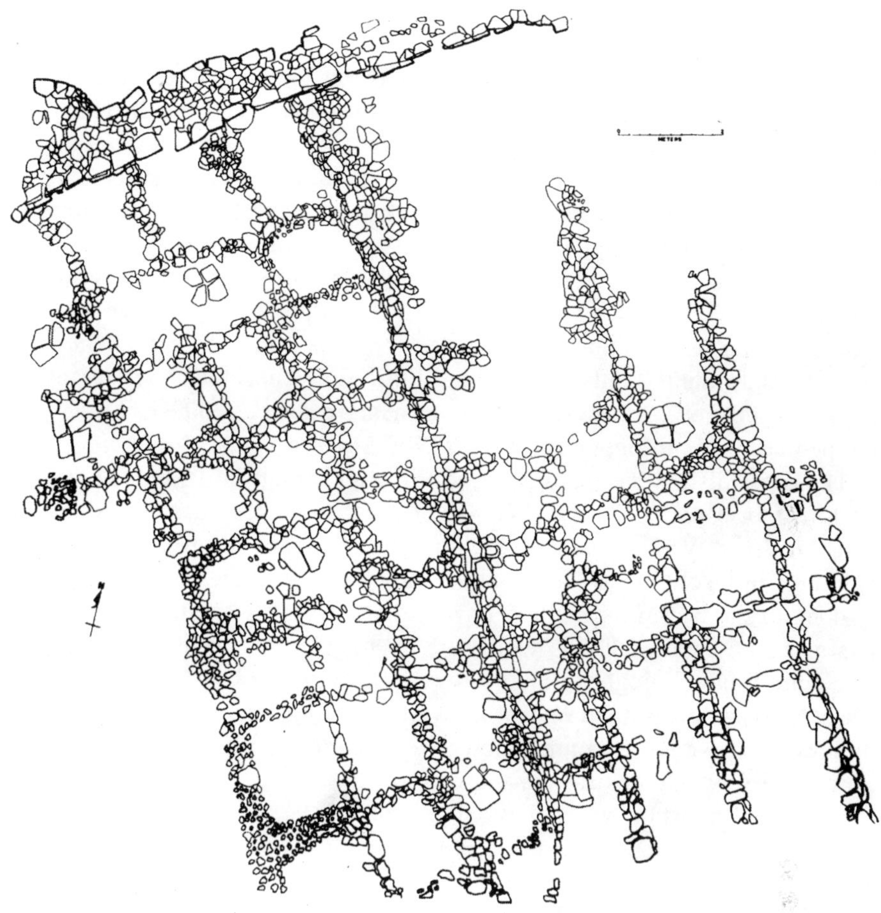

Fig. 13.5: Prabhas, structures, Period III

and others of 3.50 × 1.50 m, many of them with a large flat stone in the centre. The floor was not well-rammed and there was no indication of a hearth or anything else to indicate that it was not a residential structure. There were postholes suggesting roof above and the walls were very low, not more than 60 cm in height. The structure recalls to the mind one from Tepe Yahya in Iran which has been identified as a storage place.[24] A somewhat similar structure was exposed at Lothal which has been identified as a warehouse and the Prabhas structure may also have been used for the same purpose as Prabhas is located on the coast.[25]

[24]C.C. Martha and Lamberg-Karlovsky (1972), 'An Early City in Iran', *Old World Archaeology-Foundations of Civilization: Readings from Scientific American*, San Fransisco: Scientific American.

[25]Dhavalikar (1978), op. cit.

RANGPUR CULTURE

The Rangpur culture has been referred to as the Lustrous Red Ware culture on account of its distinctive pottery, which has been derived from the Harappan as far as forms and fabric are concerned. However, it is labelled the Rangpur culture after the site where it was first identified. Rangpur (district Limbdi, Gujarat) was known as a Harappan site and was excavated by a few reputed archaeologists. Its Harappan affinity was convincingly established by S.R. Rao[26] while the remains of the Rangpur culture were noticed in Period III dated to *c.* 1700-1400 BC. The site, located on the Bhadar River, is quite extensive and was occupied from a very early period. The first inhabitants were the late hunter-gatherers of Mesolithic times and then the Harappans (*c.* 2500-2000 BC), followed by the late Harappans (*c.* 2000-1700 BC) and the people of the Rangpur culture (*c.* 1700-1400 BC).

The most distinctive feature of the Rangpur culture is its deluxe pottery of fine fabric and bright polish, which has, therefore, been labelled the 'Lustrous Red Ware'. It is treated with a deep red slip and is decorated with paintings in black: mostly linear and geometric, sometimes with animal and bird figures. The forms include bowls, dishes, dishes-on-stand, perforated jars and stud-handled bowls which are clearly derived from the Harappan. The pottery has analogues in the cemetary ware of the late Harappan phase. Associated with it is a BRW bearing white paintings and represented mostly by bowls (probably the contribution of the Ahar culture), and coarse red and grey pottery which was for daily use.

In sharp contrast to the Prabhas culture, microliths of chalcedony, agate and jasper were used along with those of copper. Beads of semi-precious stones are present but those of faience and steatite are absent. As chank shell was available, bangles and beads were made of it. Harappan cubical chert weights were replaced by spheroid or elliptical ones which were made of dolerite. As at Prabhas, at Rangpur, too, a steatite seal was later found on the surface.[27] It is also engraved on both sides; on one side are two deer, one above the other, and on the other is a deer in the lower part above which somewhat looks like a seated human figure. It can be assigned to *c.* 1800 BC.

Structures

Mud-brick structures have been unearthed at Rangpur in which lime was used as a binding medium. The mud walls had foundation trenches in which clay was rammed. Storage jars were buried in house floors which were well-rammed. The roof was supported by wooden posts.

[26] S.R. Rao (1963), 'Excavations at Rangpur and Other Explorations in Gujarat', *Ancient India*, 18-19, Archaeological Survey of India, New Delhi, pp. 5-207.

[27] R. Bhattacharya (1991), 'Rangpur Seal: Probable Egyptian Connection of the Harappan Civilization', *ME*, 16, pp. 53-7.

CENTRAL INDIA

The Malwa region forms a distinct geographical unit on account of its physiography, as also economically and culturally. Lying almost in the heart of India, it forms a link between the Indo-Gangetic plain and the southern peninsular region. Its geology is complex and almost all the peninsular groups are represented here. It is drained by the Narmada, Tapi and Mahi which join the Arabian Sea, and the Chambal and Betwa that join the Yamuna. The climate is generally of the monsoon type with an average rainfall of about 1000 mm. The black soil, which occupies all of Malwa, is known for its fertility. It is much deeper in the Narmada basin. Very probably, the earliest settlers of Malwa, the authors of the Chalcolithic cultures, were attracted to this region because of its fertility. Even in the historical period, Malwa was the bone of contention among rival princely houses.

KAYATHA CULTURE (*c.* 2450-2000 BC)

A number of Chalcolithic sites have been discovered in Madhya Pradesh, more particularly in Malwa, which is the western part of the state, and quite a few have been excavated. The Kayatha culture has been named after the type-site, Kayatha (23°14′ N, 76°2′ E), which has been identified with ancient Kapitthaka (district Ujjain), the birthplace of the celebrated astronomer Varahamihira who lived in the fifth-sixth century AD (Wakankar 1968-9). The site is located on the Choti Kali Sindh, a tributary of the Kali Sindh, which, in turn, belongs to the Chambal system. It was occupied during the proto-historic times by the people of the Kayatha, Ahar and the Malwa cultures, as also later in the early historic period.[28]

The first settlement at the site was that of the Kayatha culture, which is characterized by distinctive ceramic industries of which the chocolate-slipped ware bears some resemblance to Harappan pottery (Fig. 13.6). It is a sturdy ware of an extremely fine fabric, is most distinctive and has, hence, been named the Kayatha ware. The forms include bowls, basins, dishes and storage jars, many of which have a ring base—but, in some cases, the bottom of the vessels is seen bulging below the rim, making the ring meaningless. Over the thick slip are painted patterns, mostly linear and geometric, in purple or dark red. The ware is available in two varieties, thick and thin.

Another ceramic is a fine, thin-walled, red painted buff ware represented mostly by the typical Indian *lotas*, with a concave profile, globular lower part and rounded base. Dishes and bowls, too, occur but rarely. Yet another pottery is the combed ware which is decorated with incised wavy lines executed by a comb-like instrument. Bowls and basins mostly occur in this ware, some of which have a dark red slip on the interior. It reminds one of

[28] Ansari and Dhavalikar (1971), op. cit.; idem (1973), *Excavations at Kayatha*, Deccan College, Poona.

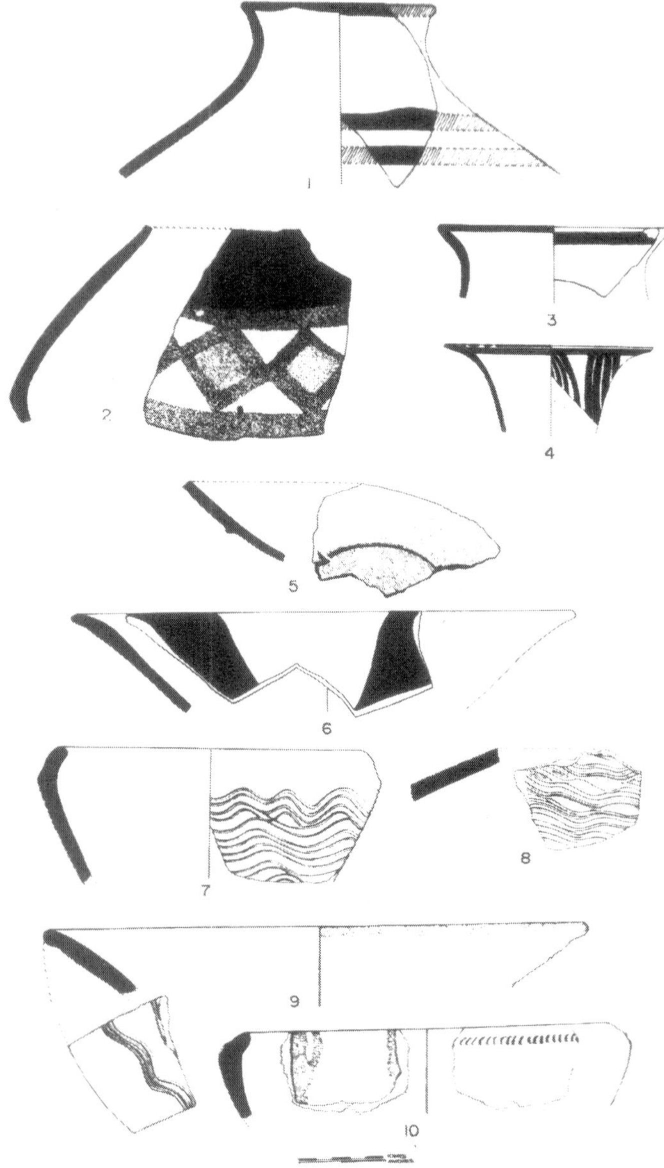

Fig. 13.6: Kayatha, pottery; 1-4 Kayatha ware, 5-6 red painted buff ware, 7-10 combed ware

the Sothi ware and Fabric D from Kalibangan which, however, has deep incised patterns. Coarse red and grey hand-made pottery occurs profusely.

The Kayatha people used a specialised made industry of chalcedony as also copper tools. Two exquisite copper axes from Kayatha are unique as they were made from moulds and hammered by hand as those from other Chalcolithic sites. Copper bangles (28 nos.) do not seem to have been used as personal ornaments but seem to represent a method of storing the metal. Besides, thousands of miniature steatite were found in a pot. More interesting are two necklaces of beads of semi-precious stones which are almost similar to those from Mohenjo-daro.[29]

MALWA CULTURE (*c.* 1700-1400 BC)

The Malwa culture was the most widely-spread Chalcolithic culture of central India. It had its origins in Malwa but it spread into Maharashtra. It was first brought to light in excavations at Maheshwar (district Nimar, MP), which has been identified as ancient Mahishmati of the Puranas, the capital of Omkar Mandhata, sacred to the Hindus because of the presence of a *Jyotirlinga.* While the excavation was in progress at Maheshwar, the Chalcolithic site of Navdatoli was discovered across the Narmada on the other bank. The latter was then excavated on a large scale but has now been submerged under the waters of the Narmada dam.

A large number of Malwa culture sites have been discovered with a heavy concentration in the Malwa region and even beyond its confines in eastern Madhya Pradesh and Maharashtra. Malwa is situated almost in the heart of India on the northern tip of the great central Indian plateau and is known for the fertility of its black soil which is watered by two great river systems; the Narmada and the Chambal. There are, however, more settlements on the tributaries than on the main rivers which are prone to high floods. The region was well-forested in the ancient past and the earliest settlers were attracted to it because of its fertile soil and natural resources. Even in the historical period, it was a bone of contention among rival powers.

Chronology

Navdatoli is probably the most extensive Malwa site and was excavated on a large scale. The Chalcolithic habitation at the site has been divided into four phases as follows:[30]

Phase I: Lime-plastered floors, Malwa ware, white painted BRW, and a cream-slipped ware.
Phase II: Lime floors and yellow silt floors, Malwa ware, the white painted BRW disappears, habitation destroyed by fire.
Phase III: Houses with wooden posts, Malwa ware and Jorwe ware. Lustrous Red Ware of the Rangpur culture, habitation destroyed by fire.
Phase IV: Wattle-and-daub houses with thatched roofs, all the pottery of Phase III continues but storage jars now have applique decoration.

[29] John Marshall (1931), *Mohenjodaro and the Indus Civilization*, 3 vols., Arthur Probsthain, London, III, Pl. CXLVIII, 6.

[30] Sankalia et al. (1971), *Chalcolithic Navdatoli*, Deccan College, Poona, pp. 35-42.

The entire Malwa culture habitation at Navdatoli can be dated on the basis of radiocarbon dates to *c*. 1900-1400 BC.

Settlement Pattern

Over two hundred Malwa settlements which have come to light so far display a particular two-level settlement pattern, viz., large and small villages, many situated on tributaries rather than on the major rivers which are prone to high floods. Navdatoli, Nagda and Eran were large villages which could have evolved into urban centres in the course of time if the environment had been favourable. Of these, Navdatoli was the largest settlement spread over an area of 300 × 240 m or about 7 ha, which is equal to that of Kalibangan or Lothal. Here, the habitation was distributed over four localities as was the case with some of the Harappan towns, as, for instance, Dholavira. It would have been interesting to excavate them to ascertain whether the division was occupational. However, a close glance at the contour plan reveals that the habitation was originally divided into two distinct areas, one in the north-west and the other in the south-east, like the citadel and lower town of the Harappans. It appears that the entire habitation was enclosed in enclosure. Evidence from the excavation shows that Navdatoli was an important religious centre which, in historical times, shifted to the other bank at Maheshwar. Nagda (district Ujjain, MP) on the Narmada was another important Chalcolithic settlement where a maze of structures was unearthed which the excavator calls 'semblances of an elaborate defence'.[31] He further adds: 'Since the defence wall was built of mud and mud-bricks on the vulnerable riverside, it was inferably not intended against floods, but possibly against extraneous attack'.[32]

This may not have been the case for the simple reason that there was no danger of any attack from the riverside because the river itself offers protection and, logically, the structure, which can be called an embankment, was, in all probability, erected for protecting the settlement from floods. At Eran (district Sagar, MP), there was a similar embankment on the riverside built completely of mud for the same purpose. Doubts have been raised about the Chalcolithic date of the Eran embankment which was 30 m wide at the base and an extant height of 6.41 m (Ghosh 1989: 134-46). There should be little doubt that it belongs to the latter half of the Chalcolithic period.[33] The site is situated on the confluence of the Betwa (ancient Vetravati) and the Bina (ancient Venna) and, hence, there was the danger of floods. A moat was excavated around the habitation and mud was used for setting up the embankment.

The Nagda evidence gives an idea of the micro-settlement pattern of the

[31] N.R. Banerjee (1986), *Nagda*, Archaeological Survey of India, New Delhi, p. 40.

[32] Ibid.

[33] U.V. Singh (1962), 'Excavations at Eran', *Journal of M.P. Itihasa Parishad*, 4, pp. 41-4.

Malwa culture. Houses were built in rows along the roads and by-lanes.[34] The roads ran straight, cutting each other at right angles and were partly cobbled with stones. The houses were multi-roomed and spacious; one room was quite large (6.70 × 5.94 m)[35] and contained a four-armed double *chulha* which is identical with that at Ahar[36] and Navdatoli.[37] The multi-roomed structures may have been occupied by extended families. The house floors were rammed hard and repaired periodically. There were pebble platforms, the exact function of which cannot be determined. At Nagda, mud-brick drains were built.

A large number of residential structures were exposed at Navdatoli, which were either rectangular or circular in plan. There were even pit-dwellings in the earliest phase.[38] Round huts were found in clusters of two, three or four, with each group representing one household. The rectangular houses were quite spacious, ranging from 3 × 3 m to 6 × 4.50 m with thick (30 to 60 cm) mud walls and wooden posts supporting the roof. One house of Phase II had a double row of posts.[39] Rectangular and round houses have also been exposed at Chichli.[40] The Malwa culture spread into Maharashtra where similar houses have been unearthed in excavations at Daimabad and Inamgaon.

Subsistence

There is fairly good evidence for the agriculture of the Malwa people. They cultivated cereals, legumes, oil seeds and fruits. Wheat (*Triticum vulgare compactum*, bread wheat), rice (*Oryza sativa*), barley (*Hordeum vulgare*) and jowar (*Sorghum vulgare*) have been reported from Malwa levels in Maharashtra. Other crops include lentil (*Lens esculenta*), black gram (*Vigna mungo*, urd), green gram (*Phaseolus mungo* or *Phaseolus radiatus*), gulabi chana (*Lathyrus sativus*) and grass pea. Linseed oil (*Linum usitatissimum*) was also used. Ber (*Zizyphus jujube*) was quite common. Hunting and fishing also supplemented food. Beef was commonly eaten as also venison. The bones of pigs, barasingha, sheep/goat and rat occur and, in all likelihood, they were eaten. Besides, there were fish, turtle and shells.

Arts and Crafts

The fine Malwa ware, which constitutes the distinguishing feature of the Malwa culture, is essentially buff or cream-slipped, with painted designs in

[34] Banerjee (1986), op. cit., Fig. 1, p. 36.

[35] Ibid., Pl. Xa.

[36] Sankalia et al. (1969), op. cit., Fig. 29.

[37] Sankalia (1971), op. cit., Fig. 26.

[38] Ibid., p. 43.

[39] Ibid., Pl. XIB and Fig. 26.

[40] S.K. Mittra and V. Shivananda (1999-2000), 'Chalcolithic Settlement at Chjichli', *Puratattva*, 30, pp. 45-9, Pls. 1 and 3.

dark brown or black. It bears some resemblance to the red painted buff ware of the Kayatha culture which, however, is of fine fabric. The Malwa ware is of coarse fabric but has a thick slip. The commonest form is the typical Indian *lota* with flaring mouth and bulbous body, which comes in different sizes, small and big. Besides, there are a variety of bowls, dishes and globular jars. More interesting are the channel-spouted bowls, cups-on-stand and chalices or stemmed goblets which occur at Navdatoli, have significant analogues in Bronze Age Iran and have, therefore, been associated by Sankalia[41] with the Aryans (Fig. 13.7). The painted repertoire of the Malwa ware is extremely rich and includes linear, geometrical, and plant and animal motifs. The ware can be divided into two varieties on the basis of its fabric. Although the bulk of the pottery is of coarse fabric, that with thin and finer fabric also occurs. It is also present at Eran and in Maharashtra. All the pottery is well-baked as the fully oxidized cores show. A pottery kiln of the Malwa period was discovered at Inamgaon in Maharashtra. It had a fire chamber down below over which the kiln, resembling a huge cauldron (diameter 1.55 m), was built in clay with radiating flues at the base.[42]

Associated pottery of the Malwa ware includes the white-painted BRW of the Ahar culture, a cream-slipped ware, coarse red/grey wares and hand-made storage jars.

Excavations of Malwa sites have yielded microlithic blade tools in profusion which are mostly made of chalcedony. Cores and waste flakes indicate that they were made at the site as and when needed. According to Sankalia, they were made in every house, and those with a sheen on their edge were used for cutting grasses and for harvesting.[43] Copper, being scarce, was used sparingly for axes, fishhooks, chisels, etc., as also for bangles and beads. A noteworthy feature of the copper axes from Chalcolithic sites is that they usually bear shallow indentations which may be those of coppersmiths. It is, therefore, likely that there was a community of itinerant coppersmiths specializing in making copper artefacts, who supplied them to the Chalcolithic people. A mid-rib dagger from Navdatoli has affinities with one from Tepe Hissar (Iran) which is noteworthy.[44] Beads of semi-precious stones were also made at Navdatoli which has yielded over 2,800 specimens in contrast to fourteen from Nagda.

Religion

The Navdatoli excavation has revealed some evidence with respect to the religious beliefs of the people. In one building (7 m^2) a carefully cut squarish

[41] H.D. Sankalia (1963), 'New Light on Indo-Iranian or Western Asiatic Relations between 1700-1200 BC', *Artibus Asiae*, 26, pp. 312-32.

[42] Dhavalikar et al. (1988), op. cit., I, 2, Fig. 9.25.

[43] H.D. Sankalia (1967), 'The Socio-economic Significance of the Lithic Blade Industry of Navdatoli, M.P., India', *CA*, 8, pp. 262-8.

[44] Sankalia (1963), op. cit., p. 329, Figs. 23-4.

Fig. 13.7: Malwa ware

pit (2.30 × 1.95 m, 15 cm deep) in the floor was noticed which was burnt red by constant use. It had a chamferred corners and a well-plastered floor, with charred wooden posts at the comers which probably supported a canopy above. Inside these were burnt wooden splinters over which was a log of wood. There were two jars, too. Sankalia identifies it as an *agnikunda*:[45]

> Thus there is little doubt that there is a deliberately made contrivance which, though called a pit, might better be called a *vedi* or *kunda* (for performing sacrifices and other rituals) in Brahmanic or later Hindu parlance.

Some of the terracotta figurines and painted ones on jars may be the representations of Chalcolithic divinities. On some big storage jars, female figures are found (Fig. 13.8). They are very inarticulate for their a pinched head, curved anus, and stumpy legs; the facial features are also not indicated. One such applique figure on a jar is flanked by a female figure on the right and a lizard on the left, by the side of which is what looks like a shrine, represented by three concentric arches. It may be stated that in the historical period, the lizard is associated with Durga, and the figurine may, therefore, be taken as proto-Durga. There are other creatures the monkey and the tortoise. Mention may also be made of a fiddle-shaped figurine from Nagda which, though fragmentary, recalls to the mind the similar, much earlier ones from Bronze Age sites in Baluchistan, which have convincingly been shown to be

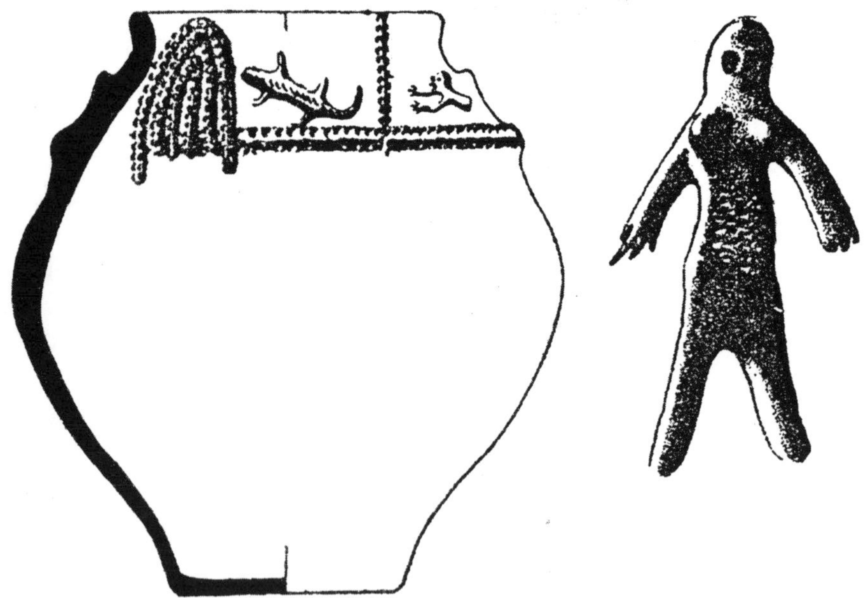

Fig. 13.8: A storage jar, Navdatoli (M.P.)

[45]Ibid., p. 49.

mother goddesses. A similar figure is reported from historical levels at Nagda itself, which may be taken as the continuity of the tradition.[46]

A male figurine occurring on a Malwa jar from Daimabad deserves special mention. He is muscular and is shown standing, surrounded by animals and birds: the peacock and deer in the upper row, and tigers in the lower (Fig. 13.9). It is a very elaborately painted scene which suggests that it may be a ritualistic vessel. Another figure painted on a channel-spouted cup from Navdatoli depicts a male figure with dishevelled hair and a spear in his right hand (Fig. 13.10). He has been identified as proto-Rudra. On the same pot

Fig. 13.9: Daimabad, painted jar of Malwa ware

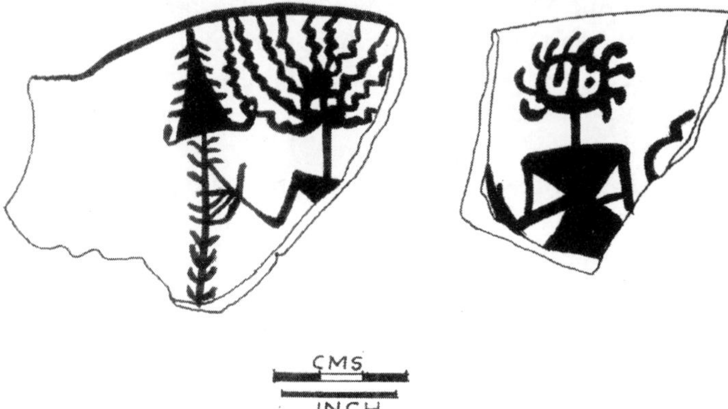

Fig. 13.10: Malwa pottery with painted human figures

[46]Bannerjee (1986), op. cit., pp. 227-8, Pl. XXVI, A2.

is another person with raised hair who may be a shaman (*mantrik*) of the community (Sankalia 1959: 185, fig. D 473, A-B).

Burials

The Malwa people in Maharashtra buried dead children in two urns placed mouth-to-mouth horizontally and adults in an extended position in the burial pit. However, Malwa burials have not been found in Malwa, the main focus of the culture; in Maharashtra, they seem to have adopted the custom from the Neolithic people of the southern Deccan.

Authorship

It is hard to hazard any opinion about the authors of the Malwa culture in the absence of any concrete evidence. Sankalia's objective was to test the historicity of the Puranic evidence when he began the Maheshwar excavations. He tentatively concluded that 'the earliest residents were most probably colonizers from the north'.[47] He was also of the opinion that the Bhils were the Chalcolithic people. They are presently to be found in Rajasthan, Malwa, Gujarat and north Maharashtra. They were driven to hilly and forest tracts by the invading Aryans.[48] Yet when West Asian influence was discerned in some of the artefacts from Navdatoli, he observed that 'It is not yet possible to say who these people were: Aryans or pre-Aryan Nagas—for instance—as the Puranic traditions imply.[49] His view of West Asian influence on the Malwa culture has been severely criticized but there should be little doubt that the West Asian parallels cited by him are not too general as has been argued but quite significant. The two cultures were thought to have been separated by a huge chronological gap but the calibrated dates now take the antiquity of the Malwa culture back to the beginning of the second millennium BC and the gap is now reduced to a considerable extent. There is a strong possibility that the genesis of the Malwa culture lies in the Kayatha culture, considering the similarity between the red painted buff ware of the Kayatha culture and the Malwa ware; at some sites in Malwa, the Malwa culture succeeds the Kayatha with an appreciable overlap, as at Dhangwada which is close to Kayatha.[50]

The Malwa people vanish from the scene by 1400 BC possibly because of the onset of aridity from the middle of the second millennium BC. The sites in MP were again occupied after nearly a thousand years in the early historical period. What happened to the Malwa people is now known; they may have resorted to pastoral nomadism.

[47] Sankalia et al. (1971), op. cit., p. 423.

[48] Ibid., pp. 423 ff.

[49] H.D. Sankalia, B. Subba Rao and S.B. Deo (1958), *Excavations at Maheshwar and Navdatoli (1952-53)*, Deccam College, Poona, pp. XII-XIII.

[50] *IAR*, 1982-3, pp. 59-61.

MAHARASHTRA

The Chalcolithic culture was first discovered in Maharashtra at Jorwe and its chronological position was determined in the excavation at Nasik. Since then, over two hundred Chalcolithic sites have been discovered and quite a few have been excavated, a couple of them on a large scale, as a result of which we now have a fairly good knowledge of the lifestyle of the early farming communities in Maharashtra. Settled life began in this region in the latter half of the third millennium BC and continued in unbroken succession till the end of the second millennium. The following is the culture sequence in Maharashtra:

1. Savalda culture (*c.* 2300-2000 BC)
2. Harappan culture (*c.* 2200-1800 BC)
3. Malwa culture (*c.* 1700-1500 BC)
4. Jorwe culture (*c.* 1500-900 BC)

Maharashtra is characterized by a plateau-like morphology, shallow stream valleys and a semi-arid monsoon climate. Basaltic rocks occupy a major part of the state, and have dolerite dykes and pockets of silicious material such as chalcedony, agate, chert and jasper. From June to October, the south-west monsoon is very high in the coastal strip (5000-7000 mm), but it decreases to about 400-700 mm eastwards in the rain-shadow region. There is hardly any winter rain and the temperature ranges between 35 to 40 °C in summer (May) and 5 °C in the winter (December). The major part of the state has black cotton soil which is known for its fertility and moisture-retaining capacity. The rivers run into deeply entrenched valleys as they traverse the rocky uplands and, hence, habitations are not really affected by floods. Although this is advantageous to the human population, the lack of fresh alluvium as in the Indo-Gangetic plains creates problems for agriculture. Agriculture, therefore, is a gamble with nature as every third year is a bad year and every fourth a famine.

SAVALDA CULTURE (*c.* 2300-2000 BC)

The culture was first identified at Savalda (district Nandurbar) but its chronological position was placed on a secure footing by the excavation at Daimabad (district Ahmednagar) where it underlies the Harappan culture[51] and can, therefore, be dated to *c.* 2300-2000 BC. About twenty-five settlements of the Savalda people have been discovered so far, most of them in the Tapi Valley. Kaothe (Tal, Sakri, district Dhule), an important site of the Savalda culture[52] is very extensive (about 30 ha) but has largely been destroyed because of modern cultivation. The cultural debris is now just 50 cm to 1 m

[51] S.A. Sali (1986), *Daimabad (1976-79)*, Archaeological Survey of India, New Delhi.
[52] M.K. Dhavalikar et al. (1990b), *Excavations at Kaothe*, Deccan College, Pune.

thick. However, it is a single culture site and, hence, there is no danger of admixture of any later material.

Dwellings

The excavation at Kaothe covered a large area of the habitational site. A number of pits, some of which were obviously used as dwellings, were exposed and others as storage pits. The largest dwelling pit (Fig. 13.11) was oval in plan (5.60 × 3.65 m and 80 cm deep). Along the periphery, it had sixteen postholes. It contained pottery and other evidence of habitation and there should, therefore, be little doubt that it was used as a dwelling pit. In its south-western end was a circular pit (diameter 1.20 m depth 1.10 m) which contained vast quantities of animal bones, ash charcoal and other refuse. It is bell-shaped with its sides broadening towards the base; the diameter at the base was 1.85 in. It is not unlikely that it was first used as a silo but was later used as a refuse pit. In the courtyard, there were smaller pits which may have been used for storage purposes; the deeper ones were, in all probability, used for storing grain but those which are shallow may have been intended for keeping poultry at night. The kitchen, located in a smaller pit, consisted of a two-armed hearth with three lumps of clay, which obviously supported the cooking vessel. The flimsy floor and the makeshift kitchen suggests that the people who lived in the pit-dwellings were probably semi-nomadic and occupied them only seasonally.

Pottery

Three different ceramic industries could be distinguished of which the most predominant is a sturdy red ware of fine fabric with painted designs in black pigment. It bears a strong resemblance to the Harappan black-on-red pottery from the adjoining Gujarat region where the Indus civilization flourished. The forms include bowls with featureless rims, globular storage jars and basins. Another distinct ceramic industry is the Savalda ware named after the type-site. It has a coarse fabric but, in the variety of painted designs, we often come across aquatic creatures such as fish and tortoises, which are shown as being hunted with harpoons and arrows. Besides, a variety of creatures such as elephants, boars, birds and reptiles also occur. Among the characteristic forms, mention should be made of rimless bowls and high-necked storage jars. Yet another ceramic is the Kayatha ware which occurs in central India, especially the Malwa region. It is a red-slipped ware bearing designs in black but has a very thick, sturdy fabric. The single radiocarbon date for Kaothe, 1920+80 BC (uncalibrated), enables us to date the habitation to *c.* 2200-2000 BC.[53] The most remarkable feature of this early fanning

[53] Ibid.

Fig. 13.11: A pit dwelling, Kaothe (*c*. 2200-2000 BC) (Maharashtra)

culture was the conspicuous absence of stone and metal tools; instead, we have a profusion of bone tools consisting of points, punches, awls and knives.

Subsistence

The inhabitants cultivated bajra-pearl millet (*Pennisetum typhoides*). This, again, constitutes a noteworthy feature because the early farming communities in central, western India and the Deccan mostly produced barley (*Hordeum vulgare*), while the Kaothe people cultivated *bajra*. It should be noted that the earliest occurrence of bajra so far is reported from Kuntasi in Gujarat in 2300 BC levels.[54] What is more, in the region around Kaothe today, the main crop is bajra and not jowar (*Sorghum vulgare*), which is grown in other parts of Maharashtra. It may be stated that the earliest *bajra* in the world is reported from South Africa where it is dated to *c.* 2400 BC,[55] and it is highly likely that millet was introduced into western India through the Persian Gulf. Hunting and fishing also formed an important part of the diet.

Burials

Five burials were encountered in the course of excavation while the sixth, one was partially destroyed by a small well which was later dug at the site. Two were adult burials whereas the remaining three were infant burials. The dead were buried in a pit especially dug for the purpose in either a supine or crouching posture. The body was kept in a north-south direction with the head towards the south. This marks a distinct variation in the Chalcolithic burials of Maharashtra in the second millennium BC in which the legs are generally found in the southern direction. Both the adult skeletons are of fully-grown individuals and their age at the time of death has been established to be around thirty to forty years. Of the two adults, one is a male and the other a female. The infant skeletons are of individuals who died around two to four years of age but the age of one infant was less than six months.[56]

HARAPPAN CULTURE (*c.* 2200-1800 BC)

The Harappans seem to have made inroads into the heartland of Maharashtra in the last quarter of the third millennium. It is highly likely that they might have been making forays into Maharashtra even earlier through the Tapi Valley for acquiring raw materials like agates and ivory. The Harappan

[54]M.K. Dhavalikar et al. (1996), *Kuntasi: A Harappan Emporium on West Coast*, Deccan College, Pune.

[55]O. Davies and G. Gray (1977), 'Tropical African Cultigens from Shongweni Excavations', *Jr. of Arch. Sc.*, 4, pp. 153-62.

[56]Dhavalikar et al. (1990), op. cit.

occupation at Daimabad came to light accidentally because of the discovery of a unique hoard of bronzes consisting of a bull chariot, an elephant, a rhino and a bison, all made of arsenic bronze. The excavation at the spot where the bronzes were found yielded evidence of Harappan occupation. The structure complex discovered at Daimabad consists of six houses (nos. 15-20) which must have formed one unit as they were enclosed in a wall. The unit must have belonged to an important, well-to-do family, perhaps the chief of the community, as is evident from the artefacts found in them. The mud-bricks used in the construction conforms to the Harappan standard of 4:2:1. The largest room in the complex measures 6.30 × 6 m. There were several pit silos for storage. Two terracotta seals engraved with Harappan characters found in the house denote the authority of the person occupying it. The bronzes also came from this area.

Bronzes

The bronzes were accidentally discovered by some shepherds when they were digging for a tree root at the ancient site. The hoard consists of a bull-chariot driven by a man (Fig. 13.12), and an elephant, rhino and buffalo (Fig. 13.13), each standing on wheels.[57] Excavations were undertaken at the spot where the hoard was found. On the basis of the evidence of pottery, the hoard can be assigned to the Harappan period (*c.* 2200-2000 BC). All the bronzes are large and so heavy that they must have been used as ritual objects. They are all movable and it is, therefore, highly likely that they were meant to be taken out in a procession. Such a procession of animals is shown on a seal from

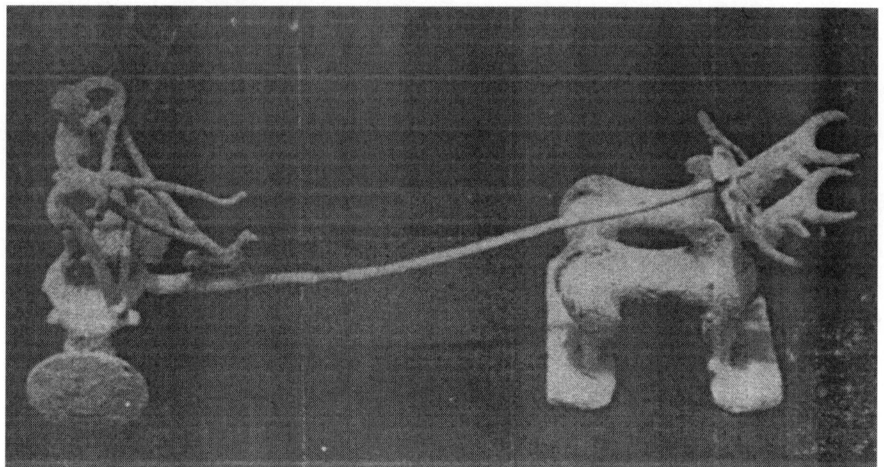

Fig. 13.12: Daimabad, bronze chariot

[57] M.K. Dhavalikar (1993), 'Daimabad Bronzes', in G.L. Possehl (ed.), *HCRP*, Oxford IBH, New Delhi, pp. 421-7.

Fig. 13.13: Daimabad, bronze bison

Mohenjo-daro on which four animals—an elephant, a rhino, a tiger and an unidentified animal—are seen in a file facing right.[58] Again, from Mohenjo-daro comes a seal amulet on one side of which is an animal in the centre—a *gharial* according to the excavator—on either side of which is a bull and, below, an elephant on the left and a tiger on the right.[59] It is, therefore, clear that these animals (the elephant, rhino, bull, buffalo, tiger, etc.) played an important role in the religious life of the Harappans.

[58]Marshall (1931), op. cit., II, p. 365, III, Pl. CXVI, 14 and CXVIII, 10.

[59]E.J.H. Mackay (1937), *Further Excavations at Mohenjodaro*, 2 vols., Manager of Publications, Delhi, I: 357; II: Pls. XCL.2a and 10.

The objects in the Daimabad hoard remind us of the well-known "Pashupati' seal from Mohenjo-daro on which is depicted a human figure seated on a stool in a yogic posture in the centre, flanked, on its right, by an elephant and on its left by a tiger, a rhino and a buffalo, while below the stool are two antelopes or goats. Although Marshall recognized the proto-type of Shiva in his aspect of Pashupati in the figure, the identification has been questioned[60] and the figure has been identified as that of a mother goddess.[61] Be that as it may, it is important to note that animals played an important role in the Harappan religion.

MALWA CULTURE (*c.* 1700-1500 BC)

The Malwa culture was also spread over Maharashtra and, at many sites, the Malwa people were the first settlers. Several Malwa sites have been found in the north and central parts. The Malwa people began to migrate into Maharashtra around 1700 BC in search of fresh pastures. At Inamgaon, where they were the first settlers, a number of houses of the Malwa period have been laid bare and this is also the case at Daimabad. The Malwa houses were quite spacious, as at Inamgaon (Fig. 13.14). They had low mud walls about 50 cm high, well-rammed floors and a partition wall dividing the house into two parts. Inside the house was a two-armed *chulha* for cooking daily meals and a large fire pit outside in the courtyard for roasting hunted animals. In the courtyard were pit silos for storing grain but, at Inamgaon, there were, in addition, circular mud platforms for storage bins. At Daimabad, a few houses were enclosed in a wall. Of the twenty-odd Malwa houses exposed at Inamgaon, a vast majority were in an east-west orientation and though they were built close together, they had an intervening space of about 1-2 m which would have served as a lane. They were all large rectangular structures (7 × 5 m) with a partition wall in between. Some people lived in round huts and some in pit-dwellings.

The characteristic Malwa ware with coarse fabric and thick slip also occurs in Maharashtra but associated with it is a finer variety of thin fabric with an orange wash over which designs are executed in black. Characteristic Malwa forms such as the *lota*, high-necked globular jar and bowl with blunt carination occurs in this finer ware. A small pottery kiln of the Malwa phase was discovered at Inamgaon.[62]

The Malwa people cultivated barley, had domestic animals, hunted wild animals (mostly deer) and fished. They worshipped a mother goddess and their god, surrounded by wild animals is depicted on a pot from Daimabad.

[60] Marshall (1931), op. cit., I:5; Pl. XII, 17.

[61] Shubhangana Atre (1987), *The Archetyal Mother: A Systemic Approach to Harappan Religion*, Ravish Publishers, Poona.

[62] Dhavalikar et al. (1988), op. cit., I, ii, Fig. 9.25.

Fig. 13.14: Inamgaon, house of Period I (Malwa)

They buried children in two urns in a pit. A few adult burials have also been reported.

JORWE CULTURE (*c.* 1500-900 BC)

The Jorwe culture named after the type-site is the most important Chalcolithic culture of Maharashtra. Over 200 Jorwe settlements discovered so far demonstrate that it was spread almost all over the present state of Maharashtra, except the coastal strip on the west and Vidarbha in the north-east. A notable feature of the Jorwe settlement organization was that there was a large centre in each region, e.g. Prakash in the Tapi Valley, Daimabad in the Pravara-Godavari Valley and Inamgaon in the Bhima Valley. There is a heavy concentration of sites in the Tapi Valley, less in the Godavari basin and sporadic in the Bhima Valley obviously depending upon the availability of rich black cotton soil in each region. The Tapi Valley is the most fertile topographic unit in Maharashtra whereas the Pravara-Godavari Valley, characterized by undulating surfaces, and the Bhima Valley have rocky uplands with a thin soil cover. Early farming communities selected those areas where arable land was available.

Houses

A vast majority of the Jorwe settlements can be classed as villages as they are usually 1 to 3 ha in extent. A few of these villages such as Songaon and Chandoli have been excavated. Bahal and Nevasa are somewhat larger whereas some like Pimpaldar are very small, hardly 1 ha in extent, Inamgaon, about 5 ha in extent, can be classed as a large village but the largest of them all was Daimabad, which was spread over 30 ha. Several houses of the Jorwe phase have been exposed at Inamgaon and some at Daimabad. Structurally, they follow the Malwa pattern: a large rectangular room, partitioned into two parts by a low mud wall, with low mud walls or wattle-and-daub walls, and a thatched roof (Fig. 13.15). There appears to be some modicum of planning at the Jorwe settlement at Inamgaon as the houses were laid out almost in rows with an open space (about 1.5 m wide) in between, which might have served as a lane. The houses measure about 5 × 3 m, with a small fire pit inside and a larger one outside in the courtyard with a flat stone in the centre daubed with mud to serve as a stand for the cooking vessel. In one case, a flat earthen pan was attached to it, obviously for baking bread. Very often, inside, and rarely outside, was a pit silo. 1-2 m in diameter and equally deep, and lined with lime for storing grain. In addition, there was a round mud platform (1.5 m diameter and 10 cm high) which served to support a storage bin. Similar mud platforms can be seen even today in the houses in Inamgaon village. The house floor was made of rammed clay and even the courtyard was well-made.

All this undergoes a sudden change in the Late Jorwe period around

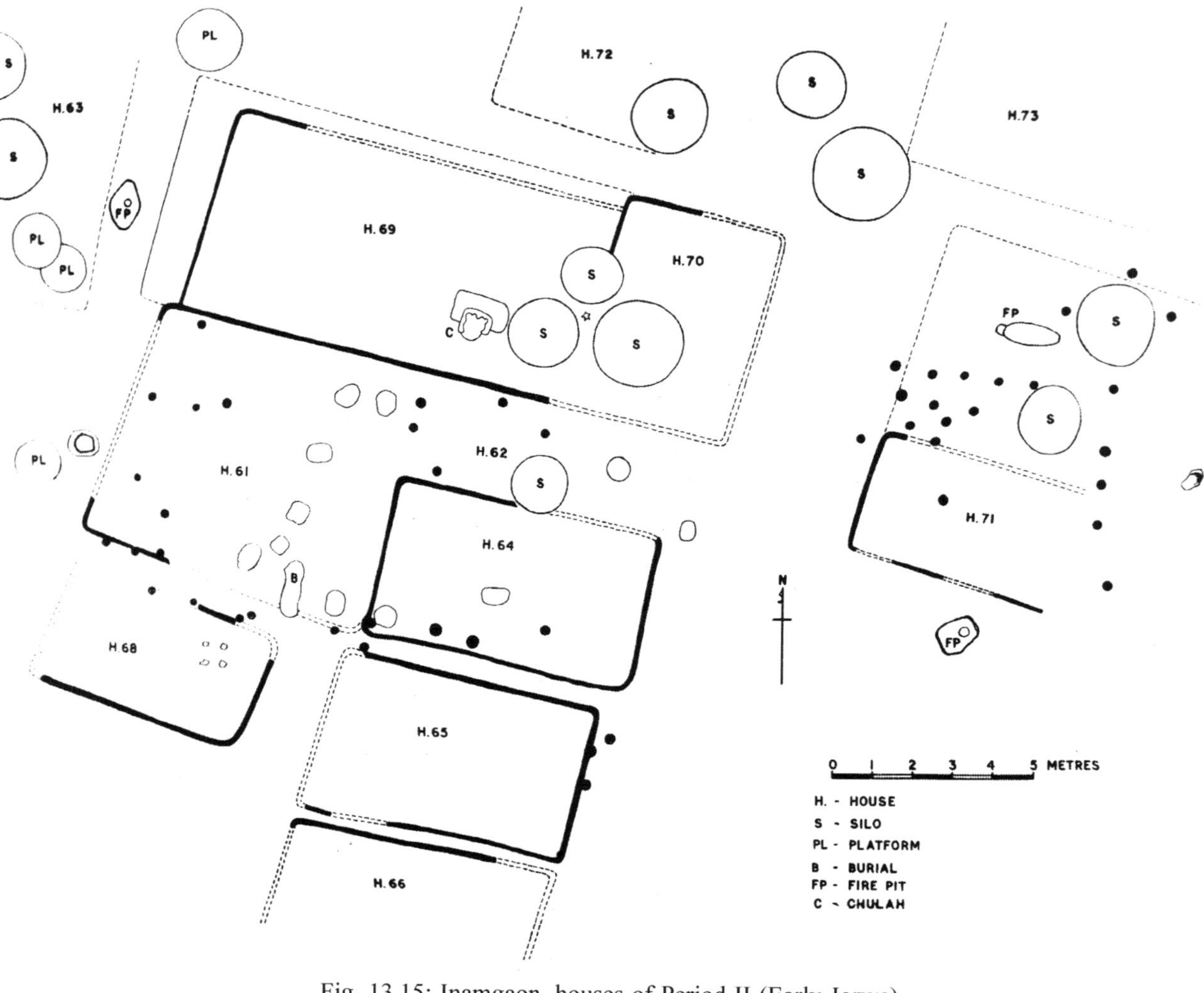

Fig. 13.15: Inamgaon, houses of Period II (Early Jorwe)

1200 BC. Increasing aridity led to the decline of agriculture and the consequent poverty is reflected in the small, round huts which replace the large, rectangular houses of the Early Jorwe period (Fig. 13.16). They were found in clusters of three and four huts. Inside, there is a small circular fire pit and outside too. The pit silos are replaced by four-legged storage jars which are supported on four flat stones. There are no mud platforms for storage bins. The round hut had a very low mud wall, some 10-15 cm high, the main function of which was to prevent rainwater getting into the hut. In the closing phase of Late Jorwe around 1000 BC, the huts become extremely flimsy with an irregular plan and without any well-made floor. There was no wattle-and-daub construction above the low mud wall only the thatched roof which was very low.

A remarkable feature of the Jorwe settlement, both Early and Late, is that the houses of artisans such as the potter, the goldsmith, the lapidary, etc., were located on the western side of the principal habitation area at Inamgaon whereas those of the well-to-do farmers were in the central part. This recalls to mind present-day villages in Maharashtra in which the houses of craftsmen are generally located near the entrance gate whereas the village chief—Patil—lives in the central part.

Subsistence

The Jorwe people cultivated a variety of crops. Their subsistence agriculture was mainly dry farming as they were living in a semi-arid region with the annual precipitation ranging around 500 m but they also had the facility of artificial irrigation as at Inamgaon. They even practised crop rotation which is well-attested at Inamgaon. The principal cereal crop was barley (*Hordeum vulgare*) but wheat (*Tricticum* spp.), where irrigation was available, and rice (*Oriza sativa* Lin) were raised in small, carefully-tended plots. Jowar (*Sorghum vulgare*) is attested to at Daimabad and Inamgaon; it must have come from Gujarat where it was probably an import from the Gulf region.[63] Mention should also be made of finger millet (ragi—*Eleucine coracana*), the origin of which has been traced to Egypt.[64] Besides, there were green peas, grass pea (*Lathyrus sativas* Linn), lentil (*Lens esculenta*) and black gram. A most interesting cultigen from Inamgaon is the hyacinth bean (*Dolichos biflorus*); it requires higher rainfall, about 800 mm, and might have been an import from the west coast.

All these Chalcolithic cultures flourished in the black cotton soil region. The black soil, which is known for its fertility and moisture-retaining capacity, is hard and compact. How was it cultivated? There is a saying that 'the black soil ploughs itself'. It develops large, deep fissures in summer which can be

[63] Weber (1991), op. cit.

[64] K.L. Mehra (1963), 'Considerations on the African Origin of Elensine coracana (1) Gaertn', *Science*, 7, pp. 301-2.

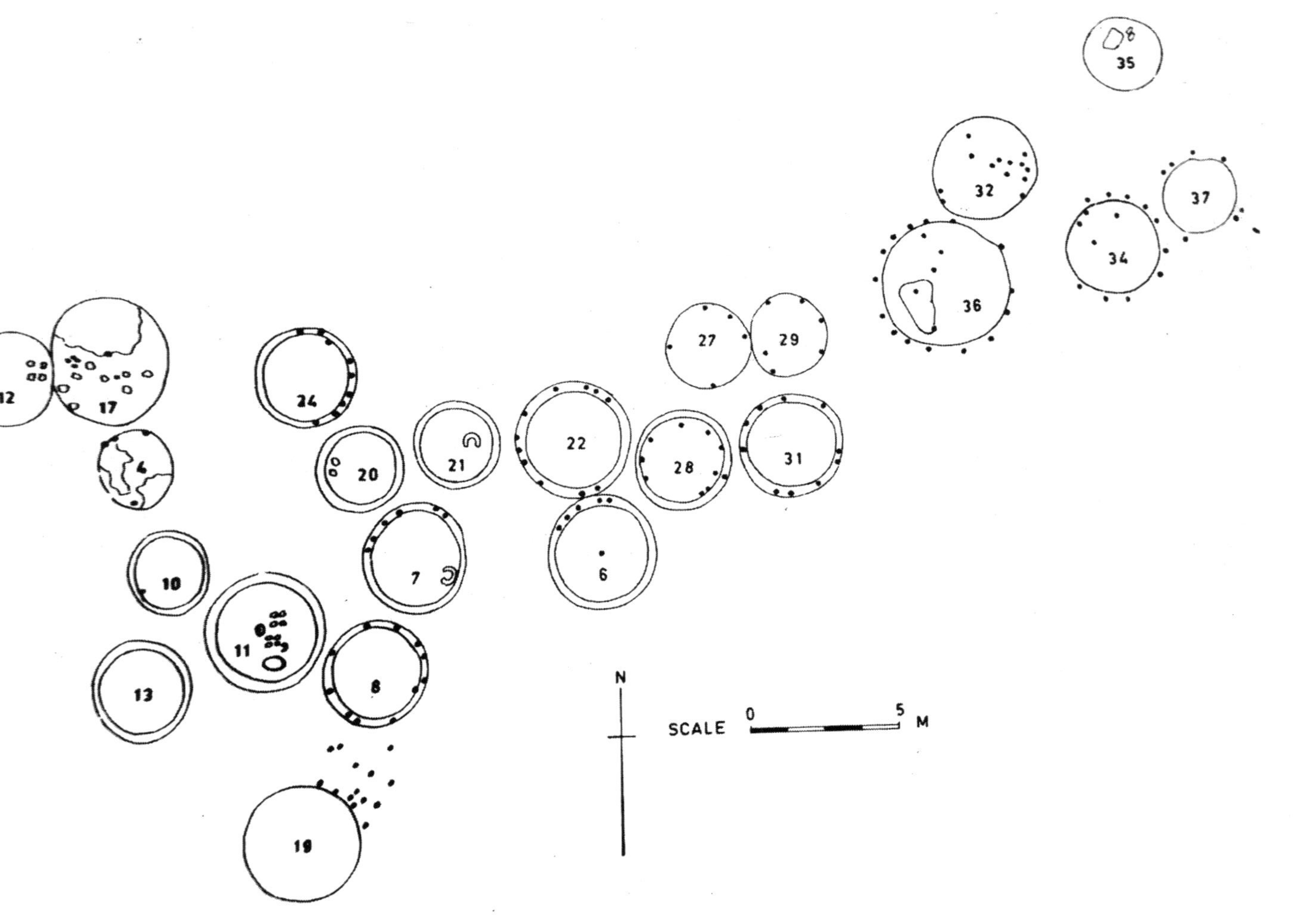

Fig. 13.16: Inamgaon, houses of Period III (Late Jorwe)

filled by a hoe and, by this means, the circulation of the soil is complete. The cracks fulfil the function of ploughing by admitting air freely into the soil. Thus, nature does the job of ploughing and, hence, the saying. A ploughshare made of the shoulder bone of cattle has been found at Walki, a Chalcolithic farmstead.[65] It resembles what was used in Neolithic times and was the prototype of the ploughshare.

There is no doubt that hunting and fishing supplemented the Chalcolithic diet. Fishhooks of copper and fish bones have been reported from excavations. The presence of fish at Inamgaon shows contact with the coastal region. Domestic animals were slaughtered for food but people seem to have developed a weakness for venison. Wild pig, too, was hunted. A multi-elemental analysis including strontium, zinc, copper and manganese of the human skeletal remains from Inamgaon indicates that, in the Early Jorwe period, people subsisted more on plant foods and agricultural products whereas the Late Jorwe people subsisted more on animal foods. This supports the inference that, in the Late Jorwe phase, agriculture was on the decline as a result of increasing aridity which set in towards the end of the second millennium. Gradually, the people resorted to sheep-goat pastoralism if the evidence of animal bones is any indication. The scientific analysis also shows that the children were fed on mothers' milk during the Malwa and Early Jorwe period till the age of about six months or one year but, in the Late Jorwe period, they were weaned at the age of two or two-and-half years.

Socio-Political Organization

Evidence from Inamgaon allows us to draw interesting conclusions about the socio-political organization of the Jorwe people. It consists of site hierarchies, certain structures and burials. The Chalcolithic communities seem to have been organized into chiefdoms and were ranked societies. The most important criterion of a chiefdom society is said to be the existence of public structures such as fortification, a temple, a granary, etc.[66] An important example of public architecture is furnished by the granary at Inamgaon which was a mud-walled structure, about 10 m^2 divided into two parts by a low mud wall. It contained many pit silos and round mud platforms for storage bins. It was located in the central part of the principal habitation area (INM-I) by the side of the largest house in the settlement, which has been identified as the residence of the most important person in the settlement, perhaps the ruling chief, due to the location of the granary by the side of his house (Fig. 13.17). He might have collected taxes in the form of grain from the people and stored them in the granary as insurance against droughts, which must have been as frequent then as they are now.

[65]M.K. Dhavalikar, V.S. Shinde, Shubhangana Atre (1990a), 'Small Site Archaeology: Excavations at Walki', *BDCRI*, 50, pp. 197-228.

[66]C.S. Peebles and S.M. Kus (1977), 'Some Archaeological Correlates of Ranked Societies', *American Antiquity*, 42, pp. 421-48.

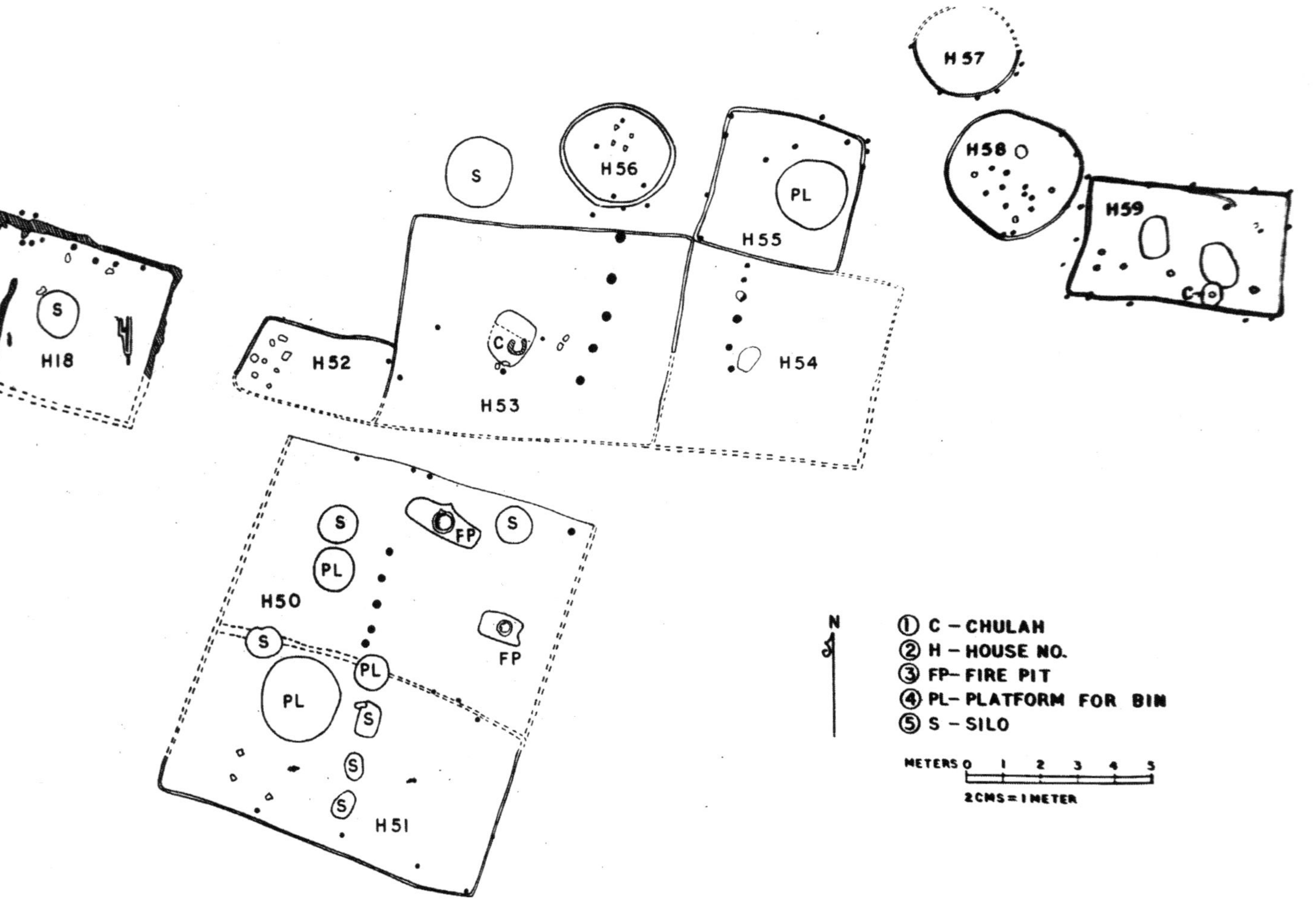

Fig. 13.17: Inamgaon, house of the chieftain, Early Jorwe Period

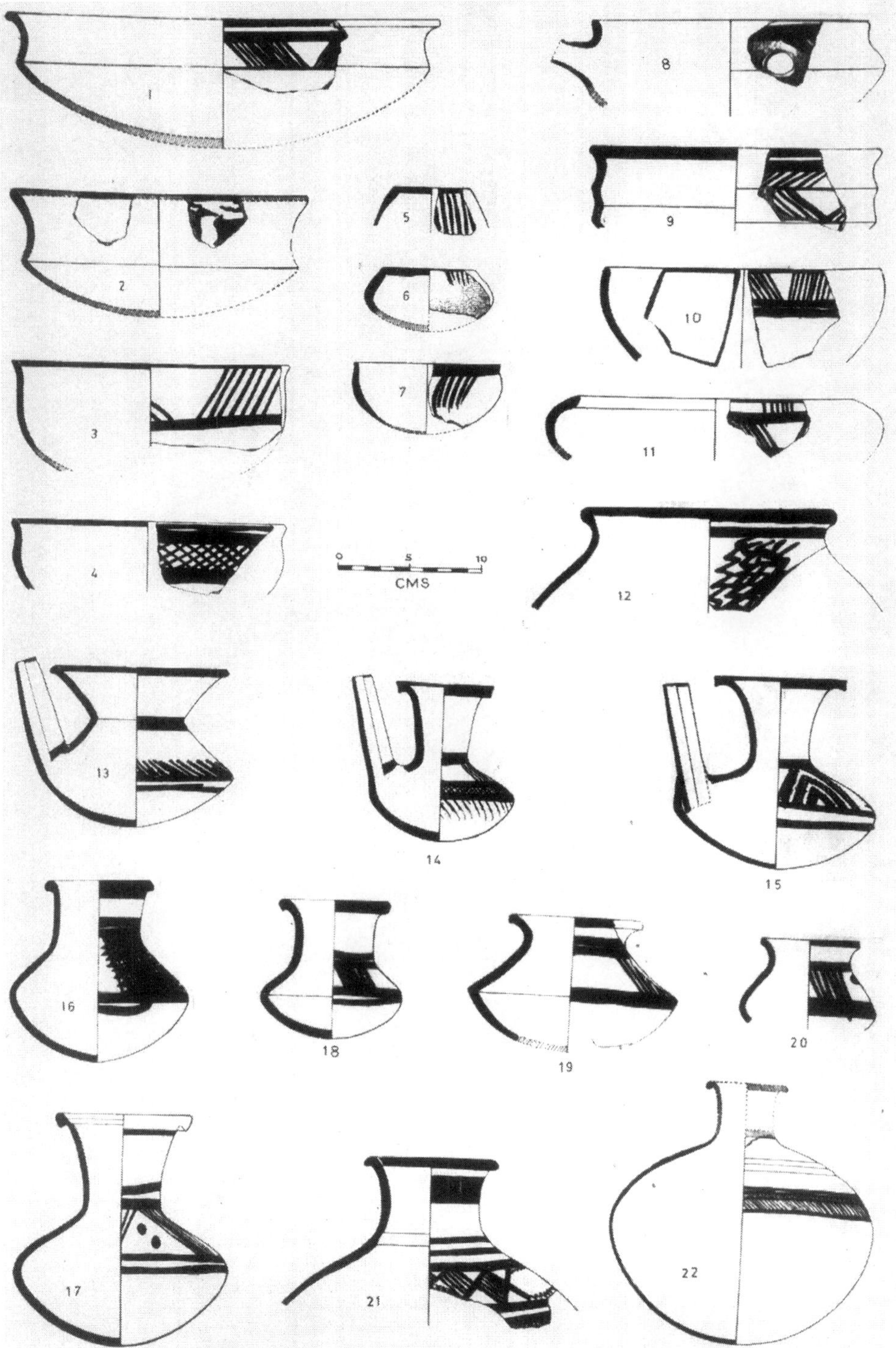

Fig. 13.18: Inamgaon, Early Jorwe (Period II) pottery

Fig. 13.19: Inamgaon, pottery kiln, Period II

Yet another example of public works from Inamgaon is the diversionary channel and the massive embankment. The construction of such hydraulic works implies a central administrative authority not only for mustering community effort but also for controlling the distribution of water.[67] This strengthens our hypothesis of a ruling chief at Inamgaon in the Early Jorwe period.

The most important evidence for a ranked society is furnished by burials. An individual's treatment at death is a reflection of the position he occupied in a status system in life. An elaborate burial would indicate what Binford calls the 'social persona' of the deceased.[68] Interesting evidence in this respect is available at Inamgaon. The Jorwe people buried children in two, placed mouth-to-mouth horizontally in a pit dug inside or outside the house (Fig. 13.20). The body of the child was placed inside with the head towards the north and legs towards the south. Small pots, probably containing food and water, were also placed in the burial pit. Adults were buried in a pit with the

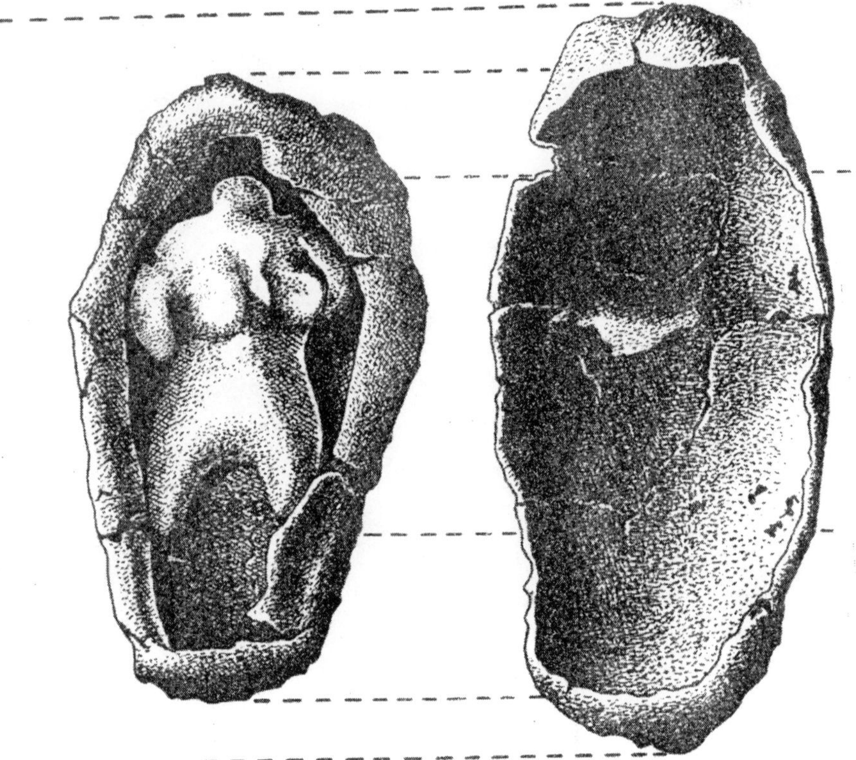

Fig. 13.20: Clay female figurine in a clay receptacle, Inamgaon (Period II)

[67]K.A. Wittfogel (1959), *Oriental Despotism: A Comparative Study of Total Power*, Yale University Press, New Haven.

[68]L.R. Binford (1972), *An Archaeological Perspective*, Seminar Press, New York, p. 225.

body placed in a supine position but before the ceremonious burial, the portion below the ankle was chopped off (Fig. 13.21). This was the normal mode but there are a couple of different examples from Inamgaon. In the courtyard of the largest house was a burial in which the dead body was placed in a seated, cross-legged posture in a four-legged jar. The skeleton was that of an adult male whose feet were not cut-off. This differential treatment is indicative of the person being different and, hence, the normal rules of the community were not applicable to him.

Yet another burial of this class was located at the same place but in the preceding level. There were two four-legged jars, one full and the other half, placed side by side, but they did not contain any skeletal remains. It was obviously a symbolic burial, probably because the dead body could not be recovered, but the status of the person was such that he deserved a cermonious burial. Both these burials were found in the largest house in the Chalcolithic settlement, which has been identified as that of the ruling chief. The evidence also shows that the chiefdom was hereditary.

Technology

The Jorwe black-on-red painted pottery is of extensively fine fabric, was made on a fast wheel and was well-fired (Fig. 13.22). The forms comprise concave-sided carinated bowl, a spouted jar with featureless mouth and a

Fig. 13.21: Inamgaon, a headless female figurine (Period II)

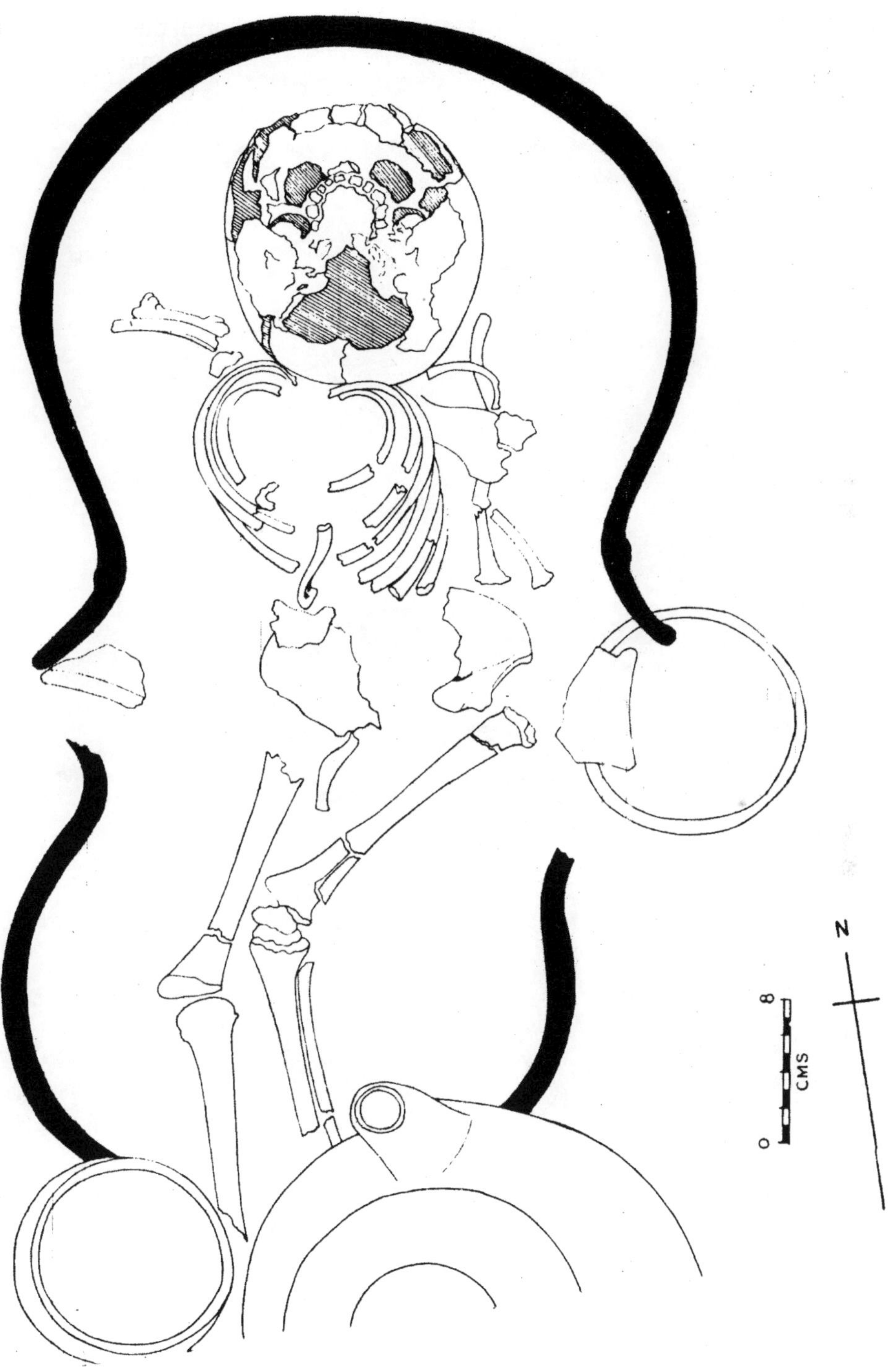

Fig. 13.22: Inamgaon, child burial.

Fig. 13.23: Inamgaon, adult burials

high-necked globular jar. The painted patterns are mostly linear and geometric but naturalistic designs also occur, though rarely. Jorwe pottery kilns have been found in excavations, two at Daimabad and one at Inamgaon (Fig. 13.19). The one at Inamgaon resembles a huge clay basin (diameter 1.7 m) with flues at the base below which was the fire chamber. The opening at the base was spanned by oblong clay cushions, which have holes in the middle and grooves on the sides through which hot gas passed upwards. The kiln at Daimabad was of a different type; it was a roughly squarish, mud structure (5 × 5 m) built on a mud platform (25 cm high). It had double walling (1.40 cm high × 50 cm thick) with ash packed in between. Inside, there was yet another wall dividing the kiln into two parts. There were oval-shaped stoke holes. The kiln contained charcoals of burnt earth, ash and vitrified pottery. If resembles present-day kilns in Maharashtra villages.

Religious Beliefs

Female figurines of clay, baked or unbaked, have been reported from Jorwe sites, among which those from Inamgaon are noteworthy. Some of them have heads but, curiously enough, some are headless. One female figurine was found inside a clay box (Fig. 13.23) over the lid of which was yet another female figure without a head and a bull, all unbaked and carefully deposited in a small hole (Fig. 13.24). The headless goddess was probably connected

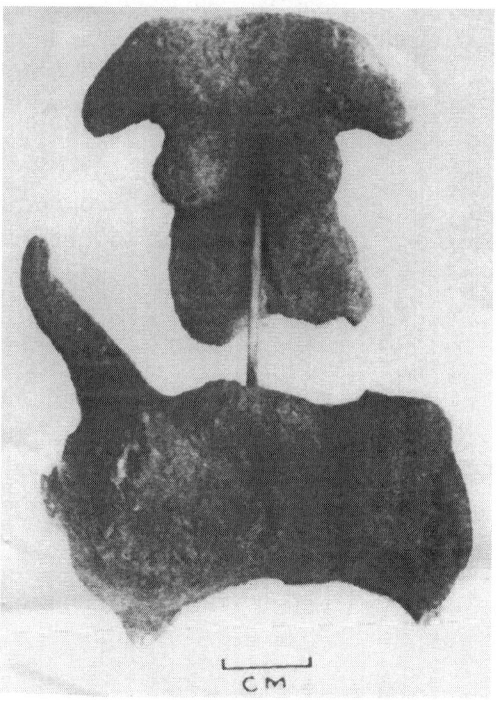

Fig. 13.24: Inamgaon, clay figurines of mother goddess without head and a bull.

with fertility and reminds us of the stone images of the headless goddess identified as Lajjagauri belonging to the early historic period, which are presently worshipped by barren women for procuring offspring. It must also be noted that a similar goddess is worshipped by the Warlis, a tribe living in the Thane district near Bombay. They call it Palghat (meaning, in the Warli language, 'the position of woman at the time of childbirth') whose pictures are painted on house walls at the time of weddings in the family.

Male figurines of unbaked clay have also been found at Inamgaon and appear to have been worshipped. A very interesting piece of evidence again comes from Inamgaon where, very close to the ancient site, is a shrine of Mhasoba. It is a large chunk of rock which is worshipped not by the local people but by Bhils who come from different parts of Maharashtra once a year whenever convenient, apply red lead to the rock, slaughter chicken and offer wooden bulls. Our enquiries revealed that the Bhils have been traditionally told by their forefathers that their ancestral god is at Inamgaon. It is, therefore, not unlikely that the shrine was established by the Chalcolithic inhabitants of Inamgaon.

Authors

It is hard to say anything about the authors of the Jorwe culture. The few skeletons which have been found and studied are said to be of the Mediterranean type with an admixture of proto-Austroloid elements, whatever that may mean. The Late Jorwe people, though of the Mediterranean type, were taller and more well-built than their predecessors in the Early Jorwe period.[69] Their dentition, too, was strong probably because of their subsistence on animal food, as Late Jorwe marks a sharp decline in agriculture and a simultaneous increase in hunting. It is also highly likely that there is some Harappan contribution in the make-up of these Chalcolithic cultures, considering the Harappan influence on the Kayatha culture out of which evolved the Malwa and, through it, the Jorwe.

End

The Chalcolithic cultures flourished during the second millennium BC and began to decline towards the last quarter; they totally died out at the end of the second millennium BC and the beginning of the first millennium BC when the entire Chalcolithic activity comes, as it were, to a grinding halt. At many of the Chalcolithic sites, there is a sterile layer which indicates a hiatus of several centuries between the Chalcolithic and early historic periods. The chemical analysis of the sterile layer from Nevasa indicates a decline in the rainfall pattern. This is also the conclusion of Gurdip Singh who has inferred

[69] R. Lukacs and G.L. Badam (1981), 'Palaeodemography of Post-Harappan Inamgaon', *JIAS*, 16, pp. 59-74.

an arid phase from *c.* 1200 BC in western India.[70] The decrease in the rainfall pattern and the consequent drought periods led to the desertion of settlements by early farming communities, which were occupied much later in the sixth-fifth century BC in the early historical period.

It has been shown that the drastic change in climate towards aridity at the end of the second millennium BC was almost a global phenomenon when many agricultural communities in the old world abandoned agriculture and resorted to pastoral nomadism.[71] This would explain why the Chalcolithic people remained a rural folk and could not attain an urban status.

UTTAR PRADESH

Interesting evidence of Chalcolithic farming communities has come to light in recent years in the lower Ganga basin. In Uttar Pradesh, it is found in the south-eastern part of the state, which roughly covers the Bundelkhand and Baghelkhand divisions. In the south, the region is delimited by the Vindhyan hills and, in the north, by the rivers Ganga and Yamuna. The Bundelkhand region is drained by some of the tributaries of the Yamuna, and the Baghelkhand region by the Ganga and the Son. The climate of the region is extreme with hot summers and cold winters, and the annual precipitation is around 1000 mm. The southern part of the Vindhyan slopes has dense forests while, in the north, it is very thin. The region has black soil which represents disintegrated basalts. A variety of wild fauna still survives here and it must have been an attractive area for early hunter-gatherers. Archaeologically, the area is considerably rich. It was occupied by hunter-gatherers from Palaeolithic times as also food-producing communities in Neolithic times. Interestingly enough, there is also clear evidence of the transition between the two epochs. It appears that the early farming communities began to occupy south-eastern Uttar Pradesh towards the close of the third and the beginning of the second millennium BC. Perhaps the only region in India where the transition from hunting-gathering to sedentary agriculture can be traced is the Vindhyan region of Uttar Pradesh.

Among the sites, two deserve special mention, viz., Mahagara and Koldihwa (district Allahabad), which are situated opposite each other on the river Belan, a tributary of the Ganga. Still earlier is the settlement of Chopani Mando, also on the Belan, which was occupied during the epi-Palaeolithic. Mesolithic and proto-Neolithic times. A blade-flake industry characterizes the first two cultural periods whereas, in the third, hand-made pottery appears for the first time. The floors of huts could also be traced from the scatter of cultural

[70]Gurdip Singh (1971), 'The Indus Valley Culture seen in the Context of Post-Glacial Climatic and Ecological Studies in Northwestern India', *Archaeology and Physical Anthropology in Oceania*, 6, pp. 177-88.

[71]A.M. Khazanov (1984), *Nomadism and the Outside World*, Cambridge University Press, Cambridge, pp. 85, 95.

debris. Bones of wild sheep and goats have been reported but there is no evidence of the domestication of plants and animals. Further development can be traced at Koldihwa where the Neolithic evolves into the Chalcolithic and Iron Age, with an appreciate overlap in between. The Neolithic is characterized by rounded celts and cord-impressed pottery, ring stones, querns, mullers and hammer stones, as also microliths. People lived in round or oval huts with wattle-and-daub walls and thatched roofs. Eighteen such floors were exposed at Mahagara. Semi-circular huts were also built. A cattle pen was unearthed at Mahagara where clusters of hoof imprints were found.

The most important discovery is that of domesticated rice which has been radiocarbon dated to *c*. 4500 BC. There are two dates: (1) 7390 + 240 BP and (2) 6480 + 185 BP, which make it the earliest evidence of rice anywhere in the world.[72] It is interesting that all the sites have yielded evidence of rice in the form of husks (used as degraissants in pottery) and charred grains, which include cultivated (*Oriza sativa*), wild annual (*Oriza nivara*) and perennial (*Oriza rufigona*) varieties. Animal bones include domestic species of cattle, sheep/goat, as also bones of wild deer, antelope and boar, and those of birds too. This would suggest that hunting was equally important. Aquifauna supplemented the diet.

The overlap between the Neolithic and Chalcolithic is evident at Koldihwa itself. This ancient site is located on the left bank of the Belan, about 80 km south-east of Allahabad. The Neolithic habitation took place on the southern and eastern parts of the mound whereas the western part came to be occupied later in the Chalcolithic period. Mahagara, which is situated on the opposite bank of the river, was also occupied during Neolithic times. There are numerous Chalcolithic sites in the Varanasi, Mirzapur, Allahabad and Banda districts of U.P. Among the excavated sites, mention should be made of Kakoria (district Varanasi), Koldihwa (district Allahabad), Banamilia, Bahera and Magha Manigara (district Mirzapur), all of which were small-scale excavations.

The Chalcolithic culture of U.P. is characterized by three distinct ceramic industries, microliths, bone tools and copper, which, although the scarce, was used on a restricted scale. Among ceramics, mention should be made of a red ware, black-and-red ware and black-slipped ware. The red ware is a nondescript, coarse ceramic but is the predominant pottery comprising two-thirds of the pottery yield. It is mostly wheel-made but a few hand-made vessels are also present. The latter is represented by big storage jars which cannot be turned on the wheel. Wheel-made forms comprise bowls (which are predominant), and dishes, basins, vases and *handies*. Perforated vessels which, too, occur are usually decorated with incised designs of dots, strokes, criss-

[72] J.N. Pal (1986), *Archaeology of Southern Uttar Pradesh: Ceramic Industry of Northern Vindhyas*, Sulabha Prakashan, Allahabad.

cross pattern, wavy lines, chevrons, lattices, zigzags and even floral patterns, as also thumb impressions and nail marks.

The other important ceramic is the black-slipped ware which, being ill-fired, is very fragile (even the slip peels off) and is devoid of any decoration. The forms include mostly bowls but there are also dishes, basins and funnel-shaped lids. The associated black-and-red ware occurs in negligible quantities (about 8 per cent). It is wheel-made but coarse in fabric due to the chopped husk mixed with the clay. It is represented mostly by bowls and, rarely, by vases, troughs and funnel-shaped lids which are not very different from the conoids occurring in south Indian megaliths. The vessels are sometimes treated with an applique decoration of the chain or rope pattern.

Chalcolithic sites in south-eastern U.P. have also yielded microliths and a few copper objects but more interesting is the bone tool industry, which is represented by points and arrowheads. From Koldihwa are reported a variety of arrowheads which occur in profusion. Besides plain specimens, there are tanged and socketed ones; the latter are decorated with incised circlets. Only a few pieces of copper were found, among which there is a blade and a ring, but beads of semi-precious stones, shell, bone and terracotta occur in a good number. Grinding stones, rubber stones and mullers constituted the kitchen equipment; stone sharpeners may have been used for sharpening copper tools, whereas those with grooves may have been bead polishers.

The mixed economy of the people was based on subsistence agriculture, stock-raising and hunting-fishing. Rice (*Oriza sativa*) is reported from Koldihwa, and the bones of domesticated animals such as cattle, sheep and goat, which bear cut marks, indicate that they supplemented the diet. The people lived in mud structures with thatched roofs. An oblong floor, well-rammed and with postholes along the periphery, was exposed at Koldihwa. The Koldihwa pottery is slightly better in fabric than that occurring elsewhere in the Vindhyan region. It is well-fired and better finished. Although the transition between the Neolithic and Chalcolithic has been noted, it has been observed that the Chalcolithic habitation at Koldihwa occurred after the Neolithic settlers at the site had deserted it.[73] This is indicative of the Neolithic and Chalcolithic settlers being two different groups of people and, moreover, suggests a break in occupation in the history of the settlement at Koldihwa. However, the similarity in ceramic ware would point to the people being culturally one but the hiatus still remains. There is, however, clear evidence of the transition into the Iron Age at the end of the Chalcolithic occupation.

The most noteworthy feature of the Vindhyan Chalcolithic is the Megalithic burials. They occur at the foot of the Hathinia hillock on the right bank of the river Chandrabhaga in the Varanasi district on the northern slopes of the

[73] Ibid., pp. 131-2.

Vindhyas at their junction with the Ganga-Yamuna, as also along the margins of different streams at the foot of the Kaimur ranges.[74] Although numerous megaliths have come to light, only a few have been subjected to excavation. They belong to two different cultural periods, viz., the Chalcolithic and the Iron Age. Those of the Chalcolithic are represented by different types and it is significant that some predominate in certain regions. Thus, in the Varanasi district, the dominant type is the cairn circle in which the burial spot is marked by a heap of earth or tumulus, surrounded by boulders arranged in a circular fashion. In the Banda district, the cist is the most common type, which is a sort of box made of flat slab-like stones in the burial pit.[75] Both the types, however, were equally well-represented at Kakoria. Of the seven megaliths which were opened, four were cairn circles and the remaining three were cists. Far more interesting were the megaliths in the Mirzapur district.[76] These were located between the villages of Banamilia and Bahera, and represented four types: (1) cairn, (2) cairn circle, (3) cist, and (4) tumulus, containing rectangular or semi-circular chambers of dressed stones with a single or multiple capstone, enclosed by a heap of stone rubble mixed with mortar, covering the capstone at times.

The pottery from these megaliths consists of an ill-fired coarse red ware, sometimes treated with a red slip, black-slipped ware and black-and-red ware, as also an over-fired red ware. All these wares, save the last one, also occur at Chalcolithic habitation sites at Kakoria and Koldihwa, and there should, therefore, be little doubt about the Chalcolithic date of these Megalithic burials. Besides, microliths, too, occur in these burials. Among the excavated sites, that at Kakoria which is located on the right bank of the Chandrabhaga has both habitation and burials. Here, a dozen megaliths were opened: eight cairns, three cists and one cist within a cairn. In one of the cairns, pottery, terracotta beads, microliths and even a gold bangle along with a few skeletal remains were found.

A vexing problem of the Megalithic culture in the south is that, while there are thousands of burial sites, there are only a few habitation sites. In U.P., however, quite a few Megalithic habitation sites have been discovered. The Megalithic habitation site at Kakoria (district Varanasi) is located just to the north-west of the burial ground. The habitation is divided into three phases on the basis of the evidence of pottery. At Magha (district Mirzapur), the habitation area and burial ground are clearly marked.[77] The people lived in thatched huts, oval in plan, with postholes along the margins. One of the huts contained a single-mouthed *chulha* similar to that found in Indian villages today. Rectangular huts with well-rammed floors have been exposed at

[74] *IAR*, 1961-2, p. 53.

[75] V.D. Misra and B.B. Misra (1977), 'Megalithic Culture in Southern U.P.', in S. Gopal (ed.), *Prof. D.D. Kosambi Commemoration Volume*, Varanasi, pp. 309-20.

[76] *IAR*, 1962-63, pp. 39-40.

[77] *IAR* 1980-81, pp. 72-3.

Koldihwa. Burnt wall lumps with reed impressions have been recovered at Munhai. The use of mud-brick has been attested at Kakoria where two rooms of a residential unit were uncovered. They measure 2.48 × 2.84 m and 2.79 × 3.47 m, respectively, with their floor paved with burnt lumps and potsherds.

The Megalithic culture was quite widespread in south-eastern U.P. as is evident from the hundreds of megaliths which have been discovered so far. Although there is not much variety in the burial types as in south India, it is apparent that, of the two types, one was more common in a particular area. Thus, in the Varanasi and Banda districts, the cist is the predominant mode of burial whereas, in the Mirzapur and Allahabad districts, the cairn is more common. According to V.D. Misra, the Kakoria-Koldihwa complex represents perhaps the earliest group whereas those in Mirzapur mark the later.[78]

Sarayupara Region

The Chalcolithic communities of U.P. also reached the Sarayupara region, which is located in the south-eastern part of U.P. in the middle Ganga basin. At Sohagaura (district Gorakhpur), where an important copperplate charter of the Mauryan period was earlier found, traces of a Neolithic-Chalcolithic habitation were found. Six cultural periods were identified at the site from the Neolithic to the medieval. The second and third represent the Chalcolithic occupation. The Neolithic inhabitants (Period I) used cord-impressed handmade pottery which also continues in the succeeding Chalcolithic (Period II) when wheel-made pottery appears, as also the BRW and grey wares. The discovery of the *tandoor*-like underground oven of this period deserves special mention. Period III is also Chalcolithic but has more varieties of painted pottery besides copper and bone tools. Several Neolithic and Chalcolithic settlements have been explored in the Gorakhpur and Basti districts where grey chert was used along with chalcedony to make blade tools. The occurrence of rice, cultivated and wild, has been reported.[79] The Chalcolithic habitation can be assigned to Period I: 1600-1300 BC and Period II: 1300-1000 on the basis of radiocarbon determinations but Chaturvedi is inclined to date them to 1900-1500 BC and 1500-900 BC, respectively.[80]

The excavation at Khairadih (district Ballia, U.P.), which is situated on the right bank of the Ghaghra, revealed the remains of a Chalcolithic habitation which, however, was confined to a very small area near the river bank. It is

[78]V.D. Misra (1977), 'Excavations at Koldihwa (Deoghat): Some Preliminary Observations', in V.D. Misra (ed.), *Some Aspects of Indian Archaeology*, Pratibha Prakashan, Allahabad.

[79]S.N. Chaturvedi (1985), 'Advance of Vindhyan Neolithic and Chalcolithic Cultures to the Himalayan Terai: Excavations and Explorations in the Sarayupara Region of Uttar Pradesh', *ME*, 9, pp. 101-8.

[80]Ibid.

characterized by BRW, black-slipped ware and painted red ware, slipped and unslipped. The people lived in mud huts with thatched roofs, cultivated rice and hunted animals. Microlithic tools are conspicuously absent but bone tools may have been used, as a tanged arrowhead of bone indicates. The Chalcolithic habitation is placed in *c.* 1100-900 BC.[81]

Narhan Culture

The excavation at Narhan (district Gorakhpur), which is located on the right bank of the Ghaghra, revealed a fivefold sequence of cultures of which the first is Chalcolithic. It is not very different from that of the Sarayupara region but could be studied in greater detail at Narhan after which the culture is named.[82] The Chalcolithic is characterized by white painted BRW, black-slipped ware sometimes decorated with white paintings, a red-slipped ware and a red ware. Black ware is represented by bowls, basins and jars but dishes are absent. The people lived in mud huts containing hearths, sometimes two-armed, similar to those at Chirand. They raised barley (*Hordeum vulgare*), wheat (*T. spha erococcum*), rice (*Oriza sativa*), pulses including pea (*Pisum sativum*), green gram (*moong*, *Vigna radiata*), besides mustard and linseed. This is the earliest occurrence of linseed in India. The occurrence of jackfruit, too, is noteworthy. The people kept domestic cattle, sheep/goat and horse, and hunted deer and antelope. They used beautiful bone tools. The culture is dated to *c.* 1300-700 BC.

BIHAR

The existence of the Chalcolithic culture has also come to light in Bihar. Evidence from excavations at Sonpur, Chirand and Oriup demonstrates that, as in south-eastern U.P., in Bihar, too, the earliest food-producing communities using ground and polished stone tools were living some time in the second quarter of the second millennium BC. As at Kakoria and Koldihwa in U.P., here, too, there was a clear overlap between the Neolithic and the Chalcolithic. In this respect, the excavations at Sonpur have proved to be of great importance. Sonpur (84° 56′ N 24° 57′ E) is a small village in the district of Gaya on the bank of the Yamuna River. Earlier known as Shonitpur, archaeological remains are found scattered on the mound known as Banasurkagadh. The excavation revealed a sequence of three cultural phases of which the first represents the proto-historic occupation, followed by the NBP and post-NBP periods.[83] The earliest cultural period (I) has been divided into two sub-phases. Of these,

[81] B.P. Singh (1987-8), 'Khairadih: A Chalcolithic Settlement', *Puratattva*, 18, pp. 28-34.

[82] Purushottam Singh (1994), *Excavations at Narhan (1984-89)*, Banaras Hindu University and B.R. Publishing Corporation, Varanasi and Delhi.

[83] B.P. Sinha and B.S. Verma (1977), *Sonpur Excavation (1956 and 1959-62)*, Patna.

phase IA represents the Neolithic habitation, characterized by a coarse black-and-red pottery and a non-descript red ware, both hand-made, and contain rice husk. BRW, which is predominant, curiously has its black portion smooth whereas the red surface is dull. It is represented by such utilitarian forms as dishes and bowls, some of which are tipped or perforated, and vases. Another interesting feature are the bone tools such as points, stylii, and arrowheads, both of the socketed and tanged varieties. This phase has been dated on the basis of radiometric dates to about *c.* 1100-1000 BC (uncalibrated) because the occupational deposit is very thin (61 cm).

The overlap between the Neolithic (IA) and the Chalcolithic (IB) is evident from the occurrence of the same ceramic ware in both phases. The only difference is that the fabric is now finer and the vessels are mostly wheel-made. The people lived in small, round huts whose plans have been traced. Besides, it is highly likely that they also had dwelling pits as some of the pits appear to be quite large. There is also a smaller circular pit, very regular in plan, which may have been a silo for storing grain.[84] The floor of the hut was well-rammed and lime-coated. The diameter of the round huts varied from 1.8 to 2.44 m and the depth was 8 cm.[85]

The tool-kit is consisted of a variety of bone tools, as in the preceding phase, but a few copper objects also appear in this phase. Many bone tools were in the manufacturing stage, indicating that they were made at the site. Besides, there are a few Microlithic and Neolithic tools. The mixed economy of the inhabitants was based on subsistence agriculture, stock-raising and hunting-fishing. The people cultivated rice, as is evident from the finds of charred rice. Their ornaments included a variety of beads of semi-precious stones, and hair-pins and antimony rods of bone. It is interesting that a few post-cremation burials have also been found. The burial pit was circular (diameter 1.82 to 2.12 m and 91 cm deep) in which a few charred human bones and some pottery vessels, probably containing food and water for the dead, were deposited. There were also perhaps a few urn burials, as some big jars containing human bones have been encountered.[86] The Chalcolithic occupation (IB) has been assigned to *c.* 1000-650 BC (uncalibrated).

The evidence recurs at other sites: Chirand (district Saran), Oriup (district Bhagalpur) and Taradih (district Gaya). All these early farming settlements were located in the vast alluvial tract of the Ganga where the soil is extremely fertile and the rainfall is quite high (44.5 inches or 1150 mm). There was an excellent forest cover in the ancient past but it is now fast-depleting. The region is rich in flora and fauna and it was, thus, an attractive area for early settlers.

The evidence from Sonpur is more or less repeated at Chirand, which has

[84]Ibid., p. 8, Fig. 4.

[85]Ibid., 1B.

[86]Ibid., p. 7.

been intermittently excavated for several reasons.[87] Chirand, located on the river Ghaghra, has revealed a threefold sequence of cultures. The earliest settlers subsisted more on hunting-gathering, lived in small, round huts enclosed by mud walls,[88] used burnished and unburnished red wares, a variety of bone tools and microliths, and cultivated rice. This phase is coeval with phase IA at Chirand and the same holds true in the case of IB. In this latter phase, copper comes into use though on a very restricted scale. The ceramic wares comprise red, blackish-grey and black-and-red. The grey ware was sometimes painted with red ochre and the red ware was decorated with applique designs. Period II marks the flowering of the Chalcolithic culture. Although the same ceramics continue, the variety of forms such as the dish-on-stand and pedestalled cup are interesting. Some vessels also bear post-firing paintings in white and yellow. There is a noteworthy change in house plans; though they are wattle-and-daub constructions with thatched roofs, they are now apsidal in plan. The large ovens at Taradih may have been used for community cooking or smelting copper.[89] The agricultural economy consisted of rice, wheat, lentil (*masur*). and moong (*Phaselus mungo*). The people worshipped a mother goddess whose terracotta representation has been found (Prasad 1980-1). Bull, bird and *naga* figurines may also be associated with their religious beliefs. The repertoire of bone tools is also varied as there is a shaft straightener and an adze.[90] Mention should also be made of a bone chisel and barbed arrowheads from Taradih (Gaya).

The series of radiocarbon dates (calibrated) indicates that the Bihar Neolithic started in about 2200 BC and continued up to *c*. 1500, and the following Chalcolithic phase can be assigned to *c*. 1500-800 BC at the end of which the Iron Age commences.[91]

BENGAL

A few Chalcolithic sites have been excavated in Bengal as well and, among these, mention must be made of Pandu Rajar Dhibi (district Burdwan), Mahishdal (district Birbhum), Mangalkot (district Burdwan), Hatikera (district Birbhum), and Dihar (district Bankura). All these were small-scale digs and not much besides pottery has been found. Pandu Rajar Dhibi is located on the southern bank of the Ajay River with a 5.75 m thick cultural deposit, divisible into three distinct cultural periods. Of these, the first represents the Neolithic occupation characterized by ill-fired pottery, including red, grey

[87] B.S. Verma (1970-1), 'Excavations at Chirand: New Light on the Indian Neolithic Culture Complex', *Puratattva*, 4, pp. 19-23.

[88] *IAR*, 1972-3, p. 50.

[89] *IAR*, 1985-6, p. 8.

[90] *IAR* 1972-3, p. 51.

[91] G.L. Possehl and P. Rissman (1992), 'India', in R.W. Elwrich (ed.), *Chronologies in Old World Archaeology*, Chicago University Press, Chicago, I, p. 481.

and black ware, mostly hand-made and containing husk impressions. People lived in thatched huts, the floors of which were rammed with pellety laterite and were, occasionally, burnt hard. Bone tools were made and one of fossil wood has also been found. A secondary burial containing a headless skeleton was encountered[92] as also a fractional burial.[93]

There does not seem to be a clear overlap between the Neolithic and the Chalcolithic (as in U.P. and Bihar) at Pandu Rajar Dhibi where the evidence shows that the Neolithic settlement was deserted by the people because of the Ajay River floods. At other sites, the Chalcolithic people were the first to settle. The Neolithic-Chalcolithic settlers of Bengal (Period I at Pandu) seem to have come from Bihar and can, therefore, be dated to the first half of the second millennium BC and the succeeding Chalcolithic phase to *c*. 1500-800 BC.

The Chalcolithic people lived in mud-plastered thatched huts with lime-plastered floors.[94] They used a variety of ceramic ware which included plain and painted BRW, and black painted lustrous red and chocolate wares, represented by carinated and lipped bowls, and channel-spouted cups. The design repertoire mostly consists of linear goemetrical patterns whereas punctured and incised decorating also occurs. The tool outfit comprised a bone industry and microlithic blade industry. A few Neolithic ground and polished celts also have been picked up. Copper was used for ornaments such as rings and bangles, as also for tools such as nail parers and celts.[95] A variety of beads of semi-precious stones were made and, among these, a specimen of *lapis lazuli* is noteworthy. Charred grains of rice have been reported from Mahishdal.[96] The remains of cattle, deer, turtle, fish and birds indicate that hunting and fishing supplemented their diet.

Human burials have been encountered at some sites. They can be divided into three distinct categories: (1) extended, (2) fractional, and (3) urn burials.

ORISSA

In recent years, excavations at Golbai Sasan (district Puri) have provided evidence of Chalcolithic habitation. The Neolithic wave probably reached Bihar from Orissa. Earlier the Kuchai excavations had yielded evidence of Mesolithic and Neolithic occupation but the Chalcolithic has been brought to light for the first time at Golbai Sasan.[97] The ancient site is situated on

[92] *IAR*, 1965-6, p. 46, Pl. XL-A.
[93] *IAR*, 1962-3, p. 43.
[94] *IAR*, 1961-2, p. 61, Pl. XCVII-A.
[95] *IAR*, 1963-4, p. 60.
[96] Ibid.
[97] B.K. Singh (1992-3), 'Excavations at Golbai Sasan, District Puri, Orissa', *Puratattva,* 33, pp. 28-50.

the left bank of the Mandakini, a tributary of the Daya which flows into the Chilka Lake. It was occupied only during the Neolithic and Chalcolithic times, and there appears to be a hiatus between the two which is represented by a sterile layer.

The Chalcolithic period has been divided into two phases, IIa and IIb (*c.* 1300-900 BC), as it was a prolonged habitation which is represented by a 5-m thick cultural debris. It is characterized by BRW, mostly hand-made, plain red ware, burnished black and chocolate ware. These sometimes bears linear and geometrical designs in red ochre. Bowls, basins, jars, dishes-on-stand and lids were the prominent forms, besides miniature pots which were used for containing medicines. Pottery crucibles were possibly meant for heating copper.

The people lived in mud huts, circular in plan, with their diameter varying from 3.90 to 7.90 m, and well-rammed floors. The largest structure may have been a public building.[98] Along with ground and polished tools such as axes, adzes and chisels, they also had a specialized bone tool-kit consisting of burins, points, adzes, chisels and needles. A long spearhead (27 cm long) and a barbed harpoon of bone deserve special mention. Subsistence was based on rice, *kulthi* (*Dolichos lablab*), and plant and animal foods. The solitary human burial, too, is unique as it was without the head, as was the case at Pandu Rajar Dhibi in Bengal. Moreover, the portion of the legs below the ankles was missing, as in the Deccan Chalcolithic. A copper bangle, a few copper rings, a chisel and a fish hook were recovered from it. Period IIB is also Chalcolithic but marks the advent of iron.

It has been observed that there is a hiatus in the occupation of sites between the Chalcolithic and early historical strata almost all over the country except for the Ganga Valley where there seems to have been an overlap. Although this is not unlikely as the environment there might not have been as arid as in other parts, yet it is necessary to carefully examine the stratigraphic position.

[98] Ibid.

Chapter 14

Ochre Coloured Pottery and Copper Hoards

Purushottam Singh

Among the several vexing questions in Indian archaeology is the problem of copper hoards and their alleged association with a class of pottery known as Ochre Coloured Pottery (OCP). Ever since the first discovery of a copper harpoon at Bithur (district Kanpur) way back in 1822, more than 1,300 objects have been documented so far.[1] Most of these artefacts were accidentally found in caches and only 26 per cent of them came from regular excavations, mostly from the Chalcolithic sites of Maharashtra. The number of objects found in a hoard varies between one and forty-seven except in association with thin sheets of silver objects, mainy oxheads (bucrania) and discs of indeterminate use. Most of these objects are massive in weight and size. The fact that all of them are well-preserved and do not bear any wear marks on their edges has led scholars to believe that these objects were valuable commodities rather than utilitarian objects of daily life.[2]

SURVEY OF LITERATURE

All though brief notes on the discovery of these hoards have appeared from time to time, the problem was critically studied for the first time by B.B. Lal who, in his brilliant paper, prepared an updated list of their findspots, commented upon their alleged association with OCP, and examined the issue of their authorship.[3] In his subsequent papers, Lal further examined this problem in the light of new data.[4] The problem also received an exhaustive treatment

[1] D.K. Chakrabarti and Nayanjot Lahiri (1996), *Copper and its Alloys in Ancient India*, Munshiram Manoharlal, New Delhi.

[2] V. Tripathi (1998) (ed.), *Archaeometallurgy in India*, Sharada Publishing House, Delhi, p. xvi.

[3] B.B. Lal (1951), 'Further Copper Hoards from the Gangetic Basin and a Review of the Problem', *Ancient India*, 7, pp. 20-39.

[4] B.B. Lal (1968), 'A Deluge? Which Deluge? Yet Another Facet of the Problem of the Copper Hoard Culture', *American Anthropologist* (5); idem (1971-2), 'A Note of the Excavations at Saipa', *Puratattva*, 5, pp. 46-9.

by S.P. Gupta,[5] Makkhan Lal[6] and Paul Yule.[7] It was discussed at length by D.P. Agrawal[8] and was briefly commented upon by a number of scholars.[9] Technical and metallurgical studies of some of these artefacts were done by Agrawal, Paul Yule, Rajam Seshadri and P.K. Chattopadhyay.[10]

DISTRIBUTION (Fig. 14.1)

Although copper hoards have been reported from various parts of the country, their main concentration is in the Ganga-Yamuna Doab, the eastern Chota Nagpur region, southern Haryana, northern Rajasthan and scattered sites in Madhya Pradesh. Thus there are seven sites in Haryana, eleven in Rajasthan, eight in Bengal, two in Orissa, eight in Madhya Pradesh, four in Bihar, eight in Jharkhand and as many as thirty-one sites in U.P., Gujarat, Maharashtra and Karnataka have yielded six sites each and two sites were recorded from Punjab. Andhra Pradesh, Kerala and Nepal are represented by one site each. A complete list of hitherto recorded copper hoard sites is given in the appendix.[11]

TYPOLOGY

Main Types (Figs. 14.2 and 14.3)

The principal types of copper hoard tools comprise anthropomorphs, swords, double-edged axes, harpoons, socketed axes, trunion axes, flat and shouldered

[5] S.P. Gupta (1963), 'Indian Copper Hoards: The Problem of Homogeneity, Stages of Development, Origin, Authorship and Dating', *Journal of the Bihar Research Society*, 49, pp. 147-66.

[6] Makkhan Lal (1984), *Settlement History and Rise of Civilization in Ganga-Yamuna Doab*, B.R. Publishing Corporation, Delhi.

[7] Paul Yule (1985), *Metal Work of the Bonze Age in India*, Munchen; idem (1989), *The Copper Hoards of the Indian Subcontinent: Preliminaries for Interpretation*, Mainz.

[8] D.P. Agrawal (1971), *The Copper Bronze Age in India*, Munshiram Manoharlal, New Delhi; idem (1982), *The Archaeology of India*, Curzon Press, London.

[9] H.D. Sankalia (1972), *Prehistory and Protohistory of India and Pakistan*, Deccan College, Poona; B. Allchin and R. Allchin (1983), *The Rise of Civilisation of India and Pakistan*, Select Service Syndicate, New Delhi; B.K. Thapar (1985), *Recent Archaeological Discoveries in India*, UNESCO, Paris, pp. 99-103; Chakrabarti and Lahiri (1996), op. cit.; M.K. Dhavalikar (1997), *Indian Protohistory*, Book & Books, New Delhi; D.K. Chakrabarti (1999), *India: An Archaeological History*, Oxford University Press, New Delhi.

[10] Agrawal (1971), op. cit.; Yule (1985), op. cit.; idem (1989), op. cit.; Rajan Seshadri (1994), 'The Metal Technology of the Harappan and the Copper Hoard Culture: Comparative Study', Ph.D. thesis (unpublished), The Maharaja Sayajirao University, Baroda; P.K. Chattopadhyay (1992), 'Archaeometallurgy in India: Studies on Technoculture in Early Copper and Iron Ages in Bihar and West Bengal', Ph.D. thesis (unpublished), Patna University.

[11] Yule (1985), op. cit., p. 108.

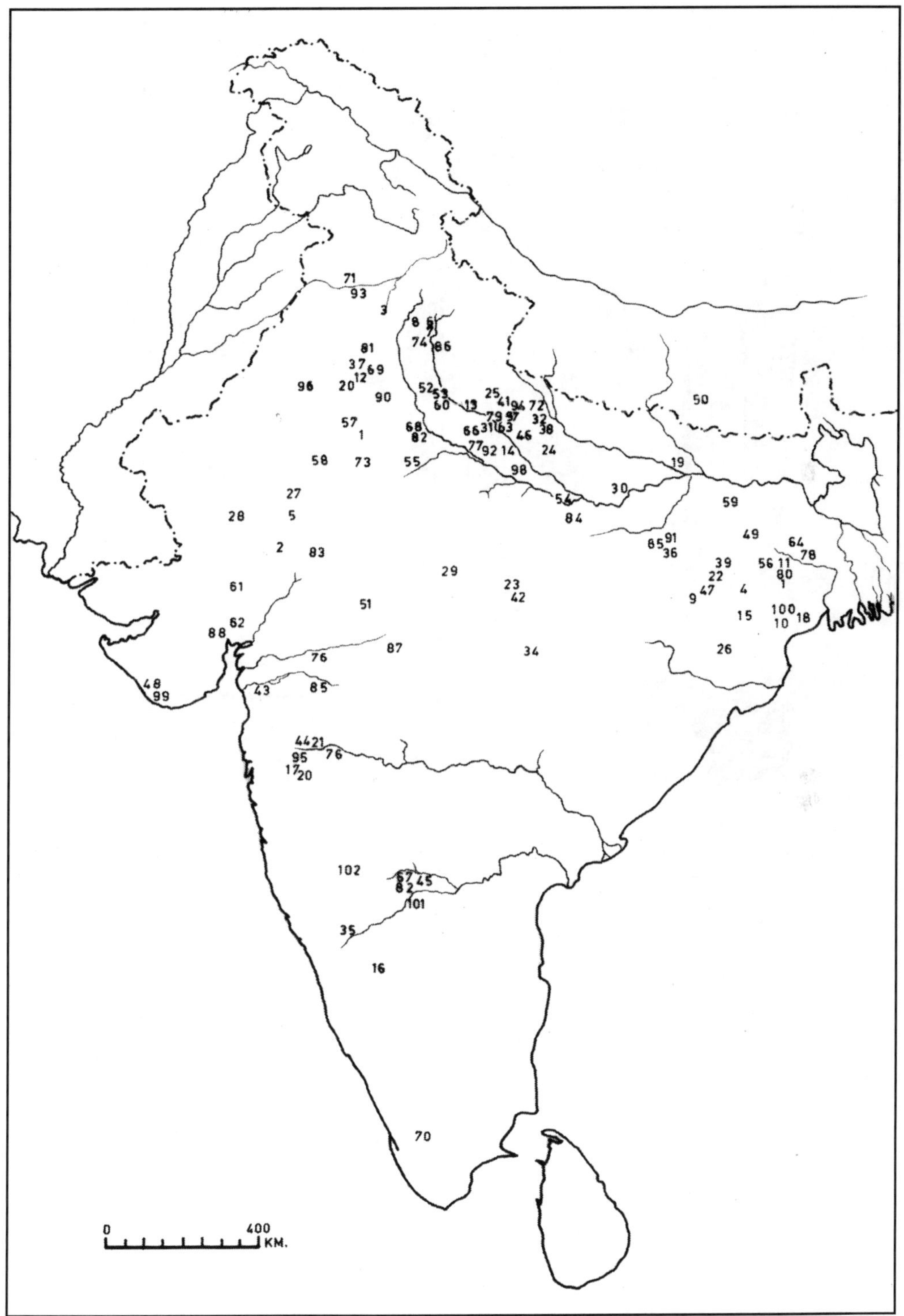

Fig. 14.1: Map showing copper hoard sites

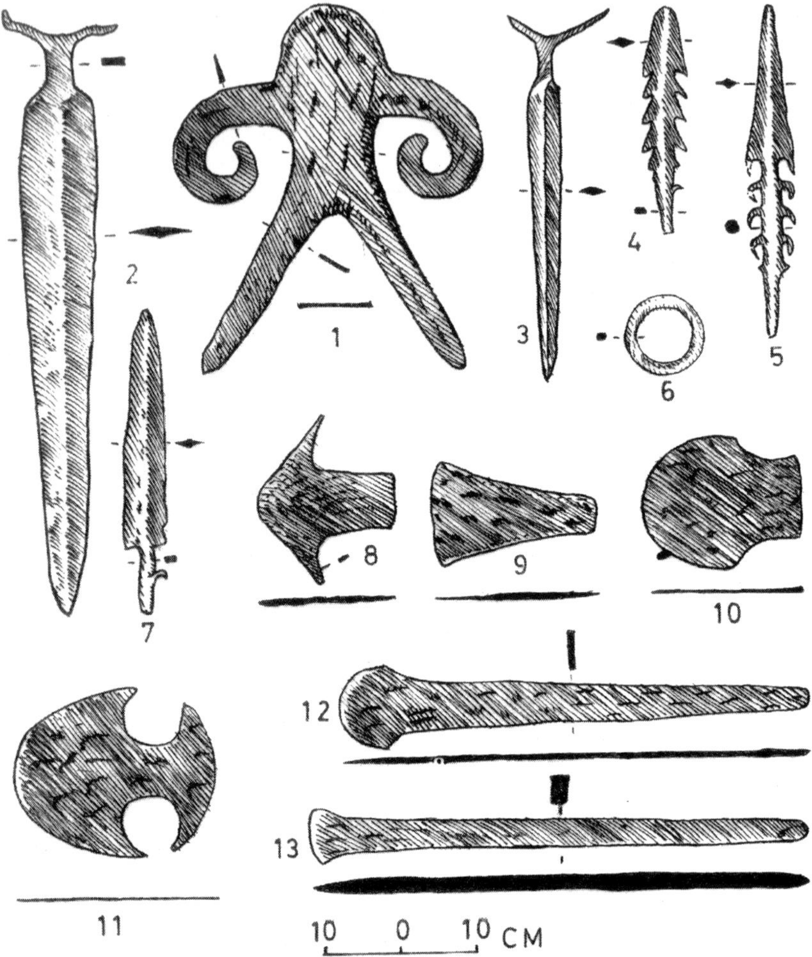

Fig. 14.2: Copper hoard objects: 1. Anthropomorphic figure, Sheorajpur; 2, 3. Antennae sword, Fatehgarh; 4-5. Harpoons respectively from Sarthauli and Bisauli; 6. Ring, Pondi; 7. Hooked spearhead, Sarthauli; 8. Hatchet (*parashu*), Sarthauli; 9. Celt, Gungeria; 10. Shouldered celt, Dunria; 11. Double-edged axe, Bhagra Pir; 12, 13. Bar celts, Gungeria

celts, and rings. Besides, there are some associated specimens found in a particular hoard or confined to a particular geographical unit. Thus, bucrania and discs of silver were found in the Gungeria hoard and arrowheads are a common feature of the Ganeshwar complex. Arrowheads are made from relatively thin strips of metal and been a superficial resemblance to several Harappan examples. Initially, there was a lot of confusion about their typology but Lal has done pioneering work in sorting out their typology. He observed that trunion axes, the Fort Munro sword, the socketed axe and the axe-adze

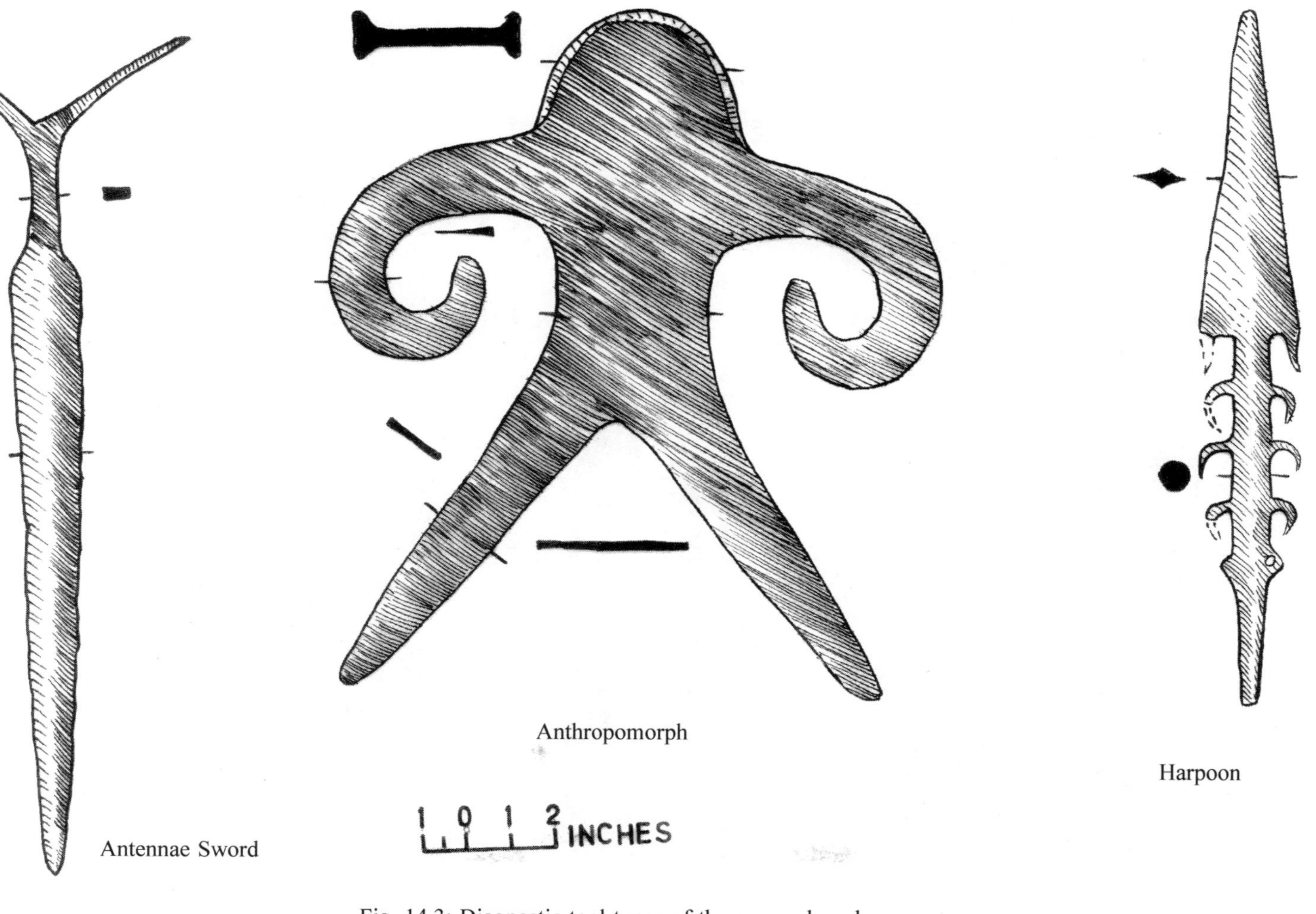

Fig. 14.3: Diagnostic tool-types of the copper hoards

are confined to the north-western part of the subcontinent. Again, the harpoon, bar celt and anthropomorphs are never found west of the *doab*.

Paul Yule has made a detailed classification of copper hoard artefacts.[12] Of these, the anthropomorph is the most diagnostic and enigmatic tool-type. As the name suggests, it represents a human form. It has externally sharpened and incurved forearms, plain hind limbs, and a thickened head. It has a restricted provenance and number. There are only thirteen known anthropomorphs, eleven of them coming from seven localities in U.P.[13] Yule divided them into two sub-types on the basis of the fact that some are more elongated and heavier than the rest. Type I has a length of 23-4 cm and of average weight of 1,260 gm while the heavier ones measure 30-7 cm with an average weight of 4,500 gm.[14]

The antennae-hilted swords have a long, broad and leaf-shaped blade (mid-ribbed and slightly concave in section) with about 6-10 cm grip and antennae hilt. Their strength ranges between 56 and 76 cm, and weight between 1,238 and 2,380 gm.

The hooked sword (generally bracketed with antennae-hilted swords) has a length of 43-7 cm, a sharply profiled mid-rib and highly concave sides in section, with a hook bent backwards in the middle of the grip. The double-axes have large violin-shaped blades and the sides curve inward at the waist. Their length varies between 23 and 46 cm, and weight between 280 and 230 gm. A variety of these double-axes have been termed *parashu*. They have, in plan, two bilaterally symmetrical cutting edges, one at each end of the bow-shaped blade. Invariably, the cutting edges are broader than the middle of the blades and are usually convex.

The simple axes have been divided into seven sub-types by Yule on the basis of their length-breadth ratio and morphological features. They have straight sides, a convex cutting edge, and a roughly flat, convex or slightly concave butt end. Their length varies from 9.8 to 16.5 cm and they weigh up to 3,700 gm. The axe-ingots are proportionately thick and often asymmetrical in profile. Some are very large and heavy and weigh up to 4,250 gm.

Harpoons have been divided into three sub-types, the commonest having a short bladed tip and 4-6 angularly disposed barbs, generally with an eyelet on one side below the barbs. Its length range is 17.5-28.6 cm and weight range is 215-915 gm.

The bars are 19.5 to 46 cm long, with sides tapering towards one end and are usually rectangular in cross-section. Their weight range is 350-1400 gm. The bar celts measure 30-10 cm with rectangular shafts in section. Their weight varies between 832 to 2,943 gm.[15] The bar celt ingots are with no

[12] Yule (1985), op. cit.

[13] Lal (1984), op. cit., p. 47.

[14] Yule (1985), op. cit., p. 52; Chakrabarti and Lahiri (1996), op. cit., p. 79.

[15] Chakrabarti and Lahiri (1996), op. cit., p. 82.

sharp edges or corners and are plano-convex in section. Chisels are much smaller than the bars and bar celts.

The bangles are heavy, large and ring-shaped. They are made of thick stock and are circular in section—the ends either meeting or with a slight space between them. Their diameter ranges between 6.5 to 10.5 cm and weight between 135-475 gm. A total of eighty rings have been found from nine localities. Typologically, the rings from Pondi (Rewa district, M.P.) differ from those of other sites.

MINOR TYPES

In the excavated objects of Ganeshwar, there are twenty-five arrowheads of a variety of shapes and sizes. Their average length is 3 cm and the mean width is 1.22 cm. The fifteen bucrania found in the Gungeria hoard are made of thin silver foil. They have downward-turned horns and a hanging semi-circular headlike form between them. Their mean dimension is 13.32 × 5.98 × 0.02 cm. The nine silver discs found in this hoard were convexly formed. They are geometrically regular and form a homogeneous group in size.

METALLURGY

The chemical analysis of copper hoard tools has shown that by and large, they are made of pure copper of up to 98 per cent purity.[16] Technological studies show that most of them were completely cast in single (open) or double (closed) moulds or both, before being finished by hammering, chiselling, filing and tempering.[17] Celts were generally cast in an open mould whereas swords and harpoons were cast in closed moulds. It is believed that the copper hoard people knew closed-casting and smelting but probably not alloying or annealing and cold work for hardening the tools.[18] Here, it needs to be emphasized that no two metal objects are identical in shape and, thus, could not have been cast in the same mould. The overall rough and grainy surface, particularly of the Chota Nagpur objects, could be the result of sand-casting. Agrawal and his colleagues carried out an analysis of forty-one copper hoard objects.[19] Of these, thirty-two came from twelve sites in U.P. and nine from five sites in Bihar. They comprised thirty-three celts, two bangles, one

[16]Lal (1951), op. cit., p. 24.

[17]Agrawal (1971), op. cit., p. 186.

[18]Ibid., pp. 242-3.

[19]D.P. Agrawal et al. (1974), 'Alloying in Copper Hoards', *Bulletin of Archaeology and Museums, U.P.*, 14, pp. 14-18; idem (1978), 'New Data on the Copper Hoards and Diamabad Bronzes', *Man and Environment*, 2, pp. 40-6; idem (1981), 'Arsenical Coppers in the Indian Bronze Age', in M.S. Nagaraja Rao (ed.), *Madhu: Shri M.N. Deshpande Volume (Festchrift)*, Agam Kala Prakashan, Delhi, pp. 9-16.

anthropomorph, two spears, two harpoons and two swords. The results of this analysis have been summarized by Makkhan Lal as follows:

Atomic absorption spectrometric analysis of 27 objects from Uttar Pradesh shows traces of tin in all specimens whereas nickel 0.005 to 0.453% iron 0.037 to 0.47%, arsenic 0.1361 to 7.844% and lead 0.0038 to 2.432% are present (Agrawal et al. 1978: Table 1). Alloying of arsenic was deliberate. The closed casting of pure copper is quite difficult and harpoons and swords show that their casting was done in closed moulds. Arsenic was added to facilitate casting and make the metal hard.

A comparative study of impurity patterns of copper hoard objects from U.P. and Bihar has been carried out by Agrawal et al. (1978: 43, Tables 2 & 3). On the basis of the presence of iron, antimony, nickel, manganese, cobalt, aluminium and chromium and absence of gold, wolfram, titanium, vanadium, and phosphorous in copper hoard objects and Rakha ores, they have concluded that the source of metal for the Uttar Pradesh copper hoard were Rakha ore mines. But in spectrophotometric analysis not a single object from Uttar Pradesh shows the presence of tin whereas it is present in the Rakha ore (Agrawal et al. 1978: Table 3).

Chemical analysis of 5 celts (Nos. 4, 6, 7, 8 and 9) from Madnapur, Hardoi district, U.P. (Misra 1976) were carried out by Thakkar (1977). The analysis shows that three celts (Nos. 7, 8 and 9) have an identical impurity pattern. They contain lead, cadmium, bismuth, arsenic, antimony, iron, manganese and zinc as impurities. Celt No. 4 fails to show bismuth, arsenic, and antimony which are present in other three celts. In celt No. 6, lead, arsenic and antimony are absent. However, this is the only celt in which lead is absent but it shows the presence of tin. Celt Nos. 4 and 6 show the presence of aluminium which is absent in celt Nos. 7, 8 and 9. The impurity pattern of the last three celts shows that they belong to the same source.

When we compare the impurity patterns of above five celts with Rakha ores we find that in Rakha ores tin, silver and cobalt are present whereas these are absent in the celts. Bismuth is not present in the ores whereas it is present in the celts.

This comparative study of the chemical analysis of Rakha copper ores and copper hoard objects shows that Uttar Pradesh copper hoards have not been made from Rakha ores. The probability of Singhbhum or Khetri ore mines as the source for Uttar Pradesh copper hoards has already been excluded by Agrawal et al. (1978). What then may be the source of the copper hoards from Uttar Pradesh? In zones A and C ores were available locally but in zone B there are no ores. So the manufacturer had to import the raw material from outside. Zones A and C could not be the source of the raw material. The nearest ore sources to zone B are the mines of the Kumaon-Garhwal region. The largest concentration of copper hoards in Uttar Pradesh is in the upper and central parts. It would be easier for the copper hoard smiths of zone B to obtain ore from the Kumaon-Garhwal region than to import it from Rajasthan and Bihar. But anything with certainty can be said only when the chemical analysis of the Kumaon-Garhwal ores is also available.[20]

In this context, mention may be made of the analysis of two copper shouldered celts from Akhuldoba and five double-edged axes from Parihati (both in district Midnapur, West Bengal) by P.K. Chattopadhyay who found that these implements were manufactured by casting in moulds with a better

[20]Lal (1984), op. cit., p. 49.

ventilation system. After casting, the edges of the implements were later finished by forging with a hammer.[21]

Recently, Rajam Seshadri has done a detailed metallurgical study of eight samples of copper hoard affiliation.[22] These were taken from a celt from south Bihar, a double-axe from Bhagrapir (Orissa), a harpoon from Raipur (M.P.), an anthropomorph from Saguna (Bihar) and a bar-celt from Hami (Bihar). Samples were also taken from two axes and a *parashu*—all from Madnapur in the district of Hardoi (U.P.). However, although Seshadri used an advanced metallurgical technique (non-destructive Energy Dispersive X-ray Fluorescence), the results were not very promising. She noted that all the samples were of pure copper and no alloys were noticed. The iron content in all is quite high as compared to the Harappan samples where it was negligible. This indicates that the smelting technology of the Harappans was superior to that of the copper hoard people. As regards smith techniques, the copper hoard specimens show evidence of annealing but do not indicate any type of cold work. The complete absence of any evidence of the latter suggests that these objects were not put to use—an observation made by other scholars too.[23] The percentage composition of copper hoard artefacts from Hami, Rewari, Bahadrabad, Nasirpur, Gungeria and several other sites was done by Hauptmann.[24] Chakrabarti and Lahiri observe that, in the present state of our knowledge, we find it difficult to accept the notion that the Chota Nagpur hoards were proto-historic and that these could be related to the upper Gangetic valley and the north Rajasthan—southern Haryana hoards in any way.[25]

FUNCTION

Before assigning any function to the copper hoards artefacts, it needs to be borne in mind that there is a conspicuous lack of ancient use-wear marks on them. Even such utilitarian types as the axes are either too small or too large, too thin or too thick, too light or too heavy, or too dull to have been used or, subsequently, cold-worked into finished axes. Similarly, the axe-ingots and bar celt-ingots from the copper-rich Chota Nagpur area show no traces of use-wear and served no obvious function. Even the exaggerated weight and size of the harpoons present grounds to doubt their primary utilitarian function. Further, Yule has doubted that they were actually used in combat or for hunting and that they can be more plausibly understood as ceremonial, cultic or ritual objects rather than as combat arms.[26]

[21] Chattopadhyay (1992), op. cit., p. 138.

[22] Seshadri (1994), op. cit.

[23] Tripathi (1998), op. cit.; Yule (1985), op. cit., p. 102.

[24] Cited in Yule (1989), op. cit.; quoted by Chakrabarti and Lahiri (1996), op. cit., pp. 87-90.

[25] Chakrabarti and Lahiri (1996), op. cit., p. 90.

[26] Yule (1985), op. cit., pp. 103-5.

As regards the three diagnostic objects of the upper Ganga Valley, viz., the anthropomorph, the sword with an antennae and the harpoon, Agrawal thought that they were all weapons of hunting. He suggested that the antennae-sword was used for killing or wounding big game by trapping as follows: 'This sword can be fixed securely in narrow clefts made in heavy wooden logs. Such logs, with antennae swords projecting out, could be placed in the bottom of big pits. The pits could be camouflaged. . . .' But Sankalia has rightly observed that this conjectural usage has no backing from the current practices of trapping big game or from historic and pre-historic practices, as deduced with the help of ethnology and the study of weapons themselves.[27]

Further, Agrawal suggested that the heavy anthropomorphs were hurled against flying birds and their sharp forearms could produce cuts in the bodies of the victims—birds or animals.[28] Yet the use of such a heavy and complicated weapon for bringing down birds is uneconomical and not expected from unsophisticated nomadic hunters.[29] Thus, in all likelihood, the anthropomorphic figures were ritualistic objects. Krishna Kumar believes that these figures represent the late Rigvedic images of Indra and, thus, are the earliest Brahmanical metal icons manufactured in Sarasvati and the Ganga valleys.[30] A similar suggestion was made by T.K. Das Gupta in 1975.[31] Vibha Tripathi believes that the copper hoard objects were valuable commodities rather than utilitarian objects of day-to-day life.[32] This is borne out by: 1. the fact that they were hoards, 2. the virtual absence of wear-marks on the edges of these well-preserved objects, 3. the massiveness of these objects in weight, height and length.

AUTHORSHIP

On the basis of a typological analysis of copper hoards and copper tools from Harappa and Mohenjo-daro and similar objects found in Egypt, Sardinia, the British Isles, Greece and Transcaucasia, Heine-Geldern[33] propounded that the copper hoards belong to the Aryans who came to India some time between 1200 and 1000 BC. Lal made a critical examination of Heine-Geldern's view

[27] Sankalia (1972), op. cit., p. 398.

[28] Agrawal (1971), op. cit., pp. 199-201.

[29] Sankalia (1972), op. cit., p. 399.

[30] Krishna Kumar (2000), 'The Protohistoric Copper/Bronze Anthropomorphs from Northern India', in S.C. Bhattacharya et al. (eds.), *Peeping Through the Past (Prof. G.R. Sharma Memorial Volume)*, Department of AIHC & Archaeology, Allahabad, p. 112.

[31] Yule (1985), op. cit., p. 105, fn. 35.

[32] Tripathi (1998), op. cit., p. xvi.

[33] R. Heine-Geldern (1936), 'Archaeological Traces of the Vedic Aryans', *Journal of the Indian Society of Oriental Art*, 4, pp. 87-113.

and showed that none of the copper hoard types have been found in the countries noted above, hence this theory is not tenable.[34]

Stuart Piggott (1944) initially supported the Aryan theory of Heine-Geldern but subsequently revised his views and assigned the copper hoards to the refugees and displaced persons from the Punjab and the Indus Valley during the time of the break-up of the Harappan empire. Similar views were expressed by Sharma. Lal ascribes these artefacts to the ancestors of proto-Australoid tribes like the Mundas and Santhals. D.P. Agrawal[35] thinks that the copper hoard people were the original inhabitants of the tangled, wooded country of the *doab* before the Painted Grey Ware people started clearing the forests with their iron tools. It is clear from the above that there is no unanimity of views on this issue and it is difficult to resolve it in the present state of our research.

COPPER HOARDS AND THE OCP (FIG. 14.4)

It was B.B. Lal who, after excavations at Bisauli and Rajpur Parsu, suggested that copper hoard implements were associated with OCP. Bisauli (district Badaun in western U.P.) had yielded three anthropomorphs, a flat axe and a harpoon, now housed in the Bharat Kala Bhavan, Varanasi. Lal excavated two trenches up to a depth of 3 ft below the ground level in October 1949. The pottery from the trenches, though limited in quantity, was divided into two classes: (a) well-fired? red slipped ware with designs executed in black colour, and (b) ill-fired thick, ochre-washed ware with worn-out edges.[36]

At the same time, Lal also excavated Rajpur Parsu in the district of Bijnor, which had yielded a hoard consisting of various axes, one axe-ingot, a bar and a harpoon way back in June 1896 (now housed in the State Museum, Lucknow). All these artefacts are supposed to have come from a mound 800 × 800 m in size and rising to 1 to 2 m. Lal excavated five small trenches on this mound in October 1949 and OCP, similar in appearance to that first found at Bisauli, was obtained.[37] Subsequently, the same ill-fired, thick, ochre-washed pottery was found by him in the lowest levels of Hastinapura near Meerut during 1950-1 and 1951-2. Thus, circumstantial evidence established the connection of copper hoard artefacts with OCP. A similar situation prevailed at Baharia which yielded a harpoon and a sword. Subsequently, this site was visited by V.D. Misra (1977: 123) who excavated a trial trench near the find-spot of the copper hoards. The total habitational deposit of about 1 m was composed of three layers. This trench yielded a few potsherds, small and rolled. As regards pottery, four types of vases and

[34] Lal (1951), op. cit.
[35] Agrawal (1971), op. cit., pp. 242-3.
[36] Lal (1951), op. cit., pp. 25-7.
[37] Ibid., p. 37.

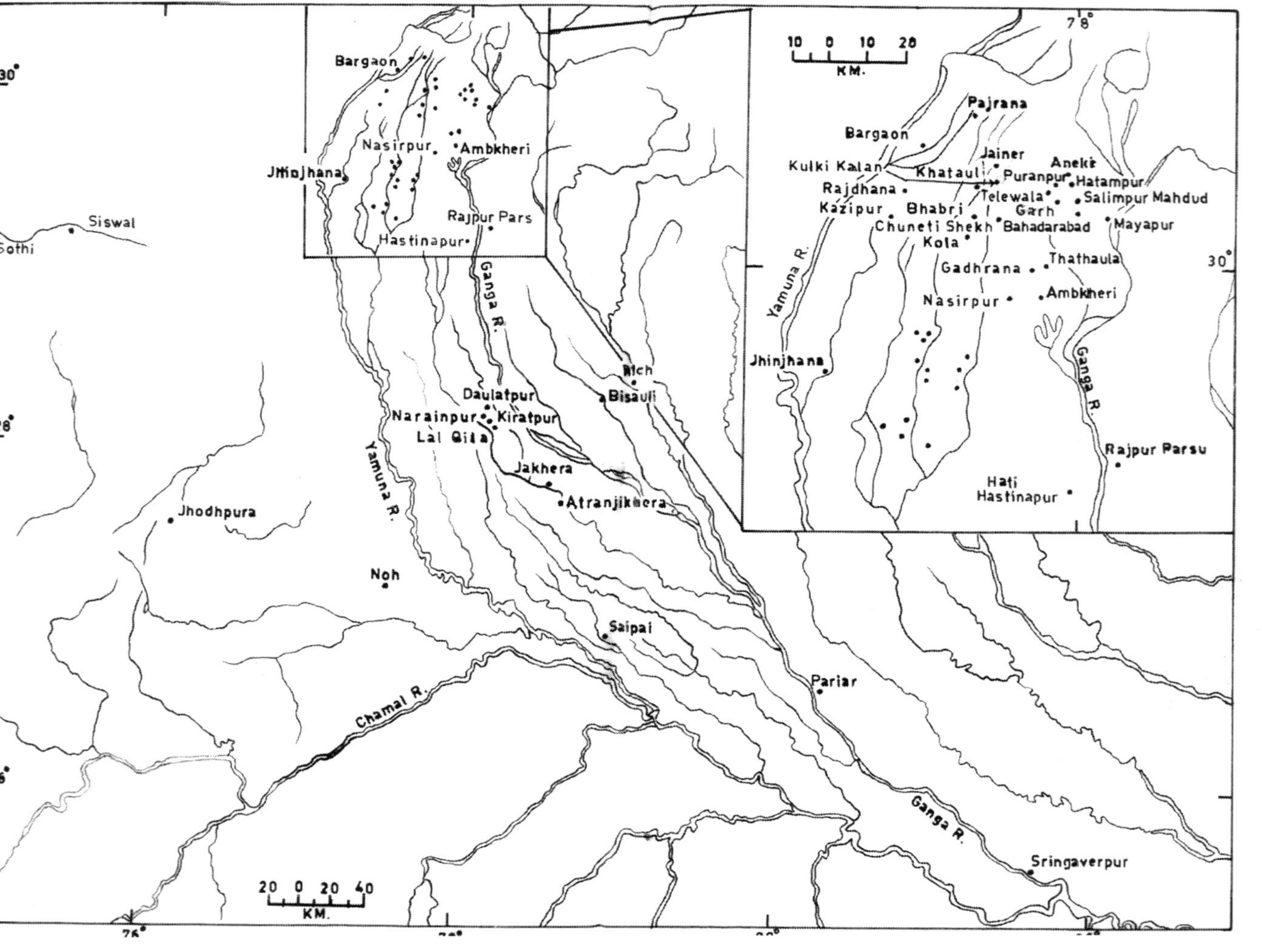

Fig. 14.4: Map showing OCP sites

shallow bowls could be identified. This association of copper hoard tools with OCP once again strengthened the belief that they are the product of one and the same people. Similar evidence comes from Bahadarabad, Nasirpur, Baragaon and Saipai.

While excavating a canal at Bahadarabad (district Saharanpur), 13 km west of Hardwar, workers came across a cache of objects consisting of copper lance heads, axes, bangles and pottery. Subsequently, Y.D. Sharma carried out a test excavation at this spot in 1952 and found OCP from a depth of 0.6 to 1.0 m. Nasirpur, located about 12 km south of Roorkee (district Saharanpur) also yielded a hoard consisting of various kinds of axes, bars, a harpoon and lanceheads in the early 1960s. Lal examined this site and found OCP sherds.

Bargaon is situated 24 km north of Saharanpur, the district headquarters. Here, Deshpande found OCP together with two copper bangles and a fragmentary chisel. However, the clinching evidence of this association, though only circumstantial, was provided by Saipai in the Etawah district. Here, a hoard of artefacts comprising a hooked sword, anthropomorphic figures, axes, bangles, bar-celts and harpoons was found in 1969. Shortly thereafter, in May 1970. L.M. Wahal carried out trial excavations near the find-spot and uncovered a lance head. Later that year, an area of 20 × 20 m was excavated and a harpoon was found in association with a OCP, establishing the definite association of copper hoards of Zone B with this pottery. Associated finds included pounders, rubbers, querns, and blades of chert and chalcedony. Traces of wattle-and-daub houses were also found.

OCHRE COLOURED POTTERY (FIGS. 14.5-14.7)

The meagre data obtained from Bisauli, Raipur Parsu and Hastinapura by Lal about this ware was supplemented by that obtained from Atranjikhera and Lal Qila. This ware has been studied in detail by Krishnadeva,[38] Gaur,[39] Makkhan Lal,[40] Indrani Dhar[41] and Poonam Chitkara.[42] Prior to the excavations at Lal Qila, it was believed that this pottery was made of medium-grained clay, was ill-fired and was given a ochrous wash of an orange red to a deep

[38] Krishnadeva (1969), 'The Problem of Ochre Coloured Pottery', in B.P. Sinha (ed.), *Potteries in Ancient India*, University of Patna, Patna.

[39] R.C. Gaur (1969), 'The OCP from Atranjikhera and Its Significance', in B.P. Sinha (ed.), *Potteries in Ancient India*, pp. 112-17; idem (1983), *Excavations at Atranjikhera*, Munshiram Manoharlal, Delhi; idem (1995), *Excavations at Lal Qila*, Publication Scheme, Jaipur.

[40] Lal (1984), op. cit.

[41] Indrani Dhar (1997), 'OCP and the Copper Hoard Problem', in V.D. Misra and J.N. Pal (eds.), *Indian Prehistory 1980*, Department of AIHC & Archaeology, Allahabad, pp. 308-12.

[42] Poonam Chitkara (1997), 'OCP in the Ganga-Yamuna Valley: A Reassessment of Possible Links', in V.D. Misra and J.N. Pal (eds.), *Indian Prehistory 1980*, pp. 313-15.

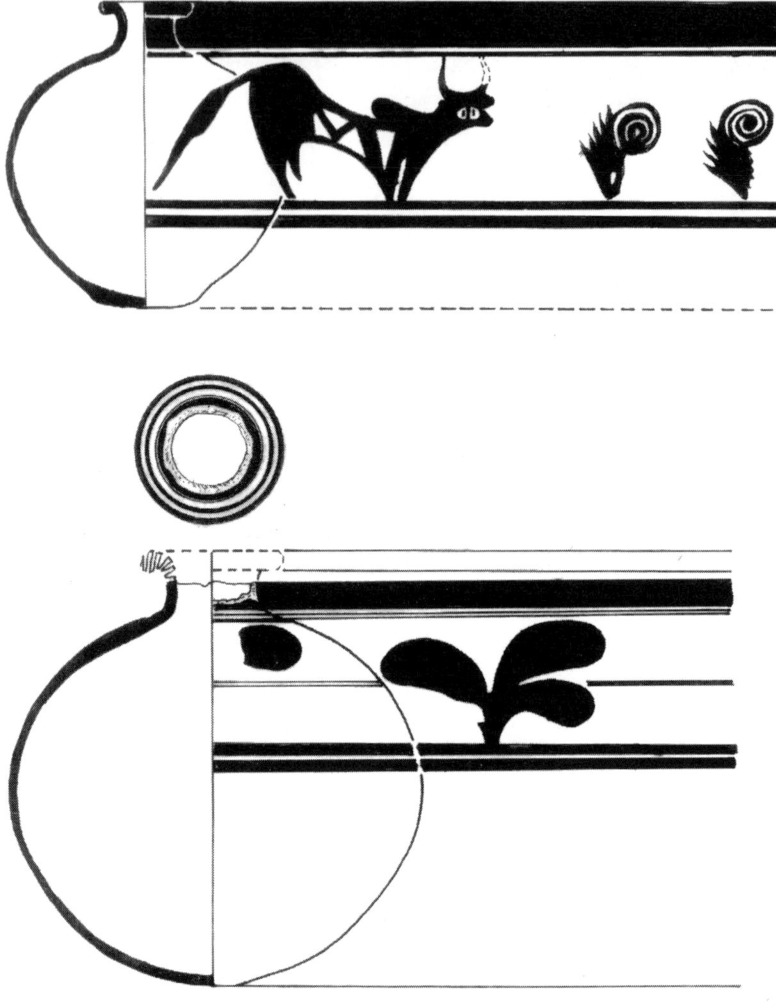

Fig. 14.5: Lal Qila OCP

red colour that has a tendency of being easily rubbed off. The OCP obtained from Atranjikhera, Baragaon and Ambakheri indicates the use of the potter's wheel for its manufacture. Now there are more than a 100 sites of this ware in western U.P.[43] and thirty-three of them have been added in the course of surface explorations from Muzaffarpur district alone. This ware is found from Aneki (district Hardwar) in the north to Noh (district Bharatpur, Rajasthan) in the south. Its western limit is Katpalon near Jullunder and Sringaverapura near Allahabad marks its eastern boundary (Fig. 14.4).

[43] V.D. Misra (1975), *Some Aspects of Indian Archaeology*, Prabhat Prakashan, Allahabad, p. 59.

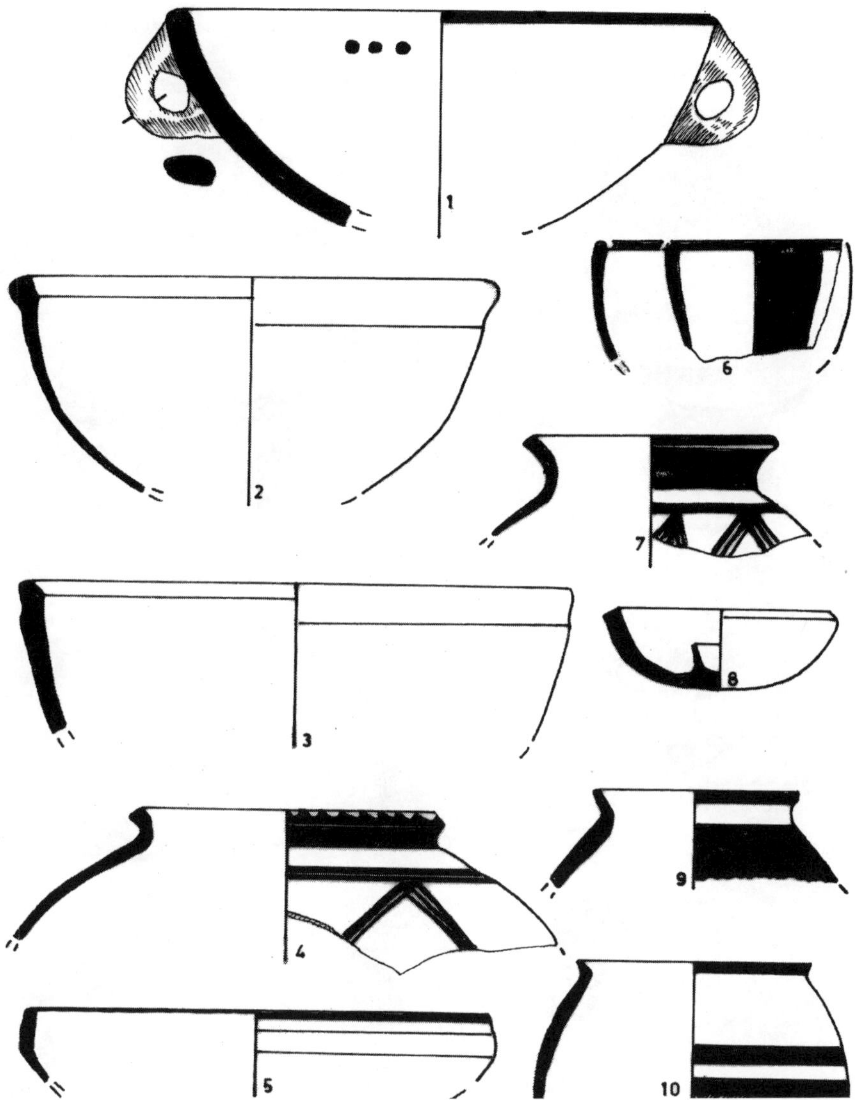

Fig. 14.6: Lal Qila: main types of OCP: 1. Basin with handles, 2. Basin without turned rim and convex sides, 3. Trough, 4. Jar, painted in black, 5. Dish with incurved rim, 6. Bowl, 7. Vase, 8. Lid with central knob, 9. Vase with painted bands, 10. Vase, painted in black

Typology

Gaur has identified eight main types in this ware. These comprise jars, vessels with out-turned rims, troughs with vertical sides, basins, bowls, dishes-on-stand, lids and pots with handles. The pottery obtained from Lal Qila located on the left bank of the Kalinadi, a tributary of the Ganga in the Anupshahr tahsil of the Bulandshahr district, is a well-preserved red ware as compared

Fig. 14.7: Pottery types of the OCP culture of Lal Qila, U.P.

to that obtained from the other sites listed above. It is not only wheel-turned and well-burnt, but is well-decorated with incised designs, graffiti marks and paintings in a black pigment over a smooth red-slipped surface, showing a high degree of sophistication.[44] A semi-naturalistic humped and long-horned

[44]Gaur (1995), op. cit., p. 23.

bull with two stylized representations of curved horns has been found painted on the ovoid body of a vase (Fig. 14.5). Post-firing graffiti marks and a variety of incised designs occur on some potsherds. The principal forms are similar to those obtained from Atranjikhera, situated on the same river system (Kalinadi, a tributary of the Ganga) as Lal Qila. The types include bowls, lids, basins, troughs, dishes, dishes-on-stand, storage jars, vases and miniature pots.

Associated Finds

The data obtained from excavations at Atranjikhera, Saipai and Lal Qila have provided some insight into the life of the OCP people. That they lived in wattle-and-daub houses and led a sedentary life has been proved by the evidence from all three sites. An interesting aspect of the wattle-and-daub houses (rice husks in mud plaster) of the OCP level at Atranjikhera is that posts of the babul, sissoo, sal and chirpine trees were used, with the chirpine coming from the Himalayan belt. There is no reason to believe that the sissoo and sal were imported too. Their present absence in the area does not mean that they were not growing there earlier.[45]

Four phases of structural activity were identified at Lai Qila. Rammed floors with clay plasters were noticed from the first two phases at this site, while a debris of mud-bricks and baked bricks together with reed and bamboo-marked burnt plaster was noticed in Phase III. A floor measuring 5 × 2.3 m was exposed in Phase IV.[46]

The small finds from Lal Qila comprise five copper objects, two human figurines of terracotta, several bangle pieces, incised and plain beads of terracotta and stone (carnelian, agate and soapstone), pestles, net-sinkers and sling balls. The bone objects comprise arrowheads, points and stylii. Faunal remains from this site include domestic cattle, buffalo, sheep, goat, pig, house dog and (wild) deer. There are three sizes of cattle and many of the bones bear cut and burn marks. Evidence from Atranjikhera[47] shows that the OCP people cultivated rice, barley, gram and khesari. suggesting that two crops were grown in a year: rice in summer and barley and legumes in winter. Stratigraphic evidence from this site suggests that rice cultivation antedates the cultivation of barley, gram and khesari.[48]

Generally, the settlements of the OCP people are found on river banks and they all are small in size (200 × 200 m). They are found at a distance of 5 to 8 km from each other and the occupational thickness varies from 0.30

[45]Chakrabarti (1999), op. cit., p. 254.

[46]Gaur (1995), op. cit., p. 17.

[47]K.A. Chowdhury et al. (1977), *Ancient Agriculture and Forestry in Northern India*, Asia Publishing House, New Delhi.

[48]Lal (1984), op. cit., p. 32.

to 1.20 m. The deposit is generally mixed with brown earth, kankar and sand.

TL Dates

Twelve pottery sherds from four sites: Lal Qila, Atranjikhera, Jhinjhana and Nasirpur, were dated by the thermoluminescence method by the Research Laboratory for Archaeology, Oxford. The results are as follows:

Sites	Sherd No.	TL age	Mean RL age	Mean deviation (%)
Atranjikhera	111 b4	1610 BC		
	b5	1180 BC		
	c1	2280 BC		
	c2	1250 BC	1690 BC	11
	c3	2130 BC		
Lal Qila	112 al	1730 BC	1880 BC	4
	a2	2030 BC		
Jhinjhana	113 a2	1990 BC		
	b1	1570 BC	2070 BC	9
	b2	2650 BC		
Nasirpur	114 al	1500 BC	1340 BC	5

Commenting upon these dates, Gaur observes:

> The precision of the TL dating at present is such that the date of the majority of the individual sherds should be within about 7 per cent of the mean TL age of a context. The spread of TL ages for Atranjikhera and Jhinjhana is appreciably more and implies that the occupation there lasted for several hundred of years. The longevity of the OCP industry is further shown by the 700-year difference in average TL age of Nasirpur compared with Jhinjhana. The TL dates from Lal Qila and Jhinjhana with average values of 1880 and 2070 BC lend strong support to the hypothesis that the early part of the OCP industry was contemporary with the late phase of the Harappan civilization.[49]

CONCLUDING REMARKS

A survey of the data presented above shows that although some doubts have been cleared, others still persist and will continue to do so for some more time. The OCP is no longer an ill-fired, ochre-washed pottery but has emerged as a sturdy wheel-turned ware with several utilitarian shapes (Fig. 14.6). A statistical analysis of some pot shapes from Lal Qila shows that the commonest

[49] Gaur (1995), op. cit., p. 211.

shapes are the vase (53 per cent), basin (nearly 22 per cent), bowls (12 per cent) and storage jars (3.5 per cent). Miniature pots and lids fall between 1 and 2 per cent while dish, trough and dish-on-stand account for less than 1 per cent.[50] The authors of this culture lived in wattle-and-daub houses but started using baked and unbaked bricks in the upper phases. Their settlements constituted small villages situated at a distance of 5 to 8 km. They cultivated two crops a year and their food was supplemented by hunting. Traces of burning and cut marks on animal bones show that meat formed an important component of their diet. TL dates put this culture around 2000-1800 BC.

Until recently, the culture was believed to have extended over an area of 300 × 200 km, mainly in the Ganga-Yamuna *doab* (Gaur 1989) and a little over seventy of its sites had been listed.[51] However, the discovery of OCP in the lower levels of Sringaverapura near Allahabad has increased its domain twofold and intensive explorations have shown that many more sites still remain to be documented. Previously, only three sites had been noticed in the district of Muzaffarnagar but as many as thirty-three additional ones have been recently documented by systematic fieldwork.[52] These include twelve sites in block Charthawal, five sites each in blocks Purkazi and Budhana, and four sites each in blocks Baghra and Shahpur. One site each was located in blocks Un, Morna and Kandhala. An interesting feature was that OCP and Harappan pottery were found on some sites together but the relationship of the two cultures is difficult to determine, although we know for certain that the Late Harappan culture flourished in this region (Alamgirpur, Hulas). Gaur (in Ghosh 1989) has divided OCP into three groups:

1. Genuine OCP as found at Atranjikhera, Saipai, Lal Qila, Noh, etc.
2. OCP with Harappan influence as found at Bahadarabad Ambkheri, etc.
3. Late Harappan ware with OCP influence as found at Alamgirpur, Bargaon, etc.

The latter two suggest that the Late Harappan and OCP people had come into contact somewhere near the western border of Uttar Pradesh and there was some mutual borrowing (Gaur in Ghosh 1989). However, it is difficult to establish which of the two cultures began earlier, although one can be certain of a chronological overlap.

Second, while discussing the extension of OCP in the west and south, one has to work out its relationship with the pottery obtained from Jodhpur (Jaipur, Rajasthan), which has been taken to belong to the OCP complex. The site

[50]Ibid., p. 23.

[51]K.N. Dikshit (1979), 'The Ochre Coloured Ware Settlement in Ganga-Yamuna Doab', in D.P. Agrawal and Dilip Chakrabarti (eds.), *Essays in Indian Protohistory*, B.R. Publishing Corporation, Delhi, pp. 285-99.

[52]O.P. Srivastav (2001), 'An Archaeological Study of District Muzaffarnagar', Ph.D. thesis (unpublished), Aligarh Muslim University, Aligarh.

has revealed four phases of this level and it seems that its final phase is manifested in the *doab* sites.[53] The four OCP phases at Jodhpur are:

Phase A: Rolled, ill-fired, undecorated OCP of indeterminate shape, cattle footprints.

Phase B: Wheel-turned, undecorated OCP.

Phase C: Round huts, red-slipped pottery with both incised and painted designs.

Phase D: Full development of OCP, the pottery shapes and decorations being comparable with Atranjikhera and Lal Qila specimens.

If, in the doab, the OCP level falls in the first half of the second millennium BC beginning around 2000 BC, its beginning at Jodhpur is considerably earlier, as its late fourth millennium calibrated BC date suggests.[54]

As regards the association of copper hoard tools OCP, the evidence from Saipai has conclusively proved that the copper hoards of the upper Ganga-Yamuna *doab* are associated with this pottery. However, the basic problem is whether all the copper hoards are homogeneous in character or whether they have regional variations and belong to different time-brackets. In the present state of our research, the latter hypothesis seems more plausible. As Lal has already pointed out, certain tool-types (Fort Munro swords, trunion celt from Shalozan, etc.) are confined to the north-western part of the sub-continent and these do not occur in the upper Ganga Valley.

On the basis of typology the copper hoard area has been divided into three zones:[55]

Zone A: It comprises Bihar, West Bengal and Orissa. Flat celts, shouldered celts, bar celts and double axes are its main tool-types.

Zone B: This zone comprises Uttar Pradesh and Haryana. The main types include anthropomorphs, antennae-swords, hooked swords and harpoons, besides the first three types of Zone A.

Zone C: This zone comprises Rajasthan. Its main types are flat celts and bar celts.

The precise function of the copper hoard artefacts are still not clear. The suggested use of anthropomorphs for killing birds is too far-fetched to merit serious consideration. Surely, the manufacture of such an elaborate tool-type with 5 kg of pure copper just to kill a small bird was neither an efficient method nor economical. Further, such a small number (only thirteen pieces) could not have catered to the needs of a hunting tribe. Again, the use of the antennae-sword, as suggested by Agrawal, for trapping big game is highly

[53] Chakrabarti (1999), op. cit., p. 254.

[54] Ibid.

[55] Lal (1984), op. cit., p. 48.

conjectural.[56] Similarly, the question of their authorship is difficult to resolve as most of these implements are chance discoveries, come from unstratified contexts and are unassociated with any cultural trait.

Appendix: List of Copper Hoard Sites

	Site	District	State
1.	Aguibani	Midnapur	West Bengal
2.	Ahar	Udaipur	Rajasthan
3.	Ambala	Ambala	Haryana
4.	Andhari	Singhbhum	Jharkhand
5.	Bagor	Bhilwara	Rajasthan
6.	Bahadarabad	Saharanpur	U.P.
7.	Baharia	Shahjahanpur	U.P.
8.	Bargaon	Saharanpur	U.P.
9.	Bartola	Ranchi	Jharkhand
10.	Bendarkala	Hardoi	U.P.
11.	Bhagra Pir	Mayurbhanj	Orissa
12.	Bhaktabundh	Bankura	West Bengal
13.	Bhiwani	Bhiwani	Haryana
14.	Bisauli	Badaun	U.P.
15.	Bithur	Kanpur	U.P.
16.	Borodanga	Singhbhum	Jharkhand
17.	Brahmagiri	Chitaldurg	Karnataka
18.	Chandoli	Pune	Maharashtra
19.	Chatla	Midnapur	West Bengal
20.	Chirand	Saran	Bihar
21.	Dadari	Bhiwani	Haryana
22.	Daimabad	Ahmednagar	Maharashtra
23.	Dargama	Ranchi	Jharkhand
24.	Debakia	Jabalpur	Madhya Pradesh
25.	Deoti	Lucknow	U.P.
26.	Dhaka	Shahjahanpur	U.P.
27.	Dunria	Dhenkanal	Orissa
28.	Ekalsimha	Ajmer	Rajasthan
29.	Elana	Jalon	Rajasthan
30.	Fran	Sagar	Madhya Pradesh
31.	Etawah	Varanasi	U.P.
32.	Fatehgarh	Farrukhabad	U.P.
33.	Gandhauli	Sitapur	U.P.
34.	Ganeshwar	Sikar	Rajasthan
35.	Gungeria	Balaghat	M.P.

[56]Sankalia (1974), op. cit., p. 398.

36. Hallur	Dharwar	Karnataka
37. Hami	Palamu	Jharkhand
38. Hansi	Hissar	Haryana
39. Hardi	Sitapur	U.P.
40. Harra Chowra Darh	Ranchi	Jharkhand
41. Inamgaon	Pune	Maharashtra
42. Indilapur	Shahjahanpur	U.P.
43. Jabalpur	Jabalpur	M.P.
44. Jokha	Surat	Gujarat
45. Jorwe	Ahmednagar	Maharashtra
46. Kallur	Raichur	Karnataka
47. Kamalpur	Hardoi	U.P.
48. Kamdara	Ranchi	Jharkhand
49. Kankasa	Junagarh	Gujarat
50. Karharbari	Hazaribagh	Jharkhand
51. Kathmandu Valley	Kathmandu	Nepal
52. Kayatha	Ujjain	M.P.
53. Khera Manpur	Bulandshahr	U.P.
54. Kiratpur	Bulandshahr	U.P.
55. Kosam	Kausambi	U.P.
56. Kota	Sawaimadhopur	Rajasthan
57. Kulgara	Purulia	West Bengal
58. Kulhade ka Johade	Sikar	Rajasthan
59. Kurada	Nagaur	Rajasthan
60. Kushaya	Monghyr	Bihar
61. Lal Qila	Bulandshahr	U.P.
62. Langhnaj	Mehsana	Gujarat
63. Lothal	Ahmedabad	Gujarat
64. Madnapur	Hardoi	U.P.
65. Mahishadal	Birbhum	West Bengal
66. Mahuadanr	Palamu	Jharkhand
67. Mainpuri	Mainpuri	U.P.
68. Maski	Raichur	Karnataka
69. Mathura	Mathura	U.P.
70. Mitathal	Bhiwani	Haryana
71. Moongalaar Tea Estate	Idukki	Kerala
72. Nagar	Jullunder	Punjab
73. Nakrahiya	Sitapur	U.P.
74. Nandalapura	Jaipur	Rajasthan
75. Nasirpur	Saharanpur	U.P.
76. Navdatoli	Nimar	M.P.
77. Nevasa	Ahmednagar	Maharashtra
78. Niorai	Etawah	U.P.

79.	Pandu Rajar Dhibi	Burdwan	West Bengal
80.	Pariar	Unnao	U.P.
81.	Parihati	Midnapur	West Bengal
82.	Pauli	Jind	Haryana
83.	Piklihal	Hyderabad	Andhra Pradesh
84.	Pind	Chittorgarh	Rajasthan
85.	Pondi	Rewa	Madhya Pradesh
86.	Prakash	Dhulia	Maharashtra
87.	Rajpur Parsu	Bijnor	U.P.
88.	Ramjipura	East Nimar	Madhya Pradesh
89.	Rangpur	Surendranagar	Gujarat
90.	Resgavaon	Mathura	U.P.
91.	Rewari	Mahendragarh	Haryana
92.	Saguni	Palamau	Jharkhand
93.	Saipai Ichchwai	Etawah	U.P.
94.	Sanghol	Ludhiana	Punjab
95.	Sarthauli	Shahjahanpur	U.P.
96.	Sastevadi	Pune	Maharashtra
97.	Saunia	Bikaner	Rajasthan
98.	Shahabad	Hardoi	U.P.
99.	Sheonajpur	Kanpur	U.P.
100.	Somnath	Junagarh	Gujarat
101.	Tamajuri	Midnapur	West Bengal
102.	Tekkalakota	Bellary	Karnataka
103.	Terdal	Bijapur	Karnataka

Chapter 15

Human Skeletal Biology

Kenneth A.R. Kennedy

A very significant but discontinuous hominid fossil record of 9 to 15 myr comes from the Siwalik range of the sub-Himalayan region which includes specimens assigned to the *Sivapithecus* group of Asian dryopithecines and to the *Gigantopithecus*. Complementary with the archaeological evidence of the hominid settlement of the Indian subcontinent by mid-Pleistocene times are skeletal remains collected from over seventy localities in India, Pakistan and Sri Lanka, which have been described by anthropologists with the publication of research results. More than twice that number of archaeological localities have yielded skeletons awaiting scientific study. This skeletal record continues to increase in size. Most specimens have been chronologically dated and are assignable to prehistoric cultural periods. Conservation in research institutions allows biological anthropologists to carry out their morphometric and statistical analyses in their investigations of hominid diversity and evolution. Catalogues and summary studies of these data are published along with comparative surveys of burial practices.[1]

PALAEOLITHIC

The distribution of Acheulian stone tools throughout the Indian subcontinent north of the Cauvery River and Sri Lanka testifies to the hominid settlement of South Asia by mid-Pleistocene times but, if the dating of quartzite artefacts to 2.2 myr from the Potwar region of Pakistan is confirmed, then an early Pleistocene period of occupation will be established. Until fossil remains of the tool manufacturers are found, it is impossible to assign them to a fossil hominid taxon. Previous claims of discoveries of Tertiary or early Pleistocene hominid fossils from South Asia are unsubstantiated, many reports never

[1] S.P. Gupta (1972), *Disposal of the Dead and Physical Types in Ancient India*, Oriental Publishers, Delhi; K.A.R. Kennedy (1980), 'Prehistoric Skeletal Record of Man in South Asia', *Annual Review of Anthropology*, 9, pp. 391-432; K.A.R. Kennedy and P.C. Caldwell (1984), 'South Asian Prehistoric Skeletal Remains and Burial Practices', in J.R. Lukacs (ed.), *The People of South Asia: The Biological Anthropology of India, Pakistan and Nepal*, Plenum Press, New York, pp. 159-97; H. Walter et al. (1991), *Anthropologie Indiens*, Gustav Fischer Verlag, Stuttgart.

receiving scrutiny by scientific experts or, if investigated, the reputed hominid bones turning out to be the remains of other faunal species. Since the first third of the nineteenth century when the search for fossil human remains began, a number of possibly genuine specimens have been recovered but, subsequently, lost or destroyed.[2]

This unfortunate history of palaeontological unfulfilment was removed in 1982 with the discovery of a hominid calvaria from Hathnora on the Narmada River in a mid-Pleistocene (*c.* 250000 BP) deposit with fossil fauna and a lower Palaeolithic (Acheulian) cultural context (Fig. 15.1). Originally named *Homo erectus narmadensis*, more recent laboratory investigations reassign the specimen as an anatomically early (archaic) *Homo sapiens* with certain morphometrie features present in early *sapiens* fossils from Dali, Ngandong (Solo) and Petralona.[3]

Fossils of anatomically modern *Homo sapiens* are dated to 30000+1900-1200 BP from the Mousterian site of Darra-i-Kur in north-eastern Afghanistan, the temporal bone sharing some morphometric features with fossils from the Mount Carmel site in Israel, which are now regarded as representatives of a modern *sapiens* population contemporary with Neanderthals, whose remains are also at this locality. More complete hominid fossils have been recovered in highland jungle caves in Sri Lanka over the past decade, the earliest from Batadomba lena dating to 28500+2150-1710 BP and from Fa Hien dating to 24470+290 BP. At Beli lena Kitulgala, human remains are dated to 12870+870 BP, the burials in the cave floor associated with microlithic tools, fauna, charcoal from hearths and plant seeds. Here, as at Batadomba lena, geometric microliths are in direct association with the burials; at Fa Hien, non-geometric microliths appear only with burials of the upper levels. The presence of a chopper tool industry on the island in a pre-microlithic cultural period and the absence of an Acheulian technological tradition indicates settlement by 74000 BP. The skeletal series of *c.* forty-five individuals from these three cave sites exhibit a number of morphometric features encountered in the aboriginal Veddas of Sri Lanka, a circumstance suggesting a biological continuum under conditions of relative genetic isolation from the late

[2]K.A.R. Kennedy (1977), 'Fossil Man in India: The Missing Link in Our Knowledge of Human Evolution in Asia', *Bulletin of the National Speliological Society*, 39(4), pp. 99-103; H.M. Rendell et al. (1989), *Pleistocene and Palaeolithic Investigations in the Soan Valley, Northern Pakistan*, British Arch Mission to Pakistan, Series 2, BAR International Series 544, Oxford.

[3]K.A.R. Kennedy et al. (1991), 'Is the Narmada Hominid an Indian *Homo Erectus*?', *AJPA*, 86, pp. 475-96; M.A. de Lumley and S. Sonakia (1985), 'Premiere decouverte dun *Homo erectus* sur le continent Indian Hathnora dans le moyenne valee de la Narmada', *Le Anthropologic*, 89(1), pp. 13-61; A Sonakia (1984), 'The Skull Cap of Early Man and Associated Mammalian Fauna from Narmada Valley Alluvium, Hoshangabad Area, Madhya Pradesh, India', *Records of the Geological Survey of India*, 113, 6d, pp. 159-72; idem (1985), 'Early Homo from India', in F. Delson (ed.), *Ancestors: The Hard Evidence*, Alan R. Riss, New York, pp. 334-8.

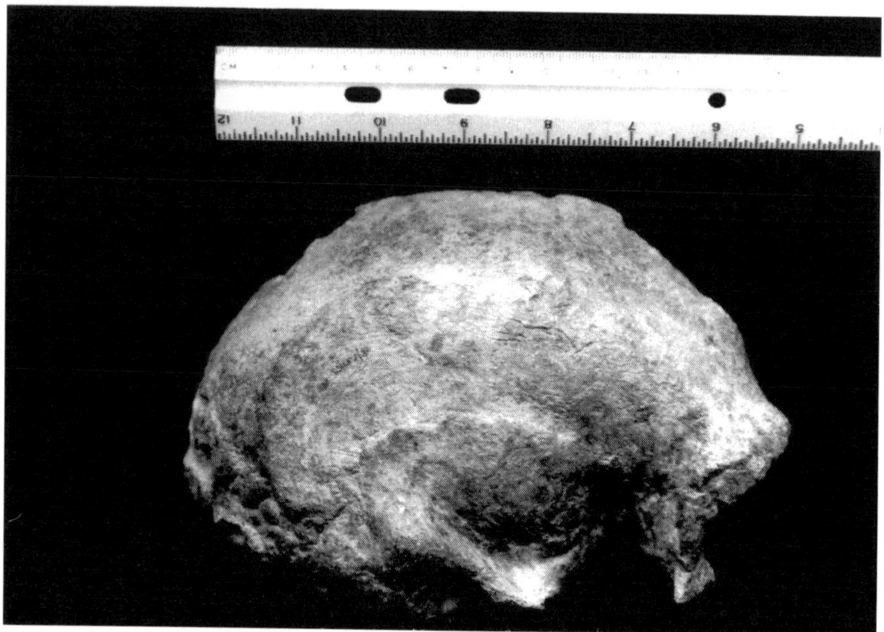

Fig. 15.1: Hathnora, (Narmada) hominid calvaria. Right lateral aspect (Courtesy: Geological Survey of India)

Pleistocene and Holocene populations of mainland India and lands bordering the Indian Ocean until the sixth century BC.[4]

Hominid skeletal remains of uncertain antiquity were recovered from Bhimbetka, the Billa Surgam caves near Kurnool, Umhut on the Koana River, Gundlakamma and Atirampakkam. Some of these may be of Pleistocene antiquity. There is a persistent myth of a fossil hominid skull found in the middle of the nineteenth century along the banks of the Narmada River but the nature of this misinterpretation of published accounts has been resolved.[5]

[4]S.U. Dereniyalgala (1992), *The Prehistory of Sri Lanka: An Ecological Perspective*, Government of Sri Lanka, Colombo; L. Dupree (1972), 'Prehistoric Research in Afghanistan', *Transactions of the American Philosophical Society*, 62, pp. 1-84; K.A.R. Kennedy and S.U. Dereniyalgala (1989), 'Fossil Remains of 28000 Year Old Hominids from Sri Lanka', *CA*, 30, 3, pp. 395-9; K.A.R. Kennedy et al. (1987), 'Upper Pleistocene Fossil Hominids from Sri Lanka', *AJPA*, 72, pp. 441-61.

[5]H.F. Blanford (1864), *Progs Journal of the Asiatic Society of Bengal*, 33, pp. 575-6; R.S. Foote (1884), 'Rough Notes on Billa Surgam and Other Caves in the Kurnool District', *Records of the Geological Survey of India*, 17, pp. 27-34; idem (1916), *The Foote Collection of Indian Prehistoric and Protohistoric Antiquities*, Madras Government Museum, Madras; A.P. Khatri (1963), 'Recent Explorations for the Remains of Early Man in India', *Asian Perspectives*, 7, 1-2, pp. 160-92; M.L.K. Murti (1974), 'A Late Pleistocene Cave Site in Southern India', *Proceedings of the American Philosophical Society*, 118, pp. 196-230;

Concerted research programmes to enhance the possibilities of finding Palaeolithic hominid remains in South Asia began with the work of the Yale-Cambridge universities team in the 1930s, the Archaeological Surveys, and the efforts of many universities since 1947 with the Independence of India and Pakistan. The Indian Council of Scientific and Industrial Research was organized in 1957. Explorations in Kashmir under the auspices of the Physical Research Laboratory, Ahmedabad, have continued since the 1980s, and there has been a long-standing programme of research at the Deccan College, Pune, since the 1930s. In collaboration with the Geological Surveys of South Asian nations, current research activities are of international scope.

MESOLITHIC

Prehistoric South Asians of terminal Pleistocene to mid-Holocene times are distinguished by the cultural achievements of microlithic tools, the bow and arrow, domestication of the dog and incipient pastoralism, successful predation of large game, extensive habitation of caves and rock-shelters as well as open-air camps, parietal art, and exploitation of diverse ecological settings. In some localities, the population size and density increased, and cultural regionalization is apparent throughout the subcontinent and Sri Lanka. The non-geometric microliths at Fa Hien which date to *c.* 34000 BP and the geometric microliths at Batadomba lena which date to *c.* 28500 BP are the earliest hallmarks of the South Asian Mesolithic and predate the occurrence of this technological tradition at Mesolithic sites elsewhere in Asia, Europe and Africa. The first discoveries of human skeletal remains with the South Asian Mesolithic were made in 1880-1 at Mahara Pahar, Uttar Pradesh, a decade later at Jalampura in Gujarat and, in the early 1930s, at Pachmarhi in Madhya Pradesh.[6]

A pioneering study of the Mesolithic peoples of Gujarat was undertaken in 1941 at Langhnaj for the purpose of resolving the question of a cultural hiatus separating the Palaeolithic from Neolithic traditions in India. In the course of several excavations from 1941 to 1963, archaeologists from the Deccan College, in collaboration with colleagues from the state of Gujarat and the University of Baroda, recovered fourteen skeletons and a copper knife of probable Harappan manufacture. This artefact, in the context of microlithic tools and human remains, suggests that Langhnaj was a late Mesolithic site occupied during the terminal period of Harappan trade activities

V.S. Wakankar (1978), *The Dawn of Indian Art*, Bharat Kala Bhavan, Ujjain; R.E.M. Wheeler (1959), *Early India and Pakistan to Asoka*, Thames and Hudson, London.

[6]A.C.L. Carlleyle (1883), 'Notes on Lately Discovered Sculptural Mounds, Cairns, Caves, Cave Paintings and Stone Implements', *PASB*, 49; S.U. Derniyalgala (1984), 'Mesolithic Stone Tool Technology at 28000 BC in Sri Lanka', *Ancient Ceylon*, 5, pp. 105-8; G.M. Moran (1936), 'Report on Human Skeletal Remains Excavated in a Rock Shelter Near Panchamarhi, Central Province', *Nagpur University Journal*, 1, pp. 1-3.

in Gujarat. A gene flow between Langhnaj and Lothal has been suggested on the basis of osteological data from these sites.[7]

Coincident with the conclusion of excavations at Langhnaj, the University of Allahabad began extensive explorations and excavations of Mesolithic sites in the Vindhya range and the Gangetic plain in Uttar Pradesh. In 1963-4, human skeletal remains were recovered in the Kaimur hills at Baghai Khor and Lekhahia ki Pahari, the latter site yielding nineteen specimens. Three Mesolithic sites on the shores of ancient oxbow lakes have provided a rich harvest of skeletal data since 1968: Sarai Nahar Rai (Figs. 15.2-15.3), Mahadaha (Figs. 15.4-15.5) and Damdama. More than eighty skeletons from these burial sites are suitable for morphometric analysis but the total number of specimens exceeds 100. Dating remains uncertain, a disputed antiquity of 10050+110 BP for Sarai Nahar Rai being discordant with a more probable date of 700-5000 BP for Damdama, 4010+120 BP for Mahadaha and a radiocarbon date of 2860+120 BP for Sarai Nahar Rai. Lekhahia ki Pahari has been dated to 4240+110 BP. These Mesolithic people of the Gangetic plain were tall and skeletally robust with low frequencies of dental caries but a higher than expected incidence of dental enamel hypoplasia than is found in prehistoric hunting-foraging populations.[8]

Rajasthan's Chalcolithic site of Bagor has a single adult human skeleton from a basal Mesolithic deposit dated to *c.* 6500 BP. It was found during the excavations of 1968-70. Several Mesolithic skeletons were found in caves at Bhimbetka, a locality discovered in 1957 and systematically excavated after 1971. Excavations at Bhimbetka have been an international effort with teams from India, Switzerland and the United States.[9]

[7]S. Ehrhardt (1960), 'Schlgspuren, Bruche and Sprunge an den Skelleten vom Longhnaj Immodlichen Gujarat Vorderindien', *Anthropologischer Anzieger*, 24, pp. 178-232; G.L. Possehl and K.A.R. Kennedy (1979), 'The Hunter-gatherer and Agricultural Exchange in Prehistory: An Example of India', *CA*, 29, 3, pp. 592-3; H.D. Sankalia (1965), *Excavations at Langhnaj 1944-63*, part 1: *Archaeology*, Deccan College Bldg. Centenary Series, 29, Poona.

[8]P.C. Dutta et al. (1971), 'Earliest Human Remains in a Late Stone Site', *Nature* 233, pp. 500-1; K.A.R. Kennedy (1990a), 'Porotic Hyperostosis in Human Remains from the Mesolithic Baghai Khor', *BDCRI*, 49, pp. 183-99; idem (1990b), 'Skeletons in the Closet: Recent Discovery of Lost Human Skeletal Remains from Iron Age Raigir', *SAS*, 6, pp. 201-26; K.A.R. Kennedy et al. (1986), *Mesolithic Human Remains from the Gangetic Plain: Sarai Nahar Rai*, Cornell University; idem (1992), *Human Skeletal Remains from Mahadaha: A Gangetic Mesolithic Site*, Occasional Papers and Theses of the South Asia Program, Cornell University; G.R. Sharma (1973), 'Mesolithic Lake Culture in the Ganga Valley', *PPS*, 39, pp. 129-46; R.K. Varma (1986), *The Mesolithic Age in Mirzapur*, Pramjyoti Prakashan, Allahabad.

[9]V.N. Misra (1973), 'Problems of Palaeo-ecology, Palaeo-climate and Chronology of the Mesolithic Cultures of Northwest India', in D.P. Agrawal and A. Ghosh (eds.), *Radiocarbon and Indian Archaeology*, Tata Institute of Fundamental Research, Bombay, pp. 58-72; J.R. Lukacs (1982), *Bagor and Tilwara: Late Mesolithic Cultures of Northwest India*, vol. I: *Human Skeletal Remains*, Deccan College, Poona.

Fig. 15.2: Sarai Nahar Rai cemetary (Courtesy: University of Allahabad)

Fig. 15.3: Sarai Nahar Rai, single and double burials (Skeleton Nos. 1973–II, Male; 1973–III, female (Courtesy: University of Allahabad)

Fig. 15.4: Mahadah cemetary (Courtesy: University of Allahabad)

Mesolithic skeletons have been found in Sri Lanka since 1908 when the floors of caves and rock-shelters inhabited by the Veddas were excavated, and yielded microliths and human bones. Since the late 1930s, concerted work by officers of the Colombo National Museum and the Archaeology Department of the Government of Sri Lanka has been rewarded with Mesolithic human remains from the caves of Alu Galge, Ravan Alle, Batadomba lena, Beli lena Kitulgala and Fa Hien, and from the open-air site of Bellanbandi Palassa, sites within the southern wet zone part of the island. The latter site with fifteen skeletons is dated to 6500+700 BP, while dates for skeletal deposits at Batadomba lena and Bela lena Kitulgala are *c*. 16000 BP and 12000 BP, respectively. Fa Hien has occupancy dates from 34000 BP to 5400 BP, the human skeletons coming from levels dated to 30060+380 BP, 6850+80 BP and 4750+60 BP. Until Iron Age times when the northern portion of the island had cultural contact with the Indian mainland, Sri Lanka constituted a zone of relative isolation as it lacked Palaeolithic, Neolithic and Chalcolithic technological traditions. There are local technological specializations of microlith manufacture without obvious parallels on the Indian mainland, hence the assignment of regional names to the Sri Lankan Mesolithic, e.g. Balangodan and Bandarawellian. Many of these lithic traditions and the hunting-foraging lifestyle continued for centuries after the colonization of Sri Lanka by Indo-European-speaking invaders in the sixth century BC.[10]

NEOLITHIC

The earliest village farming communities were established in South Asia in the north-western sector of Iran, Afghanistan and Baluchistan by the sixth millennium, the mortuary site of Mehrgarh having cultural materials of Neolithic and Chalcolithic traditions. Over eighty skeletal specimens have come from these levels, the Period I Neolithic skeletons dating before 6000 BC in an aceramic context with certain Mesolithic tool traditions persisting into a period of pottery manufacture, agriculture, and the domestication of cattle, sheep and goat. The French archaeological mission in Pakistan has been excavating in this area of the Bolan Pass since 1974 and published descriptions of the dental anthropology of the human remains have preceded any detailed studies of osteological materials.[11]

[10] P.E.P. Dereniyalgala (1963), 'An Open Air Habitation Site of *Homo sapiens balangodensis', Spolia Zeylanica*, 30, pp. 87-110; S.U. Dereniyalgala (1992), op. cit., K.A.R. Kennedy (1965), Human Skeletal Material from Ceylon with an Analysis of the Island's Prehistoric and Contemporary Populations', *Bulletin of the British Museum of Natural History* (*Geology*), 11, pp. 135-213; idem (1993), 'Recent Discoveries and Studies of the Human Skeletal Remains of Ancient Sri Lankans', in P.K. Seth and S. Seth (eds.), *New Perspectives in Anthropology*, M.D. Publications, New Delhi, pp. 299-341.

[11] J.F. Jarrige (1986), 'Excavations at Mehrgarh-Naushero', *PA*, 10-12, pp. 63-161; J.R. Lukacs (1988), 'Dental Morphology and Odentometrics of Early Agriculturists from Mehrgarh, Pakistan', in D.F. Russell et al. (eds.), *Teeth Revisited: Proceedings of the VII*

The skeletal record of early food-producing populations of central and southern India, which date from the middle to the late second millennium, was established in 1947 with excavations at Brahmagiri in Karnataka. Burials were encountered in Neolithic, Chalcolithic and Iron Age deposits, and bones of children were found in eighteen urn sarcophagi with an open burial of a juvenile receiving attention from a biological anthropologist. Also in Karnataka is Piklihal, which was discovered in 1951 and excavated nine years later, its four skeletal specimens meriting detailed study. Tekkalakota yielded nine skeletons in 1963-5 which are dated to *c.* 1800-1600 BC. T. Narsipur, the southernmost of the Karnataka sites, dated to *c.* 1500-1100 BC, a single skeleton being found there in the early 1960s. Prior to the flooding of the area of Andhra Pradesh adjacent to the Nagarjunakonda dam, a number of excavations were earned out in 1956-60 some thirteen skeletons retrieved from Neolithic cultural horizons.[12]

Early levels in Andhra Pradesh date to *c.* 2300 BC and, by, 1050 BC, copper and bronze artefacts occur with a variety of ceramic fabrics and decorative styles, which continue until the dawn of the Iron Age which is much later in peninsular India than in the central Deccan. There appears to have been demic continuity in this region of the South Asian Neolithic, as skeletal remains do not reveal any indicators of abrupt movements or replacements of populations. However, biological adaptations intrinsic to sedentary village and pastoral socio-economic lifestyles are evident in the skeletal remains with respect to tooth size reduction, higher incidence of dental pathological conditions, decrease in sexual dimorphism and overall skeletal robusticity, decrease in stature, and developmental responses to nutritional stress and a diet high in carbohydrates. Prehistoric agriculturalists and their pastoral contemporaries suffered an increase in infectious diseases and traumatic lesions, variables reflective of high population density and socio-cultural changes.[13]

International Symposium on Dental Morphology, Memories Au Museum National d'Historie Naturelle (Series C), Paris, pp. 285-303.

[12]F.R. Allchin (1960), *Piklihal Excavations*, Andhra Pradesh Govt. Arch. Series 1, Hyderabad; P. Gupta et al. (1970), Ancient Human Remains, part I: A Study of the Nagarjunakonda Skeletons, Memoirs of the Anthropological Survey of India, 20, Calcutta, pp. 1-33; K.C. Malhotra (1965), 'Human Skeletal Remains from Neolithic Tekkalkota', in M.S. Nagaraja Rao (ed.), *The Stone Age Hill Dwellers of Tekkalkota: Preliminary Report of the Excavations of Tekkalkotta*, Deccan College, Poona, pp. 109-62; idem (1967), 'Human Skeletal Remains from Chandoli', in S.B. Deo et al. (eds.), *Chalcolithic Chandoli*, Deccan College, Poona, pp. 69-90; H. Sarkar and B.N. Misra (1966), *Nagarjunakonda*, Archaeological Survey of India, New Delhi; R.E.M. Wheeler (1947-8), 'Brahmagiri and Chandravalli 1947: Megalithic and Other Cultures in Mysore State', *Ancient India*, 4, pp. 180-311.

[13]B.B. Hemphil (1992), 'Tooth Size Apportionment in Modern India: Factors of Caste, Language and Geography', *Journal of Human Ecology*, Special Issue 2, pp. 231-53; K.A.R. Kennedy (1984), 'Trauma and Disease in the Ancient Harappans: Recent Assessment of the Skeletal Record', in B.B. Lal and S.P. Gupta (eds.), *Frontiers of the Indus Civilization*,

Polished stone axes are one of the lithic hallmarks of the Neolithic in South Asia and in lands beyond the Himalayas, and by the 1860s, such tools were recognized in the archaeological record. Other technological innovations include pottery, agricultural implements, storage repositories for food, animal pens and corrals, and permanent shelters arranged according to spatial plans, reflecting social status and defence. These dynamic changes from Palaeolithic and Mesolithic lifestyles based upon predation and gathering have led to the concept of a 'Neolithic Revolution' and a frequent correlation of sudden cultural innovations with mass movements of culture-bearers into frontiers hitherto occupied by wandering hunting bands. While this scenario is difficult to document, it is nonetheless probable that the living tribal population of South Asia has genetically descended from some prehistoric populations whose habitats in fertile valleys and plains were taken over by early food-producing communities, thereby forcing these marginal groups into areas of relative isolation. A symbiotic relationship of tribal peoples with the macro-populations of the subcontinent has allowed for some gene flow, and the diffusion of ideas and material goods since the days of earliest contact.

BRONZE AGE (HARAPPAN)

Since 1921, archaeologists have recognized the existence of an advanced Bronze Age civilization in the Indus Valley region, and initial excavations at Harappa in western Punjab and Mohenjo-daro in Sind were rewarded with the recovery of human skeletal remains. The present sample stands at over 500 individuals from these two urban sites and from other localities at Chanhu-daro and Allahadino in Sind, Lothal and Rojdi in Gujarat. Rupar in eastern Punjab, Kalibangan in Rajasthan, and Nal (Sohr Damb) and Shahi Tump in Baluchistan. Some human bone fragments have been reported from Damb Bhuthi in Sind. There are over 200 known Harappan sites in India and Pakistan which have not yielded human remains but contribute to the archaeological reconstruction of a complex urban-village culture based upon agriculture, pastoralism and extensive trade networks extending over central and western Asia. The skeletal series does not constitute a genetically homogeneous Harappan population, coming, as it does, from an immense geographical portion of the subcontinent extending from northern Afghanistan and Baluchistan eastwards to the foothills of the Himalayan mountains and the Indo-Gangetic plain, and southwards to Gujarat and the Narmada Valley. The temporal period of the Harappan civilization is *c*. 2800 to 1850 BC.[14]

Books & Books, New Delhi, pp. 425-36; J.R. Lukacs (1990), 'On Hunter-Gatherers and Their Neighbours in Prehistoric India: Contact and Pathology', *CA*, 31, 2, pp. 183-6; idem (1992a), 'Dental Palaeopathology and Agricultural Intensification in South Asia: New Evidence from Bronze Age Harappa', *AJPA*, 87, pp. 133-50; idem (1992b), 'Culture, Ecology and Dental Anthropology', *Indian Society for Human Genetics*, New Delhi.

[14]G.L. Possehl (1982), *Harappan Civilization*, Oxford. IBH, New Delhi; idem (1990),

The misinterpretation of a Harappan skeletal assemblage as a single Mendelian population began with the study of the forty-six specimens from Mohenjo-daro which were unassociated with formal burial deposits at the time of their excavation in 1922-31. The disarray of skeletons at several localities within the ruins of this urban site led to a theory that they were victims of a massacre, perhaps by invading Aryan military forces, a thesis now rejected on archaeological and biological evidence. The circumstances of skeletal deposition at Mohenjo-daro are unclear but it is probable that no single catastrophic event resulted in the mass slaughter of these citizens nor did their demise occur at the same time.[15]

As for the racial identity of the Mohenjo-daro skeletons, it was claimed that they represented four of the seven racial categories of ancient and living people of India. On the basis of anthropometric analysis, a typological scheme of human physical diversity was applied. With minor modifications, this was used at a later time to classify the skeletons recovered from Harappa between 1927 and 1946 at the site localities of the mature Harappan culture (Cemetery R-37, Mound AB and Area G), and at the post-Harappan locality of Cemetery H which had been excavated between 1929 and 1934. To the 265 individuals present in the mortuary series from Harappa, another 100 specimens were added in the course of the 1987 and 1988 field seasons when Cemetery R-37 was excavated by a joint team from the University of California at Berkeley and the Archaeological Department of Pakistan (Figs. 15.6-15.7).[16]

Other skeletons associated with the Harappan civilization which have been examined by biological anthropologists include a single specimen from Chanhu-daro excavated in 1935-6, twenty-one specimens from Lothal which were recovered after 1957, eleven specimens from Kalibangan's Mature Harappan cemetery which was excavated between 1961 and 1969, a single skull recovered from Allahadino in 1973-4, over eighteen specimens from Nal recovered during field seasons in 1904-8 and 1925-6, and an uncertain number of individuals represented by fragmentary remains from Damb Bhuthi in 1930-1. Sixteen skeletons were excavated at Rupar in 1954-5 by officers of the Anthropological Survey of India. In the course of the Partition of India

---

'Revolution in the Urban Revolution: The Emergence of Indus Civilization', *Annual Review of Anthropology*, 19, pp. 261-82.

[15]George F. Dales (1964), 'The Mythical Massacre of Mohenjodaro', *Expendition*, 6, pp. 36-43; B.S. Guha and P.G. Basu (1938), 'Report on the Excavated Remains at Mohenjodaro in 1928-29', in E.T.H. Mackay (ed.), *Further Excavations at Mohenjodaro*, Government of India, New Delhi, I, pp. 613-38; Kennedy (1984), op. cit.; R.B.S. Sewell and B.S. Guha (1931), 'Human Remains', in John Marshall (ed.), *Mohenjodaro and Indus Civilization*, Arthur Probsthain, London, vol. 2, pp. 599-648.

[16]Gupta et al. (1962), op. cit.; B.B. Hemphill and J.R. Lukacs (1993), 'Hegelian Logic and the Harappan Civilization: An Investigation of Harappan Biological Affinities in the Light of Recent Biological and Archaeological Research', *SAA*, 1991, pp. 101-20; B.B. Hemphill et al. (1991), 'Biological Adaptations and Affinities of Bronze Age Harappans', in R.H. Meadow (ed.), *Harappa Excavations 1986-90*, pp. 137-82.

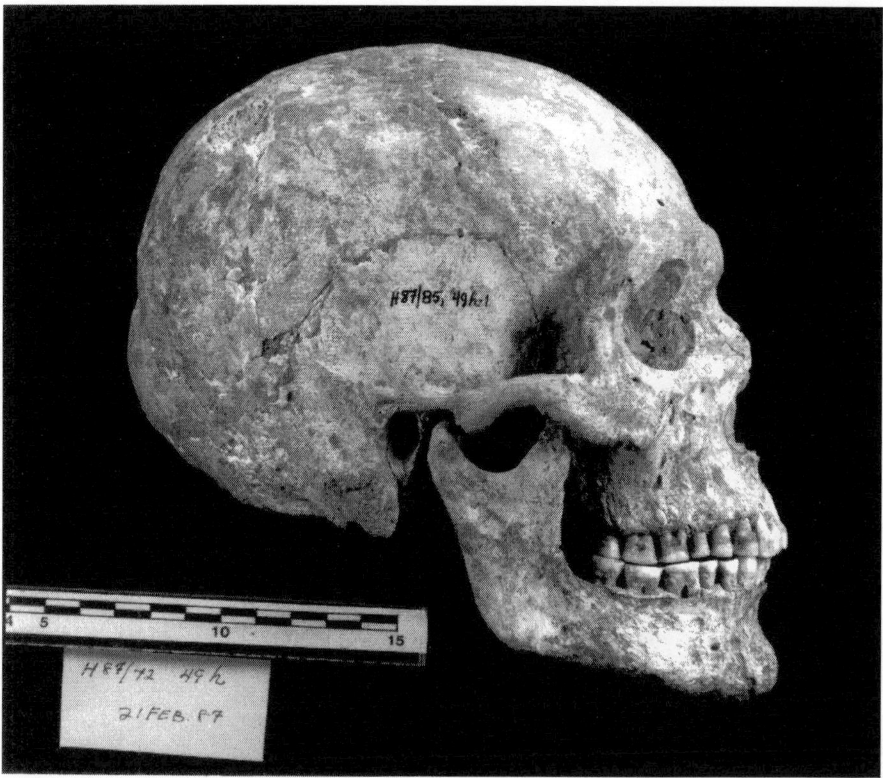

Fig. 15.6: Harappa Cemetary R-37 human skull. Right lateral aspect (Skeleton No. H 87/72-79b) (Courtesy: Richard Meadow and Archaeological Survey of Pakistan). Harappa Excavations, 1987

and Pakistan in 1947, Harappan skeletal remains were removed to India, Pakistan acquiring additional specimens during excavations in 1966 at Harappa.[17]

The earliest efforts to define the biological characteristics of the ancient Harappans were based upon univariate/bivariate statistical analyses. The goal of this employment of morphometric data was the classification of individual specimens within a typological racial model, a practice common to both Asian and Western scholars in the first half of the twentieth century. Emerging from

[17]B.K. Chatterjee and G.D. Kumar (1963), *Comparative Study and Racial Analysis of the Human Remains of Indus Valley Civilization with Particular Reference to Harappa*, Newman, Calcutta; P.C. Dutta et al. (1971), op. cit.; W.M. Krogman and W.H. Sassman (1943), 'Skull found at Mohenjodaro', in J.H. Mackey (ed.), *Chanru-daro Excavations*, New Heaven American Oriental Society, pp. 252-63; R.B.S. Sewell and B.S. Guha (1929), 'Report on the Bones Excavated at Nal', *MASI*, 35, pp. 56-96; A.K. Sharma (1969-70), 'Kalibangan Human Skeletal Remains: An Osteoarchaeological Approach, *JOI*, 19, pp. 109-13.

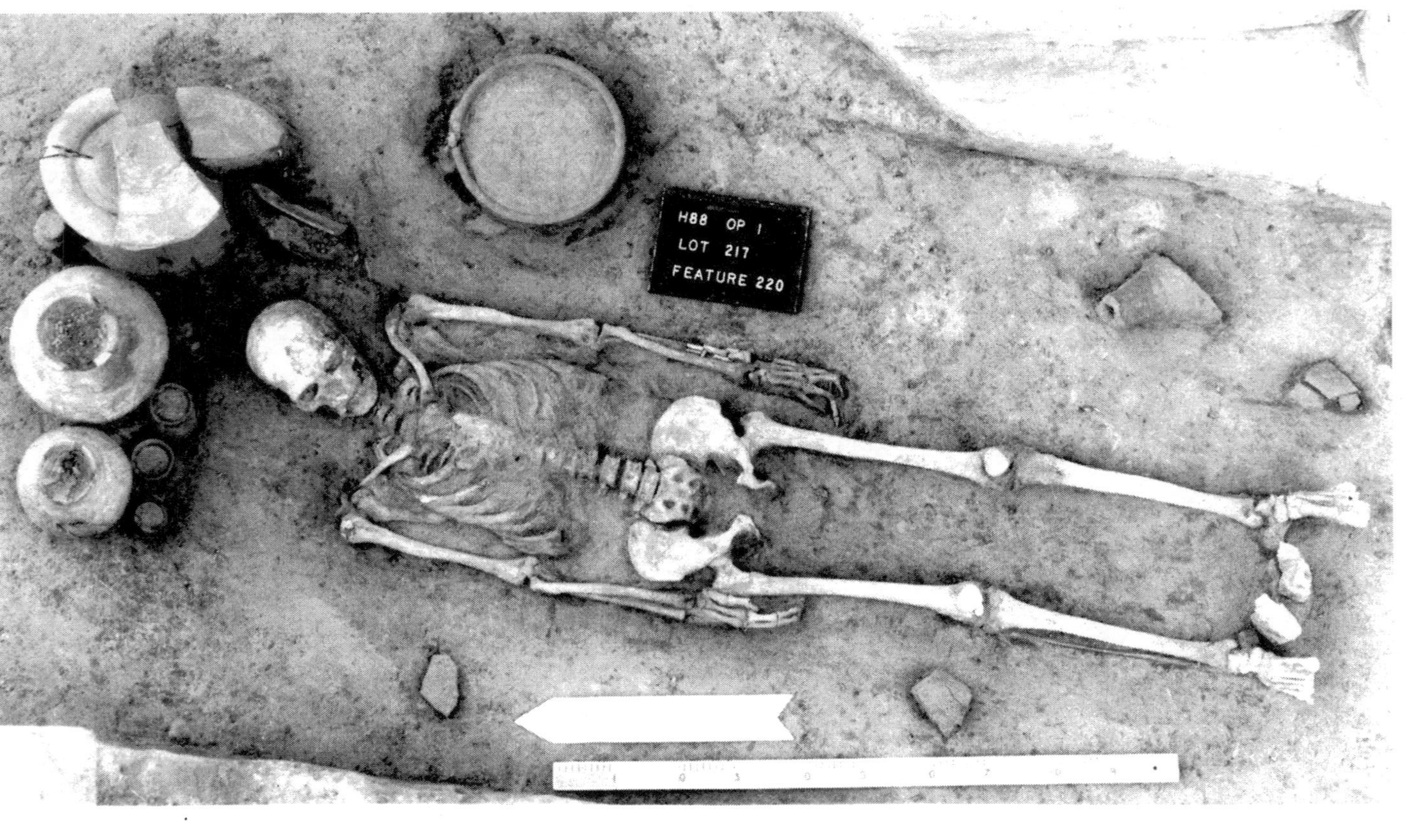

Fig. 15.7: Harappa Cemetery R-37 human skeleton (Skeleton No. H 88/217-220) (Courtesy: Richard Meadow and Archaeological Survey of Pakistan). Harappa Excavations, 1988

these studies were questions of biological affinities of Harappans to other prehistoric peoples, particularly to those represented by a preserved skeletal record in Iran and parts of Western Asia. The question of the biological profile of the 'typical Harappan' led to theories to account for variability in the shape of the cranial vault, some individuals being long and narrow-headed (dolichocranic), while others were short and broad-headed (brachycranic). It was proposed that individuals in the former cranial category were typical Harappans. Deviations from this assumed norm were attributed to the presence of submerged racial substrata assigned to autochthonous 'primitive' survivals or to the genetic ties of the Harappans to people of Negrito or Australasian races. Another approach was the employment of the Chi-square analysis along with other statistical procedures in order to resolve the issue of Harappans being a homogeneous population or a heterogeneous racially-mixed gene pool. An extreme view was that there had existed a 'Bronze Age Harappan Race' which constituted a biological sub-species of narrow genetic constitution. Although it is difficult to find agreement in these theoretical discussions, there remains the commonly held view that the Aryans of the Vedic Indian tradition were not related to the Harappans: rather, given their presumed date of entry into the subcontinent in 1500 BC, they were appointed the agents of Harappan decline and cultural extinction.

More recent interpretations of the skeletal biology and genetic affinities of the Harappans have been enhanced by various multivariate statistical analyses which use morphometric data and are not constricted by racial typologies. One discriminate analysis demonstrates that heterogeneity characterizes the interrelationships between individuals from Cemetery H at Harappa and all other individuals from the site, i.e. from Cemetery R-37 and Area G. When comparing the results of discriminate analysis in a determination of the degree of genetic distance between males from Cemetery R-37 and males from Mohenjo-daro, the two series are significantly discriminated.[18]

The results of a principal components analysis, which included a number of cranial series from widely-scattered prehistoric sites and cultural periods in South Asia, revealed a distribution of metrical traits that form clusters based upon anatomical variables that are responsive to stresses of the socio-economic and technological environments and not to criteria of racial

[18] P. Bartel (1979), 'A Discriminent Analysis of Harappan Civilization Human Population', *Journal of Archaeological Society*, 6, pp. 49-61; M. Cappieri (1971), 'Population of the Indus Civilization', in W.A. Fairservis, Jr. (ed.), *The Roots of Ancient India*, Macmillan, New York, pp. 425-43; P.C. Dutta (1972), 'The Bronze Age Harappans: A Re-examination of the Skulls in the Context of the Population Content', *AJPA*, 39, pp. 391-6; idem (1975), 'Race Concept and Palaeoanthropology: A Recent Model for Interpreting Ancient Human Remains', *Anthropologie*, 13, pp. 35-46; idem (1983), *The Bronze Age Harappans: A Bio-anthropological Study of the Skeletons Discovered at Harappa*, Anthropological Survey of India, Calcutta; S.S. Sarkar (1964), *Ancient Races of Punjab, Baluchistan and Sind*, Munshiram Manoharlal, New Delhi.

identification derived from earlier univariate and bivariate studies. No single phenotypic pattern defines the Harappans as a single Mendelian population, and the geographical separation of the skeletal series is reflected in regional anatomical dissimilarities, as between the ancient peoples of Harappa, Mohenjo-daro and Lothal. This argument for biological heterogeneity finds support from the archaeological record, as seen in the several modes of disposal of the dead at Harappan sites at different periods of time. Given the temporal distribution of Harappan cemeteries, it is probable that differences in burial practice indicate changing cultural traditions and the inclusion of enclaves of migrant families from rural and urban settings. This is what might be expected in the cosmopolitan centres of this Bronze Age culture with its far-reaching mercantile connections and political dominance in lands beyond the Indus Valley.[19]

The results of a recent research orientation towards issues of broad palaeodemographic scope and the employment of several multivariate procedures go far to support the concept of Harappan biological heterogeneity. Craniometric variables indicate a significant degree of biological distance between the inhabitants of Harappa and those of Iron Age Timargarha in Gandhara from the inhabitants of Mohenjo-daro. When the craniometric variation of these samples is compared with data for living populations from the northern and southern sectors of the subcontinent, all Harappa samples indicate the closest affinities with one another, with the exception of the Mohenjo-daro sample. Individuals buried at Cemetery R-37 have the closest affinities with open burial individuals from both Cemetery H and Timargarha. Further interpretations of these data, which include the recently excavated skeletons from Cemetery R-37 at Harappa, suggest that there were two demographic discontinuities in the north-western sector of the subcontinent: the first between 6000 and 4500 BC (a separation between the Neolithic and Chalcolithic populations from Mehrgarh), and the second between the populations of Harappa, Chalcolithic Mehrgarh and post-Harappan Timargarha, on the one hand, and the Bronze Age and early Iron Age populations of Sarai Khola in Gandhara, on the other. There is no evidence of abrupt population movements or displacements before or immediately following the decline of the Harappan civilization. While it may be argued that the Harappan culture represents an indigenous development within the region of the Indus River system, a biological continuum from the Neolithic times is not established, nor is there biological evidence to support the concept of an Aryan invasion.[20]

[19] K.A.R. Kennedy (1992), 'Biological Anthropology of Human Skeletons from Harappa: 1928-1988', *The Eastern Anthropologist*, 45, 1-2, pp. 55-85; K.A.R. Kennedy et al. (1984), 'Principal Components Analysis of Prehistoric South Asian Crania', *AJPA*, 64, pp. 105-18.

[20] G. Erdosy (1989), 'Ethnicity in the Rigveda and its Bearing on the Question of Indo-

The ancient Harappans exhibit a reduced degree of skeletal robusticity, a reduction of skeletal sexual dimorphism and the presence of markers of pathological stressers commonly encountered among other long-established agricultural and pastoral people of the old world. Prehistoric South Asians exposed to pressures of increased population size and density, sedentary lifestyles and new patterns of social organization in urban settings paid a biological cost in adapting to the socio-economic and technological transitions from hunting-foraging and village farming strategies. The increased incidence of infectious diseases, anaemias related to hemolytic, dietary or parasitic diseases, loss of the full realization of ontogenetic growth potential, and an increase in traumatic lesions are among the markers of a food-producing and urban lifestyle. Comparative studies of dental pathology and the trend towards reduction of the tooth crown size for Harappans and other prehistoric skeletal series from South Asia have been rewarding, one result being the documentation of a greater nutritional advantage for Harappan male children compared to their female counterparts (a difference based upon loci and the incidence of dental enamel hypoplasia developmental irregularities).[21]

CHALCOLITHIC

Ceramics of distinctive fabrics and decorative motifs, along with the presence of copper and bronze technology diffused from Western Asia, mark the Chalcolithic cultures which emerged in the late third and second millennia in South Asia. These food-producing societies settled in a vast area from the north-western sector of the subcontinent southwards into the Deccan and peninsular region, but never penetrated Sri Lanka. Regional cultural traditions developed of which some show affinities with the Harappan civilization. Others are the outgrowth of Neolithic communities which adopted innovative technologies. Yet other local traditions are significantly distinctive to merit separate labels of their cultural identity, e.g. Banas, Ahar, Stone Axe, etc. The occasional association of lithic artefacts called shouldered axes and faceted axes of India's eastern Neolithic in the second millennium, with copper and bronze objects, suggests an independent origin of both Neolithic and Chalcolithic cultures in this part of the subcontinent.

Covering the Mesolithic cultural horizon at Bagor, Rajasthan, is a Chalco-

---

European Origins', *SAS*, 5, pp. 35-47; Hempbill et al. (1991), op. cit.; J.G. Shaffer (1964), 'The Indo-Aryan Invasions: Cultural Myth and Archaeological Reality', in J.R. Lukacs (ed.), *The People of South Asia: The Biological Anthropology of India, Pakistan and Nepal*, Plenum, New York, pp. 77-90.

[21] J.R. Lukacs (1992a-b), op. cit.; J.R. Lukacs and M.R. Joshi (1992), 'Enamel Hypoplasia Prevalence in Three Ethnic Groups of Northwest India: A Test of Daughter Neglect and a Framework for the Past', *Journal of Palaeopathology*, 2, pp. 349-72; J.R. Lukacs and L.L. Minderman (1992), 'Dental Pathology and Agricultural Intensification from Neolithic to Chalcolithic Periods at Mehrgarh (Baluchistan, Pakistan)', *SAA*, 1989, pp. 167-79.

lithic deposit with three skeletal specimens. These are dated to 2165+105 BC and 2110+90 BC, an occupation contemporary with the Banas and Harappan cultures. Maharashtra has several Chalcolithic mortuary sites of which Nevasa was excavated in 1954-61, yielding 126 skeletons of immature individuals and four adults. One of the adult Nevasa skeletons is recent (50 BC-AD 200) but the others in the sample are dated to 1500-1000 BC. The child burials at Chandoli Khurd are from twenty-four floor graves in houses but two individuals in the sample were placed in urns. A single adult recovered in the 1961 excavation has been described. From 1968 to 1981, the site of Inamgaon was excavated, an immense habitation area of some 65 acres which includes several periods of occupation: Malwa, 1700-1400 BC; Early Jorwe, 1400-1100 BC; Late Jorwe, 1100-700 BC). Over 176 human skeletons have been recovered and described, most of them of immature individuals. A human mandible was found at Apegaon in 1976. Human skeletal remains were recovered from Daimabad in 1976-9 of which thirty-seven have been studied from the Malwa-Jorwe period. Infant and child burials predominate.[22]

Brahmagiri's Chalcolithic level contained human skeletons described with the underlying Neolithic specimens in the study cited above. Maski, another site in Karnataka with Chalcolithic and Iron Age skeletal remains, was excavated in 1935-7 and 1954, but uncertainty exists with respect to the precise cultural association and dating of these specimens. The Chalcolithic phase continued until *c.* 400 and BC over 330 skeletons are represented in the Maski series.[23]

There are some striking similarities in burial practices in the Indian Chalcolithic: urn burials, amputation of the feet of the deceased, inclusion of specific grave goods, large infant-child cemeteries, as well as burial in house floors, some consistency of burial position and compass orientation of the body, and predominance of complete burials over secondary burials. The high incidence of teeth, deciduous and permanent, from these skeletal series has encouraged progress in dental anthropology in South Asia.[24]

[22] K.A.R. Kennedy and K.C. Malhotra (1966), *Human Skeletal Remains from Chalcolithic and Indo-Roman Levels from Nevasa: An Anthropometric and Comparative Analysis*, Deccan College, Poona; J.R. Lukcas (1980), 'The Apegaon Mandible Morphology and Pathology', *BDCRI*, 39, pp. 88-95; J.R. Lukacs and G.L. Badam (1981), 'Palaeodemography of Post-Harappan Inamgaon: A Preliminary Report', *JIAS*, 16, pp. 59-74; J.R. Lukacs and R.S. Walimbe (1986), *Excavations at Inamgaon*, vol. II: *Physical Anthropology of Human Skeletal Remains*, part I: An Osteobiographic Analysis; K.C. Malhotra (1965), op. cit.; S.R. Walimbe (1986), 'Palaeo-demography of Proto-historic Daimabad', in S.A. Sali (ed.), *Daimabad 1976-79*, ASI, New Delhi, pp. 641-740; S.R. Walimbe and S.S. Kulkarni (1993), *Biological Adaptations in Human Dentition: An Odonto-metric Study on Living and Archaeological Populations in India*, Deccan College, Poona.

[23] S.S. Sarkar (1972), *Ancient Races of the Deccan*, Munshiram Manoharlal, New Delhi.

[24] J.R. Lukacs (1992a and b), op. cit.; J.R. Lukacs and B.B. Hemphill (1990), 'Traumatic

DISCUSSION

Comparative studies of South Asia's prehistoric skeletal record embrace collections from cultural contexts with iron and distinctive ceramic wares. One concentration is the Gandhar grave culture of western Pakistan which flourished between the time of the Harappan decline to the dawn of the historic period with the Achaemenid invasion of the sixth century BC. There are many skeletons recovered from these sites of which some have been the subject of laboratory analyses. A second area of early iron use is central and peninsular India and Sri Lanka where burials are frequently found in association with Megalithic monuments and subterranean tombs dating from *c.* 1100 BC to AD 50, thereby overlapping with the Chalcolithic cultures in west-central India, the early historic principalities of the peninsula and the events relating to the diffusion of Buddhism. Although these later prehistoric cultures are not covered in the present study, the laboratory analysis of the Iron Age skeletal record is relevant to a broad overview of the course of human evolution and biological diversity in South Asia.[25]

The identity of populations in this survey of skeletal data reviewed above is phenotypically South Asian with recognizable regional variations and modifications over time. Some of the phenotypic changes are adaptive responses to socio-economic and technological lifestyles, and others may be ascribed to micro-evolutionary shifts of traits under genetic control, the consequences of gene flow between regional populations, genetic drift and a random assortment of characters. Biological continua are established in a few instances but it is risky to associate certain living populations in marginal habitats to specific prehistoric skeletal series. Nonetheless, given the caveat of constructing lineages based upon the now-scientifically defunct practice of racial palaeontology, it is apparent that South Asia does not offer evidence

---

Injuries of Prehistoric Teeth: New Evidence from Baluchistan and Punjab Provinces, Pakistan', *Anthropologischer Anzeiger*, 4, pp. 3561-3; J.R. Lukacs et al. (1983), 'Crown Dimensions of Deciduous Teeth of Prehistoric and Living Populations of Western India', *AJPA*, 61, 383-7.

[25] W. Bernhard (1967), 'Human Skeletal Remains from the Cemetery of Timargarha and the Gandharva Grave Culture', *Ancient Pakistan*, pp. 289-407; idem (1969), 'Preliminary Report on the Human Skeletal Remains from the Prehistoric Cemetary of Sarai Khola', *Ancient Pakistan*, 6, pp. 100-16; K.A.R. Kennedy (1975), 'The Physical Anthropology of the Megalith Builders of South India and Sri Lanka, Canberra', Australian National Museum; idem (1986), 'Hauntings at Aditanallur: An Anthropological Ghost Story', in J. Jacobson (ed.), *Studies in the Archaeology of India and Pakistan*, Oxford-IBH, New Delhi, pp. 357-95; idem (1990a and b), op. cit., J.R. Lukacs (1983a), 'Dental Anthropology and the Origins of Two Iron Age Populations from Northern Pakistan', *Homo*, 34, pp. 1-15; idem (1983b), 'Dental Pathology and Tooth Size at Early Neolithic Mehrgarh: An Anthropological Assessment', *SAA*, Instituto Universitario Orientale, Naples, pp. 121-50; K.R. Lukacs et al. (1985), 'Dental Pathology and Dietary Patterns in Iron Age Northern Pakistan', *SAA*, pp. 475-96.

of abrupt demographic displacements and appearances of exotic phenotypic patterns introduced from outside the borders of the subcontinent (at least for the period of time since the late Pleistocene).

Beyond the temporal framework of the currently constituted skeletal record in South Asia (exclusive of the mid-Pleistocene Narmada hominid), the origins of prehistoric and contemporary populations remain unknown. The biological affinities of populations from the north-western sector with the ancient people of Western Asia and the affinities of north-western populations to central Asiatic groups are more firmly established than the question of the biological affinities of certain populations of peninsular India and Sri Lanka. Recent investigations of dental morphology suggest that prehistoric Sri Lankans evolved in relative genetic isolation from the people of the Indian mainland. A comparison of dental data indicates that, by Neolithic-Chalcolithic times, Indian populations maintained stronger genetic links with Near Eastern and European groups than with the Mesolithic Sri Lankans, the latter possessing the Sundadont dental pattern and other dental features characteristic of South-east Asian Jomon populations. The thesis of an Australasian genetic element in Sri Lanka and peninsular India is a venerable one, which may attain greater attention in the future through advances in morphometric and statistical analyses of teeth and skeletal remains.[26]

Current phylogenetic debates about modern human origins and the relevance of mitochondrial DNA as a biological clock to account for the African origins of *Homo sapiens sapiens* demand that the palaeontological record be considered for the provision of supportive or contradictory evidence. Only with the contributions of data from morphometric and statistical analyses of prehistoric human remains from Asia, including South Asia, can the questions of the Mitochondrial Eve and population displacement in Europe and Asia, or the multi-regional hypothesis of the continuity of prehistoric and modern populations in their geographically separated habitats, be resolved. India is situated in the centre of this argument, both geographically and conceptually. While the recovery of additional fossil hominid material is always welcome and necessary, the sophisticated investigation of materials now on hand by trained research scholars holds the promise of bringing current evolutionary problems to fruitful conclusions, with respect to the biological history and diversity of the ancient and modern people of South Asia. The skeletal evidence allows the historian and archaeologist to gain a different kind of knowledge of ancient populations from data not present in archival, artefactual or stratigraphic sources. Today, we are able to ascertain the palaeodemographic variables of mortality, morbidity, fecundity, population density, biological affinity, and indices of health, disease, incidence of trauma and adaptations

[26]D.F. Hawkley (1993), 'Biological Affinities of Prehistoric Sri Lankans: A Comparative Study of Dental Morphology', *AJPA*, Supplement, 16.

to changing socio-economic lifestyles through the study of the ancient skeletal record. From these beginnings in the morphometric and statistical analyses of earlier peoples are derived the broader issues of human evolution and biological diversity in all parts of the world.

Chapter 16

Prehistoric Art

V.H. Sonawane

INTRODUCTION

For a long time, the existence of prehistoric art in India was an enigma and even its very antiquity was questioned. Though its study crossed the threshold of archaeology rather late, it is now regarded as one of the prime sources for prehistoric studies. A cursory glance at the panorama of rock art is enough to reveal its diversity in time and space. It is mostly conditioned by human response to a changing environment. Most of these aesthetic works are reflections of the effects of locality and cultural contexts in their creations. From time immemorial, such creative works of human origin have been controlled by his feelings of visual space reflecting how man perceived the world. Extensive painted galleries exhibited in the hollows of rock-shelters, and engravings executed on stone, bone and ostrich eggshells are mute testimonies to prehistoric art, and attempts can be made to reconstruct the lifestyle of prehistoric societies with the integrated study of these extant works.

HISTORY OF ROCK ART RESEARCH

Rock paintings were first recorded by the pioneering discoveries made in 1867 by Archibald Carllyle in the forested region of the Kaimur ranges in the Mirzapur district of Uttar Pradesh. These paintings were discovered about twelve years prior to the discovery of the Altamira cave paintings in Spain. Though Carllyle did not publish any account of his discovery, he left his notes with a friend, and Vincent A. Smith published these in 1906. Carllyle assigned these paintings to the prehistoric period. John Cockburn, contemporary of Carllyle, not only systematically studied the rock paintings, of the Mirzapur region but also produced tracings of several of them. However, he failed to recognize their prehistoric antiquity. In 1899, he published an account of all his discoveries comparing them with those paintings found in Australia, South Africa, and North and South America.[1] Percy Brown, who visited the painted

[1] J. Cockburn (1899), 'Cave Paintings in the Kaimur Range, Northwest Provinces', *JRAS,* pp. 89-97.

shelters at Singanpur in the Raigarh district of Madhya Pradesh in 1914, was the first art expert to include prehistoric art in his book on Indian paintings.[2]

The first rock engravings of south India were known only after the visit of F. Fawcett to Kupgallu in 1892. He also acknowledged the antiquity of the same. Fawcett is better known for his discovery of the Edakal cave. Prior to this, rock bruisings were reported by Hubert Thomas Knox in the Bellary district of Karnataka. Subsequently, more rock bruisings were reported from this area by F.R. Allchin, A. Sundara and K. Paddayya.

In 1921, Manoranjan Ghosh brought to light a group of painted rock shelters at Adamgarh near Hoshangabad. In the 1930s, D.H. Gordon tried to tackle the chronological problems of rock art by observing the superimposition of paintings, their style and their technological aspects. He basically worked on the rock paintings of Pachmarhi confined to the Mahadeo hills of central India. Unfortunately, he could not imagine a long autochthonous development of Indian rock art in its original setting. Nevertheless, he was the first antiquarian to write extensively on the thematic elements shown in the rock paintings. A chapter dealing with rock art in his book on Indian Archaeology.[3]

Since then, more than 5,000 painted shelters have been reported from all parts of the Indian subcontinent. These spectacular discoveries gave a new filling to rock art studies. V.S. Wakankar who recognized its archaeological potential, was the driving force behind these recent large-scale discoveries.[4] He discovered several hundred painted rock shelters, mainly in central India, attempted a broad survey of the rock art sites of the whole country and prepared a framework to determine the chronology of the paintings based on their themes, style, superimposition and archaeological context in a historical perspective.[5] The most outstanding contribution of Wakankar to the field of rock art is the discovery of Bhimbetka in 1957. It is one of the most splendid rock art sites known in the world and has been declared as World Heritage Site by UNESCO. Contemporary researchers include S.K. Pandey;[6] Shankar Tiwari, Jagdish Gupta, R.K. Varma, A. Sundra, Erwin Neumayer[7] and Yashodhar Mathpal[8] who have contributed comprehensively to the development of a possible link between rock art and archaeological data to ascertain its prehistoric antiquity.

[2]P. Brown (1917), *Indian Painting*, YMCA Pub. House, Calcutta.

[3]D.H. Gordon (1958), *Prehistoric Background of Indian Culture,* N.M. Tripathi Pvt. Ltd., Bombay.

[4]V.S. Wakankar (1975), 'Prehistoric Cave Paintings', *Marg*, 28 (4), pp. 17-38.

[5]V.S. Wakankar and B.R.R. Brooks (1976), *Stone Age Paintings in India*, Taraporewala & Sons, Bombay.

[6]S.K. Pandey (1993), *Indian Rock Art*, Aryan Books International, New Delhi.

[7]Erwin Neumayer (1993), *Lines on Stone: The Prehistoric Rock Art of India*, Manohar, Delhi

[8]Yashodhar Mathpal (1984), *Prehistoric Rock Paintings of Bhimbetka, Central India*, Abhinav Publications, New Delhi.

Rock art studies in India, on the basis of where we stand now, are beyond any application of scientific or technological base. However, attempts are being made by young researchers to develop a multidisciplinary approach for its scientific correlation.

DISTRIBUTION AND NATURE OF ROCK ART

The vast corpus of rock art in India, confined to suitable sandstone and granite pockets, stretches from the southern parts of Kerala to the high latitudes of Ladakh and the Zanskar Valley in the north, and from Gujarat in the west to Orissa. Assam and Manipur in the east (Fig. 16.1). However, the largest concentration is to be found in the Vindhyan ranges of Madhya Pradesh and its Kaimurean extensions into Uttar Pradesh. Equally important paintings and engravings were reported from the southern Deccan in the extensive granite wilderness of the Krishna-Tungabhadra *doab*.

In the sandstone region of central India, rock paintings were found on the walls or ceilings of shelters and some time in the cavities of cliff walls or at any other suitable place where they could withstand the onslaught of different weathering agents. Bhimbetka, Jaora, Kathothia, Firengi, Kharwai, Gupha, Maser, Lakhajoar, Adamgarh and Pachmarhi are the important localities representing rock art sites of this nuclear region. The geomorphological setting of the rock art sites of south India is strikingly different from those of central India. To a large extent, the rock art of south India is mainly represented by rock bruisings but there are a few cases of paintings too. These were generally found on the shelter walls of projected ceiling hoods and, invariably, in niches developed by natural weathering. Among the many south Indian sites, the better-known are Kupgallu, Maski, Piklihal, the Edakal cave, Tekkelkotta and Badami.

As far as rock paintings are concerned, they are found in various states of preservation depending upon their location. Many of these paintings are partially faded because of the destructive action of natural and human agencies. Paintings on granite surfaces are not so durable. As a result, only those paintings located in well-protected spots or hollows that maintained the environmental balance were well-preserved. The great mass of rock paintings showed a predilection for the colour red in several shades, ranging from a rather dark violet to a yellowish brick-red. The red pigment, in most cases, was obtained from red haematite nodules called *geru*, containing iron oxide found in lateritic formations. The next most frequently used colour was white. It would have been obtained either from calcium carbonate nodules (*kankar*) or kaoline clayey deposits. Occasionally, some of the earliest paintings were depicted in green and yellow, employing mineralized chalcedony of the respective colours. Although most of the paintings were in monochrome, there were also instances of bichrome and polychrome drawings. The creators of these paintings exploited the natural resources available within the proximity

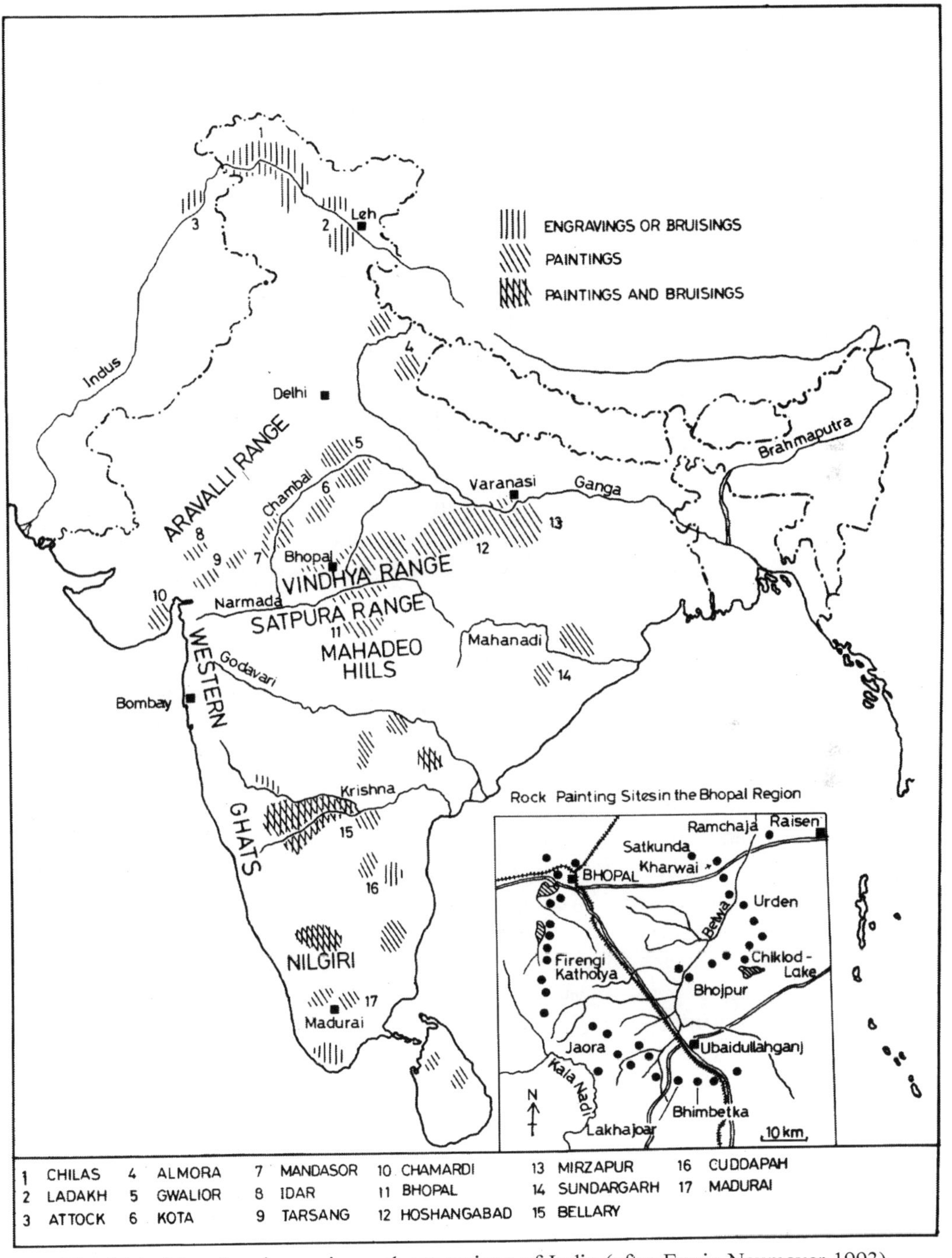

Fig. 16.1: Map showing major rock art regions of India (after Erwin Neumayer 1993)

of the rock art sites for colour pigments. At places, the rock floors of shelters show scooped-out circular depressions, often retaining traces of paints. Such 'cupmarks' were obviously intended for preparing colours for painting the rock.

No serious attempt to study the pigment has been made so far by scholars using various scientific methods. However, in the creation of rock paintings, it is proposed that the artists secured the paint either by diluting the colour in water or by tempera. They also employed the dry colour technique using crayons, stencils or the spray technique. Drawings by means other than colour are also recorded on the rock surfaces. These include engravings and carvings better specified as bruisings or petroglyphs. In the Indian context, bruisings form the most dominant part of rock art next to rock paintings. These were executed either by ribbing or pecking the rough granite surface. As a result, intended pictures in white appear clearly against the dull brown background of the rock. Such bruised works of art can withstand all weathering agencies, even on unprotected rock surfaces, and survive for a long period of time.

While discussing the prehistoric art of India, along with rock paintings and bruisings, due emphasis is also given to the role of portable artefacts in the form of stone, bone and ostrich eggshell pieces, and even unmodified objects reflecting the aesthetic taste of the prehistoric society.

CHRONOLOGY

Although rock art was discovered quite early in India, the knowledge of its existence had little influence on archaeological research until the last two or three decades. Recent attempts to find chronological indicators for rock art from associated artefacts through excavations helped, to some extent, in establishing the antiquity of some of these paintings. Such paintings, in the absence of an absolute the chronometric dating sequence, are taken into consideration for formulating a tentative stylistic criteria for the chronological sequence of Indian rock art as a broadbased working hypothesis. Besides, the rock paintings themselves are useful in establishing the relative chronology on the basis of their thematic content, superimposition, style and context. Therefore, one can use these different parameters for the chrono-cultural classification of our vast and diverse rock art treasure.

In many shelters, rock pictures are often found painted in palimpsests. In such cases, building a relative chronology of the pictures become quite easy by observing the overlapping of paints. Here, one has to observe the stylistic features of successive paintings. Thus, by correlating the relative chronology with chronologically relevant features, one can unravel the age or cultural period of the rock pictures effectively. Indian rock pictures are numerous and extremely narrative. A thematic analysis, therefore, can establish a wide-ranging picture of the technological and social conditions under which they were created. The correlation of such paintings with known archaeological data will bring us closer to a technologically well-defined periodization of Indian history. For convenience, the pictures drawn before the introduction of the Brahmi script are considered prehistoric and divided into two distinct groups: the pictures of hunters and of gatherers and agriculturalists, representing the food-gathering and food-producing societies, respectively. Pictures showing neither domesticated animals nor giving any clue about the use of metal weapons obviously belong to a class of society which did not experience these innovations. Early pictures show that the hunting and gathering groups fashioned the microliths (barbed weapons like spears and arrows) and account for the developed microlithic technology current in India from the late Upper Palaeolithic to the Mesolithic period.

Unlike the pictures of hunters and gatherers, the paintings of people practising animal domestication are shown by pictures of humped cattle, the goat and sheep. In this category, we also find yoked oxen, the two-wheeled bullock cart and many other features of an agriculture-based, settled lifestyle. In central India particularly, they resemble Chalcolithic pottery designs found on the Malwa ware. None of the south Indian bruisings can be compared to any of the Mesolithic paintings. It seems that all bruisings were executed once agriculture and animal domestication were well-established. The main subject of the bruisings and paintings of this period is cattle.

The dating of Indian rock pictures is, thus, supported by a chronological framework based on the observation of the overlapping of the successive rock pictures belonging to different stylistic groups. The periodization is further based on the thematic analysis of pictures showing patterns of subsistence, tool technology and technological innovations. Unfortunately, datable finds of carved or engraved artefacts from stratified archaeological strata are lacking in India which would have enabled the comparison of rock paintings with the design pattern found on such artefacts. Like India, most of the rock art of the world is also not securely dated. However, with the advent of AMS pigment dating, the utilization of this scientific method (at least for paintings of selected areas) to conform their chronological classification should be undertaken.

PREHISTORIC ART

In the Indian context, the antiquity of prehistoric art dates back to the Upper Palaeolithic period. However, the apparently relevant evidence begins with haematite and quartz crystals found in Acheulian deposits of the Lower Palaeolithic period. One such haematite specimen was found on the exposed floor of Locality V at Hunsgi (Karnataka) which bears a worn facet with distinctive striation marks, suggesting that it had been used as a crayon to colour or mark a rock surface. Strikingly interesting evidence came from Singi Talav (Rajasthan) where, from the base of a Lower Palaeolithic deposit, six small quartz crystals were recovered. They measured 7-25 mm in length, too small to have been used as tools, and were almost entirely unmodified. Like the Hunsgi haematite nodule, they had been brought to the site deliberately and were apparently collected for their visual qualities. Further relevant evidence comes from the site of Bhimbetka. Robert Bednarik reported two petroglyphs excavated in the Auditorium rock shelter (III F-24). They consisted of a large circular cupul and a meandering line. Their stratigraphic position within the habitation deposit suggests that they were made during the Acheulian period. Bednarik considers them the oldest known rock art specimen in the world.

Upper Palaeolithic Period

The evidence of earliest rock paintings and the systematic working of ostrich eggshells and bones in the form of engravings, cuttings and relief works of small portable artefacts comes from the Upper Palaeolithic period, indicating prolific artistic activity. In this regard, the only known engraved portable artefact of applied art is reported from Patne (Maharashtra). Out of several ostrich eggshell pieces recovered from Upper Palaeolithic levels at Patne, one of them had a simple geometric pattern forming a criss-cross hatching between two horizontal lines (Fig. 16.2). This has been dated to 25000 BP based on the C-14 dates of ostrich eggshell samples from the same stratum. Ostrich eggshells were also effectively exploited for making ornamental beads. Three such perforated disc beads together with a shell (*Olive* sp.) of estuarine origin were reported from Patne. Two more minute beads of this category were found in a burial at Bimbetka.[9] Apart from these, barrel-shaped bone beads and grooved teeth of *Bos incisors* as pendants are known from the Kurnool caves of Andhra Pradesh. The Upper Palaeolithic cave site of Muchchatala Chintamanu Gavi has furnished a TL date of *c.* 19000 BP from where one such bone bead was obtained.

These examples constitute the earliest known evidence of ornamentation in India. However, Erwin Neumayer believes that the early dates which were derived from some of the eggshell samples of Bhimbetka and Chandresal only give the age of the material and not the time when it was modified by man. Hence, while estimating the antiquity of such modified ostrich eggshell artefacts, one has to take into consideration the context in which they were found. Associated objects play a very vital role in such cases. In this context, a carved bone artefact recovered from the cemented gravel III of the Belan Valley dated to 20000 BP is quite interesting (Fig. 16.3). Though it was described as a Mother Goddess by some and a harpoon head by others, it confirms that the technique carving bone material was well-developed during this period in India.

[9] Giriraj Kumar et al. (1988), 'Engraved Ostrich Egg Shell Objects: New Evidence of Upper Palaeolithic Art in India', *Rock Art Research*, 5, 1, pp. 43-53.

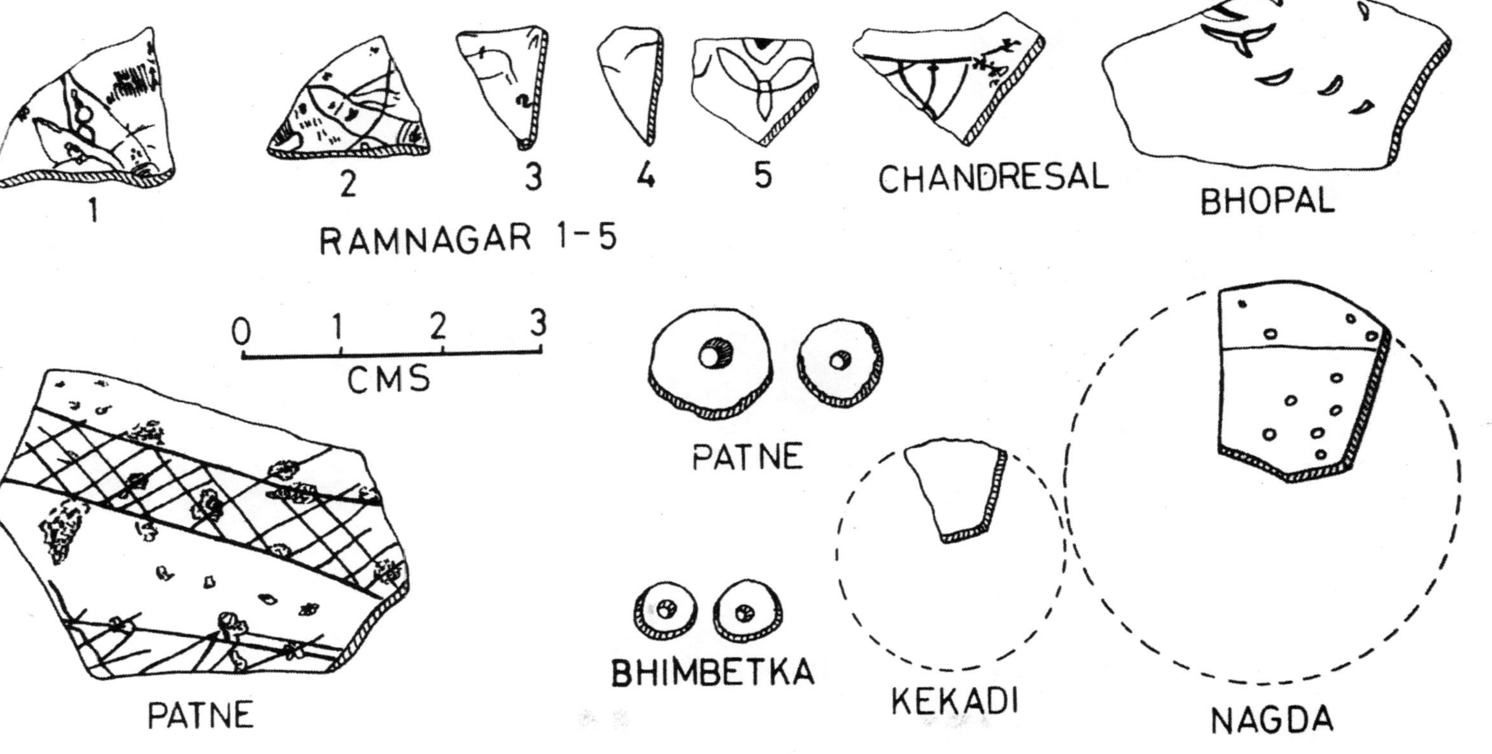

Fig. 16.2: Engraved ostrich egg-shell pieces and disc beads, Upper Palaeolithic

Fig. 16.3: Carved bone artefact from Belan Valley, Upper Palaeolithic Period

Although there is no dispute about the historicity of Mesolithic rock paintings, it is quite likely, as Wakankar believed, that some of the early depictions of rock paintings do belong to the Upper Palaeolithic phase. These include some green paintings from the earliest representations. The reason for this supposition is that green haematite faceted nodules have been found in Upper Palaeolithic deposits in one of the excavated rock shelters at Bhimbetka (III A-28Y). There is some controversy about the chronological position of these paintings. Some researchers found green paintings preceded by red. Here, emphasis is to be given to the style rather than the colour of the paintings. The green colour is most frequently found in paintings of the earliest style in the region around Bhopal. However, in this earliest style, too, most of the paintings are in red and even a few in yellow. The striking feature of this early style is the human form which is transformed to a perfect 'S' shape. The paintings do not show different activities except dancing and hunting scenes, which are characterized by vigorous dynamism which is unparalleled in the later rock art of the Indian subcontinent (Figs. 16.4-16.5).[10]

Mesolithic Period

The wide spectrum of rock art is full of descriptive details. It is surprisingly uniform in style and content all over India. There is remarkable divergence in the degree of abstraction between the depiction of human and animal forms. While animals are depicted quite naturalistically, the human forms are reduced to stick-like figures in a stylized manner. Sometimes, humans are shown wearing masks or elaborate headdresses. This difference between human and animal depiction is most visible in hunting scenes. Again, in contrast to the fragile male figures, the female form is always static with a plump, square body. As animals and women are drawn quite bulkily, there was room for body decoration. Most of the intricate design patterns like the spiral or honeycomb are seen in such paintings. There is no clear demarcation between the body pattern and 'X-ray depictions'. Both appear side by side at places within a single composition. Mesolithic paintings give a remarkably detailed account of various activities, recording minute details of a variety of game being hunted with spears and arrows, all tipped and barbed with microliths (Figs. 16.6-16.7). Hunters chasing and cornering the prey, shooting arrows at it, transporting the kill (Fig. 16.8), butchering, fishing with net traps (Fig. 16.9), catching rats using digging sticks from a burrow (Fig. 16.10), etc., throw light on hunting strategies, besides the collection of fruits and honey, and other subsistence practices. Apart from these, there are paintings which delineate other activities such as dancing, singing, playing with musical

[10]V.S. Wakankar (1992), 'Rock Paintings in India', in M. Lorblanchet (ed.), *Rock Art in the Old World*, Indira Gandhi National Centre for the Arts, New Delhi, pp. 319-36.

Fig. 16.4: A group of dancers, Lakhajoar, Upper Palaeolithic Period

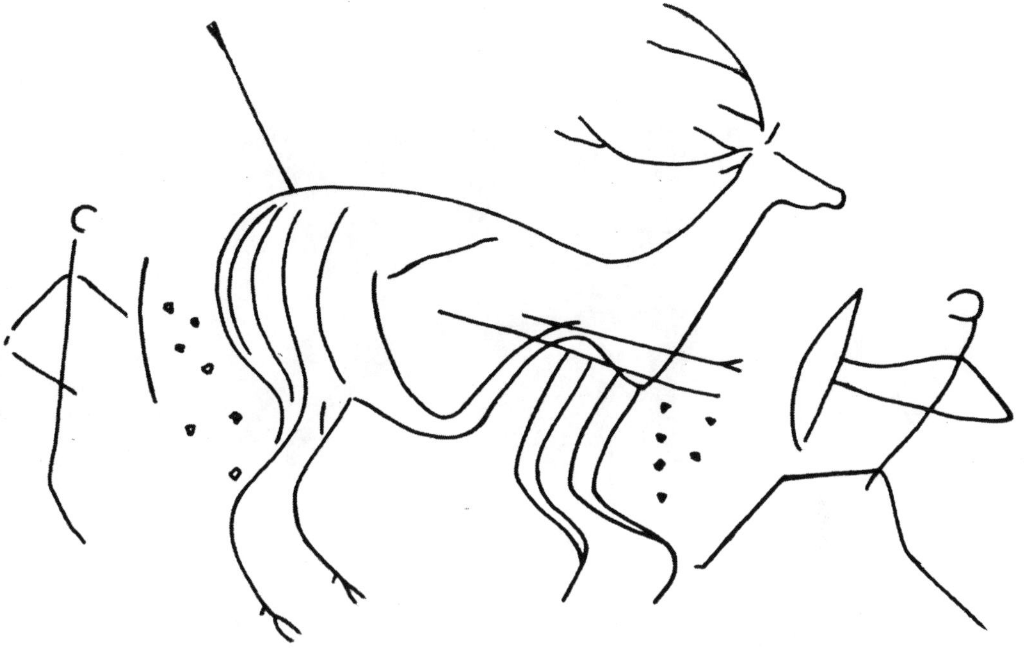

Fig. 16.5: Hunting scene, Putli Karar, Upper Palaeolithic Period

Fig. 16.6: Hunters carrying arrows set with microliths, Kharwai, Mesolithic

Fig. 16.7: Microliths set in the shaft, Lakhajoar, Mesolithic

Fig. 16.8: A hunter carrying a net containing hunted animals, Jaoro, Mesolithic

Fig. 16.9: Fishing scene, Lakhajoar, Mesolithic

Fig. 16.10: Women engaged in catching rats, Jaora, Mesolithic

instruments, and drinking and eating inside a roofed house (Fig. 16.11). A large number of paintings show subjects which may be classed as religious or cultic. Here we find mythical stories depicting deified animals chasing diminutive human beings (Fig. 16.12). Scenes narrating magical cures or medical treatment signify a deeper meaning in their creation. Most touching is the scene of a child burial where family members are shown mourning its death (Fig. 16.13).

Compared to the rock paintings, Mesolithic engravings are few and far between. Whatever is known is in the form of mere scratches, figures of animals or abstract patterns. In Orissa and Bihar, such engravings were invariably filled in with colours. Though not much is known of the portable art of these people, a solitary example obtained from Chandravati (Rajasthan) in the form of an engraved core is highly significant in this context. A rhombus type of spiral design was cut into the unscarred cortex of the core (Figs. 16.14-16.15). The execution of lines was extremely fine and delicate, and fashioned with the help of a microlithic blade.[11] Similar intricate designs have been found painted in many rock shelters (Fig. 16.16). Unfortunately, this core is a surface find and, hence, cannot be dated although the nature of the assemblage is clearly Mesolithic. Intricate designs consisting of a rhomboid as well as honeycomb patterns or variations of the 'spiral' almost constitute an index of the Mesolithic art of India.

The continuity of the tradition of engravings as a mode of expression is further supported by the discovery of bone objects recovered from Mesolithic deposits in rock shelter III A-28 of the Bhimbetka complex. They consist of simple, straight or zigzag lines and irregular parallelogrammatic designs. Apart from this, evidence of bone and antler rings used as ornamental earrings, and components of the necklace from Sarai Nahar Rai and Mahadaha (Uttar Pradesh) supply additional information on the aesthetic taste developed by these communities.

Neolithic and Chalcolithic Periods

An abrupt change is discernible in style and theme between the rock art of the hunter-gatherers and early agriculturalists. The earliest pictures of this period featuring domesticated animals are stylistically demarcated from the pictures of the preceding period. The dynamic art of the hunters and gatherers gets replaced by the progressively stiff and static art of the agriculturists and cattle-keepers, whose thematic spectrum is extremely limited and confined to the depiction of long-homed, humped cattle. However, where a hunting scene is painted, it gives a good idea about the weapons used during this period. Although the most commonly used weapons were still bows and

[11] V.H. Sonawane (1942), 'Significance of the Chandravati Core in the Light of Prehistoric Art in India', in M. Lorblanchet (ed.), *Rock Art in the Old World*, pp. 273-83.

Fig. 16.11: A family in a hut, Lakhajoar, Mesolithic

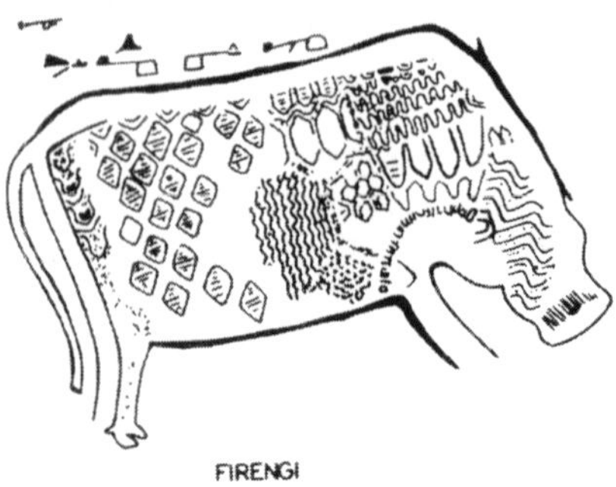

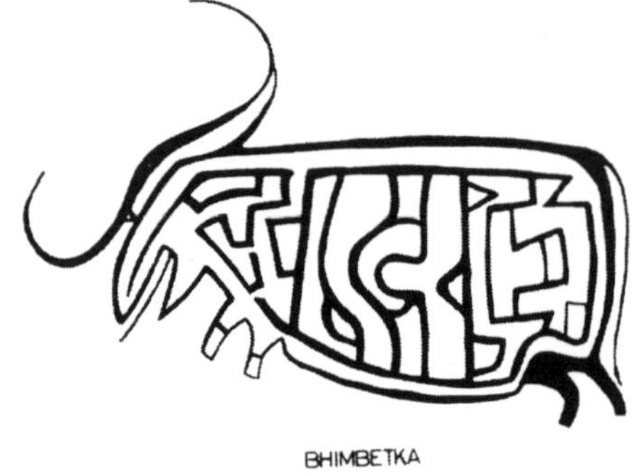

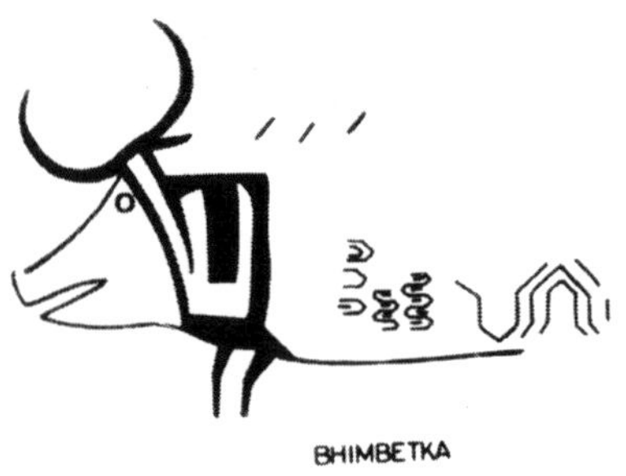

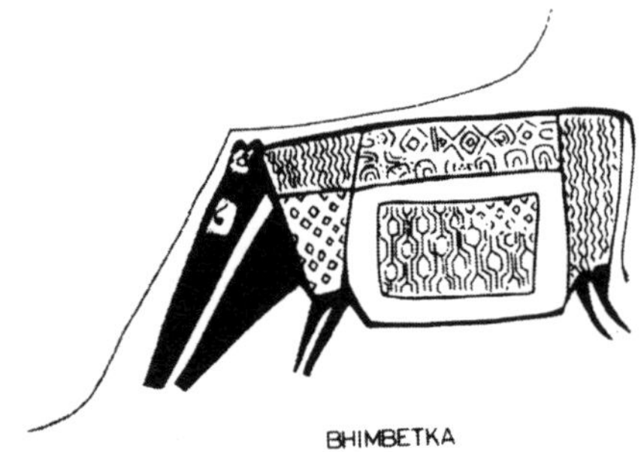

Fig. 16.12: Deified animals, Mesolithic

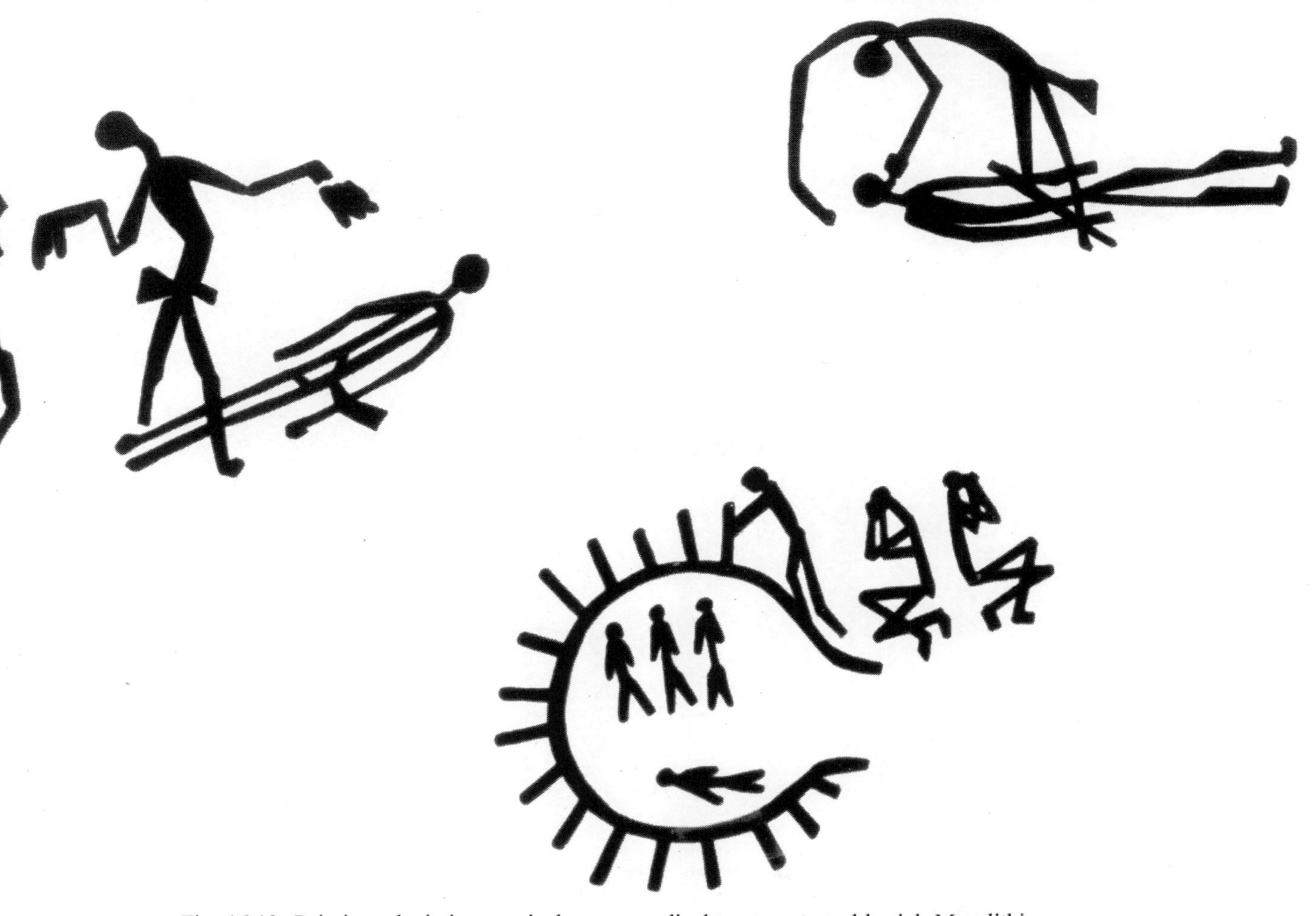

Fig. 16.13: Paintings depicting magical cures, medical treatments and burial, Mesolithic

Fig. 16.14: Engraved agate core, Chandravati, Mesolithic

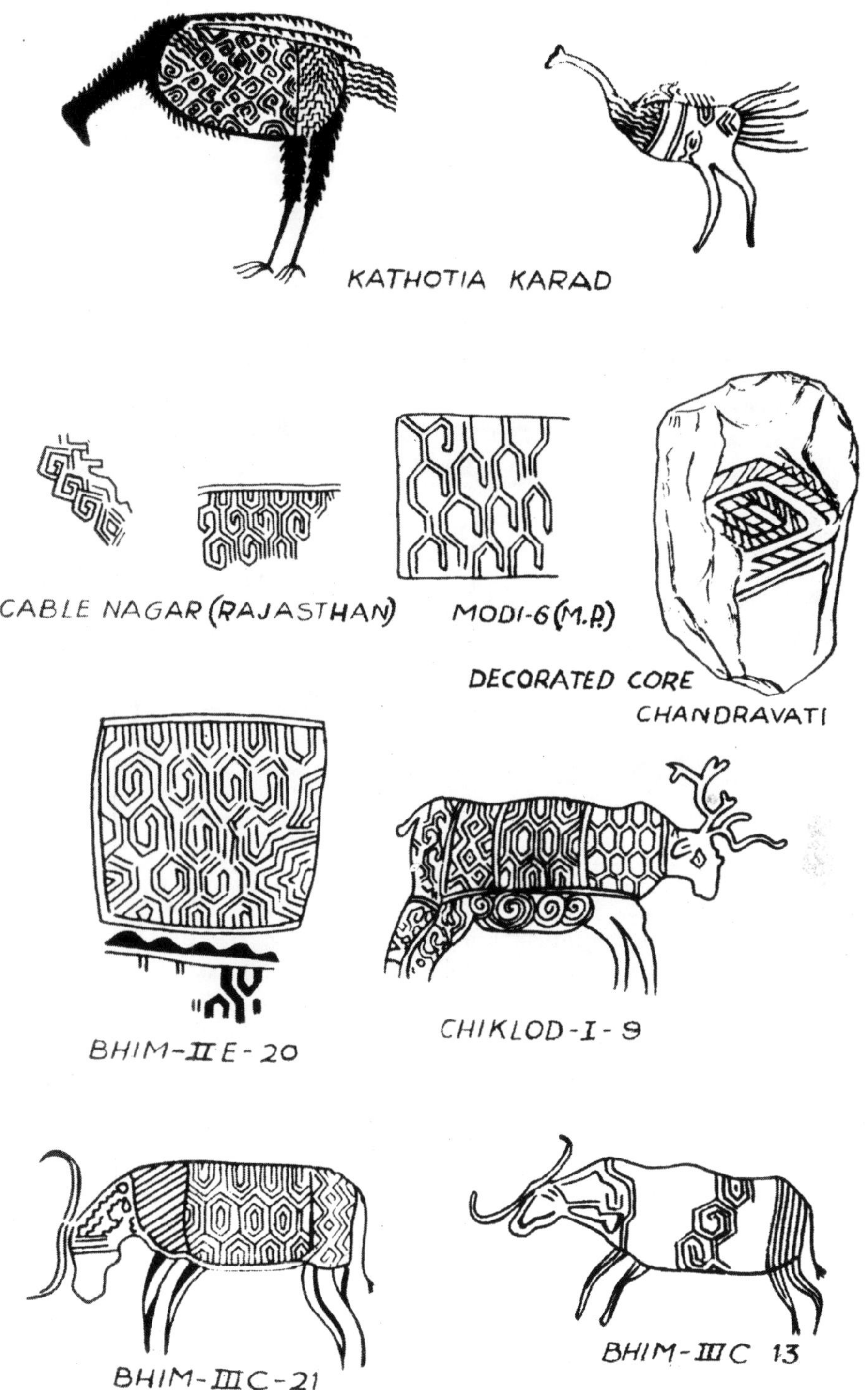

Fig. 16.15: Mesolithic rock paintings identical to the design engraved on the Chandravati core

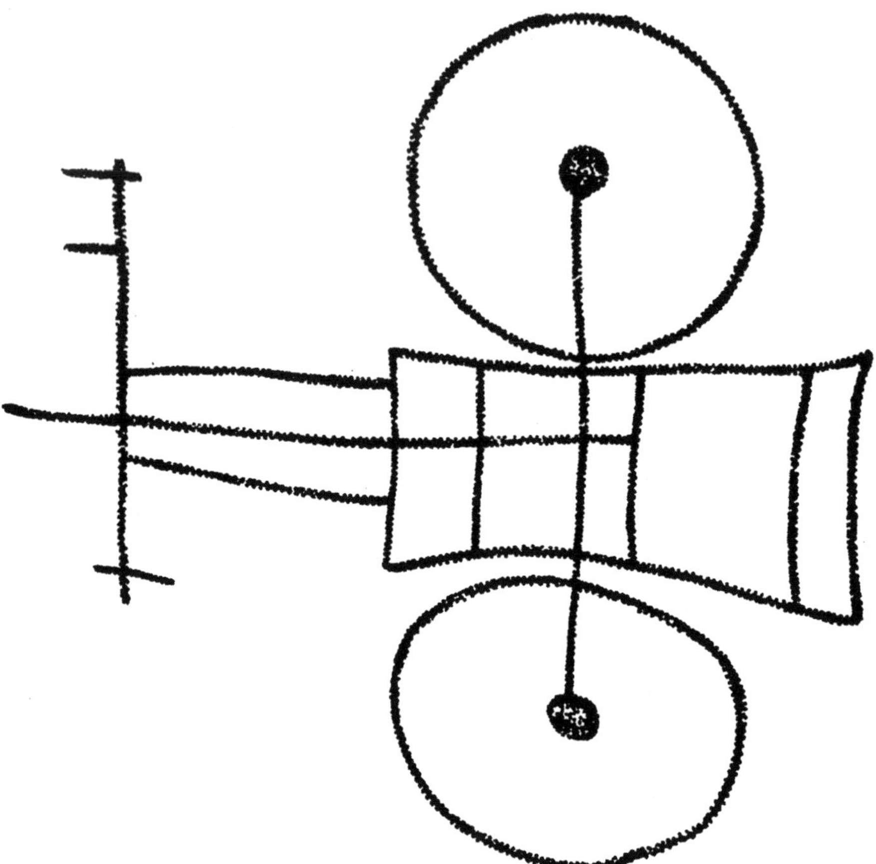

Fig. 16.16: Cart bruising, Kupgallu, Neolithic/Chalcolithic

arrows, the appearance of metal arrowheads, spears and axes heralded a fast-changing technology. The complexity of this available technology is best represented by the depiction of chariots. Several large Chalcolithic pictures show processions, accompanied by acrobats, boxers, load-carriers and musicians. In several scenes, chariots and their crew are prominently depicted, showing an advanced state of social stratification. Agriculture, the economic foundation of this period, is hardly shown in the paintings except those found at Chaturbhujnath Nala and Lakhajoar, where paintings of ploughing fanners are seen. Though hunting was a major theme, the solitary hunter and his dog encounter motionless animals standing in front of them to receive the deadly arrow. All the Chalcolithic pictures of central India represent a man's world; women are depicted very peripherally. A similar tendency is also visible in the Neolithic/Chalcolithic pictures of south India where women appear very subservient to the ithyphallic men. There are also instances of scenes depicting heterosexual intercourse in different postures.

The depiction of bullock carts as a common vehicle for transportation quite frequent. A cart bruising from Kupgallu closely resembles terracotta toy cart models reported from several Harappan sites (Fig. 16.16).. There are several indications that chariots were drawn by horses and they also appear as mounts in other paintings. Compared to this, elephant riders are very few.

The elegant long-horned bull is a special feature of Neolithic/Chalcolithic pictures of south India, taking the position of an icon. One interesting depiction comes from Kupgallu where four typical bulls are arrayed on the periphery of a circle (Fig. 16.17). In other pictures, they are placed on a T-shaped pedestal. Besides this, there are several bruisings of large implements. Compared to the size of the accompanying human figures, they are drawn as excessively large. These engravings of implements are often placed at prominent points on the granite hills, indicating thereby that they were cultic weapons. Likewise, depictions of endless knots recall the design pattern engraved on the copper tablets found at Mohenjo-daro. Of these, several rock art sites are situated in the vicinity of Megalithic burials. Obviously, some of the paintings can be related to burial practices. One such painting shows a dead person within a burial inventory in a stone circle in the Benkal forest.

Fig. 16.17: Long-horned bulls bruising, Kupgallu, Neolithic

In the same spirit, rock engravings found in the Karakoram and the Himalayas, particularly in the upper course of the Indus and its tributaries in Ladakh and Zanskar, show hunters with bows and arrows stalking the ibex, deer and bovids. These compare well with the hunting scene engraved on a stone slab recovered from a rectangular structure belonging to Neolithic phase II at Burzahom showing the hunting of a deer by two-armed persons (Fig. 16.18). Yet another slab found in the same context has an abstract design identified as a tectiform or trap, representing a hut with a thatched, domical roof.

Fig. 16.18: A hunting scene engraved on a stone slab, Burzahom, Neolithic

CONCLUSION

The aforesaid data, which are generally neglected as a source for prehistoric studies, not only reveals the antiquity and development of rock art in India but also enriches our understanding of the way of life of the prehistoric people. The works of art in any medium can tell us about the contemporary flora and fauna, hunting, gathering and other subsistence tactics, and the use of stone and metal implements, besides social and religious aspects which otherwise cannot be expected from any other branch of prehistoric research. All these works of art can be regarded as a product of the influence of their living environment. The reason for their development is still open to speculation but one should not overlook the decorative value of this form of expression. Though many of them are highly abstract, at least a few can be regarded as symbolic, while others are rich in descriptive details. In this context, evidence obtained from the Upper Palaeolithic site of Baghor I (Son valley, Madhya Pradesh) is worth recalling. Fragments of triangular-shaped natural pieces of sandstone with concentric laminations in the form of triangles were found on a slightly raised circular rubble platform. The tribal population of this area, especially the Koli's, worship similar stones as a symbol of the female principle or Mother Goddess (*Mai*).[12] Thus, by analogy with the ethnographic evidence, it has been considered the earliest cult object dating back to 10000 BP.

The motif executed on the Chandravati core and its variations found elsewhere in numerous rock paintings clearly denote some religious connotations in Mesolithic art. Kenoyer suggests that the engraved Chandravati core was prepared for some important socio-ritual activities.[13] The large and uncommon depictions of the wild boar, elephant, rhinoceros and deer, identified as 'deified animals', are also elaborately decorated with such 'spiral' patterns. These pictures are linked with mythological stories prevalent among the tribals.

According to the hypothesis set forth by Marshall, engravings found on ivory, bone, stone and shell of the prehistoric period are not purely meant for decoration but represent the earliest examples of non-verbal symbolic communication. He refers to such remarkable works of art as 'roots of civilization'.[14] Therefore, most of the graphic representations of Indian prehistoric art seem to have served as expressions of metaphysical beliefs. Hence, these are reflections of human culture as a whole which the authors had experienced, observed, believed and lived. However, knowing the weakness of the archaeological interpretation, Kenoyer has rightly pointed out that, traditionally speaking, objects or patterns of objects with no definite or identifiable utilitarian function are symbolic in function by default. The most obvious examples are rock paintings or carved objects. Therefore, one has to be very cautious while interpreting any work related to prehistoric art in any medium.

A comparison between ancient rock pictures and modern house-wall pictures often disclose strong stylistic and thematic analogies. The present-day tribal art of the indigenous population confined to the hilly tracts of the Indian subcontinent shows traditional continuity as a living pictorial tradition if analysed carefully.

[12] J.M. Kenoyer et al. (1983), 'An Upper Palaeolithic Shrine in India', *Antiquity*, 57, pp. 88-95.

[13] J.M. Kenoyer (1987), 'Ritual Artifacts of Prehistoric Hunter-Gatherers in South Asia', (unpublished).

[14] L. Gorelick and A.I. Govinett (1981), 'The Origin and Development of the Ancient Near Eastern Cylinder Seal', *Expedition*, 23, 4, pp. 21-2.

Bibliography

A. PALAEOLITHIC, MESOLITHIC AND NEOLITHIC PHASES

Agarwal, D.P. (1982), *The Archaeology of India*, Curzon Press, London.

—— (1995), 'Technology and Human Evolution', in Datta et al. (eds.), *India at the Dawn of History,* Agam Kala Prakashan, Delhi, pp. 5-8.

Agarwal, D.P. and S. Kusumagar (1974), *Prehistoric Chronology and Radiocarbon Dating in India*, Munshiram Manoharlal, New Delhi.

Agrawal, D.P. et al. (1988), 'Chronology and Significance of the Narmada Formations', *Proceedings of the Indian National Science Academy,* 54 A, pp. 418-24.

Ahmed, N. (1966), 'Stone Age Cultures of the Upper Son Valley', Ph.D. dissertation, Poona University, Poona.

Aiyappan, A. (1945), 'Mesolithic Artifacts from Sawyerpuram in Tinnevelly District, South India', *Spolia Zeylanica*, 24, 2, pp. 145-54.

Alam, D.M.S. (1990), 'Morphometric Study of Palaeolithic Industries of Bhimbetka Central India', Ph.D. dissertation (unpublished), Pune University, Pune.

Ali, A.A. (1991), 'Prehistoric Arunachal' (unpublished), Itanagar.

Allchin, B. (1958), 'Morhana Pahar: A Rediscovery', *Man*, 58, pp. 153-5

—— (1966), *The Stone Tipped Arrow: Late Stone Age Hunters of the Tropical Old World*, Barnes and Noble, London.

Allchin, B. and A. Goudie (1978), 'Climatic Change in the Indian Desert and North-West India during the Late Pleistocene and Early-Holocene', in W.C. Brice (ed.), *The Environmental History of the Near and the Middle East since the Last Ice Age*, Academic Press, London, pp. 307-18.

Allchin, B. and R. Allchin (1982), *The Rise of Civilization in India and Pakistan*, Cambridge University Press, Cambridge.

Allchin, B., A. Goudie and K.T.M. Hegde (1979), *Prehistory and Palaeogeography of the Great Indian Desert,* London: Academic Press.

Allchin, B. et al. (1978), *The Prehistory and Palaeogeography of the Great Indian Desert,* Academic Press, London.

Allchin, F.R. (1960), *Piklihal Excavations*, Government of Andhra Pradesh, Hyderabad.

—— (1961), *Utnur Excavations*, Government of Andhra Pradesh, Hyderabad.

Alur, K.R. (1980), 'Faunal Remains from the Vindhyas and the Ganga Valley', in G.R. Sharma et al. (eds.), *Beginnings of Agriculture*, Abinash Prakashan, Allahabad.

Ansari, Z.D. (1970), 'Pebble Tools from Nittur, Mysore State', *Indian Antiquary*, 4, 1-4, pp. 1-7.

Ansari, Z.D. and R.S. Pappu (1973), 'Stone Age in Kutch, Gujarat', *BDCRI* 31, pp. 150-67.

—— (1975), 'Some Observations on the Excavation of Acheulian Site, Chirki-Nevasa, District Ahmednagar, Maharashtra', *BDCRI* 35, pp. 1-8.

Badam, G.L. (1973), 'Pleistocene Fossil Studies', *Bulletin of the Deccan College Research Institute*, 33, 1-4, pp. 21-40.

—— (1976), 'Society of Vertebrate Paleontology', *News Bulletin*, 108, pp. 39-41.

—— (1977), 'First Record of a Middle Palaeolithic fossil from Gujarat, India', *Journal of the Palaeontological Society of India*, Orlo Memorial Volume, 20, pp. 314-19.

—— (1979), *Pleistocene Fauna of India with Special Reference to the Siwaliks,* Deccan College, Pune.

—— (1984), 'Pleistocene Faunal Succession of India', in R.O. Whyte (ed.), *The Evolution of East Asian Environment*, University of Hong Kong, Hong Kong, pp. 746-75.

—— (1985), 'The Late Quaternary Fauna of Inamgaon', in V.N. Misra and Peter Bellwood (eds.), *Recent Advances in Indo-Pacific Prehistory,* Oxford and IBH, New Delhi, pp. 411-15.

—— (1988), 'Quaternary Faunal Succession of India', *GSI, Special Publication II*, pp. 277-304.

—— (1989), 'Observations on the Fossil Hominid Site at Hathnora, Madhya Pradesh, India', in Ashok Sahni and Rajan Gaur (eds.), *Perspectives in Human Evolution*, Renaissance Publishing House, Delhi, pp. 153-71.

—— (2000), 'Pleistocene Vertebrate Palaeontology in India at the Threshold of the Millennium', *Journal of the Palaeontological Society of India,* 45, pp. 1-4.

—— (2002a), 'Quaternary Vertebrate Palaeontology in India: Fifty Years of Research', in S. Setter and Ravi Korisettar (eds.), *Indian Archaeology in Retrospect*, vol. III, Indian Council of Historical Research, Manohar, New Delhi, pp. 209-46.

—— (2002b), 'A Preliminary Note on the Fossils of Bhanpura Region', *Purakala,* 13, 1-2, pp. 37-8.

Badam, G.L. and C. Grigson (1990), 'A Cranium of Gaur, Bibes gausus (Bovidae, Mammalia) from the Pleistocene of India', *Modern Geology*, 15, pp. 49-88.

Badam, G.L. et al. (1986), 'Evaluation of Fossil Hominid the Maker of Late Acheulian Tools at Hathnora, Madhya Pradesh, India', *Current Science*, 55, 3, pp. 143-5.

—— (1988-9), 'Systematic study of Fossil Bovids from Nittur, District Bellary, Karnataka', *Bulletin of the Deccan College Research Institute*, 47-8, pp. 1-9.

—— (1989), 'A Preliminary Study of Pleistocene Fossils from the Middle Son Valleys, Madhya Pradesh', *ME*, 13, pp. 41-7.

Bahn, P.G. (1996), 'The First Colonisation of Europe', in B.M. Fagan (ed.), *The Oxford Companion to Archaeology*, Oxford University Press, Oxford, pp. 224-5.

Bard, E. and Wallace Smith Broecker (eds.) (1992), *The Last De-Glacialation: The Absolute and Radiocarbon Chronologies,* Springer Verlag Berlin, Heidelberg.

Basak, Bishnupriya (1997), 'Microlithic Sites in the Tarapheni Valley, Midnapur District, West Bengal: A Discussion', *ME,* XXII, 2, pp. 11-28.

Basak, Bishnupriya et al. (1998), 'Late Quaternary Environment, Palaeontology and Culture of Tarafeni Valley, Midnapur District, West Bengal: A Preliminary Study', *Journal of the Geological Society of India*, 51, pp. 731-40.

—— (in press), *Late Quaternary Environment, Palaeontology and Culture of Tarafeni Valley, Midnapur District, West Bengal: A Preliminary Study.*

Bednarik, R.G. (1990), 'Rock Art Tour of India: A Report', *Purakala*, 1, 1, p. 16.

—— (1993), 'Palaeolithic Art in India', *ME*, XVIII, 2, pp. 33-40.

—— (1993), 'Petroglyphs from Central India', *Purakala*, 2, 1, pp. 24-6.

—— (1997), 'Rock Art, Taphonomy and Epistemology', *Purakala*, 8, 1-2, pp. 53-60.

Bednarik, R.G. et al. (1991), 'Petroglyphs from Central India', *Rock Art Research*, 8, 1, pp. 33-5.

Behera, P.K. (1989), 'Archaeology of Sundargarh District with Special Reference to the Brahmani Valley, Orissa', Ph.D. dissertation (unpublished), Banaras Hindu University, Varanasi.

Bhaskaran, M. et al. (1986), 'Geochronology of Palaeolithic Cultures in the Hiran Valley, Saurashtra, India', *Journal of Archaeological Science,* 13, pp. 505-14.

Binford, L.R. (1968), 'Post-Pleistocene Adaptations', in S.R. Binford and L.R. Binford (eds.), *New Perspectives in Archaeology*, Aldine, Chicago, pp. 313-41.

Biswal, S. (2001), 'Palaeohistory of Kamakshanagar Region, District Dhenkanal', Ph.D. dissertation (unpublished), Utkal University, Bhubaneswar.

Black, G.F. (1892), 'Stone Implements from Asia and Africa', *Proceedings of the Society of Antiquaries of Scotland*, 2, pp. 407-12.

Blanford, W.T. (1869), 'On the Geology of the Taptee and Lower Berbudda Valley and Some Adjoining Districts', *Memories of the Geological Survey of India*, 6, 3, pp. 163-282.

—— (1876), 'On the Physical Geography of the Great Indian Desert with Special Reference to the Former Existence of the Sea in the Indus Valley and on the Origin and Mode of Formation of the Sand Hills', *JASB*, 45, 2, pp. 86-103.

Bordes, F. (1961) *Typology du Palaeolithic Ancien et Moyes*, 2 vols., Imprimeries Delmas, Bordeaux.

—— (1968), *The Old Stone Age*, McGraw Hill, New York, p. 59.

—— (1972), *A Tale of Two Caves,* Harper and Row, New York.

Bordes, F. and De Sounneville-Bordes (1970), 'Significance of Variability in Palaeolithic Assemblades', *World Archaeology*, 2, pp. 61-73.

Bose, N.K. and D. Sen (1948), *Excavations in Mayurbhanj*, Calcutta University, Calcutta.

Brandt, S.A. et al. (1983), 'Rockshelters with Paintings on the Top of the Kaimur Escarpment at Ghagharia and an Account of the Excavation and Analysis of the Mesolithic Occupation at the Ghagharia I Shelter', in G.R. Sharma and J.D. Clark (eds.), *The Palaeoenvironments and Prehistory in the Middle Son Valley (Madhya Pradesh, North-Central India)*, Abinash Prakashan, Allahabad, pp. 205-39.

Brock, J. Clutton (1965), *Excavations at Langhnaj 1944-63*, part II: *The Fauna*, Deccan College, Poona.

Brooks, R.R.R. and V.S. Wakankar (1976), *Stone Age Paintings in India*, D.B. Taraporevala and Sons, Bombay.

Brown, Coggin (1914), 'Grooved Hammers from Assam and the Distribution of Similar Forms in Eastern Asia', *BJAS* (New Series) 10, pp. 107-9.

—— (1917), *Catalogue Raisonne of Prehistoric Antiquities in the Indian Museum, Calcutta*, Simla, Government of India.

Brown, J.A. (1889), 'On Some Small, Highly Specialized Forms of Stone Implements Found in Asia, North Africa, and Europe, *RAI*, XVIII, pp. 134-9.

—— (1892), 'On the Continuity of the Palaeolithic and Neolithic Periods', *JRAI*, XXII, pp. 66-98.

Brown, Lt. (1872), 'A Note on the Stone Implements from the Naga Hills', *JRAI*, 1, pp. 61-2.

Calconer, F.H. (1859), *Descriptive Catalogue of the Fossil Remains of Vertabrata from the Siwalik Hills, the Nerbudda, Perim Island, etc., in the Museum of the Asiatic Society of Bengal,* Asiatic Society of Bengal, Calcutta.

Cammiade, L.A. and M.C. Burkitt (1930), 'Fresh Light on the Stone Age in South-East India', *Antiquity*, 4, pp. 327-39.

Carlleyle, A.C.L. (1883), 'Notes on Lately Discovered Sepulchral Mounds, Cairns, Caves, Cave-paintings and Stone Implements', *PASB*, 49, February', Bengal.

Chakrabarti, D.K. (1993), *The Archaeology of Eastern India*, Munshiram Manoharlal, Delhi.

Chakrabarti, D.K., A.K. Nag and S. Chakrabarti (1978-9), 'An Archaeological Reconnaissance in Birbhum', *Puratattva*, 10, pp. 25-32.

Chakrabarti, D.K. and R.K. Chattopadhyay (1984a), 'The Lithic Industries of the Tarafeni and Bhairavbanki Valleys, West Bengal', *The Calcutta Review*, 1 (2), pp. 41-63.

—— (1984b), 'Prehistoric Stratigraphy in West Bengal: The Evidence from Burdwan and Midnapur', *ME*, 8, pp. 39-60.

Chakrabarti, D.K., D.K. Bhattacharya and R.K. Chattopadhyay (1983), 'Lithic Industries of Purulia', *ME*, 7, pp. 131-41.

Chakrabarti, S. (1983), 'Acheulian Culture in Saurashtra in Relation to Pleistocene Stratigraphy: An Overview, *JIAS*, 18, 1, pp. 1-9.

—— (1990), 'The Stone Age Prehistory of Khiching, Orissa', *ME*, XV, 1-2, pp. 13-21.

—— (1995), 'Late Quaternary Stratigraphy and an Upper Acheulian Occupation Site in the Kalubhar Valley, Saurashtra', in S. Wadia et al. (eds.), *Quaternary Environments and Geoarchaeology of India*, Geological Society of India, Bangalore, pp. 277-81.

Chakrabarti, S., D.K. Bhattacharya and D.K. Chakrabarti (1982), 'The Context of Microliths at Paruldanga', *ME*, 61, pp. 150-2.

Chakravarty, D.K. (1931), 'On a Stegodon Molar from the Older Gangetic Alluvium near Benaras', *Quarterly Journal of the Geological Mineralogical and Mettalurgical Society of India,* 3, pp. 115-25.

Chakravarty, K.K. (ed.) (1984), *Rock Art in India*, Arnold Heinemann, New Delhi.

Chakravarty, K.K. and O.P. Misra, (eds.) (1997), *The Bounteous Tree-Treasures in Indian Art and Culture*, Sharada Publishing House, Delhi.

Chakravarty, K.K. and R.G. Bednarik (1997), *Indian Rock Art and Its Global Context*, Motilal Banarsidass and Indira Gandhi Rashtriya Manav Sangrahalaya, Delhi.

Chandramouli, N. (1991), 'Rock Paintings from Budagavi, Anantpur District, Andhra Pradesh, *ME*, XVI, 2, pp. 71-80.

—— (1995), 'Petroglyphs from Naidupalli, Andhra Pradesh', *Purakala*, 6, 1-2, pp. 29-34.

Chattopadhyay, I. and U. Chattopadhyay (1990), 'The Spatial Organization of Mortuary Practices in the Mesolithic Ganga Valley: Implications for Territoriality', in N.C. Ghosh and S. Chakrabarti (eds.), *Adoptations and Other Essays*, Visva-Bharati, Santiniketan, pp. 103-21.

Chaturvedi, S.N. (1985), 'Advance of Vindhyan Neolithic and Chalcolithic Cultures in the Himalayan Terai: Excavations and Explorations in the Sarangpur Region of Uttar Pradesh', *ME*, 9, pp. 101-8.

Childe, Gordon V. (1928), *The Most Ancient East*, Routledge and Kegan Paul, London.

Clark, Desmond and G.S. Khanna (1989), 'The Site of Kunjun II, Middle Son Valley and its Relevance for the Neolithic of Central India', in J.M. Kenoyer (ed), *Old Problems and New Perspectives in the Archaeology of South Asia*, Wisconsin Arch. Reports, vol. 2, University of Wisconsin, Wisconsin, pp. 29-45.

Clark, J.D. (1976), 'The African Origins of Man, the Tool Maker', in G. Isaac and E.R. McCown (eds.), *Human Origins: Louis Leakey and the East African Evidence*, W.A. Benjamin Inc, California, pp. 1-54.

Clark, J.D. and M.A. Williams (1986), 'Palaeoenvironments and Prehistory of North Central India: A Preliminary Report', in J. Jacobson (ed.), *Studies in the Archaeology of India and Pakistan*, Oxford-IBH, New Delhi, pp. 19-41.

Clark, J.D. and R. Dreiman (1983), 'An Occurrence with Small Blade Technology in the Upper Member of the Baghor Formation at the Baghor III Locality', in G.R. Sharma and J.D. Clark (eds.), *The Palaeoenvironments and Prehistory in the Middle Son Valley (Madhya Pradesh, North-Central India*), Abinash Prakashan, Allahabad, pp. 205-39.

Cockburn, J. (1879), 'Notes on the Stone Implements from the Khasi Hill and Banda and Vellor District', *JASB*, pp. 133-43.

—— (1883a), 'On the Recent Existence of *Rhinoceros indicus* in the North-West Provinces, and Description of an Archaic Rock Painting from Mirzapur, Representing the Hunting of an Animal', *JRASB*, 52, pp. 56-64.

—— (1883b), 'A Short Account of the Petrographs in the Caves and Rock Shelters of the Kaimur Range in Mirzapore District', *PASB*, pp. 125-6.

—— (1894), 'On the Flint Implements from the Kosi Ravines of South Mirzapur', *JASB*, 62, pp. 21-37.

—— (1899), 'Cave Drawings in the Kaimur Range, North-West Provinces', *JASB*, 18, pp. 89-97.

Cohen, Mark (1977), *Food Crisis in Prehistory: Overpopulation and the Origins of Agriculture*, Yale University Press, New Haven.

Colbert, E.H. (1942), 'The Geological Succession of the Proboscidea in India', in Osborn, H.F. Proboscidea, *American Museum of Natural History*, 2, pp. 1421-1521.

Cook, J. and H.E. Martingell (1994), *The Carlleyle Collection of Stone Age Artefacts from Central India*, Occasional Papers of the Department of Prehistoric and Romano-British Antiquities, no. 95, British Museum, London.

Cooper, Zarine (1983a), 'CRT-19: A Mesolithic Site in Bastar District (M.P.)', *ME*, VII, pp. 1-30.

—— (1983b), 'Adaptation Patterns During the Late Stone Age in Bastar District, Madhya Pradesh', *Bulletin of the Indo-Pacific Prehistory Association*, 4, pp. 1-9.

—— (1986), 'The Kuruk Fisherman of Bastar District, Central India', *Eastern Anthropologist*, 39, 1, pp. 1-20.

—— (1997), *Prehistory of the Chitrakot Falls, Central India*, Ravish Publishers, Pune.

Corvinus, G. (1981), *A Survey of Pravara River System in Western Maharashtra, India*, vol. 2: *The Excavations of the Acheulian Site of Chirki-on-Pravara, India,* Institute for Urgeschichte, Tubingen.

—— (1981), *A Survey of the Pravara River System in Western Maharashtra, India,* vol. 1, Verlag Archaeologia Venatoria, Tubingen.

Corvinus, G. (1994), 'Prehistoric Occupation Sites in the Dang-Deokhuri Valleys of Western Nepal', *ME*, 19, pp. 75-89.

Corvinus, G. et al. (1972/3), 'Some Observations on the Quaternary of Western Maharashtra (India)', *Quarter*, 23-4, pp. 53-69.

Crooke, W. (1896), *The Tribes and Castes of Northwestern Provinces and Oudh*, vols. I-IV, Government of India, Calcutta.

Dalton, E.T. (1872), *Descriptive Ethnology of Bengal*, Government Press, Calcutta.

Dani, A.H. (1964), 'Sanghao Cave Excavation: The First Season 1963', *Ancient Pakistan*, Bulletin of Department of Archaeology, University of Peshawar, 14, pp. 1-50.

Dasgupta, R.C. (1931), 'Bibliography of Prehistoric Indian Antiquities', *Journal and Proceedings of ASB* (New Series), 27, 1, pp. 1-96.

Dassarma, D.C. and S. Biswas (1976), 'Quaternary Deposits of the Belan-Seoti Valleys, Allahabad District, U.P.', in M.S. Srinivasan (ed.), *Proceedings of the VI Indian Colloquium on Micro-Palaeontology and Stratigraphy*, Varanasi, pp. 33-6.

Dassarma, D.C. et al. (1982), 'Fossil Vertebratres from the Late Quaternary Deposits of Bankura, Burdwan and Purulia Districts, West Bengal', *Palaeontologia Indica*, 44, pp. 1-65.

Datta, A.K. (1991a), 'Upper Palaeolithic Culture in West Bengal: A District Regional Development', in A.K. Datta (ed.), *Studies in Archaeology*, Books and Books, New Delhi, pp. 67-76.

—— (1991b), 'Blade and Blade Tool Association with Upper Palaeolithic and Mesolithic Periods: A Case Study from the "Mid-Kasai" Valley in the Jhargram Sub-division of Midnapur District, West Bengal', *ME*, 16, pp. 23-31.

Datta, A.K. and D.K. Ray (1989), 'Kattara, and Upper Palaeolithic Site in the Mid-Kasai Valley, District Midnapur, West Bengal', in D. Mitra et al. (eds.), *Studies in Art and Archaeology of Bihar/Bengal,* Sri Satguru Publications, Delhi, pp. 309-19.

Datta, A.K., D.K. Roy and B. Samanta (1984), 'Chamargora: The Microlithic Site of

Tarafeni Basin, District Midnapur', in A. Roy et al. (eds.), *The Indian Studies: Essays Presented in Memory of Prof. Niharranjan Roy*, Caxton Publications, New Delhi, pp. 21-30.

Delson, E. (1985), 'Late Pleistocene Human Fossils and Evolutionary Relationship', in E. Delson (ed.), *Ancestors: The Hard Evidence*, Alan R. Liss, Inc., New York, pp. 296-300.

Dennel, R.W. et al. (1988), 'Early Tool-making in Asia: Two Million Year Old Artefacts in Pakistan', *Antiquity*, 62, pp. 98-106.

Devraj, D.V. et al. (1995), 'The Watgal Excavations: An Interim Report', *ME*, 20, 2, pp. 57-74.

Ehrhardt, S. and K.A.R. Kennedy (1965), *Excavations at Langhnaj 1944-63*, part III: *The Human Remains*, Deccan College, Poona.

Enthoven, R.E. (1922), *Tribes and Castes of Bombay*, Government Central Press, Bombay.

Ewer, R.F. (1964), 'Large Carnivora of Bed II', in L.S.B. Leakey (ed.), *Olduvai Gorge, 1951-61*, Cambridge University Press, Cambridge, pp. 21-2.

Falconer, H. (1865), 'Fluviatile Deposits of the Ganges', *Journal of the Geological Society of London*, 21, pp. 311-89.

Foote, R. (1961), *Prehistoric and Protohistoric Antiquities of India*, Leeladevi Publications, Delhi (rpt.).

—— (1876), 'The Geological Features of the South Maratha Country and Adjacent Districts', *Memoirs of the Geological Survey of India*, 12, 1, pp. 1-265.

—— (1914), *The Foote Collection of Prehistoric and Protohistoric Antiquities: Catalogue Raisonne*, Madras Government Museum, Madras.

—— (1915), *The Foote Collection of Prehistoric and Protohistoric Antiquities: Notes on Their Ages and Distribution,* Madras Government Museum, Madras.

—— (1916), *The Foote Collection of Indian Prehistoric and Prehistoric Antiquities, Notes on their Ages and Distributions,* Government Museum, Madras.

Gaillard, C. (1985), 'Acheulian Occupation in Singi Talav, Thar Desert: A Preliminary Report on 1981 Excavation', *BDCRI*, 44, pp. 141-52.

Gaillard, C. and M.L.K. Murty (1988), 'Typo-Technological Comparison of Two Acheulian Assemblages at Renigunta, South India', *ME*, XII, pp. 125-33.

Gaillard, C. et al. (1983-5), 'Acheulian Occupation at Singi Talav in the Thar Desert: A Preliminary Report on 1982 Excavation', *ME,* VII, pp. 112-30.

—— (1986), 'Handaxe Assemblages from Didwana Region, Thar Desert, India: A Metrical Analysis', *PPS,* 52 pp. 189-214.

Ghosh, A. (1993), 'Upper Palaeolithic Blade Technology: A Preliminary Analysis of Cores from Mehtakheri', *ME*, 18, 1, pp 11-19.

Ghosh, A.K. (1970), 'The Palaeolithic Cultures of Singhbhum', *Transactions of the American Philosophical Society*, 60, 1, pp. 1-68.

—— (1974), 'Concept of Chopper/Chopping Tool Complex in India', in V.N. Misra and P. Boliwood (eds.), *Perspectives in Palaeoanthropology*, Firma K.L. Mukhopadhyay, Calcutta, pp. 221-34.

—— (1974), 'Denticulates in India: Examination of a Type Concept', *Journal of Hongkong Archaeological Society*, 5, pp. 47-56.

—— (1985), 'An Attempt to Understand the Acheulian Succession in India from Spatial Distribution', in V.M. Misra and P. Bellwood (eds.), *Recent Advances in Indo-Pacific Prehistory*, Oxford-IBH, New Delhi, pp. 29-34.

Ghosh, M. (1932), 'Rock Paintings and Other Antiquities of Prehistoric and Later Times', *MASI*, 24, Archaeological Survey of India, New Delhi.

Ghosh, R. and G. Ray (1964), 'A Technological Study of the Cleavers of Mayurbhanj', *Man in India*, 44, 1, pp. 50-74.

Goebel, T. and M. Aksenov (1995), 'Accelerator Radiocarbon Dating of the Initial Upper Palaeolithic of SE Siberia', *Antiquity*, 66, pp. 349-57.

Goebel, T. et al. (1993), 'Dating the Middle to Upper Palaeolithic Transition at Kara Bom', *CA*, 34, pp. 452-8.

Gogte, V.D. and M.L.K. Murty (1986), 'ESR Dating of Kurnool Caves, South India', *ME*, 10, pp. 135-40.

Goles, G.G. and J.R. Lukacs (1996), 'Use of Strontium Isotopic Ratios in Studies of Human Palaeodiet: An Example from Alaska and a Proposed Application to the Mesolithic of North India', in G.E. Afanas'ev et al. (eds.), *Bioarchaeology of Mesolithic India: An Integrated Approach,* Colloquium XXXIII of the International Union of Prehistoric and Protohistoric Science, ABACO Edizioni, Forli, pp. 313-19.

Gordon, D.H. (1938), 'The Microlithic Industries of India', *Man*, 38, pp. 91-100.

—— (1950), 'Stone Industries of the Holocene in India and Pakistan', *Ancient India*, 6, pp. 64-90.

—— (1958), *The Prehistoric Background of Indian Culture*, N.M. Tripathi Pvt. Ltd., Bombay.

Gorman, Chester (1971), 'The Hoabinhian and After: Subsistence Pattern in Southeast Asia during the Late Pleistocene and Early Holocene Periods', *World Archaeology*, 2, pp. 300-20.

Goswami, M.C. and T.C. Sharma (1963), 'Further Report on the Investigation into the Prehistoric Archaeology of North Kachar Hills, Assam', *Journal of Gauhati University*, 14, pp. 45-7.

Goswami, M.C. et al. (1972), 'A Typological Study of Some Prehistoric Stone Tools from Kameng District, NEFA', *Journal of Assam Research Society*, 15, pp. 29-32.

Goudeller, L.D. and Ravi Korisettar (1993), 'The First Discovery of Acheulian Bifaces in Goa: Implications for the Archaoelogy of West Coast of India', *ME*, XVIII, 1, pp. 35-42.

Guzder, Statira (1980), *Quaternary Environment and Stone Age Cultures of the Konkan, Coastal Maharashtra, India*, Deccan College, Pune.

Horn, P. et al. (1993), 'K-Ar Fission Track and Thermoluminescene Ages of Quaternary Volcanic Tuffs and Their Bearing on Acheulian Artefacts from Bori, Kukdi Valley, Pune District, India', *Zectschrift der Deutschen Geologischen Gesellschaft*, 114, pp. 326-9.

Hunter, G.R. (1935), 'Interim Report of the Excavation in the Dorothy Deep Shelter No. 1', *Nagpur University Journal*, 1, pp. 28-57.

—— (1936), 'Final Report on the Excavation in the Mahadeo Hills', *Nagpur University Journal*, 2, pp. 127-44.

Hutton, J.H. (1928), 'Prehistory of Assam', *Man in India*, 8, pp. 228-32.

—— (1946), *Caste in India: Its Nature, Function and Origins*, Cambridge University Press, Cambridge.

Ibbetson, Sir Denzil (1916), *Punjab Castes,* Punjab Government, Lahore.

Indian Archaeology: A Review (IAR), various years.

Isaac, N. (1960), 'The Stone Age Cultures of Kurnool', Ph.D. dissertation (unpublished), University of Poona, Poona.

Jacobson, J. (1970), 'Microlithic Contexts in the Vindhyan Hills of Central India', Ph.D. dissertation (unpublished), Columbia University, New York.

—— (1975), 'Early Stone Age Habitation Sites in Eastern Malwa', *Proceedings of the American Philosophical Society*, 119 pp. 280-97.

—— (1976), 'Evidence for Prehistoric Habitation Patterns in Eastern Malwa', in K.A.R. Kennedy and G. Possehl (eds.), *Ecological Backgrounds of South Asian Prehistory*, South Asia occasional papers and theses, Cornell University of New York, pp. 1-63.

—— (1980), 'Investigations of Late Stone Age Adaptations in the Central Vindhyas', *ME*, IV, pp. 65-82.

—— (1985), 'Acheulian Surface Sites in Central India', in V.N. Misra and P. Bellwood (eds.), *Recent Advances in Indo-Pacific Prehistory*, Oxford-IBH, New Delhi, pp. 49-57.

Jarrige, J.F. (1993), 'The Excavations at Mehrgarh: Their Significance for Understanding the Background of the Harappan Civilization', *HCRP*, pp. 79-84.

Jayaswal, V. (1978), *Palaeohistory of India (A Study of Prepared Core Techniques of the Palaeolithic Cultures of India)*, Agam Kala Prãkashan, Delhi.

Jayaswal, Vidula (1972-3), 'A Note on the Influence of Raw Material on the Block-debacking Technique', *Puratattva*, 6, pp. 64-70.

—— (1978), *Palaeohistory of India*, Agam Kala Prakashan, Delhi.

—— (1982), *Chopper-Chopping Component of Palaeolithic in India*, Agam Kala Prakashan, Delhi.

—— (1985), 'The Acheulian Industry of Vadamadurai', in V.N. Misra and P. Bellwood (eds.), *Recent Advances in Indo-Pocific Prehistory*, Oxford-IBH, New Delhi, pp. 73-6.

Jhaldiyal, R. (1997), 'Formation Processes of the Prehistoric Sites in the Hunsgi-Baichbal Basins, Gulbarga District, Karnataka State', Ph.D. dissertation (unpublished), University of Pune, Pune.

Joshi, R.V. (1955), *Pleistocene Studies in the Malaprabha Basin,* Deccan College, Poona.

—— (1964), 'Acheulian Succession in Central India', *Asian Perspectives*, 8, 1, pp. 150-63.

—— (1978), *Stone Age Cultures of Central India: Report on the Excavations of Rock Shelters at Adamgarh, Madhya Pradesh*, Deccan College, Poona.

—— (1994), 'Southern Asia in the Period of Homo Habitis and Homo Erectus', in S.J. de Laed (ed.), *History of Humanity*, vol. 1, *Prehistory and Beginnings of Civilization,* UNESCO, Paris, pp. 77-85.

Joshi, R.V. and A.A. Kshirsagar (1986), *Flourine and Other Chemical Studies of Quaternary Animal of India*, Deccan College, Pune.

Joshi, R.V. and A.R. Marathe (1976), 'Material Analysis of Handaxes from Chirki-on-Pravara, W. Maharashtra, India', *Puratattva*, 8, pp. 3-12.

—— (1985), 'A Comparative Study of Matrical Data on Handaxes and their Cultural Interpretations', in V.N. Misra and P. Bellwood (eds.), *Recent Advances in Indo-Pacific Prehistory,* Oxford-IBH, New Delhi, pp. 77-80.

Joshi, R.V. and B.P. Bopardikar (1972), 'Stone Age Cultures of Konkan', in S.B. Deo (ed.), *Archaeological Congress and Seminar Papers,* Nagpur University, Nagpur, pp. 47-57.

Joshi, R.V. and M.D. Khare (1966), 'Microlith-bearing Deposits of Adamgarh Rockshelters', in D. Sen and A.K. Ghosh (eds.), *Studies in Prehistory: Robert Bruce Foote Memorial Volume*, Firma K.L. Mukhopadhyaya, Calcutta, pp. 90-5.

Joshi, R.V. and R.S. Pappu (1979), 'Bhokar: An Upper Palaeolithic Factory Site from the Central Godavari Basin, Maharashtra', *ME*, 3, pp. 86-91.

Joshi, R.V. et al. (1966), 'Animal Fossil and Early Stone Age Tools from Gangapur on the Godavari River (Nasik District, Maharashtra State)', *Current Science*, 35, 13, p. 344.

—— (1975), 'Early and Middle Palaeolithic Tools, from River Terraces in the Saketi Area, Markand Valley, Himachal Pradesh', *Current Science*, 44, pp. 464-5.

—— (1978), 'Environments and Cultures of Early Man in the Northwest India: A Reappraisal, *JGSI*, 19, 2, pp. 83-6.

—— (1978), 'Fresh Data on the Quaternary Animal Fossils and Stone Age Cultures from the Central Narmada Valley, India', *Asian Perspectives*, 21, 2, pp. 164-81.

—— (1980), 'Excavations at Wadoli-Waghodi: A Middle Palaeolithic Site of the High Level Gravel of the Godavari River', *BDCRI*, 39, pp. 49-89.

—— (1980), 'Late Pleistocene Animal, Fossils and Stone Age Cultures in the Upper Mahanadi Valley, M.P.', *Eastern Anthropologist*, 33, 2, pp. 169-75.

—— (1981), 'Archaeological Studies in the Manjra Valley, Central Godavari Basin', *Bulletin of the Deccan College Research Institute*, 40, pp. 67-98.

Kajale, M.D. (1990), 'Some Initial Observations on Palaeobotanical Evidence for Mesolithic Plant Economy from Excavations at Damdama, Uttar Pradesh', in N.C. Ghosh and S. Chakrabarti (eds.), *Adaptation and Other Essays*, Visva-Bharati, Santiniketan, pp. 98-112.

—— (1996), 'Plant Resources and Diet among the Mesolithic Hunters and Foragers', in S. Afanas'ev. et al. (eds.), *Bioarchaeology of Mesolithic India: An Integrated Approach,* Colloquium XXXIII of the International Union of Prehistoric and Protohistoric Sciences, ABACO Edizioni, Forli, pp. 251-3.

Kajale, M.D. et al. (1976), 'Late Quaternary History of the Ghod Valley, Maharashtra', *Geophytology*, 6, 1, pp, 122-32.

Kale, V.S. and S.N. Rajaguru (1987) 'Late Quarternary Alluvial History of the North-Western Deccan Upland Region', *Nature,* 325, pp. 612-14.

Kale, V.S. et al. (1986), 'Discovery of an Acheulian Site at Bori, District Pune', *BDCRI,* 45, pp. 46-9.

Karve, I. and G.M. Kurulkar (1945a), *A Preliminary Report on the Human Remains Found at Langhnaj in February and December 1944*, Times of India, Bombay.

—— (1945b), *Human Remains Discovered so far*, Times of India, Bombay.

Kaw, R.N. (1979), 'The Neolithic Culture of Kashmir', in D.P. Agrawal and D.K. Chakrabarti (eds.), *Essays in Indian Protohistory*, D.K. Publishers, New Delhi, pp. 219-28.

Kennedy, K.A.R. (1973), 'Biological Anthropology of Prehistoric South Asians', *Anthropologist*, 17, 1-2, pp. 1-13.

—— (1976), 'Biological Anthropology of Prehistoric Populations in South Asia: A Summary of Current Research Efforts', in K.A.R. Kennedy and G.L. Possehl (eds.), *Ecological Backgrounds of South Asian Prehistory*, Cornell University, Ithaca, pp. 166-78.

—— (1980), 'Prehistoric Skeletal Record of Man in South Asia', *Annual Review of Anthropology*, 9, pp. 392-432.

—— (1982), 'Biological Anthropology of Human Skeletal Remains from Bagor: Osteology', in J.R. Lukacs et al. (eds.), *Bagor and Tilwara: Late Mesolithic Cultures of Northwest India*, vol. I: *The Human Skeletal Remains,* Deccan College, Poona, pp. 27-60.

—— (1984a), 'Biological Adaptations and Affinities of Mesolithic South Asia', in J.R. Lukacs (ed.), *The People of South Asia: The Biological Anthropology of India, Pakistan and Nepal*, Plenum Press, New York, pp. 29-57.

—— (1984b), 'Growth, Nutrition and Pathology in Changing', *Palaeopathology at the Origins of Agriculture*, Academic Press, Orlando, pp. 169-92.

—— (1990a), 'Porotic Hyperostosis on Human Remains from Mesolithic Baghai Khor', *BDCRI*, 49, pp. 183-98.

—— (1996), 'Skeletal Adaptations of Mesolithic Hunter-foragers of North India: Mahadaha and Sarai Nahar Rai Compared', in G.E. Afanas'ev et al. (eds.), *Bioarchaeology of Mesolithic India: An Integrated Approach*, Colloquium XXXIII of the International Union of Prehistoric and Protohistoric Sciences, ABACO Edizioni, Forli, pp. 291-300.

—— (1999), 'Palaeoanthropology of South Asia', *Evolutionary Anthropology*, 8, 5, pp. 165-85.

—— (2002), 'Skeletal Biology (Misra and Wakankar Series)', in K.A.R. Kennedy et al., *The Biological Anthropology of Human Skeletal Remains from Bhimbetka, Central India,* Indian Society for Prehistoric and Quaternary Studies, Pune, pp. 75-99.

Kennedy, K.A.R. and P.C. Caldwell (1984), 'South Asian Prehistoric Human Skeletal Remains and Burial Practices', in J.R. Lukacs (ed.), *The People of South Asia*, Plenum, New York, pp. 159-97.

Kennedy, K.A.R. et al. (1981), 'Dental Mutilations from Prehistoric India', *CA*, 22, 3, pp. 285-6.

—— (1986), *Mesolithic Human Remains from the Gangetic Plain: Sarai Nahar Rai,* Cornell University, Ithaca.

—— (1991), 'Principal-components Analysis of Prehistoric South Asian Crania', *American Journal of Physical Anthropology*, 64, pp. 105-18.

—— (1992), *Human Skeletal Remains from Mahadaha: A Gangetic Mesolithic Site*, Cornell University, Ithaca.

—— (2002), *The Biological Anthropology of Human Skeletal Remains from Bhimbetka, Central India,* Indian Society for Prehistoric and Quaternary Studies, Pune.

Kenoyer, J.M. et al. (1983), 'An Upper Palaeolithi Shrine in India', Antiquity, 57, pp. 88-94.

—— (1983), 'Preliminary Report on Excavations at the Late Palaeolithic Occupation Site at Bagor Locality', in Sharma and Clark (eds.), *Palacoenvironments and Prehistory of the Middle Son Valley,* pp. 117-48.

Khatri, A.P. (1958), 'Stone Age Cultures of Malwa', Ph.D. dissertation (unpublished), Poona University, Poona.

—— (1962), 'Mahadevian: An Oldowan Pebble Culture in India', *Asian Perspectives*, 6, pp. 186-96.

Khilar, B.K. (2001), 'Paleohistory of Parjang, District Dhenkanal', Ph.D. dissertation (unpublished), Utkal University, Bhubaneswar.

Korisettar, R. (1979), 'Prehistory and Geomorphology of the Middle Krishna Karnataka', Ph.D. dissertation (unpublished), University of Poona, Pune.

—— (1985), 'The Acheulian Site of Almatti, Karnataka', in V.N. Misra and P. Bellwood (eds.), *Recent Advances in Indo-Pacific Prehistory,* Oxford-IBH, New Delhi, pp. 65-8.

—— (1994), 'Quaternary Alluvial Stratigraphy and Sedimentation in the Upland Deccan Region, Western India', *ME*, XIX, 1-2, pp. 29-42.

Korisetter, R. et al. (1976-7), 'On the Occurrence of Plant Fossils along with Middle Palaeolithic Tools at Wajjal, District Gulbarga, Karnataka', *Bulletin of the Deccan College Research Institute,* 36, 1-4, pp. 62-5.

—— (1989a), 'Age of the Bori Volcanic Ash and Lower Palaeolithic Culture of the Kukdi Valley, Maharashtra', *BDCRI,* 47-8, pp. 135-7.

—— (1989b), 'Discovery of a Tephra Bed in the Quaternary Alluvial Sediments of Pune District (Maharashtra), Peninsular India', *Current Science,* 58, 10, pp. 564-7.

Krishnaswami, V.D. (1938), 'Environmental and Cultural Changes of the Prehistoric Man near Madras', *Journal of Madras Geographical Association*, 13, pp. 58-90.

—— (1962), 'The Neolithic Pattern of India', *Ancient India*, 16, pp. 25-64.

Krishnaswami, V.D. and K.V. Soundar Rajan (1951), 'The Lithic Tool-Industries of the Singrauli Basin, District Mirzapur', *AI*, 7, pp. 40-65.

Kshirsagar, Anupama and G.L. Badam (1990), 'Biochronology and Fluorine Analysis of Some Pleistocene Fossils from Central and Western India', *Bulletin of the Deccan College Research Institute,* 49, pp. 199-211.

Kumar, Arun (1985), 'Quaternary Studies of the Upper Godavari Valley: A Study in Environmental Archaeology', Ph.D. dissertation (unpublished), University of Poona, Pune.

—— (1989), 'Almetrical Analysis of Handaxes and Cleavers from the Acheulian Site at Gangapur, Nasik District, Maharashtra', *ME* XIII, pp. 49-64.

Kumar, Giriraj (1981a), 'Aesthetic Sense in the Prehistoric Man', in M.D. Khare (ed.), *Malwa Through the Ages*, Directorate of Archaeology and Museums, Government of Madhya Pradesh, Bhopal.

—— (1981b), 'Painted Rockshelters from Rajasthan', in V.S. Srivastava (ed.), *Cultural Contours of India: Dr. Satya Prakash Felicitation Volume*, Abhinav, New Delhi, pp. 277-85.

—— (1983), 'Ostrich Eggshells and Early Rock Paintings in India', in K.K. Chakravarty (ed.), *Indian Rock Art*, Arnold Heinemann, New Delhi, pp. 120-8.

—— (1989), 'A Unique Ritualistic Dance Composition in Indian Rock Art', *Pictogram*, 2, 3, pp. 7-8.

—— (1990), 'Ostrich Egg and the Prehistoric Man: Some More Evidence from Chambal Valley', in N.C. Ghosh and S. Chakravarti (eds.), *Adaptations and Other Essays*, Visva-Bharati, Santiniketan, pp. 69-74.

—— (1992), 'Rock Art of Upper Chambal Valley: Some Observations', *Purakala*, 3, 1-2, pp. 56-67.

—— (1995), 'Rock Art of Chambal Valley and Aravalli Hills: A Saga of the Achievements of our Ancestors', *Researcher*, 16-17, pp. 5-10.

—— (1996), 'Review of Rock Art Studies: The Post-Stylistic Era or Where Do We Go From Here?', *Purakala*, 7, 1-2, pp. 63-6.

Kumar, Giriraj and A.K. Sharma (1993), 'Sigiri-Agra Kshetra ki Shaila Chitrakala ki Kshetriya Visheshtayen evam inka Sanskritik Mahattva' (Hindi), *Purakala Souvenir*, pp. 27-8.

Kumar, Giriraj and Murarilal Sharma (1995), 'Petroglyph Sites in Kalapahar and Ganesh Hill: Documentation and Observations', *Purakala*, 6, 1-2, pp. 56-9.

Kumar, Giriraj et al. (1990), 'Archaeological Discoveries and a Study of Late Pleistocene Ostrich Eggshells and Eggshell Objects in India', *ME*, XV, 1, pp. 29-40.

—— (1992), 'Rock Art of Upper Chambal Valley: Rock Art and Rock Art Sites', *Purakala*, 3, 1-2, pp. 13-55.

Kurten, B. (1968), *Pleistocene Mammals of Europe*, Weidenfeld and Nicholson, London.

Lal, B.B. (1953), 'Pretohistoric Investigations', *Ancient India*, 9, pp. 80-102.

—— (1956), 'Palaeoliths from the Beas and Banganga Valleys, Punjab', *AI*, 12, pp. 58-92.

—— (1958), 'Birbhanpur, A Microlithic Site in the Damodar Valley, West Bengal', *Ancient India*, 14, pp. 4-48.

Lee, R.B. (1969), 'Kung Bushman Subsistence: An Input-Output Analysis', in A.P. Vaidya (ed.), *Environment and Culture Behaviour*, Natural History Press, New York, pp. 47-79.

Lele, V.S. (1989), 'Quaternary Formations in the Bhadar Valley', *BDCRI,* 47-8, pp. 165-206.

Leshnik, L.S. (1968), 'Prehistoric Exploration in North Gujurat and Parts of Rajasthan', *EW* 18, 3-4, pp. 295-310.

—— (1974), 'More Microliths from Gujarat and Some Thoughts on Langhraj', in A. Ghosh (ed.), *Perspectives in Palaeoanthropology*, Firma K.L. Mukhopadhyaya, Calcutta, pp. 249-58.

Lukacs, J.R. (1982), 'Biological Anthropology of Human Skeletal from Bagor: Dentition', in J.R. Lukacs et al. (eds.), *Bagor and Tilwara: Late Mesolithic Cultures of North-West India*, vol. 1: *The Human Skeletal Remains*, Deccan College, Poona, pp. 61-94.

—— (1985), 'Tooth Size Variation in Prehistoric India', *American Anthropologist*, 87, 4, pp. 811-25.

—— (1989), 'Biological Affinities from Dental Morphology from Neolithic Mehrgarh', in J.M. Kenoyer (ed), *OPNP*, Wisconsin Arch. Reports, Madison, pp. 75-88.

—— (1990), 'On Hunter-gatherers and Their Neighbours in Prehistoric India: Contact and Pathology', *CA*, 31, 2, pp. 183-6.

—— (1992), 'Mesolithic Hunters and Foragers of the Gangetic Plain: A Summary of Current Research in Dental Anthropology', *Dental Anthropology Newsletter*, 6, 3, pp. 3-8.

—— (2002), 'Skeletal Biology (Haas Series)', in *The Biological Anthropology of Human Skeletal Remains from Bhimbetka, Central India*, Indian Society for Prehistoric and Quaternary Studies, Pune.

Lukacs, J.R. and J.N. Pal (1992), 'Dental Anthropology of the Mesolithic Hunter-gatherers: A Preliminary Report', *ME*, XVII, 2, pp. 45-56.

—— (1993), 'Mesolithic Subsistence in North India: Inferences from Dental Attributes', *CA*, 34, 5, pp. 745-65.

Lukacs, J.R. and K.A.R. Kennedy (2002), 'The Place of the Bhimbetka Skeletal Record in South Asian Palaeoanthropology', in K.A.R. Kennedy et al. (eds.), *The Biological Anthropology of Human Skeletal Remains from Bhimbetka, Central India,* Indian Society for Prehistoric and Quaternary Studies, Pune.

Lukacs, J.R. and V.D. Misra (1997), 'The People of Lekhahia: A Bioarchaeological Analysis of Late Mesolithic Hunter-foragers of North India', in R. Allchin and B. Allchin (eds.), *SAA*, Oxford and IBH, New Delhi, pp. 873-89.

Lukacs, J.R. et al. (1982), *Bagor and Tilwara: Late Mesolithic Cultures of Northwest India*, vol. 1: *The Human Skeletal Remains*, Deccan College, Poona.

—— (1996), 'Chronology and Diet in Mesolithic North India: A Preliminary Report of New AMS C14 dates, §13C Isotope Values, and Their Significance', in G.E. Afanas'ev et al. (eds.), *Bioarchaeology of Mesolithic India: An Integrated Approach*, Colloquium XXXIII of the International Union of Prehistoric and Protohistoric Sciences, ABACO Edizioni, Forli, pp. 301-11.

Lumley, M.A. De and A. Sonakia (1985a), 'Premieve Decauverted' un Homo erectus Sur be continent Indian Hathnora, dans Moyenne Valle de la Narmada', *L'Anthropologic*, 89, pp. 13-61.

—— (1985b), 'Contexte Stratigraphique at Archeologique de l Homme de la Narmada, Hathnora, Madhya Pradesh, Inde', *L'Anthropologic*, 89, pp. 3-12.

Lydekker, R. (1886), 'The Fauna of Kurnool Caves', *Palaeontologia Indica*, Ser. C, 4, 2, pp. 23-58.

Lyer, L.K. and Anantha Krishna (1935), *The Mysore Tribes and Castes*, The Mysore University Press, Mysore.

Malhotra, K.C. et al. (1983), 'Hunting Strategies among Three Non-pastoral Nomadic Groups of Maharashtra', *Man in India*, 63, 1, pp. 21-39.

Malik, S.C. (1966), 'The Late Stone Age Industries from Excavated Sites in Gujarat, India', *Artibus Asiae*, XXVIII, pp. 167-7.

Mandal, D. (1980), 'Neolithic Cultures of the Vindhyas: Excavations at Mahagara in Belan Valley' (unpublished).

——, 'A Note on the Radiocarbon Dates from the Middle Son Valley', in G.R. Sharma and J.D. Clark (eds.) *Palaeoenvironments and Prehistory of the Middle Son Valley*, Abinash Prakashan, Allahabad, pp. 284-9.

Mandelbaum, D.G. (1972), *Society in India*, Popular Prakashan, Bombay.

Marathe, A.R. (1981), 'Middle Pleistocene Lithic Tools in Saurashtra, Western India', *BDCRI*, 40, pp. 110-22.

—— (1981), *Geoarchaeology of the Hiran Valley, Saurashtra, India*, Deccan College, Pune.

Marathe, A.R. and S.N. Rajaguru (1977), 'The Chronology of the Early Man in Saurashtra', *Recent Researchas in Geology*, 9, pp. 133-44.

Marks, A.E. (1983), 'The Middle to Upper Palaeolithic Transition in the Levant' a F. Wendorf and A.E. Close (eds.), in *Advances in World Archaeology*, Academic Press, New York, pp. 51-97.

Mathpal, Y. (1984), 'Newly Discovered Rock Paintings in the Central India showing Honey Collection', *Deewar*, 65, 3, pp. 121-6.

Mathur, S.M. (1985), 'Notice of New Microlithic Sites from the Southern Mirzapur District, U.P.', *Science and Culture*, 20, pp. 446-7.

Mathur, U.B. (1969), *Ethnographic Atlas of Rajasthan (with Special Reference to Scheduled Castes and Scheduled Tribes*, Government of India, Delhi.

Medicott, H.B. (1873), 'Note on a Celt Mound by Hackett in the Ossiferous Deposits of the Narbada Valley (Plicene of Falconer): On the Age of the Deposits and on the Associated Shells', *Records of the Geological Survey of India*, 6, 3, pp. 49-54.

Mesurier, Le (1861), *Proceedings of Asiatic Society, Bengal*, 30, 1, pp. 81-5.

Mishra, Sheila et al. (1995), 'Earliest Acheulian Industry from Peninsular India', *CA*, 36, pp. 847-51.

—— (1999), 'Late Pleistocene Aridity in the Narmada Basin', in M.P. Tiwari and D.M. Mahabey (eds.), *Quaternary of India*, Gondwana Geological Society, Nagpur, p. 338.

—— (2001), 'Quaternary Fluvial Geomorphology in Western India', *National Symposium on Role of Earth Sciences in Integrated Development and Related Societal Issues, Geological Survey of India Sp. Pub*, 65, 1, pp. ixxv-ixxxv.

Mishra, S. and S.N. Rajaguru (2001), 'Late Quaternary Palaeoclimates of Western India: A Geoarchaeological Approach', *Mausam*, 52, 1, pp. 286-96.

Mishra, S. et al. (1988), 'Relative Dating of the Quaternary Record from Upland Western Maharashtra', M.P. Patel and N. Desai (eds.), *National Seminar on Recent Quaternary Studies in India*, M.S. University, Baroda, pp. 267-8.

—— (1995), 'Chronology of the Indian Stone Age: Impact of Recent Absolute and Relative Dating Attempts', 20, 2, pp. 11-16.

—— (1998), 'Climatic Change during the Pleistocene/Holocene Transition in Upland Western Maharashtra, Western India', in A.S. Issar and N. Brown (eds.), *Water, Environment and Society in Times of Climatic Change*, Kluwer Academic Publishers, Netherlands, pp. 323-33.

—— (1999), 'Studies in the Geomorphology, Quaternary Palaeoenvironments and Archaeology of the Vel River, a Tributary of the Bhima in Western Maharashtra', *ME*, XXIV, 1, pp. 159-66.

Mishra, S.K. (1987-8), 'Stone Age Antiquities of Joshipur, Orissa: A Survey', *Man in Society*, 3, pp. 81-8.

—— (1990), 'Stone Age Remains and Palaeohuman Activities in the Burhabalang and Chipat River Valleys of Orissa', *Man in Society*, 4, pp. 21-33.

Mishra, Sheila (1985), 'Early Man and Environments in Western Madhya Pradesh', Ph.D. thesis (unpublished), Poona University.

—— (1986), 'Archaeological Assemblages and Basalt Weathering: A Re-evaluation of the Nevasian', *ME, X*, pp. 91-6.

—— (1995), 'Chronology of the Indian Stone Age: The Impact of the Recent Absolute and Relative Dating Attempts', *ME,* XX, 2, pp. 11-16.

Misra, V.D. (1977), *Some Aspects of Indian Archaeology*, Prabhat Prakashan, Allahabad.

Misra, V.D. (1996), 'History and Context of Mesolithic Research at Allahabad University, Allahabad, India', in G.E. Afanas'ev et al. (eds.), *Bioarchaeology of Mesolithic India: An Integrated Approach,* Colloquium XXXIII of the International Union of Prehistoric and Protohistoric Science, ABACO Edizioni, Forli, pp. 245-50.

Misra, V.D. et al. (1983), 'An Upper Palaeolithic Collection from Rampur', in G.R. Sharma and J.D. Clark (eds.), *Palaeoenvironments and Prehistory in the Middle Son Valley,* pp. 143-60.

Misra, V.N. (1961), 'The Stone Age Cultures of Rajputana', Ph.D. dissertation (unpublished) University of Poona, Poona.

—— (1961a), 'Palaeolithic Culture of Western Rajputana', *BDCRI*, 21, pp. 85-186.

—— (1961b) 'Palaeolithic Industry of the Banas, Eastern Rajputana', *JAS*, 34-5, pp. 138-60.

—— (1962), 'Problems of Terminology in Indian Prehistory', *Eastern Anthropologist*, 15(2), pp. 113-24.

—— (1965), 'Mesolithic Phase in the Prehistory of India', in V.N. Misra and M.S. Mate (eds.), *Indian Prehistory 1964*, Deccan College, Poona, pp. 57-85.

—— (1966), 'Stone Age Research in Rajasthan: A Review', in D. Sen and A.K. Ghosh (eds.), *Studies in Prehistory: Robert Bruce Foote Memorial Volume*, Firma K.L. Mukhopadhyay, Calcutta.

—— (1967), *Pre- and Proto-History of the Berach Basin, South Rajasthan,* Deccan College, Poona.

—— (1968), 'Late Stone Age in Rajasthan', *Proceedings of the Rajasthan History Congress,* First Session, Jaipur, pp. 16-22.

—— (1970a), 'Cultural Significance of Three Copper Arrowheads from Rajasthan, India', *JNES*, 29, 4, pp. 221-32.

—— (1970b), 'Evidence for a New Chalcolithic Culture in Rajasthan', *Indian Antiquary* (Third Series), IV, 1-4, pp. 85-95.

—— (1971a), 'Two Microlithic Sites in Rajasthan: A Preliminary Investigation', *Eastern Anthropologist*, XXIV, pp. 237-88.

—— (1971b), 'Two Late Mesolithic Settlements in Rajasthan: A Brief Review of Investigations', *Poona University Journal* (Humanities), 35, pp. 59-79.

—— (1972), 'Burials from Prehistoric Bagor, Rajasthan', in S.B. Deo (ed.), *Archaeological Congress and Seminar Papers*, Nagpur University, Nagpur, pp. 58-65.

—— (1973a), 'Bagor: A Late Mesolithic Settlement in North-west India', *World Archaeology*, 5, 1, pp. 92-110.

—— (1973b), 'Problems of Palaeoecology, Palaeoclimate and Chronology of the Microlithic Cultures of Western India', in D.P. Agrawal and A. Ghosh (eds.), *Radiocarbon and Indian Archaeology*, Tata Institute of Fundamental Research, Bombay, pp. 58-72.

—— (1973c), 'New Light on the Mesolithic Period in India from Excavations at Bagor in Rajasthan', *The Researcher*, XII-XIII, pp. 1-14.

—— (1973d), 'A New Prehistoric Ceramic from Rajasthan', *EW*, 23, 3-4, pp. 295-305.

—— (1974), 'Archaeological and Ethnographic Evidence for the Hafting and use of Microliths and Related Tools', *Puratattva*, 7, pp. 3-12.

—— (1976a), 'Ecological Adaptations during the Terminal Stone Age in Western and Central Indio', in K.A.R. Kennedy and G.L. Possehl (eds.), *Ecological Backgrounds of South Asian Prehistory*, Cornell University, Ithaca, pp. 28-51.

—— (1976b), 'Evidence of Culture Contact between Terminal Stone Age Hunter-gatherers and Contemporary Farmers', in U.V. Singh (ed.), *Archaeological Congress and Seminar: 1972*, Kurukshetra University, Kurukshetra, pp. 151-61.

—— (1976c), 'Prehistory and Palaeoenvironment in Rajasthan', in D.P. Agrawal and B.M. Pande (eds.), *Archaeology and Palaeoenvironment in Western India*, Concept, New Delhi, pp. 31-54.

—— (1978), 'The Acheulian Industry of Rock Shelter III, F-23 at Bhimbetka, Central India', *Australian Archaeology*, 8, pp. 63-106.

—— (1982), 'Bagor: The Archaeological Setting', in J.R. Lukacs et al. (eds.), *Bagor and Tilwana: Late Mesolithic Cultures of North-west India*, vol. 1: *The Human Skeletal Remains*, Deccan College, Poona, pp. 9-26.

—— (1982), 'Evolution of the Blade Element in the Stone Industries of the Rock Shelter III, F-23, Bhimbetka', in R.K. Sharma (ed.), *Indian Archaeology: New Perspectives,* Agam Kala Prakashan, New Delhi, pp. 7-13.

—— (1985), 'Microlithic Industries in India', in V.N. Misra and P. Bellwood (eds.), *Recent Advances in Indo-Pacific Prehistory*, Oxford-IBH, New Delhi, pp. 111-22.

—— (1985), 'The Acheulian Succession at Bhimbetka, Central India', in V.N. Misra and P. Bellwood (eds.), *Recent Advances in Indo-Pacific Prehistory,* Oxford-IBH, New Delhi, pp. 35-48.

—— (1987), 'Middle Pleistocene Adaptations in India', in Olga Soffer (ed.), *The Pleistocene Old World: Regional Perspectives*, Plenum Press, New York, pp. 99-119.

—— (1989a), 'Stone Age India: An Ecological Perspective', *ME*, XIV, 1, pp. 17-64.

—— (1989b), 'Mesolithic Cultures', in A. Ghosh (ed.), *An Encyclopaedia of Indian Archaeology*, vol. 1, Munshiram Manoharlal, New Delhi, pp. 37-43.

—— (1989c), 'Bagor', in A. Ghosh (ed.), *An Encyclopaedia of Indian Archaeology*, vol. 2, Munshiram Manoharlal, New Delhi, pp. 35-7.

—— (1989d), 'Bhimbetka', in A. Ghosh (eds.), *An Encylopedia of Indian Archaeology*, Munshiram Manoharlal, New Delhi, pp. 69-73.

—— (1990), 'The Van Vagris: "Lost" Hunters of the Thar Desert, Rajasthan', *ME*, pp. 89-108.

—— (1995), 'Evolution of Environment and Culture in the Rajasthan Desert during the Late Quaternary', in E. Johnson (ed.), *Ancient Peoples and Landscapes*, Texas Tech University Press, Lubbock, Texas, pp. 77-103.

—— (1995), 'Geoarchaeology of the Thar Desert, Northwest India', in S. Wadia, R. Korisettar and V.S. Kale (eds.), *Quaternary Environments and Geoarchaeology of India,* Geological Society of India, Bangalore, pp. 210-24.

—— (1996), 'Mesolithic India: History and Current Status of Research', in G.E. Afanas'ev et al. (eds.), *Bioarchaeology of Misolithic India: An Integrated Approach*, Collaquium XXXIII of thc International Union of Prehistoric and Protohistoric Sciences, ABACO, Edizioni, Forli, pp. 321-8.

—— (2001), 'Prehistoric Human Colonization of India', *Journal of Bioscience*, 26, 4, Supplement Volume, pp. 491-531.

—— (2002), 'Excavations of Human Burials', in K.A.R. Kennedy et al. (eds.), *The Biological Anthropology of Human Skeletal Remains from Bhimbetka, Central India*, Indian Society for Prehistoric and Quaternary Studies, Pune, pp. 7-25.

Misra, V.N. and Malti Nagar (1976), 'Prehistoric Background of Rajasthan', in R. Subrahmanyam and N. Rameshan (eds.), *Somasekhara Sarma Commemoration Volume* Government of Andhra Pradesh, Hyderabad, pp. 345-59.

—— (1981), 'The Microlithic Industry of Bagor, Rajasthan', in V.S. Srivastava (ed.), *Cultural Countries of India: Dr. Satya Prakash Felicitation Volume*, Abhinav, New Delhi, pp. 6-11.

—— (1997), 'From Tribe to Caste: An Ethnoarchaeological Perspective', in Dev Nathan (ed.), *From Tribe to Caste*, Indian Institute of Advanced Studies, Shimla, pp. 136-66.

Misra, V.N. and S.N. Rajaguru (1986), 'Environment et Culture de l'Homme Prehistoric dans le desert du Thar, Rajasthan, Inde', *L'Anthropologic*, 90, pp. 407-37.

Misra, V.N. and Suman Pandya (1989), 'Mesolithic Occupations Around Dhansura, Sabarkantha District, Gujarat: A Preliminary Study', *ME*, XIV, 1, pp. 123-7.

Misra, V.N. and Y. Mathpal (1979), 'Rock Art of Bhimbetka Region, Central India', *ME*, III, pp. 27-33.

Misra, V.N. et al. (1977), *Bhimbetka: Prehistoric Man and His Art in Central India*, Exhibition Souvenir, Salak Press, Poona.

—— (1980), 'Prehistory and Palaeo-environments of Jayal, Western Rajasthan', *ME* IV, pp. 9-31.

—— (1982), 'Acheullian Occupation and Evolving Landscape around Didwana in the Thar Desert, India', *ME*, VI, pp. 72-86.

—— (1988), 'Late Middle Pleistocene Environment of Acheulian Culture around Didwana, Rajasthan.

Mittre, Vishnu and Arun Sharma (1982), 'Neolithic-Chalcolithic Food Economy of Eastern Uttar Pradesh' (unpublished).

Mohanty, P. (1988-9), 'The Mesolithic Cultures of Keonjhar District, Orissa with Special Reference to the Heavy-duty Tool Component: A Functional Interpretation', *BDCRI* 47-8, pp. 227-37.

—— (1989), 'Mesolithic Settlement System of the Keonjhar District, Orissa', Ph.D. dissertation (unpublished), University of Poona, Poona.

—— (1992), 'Stone Age Research in Orissa: An Overview', *Man in India*, 72, pp. 207-32.

—— (1993), 'Mesolithic Hunter-gatherers of Keonjhar District, Orissa', *Asian Perspectives*, 32, pp. 85-104.

Mohanty, P. and B. Tripathy (1998) 'The Prehistoric, Protohistoric and the Early Historic Cultures of Orissa', *Pragdhara*, pp. 69-98.

Mohanty, P. et al. (1997), 'Stone Age Cultures of Mayurbhanj District, Orissa, *Man in India*, 77, 2-3, pp. 159-77.

Mohapatra, G.C. (1962), *The Stone Age Cultures of Orissa*, Deccan College, Poona.

—— (1966), 'Preliminary Report of the Exploration and Excavation of Stone Age Sites in Punjab', *BDCRI*, 25, pp. 221-37.

—— (1974), 'Lithic Industries of Himachal Pradesh', in A.K. Ghosh (ed.), *Perspectives in Palaeo-anthropology*, Firma K.L. Mukhopadhyay, Calcutta, pp. 199-212.

—— (1975), 'Acheulia Element in the Soan Culture Area', *Journal of the Archaeological Society of Nippon*, 80, 4, pp. 4-18.

—— (1981), 'Acheulian Discoveries in the Siwalik Frantal Rangi', *CA*, 22, 4, pp. 433-5.

—— (1982), 'Acheulian Distribution in the Siwalik of Punjab', in R.K. Sharma (eds.), *Indian Archaeology: New Perspectives*, Agam Kala Prakashan, Delhi, pp. 28-37.

—— (1985), 'The Lower Palaeolithic in India', in K.N. Dikshit (ed.), *Archaeological Perspectives of India Since Independence*, Books and Books, New Delhi, pp. 1-8.

—— (1990), 'Soanian-Acheulian Relationship', *BDCRI*, 49, pp. 251-60.

—— (1997), 'Reidentification of Acheulian Element in the Western Sub-Himalayan Lithic Complex in the Light of New Discoveries', in V.D. Misra and J.N. Pal (eds.), *Indian Prehistory: 1980*, University of Allahabad, Allahabad, pp. 43-50.

Movius, H.L. (Jr.) (1948b), 'The Lower Palaeolithic Cultures of Southern and Eastern Asia', *Transactions of the American Philosophical Society* (New Series), part IV, pp. 330-420.

—— (1957), 'Pebble Tool Terminology in India and Pakistan', *Man in India*, 37, 2, pp. 149-56.

Murty, M.L.K. (1966) 'Stone Age Cultures of Chittoor District', Ph.D. dissertation (unpublished), University of Poona, Poona.

—— (1968), 'Blade and Burin Industries near Ranigunta on the South East Coast of India', *PPS*, 35, pp. 83-101.

—— (1970), 'Blade and Burin and Late Stone Age Industries around Renigunta', *Indian Antiquary*, 1, pp. 106-27.

—— (1974), 'A Late Pleistocene Cave Site in Southern India', *Proceedings of the American Philosophical* Society 118, pp. 196-230.

—— (1975), 'Late Pleistocene Fauna of Kurnool Caves, South India', in A.T. Clason, (ed), *Archaeozoological Studies*, North Holland Publishing Company, Amsterdam and New York, pp. 132-8.

—— (1979), 'Recent Research on the Upper Palaeolithic Phase in India', *Journal of Field Archaeology*, 6, pp. 321-30.

—— (1981), 'Hunter-gatherer Ecosystems and Archaeological Patterns of Subsistence Behaviour on the South-east Coast of India: An Ethnographic Model', *World Archaeology*, 13, 1, pp. 47-58.

—— (1985), 'The Uses of Plant Foods by Some Hunter-Gatherer Communities in Andhra Pradesh', in V.N. Misra and P. Bellwood (eds.), *Recent Advances in Indo-Pacific Prehistory,* Oxford-IBH, New Delhi, pp. 329-36.

Murty, M.L.K. and K.S.V. Nambi (1983), 'An Upper Palaeolithic Fireplace in Kurnool Caves, South India, *Bulletin of the Deccan College Research Institute*, 42, pp. 110-16.

Nagar, M. (1983), 'Ethnoarchaeology of the Bhimbetka Region', *ME*, VII, pp. 61-9.

—— (1985), 'The Use of Wild Food and Plant Foods by Aboriginal Communities in Central India', in V.N. Misra and P. Bellwood (eds.), *Recent Advances in Indo-Pacific Prehistory*, Oxford-IBH, New Delhi, pp. 337-42.

Nagar, M. and V.N. Misra (1989), 'Hunter-gatherers in an Agrarian Setting: The Nineteenth Century Situations in the Ganga Plains', *ME*, XIII, pp. 65-78.

—— (1990), 'The Kanjars: A Hunting-gathering Community of the Ganga Valley, Uttar Pradesh', *ME*, XV, 2, pp. 71-88.

—— (1993), 'The Pardhis: A Hunting-gathering Community of Central and Western India', *ME*, XVIII, 1, pp. 115-40.

—— (1994), 'Survival of the Hunting-gathering Tradition in the Ganga Plains and Central India', in B. Allchin (ed.), *Living Traditions: Studies in the Ethnoarchaeology of South Asia,* Oxford-IBH, New Delhi, pp. 169-91.

Nambi, K.V.S. and M.K.L. Murty (1983), 'An Upper Palaeolithic Fireplace in the Kurnool Caves', *BDCRI*, 48, pp. 110-13.

Nanda, S.C. (1984), 'Stone Age Cultures of Indravati Basin, Koraput District, Orissa', Ph.D. dissertation (unpublished), University of Poona, Poona.

—— (1985), The Microlithic Cultures of the Indravati Valley, District Koraput, Orissa', *RAIP*, Oxford-IBH, New Delhi, pp. 159-65.

Narain, L.A. (1970), 'Neolithic Settlement at Chirand', *Journal of Bihar Research Society*, 56, pp. 16-35.

—— (1979), 'The Neolithic Cultures of Eastern India', in D.P. Agrawal and D.K. Chakrabarti (eds.), *Essays on Protohistory*, D.K. Publishers, New Delhi, pp. 301-9.

Narasimhaiah, B. (1980), *Neolithic and Megalithic Cultures in Western Tamil Nadu*, Sundeep Prakashan, Delhi.

Nesfield, J.C. (1883), 'The Kanjars of Upper India', *Calcutta Review*, LXXVII, pp. 368-98.

Neumayer, E. (1983), *Prehistoric Indian Rock Paintings*, Oxford University Press, New Delhi.

—— (1993), *Lines on Stone*: *The Prehistoric Rock Art of India*, Manohar, New Delhi.

Ota, S.B. (1982-3), 'New Research Designs in the Prehistoric Research in Orissa with Special Reference to Pebble Industry of North Boudh-Kondhmal District, Orissa', *Manav*, 1, pp. 160-8

—— (1986), 'Mesolithic Culture of the Phulbani District (Orissa): With Special Reference to the Heavy Duty Tol Implements', *BDCRI*, 45, pp. 47-56.

Paddayya, K. (1967), 'Hunsiholi: A Late Stone Age Sites in the Krishna Valley', *Eastern Anthropologist*, 20, pp. 71-8.

—— (1969), 'Hagargundi: A Fossiliferous Middle Stone Age Site on the Bhima River', *Journal of the Asiatic Society of Bengal*, 11, 1-4, pp. 12-14.

—— (1970), 'The Blade Tool Industry of Shorapur Doab, Peninsular India', *Indian Antiquary*, 4, pp. 165-70.

—— (1971), 'High-Level Gravels of the Shorapur Doab, Peninsular India', *Quarter*, 22, pp. 95-110.

—— (1973), Investigations into the Neolithic Culture of the Sharapur Doab, South India, E.J. Brill, Leiden, pp. 87-91.

—— (1975), 'Investigations into the Acheulian Phase in the Shorapur Doab, Peninsular India', *Quarter*, 26, pp. 5-11.

—— (1976), 'The Acheulian Culture of the Hunsgi Valley, South India', *CA*, 17, pp. 760-1.

—— (1977), 'The Acheulian Culture of the Hunsgi Valley, Shorapur Doab, Peninsular India', *Proceedings of the American Philosophical Society*, 121, pp. 383-406.

—— (1978), 'New Research Designs and Field Techniques in the Palaeolithic Archaeology of India', *World Archaeology*, 10, pp. 94-110.

—— (1979a), 'Excavations of a New Acheulian Occupation Site at Hunsgi, Peninsular India', *Quarter*, 29-30, pp. 134-55.

—— (1979b), 'Palaeoethnography *vis-à-vis* the Stone Age Cultures of India: Some Methodological Considerations', *BDCRI*, 38, pp. 63-90.

—— (1982), *The Acheulian Culture of Hunsgi Valley (Peninsular India): A Settlement System Perspective*, Deccan College, Pune.

—— (1985), 'Acheulian Occupation Sites and Associated Fossil Fauna from Hunsgi-Baichbal Valleys, Peninsular India', *Anthropas*, 80, pp. 653-8.

—— (1987a), 'Excavation of an Acheulian Occupation Site at Yedipur, Peninsular India', *Anthropos*, 82, pp. 610-14.

—— (1989), 'The Acheulian Culture Localities among the Fatehpur Nullah, Baichbal Valley, Karnataka, Peninsular India', in J.M. Kenoyer (ed.), *Old Problems and New Perspectives in the Archaeology of South Asia*, University of Wisconsin, Madison, pp. 21-8.

—— (1991), 'The Acheulian Culture of the Hunsgi-Baichbal Valleys, Peninsular India, a Processual Study', *Quarter*, 41-2, pp. 111-38.

—— (1993a), 'Ash Mound Investigations at Budihal, Gulbarga District, Karnataka' *Man and Environment*, 18, pp. 57-87.

—— (1993b), 'Further Field Investigations at Budihal, Gulbarga District', *BDCRI*, 53, pp. 277-322.

—— (1994), 'Investigation of Man-Environment Relationship in Indian Archaeology: Some Theoretical Considerations', *ME*, XIX, 1-2, pp. 1-28.

Pal, J.N. (1983), 'Bases of the Neolithic Cultures of the Middle Ganga Valley', *Journal of G.N. Jha Kendriya Sanskrit Vidyapith.*

—— (1984), 'Epi-Palaeolithic Sites in Pratapgarh District U.P.', *ME*, pp. 31-8.

—— (1986), 'Microlitic Industry of Damdama', *Puratattva*, 16, pp. 1-5.

—— (1986), *Archaeology of Southern Uttar Pradesh*, Swabha Prakashan, Allahabad.

—— (1988), 'Mesolithic Double Burials from Recent Excavations at Damdama', *ME*, XII, pp. 115-22.

—— (1992), 'Mesolithic Human Burials in the Gangetic Plain, North India', *ME*, XVII, 2, pp. 35-44.

—— (1994), 'Mesolithic Settlements in the Ganga Plain', *ME*, XIX, 1-2, pp. 91-102.

—— (1996), 'Lithic Use Wear Analysis and Subsistence Activities among the Mesolithic People of North India', in G.E. Afanas'ev et al., *Bioarchaeology of Mesolithic India*, pp. 267-77.

Pande, B.M. (1971), 'Neolithic Hunting Scene on a Stone Slab from Burzahom, Kashmir', *Asian Perspectives*, 14, pp. 134-7.

—— (1972), 'A Neolithic Tectiform from Burzahom, District Srinagar, Kashmir', *JRAS*, 7, pp. 175-7.

Pandey, J.N. (1990), 'Mesolithic in the Middle Ganga Valley', *BDCRI*, 49, pp. 311-16.

—— (1996), 'Burial Practices and Funerary Practices of Mesolithic India', in G.E. Afanas'ev et al. (eds.), *Bioarchaeology of Mesolithic India: An Integrated Approach*, Colloqurium XXXIII of the International Union of Prehistoric and Protohistoric Sciences, ABACO Edizioni, Forli, pp. 279-90.

Pandey, R.P. (1987), 'An Upper Palaeolithic Phase in the Upper Mahanadi Valley, M.P.', *ME,* 1, pp. 149-60.

Pandey, S.K. (1993), *Indian Rock Art*, Aryan Books International, New Delhi.

Pant, P.C. (1982), *Prehistoric Uttar Pradesh (A Study of the Old Stone Age)*, Agam Kala Prakashan, Delhi.

Pant, P.C. and V. Jayaswal (1977-8), 'Jamalpur: A Typological Variant within the Middle Palaeolithic Culture Complex of India', *Puratattva*, 9, pp. 15-33.

—— (1991), *Paisra: The Stone Age Settlement of Bihar,* Agam Kala Prakashan, Delhi.

Pappu, R.S. (1974), *Pleistocene Studies in the Upper Krishna Basin,* Deccan College, Poona.

—— (1981), 'Recent Geoarchaeological Investigations around Badami District Bijapur, Karnataka', *BDCRI*, 39-40, pp. 170-9.

—— (1985), 'Geomorphic Setting of Acheulian Sites in Peninsular India', in V.N. Misra and P. Bellwood (eds.), *Recent Advances in Indo-Pacific Prehistory*, Oxford-IBH, New Delhi, pp. 9-12.

—— (1990), 'Quaternary Environment and Palaeolithic Cultures of the Ghataprabha Basin, Karnataka', in A. Sundara (ed.), *Archaeology in Karnataka*, Directorate of Archaeology and Museums, Mysore, pp. 17-22.

—— (1995), 'The Contribution of the Earth Sciences to the Development of Indian Archaeology', in S. Wadia et al. (eds.), *Quaternary Environment and Geoarchaeology of India,* Geological Society of India, Bangalore, pp. 414-24.

Pappu, R.S. and S.G. Deo (1994), *Man-Land Relationships During Palaeolithic Times in the Kaladgi Basin, Karnataka,* Deccan College, Poona.

Pappu, Shanti (1996), 'Reinvestigation of the Prehistoric Archaeological Record in the Kortallayar Basin, Tamil Nadu', *ME*, XX, 1, pp. 1-23.

Papu, R.S. and J.V.P. Rao (1983), 'On the Problem of the Age and Origin of High Level Gravels around Moravakonda, District Kurnool, Andhra Pradesh', *BDCRI*, 42, pp. 119-30.

Patnaik, Rajeev et al. (1995), 'Discovery of Microvertebrates from the Pleistocene Deposits of the Central Narmada Valley, India', *Current Science*, 68, 8, pp. 828-30.

Peterson, T.T. and J.N.J. Drummond (1962), *Soan: The Palaeolithic of Pakistan,* Karachi, Department of Archaeology, Govt. of Pakistan.

Pilgrim, G.E. (1905), 'On the Occurrence of Elephas antiquus (namadicus) in the Godavari Alluvium with Remarks on the Species, its Distribution and the Age of the Associated Indian Deposits', *Records of the Geological Survey of India*, 32, 3, pp. 199-218.

Possehl, G. and K.A.R. Kennedy (1979), 'The Hunter-gatherer/Agricultural Exchange in Prehistory: An Example from India', *CA*, 20, 3, pp. 592-3.

Possehl, Gregory and Paul Rissman (1992), 'The Chronology of Prehistoric India: From Earliest Times to Iron Age', in R.W. Ehrich (ed.), *Chronologies in Old World Archaeologhy*, I and II, University of Chicago, Chicago, pp. 465-90 and 447-74.

Possehl, Gregory L. (2002), *Indus Civilization: A Contemporary Perspective*, Alta Mira Press, New York.

Pradhan, S. (1994), 'Painted Rockshelters of Orissa: A Case Study of Manikmoda', *Orissa Historical Research Journal*, XXXIX, 1-4, pp. 40-5.

—— (1995), 'Rock Art of Orissa: A Study of Original Style', *Purakala*, 6, 1-2, pp. 5-13.

—— (1995-6), 'Rock Engravings in the Rockshelters of Upland Orissa', *Puratattva*, 26, pp. 34-42.

—— (1997), 'Prehistoric Art', in P.K. Mishra and J.K. Samal (eds.), *Comprehensive History and Culture of Orissa*, Kaveri Books, New Delhi, pp. 46-53.

—— (1999), 'Painted Rockshelters of Orissa', in S. Pradhan (ed.), *Orissa History, Culture and Archaeology*, D.K. Printworld, New Delhi, pp. 39-46.

—— (2000), 'Rock Art of Orissa', in A.N. Tiwari (ed.), *Reference Orissa*, Enterprising Publishers, Bhubaneswar, pp. 182-7.

Prakash, P.V. (1989), 'Mesolithic Adaptations: A Case Study from Visakhapatnam Region', *Andhra Pradesh History Congress*, 13, pp. 29-31.

—— (1998), 'Vangasari: A Mesolithic Cave in the Eastern Ghats, Andhra Pradesh', *ME*, XXIII, 2, pp. 1-16.

Radhakrishna, B.P. (1952), 'The Mysore Plateau: Its Structural and Physiographic Evolution', *Bulletin of the Mysore Geologists Association*, 3, pp. 1-56.

Rajaguru, S.N. (1968), 'Some Aspects of Pleistocene Period in South Central Maharashtra', in F. Bordes and D. de Sonneville-Bordes (eds.), *La Prehistoric Problems et Tendances*, pp. 349-57.

—— (1968-9), 'Some New Fossils Discoveries from Western Maharashtra, India', *Puratattva*, 2, pp. 16-22.

—— (1969), 'On the Late Pleistocene of the Deccan', *Quaternaria,* 11, pp. 241-53.

—— (1970), 'Studies in the Late Pleistocene of the Mula-Mutha Valley', Ph.D. thesis (unpublished), Poona University.

Rajaguru, S.N. and G.L. Badam (1976), 'Litho and Bio-stratigraphy of the Quaternary Formations in the Central Godavari Valley, Maharashtra', *Seminar on Deccan Traps and Bauxites*, Geological Survey of India, Poona, p. 45.

Rajaguru, S.N. and K.T.M. Hegde (1972), 'The Pleistocene Stratigraphy of India', in S.B. Deo (ed.), *Archaeological Congress and Seminar Papers*, Nagpur University, Nagpur, pp. 69-79.

Rajaguru, S.N. and R. Korisetter (1987), 'Quaternary Geomorphic Environment and Cultural Succession in Western India', *Indian Journal of Earth Sciences*, 14, 3-4, pp. 349-61.

Rajaguru, S.N. et al. (1980), 'The Terminal Pleistocene Microlithic Industry at Inamgaon, Maharashtra', *Bulletin of the Deccan College Research Institute*, 39, pp. 150-9.

—— (1993), 'Changes in the Physical Environment of Western India During the Last 200 Kyr B.P.: A Geoarchaeological Approach', *Proceedings of International Symposium and Global Change*, Waseda University, Tokyo, pp. 599-623.

—— (1994), 'A Fresh Look at the Quaternary Lithostratigraphy of a Part of the Central Narmada Valley, Narsinghpur District, M.P', in K.R. Dikshit et al. (eds.), *India-Geomorphological Diversity*, Rawat Publishers, New Delhi, pp. 435-52.

Rajan, K. et al. (1997), *Archaeology of Tamil Nadu* (*Kongu Country*), Book India Publishing Co., Delhi.

Rajendran, P. (1983a), 'The Mesolithic Industries from South Kanara, Karnataka', *BDCRI*, 42, pp. 133-7.

—— (1983b), 'The Coastal Mesolithic Industries of South India and their Chronology', *Bulletin of the Indo-Pacific Prehistory Association*, 3, pp. 18-31.

—— (1984), 'A Preliminary Report on Tenmalai Rockshelter: A Late Mesolithic Site in Kerala, South India', *Bulletin of the Indo-Pacific Prehistory Association*, 5, pp. 20-3.

—— (1985), 'The Mesolithic Industries of North Kerala', *RAIP*, Oxford-IBH, New Delhi, pp. 165-70.

—— (1989), *The Prehistoric Cultures and Environments of Kerala,* Classical Publishing Company, New Delhi.

Rajguru, S.N. and R. Korisetter (1987), 'Late Quaternary Alluvial History of the Northwestern Deccan Upland Region', *Nature*, 325, pp. 612-14.

Rajguru S.N. et al. (1986), 'Relationship Between Sea Levels and Continentality Along Western Maharashtra During the Late Quaternary', *BDCRI*, 45, pp. 67-70.

Raju, D.R. (1985), 'Handaxe Assemblages from the Gunjana Valley, Andhra Pradesh: A Metrical Analysis', *Bulletin of the Indo-Pacific Prehistory Association,* 6, pp. 10-26.

—— (1986), 'The Upper Palaeolithic Industries of Cuddapah District', *RAIP*, Oxford and IBH, New Delhi.

—— (1988), *Stone Age Hunter-Gatherers: An Ethnoarchaeology of Cuddapah Region. South-East India,* Ravish Publishers, Pune.

—— (1989), 'The Lower Palaeolithic Culture in the Gunjana Valley on the Southeast Coast of India', *BDCRI*, 47-8, pp. 283-300.

Ramachandrayya et al. (1976), 'Jami: A Summary of Excavation Results', *Journal of the Andhra Historical Research Society*, 25.

Rao, M.S. Nagaraj (1964), 'Recent Explorations in the Tungabhadra Basin: The Chalcolithic Phase', *BDCRI*, 23, pp. 55-7.

—— (1971), *Protohistoric Cultures of the Tungabhadra Valley: A Report on Hallur Excavations*, Dharwad: The Author.

Rao, M.S. Nagaraj et al. (1965), *The Stone Age Hill Dwellers of Tekkalakota*, Deccan College, Poona.

Rao, S.N. (1966), 'Stone Age Cultures of Nalgonda', Ph.D. dissertation (unpublished), University of Poona, Poona.

—— (1974), 'The Neolithic Cultue of Sarutaru', *Bulletin of Department of Anthropology, Dibrugarh University* 2, pp. 1-9.

—— (1977), 'Excavation at Sarutaru: A Neolithic Sit in Assam', *ME*, 1, pp. 39-40.

Rao, V.V.M. (1979), 'Stone Age Cultures of Prakasham District', Ph.D. dissertation (unpublished), Andhra University, Waltair.

Ray, Ranjana (1975), 'Studies on the Blade-Bladelet Industries in India', Ph.D. dissertation (unpublished), Calcutta University, Calcutta.

—— (1985), 'The "Blade-Bladelet" Industries of India', in V.N. Misra and P. Bellwood (eds.), *RAIP*, Oxford-IBH, New Delhi, pp. 123-7.

—— (1987), *Ancient Settlement Patterns of Eastern India*, Pearl Publishers, Calcutta.

Reddy, K.T. (1968), '*Prehistoric Cultures of the Cudappah Districts, Andhra Pradesh*', Ph.D. dissertation (unpublished), University of Poona, Poona.

Reddy, K.T. (1970), 'The Vemula Industry', *Indian Antiquary*, 41.

—— (1994), 'Coastal Ecology and Archaeology: Evidence from the East Coast of India', *ME*, XIX, 1-2, pp. 43-56.

Reddy, K.T. and P. Vijay Prakash (1985), 'The Upper Palaeolithic and Mesolithic in the Gambheeram Valley, Northeastern Andhra Pradesh,' *RAIP*, Oxford and IBH, New Delhi, pp. 157-8.

Reddy, K.T. and V. Sudarsen (1978), 'Prehistoric Investigations in Sagileru Basin', *ME*, 2, pp. 32-40.

Reddy, K.T. et al. (1995), 'A Pebble Tool Assemblage on the Vishakhapattanam Coast', *ME*, XX, 1, pp. 113-18.

Reddy, V. Rami (1968), *Pre and Protohistory of South Western Andhra Pradesh,* Hyderabad, Government of Andhra Pradesh.

Rendell, H. and R.W. Dennel (1985), 'Dated Lower Palaeolithic Artefacts from Northern Pakistan', *CA*, 26, 5, p. 393.

Rendell, H.M. and R.W. Dennel (1987), 'Thermoluminiscence Dating of an Upper Pleistocene Site, Northern Pakistan', *Geoarchaeology*, 2, pp. 63-7.

Rightmire, G.P. (1983), 'The Fossil Evidence for Hominid Evolution in Southern Africa', in R.G. Klein (ed.), *South African Prehistory and Palaeoenvironment*, Rotterdam, Balkema.

Rivct-Carnac (1883), 'On Stone Implements from North Provinces of India', *JASB*, 52, I-IV, pp. 221-30.

Romesh, N.R. (1987), 'Evidence of Stone Age Culture in Pleistocene Sediments of Tripura', *Indian Journal of Earth Science*, 14, pp. 321-8.

Roy, S.C. (1925), 'Birhors, A Little Known Tribe of Chota Nagpur, Ranchi', *Man in India*.

Russell, R.V. and R.B. Hira Lal (1961), *The Tribes and Castes of the Central Provvinces of India*, Government of India Press, Delhi.

Sadakata, N. et al. (1995), 'Late Quaternary Environment, Change in the Pravara River Basin, Northwestern Deccan Upland, India', *Proceedings of the International Symposium on Palaeoenvironmental Change in Tropical, Sub-Tropical Monsoon Asia*, Hiroshima Research Centre for Regional Geography, Hiroshima University, pp. 46-56.

Sali, S.A. (1974), 'Upper Palaeolithic Research Since Independence', *BDCRI*, pp. 34-147.

—— (1980), 'Stone Age Cultures at Patne, Dist. Jalgaon, Maharashtra', Ph.D. thesis (unpublished), University of Poona, Poona.

—— (1986), 'The Upper Palaeolithic Culture of Patne, District Jalgaon, Maharashtra', *RAIP*, pp. 137-46.

—— (1989), *The Upper Palaeolithic and Mesolithic Cultures of Maharashtra*, Deccan College, Pune.

—— (1990a), 'Quaternary Environments and Cultural Change in the Central Tapi Valley', *BDCRI*, 49, pp. 375-404.

—— (1990b), *Stone Age India*, Shankar Publishers, Aurangabad.

Salim, Mohammad (1986), *The Middle Stone Age Cultures of Northern Pakistan*, Islamabad.

Sampson, C.G. (1974), *The Stone Age Archaeology of Southern Africa*, Academic Press, London, pp. 140-2.

Sankalia, H.D. (1942), 'In Search of Early Man along the Sabarmati', *Journal of Gujarat Research Society*, 4, pp. 75-80.

—— (1943), 'Pre and Protohistory of Gujarat', in K.M. Munshi (ed.), *The Glory that was Gurjar Desh,* Bharatiya Vidya Bhavan, Bombay, pp. 12-40.

—— (1944), 'The Second Gujarat Prehistoric Expedition: A Preliminary Account of the Search of "Microlithic Man" in Gujarat', *New Indian Antiquary*, 7, 1, pp. 1-5.

—— (1946), *Investigations into the Prehistoric Archaeology of Gujarat,* Baroda State Government, Baroda.

—— (1946a), 'The Age of Microlithic Culture in Gujarat', *Current Science*, 15, 1, pp. 11-13.

—— (1946b), *Investigations into the Prehistoric Archaeology of Gujarat*, Baroda.

—— (1952), *Godavari Palaeolithic Industry,* Deccan College, Pune.

—— (1955), 'Excavations at Langhraj, Gujarat', *Man*, 55, 33, p. 26.

—— (1956), 'Animal Fossils and Paleolithic Industries from the Pravara Basin at Navasa, District Ahmednagar', *Ancient India*, 12, pp. 35-53.

—— (1963), *Prehistory and Protohistory in India and Pakistan*, University of Bombay, Bombay.

—— (1964), 'Middle Stone Age Cultures in India and Pakistan', *Science*, 146, 3642, pp. 365-75.

—— (1965), 'Early Stone Age in Saurashtra Gujarat', *Miscelanes en Homenaje al Abate Henri Brenii* (*1877-1961*), T. II, Institute de Prehistoria, Barcelona, pp. 327-46.

—— (1965), *Excavations at Langhraj: 1944-63*, part I, *Archaeology*, Deccan College, Poona.

—— (1969) *Mesolithic and Pre-Mesolithic Industries from the Excavations at Sangankallu, Bellary*, Deccan College, Poona.

—— (1974), *Prehistory and Protohistory of India and Pakistan*, Deccan College, Poona.

Sankalia, H.D. and Irawati Karve (1949), 'Early Primitive Microlithic Culture and People of Gujarat', *American Anthropologist*, 51, pp. 28-34.

Sastry, M.V.A. (1968), 'Pleistocene Vertebrates from Susunia, Bankura District, West Bengal', *Indian Minerals*, 22, p. 20.

Satsangi, P.P. and A.K. Dutta (1968), 'Progress Report for the Field Season 1967-68' (unpublished), G.S.I. Report.

Semans, C.A. (1981), 'Analysis of an Acheulian Collection from Peerah Nullah, Narmada Valley, India', *ME*, V, pp. 13-31.

Sen, D. (1955), 'Nalagarh Palaeolithic Culture', *Man in India*, 35, pp. 177-84.

—— (1957), 'The Soanian and the Pebble Tool Terminology in India', *Man in India*, 37, 2, pp. 157-9

Shadaksharaiah, R.M. (1995), *Prehistoric and Early Historic Cultures in the Manjra and Karanja Valleys*, Kannada Research Institute, Karnataka University, Dharwad, pp. 107-28.

Sharma, A.K. (1967), 'Neolithic Human Burials from Burzahom, Kashmir', *JOIB*, 16, pp. 239-42.

—— (1968), 'Animal Burial from Burzahom: A Neolithic Settlement in Kashmir', *JOIB*, 18, pp. 40-4.

—— (1980-1), 'Animal Bones from Gufkral: Evidence of Human and Non-human Activities', *Puratattva*, 12, pp. 31-6.

Sharma, D.P. and M. Sharma (1987), 'A Reappraisal of the Chronology of the Mesolithic and Neolithic Cultures of the Vindhyas and Middle Ganga Valley', in B.M. Pande and B.D. Chattopadhyay (eds.), *Archaeology and History*, Agam Kala Prakashan, Delhi, pp. 57-66.

Sharma, G.R. (1965), 'Comments on Mesolithic Phase in the Prehistory of India', in V.N. Misra and M.S. Mate (eds.), *Indian Prehistory 1964*, Deccan College, Poona, pp. 76-9.

—— (1973), 'Mesolithic Lake Cultures in the Ganga Valley', *PPS* 39, pp. 129-46.

—— (1973), 'Stone Age in the Vindhyas and the Ganga Valley', in Agrawal and Ghosh (eds.), *Radiocarbon and Indian Archaeology*, TIFR, Bombay, pp. 106-10.

—— (1975), 'Seasonal Migration and Mesolithic Lake Cultures of the Ganga Valley', in G.R. Sharma (ed.), *K.C. Chattopadhyaya Memorial Volume*, K.K. Dubey, Allahabad, pp. 1-20.

Sharma, G.R. and D. Mandal (1980), *Excavation at Mahagara*, University of Allahabad, Allahabad.

Sharma, G.R. and J.D. Clark (1982), 'Palaeoenvironments and Prehistory in the Middle Son Valley, Northern Madhya Pradesh', *ME*, VI, pp. 56-62.

—— (1983b), *Palaeoenvironments and Prehistory in the Middle Son Valley, Madhya Pradesh (North Central India)*, Abinash Prakashan, Allahabad.

Sharma, G.R. et al. (1980), *Beginnings of Agriculture*, Abinash Prakashan, Allahabad.

Sharma, M.L. (1996), 'The Sahibee River Valley: A New Region of Rock Art in Rajasthan', in R.K. Sharma and K.K. Tripathi (eds.), *Recent Persepectives in Prehistoric Art in India and Allied Subjects*, Aryan Books International, New Delhi.

Sharma, T.C. (1966), 'Prehistoric Archaeology of Assam: A Study of Neolithic Culture of Assam', Ph.D. thesis (unpublished), University of London.

—— (1980), 'The Neolithic Pattern of Eastern India' (unpublished).

Sieveking, G.D.G. (1960), 'Morhana Pahar: Or the Mystery of A.C. Carlleyle', *Man*, 140, 1, pp. 98-100.

Singh, B.P. (1988), 'Early Farming Communities of Kaimur Foothills' (unpublished).

Singh, G. et al. (1974), 'Late Quaternary History of Vegetation and Climate of the Rajasthan Desert, India', *Philosophical Transactions of the Royal Society*, 267B, pp. 467-501.

Singh, J.P. Deo (1976), 'Prehistoric Cave Paintings of Jogimath Dongar', *The Orissa Historical Research Journal*, XXII, 2, pp. 21-2.

Singh, O.K. and T.C. Sharma (1969), 'On the Discovery of Stone Age Relics from Manipura', *Journal of Assam Research Society*, 12, pp. 36-48.

Singh, P.K. (1988), 'Cultural Succession of Prehistoric Cultures in Central Orissa', in K.L. Bhowmick (ed.), *Culture of the Past*, Inter India Publications, New Delhi, pp. 87-99.

Singh, Rameshwar (1965), 'Palaeolithic Industries of Northern Bundelkhand', Ph.D. dissertation (unpublished), University of Poona, Poona.

Sinha, B.P. (1979), *Archaeology and Art of India*, Sundeep Prakashan, Delhi.

Smith, V.A. (1906), 'Pigmy Flints', *Indian Antiquary*, XXXV, pp. 185-95.

Sonakia, A. (1984) 'The Skull-Cap of Early Man and Associated Mammalian Fauna from the Narmada Valley Alluvium, Hoshangabad Area, Madhya Pradesh, India', *Records of the Geological Survey of India*, 113, 6, pp. 159-72.

Sonawane, V.H. (1983), 'The Microlithic Industry of Tarsang, Gujarat', *ME*, VII, pp. 31-8.

—— (1984), 'An Important Evidence to Date Rock Paintings of Mesolithic Period', in K.K. Chakravarty (ed.), *Rock Art in India*, New Delhi.

—— (1987), 'An Engraved Mesolithic Core from Chandravati, Rajasthan', in B.M. Pande and B.D. Chattopadhyay (eds.), *Archaeology and History*, Agam Kala Prakashan, Delhi, pp. 53-6.

—— (1996), 'Rock Paintings of Gujarat', in R.K. Sharma and K.K. Tripathi (eds.), *Recent Perspectives in Prehistoric Art in India and Allied Subjects*, Aryan Books International, New Delhi.

Sondaar, P.Y. (1968), 'The Osteology of the Manus of Fossil and Recent Equidae with Special Reference to Phylogeny and Function', *Kon. Ned. Akad. Weten. Eerste Reeks-Deel*, 25, 1, pp. 22-31.

Subbarao, B. (1952), 'Archaeological Explorations in the Mahi Valley', *Journal of the M.S. University of Baroda*, I, pp. 33-72.

—— (1958), *The Personality of India*, M.S. University, Baroda.

Sundara, A. (1970), 'Neolithic Cultural Patterns and Movements in North Mysore State, *Journal of Karnataka University* (*Social Science*), 7, pp. 54-61, 109-10.

—— (1971), 'Chalcolithic Phase in the Upper Krishna Valley', *Studies, History and Culture*, P.B. Desai Felicitation Volume, Dharwad, pp. 54-61.

Supekar, S.G. (1968), 'Pleistocene Stratigraphy and Prehistoric Archaeology of the Central Narmada Basin', Ph.D. dissertation (unpublished), Poona University.

Supekar, S.G. (1985), 'Some Observations on the Quaternary Stratigraphy of the Central Narmada Valley', in V.N. Misra and P. Bellwood (eds.), *Recent Advances in Indo-Pacific Prehistory,* Oxford-IBH, New Delhi, pp. 19-28.

Susman, C. (1983), 'Preliminary Report on Excavations at the Mesolithic Occupation Site at Baghor II Locality', in G.R. Sharma and J.D. Clark (eds.), *Palaeoenvironments and Prehistory in the Middle Son Valley* (*Madhya Pradesh, North Central India*), Abinash Prakashan, Allahabad, pp. 161-96.

Szabo, B.J. et al. (1990), 'On the Age of the Acheulian Culture of the Hunsgi-Baichbal Valleys, Peninsular India', *Bulletin of the Deccan College Research Institute*, 50, pp. 317-21.

Terra, H. De and T.T. Paterson (1939), *Studies on the Ice Age in India and Associated Human Cultures,* Carnegie Institution, Washington D.C.

Thakur, Nina et al. (1988), 'Bone Tools from Senuwar' (unpublished).

Thapay, B.K. (1989), 'Kuchai', in A. Ghosh (ed.), *An Encyclopaedia of Indian Archaeology* Munshiram Manoharlal, New Delhi, p. 240.

Theobald, W. (1860), 'On the Tertiary and Alluvial Deposits of the Central Portion of the Narbudda Valley', *Memoirs of the Geological Survey of India,* 2, pp. 279-98.

—— (1862), 'Celts Found in Bundelkhand', *PASB*, p. 221.

Thomas, P.K. and P.P. Jogelkar (1994), 'Holocene Faunal Studies in India', *ME*, XX, 1-2, pp. 179-204.

Thomas, P.K. et al. (1995) 'A Preliminary Report of the Faunal Remains from Damdama', *ME*, XX, pp. 29-36.

Thripathi, K.C. (1972), 'Lithic Industries of Southwestern Orissa', Ph.D. dissertation (unpublished), Utkal University, Bhubaneswar.

—— (1973), 'South Orissan Prehistory: The First Record of Stone Age Tools', *Asian Perspectives*, 4, pp. 47-59.

—— (1977), 'Prehistoric Studies in Orissa', in M.N. Das (ed.), *Sidelights on History and Culture of Orissa*, Vidyapuri, Cuttack.

—— (1980), *Lithic Industries in India: A Study of South-Western Orissa,* Inter-India Publication, New Delhi.

Tiwari, S.C. (2002), 'Skeletal Biology (Misra Series)', in K.A.R. Kennedy et al. (eds.), *The Biological Anthropology of Human Skeletal Remains from Bhimbetka, Central India*, Indian Society for Prehistoric and Quaternary Studies, Pune, pp. 27-40.

Tod, K.R.U. (1939), 'Palaeolithic Industries of Bombay', *JRAI,* LXIV, pp. 257-72.

—— (1950), 'Microlithic Industries of Bombay', *Ancient India*, 6, pp. 4-17.

Touche, T.H.D. La (1902), 'The Geology of Western Rajputana', *MAGI*, 35, 1, pp. 1-110.

Tripathi, B. (1996-7), 'Archaeological Exploration Around Boudh District, Orissa: A Preliminary Report', *BDRI*, 56-7, pp. 41-54.

—— (2000), 'Archaeology of Boudh District: Central Orissa', in K.K. Base and P. Mohanty (eds.), *Archaeology of Orissa*, Pratibha Prakashan, New Delhi, pp. 397-416.

—— (2001), 'Archaeology of Boudh District, Orissa with Special Reference to Early Historic Settlement Pattern', Ph.D. dissertation (unpublished), Deccan College Postgraduate and Research Institute, Pune.

Tripathi, C. (1967), 'The Pleistocene Alluvial Deposits Around Nevasa, Ahmednagar District, Maharashtra', *Records of the Geological Survey of India*, 25, 2, pp. 355-66.

Tripathy, B. (1995), 'Prehistory of Boudh District, Orissa', *Boudh District Souvenir*, Satyanarayan Press, Cuttack, pp. 8-16.

Tripathy, K.C. (1970), 'Microlithic Industry of Bhubaneswar', *Prakruti, Utkal University Journal of Science*, 7, pp. 77-92.

—— (1972), 'Lithic Industries of Southwestern Orissa', Ph.D. thesis (unpublished), Utkal University, Orissa.

—— (1980), *Lithic Industries in India: A Study of South-Western Orissa*, Inter India Publications, New Delhi.

Tripathy, K.C. and U.C. Mohanty (1972) 'Lithic Industries of South-Western Orissa', *Prakruti, Utkal University Journal of Science*, 9, pp. 1-2.

Varma, K.K. (1965), 'Comments on Mesolithic Phase in the Prehistory of India', in V.N. Misra and M.S. Mate (eds.), *Indian Prehistory 1964*, Deccan College, Poona, pp. 73-6.

—— (1986), *The Mesolithic Age in Mirzapur*, Paramjyoti Prakashan, Allahabad.

Varma, R.K. et al. (1985), 'A Preliminary Report on the Excavations at Damdama (1982-4), *ME*, IX, pp. 45-65.

Verstappen, H.T. (1970), 'Aeolian Geomorphology of the Thar Desert and Palaeoclimates', *Zeitschrift fur Geomorphologie*, 10 (Supplement Band), pp. 104-20.

Vita-Finzi, C. and E.S. Higgs (1970), 'Prehistoric Economy in the Mount Carmael Area of Palestine: Site Catchment Analysis', *PPS*, 36, pp. 1-37.

Wakankar, V.S. (1962), 'Painted Rockshelters of India', *Rivista de Sciencz Perhistoriche*, 17, pp. 237-53.

—— (1973), 'Bhimbetka Excavations', *JIH*, 51, pp. 23-32.

—— (1975a), 'Bhimbetka: The Prehistoric Paradise', *Prachya Pratibha*, 3, 2, pp. 7-29.

—— (1975b), 'Prehistoric Cave Paintings', *Marg*, 28, 4, pp. 17-34.

—— (1978), *The Dawn of Indian Art*, Vishnu Bhatnagar, Ujjain.

—— (2002), 'Burial Systems in Bhimbetka', in K.A.R. Kennedy et al. (eds.), *The Biological Anthropology of Human Skeletal Remains*, pp. 1-5.

Willey, G.R. (1953), 'Prehistoric Settlement Patterns in the Viru Valley, Peru', Bulletin Bureau of American Ethnology, 155, Washington D.C.

Williams, M.A.J. and A. Royee (1983), 'Alluvial History of the Middle Son Valley, North Central India', in G.R. Sharma and J.D. Clark (eds.), *Palaeoenvironments and Prehistory in the Middle Son Valley,* Avinash Prakashan, Allahabad, pp. 9-21.

Willians, M.A.J. and M.F. Clarke (1995), 'Quaternary Geology and Prehistoric Environments in the Soanand Belan Velleys, North Central India', in S. Wadia et al. (eds.), *Quaternary Environments and Geoarchaeology of India*, Geological Society of India, Bangalore, pp. 282-308.

Wilson, T. (1894), 'Minute Stone Implements from India', *Annual Report of the Smithsonian Institution,* Washington D.C., June 1892, pp. 455-60.

Worman, E.C. (Jr.) (1949), 'The Neolithic Problem in the Prehistory of India', *Journal of Washington Academy of Sciences*, 39, pp. 181-200.

Zeuner, F.E. (1950), *Stone Age and Pleistocene Chronology in Gujarat,* Deccan College, Poona.

—— (1951), *Prehistory in India*, Deccan College, Poona.

—— (1952), 'The Microlithic Industry of Langhraj, Gujarat', *Man*, II, p. 182.

—— (1963), *Environment of Early Man with Special Reference to Tropical Regions,* M.S. University, Baroda.

Zeuner, F.E. and B. Allchin (1956), 'The Microlithic Sites of Tinnevelly District, Madras State', *Ancient India*, 12, pp. 4-20.

B. EARLY, MATURE, AND LATER BRONZE AGE

Agrawal, D.P. (1971), *The Copper Bronze Age in India*, Munshiram Manoharlal, New Delhi.

—— (1978), 'New Data on the Copper Hoards and Diamabad Bronzes', *Man and Environment*, 2, pp. 40-6.

—— (1981), 'Arsenical Coppers in the Indian Bronze Age', in M.S. Nagaraja Rao (ed.), *Madhu: Shri M.N. Deshpande Volume (Festchrift)*, Agam Kala Prakashan, Delhi, pp. 9-16.

—— (1982), *The Archaelogy of India*, Curzon Press, London.

Agrawal, D.P. et al. (1974), 'Alloying in Copper Hoards', *Bulletin of Archaeology and Museums, U.P.*, 14, pp. 14-18.

Allchin, B. and R. Allchin (1983), *The Rise of Civilisation of India and Pakistan*, Select Service Syndicate, New Delhi.

Allchin, F.R. (1960), *Piklihal Excavations*, Andhra Pradesh Govt. Arch. Series 1, Hyderabad.

Ansari, Z.D. and M.K. Dhavalikar (1971), 'New Light on the Prehistoric Cultures of Central India', *World Archaeology*, 2, pp. 337-46.

—— (1973), *Excavations at Kayatha*, Deccan College, Poona.

Anthony, D.W. (1991), 'The Archaeology of Indo-European Origins', *JIES,* 19, pp. 193-222.

Asthana, Shashi (1976), *History of Archaeology of India's Contacts with Other Countries from Earliest times to 3rd Century* BCE, B.R. Publishing Corporation, New Delhi.

Atre, Shubhangana (1987), *The Archetyal Mother: A Systemic Approach to Harappan Religion,* Ravish Publishers, Poona.

Banerjee, N.R. (1986), *Nagda*, Archaeological Survey of India, New Delhi.

Bartel, P. (1979), 'A Discriminent Analysis of Harappan Civilization Human Population', *Journal of Archaeological Society*, 6, pp. 49-61.

Bell, Barbara (1975), 'Climate and the History of Egypt', *American Journal of Archaeology*, 79, pp. 223-69.

Bernhard, W. (1967), 'Human Skeletal Remains from the Cemetery of Timargarha and the Gandharva Grave Culture', *Ancient Pakistan*, pp. 289-407.

—— (1969) 'Preliminary Report on the Human Skeletal Remains from the Prehistoric Cemetary of Sarai Khola', *Ancient Pakistan*, 6, pp. 100-16.

Bhan, Kuldeep and V.H. Sonawane (2004), 'MSU Experts Dig Up Rare Find at Harappan Site', *Indian Express News Service*, vol. I, March.

Bhan, Suraj (1971-2), 'Siswal: A Pre-Harappan Site in Drishadwati Valley', *Puratattva*, 5, pp. 44-6.

—— (1975), *Excavations at Mitathal (1968) and other Explorations in the Sutlej-Yamuna Divide*, Kurukshetra University, Kurukshetra.

—— (2000), 'Aryanization of the Indus', in Romila Thapar (ed.), *The Making of History*, Tulika, New Delhi, pp. 41-55.

Bhattacharya, R. (1991), 'Rangpur Seal: Probable Egyptian Connection of the Harappan Civilization', *ME*, 16, pp. 53-7.

Bholanath and G.V. Sreenivas Rao (1985), 'Animal Remains from Lothal Excavations', in S.R. Rao, *Lothal: A Harappan Port Town (1995-62), MASI, 78,* vol. II, ASI, p. 641.

Binford, L.R. (1972), *An Archaeological Perspective*, Seminar Press, New York.

Bisht, R.S. (1987), 'Further Excavation at Banawali: 1983-84', in B.M. Pande and B.D. Chattopadhyaya (eds.), *Archaeology and History: Essays in Memory of Shri A. Ghosh,* vol. I, Agam Kala Prakashan, Delhi, pp. 135-56.

—— (1989-90), 'Dholavira: A New Horizon of the Indus Civilization', *Puratattva*, 20, pp. 71-82.

—— (1990), 'The Harappan Settlement Patterns in the Greater Indus Valley', *PA*, 25, pp. 1-73.

—— (1991), 'Dholavira: New Horizons of the Indus Civilization', *Puratattva*, 20, pp. 71-82.

—— (1994), 'Dholavira', in J.P. Joshi and R.S. Bisht, *India and the Indus Civilization*, pp. 23-31, National Museum, New Delhi.

—— (1997), 'Dholavira Excavations: 1990-94', in J.P. Joshi (ed.), *Facets of Indian Civilization: Recent Perspectives*, Aryan Books International, New Delhi, pp. 107-20.

—— (1999), 'Harappans and the Rigveda: Points of Convergence', in G.C. Pande (ed.), *The Dawn of Indian Civilization*, PHISPC, New Delhi, pp. 393-442.

Blanford, H.F. (1864), *Proceedings: Journal of the Asiatic Society of Bengal*, 33, pp. 575-6.

Brentjes, B. (1981), 'The Mittanians and the Peacock', in M.S. Asimov et al. (eds.), *Ethnic Problems in the History of Central Asia in the Early Period*, Proceedings of the International Symposium, Dushanbe, 17-22 October 1977, UNESCO, USSR Academy of Sciences, pp. 145-8.

Brown, P. (1917), *Indian Painting*, YMCA Publishing House, Calcutta.

Bryson, R.A. et al. (1974), 'Drought and Decline of Mycenae', *Antiquity*, 48, pp. 46-50.

Burrow, T. (1963), 'On the Significance of Terms *arma/armaka* in the Early Sanskrit Literature', *JIH,* 41, pp. 159-66.

Cappieri, M. (1971), 'Population of the Indus Civilization', in W.A. Fairservis, Jr. (ed.), *The Roots of Ancient India*, Macmillan, New York, pp. 425-43.

Carlleyle, A.C.L. (1883), 'Notes on Lately Discovered Sculptural Mounds, Cairns, Caves, Cave Paintings and Stone Implements', *PASB*, 49.

Casal, J.M. (1964), *Excavations at Amri* (French edition).

—— (1964), *Fouilles d'Amri,* 2 vols., Commission des Fouilles Archeologique, Paris.

—— (1978), 'Amri: An Introduction to the History of the Indus', in D.P. Agrawal and D.K. Chakrabarti (eds.), *Essays in Indian Protohistory*, Delhi, pp. 99-112.

Catherene and J.-F. Jarrige (n.d.), *Mehrgarh: Field Reports 1974-1985, From Neolithic Times to the Indus Civilization,* Department of Culture and Tourism, Government of Sindh.

Chakrabarti, D.K. (1999), *India: An Archaeological History*, Oxford University Press, New Delhi.

Chakrabarti, D.K. and Nayanjot Lahiri (1996), *Copper and its Alloys in Ancient India*, Munshiram Manoharlal, New Delhi.

Chatterjee, B.K. and G.D. Kumar (1963), *Comparative Study and Racial Analysis of the Human Remains of Indus Valley Civilization with Particular Reference to Harappa*, Newman, Calcutta.

Chattopadhyay, P.K. (1992), 'Archaeometallurgy in India: Studies on Technoculture in Early Copper and Iron Ages in Bihar and West Bengal', Ph.D. thesis (unpublished), Patna University.

Chaturvedi, S.N. (1985), 'Advance of Vindhyan Neolithic and Chalcolithic Cultures to the Himalayan Terai: Excavations and Explorations in the Sarayupara Region of Uttar Pradesh', *ME*, 9, pp. 101-8.

Chawdhury, K.A. et al. (1977), *Ancient Agricultural and Forestry in Northern India*, Asia Publishing House, New Delhi.

Childe, G.V. (1926), *The Aryans: A Study of Indo-European Origins*, Kegan Paul, London.

—— (1937), 'On the Courses of Gray and Black Colouration in Prehistoric Pottery', *Man*, 37, p. Art. 55.

Chitalwala, Y.M. (1982), 'Harappan Settlements in Kuchchh-Saurastra Region: Patterns of Distribution and Routes of Communication', in G.L. Possehl (ed.), *Harappan Civilization*, pp. 197-204.

Chitkara, Poonam (1997), 'OCP in the Ganga-Yamuna Valley: A Reassessment of Possible Links', in V.D. Misra and J.N. Pal (eds.), *Indian Prehistory 1980*, pp. 313-15.

Cockburn, J. (1899), 'Cave Paintings in the Kaimur Range, Northwest Provinces', *JRAS*, pp. 89-97.

Dalal, Katy Feroze (1980), 'A Short History of Explorations in Bikaner and Bahawalpur Along the Lost Saraswati River', *Indica*, vol. 17, 1, March, pp. 3-46.

Dales, G.F. (1964), 'The Mythical Massacre at Mohenjo-daro', *Expedition* 6, 3, pp. 36-43.

—— (1974), 'Excavations at Balakot, Pakistan, 1973', *Journal of Field Archaeology*, 7, 1-2, pp. 1-22.

Dani, A.H. (1970-1), 'Excavations in the Gomal Valley', *Ancient Pakistan*, 5, pp. 1-177.

Dani, A.H. and V.M. Masson, eds., *History of Civilization in Central Asia*, vol. I: *The Dawn of Civilization: Earliest Times to 700 BC*, Motilal Banarsidass, Delhi.

Davies, O. and G. Gray (1977), 'Tropical African Cultigens from Shongweni Excavations', *Journal of Archaeological Society*, 4, pp. 153-62.

Dereniyalgala, P.E.P. (1963), 'An Open Air Habitation Sitre of *Homo sapiens balangodensis*', *Spolia Zeylanica*, 30, pp. 87-110.

Derniyalgala, S.U. (1984), 'Mesolithic Stone Tool Technology at 28000 BC in Sri Lanka', *Ancient Ceylon*, 5, pp. 105-5.

—— (1992), *The Prehistory of Sri Lanka: An Ecological Perspective*, Government of Sri Lanka, Colombo.

Dhar, Indrani (1997), 'OCP and the Copper Hoard Problem', in V.D. Misra and J.N. Pal (eds.), *Indian Prehistory 1980*, Department of AIHC & Archaeology, Allahabad, pp. 308-12.

Dhavalikar, M.K. (1978), 'An Early Warehouse on West Coast', *Puratattva*, 9, pp. 100-3.

—— (1993), 'Daimabad Bronzes', in G.L. Possehl (ed.), *HCRP*, Oxford and IBH, New Delhi, pp. 421-7.

—— (1997), 'Meluhha: The Land of Copper', *South Asian Studies,* 13, pp. 275-79.

—— (1997), *Indian Protohistory*, Books and Books, New Delhi.

Dhavalikar, M.K. et al. (1990b), *Excavations at Kaothe*, Deccan College, Pune.

—— (1996), *Kuntasi: A Harappan Emporium on West Coast,* Deccan College, Pune.

Dhavalikar, M.K., H.D. Sankalia and Z.D. Ansari (1988), *Excavations at Inamgaon*, Deccan College, Poona, vol. I, pts. 1 and 2.

Dhavalikar, M.K., V.S. Shinde and Shubhangana Atre (1990a), 'Small Site Archaeology: Excavations at Walki', *BDCRI,* 50, pp. 197-228.

Dikshit, K.N. (1979), 'The Ochre Coloured Ware Settlement in Ganga-Yamuna Doab', in D.P. Agrawal and Dilip Chakrabarti (eds.), *Essays in Indian Protohistory*, B.R. Publishing Corporation, Delhi, pp. 285-99.

—— (1982), 'Hulas and the Late Harappan Complex in Western Uttar Pradesh', in G.L. Possehl (ed.), *Harappan Civilization: A Contemporary Perspective*, Oxford and IBH, New Delhi, pp. 339-51.

—— (1984), 'The Sothi Complex: Old Records and Fresh Observations', in B.B. Lal and S.P. Gupta (eds.), *Frontiers of Indus Civilizations*, Books and Books, New Delhi, pp. 531-7.

—— (1993), 'Hulas and the Late Harappan Complex in Western Uttar Pradesh', in Gregory L. Possehl (ed.), *Harappan Civilization*, 2nd rev. edn., Oxford and IBH, New Delhi, pp. 399-412.

Dimri, Kiran (1998-9), 'Assessing the Distribution of Harappan Culture in North-Eastern Saurastra: A Preliminary Report', *Praghdara*, 9, pp. 27-44.

Dupree, L. (1972), 'Prehistoric Research in Afghanistan', *Transactions of the American Philosophical Society*, 62, pp. 1-84.

Durrani, F.A. et al. (1991), 'Further Excavations at Rehman Dheri', *Ancient Pakistan*, 7, pp. 61-146.

Durrani, Farzand Ali (1988), *Excavations in the Gomal Valley-Rehman Dheri Excavations*, Department of Archaeology, University of Peshawar.

Dutta, P.C. (1972), 'The Bronze Age Harappans: A Re-examination of the Skulls in the Context of the Population Content', *AJPA*, 39, pp. 391-6.

—— (1975), 'Race Concept and Palaeoanthropology: A Recent Model for Interpreting Ancient Human Remains', *Anthropologic*, 13, pp. 35-46.

—— (1983), *The Bronze Age Harappans: A Bio-anthropological Study of the Skeletons Discovered at Harappa*, Anthropological Survey of India, Calcutta.

Dutta, P.C. et al. (1971). 'Earliest Human Remains in a Late Stone Site', *Nature* 233, pp. 500-1.

Ehrhardt, S. (1960), 'Schlgspuren, Bruche and Sprunge an den Skelteten vom Longhnaj Immodlichen Gujarat Vorderindien', *Anthropologiseher Anzieger*, 24, pp. 178-232.

Erdosy, G. (1989), 'Ethnicity in the Rigveda and Its Bearing on the Question of Indo-European Origins', *SAS*, 5, pp. 35-47.

——, ed. (1995), *The Indo-Aryans of Ancient South Asia: Language, Material Culture and Ethnicity*, Munshiram Manoharlal, New Delhi.

Fairservis, W.A. (1956), *Excavations in the Quetta Valley, West Pakistan*, Anthropological Papers of Amercan Museum on Natural History, vol. 45, pt. 2, pp. 169-402.

—— (1992), *The Harappan Civilization and Its Writing*, Oxford and IBH, New Delhi.

Flam, Louis (1982), 'Towards an Ecological Analysis of Prehistoric Settlement Patterns in Sind, Pakistan', *Sindhological Studies*, Summer, pp. 5-6.

Foote, R.S. (1884), 'Rough Notes on Billa Surgam and Other Caves in the Kurnool District', *Records of the Geological Survey of India*, 17, pp. 27-34.

—— (1916), *The Foote Collection of Indian Prehistoric and Protohistoric Antiquities*, Madras Government Museum, Madras.

Francefort, H.P. (1979), 'The World Economic of West Asia in the Third Millennium BCE', *SAA*, Naples, pp. 55-85.

—— (1992), 'New Data Illustrating the Early Contacts Between Central Asia and North-West of the Subcontinent', *SAA*, Madison Wisconsin, pp. 97-102.

Gaur, R.C. (1969), 'The OCP from Atranjikhera and Its Significance', in B.P. Sinha (ed.), *Potteries in Ancient India*, pp. 112-17.

—— (1983), *Excavations at Atranjikhera*, Munshiram Manoharlal, Delhi.

—— (1995), *Excavations at Lal Bila*, Publication Scheme, Jaipur.

Geldern, R. Heine (1936), 'Archaeological Traces of the Vedic Aryans', *Journal of the Indian Society of Oriental Art*, 4, pp. 87-113.

Ghosh, A. (1952), 'The Rajputana Desert: Its Archaeological Aspect', *Bulletin of the National Institute of Science of India*, I, pp. 37-42.

—— (1989), *Encyclopaedia of Indian Archaeology,* 2 vols., Munshiram Manoharlal, New Delhi.

—— (1994), 'A Note on the Homeland of the Painted Grey Ware', in R.C. Gaur, *The Painted Grey Ware—Proceedings of a Seminar*, Jaipur, Publication Scheme, pp. 25-8.

Gimbutas, Marija (1965), *Bronze Age Cultures of Central and Eastern Europe*, Mouton, The Hague.

Gordon, D.H. (1958), *Prehistoric Background of Indian Culture*, N.M. Tripathi Pvt. Ltd., Bombay.

—— 'The Pottery Industries of the Indo-Iranian Border: A Re-Statement and Chronology', *AI*, 10-11, ASI, pp. 157-70.

Gorelick, L. and A.I. Govinett (1981), 'The Origin and Development of the Ancient Near Eastern Cylinder Seal', *Expedition*, 23, 4, pp. 21-2.

Guha, B.S. and P.G. Basu (1938), 'Report on the Excavated Remains at Mohenjodaro in 1928-29', in E.T.H. Mackay (ed.), *Further Excavations at Mohenjodaro*, Government of India, New Delhi, I, pp. 613-38.

Gupta, P. et al. (1970), *Ancient Human Remains*, part I: A *Study of the Nagarjunakonda Skeletons, Memories of the Anthropological Survey of India*, 20, Calcutta, pp. 1-33.

Gupta, S.P. (1963), 'Indian Copper Hoards: The Problem of Homogeneity, Stages of Development, Origin, Authorship and Dating', *Journal of the Bihar Research Society*, 49, pp. 147-66.

—— (1972), *Disposal of the Dead and Physical Types in Ancient India*, Oriental Publishers, Delhi.

—— (1979), *Archaeology of Soviet, Central Asia and the Indian Borderlands*, 2 vols., B.R. Publishing Corporation, New Delhi.

—— (1996), *The Indus-Sarasvati Civilization*, Pratibha Prakashan, Delhi.

—— (1999), 'The Indus-Saraswati Civilization Beginnings and Developments', in G.C. Pande (ed.), *The Dawn of Indian Civilization* (*up to c. 600* BC), Centre for Studies in Civilizations, New Delhi.

Hargreaves, H. (1954-5), 'Excavations in Baluchistan, 1925', in *MASI*, 35, Calcutta.

Hawkley, D.F. (1993), 'Biological Affinities of Prehistoric Sri Lankans: A Comparative Study of Dental Morphology', *AJPA*, Supplement, 16.

Hegde, K.T.M. et al. (1988), 'Excavations at Nagwada – 1986-87: Preliminary Report', *ME*, 12, pp. 55-65.

Helbaek, Hans (1959), 'Domestication of Food Plants in the Old World', *Science,* 130, 14, August, p. 370.

Hemphil, B.B. (1992), 'Tooth Size Apportionment in Modern India: Factors of Caste, Language and Geography', *Journal of Human Ecology*, Special Issues, pp. 231-53.

Hemphill, B.B. and J.R. Lukacs (1993), 'Hegelian Logic and the Harappan Civilization: An Investigation of Harappan Biological Affinities in the Light of Recent Biological and Archaeological Research', *SAA*, 1991, pp. 101-20.

Hemphill, B.B., J.R. Lukacs and K.A.R. Kennedy (1991), 'Biological Adaptations and Affinities of Bronze Age Harappans', in R.H. Meadow (ed.), *Harappan Excavations 1986-1990: A Multi-disciplinary Approach to Third Millennium Urbanism*, Prehistory Press, Madison, Wisconsin, pp. 137-82.

Hojlund, Fleming (1985), 'Some New Evidence of Harappan Influence in the Arabian Gulf', *SAA*, pp. 49-54.

Hours, S.J. Francis (1994), 'Western Asia in the Period of Homo Habilis and Homo Erectus', in E.J. De Laet (ed.), *History of Humanity*, vol. I, UNESCO, pp. 62-77.

Indian Archaeology: A Review (IAR)—various years.

Jarrige, J.F. (1979), 'Economy and Society in the Early Chalcolithic/Bronze Age of Baluchistan: New Perspectives from Recent Excavations at Mehrgarh', *SAA*, pp. 93-114.

—— (1979), 'Excavations at Mehrgarh-Pakistan', *SAA*, pp. 76-87 and 93-114.

—— (1981), 'Chronology of the Earlier Periods of the Greater Indus as Seen from Mehrgarh, Pakistan', *SAA*, pp. 21-9.

—— (1986), 'Excavations at Mehrgarh-Naushero', *PA*, 10-12, pp. 63-161.

—— (1992), 'Excavations at Mehrgarh: Their Significance for Understanding the Background of the Harappan Civilization', in G.L. Possehl (ed.), *Harappan Civilization: A Recent Perspective*, pp. 79-84.

Jha, N. (1996), *Vedic Glossary on Indus Seals,* Ganga Kaveri Publishing House, Varanasi.

Joshi, J.P. (1990), 'Excavations at Surkotada and Exploration in Kutch', *MASI*, 87.

—— (1993), *Excavations at Bhagwanpura 1975-76 and other Excavations and Explorations in Haryana, Jammu and Kashmir and Punjab*, ASI, New Delhi.

Joshi, J.P. et al. (1984), 'Indus Civilization: A Reconsideration on the Basis of Maps', in B.B. Lal and S.P. Gupta (eds.), *Frontiers of Indus Civilization*, Books and Books, Delhi, pp. 516, 522-3.

Kajale, M.D. (1991), 'Current Status of Indian Palaeo-ethnobotany', J. Fenfrew (ed.), *New Light on Early Farming: Recent Development in Palaeoethnobotany*, Edinburgh University Press, Edinburgh, pp. 155-89.

Kakar, Fazal Dad (1992), 'The Antiquity of Human Settlements in the Quetta Valley', *PA*, 27, pp. 1-14.

Karlovsky, C.C. Lamberg and Martha (1972), 'An Early City in Iran', *Old World Archaeology-Foundations of Civilization: Readings from Scientific American,* San Fransisco, Scientific American.

Karlovsky, Lamerg (1967), 'Archaeological and Metallurgical Technology in Prehistoric Afghanistan, India and Pakistan', *AA,* 69, pp. 145-62.

Kazanas, Nicolas (2000), 'The Rgveda and the Indo-Europeans', *ABORI,* 80, pp. 15-42.

Keith, A.B. and A.A. Macdonall (1982), *Vedic Index*, 2 vols., Motilal Banarsidass, Delhi.

Kennedy, K.A.R. (1965), 'Human Skeletal Material from Ceylon with an Analysis of the Island's Prehistoric and Contemporary Populations', *Bulletin of the British Museum of National History* (*Geology*), 11, pp. 135-213.

—— (1973), 'Biological Anthropology of Prehistoric Populations in South Asia: A Survey of Current Research Efforts', in K.A.R. Kennedy and G.L. Possehl (eds.), *Ecological Background of South Asian Prehistory*, Cornell University, pp. 116-78.

—— (1975), 'The Physical Anthropology of the Megalith Builders of South India and Sri Lanka, Canberra', Australian National Museum.

—— (1977), 'Fossil Man in India: The Missing Link in Our Knowledge of Human Evolution in Asia', *Bulletin of the National Speliological Society* 39(4), pp. 99-103.

—— (1980), 'Prehistoric Skeletal Record of Man in South Asia', *Annual Review of Anthropology*, 9, pp. 391-432.

—— (1984), 'Trauma and Disease in the Ancient Harappans: Recent Assessment of the Skeletal Record', in B.B. Lal and S.P. Gupta (eds.), *Frontiers of the Indus Civilization*, Books & Books, New Delhi, pp. 425-36.

—— (1986), 'Hauntings at Aditanallur: An Anthropological Ghost Story', in J. Jacobson (ed.), *Studies in the Archaeology of India and Pakistan*, Oxford-IBH, New Delhi, pp. 357-95.

—— (1990a), 'Porotic Hyperostosis in Human Remains from the Mesolithic Baghai Khor', *BDCRI*, 49, pp. 183-99.

—— (1990b), 'Skeletons in the Closet: Recent Discovery of Lost Human Skeletal Remains from Iron Age Raigir', *SAS*, 6, pp. 201-26.

—— (1992), 'Biological Anthropology of Human Skeletons from Harappa: 1928-1988', *The Eastern Anthropologist*, 45, 1-2, pp. 55-85.

—— (1992), *Human Skeletal Remains from Mahadaha: A Gangetic Mesolithic Site*, Occasional Papers and Theses of the South Asia Program, Cornell University.

—— (1993), 'Recent Discoveries and Studies of the Human Skeletal Remains of Ancient Sri Lankans', in P.K. Seth and S. Seth (eds.), *New Perspectives in Anthropology*, M.D. Publications, New Delhi, pp. 299-341.

—— (1995), 'Have Aryans been Identified in Prehistoric Skeletal Record from South Asia? Biological Anthropology and Concepts of Ancient Races, in G. Erodosy, ed., *The Indo-Aryans of Ancient South Asia: Language, Material Culture and Ethnicity*, pp. 32-66.

—— (2002), *God Apes and Fossil Men: Paleoanthropology in South Asia*, The University of Michigan Press, Ann Arbor.

Kennedy, K.A.R. and P.C. Caldwell (1984), 'South Asia Prehistoric Skeletal Remains and Burial Practices', in J.R. Lukacs (ed.), *The People of South Asia: The Biological Anthropology of India, Pakistan and Nepal*, Plenum Press, New York, pp. 159-97.

Kennedy, K.A.R. and S.U. Dereniyalgala (1989), 'Fossil Remains of 28000 Year Old Hominids from Sri Lanka', *CA*, 30, 3, pp. 395-9.

Kennedy, K.A.R. and S.U. Malhotra (1966), *Human Skeletal Remains from Chalcolithic and Indo-Roman Levels from Nevasa: An Anthropometric and Comparative Analysis*, Deccan College, Poona.

Kennedy, K.A.R. et al. (1984), 'Principal Components Analysis of Prehistoric South Asian Crania', *AJPA*, 64, pp. 105-18.

—— (1986), *Mesolithic Human Remains from the Gangetic Plain: Sarai Nahar Rai*, Cornell University.

—— (1987), 'Upper Pleistocene Fossil Hominids from Sri Lanka', *AJPA*, 72, pp. 441-61.

—— (1991), 'Is the Narmada Hominidian Indian *Homo Erectus*?', *AJPA*, 86, pp. 475-96.

Kenoyer, J.M. (1987), 'Ritual Artifacts of Prehistoric Hunter-Gatherers in South Asia', (unpublished).

—— (1992), 'The Harappan Craft Specialization and the Question of Urban Organization and Segregation', *The Eastern Anthropologist,* 45, pp. 88-94.

—— (1998), *Ancient Cities of the Indus Civilization,* Oxford University Press, New Delhi.

—— (2008), 'Regional Cultures of the Greater Indus Valley: The Ravi and Kot Diji Phase', in *Cultural Relations Between The Indus and the Iranian Plateau During the*

Third Millennium BCE, Indus Project, Research Institute for Humanity and Nature, Kyoto, Japan, 7-8 June 2008, pp. 46-51.

Kenoyer, J.M. et al. (1983), 'An Upper Palaeolithic Shrine in India', *Antiquity*, 57, pp. 88-95.

Khan, F.A. (1965), 'Excavations at Kot Diji', *Pakistan Archaeology*, 2, pp. 13-85.

Khatri, A.P. (1963), 'Recent Explorations for the Remains of Early Man in India', *Asian Perspectives*, 7, 1-2, pp. 160-92.

Khatri, J.S. and M. Acharya (1995), 'Kunal: A New Indus-Saraswati Site', *Puratattva*, 25, pp. 84-6.

Khazanov, A.M. (1984), *Nomadism and the Outside World*, Cambridge University Press, Cambridge.

Kochchar, Rajesh (2000), *The Vedic People: Their History and Geography*, Orient Longman, Hyderabad.

Kohl, Philip (1978), 'Western Asian Trade in the Third Millennium BCE', *Current Anthropology*, 19, pp. 463-92.

Krishnadeva (1969), 'The Problem of Ochre Coloured Pottery', in B.P. Sinha (ed.), *Potteries in Ancient India*, University of Patna, Patna.

Krogman, W.M. and W.H. Sassman (1943), 'Skull Found at Mohenjodaro', in J.H. Mackey (ed.), *Chahnru-daro Excavations*, New Haven Conn., American Oriental Society, pp. 252-63.

Kumar, Giriraj et al. (1988), 'Engraved Ostrich Egg Shell Objects: New Evidence of Upper Palaeolithic Art in India', *Rock Art Research*, 5, 1, pp. 43-53.

Kumar, Krishna (2000), 'The Protohistoric Copper/Bronze Anthropomorphs from Northern India', in S.C. Bhattacharya et al. (eds.), *Peeping Through the Past (Prof. G.R. Sharma Memorial Volume)*, Department of AIHC & Archaeology, Allahabad, p. 112.

Kuzmina, E.E. (1995), 'The Cultural Connections Between the Shepherds of the Steppes and South Central Asia, Afghanistan and India in the Bronze Age', *South Asian Archaeology*, Oxford, pp. 279-90.

Lal, B.B. (1951), 'Further Copper Hoards from the Gangetic Basin and a Review of the Problem', *Ancient India*, 7, pp. 20-39.

—— (1960), 'From the Megalithic to the Harappan: Tracing Back the Graffiti on the Pottery', *Ancient India*, 16, pp. 4-24.

—— (1963), 'The only Indian Expedition in Threatened Nubia: Work by Indian Mission in Afyeh and Tumas', *Illustrated London News*, 20, 4, p. 580.

—— (1968), 'A Deluge? Which Deluge? Yet Another Facet of the Problem of the Copper Hoard Culture', *American Anthropologist*, (5).

—— (1970), 'Some Observations on the Harappan Script', in L. Chandra et al. (eds.), *India's Contribution to World Thought and Culture*, Madras, pp. 189-202.

—— (1970-1), 'Perhaps the Earliest Ploughed Field so far Excavated Anywhere in the World', *Puratattva*, 4, pp. 1-3.

—— (1971-2), 'A Note of the Excavations at Saipa', *Puratattva*, 5, pp. 46-9.

—— (1974), *Has the Indus Script been Deciphered? An Assessment of Two Latest Claims*, Indian Institute of Advanced Study, Shimla.

—— (1983), 'Reading the Indus Script', *Indian and Foreign Review*, 20, 13, pp. 33, 36.

—— (1984), 'The Earliest Datable Earthquake in India', *Science Age* (October), Nehru Centre, Bombay, pp. 8-9.

—— (1992), 'Antecedents of the Signs used in the Indus Script: A Discussion', in G.L Possehl (ed.), *South Asian Archaeology Studies*, Oxford and IBH Publishing Co., New Delhi, pp. 45-55.

—— (1996), 'The Direction of Writing in the Harappan Script', *Antiquity,* XL, 157, pp. 52-5.
—— (1996), *The Indus-Saraswati Civilization*, Pratibha Prakashan, Delhi, 1996.
—— (1997), *The Earliest Civilization of South Asia*, Aryan Books International, New Delhi.
—— (1998), *India 1947-1997: New Light on the Indus Civilization,* Aryan Books International, New Delhi.
—— (2002), 'The Earliest Civilization of the Indian Subcontinent: Who could Have its Authors? A Fresh Look', *ICHR* (xerox copy), Foundation Day Lecture delivered in New Delhi on 27 March, p. 3.
—— (2002), *The Sarasvati Flows on: The Continuity of Indian Culture*, Aryan Books International, New Delhi.
Lal, B.B. et al. (2003), '*Excavations at Kalibanga: The Early Harappa* (1960-69)', *MASI*, ASI, New Delhi.
Lal, B.B., B.K. Thapar and J.P. Joshi (2003), *Excavations at Kalibangan*, vol. I: *Early Harappan*, Archaeological Survey of India, New Delhi.
Lal, Makkhan (1984), *Settlement History and Rise of Civilization in Ganga-Yamuna Doab*, B.R. Publishing Corporation, Delhi.
Lorenzo, Constantini (1981), 'The Beginning of Agriculture in Kachi Plain: The Evidence from Mehrgarh', *SAA*, p. 31.
Lukacs, J.R. (1980), 'The Apegoan Mandible Morphology and Pathology', *BDCRI*, 39, pp. 88-95.
—— (1982), *Bagor and Tilwara: Late Mesolithic Cultures of Northwest India*, vol. I: *Human Skeletal Remains*, Deccan College, Poona.
—— (1983a), 'Dental Anthropology and the Origins of Two Iron Age Populations from Northern Pakistan', *Homo*, 34, pp. 1-15.
—— (1983b), 'Dental Pathology and Tooth Size at Early Neolithic Mehrgarh: An Anthropological Assessment', *SAA*, Instituto Univerisitario Orientale, Naples, pp. 121-50.
—— (1988), 'Dental Morphology and Odentometrics of Early Agriculturists from Mehrgarh, Pakistan', in D.F. Russell et al. (eds.), *Teeth Revisited: Proceedings of the VII International Symposium on Dental Morphology*, Memories An Museum National d'Historie Naturelle (Series C), Paris, pp. 285-303.
—— (1990), 'On Hunter-Gatherers and Their Neighbours in Prehistoric India: Contact and Pathology', *CA*, 31, 2, pp. 183-6.
—— (1992a), 'Dental Palaeopathology and Agricultural Intensification in South Asia: New Evidence from Bronze Age Harappa', *AJPA*, 87, pp. 133-50.
—— (1992b), 'Culture, Ecology and Dental Anthropology', *Indian Society for Human Genetics*, New Delhi.
Lukacs, J.R. and B.B. Hemphill (1990), 'Traumatic Injuries of Prehistoric Teeth: New Evidence from Baluchistan and Punjab Provinces, Pakistan', *Anthropologischer Anzeiger*, 4, pp. 3561-3.
Lukacs, J.R. and G.L. Badam (1981), 'Palaeodemography of Post-Harappan Inamgaon: A Preliminary Report', *JIAS*, 16, pp. 59-74.
Lukacs, J.R. and L.L. Minderman (1992), 'Dental Pathology and Agricultural Intensification from Neolithic to Chalcolithic Periods at Mehrgarh (Baluchistan, Pakistan)', *SAA*, 1989, pp. 167-79.
Lukacs, J.R. and M.R. Joshi (1992), 'Enamel Hypoplasia Prevalence in Three Ethnic Groups of Northwest India: A Test of Daughter Neglect and a Framework for the Past', *Journal of Palaeopathology*, 2, pp. 349-72.

Lukacs, J.R. and R.S. Walimbe (1986), *Excavations at Inamgaon*, vol. II: *Physical Anthropology of Human Skeletal Remains*, part I: An Osteobiographic Analysis, Deccan College, Pune.

Lukacs, J.R. et al. (1983), 'Crown Dimensions of Deciduous Teeth of Prehistoric and Living Populations of Western India', *AJPA*, 61, 383-7.

—— (1985), 'Dental Pathology and Dietary Patterns in Iron Age Northern Pakistan', *SAA*, pp. 475-96.

Lukacs, R. and G.L. Badam (1981), 'Palaeodemography of Post-Harappan Inamgaon', *JIAS*, 16, pp. 59-74.

Lumley, M.A. de and S. Sonakia (1985), 'Premiere decouverte dun *Homo erectus*sur le continent Indian Hathnora dans le moyenne valce de la Narmada', *Le Anthropologic*, 89(1), pp. 13-61.

Lyonnat, Bertille (1993), 'Relations Between Central Asia and the Indian World: New Interpretations in the Light of Comprehensive Study of Ceramics, *ME*, XVIII, 2, pp. 75-86.

Mackay, E.J.H. (1937), *Further Excavations at Mohenjodaro*, 2 vols., Manager of Publications, Delhi, I: 357; II: Pls. XCL.2a and 10.

—— (1938), *Further Excavations at Mohenjo-daro*, 2 vols., Government of India, Delhi.

—— (1943), *Chanu-daro Excavation, 1935-36*, American Oriental Society, New Haven, Connecticut.

Mahadevan, I. (1977), 'The Indus Script: Text, Concordance and Tables', *Mem. Arch. Surv. of India (MASI)*, no. 77, ASI, New Delhi.

Majumdar, Abhijit (1998-9), 'Early Harappan Settlements in Gujarat', *Pragdhara*, 9, Lucknow, pp. 15-25.

Majumdar, N.G. (1934), 'Explorations in Sind', *MASI*, no. 48, ASI, New Delhi, pp. 24ff.

Malhotra, K.C. (1965), 'Human Skeletal Remains from Neolithic Tekkalkota', in M.S. Nagaraja Rao (ed.), *The Stone Age Hill Dwellers of Tekkalkota: Preliminary Report of the Excavations of Tekkalkotta*, Deccan College, Poona, pp. 109-62.

—— (1967), 'Human Skeletal Remains from Chandoli', in S.B. Deo et al. (eds.), *Chalcolithic Chandoli*, Deccan College, Poona, pp. 69-90.

Mallory, James (1989), *In Search of Indo-Europeans: Language, Archaeology and Myth*, Thames & Hudson, London.

Marshall, John (1931), *Mohenjodaro and the Indus Civilization*, 3 vols., Arthur Probsthain, London.

Mathpal, Yashodhar (1984), *Prehistoric Rock Paintings of Bhimbetka, Central India*, Abhinav Publications, New Delhi.

Meadow, Richard H., Jonathan Mark Kenoer and Rita P. Wright (1991ff.), Yearly Reports on Harappa Excavations, submitted to the Director General of Archaeology, Government of Pakistan and privately circulated.

Meena, B.R. and Alok Tripathi (2000), 'Further Excavation at Ojiyana', *Puratattva*, 31, pp. 73-8.

Mehendale, M.A. (1978-9), 'Prof. Thieme's Etymology of Sk. *asi* and Its Bearing on the Iron Age in India', *Puratattva*, 10, pp. 79-80.

Mehra, K.L. (1963), 'Considerations on the African Origin of *Eleusine coracana (1)* Gaertn', *Science*, 7, pp. 301-2.

Mehta, R.N. (1982), 'Some Rural Harappan Settlements in Gujarat', in Gregory L. Possehl (ed.), *Harappan Civilization*, Oxford and IBH Publishing Co., New Delhi, pp. 167-74.

Mellart, J. (1975), *The Neolithic of the Near East,* Thames & Hudson, London, pp. 70-90.

Minorov, N.D. (1933), 'Aryans Vestiges in the Near East in the Second Millennium BC', *Acta Orientalia*, 11, pp. 140-217.

Misra, S.S. (1992), *The Aryan Problem: A Linguistic Approach*, Munshiram Manoharlal, New Delhi.

Misra, V.D. (1975), *Some Aspects of Indian Archaeology*, Prabhat Prakashan, Allahabad.

—— (1977), 'Excavations at Koldihwa (Deoghat): Some Preliminary Observations', in V.D. Misra (ed.), *Some Aspects of Indian Archaeology*, Pratibha Prakashan, Allahabad.

Misra, V.D. and B.B. Misra (1977), 'Megalithic Culture in Southern U.P.', in S. Gopal (ed.), *Prof. D.D. Kosambi Commemoration Volume,* Tara Pub. Works, Varanasi, pp. 309-20.

Misra, V.N. (1973), 'Problems of Palaeo-ecology, Palaeo-climate and Chronology of the Mesolithic Cultures of Northwest India', in D.P. Agrawal and A. Ghosh (eds.), *Radiocarbon and Indian Archaeology*, Tata Institute of Fundamental Research, Bombay, pp. 58-72.

—— (1993), 'Indus Civilization and the Rigvedic Saraswati', *SAA,* Helsinki, pp. 511-55.

—— (1997), 'Balathal: A Chalcolithic Settlement in Mewar, Rajasthan, India—Result of First Three Seasons' Excavations', *SAS*, 13, pp. 251-73.

Mittra, S.K. and V. Shivananda (1999-2000), 'Chalcolithic Settlement at Chjichli', *Puratattva*, 30, pp. 45-9, Pl. 1 and 3.

Moran, G.M. (1936), 'Report on Human Skeletal Remains Excavated in a Rock Shelter Near Panchamarhi, Central Province', *Nagpur University Journal*, 1, pp. 1-3.

Mughal, M.R. (1992), 'The Consequences of River Changes for the Harappan Settlements in Cholistan', *The Eastern Anthropologist*, vol. 45, 1 & 2, pp. 105-6.

—— (1980), 'New Archaeological Evidence from Bahawalpur', *ME*, IV, New Delhi, pp. 93-8.

—— (1982), 'Recent Archaeological Researches in Cholistan', in G.L. Possehl (ed.), *Harappan Civilization*, Oxford-IBH, New Delhi, pp. 85-96.

—— (1990), 'Archaeological Field Research Since Independence', *Sindhological Studies*, Summer-Winter, pp. 31-8.

—— (1991), 'The Cultural Patterns of Ancient Pakistan and Neighboring Regions Circa 7000-1500 BC', *PA*, 26, p. 200.

—— (1997), *Ancient Cholistan: Archaeology and Architecture*, Feroz Sons, Lahore.

Mujumdar, G.G. (1969), 'Problem of Megalithic Black and Red Ware: A Technological Approach', in A.K. Narayan (ed.), *Seminar Papers on the Problem of Megaliths in India,* Banaras Hindu University, Varanasi, p. 90.

Müller, F. Max (1890), *Physical Religion,* Asian Educational Service, New Delhi, rpt. 1979.

Murti, M.L.K. (1974), 'A Late Pleistocene Cave Site in Southern India', *Proceedings of the American Philosophical Society*, 118, pp. 196-230.

Nanavati, J.M. et al. (1971), *Somnath (1965): Ahmedabad and Baroda*, Gujarat Government and M.S. University, Baroda.

Nath, Amarendra (1997-8), 'A Harappan Metropolis in the Sarasvati-Drishadvati Divide', *Puratattva*, 28, pp. 39-45.

—— (1998-9), 'Further Excavations at Rakhigarhi', *Puratattva*, 29, pp. 46-9.

Neumayer, Erwin (1993), *Lines on Stone: The Prehistoric Rock Art of India,* Manohar, New Delhi.

Oldham, R.D. (1987), 'On Probable Changes in the Geography of the Punjab and Its Rivers', *JASB*, 55, pp. 322-43.

Pal, J.N. (1986), *Archaeology of Southern Uttar Pradesh: Ceramic Industry of Northern Vindhyas*, Sulabha Prakashan, Allahabad.

Pandey, S.K. (1993), *Indian Rock Art*, Aryan Books International, New Delhi.

Parpola, Asko (1969), *Decipherment of the Proto-Dravidian Inscriptions of the Indus Civilization,* Copenhagen.

—— (1988), The Coming of the Aryans to Iran and India and the Cultural and the Ethnic Entity of the Dasas', *International Journal of Dravidian Linguistics*, 17, pp. 85-229.

—— (1994), *Deciphering the Indus Script*, Cambridge University Press, Cambridge.

Peebles, C.S. and S.M. Kus (1977), 'Some Archaeological Correlates of Ranked Societies', *American Antiquity*, 42, pp. 421-48.

Piggot, Stuart (1946), 'The Chronology of Prehistoric Northwest India', *AI*, I, ASI, New Delhi, rpt. 1983, p. 11.

Piperno, Macello (1973), 'Micro-drilling at Shahr-i-Sokhta: The Making and Use of Lithic Drill-heads', *SAA*, Duckworth, pp. 119-30.

Possehl, G.L. (1982), *Harappan Civilization*, Oxford-IBH, New Delhi.

—— (1990), 'Revolution in the Urban Revolution: The Emergence of Indus Civilization', *Annual Review of Anthropology*, 19, pp. 261-82.

—— eds. (1990), *Radiocarbon Dates for South Asian Archaeology*, The University Museum, University of Pennsylvania, Philadelphia.

—— (1996), *Indus Age: The Writing System*, Oxford and IBH, New Delhi.

Possehl, G.L. and K.A.R. Kennedy (1979), 'The Hunter-gatherer and Agricultural Exchange in Prehistory: An Example of India', *CA*, 29, 3, pp. 592-3.

Possehl, G.L. and M.H. Rawal (1989), *Harrappan Civilization and Rojdi*, Oxford and IBH, New Delhi.

Possehl, G.L. and P. Rissman (1992), 'India', in R.W. Elwrich (ed), *Chronologies in Old World Archaeology*, Chicago University Press, Chicago, I, p. 481.

Raikes, Robert (1968), 'Kalibangan: Death from Natural Causes', *Antiquity*, XLII, pp. 286-91.

Rao, L.S. et al. (2003-4), 'Unearthing Harappan Settlement at Bhirrana (2003-04)', *Puratattva*, 34, p. 23.

Rao, M.V.N. Krishna (1982), *Indus Script Deciphered*, Agam Kala Prakashan, Delhi.

Rao, S.R. (1962-3), 'Excavation at Rangpur and Other Explorations in Gujarat', *Ancient India,* 18-19, pp. 5-207.

—— (1963), 'Excavations at Rangpur and Other Explorations in Gujarat', *Ancient India*, 18-19, Archaeological Survey of India, New Delhi, pp. 5-207.

—— (1973), *Lothal and the Indus Civilization,* Asia Publishing House, New Delhi.

—— (1979), *Lothal: A Harappan Port Town (1955-62),* vol. I, Archaeological Survey of India, New Delhi.

—— (1982), *The Decipherment of the Indus Script*, Asia Publishing House, Bombay.

—— (1985), *Lothal: A Harappan Port Town (1955-62),* vol. II, Archaeological Survey of India, New Delhi.

—— (1990), *The Dawn and Devolution of the Indus Civilization*, Aditya Prakashan, New Delhi.

Ratnagar, Shereen F. (1981), *Encounters: The Westerly Trade of the Harappa Civilization*, New Delhi.

—— (1991), 'Pastoralism as an Issue in Historical Research', *Studies in History*, 7, 2 (NS), pp. 181-94.

—— (1991), *Enquiries into the Political Organization of Harappan Society*, Ravish, Pune.

—— (1996), 'Revisionist at Work: A Chauvinistic Approach of the Aryan Theory', *Frontline*, 9 February, pp. 74-80.

—— (2000), *The End of The Great Harappan Tradition*, Manohar, New Delhi, 2000.

—— (2003), 'Theorising Bronze Age Inter Cultural Trade: The Evidence of Weight', *Palaeorient*, vol. 29, 1, pp. 79-92.

—— (2004), *Trading Encounters*, Oxford University Press, New Delhi.

—— 'Ancient River Basin Agriculture (The Bronze Age)', xeroxed copy, p. 7.

Rendell, H.M. et al. (1989), *Pleistocene and Palaeolithic Investigations in the Soan Valley, Northern Pakistan*, British Arch Mission to Pakistan, Series 2, BAR International Series 544, Oxford.

Renfrew, Colin (1987), *Archaeology and Language: The Puzzle of Indo-European Origins*, Jonathan Cape, London.

—— (1988), *Archaeology and Language,* Cambridge University Press, New York.

Roux, George (1992), *Ancient Iraq*, 3rd edn., Penguin, Harmondsworth.

Sali, S.A. (1986), *Daimabad (1976-79)*, Archaeological Survey of India, New Delhi.

Sankalia, H.D. (1963), 'New Light on Indo-Iranian or Western Asiatic Relations between 1700-1200 BC', *Artibus Asiae*, 26, pp. 312-32.

—— (1965), *Excavations at Langhnaj 1944-63*, part 1: *Archaeology*, Deccan College Bldg. Centenary Series, 29, Poona.

—— (1967), 'The Socio-economic Significance of the Lithic Blade Industry of Navdatoli, M.P., India', *CA*, 8, pp. 262-8.

—— (1972), *Prehistory and Protohistory of India and Pakistan*, Deccan College, Poona.

—— (1972-3), 'The Cemetery-H Culture', *Puratattva*, 6, pp. 12-19.

Sankalia, H.D. et al. (1971), *Chalcolithic Navdatoli*, Deccan College, Poona.

Sankalia, H.D., B. Subba Rao and S.B. Deo (1958), *Excavations at Maheshwar and Navdatoli (1952-53)*, Deccan College, Poona, pp. XII-XIII.

Sankalia, H.D., S.B. Deo and Z.D. Ansari (1969), *Excavations at Ahar (Tambavati)*, Deccan College, Poona.

Santoni, Marielle (1981), 'Sibri the South Cemetery of Mehrgarh: Third Millennium Connections, between Northern Kachhi Plain and Central Asia', *SAA*, p. 52.

Saran, S.C. and U. Sant (1994), *Harappan Elements in Neo-Chalcolithic Context of the Middle Ganga Plain*, paper read at IV World Archaeology Congress, New Delhi.

Sarkar, H. and B.N. Misra (1966), *Nagarjunakonda*, Archaeological Survey of India, New Delhi.

Sarkar, S.S. (1964), *Ancient Races of Punjab, Baluchistan and Sind*, Munshiram Manoharlal, New Delhi.

—— (1972), *Ancient Races of the Deccan*, Munshiram Manoharlal, New Delhi.

Seshadri, Rajan (1994), 'The Metal Technology of the Harappan and the Copper Hoard Culture: Comparative Study', Ph.D. thesis (unpublished), The Maharaja Sayajirao University, Baroda.

Sewell, R.B.S. and B.S. Guha (1929), 'Report on the Bones Excavated at Nal', *MASI*, 35, pp. 56-96.

—— (1931), 'Human Remains', in John Marshall (ed.), *Mohenjodaro and Indus Civilization*, Arthur Probsthain, London, vol. 2, pp. 599-648.

Shaffer, J.G. (1964), 'The Indo-Aryan Invasions: Cultural Myth and Archaeological Reality', in J.R. Lukacs (ed.), *The People of South Asia: The Biological Anthropology of India, Pakistan and Nepal*, Plenum Press, New York, pp. 77-90.

Sharma, A.K. (1969-70), 'Kalibangan Human Skeletal Remains: An Osteoarcheaological Approach, *JOI*, 19, pp. 109-13.

—— (1993), 'The Harappan Horse was Buried under the Dune of . . .', *Puratattva*, 23, pp. 30-4.

Sharma, N.L. (1968), 'A Note on the Old Copper Workings of Amba Mata Near Abu Road Station, Gujarat', in *Copper: Progress on Symposium on Copper*, Geological Survey of India, Manager of Publication, Calcutta.

Sharma, R.S. (1995), *Looking for the Aryans in India*, Orient Longman, Madras.

—— (1999), *Advent of the Aryans in India*, Manohar, New Delhi.

—— (2002), 'Rgvedic and Harappan Cultures: Lexical and Archaeological Aspects', *Social Scientist*, vol. 30, nos. 7-8, July-August, pp. 1-11.

Sherrat, Andrew (1999), 'Sedentary Agriculture and Nomadic Pastoral Populations (3000-7000 BC)', in A.H. Dani (ed.), *History of Humanity*, UNESCO, vol. II, pp. 40-1.

Shinde, V.S. (1992), 'Padri and the Indus Civilization', *South Asian Studies*, 8, pp. 55-6.

—— 'Excavation at Padri (1990-91): Preliminary Report', *ME*, 17, I, pp. 79-86.

Shinde, V.S. and G.L. Possehl (2001), 'A Report on the Excavations at Gilund 1999-2001', *SAA*, Paris.

Shinde, V.S., G.L. Possehl and Shweta Sinha Deshpande (2001-2), 'The Ceramic Assemblage in Protohistoric Mewar Rajasthan with Special Reference to Gilund and Balathal', *Puratattva*, 32, pp. 5-24.

Singh, B.K. (1992-3), 'Excavations at Golbai Sasan, District Puri, Orissa', *Puratattva,* 33, pp. 28-50.

Singh, B.P. (1987-8), 'Khairahdi: A Chalcolithic Settlement', *Puratattva*, 18, pp. 28-34.

Singh, Bhagwan (1995), *The Vedic Harappans*, Aditya Prakashan, New Delhi.

Singh, Gurdip (1971), 'Indus Valley Culture Seen in the Context of Post-Glacial Climatic and Ecological Studies in North-Western India', *Archaeology and Physical Anthropology of Oceania,* 6, pp. 177-88.

Singh, Purushottam (1994), *Excavations at Narhan (1984-89)*, Benaras Hindu University and B.R. Pubishing Corporation, Varanasi and Delhi.

Singh, U.V. (1962), 'Excavations at Eran', *Journal of M.P. Itihasa Parishad,* 4, pp. 41-4.

Sinha, B.P. and B.S. Verma (1977), *Sonpur Excavation (1956 and 1959-62)*, Patna.

Sonawane, V.H. (1942), 'Significance of the Chandravati Core in the Light of Prehistoric Art in India', in M. Lorblanchet (ed.), *Rock Art in the Old World*, pp. 273-83.

—— (1998-9), 'Harappan Civilization in Gujarat: A Recent Perspective', *Pragdhara*, 9, Uttar Pradesh State Archaeology Department, Lucknow, pp. 1-14.

Sonakia, A. (1984), 'The Skull Cap of Early Man and Associated Mammalian Fauna from Narmada Valley Alluvium, Hoshangabad Area, Madhya Pradesh, India', *Records of the Geological Survey of India* 113, 6d, pp. 159-72.

—— (1985), 'Early Homo from India', in F. Delson (ed.), *Ancestors: The Hard Evidence*, Alan R. Riss, New York, pp. 334-8.

Srivastav, O.P. (2001), 'An Archaeological Study of District Muzaffarnagar', Ph.D. thesis (unpublished), Aligarh Muslim University, Aligarh.

Stacul, Giorgio (1989), 'Swat, Pirak and Connected Problems (Mid-2nd Millennium BC)', *SAA*, pp. 268-9.

Stein, A. (1929), 'An Archaeological Tour in Waziristan and Northern Baluchistan', *MASI*, no. 37, Calcutta.

—— (1931) 'An Archaeological Tour in Waziristan and Northern Baluchistan', *MASI*, no. 43, Calcutta.

—— (1942), 'A Survey of Ancient Sites Along the Lost Saraswati River', *Geographical Journal*, 99, pp. 73-182.

Talageri, S.G. (1993), *The Aryan Invasion Theory: A Re-Appraisal*, Aditya Prakashan, New Delhi.

—— (2000), *The Rigveda: A Historical Analysis*, Aditya Prakashan, New Delhi.

Thakran, R.C. (1998), 'Protohistoric Settlement Patterns in Haryana', in K.M. Shrimali (ed.), *Reason and Archaeology*, Manohar, New Delhi, 1998, pp. 29-62.

—— (2003), 'The Myth of Saraswati Civilization: A Locational Analysis of Harappan Sites', in Kesavan Veluthat and P.P. Sudhakaran (eds.), *Advances in History*, Calicut, pp. 22-43.

—— (2006), 'Was The River Water a Precondition for Human Existence?: Perspectives from Recent Explorations in Rajasthan', paper presented at *The International Conference of the Association of South Asian Archaeology*, held at Bombay University, Mumbai, 15-17 December.

—— (2006-7), 'Recent Archaeological Explorations Along the Ghaggar in Rajasthan', *PIHC*, Delhi, pp. 992-1000.

—— (2009), 'Rivers and Protohistoric Settlements: Negotiating Contrasting Perceptions in the Light of Recent Explorations in Rajasthan', in *Changing Perspectives in South Asian Archaeology*, K.P. Jayaswal Research Institute, Patna.

—— (2009), 'Was the Saraswati a Mighty Perennial River: An Archaeo-geohydrological Perspective', *Social Science Probings,* pp. 1-18.

Thakran, R.C. et al. (2009), 'Excavations at Harappan Site of Badali, District Jhajjar, Haryana', *Puratattva*, 39, New Delhi, 2009, pp. 165-71.

—— 'The Sequel to the Indus Civilization in the Greater Indus Valley', unpublished M. Phil dissertation, Jawaharlal Nehru University, New Delhi.

—— (2010), 'Manheru Excavations and Explorations in its Environs', *Journal of Ancient History Culture and Archaeology*, vol. I, M.J.P. Rohilkhand University, Bareilly, pp. 128-61.

Thapar, B.K. (1985), *Recent Archaeological Discoveries in India*, UNESCO, Paris.

Thapar, Romila (1969), 'Presidential Address', *PIHC*, Varanasi, pp. 15-39.

Thomas, D.K. and P.P. Joglekar (1994), 'Holocene Faunal Studies in India', *ME*, 19, 1-2, pp. 179-203.

Tilak, B.G. (1972), *The Orion Researches into the Antiquity of the Vedas*, Tilak Bros, Poona.

Tripathi, V., ed. (1998), *Archaeometallurgy in India,* Sharada Publishing House, Delhi.

Ushanas, E. Richter (1992), *The Fifth Veda: The Indus Seals in Comparison with the Rigveda*, Germany.

Varma, R.K. (1986), *The Mesolithic Age in Mirzapur*, Pramjyoti Prakashan, Allahabad.

Vats, M.S. (1939-40), *Excavation at Harappa*, 2 vols., Government of India, New Delhi.

Verma, B.S. (1970-1), 'Excavations at Chirand: New Light on the Indian Neolithic Culture Complex', *Puratattva*, 4, pp. 19-23.

Wakankar, V.S. (1975), 'Prehistoric Cave Paintings', *Marg*, 28 (4), pp. 17-38.

—— (1978), *The Dawn of Indian Art*, Bharat Kala Bhavan, Ujjain.

—— (1992), 'Rock Paintings in India', in M. Lorblanchet (ed.), *Rock Art in the Old World*, Indira Gandhi National Centre for the Arts, New Delhi, pp. 319-36.

Wakankar, V.S. and B.R.R. Brooks (1976), *Stone Age Paintings in India,* Taraporewala & Sons, Bombay.

Walimbe, S.R. (1986), 'Palaeo-demography of Proto-historic Daimabad', in S.A. Sali (ed.), *Daimabad 1976-79*, Archaeological Survey of India, New Delhi, pp. 641-740.

Walimbe, S.R. and S.S. Kulkarni (1993), *Biological Adaptations in Human Dentition: An Odonto-metric Study on Living and Archaeological Populations in Indian*, Deccan College, Poona.

Walter, H. et al. (1991), *Anthrfopologie Indians*, Gustav Fischer Verlag, Stuttgart.

Weber, S.A. (1991) *Plants and Harappan Subsistence*, Oxford-IBH, New Delhi.

Wheeler, Mortimer (1984), 'Harappa 1946: The Defences and Cemetery R-37', *AI*, 3, Archaeological Survey of India, pp. 58-130.

Wheeler, R.E.M. (1947), 'Harappa 1946: The Defences and Cemetery R-37', *Ancient India*, 3, pp. 58-130.

—— (1947-8), 'Brahmagiri and Chandravalli 1947: Megalithic and Other Cultures in Mysore State', *Ancient India*, 4, pp. 180-311.

—— (1959), *Early India and Pakistan to Asoka*, Thames and Hudson, London.

—— (1968), *The Indus Civilization*, Cambridge University Press, 3rd edn.

Wittfogel, K.A. (1959), *Oriental Despotism: A Comparative Study of Total Power*, Yale University Press, New Haven.

Witzel, M. (1999), 'Aryan and Non-Aryan Names in Vedic India', in Bronchorst and Deshpande (eds.), pp. 337-404.

Witzel, M. and S. Farmer (2000), 'Horseplay in Harappa', *Frontline,* 17, 19, pp. 4-16.

Witzel, Michael and Steve Farmer (2000), 'Piltdown Horse in Harappa', *Frontline*, 13 October, pp. 1-4.

Yule, Paul (1985), *Metal Work of the Bonze Age in India*, Munchen.

—— (1989), *The Copper Hoards of the Indian Subcontinent: Preliminaries for Interpretation,* Mainz.

Index